Handbook of Psychology
in
Legal Contexts

Second Edition

Handbook of Psychology in Legal Contexts

Second Edition

Edited by

David Carson

University of Southampton, UK

and

Ray Bull

University of Portsmouth, UK

WILEY

Other Wiley Editorial Offices

John Wiley & Sons Inc., 111 River Street, Hoboken, NJ 07030, USA

Jossey-Bass, 989 Market Street, San Francisco, CA 94103-1741, USA

Wiley-VCH Verlag GmbH, Boschster. 12, D-69469 Weinheim, Germany

John Wiley & Sons Australia Ltd, 33 Park Road, Milton, Queensland 4064, Australia

John Wiley & Sons (Asia) Pte Ltd, 2 Clementi Loop #02-01, Jin Xing Distripark, Singapore 129809

John Wiley & Sons Canada Ltd, 22 Worcester Road, Etobicoke, Ontario, Canada M9W 1L1

Wiley also publishes its books in a variety of electronic formats. Some content that appears
in print may not be available in electronic books.

Library of Congress Cataloging-in-Publication Data

Handbook of psychology in legal contexts / edited by David Carson and Ray Bull.
    p.   cm.
Includes bibliographical references and index.
ISBN 0-471-49874-2 (alk. paper)
1. Law–Psychological aspects.   2. Psychology, Forensic   I. Carson, David   II. Bull, Ray.

K346 .H36   2003
347′.066′019–dc21   2002033069

British Library Cataloguing in Publication Data

A catalogue record for this book is available from the British Library

ISBN 0-471-49874-2

Typeset in 10/12pt Times New Roman and Optima by TechBooks, New Delhi, India
Printed and bound in Great Britain by Antony Rowe Ltd, Chippenham, Wiltshire
This book is printed on acid-free paper responsibly manufactured from sustainable forestry
in which at least two trees are planted for each one used for paper production.

Contents

PART 3   PERSPECTIVES ON COURTS: TRIALS AND DECISION MAKING

About the Editors

David Carson

David Carson is Reader in Law and Behavioural Sciences in the Faculty of Law at the University of Southampton. He tries to be practical, preventive and interdisciplinary in his teaching and writing, and to promote those goals in his organisational work. He has developed courses on how to be skilful as an expert witness in court and how to reduce the likelihood of being criticised or sued for poor risk-taking, particularly in child protection and mental disorder contexts, simultaneously producing both valuable evidence for courts and better risk decisions. These have been provided, many times, for experienced practitioners.

He was organiser of the first international 'Psychology and Law' conference, sponsored by the American Psychology-Law Society and the European Association of Psychology and Law, which took place in Dublin in 1999. He was also invited to organise a second such conference, which are to become regular events, now also sponsored by the Australian and New Zealand Association of Psychiatry, Psychology and Law. The second conference takes place in Edinburgh in 2003.

Ray Bull

Ray Bull is Professor of Criminological and Legal Psychology in the Department of Psychology at the University of Portsmouth. He has published extensively on research topics at the interface of psychology with legal contexts, especially investigative interviewing.

In 1995 he was awarded a higher doctorate (Doctor of Science) in recognition of the quality and extent of his research publications. He is regularly asked by lawyers to write expert reports in connection with criminal and civil proceedings (over 60 to date) and has testified as an expert witness in a number of trials. In 2001/2 he was a member of the small team that was commissioned by the government to write *Achieving Best Evidence in Criminal Proceedings: Guidance for Vulnerable or Intimidated Witnesses, including Children*.

List of Contributors

Terry Bartholomew
Lecturer in Psychology, Deakin University, Melbourne Campus, 221 Burwood Highway, Burwood, Victoria, VIC 3125, Australia.

Brian H. Bornstein
Post-Doctoral Fellow, Law–Psychology Programme, Department of Psychology, Burnett Hall, University of Nebraska-Lincoln, Lincoln, Nebraska NE 68588-0308, USA.

Jennifer Brown
Professor of Forensic Psychology, Department of Psychology, University of Surrey, Guildford, Surrey GU2 7XH, UK.

Richard A. Bryant
Associate Professor, School of Psychology, University of New South Wales, Sydney, NSW 2052, Australia.

Ray Bull
Professor of Criminological and Legal Psychology, Department of Psychology, University of Portsmouth, King Henry Building, King Henry 1 Street, Portsmouth PO1 2DY, UK.

David Canter
Professor of Psychology, Centre for Investigative Psychology, University of Liverpool, Department of Psychology, Eleanor Rathbone Building, Liverpool L69 7ZA, UK.

David Carson
Reader in Behavioural Sciences and Law, Faculty of Law, The University, Southampton SO17 1BJ, UK.

Isabel C.H. Clare
Consultant Clinical and Forensic Psychologist, Department of Psychiatry (Section of Developmental Psychiatry), University of Cambridge, 18b Trumpington Road, Cambridge CB2 2AH, UK.

Brian Clifford
Professor of Psychology, Department of Psychology, University of East London, Romford Road, London E15 4LZ, UK.

John B. Davies
Professor of Psychology, Centre for Applied Social Psychology, University of Strathclyde, Graham Hills Building, 40 George Street, Glasgow
G1 1QE, UK.

Eric Y. Drogin
Forensic Psychologist/Attorney, Franklin Pierce Law Center, 2 White Street, Concord, New Hampshire 03301, USA.

David L. Faigman
Professor of Law, University of California at Hastings, 200 McAllister Street, San Francisco, California CA 94102, USA.

Katarina Fritzon
Lecturer in Forensic Psychology, University of Surrey, Department of Psychology, Guildford, Surrey GU2 7XH, UK.

Edith Greene
Professor of Psychology, Department of Psychology, University of Colorado, 1420 Austin Bluffs Parkway, Colorado Springs, Colorado 80933-7150, USA.

Clara Gumpert
Division of Forensic Psychiatry, Karolinska Institute, PO Box 4044, 141 04 Huddinge, Sweden.

Kirk Heilbrun
Professor and Chair, Department of Clinical and Health Psychology,
Drexel University, MS 626, 245 N. 15th Street, Philadelphia, PA 19102-1192, USA.

Emily Henderson
Mother/freelance researcher, 27 Victoria Road, Cambridge CB4 3BW, UK.

Mark E. Howard
Assistant United States Attorney, District of New Hampshire; Adjunct Professor of Criminal Law, Franklin Pierce Law Center, 2 White Street, Concord, New Hampshire 03301, USA.

Friedrich Lösel
Professor of Psychology, University of Erlangen-Nuremberg, Department of
Psychology I, Lehrstuhl, Bismarckstrasse 1, 91054 Erlangen, Germany.

Bradley D. McAuliff
Post-Doctoral Fellow, Law–Psychology Programme, Department of Psychology,
Burnett Hall, University of Nebraska-Lincoln, Lincoln, Nebraska NE 68588-0308,
USA.

Rebecca Milne
Senior Lecturer, Institute of Criminal Justice Studies, University of Portsmouth,
Ravelin House, Museum Road, Portsmouth PO1 2QQ, UK.

Glynis H. Murphy
Professor of Clinical Psychology of Learning Disability, Tizard Centre, University
of Kent, Canterbury, Kent CT2 7LZ, UK.

Robert J. Nemeth
Doctoral Student, Department of Psychology, 236 Audubon Hall, Louisiana State
University, Baton Rouge, LA 70803, USA.

Francis Pakes
Senior Lecturer, Institute of Criminal Justice Studies, University of Portsmouth,
Ravelin House, Ravelin Park, Museum Road, Portsmouth PO1 2QQ, UK.

Steven D. Penrod
Distinguished Professor, Department of Psychology, John Jay College of Criminal
Justice, City University of New York, 445 West 59th Street, New York, NY
10019-1199, USA.

Carrie J. Petrucci
Assistant Professor, California State University Long Beach, 1250 Bellflower Blvd.,
Long Beach, CA 90840, USA.

Janette Porteous
Barrister and Senior Lecturer in Law, University of Lincoln, Brayford Pool, Lincoln
LN6 7TS, UK.

Martine B. Powell
Senior Lecturer in Psychology, Deakin University, Melbourne Campus, 221
Burwood Highway, Burwood, Victoria, VIC 3125, Australia.

Michael J. Saks
Professor of Law and Psychology, Arizona State University, College of Law, Box
877906, Tempe, Arizona AZ 85287-7906, USA.

Stephen P. Savage
Professor, Institute of Criminal Justice Studies, University of Portsmouth, Ravelin
House, Ravelin Park, Museum Road, Portsmouth PO1 2QQ, UK.

Leonore M.J. Simon
Associate Professor, Department of Criminal Justice and Criminology, East
Tennessee State University, PO Box 70555, Johnson City, Tennessee TN 37614,
USA.

William C. Thompson
Professor, Department of Criminology, Law and Society, University of California at
Irvine, Irvine, California 92697-7080, USA.

Judith Trowell
Consultant Psychiatrist, Tavistock Clinic, 120 Belsize Lane, London NW3 5BA, UK.

Eileen Vizard
Consultant Child and Adolescent Psychiatrist and Honorary Senior Lecturer,
University College London, The Young Abusers Project, The Peckwater Centre, 6
Peckwater Street, London NW5 2TX, UK.

Aldert Vrij
Professor of Applied Social Psychology, University of Portsmouth, Psychology
Department, King Henry Building, King Henry 1 Street, Portsmouth PO1 2DY, UK.

Andrea Watts
Crime Analyst, Serious Crime Analysis Section, National Crime Faculty, Centrex,
Bramshill, Hook, Hampshire RG27 0JW, UK.

David B. Wexler
Lyons Professor of Law and Professor of Psychology, University of Arizona, and
Professor of Law and Director, International Network on Therapeutic
Jurisprudence, University of Puerto Rico, College of Law, University of Arizona,
PO Box 210176, Tucson, Arizona 85721-0176, USA.

John Williams
Professor of Law, Department of Law, University of Wales, Hugh Owen Building,
Penglais, Aberystwyth, Ceredigion SY23 3DY, UK.

Tom Williamson
Senior Research Fellow, Institute of Criminal Justice Studies, University of
Portsmouth, Ravelin House, Ravelin Park, Museum Road, Portsmouth PO1 2QQ,
UK.

Bruce J. Winick
Professor of Law, University of Miami School of Law, 1311 Miller Drive, Coral
Gables, Florida 33146, USA.

Lawrence Wrightsman
Professor of Psychology, Department of Psychology, University of Kansas, Lawrence, Kansas KS 66045, USA.

A. Daniel Yarmey
Professor of Psychology, Department of Psychology, University of Guelph, Guelph, Ontario N1G 2W1, Canada.

Peter Yates
Consultant Child and Adolescent Forensic Psychiatrist, Stamford House, Cathnor Road, Hammersmith, London W12 9PA, UK.

Donna Youngs
Centre for Investigative Psychology, University of Liverpool, Department of Psychology, Eleanor Rathbone Building, Liverpool L69 7ZA, UK.

Preface

To be asked to edit one edition was impressive enough, but to be asked to edit a second edition is ... well ... also impressive. And it is not really a second 'edition'. While some authors from the first edition have kindly joined us in this second, and some topics are similar, most chapters and authors are entirely new and fresh.

The organising principles of this edition are different from the first, in which we sought to stress the legal contexts and links between psychology and law. In this edition we have tried to highlight developments in, and roles for, psychology and law, but a number of principles remain common to both editions. We believe that there must be a 'dialogue' between the disciplines and professions, explicitly from a level starting point. Law may have been both an independent discipline and a profession for much longer than psychology, but it does not follow that the latter must adopt the former's perspectives or assumptions, let alone perpetuate them. There is an important role for psychology in the provision of expert evidence to the courts in individual cases. But that is neither the beginning nor the end of psychology's role! We must accept the reality of the law, and we must accept that that is what the courts will decide and enforce, but we are not obliged to accept that that is how it must be when psychological research or insights tell us otherwise. So, for example, several chapters in these *Handbooks* emphasise the potential of psychology to inform law reform.

We are also concerned about an artificial and premature narrowing of 'psychology and law'. For many the phrase seems to refer to psychologists interested in the law and practice as it relates to criminal justice and mental health matters. We consider that to be frighteningly narrow. We believe that psychology has a great deal to offer to all areas of law, civil as well as criminal, procedural as well as substantive. Professional issues, for example distinguishing clinical from educational and occupational, or disciplinary distinctions, for example abnormal from social psychology, should not restrict the development of an understanding of how the behavioural sciences can inform and improve the law and laws. It is not just that social and occupational psychologists and other behavioural scientists, for example, should be welcomed at psychology and law conferences and be represented in such books and journals, but that this developing interest and topic will be diminished by their absence.

We believe that psychology and law is not just a theoretical and applied subject but has considerable opportunity for both reflecting and advocating change. And this edition particularly reflects this belief. There are several chapters, particularly in Parts 3 and 4, which relate the dramatic organisational developments in our subject area. For example, important and exciting developments, which challenge many preconceptions about how our courts should operate, are taking place in the growth of restorative justice interventions around the world and in problem-solving courts in the USA in particular. Whether psychology and law should, explicitly, recognise that it is inevitably concerned with the promotion of justice, albeit granting that that will involve value disputes, is discussed, by one of us, in the opening chapter.

Part 1 of this *Handbook* considers psychology in, perhaps, its most traditional context—that is, providing information for the courts. Murphy and Clare update their chapter in the first edition, examining when and how psychology can, or could, help the courts to decide who is capable of making which legal decisions. Then Vrij examines what courts and judicial agencies might learn about how to assess and detect deception, and Bryant examines issues involved when assessing individuals for compensation purposes. We would ask readers to question whether the law and courts, in their particular countries, allow themselves to know about and be informed sufficiently on these topics.

Part 2 examines examples of how psychology is being, and could further be, developed to assist a wide range of professionals and practitioners in undertaking tasks which could have legal implications, particularly if not well performed. Milne and Bull consider police interviewing techniques. If this task is poorly performed what hope can there be for the later stages in the criminal process? Heilbrun examines what we know about assessing and managing dangerous people. But the emphasis is on how we use and manage the information we gain and not just how we might present it to courts. Carson follows this with an appeal for greater interdisciplinary cooperation on the understanding and practice of risk-taking. While courts and lawyers need to know more about the topic, he suggests that psychologists could end up victimised if they do not consider the implications of their roles in the total process.

There follow three chapters identifying the potential of psychology to better inform understanding and practice in criminal justice and policing. Canter and Youngs articulate the case for not restricting the subfield to offender profiling but rather recognising that as an example of how psychology can help investigations. Williamson identifies the many problems that arise when that most basic of needs for any organisation, clear data, is not provided. He refers to data on crime which is regularly misused by other actors. Fritzon and Watts then consider the potential of psychology to inform action to prevent crime, not just to identify and respond to it. This prevention theme, which we suggest is not usually given the prominence it deserves, is also taken up by Lösel who examines a wealth of sources to identify key factors both predictive and protective of childhood delinquent conduct. Part 2 then ends with chapters by Trowell, on the implications of disputes for children, and child psychiatrists Yates and Vizard, on the debate surrounding the competence of children to commit crimes.

Part 3 focuses on trials. McAuliff, Nemeth, Bornstein and Penrod examine the potential for assisting those who have to make decisions about disputed facts. Greene and Wrightsman compare such decision-making by country and between judges and juries. Saks and Thompson place the focus on the disputed evidence. Faigman considers the contribution of expert evidence to court decisions, and the rationale that should underpin the process. Carson and Pakes identify some of the mechanisms that lawyers can use to encourage witnesses to say what they want the courts to hear. This Part ends with a discussion of restorative justice developments in the USA and the UK by Drogin, Howard and Williams, and a description of the proactive judges in the problem-solving courts which have been developing, particularly in the USA. There are those who decry the relative absence of lawyers in the psychology and law 'movement'. We would suggest that such critics should consider such developments as those which are often led by judges and lawyers. They demonstrate a willingness, by many, to think and to act radically. The real problem may be those who restrict their image of the developing field to the traditional one of experts, accepting the law's limited perspective, to inform them about a particular case. Much more is going on and, as this Part demonstrates, much more could take place.

Part 4 identifies the role of psychology as a major contributor to debates about the law, and its potential for reform. The controversy surrounding 'recreational' drugs is one which deserves information and challenge. And Davies does that. Meanwhile Henderson, a lawyer, examines the perceptions with which lawyers approach child witnesses in sexual abuse trials. Again, if we do not consider our own and others' perceptions of the issues we both work on, then we are unlikely to communicate efficiently. Gumpert provides a Swedish perspective on allegations of child sexual abuse and how expert testimony is utilised. Eye-witnessing remains, and is likely to remain, a cornerstone of evidence in many criminal trials. It is also a source of much valuable research. Yarmey reviews this. Is it not time that we acknowledged how much is already known, and the potential for developing both 'consensus statements' and agreement to promote them with different governments? Brown and Porteous, psychologist and lawyer, examine developments in England and Wales, in particular, on the causation and extent of workplace stress. Compensation claims had been growing. Ironically, once the chapter was completed, the Court of Appeal for England and Wales greatly restricted previous decisions. The Part ends with a description of the extensive work that has been undertaken, under a therapeutic jurisprudence perspective (or 'lens'). Most of that work has been undertaken by lawyers and, again, demonstrates an openness to learning from the behavioural sciences. Petrucci, Winick and Wexler (the latter two being the originators of the approach) invite social scientists to try the perspective in their writing about law and practice.

Part 5 seeks to ask broader questions about the relationship between psychological and other methodologies. Clifford extends his valuable analysis in the first edition with another chapter which examines the problems facing collaboration between psychologists and lawyers. Powell and Bartholomew consider professional and practical issues of good practice when working with clients from different cultural backgrounds. Finally Savage, a sociologist, addresses important questions surrounding whether psychology and law pays sufficient attention to the social sciences. Is sufficient attention being given to such issues as class, power, ethnicity in a psychology and law which often seems to assume an individualistic analysis?

It was most gratifying that the first edition not only sold well but led to a paperback edition. We hope the same for this edition and thank our publishers for their hopes. We thank our contributors, with a sincerity and depth of feeling which we are unlikely to have communicated in that to and fro—over dates and lengths and editorial changes sought—which is an inevitable feature of the publishing process. Thank you! We must not assume that any of them wish to be identified with our particular vision of the potential of psychology and law, but we admire their willingness to take up the challenge we offered them. Finally, we believe in the internationalism of psychology and law. This second edition, as the first, surely demonstrates how it is developing in so many countries. That can only be beneficial.

David Carson
Winchester

Ray Bull
Chichester

Introduction

Psychology and Law: A Subdiscipline, an Interdisciplinary Collaboration or a Project?

David Carson[*]
University of Southampton, UK

Which is it? Is psychology and law a subdiscipline and, if so, of psychology, of law or both? Is it an example of two disciplines collaborating towards greater understanding of their interrelationship, and if so is it best described as psychology in law, law in psychology or psychology and law? Should it be broadened to 'behavioural sciences' rather than just 'psychology'? Or is it a coming together, a commitment, of psychologists and lawyers to improve the quality and efficiency of our laws and legal systems? Clearly we do not have a consensus on such issues. Does that matter? Do we need to decide? Are we missing anything by not identifying, debating and tackling such issues?

This *Handbook* contains chapters that exemplify each of the three approaches: subdiscipline, collaboration and 'project'. But it does not follow that the authors would argue that their approach is the only appropriate position or approach. How we 'do', or what we write, in psychology and law does not, necessarily, reflect what we would like to see happening at the macro or organisational level. As individuals and groups we tend to focus on a narrow range of topics, with a view to gaining recognition for our expertise. This chapter will argue that we have not, to our loss, paid sufficient attention to the structural and thematic issues in this developing interest area. Organisational arrangements, particularly internationally (between national and regional bodies) and structurally (between researchers and practitioners but also between psychologists and

---

[*] I am most grateful to Ray Bull for his comments on drafts of this chapter, but he must not be assumed to agree with any of it.

Handbook of Psychology in Legal Contexts, Second Edition
Edited by D. Carson and R. Bull. © 2003 John Wiley & Sons, Ltd.

lawyers), are poorly developed. Where 'psychology and law' is going, and should go, is still a matter of conjecture. Important opportunities will be lost unless we attend to these topics.

Psychology and the law are both inherently concerned with the analysis, explanation, prediction and, sometimes, the alteration of human behaviour. Of course there is much more to the study and practice both of psychology and of law. But there is this enormous overlap in interests, in clients, in topics, in issues: from identifying (e.g. see chapter by Yarmey in this volume) who has committed a particular crime to understanding why he or she did it and deterring or preventing (see Fritzon and Watts, in this volume) its repetition; from interviewing people (e.g. see chapter by Milne and Bull in this volume), in order to learn more about past events of which they may have recall, through assessing the credibility and reliability of what they say (e.g. see chapter by Vrij in this volume), to making complex decisions based on that information. Some emphasise the overlap to demonstrate how great is the common interest (e.g. Lloyd Bostock, 1988; Schuller and Ogloff, 2001). We could also list successes, for example on identification evidence, assessments of capacity to make legal decisions (e.g. see chapter by Murphy and Clare in this volume) on interviewing witness to collect more useful information about a past event, to demonstrate how much has been achieved. But that would also serve to emphasise how remarkably little use is made of that knowledge base. Legislatures and courts do not rush, or even have systems, to ensure that they take account of the latest research on, for example, identification evidence or false confessions, despite its importance for improving justice and confidence in the legal system.

Are the relations between lawyers and psychologists underdeveloped? We cannot agree an answer to that question without a consensus on what is possible. But its impact has been limited, it is submitted, when we consider what could have been achieved by now. For example, are psychologists or behavioural scientists regularly appointed members of law reform commissions, or similar? Do all lawyers have some education in the scientific analysis, prediction or shaping of human behaviour? So why has psychology and law so relatively little to show? Why, when the potential for valuable and practical collaboration is so great, is the ambition so restrained? This chapter will encourage debate about such questions. It will suggest that a more adventurous and challenging programme for relating the disciplines and professions could, and should, be adopted. It will argue that psychology and law should be a 'project', as well as a 'collaboration' and subdiscipline. It will differ from other overviews of the developing relationship between the disciplines (e.g. Kapardis, 1997; Haney, 1980; Schuller and Ogloff, 2001). The basis for interdisciplinary cooperation and intraprofessional collaboration is recognition of a need for, and a commitment towards achieving, greater (quality, quantity, efficiency and effectiveness) justice. To the extent that this necessarily involves value choices, it is political. Thus it is inimical to those who perceive 'science' as pure and objective. But this is inevitable and a feature of the subject-matter. As such it should be acknowledged openly.

TERMINOLOGY

'Psychology' or 'Behavioural Sciences'?

The area of interest is generally known as 'Psychology and Law'. Should it be? Those are the terms used by two of the three major associations with interests in this area: the American Psychology-Law Society (AP-LS), the European Association of Psychology and Law (EAP&L), and the Australian and New Zealand Association of Psychiatry, Psychology and Law (ANZAPPL). By contrast the main academic journals associated with the area often use broader terms: for example, primarily associated with (although not always edited or published within) North America are: *Law and Human Behavior*, *Behavioral Sciences and the Law*, *Psychology, Public Policy and the Law* (which is also registered as a law journal within the United States tradition). In Europe there are: *Psychology, Crime and Law* and *Legal and Criminological Psychology* and there was *Expert Evidence*, arguably the most interdisciplinary in its original design (by the editors of this volume) and format. In Australia there is *Psychiatry, Psychology and Law*. Perhaps the goal, with journals, is to have as broad a title as is possible, without losing sight of the core topic. Relevance to other disciplines—for example, lawyers, criminologists, psychiatrists—is suggested by several journals, but the core audience is psychologists. Membership of editorial boards is predominantly by psychologists. Many are dually qualified as lawyers but known, predominantly, as psychologists. But this is not dissimilar from other journals. For example the *International Journal of Evidence and Proof*, which has attracted some important papers from psychologists and might be thought to be interdisciplinary by virtue of title and topic, only has lawyers on its Editorial Board. The 'marketing truth' would appear to be that, however open and broadly based a journal may appear in terms of its title and organisation, it needs to be written for a discrete disciplinary audience. It is 'nice' if other disciplines read it but its economy must not be based upon an assumption that it will be.

The organisers of conferences are keen to distinguish their area from others, to be different, and this can cause problems of perception. For example, many if not most members of the EAP&L are interested in criminology. But neither the EAP&L's objectives nor meetings are usually limited to such topics. So membership of more explicitly criminological associations, or narrowing of conferences to such topics, may prove attractive at least until psychology and law becomes as recognised a subdiscipline as it now is in North America. There is certainly a great danger, particularly within the EAP&L and the journals published in Europe, that 'psychology and law' is perceived as limited to criminal justice issues, albeit sometimes widened to include mental health law. There is a particular risk that the potential of psychology to inform issues in civil law will be underinvested. But, perhaps, it is the inexplicit which will cause the greatest damage to 'psychology and law' conferences. Nowhere is it stated that practitioners are not welcome. However, at least by reference to recent meetings of the AP-LS and EAP&L, practitioners have been grossly underrepresented. It is not just that this area has such potential for practical application, but also that it is relevant to so many professions. Why do so few police officers, for example, attend psychology and law conferences? Psychiatrists, nurses, prison governors, etc.?

Why is it not 'Behavioural Sciences and Law'? If the focus, or the engine powering, of the interest in this area was interdisciplinarity, or the concern was intraprofessional collaboration then, it is submitted, it would be. The judge or other lawyer, whether a practitioner or an academic, is unlikely to care about the disciplinary and occupational distinctions which separate psychologists and psychiatrists, for example. Both of the disciplines and professions—psychology and psychiatry—have useful information to offer to courts and to law reform organisations. And many other disciplines and professions have much that is very important to offer. For example, consider the contribution of economists, such as Nobel prize winner Herbert Simon (1959, 1960), to our knowledge of how and why human beings make the decisions they do. Consider its potential impact on judicial decision-making, on reducing miscarriages of justice, if only we could better develop the links both in research and application.

Psychology cannot—and nobody realistically suggests that it does or could—explain all, completely or sufficiently, areas of human behaviour occurring in legal contexts. An understanding of the behaviour of tenants (of a housing complex), for example, needs to include contributions from economics, sociology and politics, at the very least. While psychology has contributed significantly to our current understanding of criminal behaviour it would be inappropriate to ignore the contributions of several other disciplines, traditions and methodologies. The critical question is whether focusing, relatively narrowly, on 'psychology' hinders inquiries, limits theories or falsifies conclusions.

So Should it be Psychiatry, Psychology and Law?

Psychiatrists, in contrast with psychologists (although they have overlapping interests in physiology and neurology), undertake a medical education and have a medical qualification. Medical education, largely because of its duration and consequent cost, is broadly perceived as a 'professional education'. It is undertaken with a view to becoming a practitioner. In that regard there is a similarity with the study of law. In the United States law is a post-graduate degree. In the United Kingdom, at least, a law degree exempts its holders from part of their professional training. In both countries students invariably choose the course with an expectation of practising. Law and psychiatry courses are rarely undertaken purely out of intellectual curiosity, perhaps unfortunately. That is more likely to be the case with the study of psychology. Indeed, in popular formats, articles on psychological topics help to sell many popular magazines and books. Indeed popularised psychology may be as important to magazines and general bookshops as law, law enforcement and the courts are to the visual media of television and film.

A greater 'affinity' between judges, practising lawyers and psychiatrists may be perceived. Various explanations may be offered. For example, both law and medicine are much older professions and have been recognised subjects for study in universities for much longer than psychology. There are, also, similarities and differences in social status and earnings between the three groups in many countries. But, it is submitted, a very important factor is the role that psychiatrists play in court. Unlike most other professions appearing before courts, psychiatrists often hold a 'key' to the disposal of the case. By giving evidence that a psychiatric disposal is appropriate, and being able to offer a service (a hospital bed or outpatient treatment), the psychiatrist can remove a difficult human problem from the courts. On other occasions, by affirming that a particular test applies, the psychiatrist can provide the judge with a solution to a case. For example, a psychiatrist may give evidence that a defendant was suffering from 'diminished responsibility' even when, as in England and Wales at least, the tests are legal and moral rather than medical (Gunn et al., 1993). Such evidence allows a judge to deal with the case in a particular manner, a conviction for manslaughter rather than murder in England and Wales (Homicide Act 1957, s. 2). Redding, Floyd and Hawk (2001) provide empirical support for this. In their study lawyers preferred psychiatrists' evidence to that of psychologists and sought evidence on the ultimate legal issue even though it was legally prohibited!

A problem with 'psychiatry and law' is that it connotes, and regularly appears to be limited to, 'mental health law'. Certainly that is a significant and substantial area of law. It encompasses many important topics: liberty of the individual through detention issues, freedom of decision and action through decisions about capacity. But it over-whelmingly focuses on solving problems with or for individuals. Should a particular person be detained because mentally disordered and with certain kinds and degrees of problems? Should treatment be imposed because of mental disorder, lack of capacity and perceived need? Mental health law is very applied. That is not a criticism! The point is that by limiting 'psychiatry and law' to, or equating it with, 'mental health law' we close off or reduce opportunities for enriching our understanding of human behaviour, individual and social, through psychiatric research and insights. And any limits in our understanding of human behaviour will, consequentially, follow through into less than ideal legal responses. 'Psychiatry and law' ought not to be limited to mental health law. A greater understanding of the brain and mind could challenge and invigorate several legal assumptions about human behaviour. New techniques for mapping brain activity are leading to major questions being asked about such assumptions as free will, consciousness, subjectivity (e.g. see Libet, Freeman and Sutherland, 1999). These have major implications for law.

The distinctions, and divisions, between psychiatry and psychology may be exagger-ated. Organisational differences, based upon education routes, may be more important than is necessary for the functional duties. It has been suggested that psychologists are as (or more) competent to treat neuroses, the more behavioural mental disorders. Psychiatrists could specialise on the psychoses. Psychologists are increasingly being recognised as the lead discipline with regard to treating, or responding to, personality disorders (Blackburn, 1993). They have certainly been prominent in the analysis and prediction of dangerousness (Monahan et al., 2001). An official inquiry into abuses at a secure mental health hospital in England, chaired by a judge, readily meted out criticism of individuals (Fallon et al., 1999). It received a recommendation that the principal provider of therapy, for those with personality disorders only, should be forensic psychologists. But it dismissed the proposal insisting that medical supervision and leadership was necessary (paras. 4.5.6–4.5.9). Its reasoning was cursory, which was all the more surprising giving its finding that there were major problems with the quality of medical supervision. It should not be impossible to devise a scheme whereby a psychologist is the responsible clinician, in practice and law, even if he or she is required by legislation, or just by the implications of the ordinary law of negligence, to have regard to psychiatrists' and other doctors' analyses, assessments and recommendations. But the problems start further back. The terms 'treatment' and 'patient' tend to prejudge the issue. We do not have to accept that people require 'treatment' for their behaviour. That approach presupposes a medical model and context that is rarely given. Unfortunately such issues are not taken up when we limit 'psychiatry and law' to 'mental health law'.

A distinction is regularly drawn between normal and abnormal psychology. The former is concerned with understanding and predicting the behaviour of 'ordinary' people, those who would not be considered patients or criminals, for example. 'Normal' psychology might be utilised when seeking an understanding of, for example, decision-making by jurors. After all, jurors are supposed to be representative of the broader community. But then the legal context, of trials and jury rooms, are hardly normal experiences. It is very difficult to replicate conditions equivalent to a trial, and the experience of a jury, in jury research (see chapter by Greene and Wrightsman, in this volume). Indeed the legal contexts for human behaviour can create a number of unique circumstances making inference and generalisation very difficult. So it is submitted that both 'psychiatry' and 'psychology' are far too narrow perspectives for analysing human behaviour in legal contexts and that 'behavioural sciences' is to be preferred. However, while 'behavioural sciences' is a broad enough expression it does not actively involve, or recognise the need for the perspectives and support of, social sciences such as sociology, economics, politics, cultural studies and history.

A 'Behavioural' or a 'Social' Science?

Psychiatry and clinical psychology are alike in their tendency to focus on individuals, although 'individual', here, could include families and similar small units. It is not just that their knowledge base is built upon studies of individuals but also that the clients of practitioners are individuals. The economy for psychological and psychiatric services involves individuals, not groups or communities. Which is the egg and which the chicken? That there is an economic demand for 'individual psychology' must feed through into an impetus, or value imperative, for research that will prove useful to that form of treatment and action. There are subdisciplines of social psychology and social psychiatry. Few clinical psychologists and psychiatrists would deny or diminish the importance of community and social contexts in explaining or treating their patients' problems. Social, or community, psychology and psychiatry have a contribution to make. But 'sick' housing estates do not have a procedure, provision or account to pay for community psychological or psychiatric services. Practitioners are likely to focus on the perceived problems and/or needs of an individual within a family before, if ever, deciding that it is more appropriate to analyse and deal with the problems in terms of family or other group dynamics or problems.

But there have to be limits, in practice. Forever arguing that there are alternative perspectives is easy. We would quickly tire of (and be unable and unwilling to pay) the medical practitioner who, rather than telling us what our problem was, let alone providing treatment, insisted on discovering the views of doctors from other medical specialities—nurses, professions allied to medicine, psychologists, complementary practitioners, and yet more. Alternative perspectives, theories, methods may have something to contribute but it is a case of core and penumbra. Some alternative disciplines, perspectives, theories and methods will more often have/more to offer, in practice. But it is critical that we do not close the door on, or exclude, alternative perspectives, disciplines, etc. And a key question is whether, in the development of interest in 'psychology and law', doors are being closed intentionally or otherwise.

The 'tension' between 'psychology and law' groups, for example in conferences, in courses with different emphases, journals, books, and criminology or 'deviancy study' groups, may be seen as a product of this issue. The former 'groups' are 'happier' with the more individualistic approaches of psychology while the latter 'assume' or emphasise the importance of social explanations. The tension is inevitable and, intellectually over time, will prove productive. But are the developing relationships in and expectations of 'psychology and law' counter-productive because they avoid, deny or do not sufficiently 'speak' of and acknowledge these 'tensions'?

For example, those who would call themselves 'forensic psychologists' or just psychologists interested in psychology and law would, overwhelmingly, be psychologists trained or practising in clinical or penal settings, or in child or family services. It is a large group but where are the educational, occupational and social psychologists? Their work is also intimately tied up with the law, in many more senses than just the legal regulation of their professional bodies. The 'psychology and law' journals, courses, conferences, books (of which this *Handbook* seeks to be an exception), are dominated by clinical and 'forensic' psychology. Indeed the word 'forensic', which originally simply meant connected with the law and legal system, appears to have been appropriated, at least in the UK, to a particular professional usage. Many still seem to assume that 'psychology and law' is limited to interests in and interaction with the criminal justice system, even when mental health law applications concern the civil law. Educational psychologists, at least in the UK, have a major legal role. Their reports can influence, even if not determine in as powerful a manner as can psychiatrists' reports, how much special provision a child will obtain to help with his or her education. And if the child's parents do not like the report then the psychologist can find himself, or herself, before a special tribunal defending the report and its recommendations. This is as much about law as mental health or prison parole legislation! Occupational psychologists could find their analyses challenged and/or adopted in and by industrial tribunals. And yet these psychologists do not seem to perceive 'psychology and law' as relevant to them. Why do they not wish to come to the party; or have they not been invited? Why should lawyers respect and be interested in the development of 'psychology and law' if it is partial, with regard to the psychologists involved, and the range of explanations offered?

'Law' and What?

'Law' tends, naturally enough, to suggest lawyers. That includes judges and legal practitioners, as well as law academics. But many other disciplines are involved with 'the law'. Police and social workers, for example, give effect to discrete areas of the law. They often know the law affecting their area of work better than many lawyers, at least until a case gets into the courts. But they are not 'lawyers'. And those legislators who make the law, even if they rarely draft (particularly draft well) the law, are not thought of as 'lawyers'. Is this significant? In terms of the model with which this chapter began, it is not significant if 'psychology and law' is considered only to be a subdiscipline. It should be significant if 'psychology and law' is to involve collaboration between disciplines. And it, most certainly, is very significant if it is to be a project wherein the goal, by developing the disciplines and working together, is to increase and improve the quantity and quality of justice experienced.

In all three senses—'psychology and law' as a subdiscipline, as collaboration or as a project—'law' is clearly the junior partner. Lawyers, certainly in the narrow sense, are rarely to be seen at psychology and law conferences, whether national or international. They are rarely represented on the editorial boards of the relevant journals, and more rarely still have editorial roles. And yet the interest is said to be in 'psychology *and* law' (rather than 'psychology *in* law') and lawyers are, or could be, major consumers of behavioural science. Most obviously they can introduce behavioural science, as expert evidence, into court proceedings. But they could draw upon behavioural science for the skills they need to improve their competence as lawyers, such as in interviewing clients, testing evidence and making decisions. And they could, and should, use behavioural science to inform the legislation they draft.

Psychology and law might be represented as a subset of the socio-legal approach, along with economics and law, history and law, etc. But the expression 'socio-legal' seems to be used in both broader and narrower senses (Cotterrell, 1984). In its broader sense it includes every approach to understanding law which includes its social setting. In this sense it includes behavioural sciences and law, as well as psychology and law. In its narrower sense it refers just to sociology and law which, depending upon particular theoretical approaches (e.g. Marxist), could include other social sciences such as economics and politics. In the broader sense behavioural sciences and law appears to be accepted as a subset of socio-legal studies, rather than the converse. Social factors, such as the distribution of power and other resources, cultural perceptions and understandings, are the context, or macro level, for understanding the more specific, or micro level, human behaviour.

Interest in socio-legal studies appears to have been (particularly in the sense of having active, interested and supportive organisations rather than isolated individuals), more long-standing than interest in behavioural sciences and law. Of course this depends upon what is to be included within the terms. For example, realist approaches to law pre-date regular use of the term 'socio-legal' (Hunt, 1978). Realist approaches emphasise what 'really' happens in fact, in practice, rather than what is stated in the rules in the statute or case law. What, really, is the speed limit that the police will act upon rather than what is it stated to be in the formal legislation giving them their powers to intervene? (In the UK it seems to be 10% higher than the sign-posted limits.) The realists' interest was in the effects of law rather than in the more traditional, for academic lawyers, interest in the detailed analysis of legal doctrine and terminology in legislation and precedent cases. But realism was a product of lawyers, including judges, looking 'outwards' rather than other disciplines looking 'inwards' to law and legal practice. It was an initiative by lawyers (Haney, 1980). Does that count, given that realist studies, even if empirical, are not necessarily or particularly interdisciplinary?

The interest in socio-legal studies in the United Kingdom, for example, if measured by the establishment of facilitating organisations or the creation of new journals, preceded the interest in psychology and law by about two or three decades. Is this significant? Well, consider the comparative competence of socio-legal and psychology and law studies to deliver robust research findings of practical value to government and research funding bodies. It is submitted that we ought to expect a greater interest in behavioural sciences and law than in socio-legal studies, from those agencies. It has a greater potential for research based upon a rigorous methodology, particularly in the control of variables. This is certainly not to question the value of socio-legal research or its potential for scientific credibility within the limits of ethically possible research. It is just to comment that the comparative interests in, and funding of, research between behavioural sciences and law and socio-legal studies is counter-intuitive. Again any testing of this hypothesis will depend upon agreement about terms. Is research by psychologists on legal topics—for example, children's experience of being witnesses in court proceedings—psychological or interdisciplinary research? However we answer such questions the key point remains, it is submitted that there is nowhere near as much behavioural science research as might be expected, particularly in comparison with socio-legal research. This is particularly true of research emanating from law schools.

Within socio-legal studies law is the senior partner to other disciplines. The journal editors and conference organisers are in law departments. It is the product of a broadening of law, an adoption of a wider perspective, the recognition of a much wider range of factors and influences as relevant to understanding law in both its statement and its practice. A lack of training in research methodology handicaps many academic, socio-legal lawyers who might otherwise wish to undertake empirical research. In marked contrast with the USA, law is an undergraduate degree in the UK. That degree is focused on acquiring knowledge of substantive rules and a relatively narrow range of intellectual techniques for handling legal materials. It rarely contains training in research methodology, whether to enable its graduates to undertake appropriate empirical research or even to recognise good and bad science. Consequently, much socio-legal writing is more theoretical, or involves policy analysis, than is empirical. The objectives of socio-legal research are, perhaps, not as pragmatic as might be expected.

There are separate national and international organisations that proclaim a focus on psychology and law, psychiatry and law, and sociology and law, although the Australian and New Zealand Association of Psychiatry, Psychology and Law differs, slightly. There are separate conferences and journals. Assuredly there is some overlap in substantive topics. In particular there is extensive overlap where the focus is criminal justice, although different terms, such as 'criminology' and 'deviancy studies', betray different emphases. Perhaps the pragmatic and professional contexts have hastened this. There are some key figures, in psychology and law, who would be invited to speak at psychiatry, criminology, penology or, less likely, law conferences. And judges are likely to be invited to speak at other disciplines' meetings and conferences although, it is submitted, that would be more due to their status and role in the legal system than to their intellectual discipline. But the rank and file adherents tend to 'stick to their own'. There are, for example, among those interested in the causes of and responses to criminal conduct, separate groups for lawyers, psychologists, social scientists, and that is not counting professional groupings, such as prison psychologists.

There is a good economic reason why practising lawyers should not attend psychology and law conferences. Most are self-employed or must earn fees for their firm. Academics, and others who are salaried, continue to be paid whilst they attend a conference (or just a few). Indeed they will often be able to reclaim some of their expenses. Not only is time spent at a conference time when practising lawyers are not earning, but also they are unlikely to receive expenses to meet the costs of their attendance. The same appears largely true with judges even though they are salaried. But then what are these lawyers likely to learn at a 'psychology and law' conference that is useful to them? Critiques of a law—for example, tests for assessing the competence of a person with a mental disorder, or descriptions of a legal practice such as interviewing—may be interesting but they are not useful to them in their jobs. Lawyers do not have an economic interest in descriptions, particularly critical, of the law or legal practice. That too much faith is placed in the competence of eyewitnesses is of no economic interest to them while the law remains the same. They have a vested interest in the status quo for that is what they operate. They need to call and examine eyewitnesses (where this is permitted by the national law), operate tests of capacity, or persuade judges and juries by further elaboration of the skills of advocacy. Of course this does not stop individual lawyers being interested in and very concerned about, for example, the calibre of eyewitnesses. And they may be so concerned that they will spend time and money pressing for law reform. But it is not in their immediate economic interests. Indeed, if the law is changed they will have to spend time, which is not directly compensated, in learning the new rules. They have an economic interest in the law *not* being changed.

The point may be clearer if a comparison is made. Doctors, for example, have an interest in knowing about recent research. If a new diagnostic test or treatment becomes available for meningitis and it merits sufficient credibility and interest to be described in medical journals, then doctors, or at least those with patients who may present with meningitis, need to know about those developments. If they do not know about that research then they may, in due course, be found to have been negligent and professionally incompetent. They have a professional and economic interest, at least to avoid legal liability, in being up-to-date with recent research. By comparison, consider that some new research has been published on interviewing—for example, on how a cognitive interview may increase memory of past events without increasing errors, or research on how and why people tend to make erroneous decisions. That might be thought to be useful and relevant research for lawyers to know about, but they do not have the same interest, economic or otherwise, in learning about it and extending their professional skills. Interviewing may be a key legal skill for many lawyers but few have demonstrated any interest in learning about it (however, see Heaton-Armstrong, Shepherd and Wolchover, 1999, for evidence of interest by practising lawyers in the UK). The fact that one lawyer interviewed a witness utilising a cognitive interview is not going to give him or her any economic or professional advantage over another lawyer who continued to use traditional interviewing techniques. Indeed the former is likely to be at a disadvantage in that cognitive interviews are liable to take longer than traditional legal interviews. They do not have the same interest as, for example, doctors in learning about such developments. Within the present system there is little to reinforce or encourage practising lawyers to learn more about the behavioural sciences. It is, unfortunately, fanciful to think in terms of them being sued, in the law of negligence, for not knowing sufficient about, for example, the unreliability of confessions and how they might best be tested. And yet their ignorance could lead to their client being imprisoned and, in some jurisdictions, executed. For them, continuing education concerns lawyers' law, changes and other developments in the statement of the law.

And, Of, With, In

Is it psychology 'and' law, the psychology 'of' law, psychology 'in' law or 'legal psychology'? Does it matter? This is not a question about the correct use of words or grammar but the perception of the 'psychology/law' area/interest/enterprise. The key question is whether it is an interdisciplinary project or just a subdiscipline. 'Legal psychology', 'forensic psychology' and the 'psychology of law' are merely the study of psychology as applied to the law and the legal system. 'Forensic psychology' is a subspeciality. The term is often coined with a view to developing courses relevant to psychologists wishing to work in such legal settings as prisons, forensic hospitals or with the police. Those professionals' interests are in research that will help them to perform their jobs more effectively and efficiently, and which will make their contribution and role more distinctive. They need to know the law, and about the legal system, to the extent that it provides organisational structures and working practices for their work. They have no particular interest, as a subprofession or discipline, in the content of the law, or its reform, although they may take an interest as individuals or a group. The other terms are wider and would, for example, embrace those interested in legal topics or procedures—for example, identification procedures, interviewing witnesses, jury decision-making. But there is nothing necessarily interdisciplinary, or intraprofessional, about those projects. How good or bad for example, and in which circumstances, using which methods, people are good or bad at identifying others they have observed in the past, can be studied and researched without ever talking to a lawyer, even without studying what are the current national rules and procedures governing identification evidence. So what? Many psychologists focus on a particular aspect of current life, for example sport, animal behaviour, education. These psychologists are doing something very similar, just choosing a focus of the law, legal procedures and legal system. Is psychology *and* law different? Yes! (See below.) It has the possibility of denoting and becoming a genuinely inter-disciplinary project.

So, it is submitted, of the model or three categories or 'levels' of relationship suggested at the start of this chapter, the current state of 'psychology and law' is closest to 'subdiscipline'. And it is 'psychology' rather than 'behavioural science'. While there are examples of collaboration, that is not the order of the day. Whilst there is evidence of researchers being concerned about the state of the law and the practice, with regard to their specialist topics, there is little evidence in the books, journals, courses or conferences, of a commitment to seeking change, improvement, of using their research and insights to promote greater or more efficient justice for more people. It may be referred to as 'psychology and law' but that, currently, is a misnomer.

> In times past, little enduring has come from the collaboration between psychologists and lawyers, periods of mutual interest have been sporadic and unsustained.... We study the law to understand but also to improve it, and hopefully to make it more fair and more just. The time has come to think explicitly about whether and how this can be done.
> (Haney, 1980, p. 150)

WHY: WHOSE FAULT?

Is Collaboration Possible?

It has been suggested that law and the social sciences will never be able to collaborate effectively. The argument is that the assumptions and methods, adopted by the disciplines, are inconsistent. Campbell (1974, building on Aubert, 1963), argues that legal thinking is distinctively different from social scientific. Social science seeks to make general rules; law is concerned with applications to specific cases. Lawyers dichotomise whilst scientists recognise that issues are relative. Social scientific thought is probabilistic; law is not. Legal thought is retrospective, it refers back to past events whereas social science aims to make statements about the future. Law is not causal, in a scientific sense; relationships are attributed by rules rather than by findings of fact. Similar points are made by other writers; but they are all mistaken. These alleged differences are a product of a misconception of law and lawyers' work, or the differences are of degree rather than nature.

Lawyers dichotomise, it is said, that is they divide people and the world into mutually exclusive alternative categories such as mentally ill or not, child or adult, possessing capacity or incapable. Psychologists, however, appreciate the relative. This appears to be a good point; but a little thought should show that it involves a gross misunderstanding of what lawyers do. Lawyers do dichotomise. But so do many others, including psychologists, such as when they give expert evidence at trials where the issue is whether someone fits into one category or another, e.g. dangerous or not dangerous. Everyone who has to make a decision—does this patient get this treatment, does this client get that service, if this child placed for adoption—does it. And lawyers are as capable as anyone else in recognising that pain and injury involve a matter of degree, that some litigants have more capacity than others. They try to get more severely injured litigants greater compensation. They dichotomise when the law and legal system requires it, for example when only some people, depending on the degree of their mental disorder and the degree of their need for medication, can lawfully be detained in a hospital. Note that this, like many of the following points, assumes that lawyers are only lawyers when they are in court which is, to be polite, manifestly absurd. Psychologists, psychiatrists and all other manner of behavioural scientists, remain such even when they are not dealing with individual clients. Now if the complaint was that lawyers tend to inappropriately dichotomise when they do not need to do so, and ought not to do so, that their education does not alert them to the misuse of dichotomies, then that would be a good point, although it would deserve empirical verification. They would be guilty of oversimplifying reality. But then dichotomising, and categorising, is a requirement of communication. When is it a thread, a piece of string, or a length of rope? We all do it. The skill, as with careful thinking and reasoning, is to know when it is appropriate and when inappropriate.

Lawyers focus on the past, for example on the incident which led to the court proceedings. And they argue by reference to the precedent cases of past courts. They concentrate upon the past. Psychologists look to the future; they wish to predict. Again, however superficially attractive this distinction may appear, and however superior it might make psychologists feel, it is wrong. Yes lawyers examine past events, say when their client is alleged to have committed an offence, for that is (part of) their job. So do psychologists. What did the child do at school? Why has the child missed school 20 times in the past two months? They too examine the past in order to decide whether and what extra educational services are required. What prior violence has he or she committed? The forensic psychologist needs to know in order to make competent assessments of the likelihood of repeated violence? Lawyers also spend a lot of time looking to the future. The drafting of a contract or a will is an attempt to control the future! What might happen? Right, let us provide that this happens in that event. Again the fallacy is to assume that all lawyers are involved in, and that all law work involves, contested trials. Perhaps people are watching too much television!

Lawyers focus on individual cases, individual clients, which psychology is concerned with groups, patterns, general principles. Lawyers are concerned about a series of individual cases, individualised justice. However psychologists wish to make general pronouncements about the future. They wish to generalise about a range of people, the more the better. Again it is a case of no, and yes. Lawyers do indeed work for individual clients, on specific cases, although they can also work for an organisation and on a group or representative basis. But so do psychologists. They see, examine, and treat, whether on a salaried or other basis, individual patients and clients. It is their job, their means to obtaining payment. The error here, repeated in examples below, is to assume that the only lawyers are practitioners and that the only psychologists are academics and/or researchers. Haney (1980) makes the same distinction; law is idiographic whilst psychology is nomothetic. But he concedes that clinical psychology is idiographic (p. 164). And lawyers can make general statements, are very keen to make broad statements, for example: 'To be guilty of a crime the defendant must have had the proscribed mental state at the time he or she caused the prohibited behaviour or outcome.' The law, particularly in text books, is full of general statements. Often there are narrower rules or statements about when there are exceptions to the general rule. Indeed, in that sense, they are similar to behavioural science and other text books.

Haney (1980), whose arguments are adopted by Schuller and Ogloff (2001) and, to a less explicit extent, by Kapardis (1997), argues that whilst law is applied, psychology is academic. It is true that many, indeed most, lawyers earn their salary from being legal actors. As such they apply the law. But there are academic lawyers, legal researchers and law reform commissioners who are not constrained by processing individual cases and disputes. And even practising lawyers can spend some time examining the law in a general, reflective, even theorising manner. Equally there are practising psychologists. They help or advise clients. They apply their knowledge. Perhaps publishing research is more highly regarded by psychologists, but this distinction between operational and academic is between practitioners and researchers rather than between lawyers and psychologists. If we are going to compare then it should be on a fair basis. Then we will discover that there are academic lawyers, many of whom love to theorise (jurisprudence has a very long and established tradition), and others who see their role as generalising from the particular or recommending changes in broad legal rules. Also there are legal practitioners. There are academic psychologists who seek to find general truths or patterns through their research. And there are practitioner psychologists who apply the information, developed by their academic colleagues, in individual cases.

It is also suggested that law is reactive and psychology proactive. Lawyers have to respond to the problems which their clients bring them, whilst psychologists have considerable control over the areas they research. No. It is the same error. Even forensic psychologists have to provide psychological services for their patients and clients. If they are in private practice they may be so successful that they can afford to pick and choose which clients. But practising psychologists are just like practising lawyers. Academic lawyers, including those interested in behavioural science, have considerable control over their research and special interest topics, just like academic psychologists. The distinction is between practitioners and academics, not between lawyers and psychologists.

Haney (1980) argues that lawyers are concerned with finality, with making decisions which determine the issue or dispute. This may appear true but, once again, only with regard to practising, litigation, lawyers. And it has to be qualified. There can be several hearings before a case finally 'gets to court'. Then, after that 'final' decision there can be several appeals. Even after that, in some jurisdictions there are possibilities of further reviews when miscarriages of justice are suspected, or reprieves. Many would complain that there is not enough finality in legal proceedings, that there are as many 'revolving door' or repeat litigants as there are patients. Many child custody cases are before the courts and other legal actors many times. Indeed 'problem-solving', or speciality courts (see the chapter by Simon in this volume), have developed, in part, because of the repetitive nature of so much legal practice. They use these repeated appearances by defendants as a means of monitoring their compliance with court orders, for example, to desist from drug taking. And law is not very different. Many practising psychologists and psychiatrists also want finality. They want the treatment, or action, that 'solves' or 'cures' their client. As with the courts it may take some time before the plan of action is determined, but these practitioners are working towards a form of finality, a resolution. At most this is a difference of degree rather than of kind. And it involves adopting a theory about law rather than recognising its practice. It certainly does not justify the comment of Schuller and Ogloff (2001, p. 10):

> The model adopted in law is one of legal precedent. In contrast, in psychology the model is one of innovation, and psychologists, in both their research and theorizing, are encouraged to explore novel ideas and methods.

Law is said to be prescriptive, psychology descriptive (Haney, 1980). Again, this appears to be a valid observation, but it involves choosing a limited perspective and claiming that it is representative of the whole. Law, in the guise of legislation, certainly is prescriptive. There are penalties for breach if anyone notices and cares to take action. A contract may also be considered prescriptive as it declares reciprocal obligations. Perhaps that is why so many psychiatrists and psychologists like to use contracts when working with their patients and clients. Is a will descriptive because it describes who is to get what, or is it prescriptive because the courts will have their interpretation enforced, if necessary? Prescription involves telling people what to do. Description simply involves noting what they do. But is that what psychologists do? Just describe what their clients do? Do they never, explicitly or implicitly, indicate what their clients ought to do? Do they do not tell patients how they should manage their symptoms, control their anger, respond to their children, interview witnesses, analyse statements? No, lets face it; psychology also involves 'prescription'. If it didn't there would be no point in employing psychologists. This is another difference of degree—although it is lawyers who are supposed to be the ones who inappropriately dichotomise— rather than of kind. True, psychologists cannot make decisions which the police will enforce, using legal force if necessary. But then their reports may be the reason why someone else, for example a judge, decides that a child is to be removed from one parent and placed with another, or a prisoner is to be refused parole. And the police will enforce, using force if necessary, those orders which the psychologists did not make, just caused.

Law is hierarchical; psychology is empirical (Haney, 1980). Yes, it is true that a higher court can overturn a lower court, that a rule laid down in one precedent case can be overturned by a higher level appeal court. And that, too, can be overturned by legislation. But we are, here, writing of choices, of normative propositions. One court decides, as had been thought to be the rule for centuries, that children between the ages of 10 and 14 can only be guilty of a crime if, in addition to all the other requirements for that particular offence, he or she demonstrates 'mischievous discretion'. But another court thinks that is not the case; either it never was or no longer is (*C.* (*A Minor*) v. *D.P.P.* [1994] 3 WLR 888). Then another, higher, court decides that mischievous discretion is required, that the lower court had no power to deny it, even though it was wise to challenge the need for such a rule (*C.* v. *Director of Public Prosecutions* [1996] 1 AC 1). Finally legislation decides that mischievous discretion is no longer required (Crime and Disorder Act 1998, s. 34). So, yes, a hierarchy is in operation. But, notice, at no stage did anyone state or decide that children between 10 and 14 are no different from adults or from children over 14. Several did state that they thought such children should not be treated as different, that any differences were not sufficiently distinctive to merit a separate and extra legal test. It is about what *ought* to be the position and, because it will have the force of law behind it, it is about what *will* be the position because it would be a waste of time and money, in England and Wales, to go against the courts and then parliament's decision on this issue. However, there is no objection or obstacle to the behavioural scientists, of the world, rising as one and declaring that, empirically, there *is* a difference between these age bands. The most supreme of courts may have spoken, the most democratic of legislatures may have declared, but it doesn't follow that they are, empirically, scientifically, or morally correct. Even lawyers can protest and work towards the day when we, once again, recognise that there is sufficient difference between 10 to 14 year olds and their elders to justify treating them differently, in terms of criminal liability. It is not a case of psychology (science) and law (norms) being incompatible or incapable of collaboration, but rather, as in this example, a demonstration of their potential—and need—to work together, when we do not make normative fallacies.

Law is adversarial; psychology is experimental (Haney, 1980). The adversarial system of justice is based on the premise that the truth is more likely to be discovered if the parties are allowed to argue their cases to the maximum (McEwan, 1998). The premise deserves challenge and investigation. It should be experimented upon. But, again, the distinction between law and psychology is overstated to the point of misrepresentation. Law, in certain legal systems (i.e. not all), is adversarial but only in court proceedings. The experimental method is alive and kicking, even if not very scientific or rigorous, in other legal contexts. Some lawyers find that, for example, writing more individualised and understanding letters gets a better response from debtors they are acting against. Many litigation lawyers will know, from experience if not report, the importance of getting particular kinds of case away from, or before, particular judges. Quite simply law is not synonymous with litigation! There is much more to law than courts. Indeed it is a minority of disputes that ever appear before the courts. The courts could not cope if all the disputes referred to lawyers had to appear before them. And psychology, or part of it, is adversarial. A premise of academic and research psychology is, at least, that the best way of achieving the best science is via competitive publishing. Publish one set of results, after critique by a number of referees. Now others can attack that paper, and criticise the methods, premises and reasoning. And others can join the fray, each advocating their position over those who have gone before. But that is the scientific method, people protest. Indeed they may point out (interestingly given the previously assumed incompatibility with law) that it has been approved and adopted by the Supreme Court of the United States (*Daubert* v. *Merrell Dow Pharmaceuticals, Inc.*, 579 US 563 (1993); see the chapter by Faigman in this volume). The adversarial legal system does not deserve uncritical adoption and preference. But then nor does adversarial publishing of research results. For example 'blind refereeing' is rarely blind. Step 1: identify the most frequently cited author in the list of references. Step 2: who do you know who adopts these methods and has these views, given you should know since you have been asked to referee the paper as a fellow specialist? So often it is not the quality of the contents of the paper, which matter, but the reputation of the journal it is published within. And, no matter how important it is that studies are replicated, journals are not keen to publish papers which simply confirm earlier studies.

Who has the Wrong Idea of Law?

Law is a distinctive discipline. Many note its professional associations. There is an expectation that studying law will lead to professional practice. It may not be as strong an expectation as with the study of medicine, which takes longer, but it is nevertheless strong. Law is not studied in the abstract. Examination of the nature of justice or equality, or the conditions necessary for fairness or independence come, at best, second to study of what the current rules in the local jurisdiction are on a range of topics. Law students are quickly socialised into perceiving instruction on what the current law *is*, and only in their jurisdiction, as being relevant. Instruction on what might be, on when it was, and why it is, are at best less relevant. Separate jurisprudence or legal philosophy courses exist for broader questions about law, justice, etc., to be debated. Such courses may be marketed on the basis that they will provide much needed 'thinking skills' but are often taught, and represented in textbooks, as little more than knowledge of a set of schools of thought which has to be learnt and understood for restatement in answers to examination questions.

Legal education is structurally conservative. Perhaps that is an important aspect of its appeal to many people. But 'law' is not. All right we are back to verbal disputes; it all depends upon what we mean by 'law'. Here 'law' includes reference to the whole enterprise associated with the legal system. Here 'law' does not presuppose an application in statute, case law, a practical value or economic interest for current practising 'lawyers'. It includes interest in the nature and achievement of fairness, equality, justice and other concepts intrinsically associated with 'law'. It includes the making of 'law' from formal statutes and precedents in courts right through to the drafting of agreements and the vast array of rules, whether binding or not, that structure our lives. Just because law courses are not interested in, or provided on, bullying in schools or in-family disputes, it does not follow that they are not legal topics or are not concerned with law. (No claim is being made that they are exclusively legal topics.) Maybe we should keep the courts out of family life, for example, but sometimes (often too late?) they are involved. Fairness, for example, is a basic expectation (and right?) of children as they develop. Should not 'the law' be interested in how this concept or value is developed, shaped, inhibited, even if it is not an issue of economic interest to practising lawyers? In this sense Piaget, and other developmental psychologists, have a great deal with which to inform those interested in law. And, it is submitted, that should be—not least because of the universality of childhood—a core interest of law.

Quite simply 'law' is not synonymous with, or circumscribed by, legal practice or legal education. 'Law' is not limited to what lawyers do. And yet so many act as if it is. Indeed, it is submitted, the critical problem for the future of psychology and law is that so many behavioural scientists are adopting the narrow, and conservative, image or remit of law propagated by practising lawyers and their teachers. If it is to be a genuinely interdisciplinary project then it must be behavioural science 'and' law, not 'of', 'with', 'in' or 'by'.

BEHAVIOURAL SCIENCES AND LAW: AN INTERDISCIPLINARY PROJECT?

The model suggested, at the start of this chapter, identified 'psychology and law' as (a) a subdiscipline, (b) a collaboration and/or (c) a project. Currently, there is more interest in developing psychology and law, or behavioural sciences and law, as a subdiscipline than as a collaboration or a project. In large measure this is an unconscious choice by the psychologists involved. They have considered neither the implications nor the choices. They want to 'do', to be authorities 'in', psychology as it applies in certain particular legal contexts, for example mental health or prisons. There is nothing shameful about this. It is perfectly understandable that individual psychologists, and other behavioural scientists, whether practitioners or researchers, wish to specialise. It is inevitable. It is the route to publication, preference and promotion. Specialist knowledge is valued over generalist. But we should not pretend that it is collaborative, interdisciplinary or international in any meaningful sense. And we should admit and recognise that the potential of psychology and law is not being sought, let alone realised.

However: The Need to Collaborate

Without a genuine attempt at collaboration psychology and law will remain a 'subdiscipline'. That is perfectly justifiable in academic terms—research for its own sake. Ever more detailed research, with ever more powerful conclusions, will be produced, but it will lack salience and value and will not be pertinent to legal issues. We may learn more about identification evidence, for example, but it will not be relevant to or useful in legal contexts unless it engages with legal criteria, even if very critically. The findings will not be usable by the police or other legal actors. The behavioural science will be regarded as irrelevant or impractical. Courts and legislatures will continue to make their assumptions about human behaviour without fear of being contradicted, because there are no mechanisms for them to learn what is known or knowable, and the dangerous consequences of their ignorance. A negative spiral will continue. If the research is not relevant, directly or indirectly, to practical issues then who will fund it? If the research is not undertaken then its potential is not appreciated. In reality psychology and law are condemned to grow in collaboration or fail through desuetude.

Avoidance of Employer and Employee Relations

There is a need for collaboration, but an employer–employee relationship must be avoided. Too often and too readily psychology drifts into an employee role to law. Psychology should not limit itself to lawyers' agendas, needs or perspectives. The law, for example, may be that when assessing an adult's capacity to make a legal decision, no account is to be taken of the complexity of the manner in which the issues are posed. Perhaps the lawyers responsible for creating the test were ignorant of the psychology on the topic; see the reports of the Law Commission for England and Wales on the capacity of people with a mental disorder to make a legal decision (Law Commission, 1995, and earlier reports cited therein). However, once proposals arc adoptcd into law they create a reality. But that does not make the law good, wise, sensible, informed or 'just'. In one sense we have to accept the reality of the status quo. In another sense we are duty bound to rebel, to protest, to complain that the law is not as good, wise, sensible, informed or as 'just' as it could be. Behavioural scientists, as practitioners, could find that they are expected to apply psychologically misinformed laws and procedures.

Lawyers are, in one sense, right to ask expert witnesses inappropriate questions. They may be trying to convince a court about a legal test or distinction which is based upon poor psychology. It may be an inappropriate dichotomy. 'Is this defendant dangerous or not; it is a simple question?' They may ask the expert to draw conclusions about a specific individual when the witness can only draw inferences from the behaviour of a research group of people with some similar features. Their excuse may be that the current law is formulated in such a way as to make the question 'appropriate'. The expert witness, it is submitted, is not right to answer those questions, except under protest (see the chapter on risk by Carson in this volume). The lawyer may fairly claim to be doing his or her job. The witness is not similarly excused when he or she, by answering the inappropriate questions, not only provides the information question sought but also implies that it is appropriate to seek and use the information in the manner the court or lawyer proposes. Every answer, by an expert witness, has two aspects. One is the information sought; the other is a validation of the enquiry and its methods of using the information.

Ah, But: Acknowledging it is Not Perfect

Ah but, come the excuses. We do not know, the behavioural scientists will excuse, all that there is to know about identification, deceit, discrimination, attachment or whatever. And there will always be more to learn. We can only, at best, tell the courts, law reformers and parliaments, what is currently known about these and other topics. And we may be proved wrong in the future. And, what is more, many of these topics involve value judgements, policy choices, which are not 'rational', and are beyond science. To take perhaps the most basic example; is 'truth' the objective of our courts? Are our criminal courts designed as the best knowable means of producing the greatest number of accurate decisions, or at least the fewest erroneous guilty verdicts? Or, in reality, do they have other objectives which impede these goals, such as providing public assurance that justice appears to be being done and satisfying people that the system is 'fair' because it will allow lawyers to fight for you should you be accused of an offence? Is the cost of achieving justice always irrelevant? When we seek to distinguish those people who are capable of making legal decisions, and those who are not, are issues of efficiency, such as a perceived need to get decisions made, irrelevant?

And there is the more classic complaint that, anyway, behavioural scientists cannot really help the courts. The courts want to know about the particular case. 'Is witness X's identification evidence/confession/opinion reliable?' The expert witness may insist, to the court or to himself or herself, that he or she can only give evidence about witnesses with some similar characteristics. So some psychologists do not like giving expert evidence, because the courts will misuse their evidence, and possibly them. Others do not mind because they are only giving the court general information and leaving it to the judges to apply it in the specific case. But these arguments to do not satisfy. Those who will not give evidence, because the courts will/may misuse it, are nevertheless deciding that it is acceptable for the courts to make a decision without the benefit of their evidence. Either way they are condemned to participating in a likely error by a court. Those who give evidence, but place responsibility on the court for its use, are avoiding responsibility. What would they do, if they were the 'treating' professionals, or otherwise were decision makers with practical consequences (such as to release an offender or suspect), in the specific case? Which way would they decide? And how would they decide? They would draw upon studies of people with similar characteristics. They would do what the court would do, infer to the specific from the general. That is what practitioners are condemned to do. And, being more knowledgeable of the limits of their knowledge and decision-making pitfalls, they may do it better than the courts.

And even if there is a good excuse for reluctance to give the courts expert evidence—for example, concern about the experience of being questioned in court—there are none for failure to inform law commissions, and other law reform organisations, as well as legislatures, about the best, current, behavioural science. Indeed it is professionally perverse, given the concerns expressed about inferring from general knowledge to specific cases, for the modal contribution of psychology to law to be via the giving of expert testimony in individual trials. Those concerns do not exist when the issues are what should the general legal tests, law, be?

THE NEED FOR A BEHAVIOURAL SCIENCE AND LAW 'PROJECT'

Collaborating for 'Justice'

'Psychology and law' are condemned to collaborate, or fail entirely. It is an illusion that a value-free, methodologically perfectly proper, science of psychology of law can be created (King, 1986). At the very least law is contextual and changeable. However, so much can be done to inform law and enable legal actors to be more effective, efficient and just. Collaboration is insufficient. It is not just that it will, inevitably, be unequal but also that it will be driven by differences. It arises out of, and reinforces, the fact that the lawyer and the behavioural scientist have different backgrounds, disciplines, methods and goals. Collaboration also tends to be topic specific; for example, the psychologist is keen to know ever more about the recall of past events. A practising lawyer will be interested in recall of evidence, which will only be parts of recall of specific past events, by particular witnesses. Research lawyers, seeking to critique and/or propose alternative rules, may want to know about recall for general evidentiary purposes. The reasons for legal interest are instrumental; they concern current legal systems, practices and interests. Frameworks of past practice and assumptions get taken for granted. Collaboration is not systematically critical.

What is needed is a 'project', and this should be for further and deeper, more effective and efficient, justice. Yes, this implies adopting a value base, acknowledging a goal, but not uncritically. It would automatically be acknowledged that what 'justice' constitutes is not just vague but controversial. It could mean very different things for different people—for example, the distinctions between formal or procedural justice and substantive or distributive justice, the acceptability of legal executions. Such differences could provide some difficulties but also many opportunities for more rigorous debate about goals and outcomes. Such debates would become explicit rather than remain implicit or, worse, be ignored because uncomfortable or not considered. 'Justice' would be a goal, requiring explanation and elaboration, just as 'science' is a goal, requiring explanation and justification of the specific methodology adopted.

Justice is not the preserve of lawyers or the courts. It is not necessarily their business or trade. So collaboration in such a project is a common interest, a combination of methods and interests to a shared goal—albeit in dabatable detail. Declaring and applying the law may have very little to do with achieving justice in the opinion of many people. Neither lawyers nor behavioural scientists can claim any prior rights to, knowledge of, or skills in achieving justice. And yet, whether in researcher, teacher, policy-maker or practitioner roles, both lawyers and behavioural scientists can have interests in achieving more of it. It is what can unite them. They can ignore it, if they wish. They can research legal issues in isolation of legal contexts and perspectives. Law practitioners can simply apply the law, seeking to maximise their clients' interests, irrespective of the merits of the case either because they do not care about justice or because they believe that playing that role is the best means of achieving justice (for example, they believe in the adversarial system). But, ultimately, a disinterest in the promotion of justice will damage the disciplines and professions involved, as much as a disinterest in methodology. It is one thing to seek and argue for a particular meaning of justice; it is very different to be disinterested in it.

Conditions for the Development of the 'Psychology and Law' Project

Drawing upon the discussion above it is submitted that the development of a genuinely interdisciplinary and intraprofessional 'psychology and law' should be based upon the following understandings.

1. It should be 'behavioural sciences and law' rather than 'psychology and law', and it should not just be open to, but encourage review by, the social sciences and their contributions (see the chapter by Savage in this volume). The focus should be upon greater understanding of human behaviour, irrespective of professional or disciplinary distinctions developed for other reasons. Law collaborators have no need of frustration by disciplinary distinctions and professional rivalries. The need, for example, is to predict violence by people diagnosed as having a personality disorder. Whether that comes from a psychiatrist, a psychologist, or someone else is unimportant, although the quality of the science most certainly is. That is not to deny that law collaborators may need to understand how different disciplinary or professional backgrounds can lead to different approaches and analyses. And this does not deny the meaningfulness and value of the distinctions that have developed. It may continue to be more productive to have, for example, psychology and law conferences than behavioural sciences and law conferences. There may be occasions when it is useful to examine the specific contribution of psychology. But conferences, journals, books, courses, etc., should be open to those interested in understanding, explaining, predicting and altering human behaviour, be they police officers, prison governors, law reformers or whatever.

2. We should recognise that the project is applied as well as theoretical, and practical as well as principled. Research psychologists are not the only behavioural scientists. Very many disciplines and professions have, at least, overlapping interests in the development of this project. Particularly because the project is so open to debate and controversy, to value disputes and to different interpretations of 'justice', it is critical that the best contemporary methods of research are utilised wherever possible. But a different range of methods must be recognised as inevitable. There is a place for single case studies and qualitative analyses (see King, 1986).

3. The 'law' must not be limited to legislation or case law precedents. Better-understood 'law' is pervasive and more general than its specific and relatively narrow manifestations in legislation and case law would suggest. We can be the only car approaching the junction and yet we obey the traffic signal which tells us to stop. Law is but one system of regulating human behaviour and not necessarily the most important or effective. Why resort to expensive legislation if the same effects can be achieved by other routes? In particular our enquiries should include codes, norms and agreements. We acquiesce in the authority, perhaps more frequently, of many more people than just judges. The mystique of 'law' should be tackled. Law is, for example, just one example of how to maintain order. We all, at one time or another, make and seek to enforce rules. These could be rules for our children or subordinates at work. We all read rules, including instructions on how to use appliances. And, beyond that, there are norms, standards and expectations. Of course it will be objected that this is giving 'law' such a wide meaning as to have no value. No, whilst it is not contended that these rules are as important as those passed at great expense by parliaments, they still have significance for the people involved. Indeed such rules may be more significant. Office rules, for example, may impact on our lives more than statutes.

The point is that rules, rule-making, rule-breaking, is a legitimate and valuable subject for study irrespective of the power, authority and legitimacy of the rule-maker. The presence of norms about proper conduct, expectations and standards is often sufficient to mean that formal rules are unnecessary. (Self-regulation, for example, is often cited as a core feature of a profession that entitles it to be independent of state regulation; Johnson, 1972.) We often wonder at why we stop and wait at red traffic lights even when there is nobody else around either to have a prior right to use the junction or to observe our criminal conduct. Perhaps we would understand more, and propagate more effective laws, if we studied norm and rule observance generally, not just formal laws. Certainly we can analyse and generalise about the features of clear and easily comprehensible laws. Drafting clear rules is a skill that can be analysed and taught. Lawyers are not the only people who would benefit from such skills. Why, when practitioners find contracts an effective and efficient means of working with, for example, mentally disordered people, does our law not seize on that experience and develop them (Carson, 1999)?

4. The psychology and law project should not limit itself to the formal courts and tribunals propagated by the state authority. There are, and need to be, so many other venues where disputes can be aired and resolved. Courts and trials are dramatic. They are a staple of the diet of television schedules. But many of us (well the non-lawyers amongst us) get through life, and more desperately want to get through life, without going anywhere near a court. So many tips of icebergs, so many misleading impressions, are involved. Contested criminal trials are atypical; the vast majority of people plead guilty! It is a very small percentage of civil claims, 1% in England and Wales, which reach full trial. And further reforms, towards more alternative dispute resolution, are advocated as necessary to maintain the legal system. A much higher proportion of cases affecting children and families will get to court. Active judicial choice or supervision is required for many of those decisions. That is admitted. But what of the family disputes that do not get to court? We know or suspect that the violence against partners and children, which reaches the courts, is another tip of another iceberg. Problem-solving judges (see chapter by Simon in this volume) are responding to the criticism that the courts make no or too little difference. They are concerned with efficacy as well as procedural and substantive correctness. That is greatly to be applauded. But how are the courts, or the law, to impact upon the hidden violence, especially when family life is so highly regarded and protected? The family, like the school, contributes greatly to our understandings, assumptions and expectations of how disputes are to be perceived and tackled. And yet the predominant focus of psychology and law is on formal trial procedures. We need to examine law, procedures and legal systems as being akin to technology. In a world where knowledge, science and technology have and are developing at considerable pace we rely upon a technology of law that has changed very little, particularly in comparison with those other areas of endeavour. The 'mystery' and 'magic' of it being 'law' and concerning 'justice' has, for far too long, discouraged us from conceiving of it as merely a way of doing a particular kind of business, producing a particular product, albeit exceptionally important.

5. We need to focus on prevention as well as pathology. Psychologists and other behavioural scientists have aped lawyers' preoccupation with sorting out problems which have gone wrong, crimes committed, contracts broken, injuries inflicted. Obviously some lawyers must work in that area. It is also the obvious context for their remuneration. Specialist services are required; knowledge is both power and a source of income. But the prevention of disputes should command much greater attention and resources than it does. People used to be laughed at for suggesting that couples should prepare, and agree, detailed contracts before they decided to get married. Now the practice is much more common although, unfortunately, it is primarily associated with financial settlements among the wealthy media community. Whilst questionnaires and articles about whether couples are compatible with each other will be read avidly, the notion that better science should be called in to help to ensure that a married couple behave more mutually towards each other is still regularly dismissed. And yet, by the time of divorce, there may well be children who are liable to experience adjustment problems and be partners who have been violated emotionally, sexually and physically. The usual first objection, to the very idea of relationship or marriage contracts, is the thought of them being fought over in a court. Almost invariably and immediately people contemplate traditional legal outcomes even though they are atypical! A contract is viewed in terms of its breach, what happens in court, rather than what it helps people to achieve before—if!—there is a sufficient breach to require such a response. We focus on the dramatic, the visible, and not on the great good work that legal interventions might achieve via prevention.

How could psychologists and other behavioural scientists work with lawyers to develop a technology of prevention? For example, committees of inquiry, say into child abuse or the apparently inappropriate discharge of a patient or prisoner, regularly conclude that there was a 'system failure'. The phrase often seems to be used as a means of concluding that something went wrong and is to be condemned, even if no individual can be pinpointed with blame. It is more than a breakdown in communication, another favourite finding. But what are these 'system failures' and why do these reports fail to analyse them more closely to provide practical advice on their avoidance? Most of these reports, substantially it is suggested because they are chaired by lawyers or because they are undertaken with 'legal techniques' or 'technology', adopt an individualistic analysis. What did each person do, and how did that interact with another person's contribution, to which ends? That approach is, it must be admitted, very popular with the aggrieved parties (provided it blames someone) and the media. But it is very inadequate. Social, cultural, organisational approaches and assumptions, etc., are relatively poorly understood or illuminated. The focus is on explicit decisions, actions, and yet we know from our experience of daily life that much occurs that is unplanned, not thought about, automatic. We seem surprised that a detailed forensic review of a past short period of time will produce findings that people were not as alert, insightful or knowledgeable as they might have been. But, perhaps we are beginning to see a greater focus on prevention and systems with the new approach to risk, which emphasises its management as well as assessment. (See the chapter by Heilbrun and Kramer in this volume.)

6. The project should, explicitly, be international. First, the role and importance of international law, international tribunals and international crime are increasing, but 'psychology and law' has not responded. The practical focus has led to a national focus, albeit often more implicit rather than explicit; what is 'dangerous' as understood in our legal system or who has 'capacity' under our national legal test? But science should be international, not constrained by particular national contexts. It may lead to controversy over which types of legal system should be adopted but psychology and law should have a voice. Secondly, why should every country have to re-invent legislative wheels? A great deal is already known on a range of psychology and law topics, for example identification. That knowledge could be turned into a 'consensus statement'. It would have to include qualifications about, for example, future research and the importance of social and cultural contexts. It could receive an official ac-knowledgement, an *imprimatur*, from an international organisation, for example the existing three psychology and law associations. That should carry considerable weight with legislatures and law reform bodies. It could help national psychology and law societies to establish themselves. It would demonstrate the relevance of the subdisci-pline and its project. It could emphasise the 'international market' for science; there is no good reason why expert witnesses should only give evidence in the courts of the countries where they live and/or work. And it could speed up moves to improve the justice experienced by people around the world. It is not enough, for example, that the examination of children's evidence is improved in some countries but ignored in others. Thirdly, there is so much to be learnt from a comparative perspective, both experimentally and in terms of comparing substantive laws and procedures.

7. The project should be concerned with reality as well as formality, with what happens in practice and not just what should happen in theory. It should recognise that what happens in the courts may be unrepresentative of what happens in similar cases. What is the point in having, for example, a very refined and research informed test of capacity of mentally disordered people to make legal decisions if, in practice, very few get a chance to make those decisions because family or staff take the decisions for them in the names of charity and efficiency?

The Project has Begun

It is submitted that aspects of such a behavioural sciences and law project are already developing. It is exemplified by interest in and action on such topics as restorative and community justice and in therapeutic jurisprudence. Both are concerned with visions of justice and, most interestingly, are challenging traditional legal 'technologies'. Restorative justice (see the chapter by Drogin, Howard and Williams in this volume) expresses concern for the interests of victims, witnesses and affected communities, as well as perpetrators, and the families of all. But it is not just a value judgement or pressure group. It is demonstrating greater effectiveness than more traditional ways of 'doing justice'. And the rich literature on therapeutic jurisprudence (see chapter by Petrucci, Wexler and Winick in this volume) is testament to how laws and procedures regularly have anti-'therapeutic' effects.

CONCLUSION

But we do not, yet, have a common project. There are enthusiasts for restorative justice, for therapeutic jurisprudence, just as there are for traditional research on specific topics with 'psychology and law'. It is a loose collection of interest groups and the overarching perspectives and links are, as yet, weak. Interest in 'psychology and law' is defined by interest in a specific topic or method within the topic rather than by a more general interest in promoting better laws and greater justice by harnessing an understanding of the behavioural sciences. Perhaps it is too embarrassing, as an individual researcher on a narrow topic or a practitioner responding to what daily life throws up, to admit to an interest in something as apparently grand and/or amorphous as 'justice'. But, provided minds are kept open and respectful critique is always encouraged, it is not a bad thing. It is what unites us as a community of behavioural scientists and lawyers, both researchers and practitioners.

Haney (1993) fears that psychology and law has lost its momentum. He poses many important questions which have not been identified, let alone developed, here. He refers to psychology and law as a change discipline, as rightly being concerned with producing change.

> We are still plagued, I think, by fundamental, lingering doubts about a commitment to social and legal change. (p. 392)

Perhaps, if we can be more explicit—it concerns law reform and not mere change—and acknowledge that it is of the nature of this area of knowledge, particularly if it is to be interdisciplinary and intraprofessional, we can regain some of the excitement of psychology—sorry, behavioural sciences—and law.

REFERENCES

Aubert, V. (1963). The structure of legal thinking. In J. Andenses (ed.), *Legal essays: A tribute to Fride Castberg on the occasion of his 70th birthday*. Boston: Universitetsforlaget.

Blackburn, R. (1993). *The psychology of criminal conduct: Theory, research and practice*. Chichester: John Wiley & Sons.

Campbell, C. (1974). Legal thought and juristic values. *British Journal of Law and Society, 1*, 13–31.

Carson, D. (1999). From status to contract: A future for mental health law. *Behavioral Sciences and the Law, 17* (5), 645–660.

Cotterrell, R. (1984). *The sociology of law: An introduction*. London: Butterworths.

Fallon, P. (His Honour), Bluglass, R., Edwards, B. and Daniels, G. (1999). *Report of the Committee of Inquiry into the Personality Disorder Unit, Ashworth Special Hospital* (vol. 1). London: HMSO.

Gunn, J., Briscoe, O., Carson, D., 'Orban, P., Grubin, D., Mullen, P., Stanley, S. and Taylor, P.J. (1993). The law, adult mental disorder, and the psychiatrist in England and Wales. In J. Gunn and P.J. Taylor (eds), *Forensic psychiatry: Clinical, legal and ethical issues*. Oxford: Butterworth-Heinemann.

Haney, C. (1980). Psychology and legal change: On the limits of a factual jurisprudence'. *Law and Human Behavior*, *4* (3), 147–199.

Haney, C. (1993). Psychology and legal change: The impact of a decade. *Law and Human Behaviour*, *17* (4), 371–398.

Heaton-Armstrong, A., Shepherd, E. and Wolchover, D. (1999). *Analysing witness testimony*. London: Blackstone.

Hunt, A. (1978). *The sociological movement in law*. London: Macmillan.

Johnson, T.J. (1972). *Professions and power*. London: Macmillan.

Kapardis, A. (1997). *Psychology and law: A critical introduction*. Cambridge: University Press.

King, M. (1986). *Psychology in and out of court: A critical examination of legal psychology*. Oxford: Pergamon Press.

Law Commission (1995). *Mental incapacity*. London: HMSO (Law Com. No. 231).

Libet, B., Freeman, A. and Sutherland, K. (Eds) (1999). *The volitional brain: Towards a neuroscience of free will*. Thorverton, UK: Imprint Academic.

Lloyd-Bostock, S. (1988). *Law in practice*. Leicester: British Psychological Society.

McEwan, J. (1998). *Evidence and the adversarial process: The modern law* (2nd edn). Oxford: Hart.

Monahan, J., Steadman, H.J., Silver, E., Appelbaum, P.S., Clark Robbins, P., Mulvey, E.P., Roth, L.R., Grisso, T. and Banks, S. (2001). *Rethinking risk assessment: The MacArthur study of mental disorder and violence*. New York: Oxford University Press.

Redding, R.E., Floyd, M.Y. and Hawk, G.L. (2001). What judges and lawyers think about the testimony of mental health experts: A survey of the courts and bar. *Behavioral Sciences and the Law*, *19*, 583–594.

Schuller, R.A. and Ogloff, J.R.P. (2001). An introduction to psychology and law. In R.A. Schuller and J.R.P. Ogloff (eds), *Introduction to psychology and law: Canadian perspectives*. Toronto: University of Toronto Press.

Simon, H.A. (1959). Theories of decision making in economics and behavioral science. *American Economic Review*, 49, 253–283.

Simon, H.A. (1960). *The new science of management decision*. New York: Harper & Row.

Part 1

Psychological Assessments
for the Courts

Chapter 1.1

Adults' Capacity to Make Legal Decisions

Glynis H. Murphy
University of Kent, UK
and
Isabel C.H. Clare
University of Cambridge, UK

INTRODUCTION

Respect for individual decision-making has assumed increasing importance recently, although the extent of choice available to marginalised and vulnerable men and women has, in practice, often been limited. Such limitations to individual choice have been experienced, and continue to be experienced, by many different groups but have most seriously affected the lives of people with a 'mental disorder'. The term 'mental disorder' is generic, but includes intellectual disability (previously known in the UK as 'mental handicap' and currently referred to as 'mental retardation' or 'developmental disabilities' in the USA), serious mental health problems such as a 'mental illness', and dementia. During the eugenics era, in particular, but also at other times, the rights of individuals with a 'mental disorder' have frequently been seriously violated (e.g. Fennell, 1996; Thomson, 1998; Walsh and Murphy, 2002). Nowadays, more care is purportedly taken to enable people to have greater control over their own lives, but increased autonomy can leave individuals vulnerable to exploitation, particularly in circumstances in which they may not have the ability, or 'capacity', to make relevant decisions for themselves.

In English law (i.e. the law in England and Wales), as in many other jurisdictions, there is a general presumption that adults have capacity. However, this presumption is rebutable. Considerable attention has been given to the approaches which might be used to assess capacity in such situations, with three broad approaches being distinguished: 'outcome', 'diagnostic' and 'functional' (see review by Wong et al., 1999).

Handbook of Psychology in Legal Contexts, Second Edition
Edited by D. Carson and R. Bull. © 2003 John Wiley & Sons, Ltd.

The outcome approach argues that, where an individual makes a decision that differs from most other people's, his or her capacity should be called into question. This approach does not really respect individual freedom to make a choice and it has been rejected by the case law in most jurisdictions. In English law it might contravene the Human Rights Act 1998. Nevertheless, examples of occasions where an outcome approach has been taken in decision-making continue to come to light. For example Ms B, a social worker in the UK who became paralysed from the neck down and was dependent on a ventilator, was judged by medical staff to lack the capacity to make the decision to turn off the equipment that supported her life. Ms B had to resort to the High Court where the judge, Dame Butler-Sloss, held that, given that she was capable, she had an absolute right to make this decision. That her doctors might consider her decision unreasonable, irrational or inadvisable was irrelevant (*Re B* (*Consent to Treatment: Capacity*), [2002] EWHC 429).

A diagnostic (or status) approach involves inferences based on a person's membership of a specific population sharing some characteristic, such as gender, age, 'race' or sexual orientation. Historically, this approach has also been widely used to limit the decision-making of men and women who need or receive treatment and/or support because of a 'mental disorder' but it has been increasingly criticised (see Grisso, 1986, pp. 8ff. for a summary of the main arguments). One of the most salient objections has been that it may be irrelevant to consider clinical diagnosis, since it provides no direct information about the capacity of a specific individual to make decisions within a particular legal context (Grisso and Appelbaum, 1998).

In contrast, a functional approach, which now has most informed support (Grisso, 1986; Law Commission (England and Wales) hereafter Law Commission, 1995; Lord Chancellor's Department, 1997, 1999; Adults with Incapacity Act (Scotland) 2000; Grisso and Appelbaum, 1998) is based on establishing:

(1) a person's 'functional abilities, behaviors or capacities' (Grisso, 1986, p. 15), that is, what he or she understands, knows, believes, or can do that is *directly* relevant to the legal context at issue (such as capacity to manage the role of a defendant in a trial);

(2) the extent to which these functional abilities meet the demands of a particular situation within a given legal context (for example, within the context of a trial, a brief and simple trial versus one which is likely to be lengthy and involve complex issues).

While the diagnostic approach focuses exclusively on the person, the functional approach emphasises that capacity reflects the interaction between a person's functional abilities and a given situation. The implication is that, before making any declaration of incapacity, consideration needs to be given as to whether it would be possible either to improve the person's relevant functional abilities (for example, by ensuring that he or she is offered education or additional support), and/or to simplify or otherwise amend the situation, to improve the person's capacity.

However, though a functional approach rejects the making of inferences about an individual's capacity on the basis of his or her diagnostic label, it does not suggest that evidence concerning the factors contributing to the person's difficulties is irrelevant. Instead, as Grisso (1986, p. 30) notes, evidence about the population of which the individual is a member is a source of 'supplemental data with which to assist courts in addressing causal, predictive, and remediation questions about . . . functional abilities'.

This chapter has two objectives. First, to provide an introduction to some of these 'supplemental data' through an overview of the psychological functioning of three groups who, compared with their general population peers, are more likely to have their decisions scrutinised. These are people with (a) intellectual disabilities, (b) mental illness or (c) dementia. The second objective is to consider some of the issues and specific tests which psychologists, and others adopting a psychological perspective, may take into account in a functional assessment of capacity, using three illustrative contexts:

- consent to treatment

- consent to sexual intimacy

- capacity to stand trial.

There are a number of other contexts in which adults make legally significant decisions and where capacity to make decisions may become an issue. These include dealing with financial affairs, making a will, making a gift, suing someone, entering into a contract, voting, becoming a parent, consenting to research (British Medical Association and The Law Society, 1995). The three contexts chosen have been selected to illustrate some of the most controversial and well-examined issues.

PSYCHOLOGICAL FUNCTIONING IN PEOPLE WITH INTELLECTUAL DISABILITIES, MENTAL ILLNESS, AND DEMENTIA

The definitions of 'intellectual disabilities' and 'mental illness' continue to be debated. For the moment there is agreement that intellectual disabilities should be defined as a developmental difficulty involving significant impairments of intellectual and social functioning/adaptive behaviour. However there are debates about the degree to which all areas of social functioning need to be impaired (American Association on Mental Retardation, 1992; British Psychological Society, 2001).

The term 'mental illness' is more difficult to define. Though *mental health* problems are endemic, at least in England, Wales and Northern Ireland (Singleton et al., 2001), the term *'mental illness'* seems to be restricted to the subset of problems which are associated, normally transiently, with abnormal psychological phenomena (or 'psychotic symptoms') such as hallucinations ('hearing voices'), delusions ('irrational' beliefs) and disordered thinking. These phenomena are most frequent among persons with a diagnosis of schizophrenia (or one of its variants) or an affective disorder (such as severe depression), or bipolar disorder (manic depression). (For details of the clinical features of these conditions, see sections 4 and 5, of Gelder et al. (2000). For personal accounts of the experience of mental illness, see British Psychological Society (2000) and Solomon (2002)). About 40% of people who experience a single episode of mental illness recover fully. Most of the remainder make at least a partial recovery, although they may continue to need treatment and support at times; only a small minority require assistance for almost all their lives (Kuipers and Bebbington, 1987).

'Dementia', on the other hand, usually occurs after a period of normal functioning and involves 'the global impairment of higher cortical functions' (Royal College of Physicians, 1981), affecting memory, thought, language, emotion, personality and behaviour, as well as motor and sensory abilities. Dementia may arise from a number of underlying conditions, but the most frequent causes in 'elderly' people (i.e. persons aged 65 years or more), such as Alzheimer's disease (the commonest form), are progressive and irreversible (see Jacoby and Oppenheimer, 2002; Gelder et al., 2000, for further details).

Each of the broad diagnostic labels being used here refers to a heterogeneous popula-tion, and the variation between different individuals within the same group can hardly be overstated. Within each group, there are many individuals who resemble the gen-eral population much more than other persons with the same diagnosis. For example, the overwhelming majority of people with intellectual disabilities have difficulties which are subtle and are not easily recognised (see Emerson et al., 2000). Only a very small proportion is unlikely to be able to use verbal language or to carry out simple tasks of everyday living (such as eating independently, washing and dressing) without support (Hogg and Sebba, 1986). In addition to this inter-individual variation, there may be major intra-individual fluctuations over even quite brief periods of time. These may arise from changes in the person's physical state (for example, as a result of pain or fatigue) or psychological functioning (for example, following unwanted events in everyday life).

While the nature of decision-making continues to be debated, theoretical analyses (for example, Appelbaum and Grisso, 1995; Law Commission, 1995; Lord Chancellor's Department, 1997, 1999; Grisso and Appelbaum, 1998) have suggested that legal decision-making involves at least three main stages: (a) understanding the nature of the choice to be made, (b) making the decision, and (c) communicating the decision to others. These stages indicate the areas of psychological functioning which may be relevant in providing 'supplemental data'. They will be discussed under two main headings: cognitive and emotional factors, and social factors.

Cognitive and Emotional Factors

By definition, the intellectual functioning of people with intellectual disabilities or dementia is impaired. Similarly, overall intellectual impairment may temporarily accompany mental illness, at least while there is evidence of psychotic symptoms. Over the last 10 years, however, it has become increasingly apparent that, even when a well-established, global, measure of overall intellectual ability is used (for example, the *Wechsler Adult Intelligence Scale* (3rd edition); Wechsler, 1999), it is an inadequate predictor of the ability to make a particular decision. Indeed, even the verbal parts of such assessments, though they normally correlate positively with judgements of capacity, do not accurately predict decision-making ability (Grisso et al., 1995; Wong et al., 2000). This is, perhaps, not surprising since each subtest normally reflects a variety of skills, including abstract ability, attention, motivation, and educational background (Kaufman and Lichtenberger, 1999). As a result, similar scores, even on a single subtest and in people with the same diagnosis, may reflect different underlying patterns of skills and difficulties. Nevertheless, this type of global information on intellectual ability, and in particular, detailed analysis of the person's responses, provide a useful starting point for further exploration of specific cognitive abilities such as memory, communication, and problem-solving (planning, reasoning, and other tasks of 'executive functioning'; Pennington and Ozonoff, 1996) which appear to be related to decision-making. For reviews relating to intellectual abilities see Clements, 1987; for schizophrenia see David and Cutting, 1994; Evans et al., 1997; Nuechterlein and Subotnik, 1998; for dementia see Morris, 1997; and see Grisso and Appelbaum, 1998.

Increasingly, it has been recognised that even each of these specific cognitive abilities itself comprises complex processes. 'Memory', for example, involves the acquisition, retention and retrieval of information (Loftus, 1979). Acquisition refers to a process involving (a) the perception of the material by a sensory register, where it is retained for a very brief period, before being transferred to (b) working memory (Baddeley, 1986). The material is stored for only as long as it receives attention in the form of rehearsal or other conscious routines. It is related to current knowledge of the world imported from long-term memory before passing to (c) long-term, more permanent, memory. Retention refers to the period of time between encoding and recollection, while retrieval involves the person bringing the information from short-term or long-term memory back into awareness.

Memory problems may therefore reflect one or a number of difficulties at different stages: for example, inadequate rehearsal in working memory—itself arising from a variety of factors—leading to a loss of the material before it reaches long-term memory (severe intellectual disabilities, Hulme and MacKenzie, 1992; schizophrenia, Nuechterlein and Dawson, 1984; depression, McAllister, 1981), inefficient encoding from working memory into long-term memory (dementia, Morris, 1997), and inefficient retrieval strategies (schizophrenia, Gray et al., 1991). Enumerating the impairments that define, and are associated with, a person's diagnosis (for example, short-term memory impairments in someone with dementia) is not sufficient; a comprehensive functional assessment would include detailed information about the probable causes and location of the individual's particular difficulties. Such an assessment would suggest strategies that, even if they did not alleviate the person's impairments, might at least maximise his or her participation in the decision to be made.

Assessments of decision-making have been criticised (Bursztajn et al., 1991) for focusing on cognition, with little attention on the role of emotional factors, except insofar as they define and are associated with a particular 'mental disorder.' Examples include the negative views of the self, current experiences and the future, which characterise depression. (See section 5 of Gelder et al., 2000, and Grisso and Appelbaum, 1998, p. 53). In clinical practice, however, feelings of shame, guilt and low self-esteem are widely expressed by people with a range of conditions (for example, mental illness (British Psychological Society, 2000); intellectual disabilities (Jahoda et al., 1988; Sinason, 1992); dementia (Jacoby and Oppenheimer, 2002). It would not be surprising if these affected their ability to make decisions. Many such feelings are likely to reflect social factors.

Social Factors

Some of the social factors which affect people with intellectual disabilities, mental illness or dementia, are part of the condition itself (for example, the change in personality, often affecting attention to personal hygiene, social skills, emotional control, and sensitivity to others, found among men and women with dementia (Jacoby and Oppenheimer, 2002). Other social factors, however, arise as a consequence of being known as a person with a 'mental disorder'.

People with such disorders experience innumerable social disadvantages, ranging from poverty, limited access to employment, social isolation, neglect, and unequal treatment by statutory services to financial, verbal and physical, and sexual, victimisation (Sobsey, 1994; Brown et al., 1995; Hirsch and Vollhardt, 2002; Mencap, 1999; Williams and Keating, 1999; Glendenning, 1999; British Psychological Society, 2000; Davis and Hill, 2001; Nosek et al., 2001). The extent of different forms of victimisation among the three groups is unclear, and reported rates vary greatly. In part this is likely to reflect different definitions of victimisation and variation in the ways in which the populations are defined. (See Brown and Turk (1992) for a discussion of these issues in relation to the sexual abuse with people with intellectual disabilities.) Furthermore the likelihood of sexual, and other, victimisation coming to light in people with a mental disorder may be much lower than for the general population (James, 1988, cited in Tharinger et al., 1990). Even when the person is able to communicate his or her experiences effectively, he or she may not be taken seriously. For example, the majority (75%, $N = 904$) of respondents with intellectual disabilities who had been 'bullied' reported that they informed a family member, staff, or the police; fewer than half of these reports resulted in the termination of the incidents (Mencap, 1999). As a result, most prevalence or incidence rates are likely to be gross underestimates. Given the methodological difficulties, it is not surprising that reported rates have varied widely (for example, for sexual abuse of people with intellectual disabilities: 2 to 5% (Chamberlain et al., 1984); 8% (Buchanan and Wilkins, 1991); around 4% (Cooke, 1990)). Nevertheless the figures are consistent in indicating a significant problem. Similarly, while the prevalence of sexual and other abuse among people with dementia is uncertain, the estimated rate of 2–5% (Allen, 2001) for abuse of the ordinary elderly population is likely to be overly conservative, particularly as mental frailty appears to be a risk factor (see review by Glendenning, 1997a). Among women, in particular, a high proportion of whom have a history of trauma prior to the onset of serious mental health problems, including mental illness (Allen, 2001), a significant minority experience sexual abuse during admission to hospital for treatment (Nibert et al., 1989). The available data indicate, consistently, that a very substantial proportion of victimisation of all three groups is carried out by people with some presumed 'caring' relationship, including family members [intellectual disabilities (Sobsey, 1994; Brown et al., 1995); serious mental disorder, (Allen, 2001); elderly persons (Decalmer, 1997)], 'friends' [intellectual disabilities (Sobsey, 1994)] or paid carers [intellectual disabilities (Sobsey, 1994; Brown et al., 1995); elderly persons (Glendenning, 1997b)].

These experiences may affect the extent to which, even when they have understood the relevant information and made a decision, people with intellectual disabilities, mental illness, or dementia will be able to express their own views, rather than those indicated to them, albeit inadvertently, by other people. Increasingly, as understanding of the psychological processes of acquiescence, interrogative suggestibility and compliance develop (for a comprehensive review, see Gudjonsson, 2002), it has been accepted that attention is needed regarding the way in which decisions are elicited. Recently, Finlay and Lyons (2001, 2002) have suggested a number of practical strategies to assist in these processes; though focused on people with intellectual disabilities, they are likely also to be relevant to other groups of men and women. In addition, though, the broader social context, in which imbalances of power between the person presenting or requesting a decision, and the decision-maker with a 'mental disorder', are likely to exist, needs to be considered.

Summary

While the heterogeneity of the populations means that impaired decision-making should not be assumed, individuals with intellectual disabilities, mental illness and dementia are at increased risk of experiencing difficulties. However, the possible difficulties are multiple and complex, and need careful individual assessment.

SPECIFIC DECISIONS AND TESTS OF CAPACITY

Consent to Treatment

In English law and in Canada and the USA, adults must give consent to any treatment they receive. With the exception of certain circumstances (see below), an individual has an absolute right to refuse treatment, even if his or her decision seems unreasonable to others (as, for example, in the case of Ms B, see above). While most discussions of consent to treatment focus on medical treatment (which is usually taken to include nursing care, such as turning the person to avoid bed-sores, attending to bruises), other treatments should also be included (such as psychological treatments). These can also interfere with people's rights and have been the subject of controversy from time to time (Wexler, 1973; Repp and Singh, 1990; Murphy, 1993).

According to Grisso and Appelbaum (1998), the historical record regarding consent to treatment begins with the case of *Slater* v. *Baker and Stapleton* in 1767 (95, Eng. Rep. 860 (KB 1767)). At that time, as they noted, only 'simple consent' was required for treatment and no one considered precisely what the person should be told or whether he or she had understood what was said, could remember it, and weigh it in the balance to arrive at a decision. Nowadays, in most jurisdictions, there is a requirement for informed consent of some kind from those who have the capacity to make decisions and there are increasingly sophisticated ways of assessing whether someone does have capacity.

In practice, when people with intellectual disabilities, mental illness or dementia, are in contact with health services, assumptions may sometimes be made about their capacity on the basis of their diagnosis. This diagnostic (or status) approach to capacity has not been supported in recent case law (see, for example, *Re C (Adult: Refusal of Medical Treatment)* ([1994] n All ER 819), where a patient in a psychiatric hospital with a diagnosis of paranoid schizophrenia was judged to have the capacity to refuse amputation of his gangrenous leg). Research evidence has also consistently shown that many people with intellectual disabilities, mental illness, or dementia certainly have the capacity to make healthcare decisions (Roth et al., 1982; Grisso and Appelbaum, 1991, 1998; Morris et al., 1993; Marson et al., 1995; Arscott et al., 1999; Fazel et al., 1999; Wong et al., 2000).

Equally, there are probably also many occasions on which people with disabilities or mental disorders appear to consent to treatment (or at least do not actively refuse it) without having understood fully what is involved. Consent is assumed to be valid simply because the decision seems sensible to a medical practitioner or another powerful professional. This outcome approach to capacity is also inappropriate and, in a recent English case *(R v. Bournewood Community and Mental Health NHS Trust, ex parte L* [1998] 3 All ER 289), the Court of Appeal ruled that an NHS trust acted illegally in detaining a man with autism, because he lacked the capacity to give or withhold consent (Eastman and Peay, 1998). The House of Lords overruled the Appeal Court but its decision has been heavily criticised as being based more on the likely financial and resource issues than ethical treatment, particularly in relation to the probable costs in relation to people with dementia (Shah et al., 1999; Mukherjee and Shah, 2001; Jacoby, 2002). A similar judgement to that of the English Court of Appeal was made in *Zinermon* v. *Burch* ((1990) 494 US 113) by the US Supreme Court (Poythress et al., 1996).

In most jurisdictions it is now considered that the functional approach must be taken with respect to treatment decisions (Wong et al., 1999) and this means that the person in question must be able to understand what he or she is consenting to, must be able to remember the information, appreciate that it applies to him or her and weigh the information to arrive at a decision. For a person's consent to be valid (Department of Health, 2001), the person must be:

- capable of taking that decision ('competent');

- acting voluntarily; and

- provided with enough information to enable him or her to make the decision.

In English law, an individual is required only to understand the nature and purpose of the treatment to which he or she is consenting 'in broad terms'. The vagueness of this may help to preserve the autonomy of people with intellectual disabilities, mental illness, or dementia.

Health care professionals in England and Wales are responsible for providing adequate information for consent. Adequacy is judged by whether the information provided conformed to what would have been considered sufficient by a responsible body of medical opinion 'skilled in the particular form of treatment in question' (Gunn, 1985; Mackay, 1990a). This is the so-called 'Bolam' test. (See the case of *Bolam* v. *Friern Hospital Management Committee* [1957] 2 All ER 118, and *Sidaway* v. *Board of Governors of Bethlem Royal and Maudsley Hospital* [1984] 1 All ER 643.) While there is, as yet, no legal requirement for medical practitioners and others to provide a warning of a risk which a 'prudent patient' would consider significant (Lord Scarman's suggestion in the *Sidaway* case), nevertheless recent case law on negligence has suggested that the court is the final arbiter of what constitutes 'responsible practice' and courts are willing to be critical of medical opinion (*Bolitho* v. *City and Hackney Health Authority* [1998] AC 232). It is therefore 'advisable' to include information on 'material' or 'significant' risks in the proposed treatment, the alternatives to it and the risks incurred by doing nothing (Department of Health, 2001).

In the USA people have to give 'informed consent' to treatment. This requires knowledge of the information relevant to a treatment decision, voluntarily exercising choice and having the capacity to make the decision (Grisso, 1986), much as is now advised by the Department of Health in England. The 'knowledge' element was defined in *Natanson* v. *Kline* (350 P.2d 1093 (1960)) in 1960 in the Kansas courts (Grisso and Appelbaum, 1998, pp. 7–8). It was held that patients should be told:

- the nature and purpose of the proposed treatment or procedure;

- its potential benefits and risks; and

- the alternative approaches and their benefits and risks.

The *Natanson* court held that the adequacy of the information provided would be judged by how it compared to what a reasonable member of the profession would disclose in a similar situation, i.e. there was a 'professional standard' for disclosure, much like the English *Bolam* test. Nevertheless, Grisso and Appelbaum (1998, pp. 7–8) have noted that, as time has gone on, 'more and more courts embraced an alternative patient-oriented standard of disclosure', such that information must be disclosed that a reasonable patient would find material to his or decision (the so-called 'material standard').

The 'capacity' element of informed consent has been much debated and a universally accepted definition has not yet been produced. Nevertheless a consensus is beginning to emerge about the essential abilities that make up capacity (Law Commission, 1995; Grisso and Appelbaum, 1998; Wong et al., 1999):

- communicating a choice;

- understanding relevant information;

- retaining the information;

- appreciating the personal significance of the information; and

- reasoning and rational manipulation of information to arrive at a decision.

There are two controversial elements in this list. First, some people have argued that the item on retention of information is redundant since, if it is a problem for an individual, then other elements will be problematic anyway. (So this item does not appear in Grisso and Appelbaum's list (1998, p. 31)). Second, the need for the term 'rational' in considerations of how information is weighed to arrive at a decision has been debated, since this may allow a 'back door' adoption of an outcome approach (see Wong et al., 1999, for a discussion of these points).

Assessing Capacity to Consent to Treatment

In most jurisdictions there is a presumption of capacity. Once outcome and diagnostic (or status) approaches are rejected, it becomes a more difficult to ascertain when capacity to consent to treatment should be assessed. Grisso and Appelbaum (1998, ch. 4) recommend that there are four circumstances in which this should be considered:

- when there are abrupt changes in a person's mental state;

- when a person refuses a recommended treatment;

- when a person consents to a very risky and invasive treatment; and

- when a person has one or more risk factors for impaired decision-making (such as a 'mental disorder').

This 'mental disorder' threshold has been the approach adopted in the proposed changes to English law (Lord Chancellor's Department, 1999). Although the presumption of capacity will remain, a 'mental disorder' (so-called 'mental disability') may 'trigger' a functional assessment.

When considering how to assess capacity, Grisso (1986) argued that capacity could be understood either as the *general* ability to understand and decide upon information or that it could be seen as a *particular* understanding of the facts and ability to decide in a specific case. Subsequently, several different measures of capacity to make treatment decisions were developed. In some the individual is presented with hypothetical information on several disorders and possible treatments, and the person's capacity to understand the information, weigh the risks and benefits, and appreciate the consequences is assessed (e.g. Grisso and Appelbaum, 1991; Morris et al., 1993; Marson et al., 1995; Arscott et al., 1999). Other tests (e.g. Roth et al., 1982; Wong et al., 2000; Mukherjee and Shah, 2001) are more specific and relate to the precise treatment decision the person is needing to make. Some examples of each type are outlined below.

Grisso and Applebaum (1991) developed a procedure (originally called the MUD, Measuring Understanding of Disclosure, but now known as the UTD, Understanding Treatment Disclosures) for assessing the understanding of hypothetical information for people admitted to hospital with a diagnosis of schizophrenia or depression. Participants (in four groups: those with depression, schizophrenia, heart disease, and a not unwell group) were presented verbally with two 'disclosures' (one about a mental illness and one about heart disease). Each disclosure consisted of five paragraphs of information relating to the disorder, its symptoms, commonly prescribed medication, the benefits and side effects of the medication, and alternative treatments. Assessment of participants' understanding was tested in three ways: (a) *uninterrupted disclosure*, where standardised questions were asked after the information was presented to elicit the participant's paraphrased recall of all the material, (b) *single unit disclosure*, where questions to elicit paraphrased recall followed each paragraph, and (c) *single unit recognition*, where each paragraph was again taken separately and the participant was asked to identify which of four statements were the same as, and which different from, the information which was presented. Grisso and Appelbaum found that, in general, people with schizophrenia had more difficulties than the other groups in understanding the disclosures, though some of the people in the group with schizophrenia did as well as people without mental illness. The depressed group only had trouble on some aspects of understanding (mainly related to the medical disorder, with which they were not familiar). All the groups did better when single unit disclosures were used (as opposed to uninterrupted disclosures) and most groups did better under the 'recognition' condition (compared to the other two conditions).

A variation of the hypothetical information procedure has been used with people with intellectual disabilities. Morris et al. (1993) designed the Ability to Consent Questionnaire (ACQ) with three hypothetical treatment dilemmas (concerning consent to behavioural treatment, surgery, and psychotropic medication) and presented one example of each to adults of average intellectual ability and to adults with mild or moderate intellectual disabilities. Interviews were then carried out using probe questions (and follow-up questions as necessary) regarding understanding of the problem, the proposed treatment, its risks and benefits, and its alternatives, their understanding of the right to choice, and ability to arrive at a rational decision. The results indicated that less than half of the people with mild intellectual disabilities had capacity to make decisions. It was also apparent, for both groups of participants, that some of the tasks involved in capacity to consent were more difficult than others. For example, participants found it much easier to understand the nature of the treatment than their rights and choices in relation to it. Arscott, et al. (1999) in a similar study with adults with intellectual disabilities adapted the materials used by Morris et al., by simplifying the language in the vignettes, using pictorial aids and smaller 'chunks' of information. They found that 65% of the participants had capacity to consent to at least one vignette (the surgical vignette was found easier than the medical one, which in turn was easier than the restraint vignette).

One of the difficulties with these 'hypothetical vignettes' approaches is that they provide information about whether a person has the capacity to consent to a treatment that may be irrelevant or only partially relevant to them personally. Since capacity is decision-specific and time-specific, a person may appear unable to make a decision about an unfamiliar form of treatment (i.e. a vignette), but be perfectly well able to give or withhold consent to another treatment which may be simpler or more familiar. Consequently some researchers have been at pains to use methods of assessing capacity that are relevant to the actual treatment decision the person has to make.

Roth and his colleagues (1982), for example, used this method to examine capacity to consent to electro-convulsive therapy (ECT) among persons being offered this treatment in one psychiatric hospital, using the Two-Part Consent Form for ECT (TCF-ECT). After answering standardised written questions regarding their understanding of the information about ECT, given on a standard hospital consent form, participants received a semi-structured interview during which the procedures were explained more simply, and understanding was reassessed. The interviews were videotaped and rated by experts with no knowledge of the participants' scores on the earlier test. The raters judged as competent all of those who gained high scores (indicative of competence) on the standardised written questions. However, almost half of those persons who had obtained scores below 50% on the earlier test (and therefore seemed incompetent) were judged 'likely competent' on the basis of their videotaped responses following the simplified explanation.

Wong et al. (2000) is one of the few studies that has examined decision-making among three groups of people with different forms of mental disorder (mental illness, dementia and intellectual disabilities) and a general population comparison group, and has used a decision (whether or not to have a blood test which was clinically indicated) about a healthcare intervention of real importance. Drawing on previous research (Grisso et al., 1995; Grisso and Appelbaum, 1998), they designed an information sheet about the blood test and a decision-making assessment measure. Participants were asked to give four different kinds of responses: a spontaneous account about the blood test (before any information disclosure), uninterrupted disclosure (a paraphrased recall after hearing the whole information sheet read once); element disclosure (paraphrased recall after each element of information), recognition (recognising correct and incorrect statements about the blood test) and non-verbal demonstration (selecting the items to be used in the procedure for a blood test). Participants' verbal responses were rated with respect to understanding the purpose of the test, its nature, its risks, the risks of not having it and voluntariness. Using the legal criteria for incapacity, which form part of the proposed changes to English law (see below; Lord Chancellor's Department, 1999), Wong et al. found that, in contrast to all the men and women in the 'general population' group and almost all of those with a mental illness, only 65% of those with intellectual disabilities and 33% of those with dementia were able to give or withhold consent to the blood test. Simplifying the demands of the decision-making task was successful in increasing the numbers of people judged competent (as, at least for those with intellectual disabilities; Gunn et al., 1999). As might be expected, the three groups had somewhat different difficulties with decision-making. Those with dementia and with intellectual disabilities often had difficulty understanding and retaining information. Also, some aspects of the decision posed more problems than other aspects (e.g. the rights and risks of saying 'no' seemed to be the hardest issues, as Arscott et al., 1999, also found).

In summary, these studies suggest that, as would be expected from the overview of psychological functioning (see above), capacity to consent is likely to depend on at least the manner in which information is presented and tested, and the complexity of the task required. Breaking-up information into smaller 'chunks', using simpler language, and even non-verbal measures are clearly helpful for people with intellectual disabilities (Arscott et al, 1999; Wong et al. 2000), mental illness (Grisso and Appelbaum, 1991; Roth et al., 1982; Wong et al. 2000) and dementia (Wong et al., 2000). It is clear that some scenarios are more difficult to decide than others and some aspects of the decision-making process are more difficult than others (e.g. Arscott et al., 1999; Wong et al., 2000), as would be expected from a functional approach.

Many of the above instruments for assessing capacity were developed as research tools and Grisso and Appelbaum (1998) have since developed an assessment instrument, the MacArthur Competence Assessment Tool (MacCAT-T) which can be used to assist in making judgements about capacity in a variety of clinical situations. The MacCAT-T is a structured interview that takes about 15 to 20 minutes to complete and guides the clinician through a disclosure of treatment options, requiring feedback from the interviewee at various points, to demonstrate whether he or she has understood the information, appreciates that it applies to him or her, and can reason with the information in order to make a choice. The framework includes a system for rating the responses (Grisso and Appelbaum, 1998, pp. 120–126) and guidance is provided to help the clinician reach a clinical judgement.

When Consent is not Required

A controversial issue concerns the provision of medical treatment for adults who cannot, or do not, consent. At present, in England and Wales, for example, there is no clear procedure for this (except through the Mental Health Act 1983, which provides a legal framework to enable people to be detained in hospital for the assessment and treatment for a mental disorder), since parents and/or carers cannot legally consent to treatment in place of an adult. It has sometimes been asserted that this difficulty means that some people will be refused treatment because of uncertainties about its lawfulness (Mencap, 1989). While this is not necessarily true (Murphy and Clare, 1997), nevertheless, it is clear that, when adults lack capacity:

- sometimes treatment is refused when it should not be, and

- sometimes inappropriate treatment of a questionable kind does take place.

In England and Wales, these dilemmas have been highlighted by several cases regarding girls and women with intellectual disabilities. In the first case (*Re D* [1976] 1 All ER 326) the mother, General Practitioner, paediatrician and gynaecologist of a girl aged 11 years, with Soto's syndrome, proposed that she be sterilised. However the Court ruled that sterilisation would be unlawful since it was being proposed for non-therapeutic reasons, was not in the girl's best interests and would prevent her from exercising her basic human right to reproduce. In the second case (*Re B* [1987] 2 All ER 206), the Court considered whether a young woman with a severe intellectual disability, who was still a minor (17 years old), could be sterilised when she was believed to be unable to consent herself. Sterilisation was authorised on the debatable grounds that it was a relatively minor operation with few side effects and would provide a high degree of protection from pregnancy. However, it was also stated that no sterilisation would be authorised for eugenic or social purposes. In the third case (*Re F* [1990] 2 AC 1), sterilisation was sought for a woman aged 35 years, who had a severe intellectual disability, was living in an institution, had an active sexual relationship with a man who also lived in the hospital and had a severe intellectual disability. In this case, the House of Lords ruled that those providing treatment for someone unable to consent would not be subject to accusations of unlawful action, provided that they acted in the person's best interests and in accordance with a responsible and competent body of relevant professional opinion.

With regard to both *Re B* and *Re F*, however, it has been argued (e.g. Baum, 1994) that sterilisation was undertaken far too lightly. In the case of *Re B*, there was no current, active, sexual relationship and the nature of the sexual activity in *Re F* was not clearly established. In addition, certain forms of contraception were dismissed very readily (and seem not to have been considered at all for the male partner in *Re F*). Moreover, little attention was given to the possibility of a period of sex education for the women. Both of them had communication difficulties but a level of comprehension that might have made basic sex education feasible. That may have assisted them to become sufficiently aware of the relevant issues to become capable of consent. In addition, however, in neither *Re B* nor *Re F* did the courts seem concerned about the women having sexual relationships (see also below), with their attendant risks (for example, of exploitation and sexually transmitted diseases), but only about the possibility of pregnancy. This suggests that the decisions may, in part, have been motivated by eugenic considerations.

Following these (and a number of other cases) in England and Wales, the Law Commission made proposals (Law Commission, 1995) for a statutory definition of incapacity and a procedure for making health care and other decisions for those deemed not to have capacity. These were subsequently largely accepted by the government (Lord Chancellor's Department, 1999). Though these proposals have not yet become law, similar provision has now been introduced in Scotland (Adults with Incapacity Act (Scotland) 2000). According to the proposals, a person should be defined as not having capacity at the time a particular decision needs to be made if:

- he or she is 'unable by reason of *mental disability* to make a decision on the matter in question or unable to communicate a decision on that matter' and where

- *'Mental disability'* is 'any disability or disorder of the mind or brain, whether permanent or temporary, which results in an impairment or disturbance of mental functioning' and where

- *'Unable to make a decision'* means that the person was 'unable to understand or retain the information relevant to the decision, or unable to make a decision based on that information' (Lord Chancellor's Department, 1999, para. 1.6).

If an individual does lack capacity, decision-making would be delegated to a nominated, or appointed, person who would be able to make some decisions on that individual's behalf, in his or her 'best interests' (for details, see Lord Chancellor's Department, 1999, ch. 2). The proposals emphasise the need to ascertain the past and present wishes of the person, permitting and encouraging the person to participate in making the decision, and taking the least restrictive action possible.

The Law Commission and Lord Chancellor's Department also considered advance directives (advance healthcare statements), but no decision has been made on these. According to Wong et al. (1999), such directives are currently only lawful in some circumstances (advance refusals of treatment can be lawful; euthanasia remains unlawful). Nevertheless, there is an increasing interest in the possibility of advance requests or 'crisis cards' for men and women who currently have capacity but believe that they may become unable, temporarily or permanently, to make decisions about their treatment and/or support (Fazel et al., 1999).

Other countries have approached consent to treatment for persons who are incapacitated by appointing guardians, sometimes family members, sometimes public guardians and occasionally professional guardians (for a review of provision in Europe, see Gove and Georges, 2001). In the USA, where the majority of guardians are appointed for elderly persons, there are great variations between States in the definitions of capacity and types of capacity decisions possible (for example some States will only provide categorical decisions about capacity or incapacity, while others accept the concept of limited capacity), the extent to which the person is represented in hearings and the provisions for review (Grisso, 1986; Kapp, 1999; Wilber and Zarit, 1999; O'Sullivan, 1999; Wilber, 2001; Kapp, 2001). The provision of guardians has not always been satisfactory and professional guardians in particular have been subject to criticism, as a result of some well-publicised scandals involving financial exploitation, although one recent study in Florida found there was little evidence of abuse (Reynolds and Carson, 1999). A better solution, perhaps, is that adopted in Sweden, where special representatives (Social Workers), who are independent of carers and treatment providers, assist persons with difficulties to make decisions, without removing capacity from them.

Consent to Sexual Intimacy

Attitudes to Sexuality, Abuse and Protection

Historically, especially in the early 1900s, there was a great deal of concern in the UK, the USA and elsewhere about the reproduction of a number of groups, including people with intellectual disabilities or a mental illness, who were deemed to be 'unfit' (Barker, 1983; Showalter, 1985, p. 110; Fennell, 1996). Reflecting this concern, 'patients' in psychiatric and 'mental handicap' hospitals were very strongly discouraged from having sexual relationships (although illicit and abusive sexual activities were far from unknown). For example, wards were segregated by gender and no contraceptive or sexual advice was offered, even in long-stay hospitals. The advent of the normalisation movement (Nirje, 1980; Wolfensberger, 1980, 1983; Emerson, 1992) and the rights movement (Rioux, 1997; Shakespeare, 2000; Cook, 2000), with its associated legislation (e.g. Daw, 2000) radically changed views about the opportunities which should be offered to people with disabilities and/or mental health needs, providing a new emphasis on age-appropriate and culturally normative experiences. For people with intellectual disabilities, there was a recognition that sex education should be offered (Craft and Craft, 1983; Murphy et al., 1983; McCarthy, 1999, pp. 61–67) and, increasingly, there was a move to more ordinary living conditions in the community (Mansell and Ericsson, 1996). Similar deinstitutionalisation took place in regard to people with a diagnosed mental illness and hospitals themselves became less prohibitive about sexual matters: most wards began to contain men and women (though this has resulted in concerns about sexually abusive behaviour by men—see below).

In most jurisdictions, despite this evidence of attitudes opposing the expression of sexuality for marginalised groups, there was a legal presumption of capacity to consent to sexual relationships, so that everyone above the age of consent (with very few exceptions) was considered competent to consent to sexual activity. Most countries had laws to protect people from unwanted sexual encounters, though, and there were often added protections for those who were regarded as unable to consent (such as for men and women with severe intellectual disabilities in England and Wales; for the relevant law, see Gunn, 1996). Nevertheless, the law normally only concerned itself with situations where it was reported that a person did not or could not consent. Where consent appeared to have been given, the law did not usually seem concerned with the *reason* why consent was given, enabling people to consent to sex for all sorts of reasons including sexual gratification, affection, duty, money, physical closeness, physical comfort or fear. As a result, in cases where a man or woman had consented to sexual activities for a small gift, such as a cigarette, there could usually be no prosecution, even though others may have felt that he or she had been exploited.

People with intellectual disabilities, physical disabilities, a mental illness, or dementia are all thought to be at increased risk of sexual exploitation and/or sexual abuse because of their social and/or cognitive disadvantages (Sobsey, 1994; Brown et al., 1995; Williams and Keating, 1999; Glendenning, 1999; Nosek et al., 2001). Nevertheless, discussions about capacity to consent to sexual relationships normally only occur in relation to people with intellectual disabilities and these debates tend to be about the degree of sexual knowledge required to indicate capacity.

For all vulnerable groups, however, there has been a rising concern about how to provide them with protection, without wishing to remove their right to consenting sexual relationships. It has been suggested (e.g. Copperman and Burrowes, 1992) that mixed gender wards in psychiatric hospitals place women with mental illness or other mental health problems at risk of sexual abuse and that single sex provision should routinely be available (a similar argument might be made for women with intellectual disabilities or dementia living in hospital or community services). In addition, local policy guidelines on personal and sexual relationships and adult protection procedures have been drawn up by and for staff in residential and day care facilities for vulnerable people (Booth and Booth, 1992; Brown and Stein, 1998). Most of the guidelines assert that such persons have the same right to consenting sexual expression as other people but that they also have a right to be protected from abuse and exploitation. The majority of guidelines are then mainly concerned with procedures to be followed when abuse comes to light; they tend to provide no guidance on what constitutes consent.

What Constitutes Capacity to Consent to Sexual Relationships?

Precisely what constitutes capacity to consent to sexual activity is unclear in many jurisdictions, even though the definition of capacity is crucial in establishing a balance between a proper empowerment to exercise sexual rights and effective protection from abuse. Clearly, the higher the requirement for knowledge and understanding, the better protection from abuse but the more that people with a 'mental disorder' may be prevented from exercising their sexual rights.

In most European countries, there is no requirement that someone engaging in sexual activity should exercise 'informed consent' of the kind required for medical treatment (i.e. to be informed and to choose voluntarily). As a result, there seems to be no need, in law, for a person to demonstrate that he or she understands the nature of sexual activity, its benefits and risks and possible alternatives. If there were such requirements, people would presumably need to understand and differentiate between sexual intercourse, masturbation and procreation. They would also need to understand the risks of pregnancy and sexually transmitted diseases, particularly HIV. In addition, they would need an understanding of alternative forms of contraception and of how to gain the benefits of sexual behaviour by other means (for example, if they are going to engage in sexual intercourse for a material object, such as cigarettes, they need to know how else these might be obtained). Realistically, to make a voluntary choice, many people would also need assertiveness training, so that they did not simply submit to sexual activity because of compliance.

Guidance on mental capacity in England, drawn up by the British Medical Association and The Law Society (British Medical Society and the Law Society, 1995) has considered the issue of how to define capacity to consent to sexual relationships. They asserted that the common law test was that the person concerned:

- 'must be capable of understanding what is proposed and its implications; and

- must be able to exercise choice. (It is important to consider whether one party is in a position of power which will influence the ability of the other party to consent.)'

This implied that, at a minimum, people would need to understand what sexual intercourse was, and that pregnancy and/or sexually transmitted diseases were risks (as well as being able to make a free choice). This definition of capacity was not always accepted in the courts, however (see, for example, Murphy, 2000) and sometimes it was argued that setting the 'sexual knowledge' criterion this high would disadvantage people with more severe disabilities from exercising their sexual rights. Other jurisdictions, have proposed similar but less stringent tests, such as that of the Supreme Court of Victoria, in the case of *Morgan* ((1970) VR 337) (where consideration of the consequences of sexual acts appears to have been excluded):

It must be proved that she has not sufficient knowledge or understanding to comprehend:

(a) that what is proposed is the physical act of penetration of her body by the male organ; or if that is not proved,

(b) that the act of penetration proposed is one of sexual connection as distinct from an act of a totally different character.

The English Home Office (2000, paragraphs 4.5.8 and 4.5.13), when reviewing the sexual offences legislation, considered that understanding the consequences of sexual acts was important. It proposed that a person should be regarded as lacking capacity if they were unable to communicate a decision or if they had a mental disability and were unable to make a decision because:

He or she is unable to understand:

i) the nature and reasonably foreseeable consequences of the act and

ii) the implications of the act and its reasonably foreseeable consequences.

In the USA different States have different criteria for capacity to consent to sexual relationships and, in general, courts have tended to rely heavily on professional judgements (Stavis, 1991). According to Sundram and Stavis (1994) and Stavis and Walker-Hirsch (1999), some States require people to understand:

- the nature of sexual conduct;

- the consequences of their actions, and

- the moral aspects of their decisions.

Other States require only the first criterion (for example, New Jersey) or the first two criteria to be fulfilled. Stavis and Walker-Hirsch (1999) go on to suggest that it is incorrect to consider capacity to consent to sexual activity an all-or-nothing ability. Instead, they argued, some activities required very little understanding or regulation (apart from mutual consent), whereas others (e.g. sexual intercourse) did require assessment of capacity according to State laws. They then provide a very long list of requirements for full capacity which would be rather restrictive if enforced.

Research has shown that people with intellectual disabilities often have more limited sexual knowledge than other people (McCabe, 1999; McCabe and Cummins, 1999; O'Callaghan and Murphy, 2002) and are more vulnerable to abuse than others (Wilson et al., 1996; Khemka and Hickson, 2000; O'Callaghan and Murphy, 2002). Attempts to operationalise the English definitions of capacity have suggested that about half of the people involved in one research project would have been unable to consent to sexual relationships because they did not understand about pregnancy and/or sexually transmitted diseases (O'Callaghan and Murphy, 2002). The same project found that people who had had sex education were more knowledgeable and less vulnerable than those who had not. They concluded that it was essential for people to be offered life-long sex education (as opposed to the 'one shot' variety).

Not surprisingly, staff in community care services for people with intellectual disabilities are often unsure about whether (and how) to determine if people with intellectual disabilities have the capacity to consent to sexual relationships (O'Callaghan and Murphy, 2002). They frequently respond by not intervening when they see sexual behaviour between residents and not reporting sexually abusive behaviour (Sundram and Stavis, 1994). Some staff tend to consider themselves 'enlightened' in 'allowing' sexual intercourse between people with intellectual disabilities, without really considering the potential of one person to abuse the other; other staff remain quite restrictive in their views. Often staff make judgements about whether to 'allow' relationships by considering whether the two people in question actively seek each other out, spend time together, share leisure activities and restrict activities with other partners. These characteristics may be good guides as to whether relationships are consenting but they tend to be tinged with value judgements about how such intimate relationships should be conducted (i.e. that people should only have sex together if they also like spending other time together; that people should not have sex with lots of different partners, and so on).

One study examined the views of over 300 psychologists (from a variety of fields) on the subject of capacity to consent to sexual relationships by asking participants to grade 56 statements from five (most important) to one (least important) for judging capacity (Kennedy and Niederbuhl, 2001). The results suggested that the following eight abilities were judged absolutely necessary (mean rating of 4.5 or more) to demonstrate capacity.

- Individual can say or demonstrate 'no'.

- Individual knows that having intercourse can result in pregnancy.

- When given options the individual can make an informed choice.

- Individual knows that having intercourse or other sexual relations can result in obtaining a disease.

- Individual can differentiate between appropriate and inappropriate times and places to engage in intimate relations.

- Individual can differentiate between males and females.

- Individual can recognise individuals or situations which might be a threat to him or her.

- Individual will stop behaviour if another person tells him or her 'no.'

Interestingly, these go considerably beyond the minimal criteria proposed by the English Home Office. They also fall short of the more restrictive criteria of some States in the USA (e.g. the 'moral dimension' item was not rated as absolutely necessary for capacity).

Practice Issues

In practice, where a sexual relationship involving a person who is believed to have an intellectual disability, a mental illness, or dementia, has begun or appears imminent, then families, carers and professionals should consider the following issues.

- Is there a major imbalance of power between the two persons (for example, is one physically frail or a subservient partner)? If so there is a much greater risk of an abusive relationship.

- Is the sexual relationship rewarding in itself, or is one person offering inducements to the other (such as cigarettes or car rides)? If one partner always gives tangible inducements to the other then there is a far greater risk of the relationship being abusive.

- If the relationship is heterosexual, do both partners understand (at least) that pregnancy can result from sexual intercourse?

- Where the relationship is heterosexual, do both know what contraception means and how to use methods of contraception?

- Do both partners understand that there is a risk of sexually transmitted diseases, particularly when the sexual activity includes oral or anal penetration, and know how to engage in safer sex?

- If pregnancy is a possibility, have both people been given adequate access to genetic counselling and have they been informed and understood issues relating to parenting (including the reality that fostering may be required)?

- Have both people been offered sex education?

In some cases, where the answer to any of these questions is 'No', then one or both persons may need counselling and/or further sex education, possibly with assertiveness training if the relationship appears exploitative. There are a number of sex education packages available for people with intellectual disabilities (Craft and Brown, 1994) and/or autism (Koller, 2000), including both slide and pictorial packages, many of which can be employed in either group or individual training (e.g. Kempton, 1988; Hingsburger, 1995; McCarthy and Thompson, 1998). Most of these would also be appropriate for other adults who may be more vulnerable than the general population.

It may be necessary to assess a person's understanding both before and after the training. Ideally this ought to be done in a standard way, using the same questions each time, to see what the person has gained from the training. There are a number of tests of sexual knowledge available for this kind of assessment, some of which include questions about social interaction issues (as well as sexual facts), and which have been designed specifically for a particular population (e.g. Fischer et al., 1973; Wish et al., 1979; Bender et al., 1983; McCabe, 1999). If the two people appear not to be able to understand or retain information from the sex education sessions, even though pictorial, signed and other forms of communication have been used, then consent may not be possible. Many carers, however, would still consider that the couple had a right to be sexual (Craft and Brown, 1994) if it appeared that they had a genuine affection for each other and there was no clear evidence of exploitation. In such circumstances it may be possible for carers to assist the couple in obtaining protection from any risk of pregnancy; however, limiting the risk of sexually transmitted diseases is much more problematic (practical guidance on this issue is given by McCarthy and Thompson, 1994). In the absence of apparent affection between the two people, some carers would argue that a sexual relationship should be discouraged if informed consent is not possible. This may mean that some people have less likelihood of establishing a sexual relationship (for example, people with autism are unlikely to display affectionate behaviour in a normal way). Meanwhile, Carson (1994) in the UK has argued that what is needed is a change in the law, creating a new offence of serious exploitation of a person with a 'mental disorder', as defined in Section 1 of the Mental Health Act 1983. This would provide some legal recourse for vulnerable persons (and might serve some protective role, through acting as a deterrent to potential abusers) but enable those with severe learning disabilities to engage in non-exploitative sexual relationships.

Capacity to Stand Trial

The Early Years

In many jurisdictions it is considered unjust for someone to stand trial if they are unfit to plead or lack the capacity to stand trial. In England and Wales, the concept dates back to the fourteenth century, according to Grubin (1996): it was thought that a criminal prosecution could not proceed against someone who had not entered a plea and it was recognised that defendants could be 'mute of malice' (i.e. deliberately silent) or 'mute by visitation of God' ('deaf' or 'insane'). The legal criteria for incompetence were laid down in the case of *Pritchard*, in 1836, who was accused of bestiality. As he was 'deaf-mute' he was considered unable to plead and was exempted from trial (Mackay, 1990b; Grubin, 1991a). The court in *R* v. *Pritchard* ((1836) 7 C&P 303) held that the accused must be able to plead and be 'of sufficient intellect to comprehend the course of proceedings in the trial so as to make a proper defence, to challenge a juror to whom he might wish to object and comprehend the details of the evidence' (Mackay, 1990b).

Nowadays, the criteria for judging capacity to stand trial vary from jurisdiction to jurisdiction. In England and Wales, 'fitness to plead' is judged by the court and is considered to be a function of five criteria (Grubin, 1991a; Mackay and Kearns, 2000):

- ability to plead;

- ability to understand evidence;

- understanding the court proceedings;

- ability to instruct a lawyer; and

- knowing that a juror can be challenged.

Occasionally these criteria are varied slightly and/or expanded (see James et al., 2001, below).

In the USA the well-known legal standard for determining fitness to plead or 'competency to stand trial' was given in the *Dusky* case (*Dusky* v. *United States* (1960) 362 US 402). The person must have 'sufficient present ability to consult with his lawyer with a reasonable degree of rational understanding' and must have a 'rational as well as a factual understanding of proceedings against him' (Grisso, 1986). Since then, according to Grisso (1986), there have been a number of somewhat different lists of competencies, amplifying the *Dusky* criteria, provided by courts. For example, in the case of *Wieter* v. *Settle* in 1961 (193 F. Supp. 318 (WD Mo., 1961), quoted in Grisso, 1986) it was held that the person must comprehend that:

- he is in court, charged with an offence;

- there is a judge;

- a prosecutor will try to convict him;

- a lawyer is present to defend him;

- he will be expected to tell his lawyer the facts in relation to the alleged offence;

- the jury will decide on his guilt or innocence; and

- he has sufficient memory to relate what happened to him.

As Grisso (1986) pointed out, many States in the USA (though not all) required that the person also had a mental disability, in order to be judged not competent to stand trial. However mental disability alone was not sufficient to qualify anyone as not competent (i.e. the test was functional, not diagnostic). Canada has also had an 'insanity' requirement and, as Mackay (1990b) argued, this has led to difficulties in the past, in relation to the precise definition and limits of 'insanity'. The Canadian test for unfitness, however, has been very like the English one (Mackay, 1990b).

In many jurisdictions the issue of fitness to plead or competency to stand trial could be raised by the defence, the prosecution or the court and the judge could order the issue to be tried immediately (Grisso, 1986; Mackay, 1990b). In the USA and Canada there tended to be very large numbers of competency evaluations (for example, over 6000 in the USA for an estimated 25,000 defendants, according to Steadman et al., 1982), whereas there were far fewer in Scotland and England (Grubin, 1996; Mackay and Kearns, 2000). Studies in the USA and elsewhere have tended to show that people who are referred for competency evaluations are overwhelmingly male, often from minority ethnic groups, usually with poor education, a history of psychiatric hospitalisation, previous offences and an index charge of a violent offence (Nicholson and Kugler, 1991; James et al., 2001). Several studies have demonstrated that the presence of psychosis (including delusions, hallucinations, impaired memory, thought or communication and disturbed behaviour) raised the likelihood of a finding of unfitness or incompetency (Nicholson and Kugler, 1991; Mackay and Kearns, 2000; James et al., 2001). Nevertheless, as Grisso (1986) commented, the level of impairment required in relation to competency criteria was not really defined, so that it was always a matter of opinion when a defendant was not able to stand trial.

In the early years, if the defendant was found unfit to plead, the outcome in most jurisdictions was to require the defendant to be sent to hospital. In the USA, in the

1960s and 1970s, it was found that those ruled incompetent to stand trial tended to experience extremely long periods in hospital. For example, Hess and Thomas (1963) estimated that more than 50% of those found unfit in Michigan would never be released from hospital and McGarry (1971) found that, after being found incompetent to stand trial, more people had left a Massachusetts hospital by dying than by any other route.

Similarly in England and Wales and Canada, until recently, a finding of 'unfit to plead' led to compulsory hospitalisation for an indeterminate period, the intention being that those who recovered would be returned to court for trial (Mackay, 1990b; Grubin 1991a). However it transpired that, in both England and Canada as in the USA, this sometimes resulted in people being detained in hospital for very long periods without ever being able to establish their innocence, even when the original charge had sometimes been quite trivial (Savage, 1981; Grubin, 1991a). This especially applied to people with intellectual disabilities who, of course, were unlikely to 'recover' their fitness to plead. There seems to be no evidence that anyone, in the hospitals, even considered attempting to teach them about the criminal justice issues they had not grasped at the time of the court hearing. Thus, according to Grubin (1991a), there were 295 people who were found unfit to plead in England and Wales between 1976 and 1988. Of these, 23% were deemed to have intellectual disabilities, 58% schizophrenia, 8% had other psychoses, 3% had dementia, 2% were deaf and the remainder had a variety of diagnoses. A third of the original charges were for 'nuisance' or 'mild' offences and a number of defendants protested their innocence, yet all the defendants were sent to hospital for an indefinite period, since this was what the legislation (Criminal Procedure (Insanity) Act 1964) at the time required. Overall less than half of those detained (46%) were considered to have regained fitness to plead and most of these proceeded to trial. Of those (54%) who appeared to remain unfit, many stayed in hospital for a considerable time (an average of six years) and they were disproportionately likely to have been diagnosed as having intellectual disabilities (Grubin, 1991b).

Recent Developments

As a result of these injustices, following a Supreme Court ruling in the USA (in 1972) and various government reports in England and Canada (e.g. Home Office/Department of Health and Social Security, 1975; Law Commission of Canada, 1987), a number of changes occurred (Grisso, 1986; Grubin, 1991a; Mackay, 1995; Grisso, 1996). In the USA, in the case of *Jackson* v. *Indiana* in 1972 ((1972) 406 US 715), the US Supreme Court ruled that those held in hospital following an incompetency finding could not be kept in hospital for an unreasonable length of time (Grisso, 1986, 1996). Thereafter, courts were required to determine whether defendants' mental disorders were treatable. Where they were not treatable courts were required not to proceed with a trial and the state had to either drop the charges or proceed with a civil commitment (Grisso, 1986, p. 68). Where they were treatable defendants were often committed to hospital for treatment (some States had 'least restrictive facility' requirements). After 1972, therefore, far greater efforts were made to return people to trial once they were deemed fit and the average length of time in hospital following incompetency rulings fell to around six months to a year (Williams and Miller, 1981; Steadman et al., 1982). Finally, in the USA, there were some disputes about whether a higher level of competence than that defined by the *Dusky* criteria was required for certain legal decisions (such as to waive the right to be represented by counsel in court). Some courts held that such decisions required the capacity to make a 'reasoned choice', while others held that this was not so (Grisso, 1996). However, in 1993, the US Supreme Court ruled in the case of *Godinez* v. *Moran* ((1993) 113 S.Ct 2680) that no higher capacity was necessary for such decisions (Grisso, 1996).

In England the changes to fitness to plead procedures were legislative. The Criminal Procedure (Insanity and Fitness to Plead) Act 1991 came into force in 1992. No changes were made to the criteria for fitness to plead but courts were required, when finding someone unfit to plead, to have a trial of the facts. This ensured that the jury was satisfied that the defendant committed the acts of which he was charged, before he was subject to the court's powers of disposal. Moreover, the new Act allowed both community and hospital disposals for those found unfit, instead of the rigid indefinite hospital orders of the previous legislation. Similar changes in relation to establishing the defendants' guilt and to preventing indeterminate hospitalisation occurred in Canada, following the cases of *Swain* ((1991) 63 CCC (3d) 481) and *Taylor* ((1993) 11 OR (3d) 323)—see Mackay (1995).

Mackay and Kearns (2000) reported that, in England as a result of the legislative changes, findings of unfitness rose (from about 12 per year to about 33 per year). The diagnostic categories remained much as before (44% of those found unfit were diagnosed as having schizophrenia, 24% as having intellectual disabilities, 10% as having dementia, 6% as having other psychoses, 4% as having brain damage with the remainder having a variety of diagnoses). The disposals were more varied than previously, although still only 19% were community based (Guardianship Orders or Supervision and Treatment Orders). And in the vast majority of cases (110 out of 125), in the trial of the facts, the defendant was found to have committed some or all of the acts with which he was charged.

What Constitutes Fitness to Plead?

The basic legal criteria of fitness to plead or competence to stand trial, arising from the cases of *Pritchard* in England and *Dusky* in the USA remain substantially unchanged, although *Jackson* v. *Indiana* did bring treatability issues into the USA criteria, and Gray et al. (2001) have argued that ability to give evidence may become part of the fitness to plead criteria in England, since the abolition of the right to silence. In both England and the USA courts have taken advice from psychiatrists and psychologists about fitness to plead, although in the USA they are not obliged to do so (Grisso, 1986).

In England there have been no standardised tests of fitness to plead, although there have been several analyses of the criteria which mental health professionals use. Grubin (1991a), for example, found that in his examination of the 295 reports of cases of fitness to plead between 1976 and 1988:

- 195 mentioned ability to instruct legal advisers,

- 144 discussed ability to comprehend court proceedings, and

- 98 commented on ability to challenge a juror.

Other reasons mentioned in reports included delusional thinking, lack of understanding of what the sentence might mean, and likelihood of making misleading statements.

In Mackay and Kearns' (2000) more recent analysis of 125 cases of fitness to plead in England, their examination of the 197 psychiatric reports showed that only 21 examined all five of the accepted criteria (see above), while 28 simply (and incorrectly) used a diagnostic criterion for fitness to plead. The frequency with which the five criteria were addressed was as follows.

- 73 reported on ability to instruct counsel (64 competent; 8 not competent, 1 uncertain).

- 60 considered ability to understand the court proceedings (54 competent, 6 not competent).

- 46 reported on understanding the plea (25 competent, 19 not competent, 2 uncertain).

- 31 considered ability to challenge a juror (27 competent, 3 not competent, 1 uncertain).

- 26 commented on ability to understand evidence (24 competent and 2 not competent).

Other issues were also addressed in 49 reports, including the defendants' understanding of the charges, their apparent amnesia with regard to the offence, their likely behaviour in court, and their understanding of the consequences of a guilty finding.

In James et al.'s (2001) prospective study of 479 referrals to a psychiatric service at a magistrates court, a standard set of data were gathered using a 170 item semi-structured interview. This included the extent to which two psychiatrists both judged the defendant fit or unfit on six criteria (ability to understand the nature of the charge, understand the meaning of a plea, understand the consequences of a plea, instruct his or her lawyers, understand the details of the evidence, and follow the proceedings so as to make a proper defence, e.g. challenging a juror). It transpired that, of the 466 cases where full data were available, 80 (17%) were judged unfit to plead. Only a few (10%) failed on one legal criterion, 18% failed on two, 38% on three, 13% on four, 10% on five, and 13% on all six criteria. The least difficult criteria to pass appeared to be the understanding of the charge, the understanding of the plea, and the understanding of the consequences of the plea (5% failed on each of these criteria). In contrast, between 13% and 18% failed the other three criteria. The criterion of ability to follow the proceedings in court was the best predictor of judgements of fitness to plead. No measures of inter-rater reliability were given, as James and colleagues required their psychiatrists to come to joint decisions.

In the USA, in contrast, a series of possible tests of competency to stand trial have been developed, including screening tests (such as the Competency Screening Test of Lipsitt et al., 1971). A number of the older ones have been described in detail in Grisso (1986, pp. 78–104) and some are reviewed in Nicholson et al. (1988). Four examples of tests (two older and two more recent) will be described here.

One of the first tests in the USA was that of McGarry (1973) and others: the Competency to Stand Trial Assessment Instrument (CAI). The test consisted of a series of questions, designed to assess defendants' competence in 13 areas, the response to each question being rated on a scale of 1 (lack of capacity) to 5 (full capacity). The questions covered the following.

- Appraisal of legal defences available.

- Ability to manage own behaviour in court.

- Ability to relate to the attorney.

- Ability to participate with the lawyer to plan a legal strategy.

- Understanding of the roles of various court personnel.

- Understanding of court procedure.

- Appreciation of the charges.

- Appreciation of the nature and range of possible penalties.

- Appraisal of the likely outcome of the trial.

- Ability to provide the lawyer with relevant facts.

- Ability to challenge prosecution witnesses.

- Capacity to testify relevantly.

- Motivation to defend oneself.

The CAI provided no specific criteria for the (1 to 5) ratings of answers and reliability was therefore compromised, especially with inexperienced raters (Grisso, 1986, p. 82). According to Schreiber (1983; quoted in Grisso, 1986, p. 83), the CAI was rather stricter than other instruments, finding rather more people not competent. It was criticised by some for not including any measures of psychopathology (see below).

The Interdisciplinary Fitness Interview (Golding et al., 1984) attempted to improve on the CAI by including mental disorder issues as well as legal issues, and by having a lawyer and a mental health professional jointly make the judgements. The interview was semi-structured and divided into two parts: legal issues and psychopathological symptoms. The legal section included questions about capacity to appreciate the nature of the crime, disclose the relevant facts, relate to the lawyer, anticipate court-room requirements of demeanour, and conduct and appreciate the consequences of various legal options. These items could also be weighted for importance to the final competency judgement. The second section concerned mental disorder and consisted of questions to establish the presence of thought disturbance, communication disturbance, delusions and hallucinations, disturbed behaviour, affective disturbances, memory and/or consciousness disturbances, the presence of intellectual disabilities, and impairments of judgement and/or insight. Reliability data for the overall competency rating were good (97% agreement between mental health professionals and lawyers), though the reliability of individual items was lower, of course (Golding et al., 1984).

The Competence Assessment for Standing Trial for Defendants with Mental Retardation, CAST-MR (Everington, 1990) was developed specifically to assess the capacity of people with intellectual disabilities to stand trial because other measures were inappropriate. For example, many people with intellectual disabilities would not have symptoms of mental illness and therefore the Interdisciplinary Fitness Interview would have been inappropriate. The CAST-MR consisted of three sections.

- Section I contained 25 multiple choice items examining the defendant's vocabulary and concepts.

- Section II contained 15 multiple choice items to assess the defendant's ability to assist in his/her own defence and to understand proceedings in court.

- Section III contained 10 open-ended questions examining the defendant's ability to relate factual events and understand the charges.

Measures of internal consistency and test–retest reliability were high, as were measures of content validity. A comparison of the scores for defendants with and without intellectual disabilities (of whom some were with and some without capacity to stand trial, as judged by forensic evaluators) demonstrated good construct validity and an analysis of the 'hit rate' showed that 70% of defendants were correctly classified. Later research showed that people's language skills and IQ were correlated with their CAST-MR scores, as might be expected (Everington et al., 2000).

The MacArthur Adjudicative Competence Assessment (MacCAT-CA) is probably the most sophisticated instrument for measuring competence to stand trial. It was derived from an earlier prototype, the MacArthur Structured Assessment of the Competencies of Criminal Defendants or MacSAC-CD (Hoge et al., 1997). The MacSAC-CD was developed because other measures were found wanting in terms of their legal under-pinning, their reliance on current knowledge rather than true capacity, and in some cases inadequate administration and scoring criteria. The new measure was based on Bonnie's (1992) hypothesis that what mattered in adjudicative competence was two main skills: ability to assist counsel and decision-making competence. Competence to assist counsel (CAC) was measured using a vignette to assess understanding (CAC-U) and reasoning (CAC-R) in relation to court procedures and six items about the defendant's beliefs were used to assess appreciation (CAC-A). Decisional competence (DC) examined the defendant's capacity in relation to the two most likely decisions to be made, i.e. to pleading guilty and to waiving a jury trial. It also examined, in each case, the extent to which defendants could understand relevant information (DC-U), could reason with or weigh that information (DC-R), could appreciate their situation (DC-A), and express a choice (DC-C). The measure appeared to have good internal consistency; it distinguished between 'competent' and 'incompetent' groups, it reflected changes for hospitalised defendants who went from 'incompetent' to 'competent' and correlated, as expected with symptoms of psychoticism. However, it was also lengthy and the researchers proceeded to develop a shortened 22-item version, the MacCAT-CA, which has recently been published and has normative data to aid interpretation.

Interestingly, despite the availability of tests of capacity to stand trial, some reviewers have found that tests are rarely used. Nicholson and Kugler (1991), for example, reviewed 30 published studies but reported that only about half used any kind of competency test, 11 of the 30 only employing the Competency Screening Test and seven employing more detailed measures. One of the reasons for this may be the speed of administration: some of the measures take as much as two hours to administer. Another reason may be that, at the end of the day, courts require a yes/no decision and not all of the tests lead to such a decision (indeed Hoge et al., 1997, argued that this would be inappropriate). Of course, the real test of these competency assessments is whether they predict defendants' ability to meet the *Dusky* (or other relevant) legal criteria. In fact, though, when construct validity has been addressed, it has almost always been concerned with whether the test results correlate well with other court findings of competency, rather than whether the people declared fit to stand trial can really exercise the abilities intended.

CONCLUSIONS

Two major conclusions may be drawn from the material presented in this chapter. First, it appears from research carried out by psychologists, and by others with a psychological perspective, that the factors involved in adults' decision-making are very complex. Any particular decision is likely to reflect an interaction between, at the least, the individual's cognitive and emotional functioning, his or her knowledge and experience of the background to the decision, the way in which information about the decision is presented and sought, the specific tasks relating to the decision, and the nature of the relationship between the presenter and the decision-maker. The implication of this complexity is that an approach to assessment based simply on diagnosis is quite inadequate, and that the criticisms to which the diagnostic approach has been subjected are justified. Instead, lawyers should expect that, when psychologists are involved in the determination of the capacity of a specific individual within a particular legal context, they will provide the detailed information which is demanded by a functional approach. Included in this should be evidence that the psychological literature has been used to attempt to locate the source(s) of any discrepancy between the person's abilities and a given situation, and that an effort has been made to provide appropriate remedial strategies or at least to maximise the person's participation in the decision.

The second general conclusion, highlighted by a consideration of the three specific contexts, is that the contribution which psychologists may make to the above task is increasingly important. A functional approach to the determination of capacity is prominent in the USA, but remains underdeveloped in the UK. For a number of legal contexts, there are increasing numbers of standardised and agreed psychological measures which permit assessment of individuals' functional abilities (particularly of those whose functioning differs markedly from that of the general population) and the extent to which these meet the demands of the specific context. Over the next 10 years it is to be hoped that the development and use of such measures will increase and that there will be a burgeoning literature on how to assist and support people whose decision-making may be compromised to make decisions and choices that fit with their own wishes, rather than the wishes of professionals or family members.

REFERENCES

Allen, J.G. (2001). *Traumatic relationships and serious mental disorders*. Chichester: John Wiley & Sons.

Appelbaum, P.S. and Grisso, T. (1995). The MacArthur Treatment Competence Study. I Mental illness and competence to consent to treatment. *Law and Human Behavior, 19*, 105–126.

American Association on Mental Retardation (1992). *Mental retardation: Definition, classification and systems of supports*. Washington, DC: American Association on Mental Retardation.

Arscott, K., Dagnan, D. and Kroese, B. (1999). Assessing the ability of people with a learning disability to give informed consent to treatment. *Psychological Medicine, 29*, 1367–1375.

Baddeley, A.D. (1986). *Working memory*. Oxford: Oxford University Press.

Barker, D. (1983). How to curb the fertility of the unfit: The feeble-minded in Edwardian Britain. *Oxford Journal of Education, 9*, 197–211.

Baum, S. (1994). Interventions with a pregnant woman with severe learning disabilities: A case example. In A. Craft (ed.), *Practice issues in sexuality and learning disabilities* (pp. 217–236. London: Routledge.

Bender, M., Aitman, J.B., Biggs, S.J. and Haug, U. (1983). Initial findings concerning a sexual knowledge questionnaire. *Mental Handicap, 11*, 168–169.

Bonnie, R.J. (1992). The competence of criminal defendants: A theoretical formulation. *Behavioral Sciences and the Law, 10*, 291–316.

Booth, T. and Booth, W. (1992). Practice in sexuality. *Mental Handicap, 20*, 64–69.

British Psychological Society (2000). *Recent advances in understanding mental illness and psychotic experiences.* A report by The British Psychological Society Division of Clinical Psychology. Leicester: The British Psychological Society.

British Psychological Society (2001). *Learning disability: Definitions and contexts.* Leicester: British Psychological Society.

British Medical Association and The Law Society (1995). *Assessment of mental capacity: Guidance for doctors and lawyers.* London: British Medical Association.

Brown, H. and Stein, J. (1998). Implementing adult protection policies in Kent and East Sussex. *Journal of Social Policy, 27*, 371–396.

Brown, H., Stein, J. and Turk, V. (1995). The sexual abuse of adults learning disabilities: Report of a second two year incidence survey. *Mental Handicap Research, 8*, 3–24.

Brown, H. and Turk, V. (1992). Defining sexual abuse as it affects adults with learning disabilities. *Mental Handicap, 20*, 44–55.

Buchanan, A. and Wilkins, R. (1991). Sexual abuse of the mentally handicapped: Difficulties in establishing prevalence. *Psychiatric Bulletin, 15*, 601–605.

Bursztajn, H.J., Harding, H.P., Gutheil, T.G. and Brodsky, A. (1991). Beyond cognition: The role of disordered affective states in impairing competence to consent to treatment. *Bulletin of the American Academy of Psychiatry and Law, 19*, 383–388.

Carson, D. (1994). The law's contribution to protecting people with learning disabilities from physical or sexual abuse. In J. Harris and A. Craft, *People with learning disabilities at risk of physical or sexual abuse* (pp. 133–143). Kidderminster: BILD.

Chamberlain, A., Rauh, J., Passer, A., McGrath, M. and Burket, R. (1984). Issues in fertility control for mentally retarded female adolescents: I, Sexual activity, sexual abuse and contraception. *Pediatrics, 73*, 445–450.

Clements, J. (1987). *Severe learning disability and psychological handicap.* London: John Wiley & Sons.

Cook, J.A. (2000). Sexuality and people with psychiatric disabilities. *Sexuality and Disability, 18*, 195–205.

Cooke, L.B. (1990). Abuse of mentally handicapped adults. *Psychiatric Bulletin, 14*, 608–609.

Copperman, J. and Burrowes, F. (1992). Reducing the risk of assault. *Nursing Times, 88*, 64–65.

Craft, A. and Brown, H. (1994). Personal relationships and sexuality: The staff role. In A. Craft (ed.), *Practice issues in sexuality and learning disabilities* (pp. 1–22). London: Routledge.

Craft, A. and Craft, M. (1983). *Sex education and counselling for mentally handicapped people.* Tunbridge Wells: Costello.

Davis, A. and Hill, P. (2001). *Poverty, social exclusion and mental health. A resource pack.* London: Mental Health Foundation.

David, A. and Cutting, J. (eds) (1994). *The neuropsychology of schizophrenia.* Hove: Erlbaum Associates.

Daw, R. (2000). *The impact of the Human Rights Act on disabled people.* London: Disability Rights Commission.

Decalmer, P. (1997). Clinical presentation and management. In P. Decalmer and F. Glendenning, (eds), *The mistreatment of elderly people* (2nd edn; pp. 42–73). London: Sage Publications.

Department of Health (2001). *Reference guide to consent for examination or treatment.* London: Department of Health.

Eastman, N. and Peay, J. (1998). Bournewood: An indefensible gap in mental health law. *British Medical Journal, 317*, 94–95.

Emerson, E. (1992). What is normalisation? In H. Brown and H. Smith (eds), *Normalisation: A reader for the nineties* (pp. 1–18). London: Routledge.

Emerson, E., Hatton, C., Felce, D. and Murphy, G. (2000). *Learning disabilities. The fundamental facts.* London: The Foundation for People with Learning Disabilities.

Evans, J.J., Chua, S.E., McKenna, P.J. and Wilson, B.A. (1997). Assessment of the dysexecutive syndrome in schizophrenia. *Psychological Medicine, 27*, 635–646.

Everington, C. (1990). The Competence Assessment for Standing Trial for Defendants with Mental Retardation (CAST-MR): A validation study. *Criminal Justice and Behaviour*, *17*, 147–168.

Everington, C., DeBerge, K. and Mauer, D. (2000). The relationship between language skills and competence to stand trial abilities in persons with mental retardation. *Journal of Law and Psychiatry*, *28*, 475–492.

Fazel, S., Hope, T. and Jacoby, R. (1999). Dementia, intelligence, and the competence to complete advance directives. *The Lancet*, *354*, 48.

Finlay, W.M.L. and Lyons, E. (2001). Methodological issues in interviewing and using self-report scales with people with mental retardation. *Psychological Assessment*, *13*, 319–335.

Finlay, W.M.L. and Lyons, E. (2002). Acquiescence in interviews with people who have mental retardation. *Mental Retardation*, *40*, 14–29.

Fischer, H.L., Krajicek, M.J. and Borthick, W.A. (1973). *Sex education for the developmentally disabled: A guide for parents, teachers and professionals.* Baltimore: University Park Press.

Fennell, P. (1996). *Treatment without consent. Law, psychiatry and the treatment of mentally disordered people since 1845.* London: Routledge.

Gelder, M.G., Lopez-Ibor, J.J. and Andreasen, N.C. (eds) (2000). *New oxford textbook of psychiatry*, Vols 1 and 2. Oxford: Oxford University Press.

Glendenning, F. (1997a). What is elder abuse and neglect? In P. Decalmer and F. Glendenning (eds), *The mistreatment of elderly people* (2nd edn; pp. 13–41). London: Sage Publications.

Glendenning, F. (1997b). The mistreatment and neglect of elderly people in residential centres: research outcomes. In P. Decalmer and F. Glendenning (eds), *The mistreatment of elderly people* (2nd edn; pp. 151–162). London: Sage Publications.

Glendenning, F. (1999). The abuse of older people in institutional settings. In N. Stanley, J. Manthorpe and B. Penhale (eds), *Institutional abuse: Perspectives across the life course* (pp. 173–190). London: Routledge.

Golding, S., Roesch, R. and Schreiber, J. (1984). Assessment and conceptualisation of competency to stand trial: Preliminary data on the Interdisciplinary Fitness Interview. *Law and Human Behaviour*, *8*, 321–334.

Gove, D. and Georges, J. (2001). perspectives on legislation relating to the rights and protection of people with dementia in Europe. *Aging and Mental Health*, *5*, 316–321.

Gray, J.A., Feldon, J., Rawlins, J.N.P., Hemsley, D.R. and Smith, A.D. (1991). The neuropsychology of schizophrenia, *Behavioral and Brain Sciences*, *14*, 1–20.

Gray, N.S., O'Connor, C., Williams, T., Short, J. and McCulloch, M. (2001). Fitness to plead: implications from case-law arising from the Criminal Justice and Public Order Act, 1994. *Journal of Forensic Psychiatry*, *12*, 52–62.

Grisso, T. (1986). *Evaluating competencies: Forensic assessments and instruments.* New York: Plenum Press.

Grisso, T. (1996). Pre-trial clinical evaluations in criminal cases: past trends and future directions. *Criminal Justice and Behavior*, *23*, 90–106.

Grisso, T. and Appelbaum, P. (1991). Mentally ill and non-mentally ill patients' abilities to understand informed consent disclosures for medication. *Law and Human Behaviour*, *15*, 377–388.

Grisso, T. and Appelbaum, P. (1998). *Assessing competence to consent to treatment: A guide for physicians and other health professionals.* New York: Oxford University Press.

Grisso, T., Appelbaum, P.S., Mulvey, E.P. and Fletcher, K. (1995). The MacArthur Treatment Competence Study. II Measures of abilities related to competence to consent to treatment. *Law and Human Behavior*, *19*, 127–148.

Grubin, D.H. (1991a). Unfit to plead in England and Wales, 1976–1988: A survey. *British Journal of Psychiatry*, *158*, 540–548.

Grubin, D.H. (1991b). Unfit to plead, unfit for discharge: Patients found unfit to plead who are still in hospital. *Criminal Behaviour and Mental Health*, *1*, 282–294.

Grubin, D.H. (1996). *Fitness to Plead in England and Wales.* (Maudsley Monograph N bo. 38). Hove: Psychology Press.

Gudjonsson, G.H. (2002). *The psychology of interrogations and confessions: A handbook.* Chichester: John Wiley & Sons.

Gunn, M.J. (1985). The law and mental handicap: 3 The Mental Health Act, 1983—consent to treatment. *Mental Handicap, 13,* 70–72.

Gunn, M.J. (1996). *Sex and the law: A brief guide for staff working with people with learning difficulties* (4th edn). London: Family Planning Association.

Gunn, M.J., Wong, J.G., Clare, I.C.H. and Holland, A.J. (1999). Decision-making capacity. *Medical Law Review, 7,* 269–306.

Hess, J.H. and Thomas, H.E. (1963). Incompetency to stand trial: Procedures, results and problems. *American Journal of Psychiatry, 119,* 713–720.

Hingsburger, D. (1995). *Just say Know!: Understanding and reducing the risk of sexual victimisation of people with developmental disabilities.* Quebec: Diverse City Press.

Hirsch, R.D. and Vollhardt, B.R. (2002). Elder maltreatment. In R. Jacoby and C. Oppenheimer (eds), *Psychiatry in the elderly* (3rd edn; pp. 896–918). Oxford: Oxford University Press.

Hoge, S.K., Bonnie, R.J., Poythress, N., Monahan, J., Eisenberg, M. and Fuecht-Havier, T. (1997). The MacArthur adjudicative competence study; development and validation of a research instrument. *Law and Human Behaviour, 21,* 141–179.

Hogg, J. and Sebba, J. (1986). *Profound retardation and multiple impairment,* Volume 1, Development and Learning. London: Croom Helm.

Home Office (2000). *Setting the boundaries: Reforming the law on sex offences.* London: Home Office Communication Directorate.

Home Office/Department of Health and Social Security (1975). *Report of the Committee on Mentally Abnormal Offenders. Cmnd. 6224.* London: HMSO.

Hulme, C. and MacKenzie, S. (1992). *Working memory and severe learning difficulties.* Hove: Lawrence Erlbaum Associates.

Jacobson, A. and Richardson, B. (1987). Assault experience of 100 psychiatric inpatients. Evidence of the need for routine inquiry. *American Journal of Psychiatry, 144* (7), 908–913.

Jacoby, R. (2002). Old age psychiatry and the law. *British Journal of Psychiatry, 180,* 116–119.

Jacoby, R. and Oppenheimer, C. (eds) (2002). *Psychiatry in the Elderly* (3rd edn). Oxford: Oxford University Press.

Jahoda, A., Markova, I. and Cattermole, M. (1988). Stigma and the self-concept of people with a mild mental handicap. *Journal of Mental Deficiency Research, 32,* 103–115.

James, D.V., Duffield, G., Blizard, R. and Hamilton, L.W. (2001). Fitness to plead: A prospective study of the inter-relationships between expert opinion, legal criteria and specific symptomatology. *Psychological Medicine, 31,* 139–150.

Kapp, M.B. (1999). From medical patients to health care consumers: decisional capacity and choices to purchase coverage and services. *Aging and Mental Health, 3,* 294–300.

Kapp, M.B. (2001). Legal interventions for persons with dementia in the USA: Ethical, policy and practical aspects. *Aging and Mental Health, 5,* 312–315.

Kaufman, A.S. and Lichtenberger, E.O. (1999). *Essentials of WAIS-III Assessment.* New York: John Wiley & Sons.

Kempton, W. (1988). *Life horizons I and II: Sex education for persons with special needs.* Santa Monica, CA: James Stanfield & Company.

Kennedy, C.H. and Niederbuhl, J. (2001). Establishing criteria for sexual consent capacity. *American Journal on Mental Retardation, 106,* 503–510.

Khemka, I. and Hickson, L. (2000). Decision-making by adults with mental retardation in simulated situations of abuse. *Mental Retardation, 38,* 15–26.

Koller, R. (2000). Sexuality and adolescents with autism. *Sexuality and Disability, 18,* 125–135.

Kuipers, E. and Bebbington, P. (1987). *Living with mental illness: A book for relatives and friends.* London: Souvenir Press.

Law Commission (England and Wales) (1995). *Mental incapacity.* Report No. 231. London: HMSO.

Law Commission of Canada (1987). *Recodifying criminal law.* Report 31. Ottawa: Canada.

Lipsitt, P.D., Lelos, D. and McGarry, A.L. (1971). Competency for trial: A screening instrument. *American Journal of Psychiatry*, *128*, 105–109.

Loftus, E.F. (1979). *Eyewitness testimony*. London: Harvard University Press.

Lord Chancellor's Department (1997). *Who Decides? Making decisions on behalf of mentally incapacitated adults*. London: The Stationery Office.

Lord Chancellor's Department (1999). *Making decisions*. London: The Stationery Office.

McAllister, T.W. (1981). Cognitive functioning in the affective disorders. *Comprehensive Psychiatry*, *22* (6), 572–586.

McCabe, M.P. (1999). Sexual knowledge, experience and feelings among people with disability. *Sexuality and Disability*, *17*, 157–170.

McCabe, M.P. and Cummins, R. (1999). Sexual knowledge, experience, feelings and needs of people with mild intellectual disability. *Mental Retardation and Developmental Disabilities*, 13–21.

McCarthy, M. (1999). *Sexuality and women with learning disabilities*. London: Jessica Kingsley.

McCarthy, M. and Thompson, D. (1998). *Sex and the 3 Rs: Rights, responsibilities and risks* (2nd edn). Brighton: Pavilion Publishing.

McCarthy, M. and Thompson, D. (1994). HIV/AIDS and safer sex work with people with learning disabilities. In A. Craft (ed.), *Practice issues in sexuality and learning disabilities* (pp. 186–201). London: Routledge.

McGarry, A.L. (1971). The fate of psychotic offenders returned for trial. *American Journal of Psychiatry*, *127*, 1181–1184.

McGarry, A.L. (1973). *Competency to stand trial and mental illness*. Rockville, MD: Department of Health Education and Welfare.

Mackay, R. (1990a). Consent to treatment. In R. Bluglass and P. Bowden (eds), *Principles and Practice of Forensic Psychiatry* (pp. 1149–1162). Edinburgh: Churchill Livingstone.

Mackay, R.D. (1990b). Insanity and fitness to stand trial in Canada and England: A comparative study. *Journal of Forensic Psychiatry*, *1*, 277–303.

Mackay, R.D. (1995). Insanity and fitness to stand trial in Canada and England: A comparative study of recent developments. *Journal of Forensic Psychiatry*, *6*, 121–138.

Mackay, R.D. and Kearns, G. (2000). An upturn in unfitness to plead? Disability in relation to the trial under the 1991 Act. *Criminal Law Review*, 532–546.

Mansell, J. and Ericsson, K. (1996). *Deinstitutionalisation and community living: intellectual disability services in Britain, Scandanavia and the USA*. London: Chapman & Hall.

Marson, D.C., Imgram, K.K., Cody, H.A. and Harrell, L.E. (1995). Assessing the competency of patients with Alzheimer's disease under different legal standards: a prototype instrument. *Archives of Neurology*, *52*, 949–954.

Mencap (1989). *Competency and consent to medical treatment*. London: Mencap (Royal Society for Mentally Handicapped Adults and Children).

Mencap (1999). *Living in fear. The need to combat bullying of people with a learning disability*. London: Mencap.

Morris, C.D., Niederbuhl, J.M. and Mahr, J.M. (1993). Determining the capability of individuals with mental retardation to give informed consent. *American Journal on Mental Retardation*, *98*, 263–272.

Morris, R.G. (1997). Cognition and ageing. In R. Jacoby and C. Oppenheimer (eds), *Psychiatry in the Elderly*. (2nd edn; pp. 37–62). Oxford: Oxford University Press.

Mukherjee, S. and Shah, A. (2001). The prevalence and correlates of capacity to consent to a geriatric psychiatry admission. *Aging and Mental Health*, *5*, 335–339.

Murphy, G.H. (1993). The use of aversive stimuli in treatment: the issue of consent. *Journal of Intellectual Disability Research*, *37*, 211–219.

Murphy, G. (2000). Justice denied. *Mental Health Care*, *8*, 256–257.

Murphy, G.H. and Clare, I.C.H. (1997). Consent issues. In J. O'Hara and A. Sperlinger (eds), *Adults with Learning Disabilities: A Practical Approach for Health Professionals* (pp. 171–185). Chichester: John Wiley & Sons.

Murphy, W.D., Coleman, E.M. and Abel, G.G. (1983). Human sexuality in the mentally retarded. In J.L. Matson and F. Andrasik (eds), *Treatment Issues and Innovations in Mental Retardation* (pp. 581–642). New York: Plenum Press.

Nibert, D., Cooper, C. and Crossmaker, M. (1989). Assaults against residents of a psychiatric institution. *Journal of Interpersonal Violence, 4* (3), 343–349.

Nicholson, R. and Kugler, K.E. (1991). Competent and incompetent criminal defendants: A quantitative review of comparative research. *Psychological Bulletin, 109*, 355–370.

Nicholson, R., Robertson, H., Johnson, W. and Jensen, G. (1988). A comparison of instruments for assessing competency to stand trial. *Law and Human Behavior, 12*, 313–321.

Nirje, B. (1980). The normalisation principle. In R.J. Flynn and K.E. Nitsch (eds), *Normalisation, Social Integration and Community Services*, (pp. 71–116). Austin, TX: Pro-ed.

Nosek, M.A., Foley, C.C., Hughes, R.B. and Howland, C.A. (2001). Vulnerabilities for abuse among women with disabilities. *Sexuality and Disability, 19*, 177–189.

Nuechterlein, K.H. and Dawson, M. (1984). Information processing and attentional functioning in the developmental course of schizophrenic disorders. *Schizophrenia Bulletin, 10*, 160–203.

Nuechterlein, K.H. and Subotnik, K.L. (1998). The cognitive origins of schizophrenia and prospects for intervention. In T. Wykes, N. Tarrier and S. Lewis (eds), *Outcome and Innovation in Psychological Treatment of Schizophrenia*. Chichester: John Wiley & Sons.

O'Callaghan, A.C. and Murphy, G.H. (2002). *Capacity to consent to sexual relationships in adults with learning disabilities*. Final report to the Nuffield Foundation.

O'Sullivan, J.L. (1999). Adult guardianship and alternatives. In R.D. Dinerstein, S.S. Herr and J.L. O'Sullivan (eds), *A Guide to Consent* (pp. 7–38). Washington, DC: American Association on Mental Retardation.

Pennington, B.F. and Ozonoff, S. (1996). Executive functions and developmental psychopathology. *Journal of Child Psychology and Psychiatry, 35*, 29–72.

Poythress, N.G., Cascardi, M. and Ritterband, L. (1996). Capacity to consent to voluntary hospitalisation: searching for a satisfactory Zinermon screen. *Bulletin of the American Academy of Psychiatry and Law, 24*, 439–452.

Repp, A. and Singh, N. (1990). *Perspectives on the use of non-aversive and aversive interventions for persons with developmental disabilities*. DeKalb, IL: Sycamore Press.

Reynolds, S.L. and Carson, L.D. (1999). Dependent on the kindness of strangers: Professional guardians for older adults who lack decisional capacity. *Aging and Mental Health, 3*, 301–310.

Rioux, M. (1997). Disability: The place of judgement in a world of fact. *Journal of Intellectual Disability Research, 4*, 102–111.

Roth, L.H., Lidz, C.W., Meisel, A., Soloff, P.H., Kaufman, K., Spiker, D.G. and Foster, F.G. (1982). Competency to decide about treatment or research: An overview of some empirical data. *International Journal of Law and Psychiatry, 5*, 29–50.

Royal College of Physicians (1981). Organic mental impairment in the elderly: Implications for research, education and the provision of services. Report of the Royal College of Physicians by the College Committee on Geriatrics. *Journal of the Royal College of Physicians of London, 15*, 141–167.

Savage, H.S. (1981). The relevance of the fitness to stand trial provisions of persons with mental handicap. *Canadian Bar Review, 59*, 319–336.

Showalter, E. (1985). *The female malady: Women, madness and English culture, 1830–1980*. London: Virago.

Shah, A., Foli, S. and Odutoye, K. (1999). Capacity to consent in dementia and the additional costs of implementing the Bournewood judgement in geriatric psychiatry. *Aging and Mental Health, 3*, 153–157.

Shakespeare, T. (2000). Disabled sexuality: Towards rights and recognition. *Sexuality and Disability, 18*, 159–166.

Sinason, V. (1992). *Mental handicap and the human condition*. London: Free Association Books.

Singleton, N., Bumpstead, R., O'Brien, M., Lee, A. and Meltzer, H. (2001). *Psychiatric morbidity among adults living in private households 2000*. London: The Stationery Office.

Sobsey, D. (1994). Sexual abuse of individuals with intellectual disability. In A. Craft (ed.), *Practice Issues in Sexuality and Learning Disabilities* (pp. 93–115). London: Routledge.

Solomon, A. (2002). *The noonday demon. An anatomy of depression*. London: Vintage.

Stavis, P.F. (1991). Harmonising the right to sexual expression and the right to protection from harm for persons with mental disability. *Journal of Sexuality and Disability*, *9*, 131–141.

Stavis, P.F. and Walker-Hirsch, L.W. (1999). Consent to sexual activity. In R.D. Dinerstein, S.S. Herr and J.L. O'Sullivan (eds), *A Guide to Consent* (pp. 57–67). Washington, DC: American Association on Mental Retardation.

Steadman, H.J., Monahan, J. and Hartson, E. (1982). Mentally disordered offenders: A national survey of patients and facilities. *Law and Human Behaviour*, *6*, 31–38.

Sundram, C.J. and Stavis, P.F. (1994). Sexuality and mental retardation: Unmet challenges. *Mental Retardation*, *32*, 255–264.

Tharinger, D., Horton, C.B. and Millea, S. (1990). Sexual abuse and exploitation of children and adults with mental retardation and other handicaps. *Child Abuse and Neglect*, *14*, 301–312.

Thomson, M. (1998). *The problem of mental deficiency*. Oxford: Clarendon Press.

Walsh, P.N. and Murphy, G.H. (2002). Risk and vulnerability: Dilemmas for women with intellectual disabilities. In P.N. Walsh and T. Heller (eds), *Health of women with intellectual disabilities*. Oxford: Blackwell Science.

Wexler, D.B. (1973). Token and taboo: Behaviour modification, token economies and the law. *California Law Review*, *61*, 81–109.

Wilber, K.H. and Zarit, S.H. (1999). To decide or not to decide for others: Competency, choice and consequences. *Aging and Mental Health*, *3*, 277–280.

Wilber, K.H. (2001). Decision-making, dementia and the law: Cross national perspectives. *Aging and Mental Health*, *5*, 309–311.

Wechsler, D. (1999). *Wechsler Adult Intelligence Scale* (3rd edn). London: The Psychological Corporation.

Williams, J. and Keating, F. (1999). The abuse of adults in mental health settings. In N. Stanley, J. Manthorpe and B. Penhale (eds), *Institutional Abuse: Perspectives Across the Life Course* (pp. 130–151). London: Routledge.

Williams, W. and Miller, K. (1981). The processing and disposition of incompetent mentally ill offenders. *Law and Human Behaviour*, *5*, 245–261.

Wilson, C., Seaman, L. and Nettlebeck, T. (1996). Vulnerability to criminal exploitation: influence of interpersonal competence differences among people with mental retardation. *Journal of Intellectual Disability Research*, *40*, 10–19.

Wish, J., McCombs, K.F. and Edmonson, B. (1979). *Manual for the socio-sexual knowledge and attitudes test*. Chicago: Stoelting Corporation.

Wolfensberger, W. (1980). The definition of normalisation. In R.J. Flynn and K.E. Nitsch (eds), *Normalisation, Social Integration and Community Services* (pp. 71–116). Austin, TX: Proed.

Wolfensberger, W. (1983). Social role valorisation: A proposed new term for the principle of normalisation. *Mental Retardation*, *21*, 234–239.

Wong, J.G., Clare, I.C.H., Gunn, M.J. and Holland, A.J. (1999). Capacity to make health care decisions: Its importance in clinical practice. *Psychological Medicine*, *29*, 437–446.

Wong, J.G., Clare, I.C.H., Holland, A.J., Watson, P.C. and Gunn, M.J. (2000). The capacity of people with a 'mental disability' to make a health care decision. *Psychological Medicine*, *30*, 295–306.

Chapter 1.2

The Assessment and Detection of Deceit

Aldert Vrij[1]
University of Portsmouth, UK

INTRODUCTION

When criminal justice investigators (police officers, lawyers, prosecutors, judges, juries, and so on) assess statements made by suspects, victims and witnesses, they are almost always confronted with an age old dilemma: how to distinguish between those who are telling the truth and those who are not. One way to examine this is by observing people's behaviour and analysing their speech content. This chapter reviews research findings on (i) differences in behaviour and speech content between liars and truth tellers, and (ii) people's ability to detect deceit while observing someone's behaviour and analysing someone's speech. The first part of this chapter addresses the relationship between behaviour and deception. This part will demonstrate that, although no single pattern of behaviour is uniquely related to deception (Pinocchio's nose does not exist), some behaviours are more likely to occur during deception than others. Also, it shows that people are generally not very good at detecting deceit when paying attention to someone's behaviour. Several reasons to explain this poor lie detection ability and some ideas how to improve behavioural lie detection will be discussed.

The second part considers the relationship between speech content and deception. Although analyses of non-verbal behaviour are never formally used as evidence in criminal courts, verbal assessments sometimes are. This part of the chapter discusses the most popular verbal detection technique used in court to date: Statement Validity Assessment (SVA). Research has shown that some of the speech content criteria that SVA experts examine do differentiate between liars and truth tellers. Also, we will see that experts who employ this technique are able to detect lies and truths above the

---

[1] Correspondence should be addressed to: Aldert Vrij, University of Portsmouth, Psychology Department, King Henry Building, King Henry 1 Street, Portsmouth PO1 2DY, United Kingdom or via email: aldert.vrij@port.ac.uk

---

Handbook of Psychology in Legal Contexts, Second Edition
Edited by D. Carson and R. Bull. © 2003 John Wiley & Sons, Ltd.

level of chance. However, their lie detection skills fall short to the level required for using their assessments as reliable evidence in criminal courts. Some limitations of SVA and ideas how to improve speech content lie detection will be discussed.

Throughout this chapter methodological problems in deception research will be addressed. These are important as they raise questions about the generalisability of the research findings to legal settings. I will conclude with discussing some implications of the research findings for lie detection in legal settings.

NON-VERBAL BEHAVIOUR AND DECEPTION

The Behaviour of a Liar

Researchers have examined a variety of different non-verbal behaviours, including gaze aversion (looking away from the conversation partner), smiling, illustrators (hand and arm movements that accompany speech and illustrate it), self-manipulations (touching or scratching body or face, playing with own hair, playing with objects), subtle movements of hands and fingers, speech rate, pauses in speech, speech latency (period between question being asked and answer being given), speech fillers (um's and er's), stutters (repetitions of words, correcting sentences, and so on), and pitch of voice. Vrij (2000) reviewed more than 40 studies concerning such behavioural indicators of deception. The review revealed that deception is not related to a unique pattern of specific behaviours. In other words, there is nothing like Pinocchio's nose. Some behaviours, however, are more likely to occur during deception than others. Liars tend to speak with a higher-pitched voice, speak slower, pause longer while they speak, and display a decrease in illustrators, hand/finger movements, and leg and foot movements (Vrij, 2000).

Three theoretical approaches are usually offered to explain these findings: the emotional approach, the cognitive approach, and the attempted control approach (Burgoon et al., 1989; DePaulo, 1988, 1992; DePaulo and Kirkendol, 1989; DePaulo, Stone and Lassiter, 1985a; Ekman, 1989, 1992; Ekman and Friesen, 1972; Goldman-Eisler, 1968; Knapp, Hart and Dennis, 1974; Köhnken, 1989, 1990; Riggio and Friedman, 1983; Vrij, 1998, 2000; Zuckerman, DePaulo and Rosenthal, 1981). Although deception *in itself* does not lead to specific behaviour, liars may experience emotional, content complexity, and controlling processes, which may influence their behaviour. Each process emphasises a different aspect of deception and deceptive behaviour. However, the distinction between them is artificial. Lies may well feature all three aspects, and the three approaches should not be considered as different camps.

The emotional approach proposes that deception can result in various emotions. The three most common types of emotion associated with deceit are guilt, fear and excitement (Ekman, 1992). People may feel *guilty* while lying, because they realise that it is morally wrong to deceive; they might also be *afraid*, because they might be worried that someone will find out that they are lying; they might become very *excited* because they might enjoy the opportunity to fool someone. The strength of these emotions depends on the personality of the liar and on the circumstances in which the lie takes place (Ekman, 1992; Vrij, 2000). The higher-pitched voice during deception might be the result of the emotions that liars experience (Ekman, Friesen and Scherer, 1976). However, differences in pitch between liars and truth tellers are usually very small, only a few Hertz, and therefore usually only detectable with sophisticated equipment.

The content complexity approach emphasises that lying can be a cognitively complex task (Vrij, 2000). Liars have to think of plausible answers, should not contradict themselves, should tell a lie that is consistent with everything which the observer knows or might find out, and should avoid making slips of the tongue. Moreover, they have to remember what they have said, so that they can say the same things when someone asks them to repeat their story. People engaged in cognitively complex tasks speak slower and pause more (Goldman-Eisler, 1968). Cognitive complexity also leads to fewer movements, due to the fact that a greater cognitive load results in a neglect of body language, reducing overall animation (Ekman and Friesen, 1972).

So far, the predictions of how liars behave have been straightforward. A liar may experience emotions or may find it difficult to lie, and this will result in behaviourial signs of emotion and content complexity. However, the situation is more complicated than this. Liars may be afraid that several cues will give their lies away, and therefore try to suppress such signs in order to avoid getting caught. This is emphasised in the attempted behavioural control approach (Vrij, 2000). Hocking and Leathers (1980) argued that liars' attempts to control their behaviour will focus on those behaviours that fit the cultural stereotype of liars. For example, if there is a widespread belief that liars look away, increase their movements and stutter, then liars will try to maintain eye contact, refrain from making too many movements, and will try to speak smoothly. When people try to do this, they sometimes tend to overcontrol themselves, which results in behaviour that looks too rehearsed and too rigid (i.e. decrease in movements) (Vrij, 2000).

Vrij's (2000) literature review showed a conflicting pattern concerning speech fillers and stutters. In most studies an increase in speech fillers and stutters were found, but some studies revealed the opposite pattern (a decrease in speech fillers and stutters). Vrij and Heaven (1999) found in their study that variations of lie complexity are responsible for these conflicting findings. When the lie was easy to fabricate, a decrease in speech errors and stutters occurred, whereas the opposite pattern occurred when the lie was difficult to fabricate. Vrij and Heaven (1999) suggested that, in line with the attempted behavioural control approach, liars will try to avoid making speech errors and stutters while lying. However, they only achieve this when the lie is easy to formulate. When the lie is difficult to fabricate an increase in speech errors and stutters occurs, due to the cognitive load required to fabricate the lie.

Perhaps the most interesting aspect of the literature review was the absence of several signs of nervousness as indicators of deception. For example, nervous behaviours such as gaze aversion and fidgeting are not related to deception (see also DePaulo et al., 2000). This is remarkable as most people, often including professional lie detectors such as the police and customs officers, believe that liars fidget and look away (Akehurst et al., 1996; Vrij and Mann, 2001a; Vrij and Semin, 1996).

One possible reason why liars don't show clear patterns of nervous behaviour is that the stakes (the positive and negative consequences of getting caught) are not high enough for the liar in (most of the) deception studies to elicit clear nonverbal cues to deception (Mann, Vrij and Bull, 2002; Miller and Stiff, 1993; Vrij, 2000). The vast majority of deception studies are experimental studies: laboratory studies in which participants (usually university students) are requested to lie or tell the truth for the sake of the experiment. The research designs typically involve asking a participant to lie about various issues. People lied or told the truth about beliefs and opinions (DePaulo and Rosenthal, 1979; DePaulo, Stone and Lassiter, 1985b), about personal facts such as the course they study (Vrij and Holland, 1998), about videofilms or pictures they had just seen (Bell and DePaulo, 1996; Ekman and Friesen, 1974; Vrij and Heaven, 1999), about feelings about an object or person (DePaulo, Lanier and Davis, 1983; DePaulo, LeMay and Epstein, 1991; DePaulo, Stone and Lassiter, 1985b; Ekman and Friesen, 1974; Frank and Ekman, 1997; Riggio, Tucker and Throckmorton, 1988), or about the possession of an object (Vrij, 1995; Vrij, Akehurst and Morris, 1997). Also, people were induced to cheat and then to lie about it (deTurck and Miller, 1985), or were given the opportunity to take money and, if taken, to lie about this in a subsequent interview (Frank and Ekman, 1997).

In order to raise the stakes in laboratory experiments, participants are offered money if they successfully get away with their lies (Vrij, 1995), or researchers tell participants (nursing students) that being a good liar is an important indicator of being successful in a future career (Vrij, Edward and Bull, 2001a, c).[2] In some studies, participants are told that they would be observed by a peer who will judge their sincerity (DePaulo, Stone and Lassiter, 1985b). Obviously, the stakes in these experimental studies are still lower than the stakes in several real-life situations. Frank and Ekman (1997) therefore raised the stakes even further. In their study, participants were given the opportunity to take 50 dollars. If they could convince the interviewer that they had not taken the money, they could keep the 50 dollars. If they took the money and the interviewer judged them as lying, they had to give the 50 dollars back and also lost their 10 dollars per hour participation fee. Moreover, some participants faced an additional punishment while lying. They were told that they would have to sit on a cold, metal chair inside a cramped, darkened room labelled ominously XXX, where they would have to endure anywhere from 10 to 40 randomly sequenced, 110-decibel starting blasts of white noise over the course of one hour. These participants were given a sample of this punishment prior to engaging in the task. However, no participant who was judged lying actually received the punishment (Frank and Ekman,

[2] This information is based on evidence. Ekman and Friesen (1974) have found that nurses' ability to conceal negative emotions (when they interact with patients who are terminally ill, or with patients with severe burns, and so on) is very useful in their jobs.

1997, pp. 1431/1432). Although this laboratory study might be a good example of a high stake study, it also raises serious ethical concerns. To what extent is it ethically acceptable to threaten people so much, just for the sake of an experiment? See Vrij (2002b) for a discussion concerning ethical issues in deception research.

Whatever researchers try, the best insight into deceptive behaviour in real-life situations will be obtained by examining people's behaviour in such situations. This is exactly what some researchers recently did (Davis and Hadiks, 1995; Vrij and Mann, 2001b; Mann et al., 2002). For example, Vrij and Mann (2001b) examined videotapes of a murderer when he was questioned by the police regarding his crime. The man initially denied having committed the crime, but confessed following the presentation of indisputable evidence. Davis and Hadiks (1995) analysed Saddam Hussein's behaviour while he was interviewed by CNN during the Gulf War. Interestingly, the murderer in Vrij and Mann's study did not show a clear pattern of nervous behaviours, neither did Saddam Hussein while he lied during his CNN interview. An explanation why nervous behaviours might still not be present in high-stakes lie situations is that liars probably will experience increased cognitive load and/or attempted behavioral control, which will negate their nervous behaviours. In the most extensive study examining the behaviour of authentic high-stake liars to date, Mann et al. (in submission) analysed, amongst others, the behaviour of 13 male suspects during their police interviews. The strongest indicator for deceit in that study was eye blinking, with 11 out of the 13 male suspects (85%) showing less eye blinking while lying. This is an interesting finding since research on eyeblinks has shown that these decrease as a result of cognitive load (Bagley and Manelis, 1979; Bauer et al., 1985; Wallbott and Scherer, 1991), but increase as a result of stress (Harrigan and O'Connell, 1996; Tecce, 1992). In other words, our finding suggests that these suspects experienced more cognitive load than stress during their interviews. However, since we did not directly test this hypothesis, this conclusion should be drawn with caution.

In summary, the authentic high-stakes studies conducted so far do not support the idea that liars show nervous behaviours. Instead, liars tend to show behaviours which indicate cognitive load or attempted behavioural control. However, we have to be careful with drawing this conclusion. The studies examining behaviour during authentic high-stakes lies have only examined behaviours shown by criminals (and Saddam Hussein). Obviously, there is a difference between this sample of participants and the population at large, limiting the generalisability of the findings. For example, it might be that the people examined in these studies experienced less guilt or fear, might have been more experienced liars, or might care less about the consequences than other people (such as victims and witnesses) who are involved in high-stakes lie situations.

Detecting Lies by observing Someone's Behaviour

In scientific studies concerning detection of deception, observers are typically given videotapes or audiotapes and asked to judge whether each of a number of people is lying or telling the truth. Statements of liars and truth tellers are usually taken from the laboratory studies described above. Vrij (2000) examined the percentages of lie detection (the 'accuracy rate') of 37 studies. Included were studies in which judges were university students who tried to detect lies and truths told by people they did not know.

The total accuracy rate was 54.6%, when 50% accuracy is expected by chance alone. (Guessing whether someone is lying or not gives a 50% chance to be correct.) People were to some extent capable of detecting truths (67% accuracy rate) but particularly poor at detecting lies (44% accuracy rate). In fact, 44% is below the level of chance. In other words, people would be more accurate at detecting lies by simply guessing!

It could be argued that university students do not habitually detect deception. Perhaps professional lie catchers, such as police officers or customs officers, would obtain higher accuracy rates than lay persons. It might be that their experiences at interviewing people and catching liars has a positive influence on their skills to detect deceit. In several studies professional lie catchers participated as judges—see Vrij (2000) and Vrij and Mann (2001a) for details concerning these studies. Most of the professional lie catchers' accuracy rates fall in the 45–60% range, which was also found in studies with university students as observers. This suggests that professional lie catchers are not better in detecting deception than are university students. DePaulo and Pfeifer (1986), Ekman and O'Sullivan (1991) and Vrij and Graham (1997) directly tested this idea by including both lay persons and professional lie catchers as observers in their experiments. DePaulo and Pfeifer (1986) and Vrij and Graham (1997) found that police officers were as (un)successful as university students in detecting deception. Ekman and O'Sullivan (1991) found that police officers and polygraph examiners obtained similar accuracy rates to university students, whereas members of the Secret Service were better at detecting lies than university students. The latter finding suggests that some groups of police officers are better at detecting lies than others, a finding which was supported by a study conducted by Ekman, O'Sullivan and Frank (1999). Federal officers (police officers with a special interest and experience in deception and demeanour) and sheriffs (police officers who were identified by their department as outstanding interrogators) were considerably better at detecting lies than mixed law-enforcement officers (officers who had not been chosen because of their reputation as interrogators).

Moreover, DePaulo and Pfeifer (1986) investigated how confident observers were in the decisions they made. They found that police officers were more confident than university students, which suggests that being a professional lie catcher may increase self-confidence in the ability to detect deceit, but does not increase accuracy. The tendency to be overconfident is not unique for police officers, it is common amongst many different groups of professionals (Allwood and Granhag, 1997).

The fact that professional lie catchers seem to be as inaccurate as lay persons at detecting lies, indicates that professional lie catchers do not seem to learn how validly to interpret non-verbal behaviour from their daily work experience. One explanation is in connection with the feedback they usually receive about the accuracy of the decisions they make. It may be that daily-life experience in detecting lies results in better insight among professional lie catchers only when they receive adequate outcome feedback, that is, adequate information regarding whether their true/lie judgements are either right or wrong. In daily-life such outcome feedback is usually lacking (DePaulo and Pfeifer, 1986). Take, for example, customs officers. Good feedback in their occupation means that they get insight into how many travellers they stopped and searched, did actually try to smuggle, but also how many travellers they did *not* stop tried to smuggle. The latter form of feedback is usually lacking. They will almost never find out whether or not the travellers they did not search were smuggling goods, and they therefore cannot learn from these cases. It may well be the case that a customs officer who has caught many smugglers in his career and therefore believes himself to be good at detecting lies, turns out to be less successful when taking into account the number of smugglers who managed to dupe this particular officer.

However, how realistic are these findings of scientific lie detection studies? Clearly, there are many differences between lie detection in scientific deception studies and lie detection in real life. For example, in deception studies observers watch videotapes of liars and truth tellers, whereas in real life they often actually interview people. Police officers, judges and prosecutors believe that it easier to detect lies in real interviews than when they are watching a video (Granhag and Strömwall, 2001, in press). Researchers also regularly criticise the lack of interaction between interviewers and potential liars in (detection of) deception research (Burgoon and Buller, 1994; Burgoon et al., 1999; Burgoon and White, 1997; Seiter, 1997). However, it is doubtful whether having the opportunity to interview the potential liar improves detection accuracy. Several researchers compared the accuracy scores of observers who actually interviewed potential liars with those who observed the interviews but did not interview the potential liars themselves (Buller, Strzyzewski and Hunsaker, 1991; Feeley and deTurck, 1997; Granhag and Strömwall, 2001). In all three studies it was found that observers were more accurate in detecting truths and lies than were interviewers. These findings suggest that actually interviewing someone is a disadvantage, and not an advantage in detecting deceit. This finding is perhaps not surprising. First, interviewers need to concentrate on the interview itself. For example, they have to decide what to ask, how to phrase their questions, and at what moment in the interview they are going to ask these questions. Additionally, they must listen to the interviewees and reply to what they say. This requires cognitive energy which can not be used for the lie detection task. Observers on the other hand do not have to think about the flow of the conversation and can fully concentrate on the lie detection task (Vrij, 2000).

I believe that there are several reasons why people are generally poor at detecting deceit. For example, lie detectors face many difficulties. Also, there are opportunities to improve someone's ability to detect deceit. Elsewhere I have discussed numerous difficulties and opportunities (Vrij, 2000). I will here briefly mention just a few, starting with three difficulties which lie detectors face.

First, differences between liars and truth tellers are usually very small (Vrij, 1994). Freud's (1959) view that 'betrayal oozes out of liars at every pore' is incorrect. Obviously, the smaller the differences, the more difficult it will be to detect them.

Second, as mentioned above, there is no such thing as typical deceptive behaviour. The fact that generic deceptive behaviour does not exist makes it difficult for observers to decide what to look for. Third, truth tellers may show identical behaviour as liars, because they may experience the same processes. For example, innocent (truthful) suspects who are worried that they will not be believed by a police officer may, because of that fear, show the same nervous behaviours as guilty liars who are afraid of being caught (Bond and Fahey, 1987). Ekman (1992) labelled this phenomenon the *Othello error*, after Shakespeare's play. Desdemona (Othello's lover) is falsely accused of infidelity. Realising that she cannot prove her innocence, Desdemona reacts with an emotional outburst that seems to confirm the accusation. The Othello error is important because it is one of the main reasons why people are often poor at detecting deceit.

However, there are opportunities to improve people's ability to detect deceit. First, lie detectors could apply the baseline method. Knowing someone's natural truthful behaviour (so-called baseline behaviour) could facilitate lie detection, as comparisons can be made between this natural behaviour and the behaviour under investigation. During a videotaped real-life police interview a man was asked to describe his activities during a particular day (Vrij and Mann, 2001b). The murder suspect gave descriptions of his activities during the morning, afternoon and evening. Detailed analyses of the videotape revealed a sudden change in behaviour as soon as he started to describe his activities during the afternoon and evening. One possible reason for this may have been that he was lying. Evidence supported this view. Police investigations could confirm his story about his morning activities, but revealed that his statement about the afternoon and evening were fabricated. In reality, he met the victim and killed her later on that day. Crucial in the use of the baseline technique is that the correct parts of the interview are compared. One should not compare apples with oranges. Unfortunately that happens often in police interviews (Moston and Engelberg, 1993). Small talk at the beginning of the interview is used to establish a baseline, which is then compared with the behaviour shown in the actual interview. This is an incorrect way of employing the technique as small talk and the actual investigating part of the police interview are totally different situations. Not surprisingly, both guilty and innocent people tend to change their behaviour the moment the actual interview starts (Vrij, 1995). In the case of the murderer, we were able to make a good comparison. There seemed no other reasons why different behaviours would emerge while describing the morning or the afternoon and evening. Interestingly, the question on which we based the baseline method 'What did you do that particular day?' could be asked in many police interviews.

Second, there is evidence that people know more about deception than it appears when they are asked directly whether they think someone is lying (DePaulo, 1994). When people are asked to detect deception both in a direct way (i.e. 'Is the person lying?') and in an indirect way (i.e. 'Does the speaker sincerely like the person (s)he just described?'), they are usually more accurate using the indirect way (Anderson, DePaulo and Ansfield, 2002; DePaulo et al., 1982a, 1982b; Hurd and Noller, 1988). This might be the result of conversation rules which regulate politeness. Observers are often unsure as to whether someone is lying to them. In such instances it will be impolite, or for other reasons undesirable, to accuse someone of being a liar, but it might be possible to challenge the words of a speaker more subtly. In other words, it is more difficult to say 'I do not believe you' than to say 'Do you really like that person so much?'. Alternatively, people might look at different cues when directly trying to detect lies than when applying an indirect method. In Vrij et al. (2001b) study, police officers watched a number of videotaped interviews of truth tellers and liars. Some participants were asked whether each of these people was lying, others were asked to indicate for each person whether that person 'had to think hard' (they were not informed that some people were actually lying). Police officers distinguished between truths and lies, but only when using the indirect method. Only in the indirect method did they pay attention to the cues which actually discriminated between truth tellers and liars on the videotape, such as a decrease in hand movements.

Finally, although on average people are not very good at detecting lies, there are exceptions. Perhaps, if some people are good at it, others might improve their skills by copying the methods used by good lie detectors. Ekman and O'Sullivan (1991) found that, compared to inaccurate observers, accurate observers more frequently mentioned both verbal and non-verbal cues to arrive at their decision whether someone was lying. Vrij and Mann (2001b) found that those observers (police officers) endorsing popular stereotypical views on deceptive behaviour, such as 'liars look away' and 'liars fidget' were the poorest lie catchers. In their study with undergraduate students as lie detectors, Frank and Ekman (1997) found that good lie detectors are also good at spotting facial micro-expressions of emotions (facial expressions of emotions which last less than a quarter of a second).

In summary, on average people are rather poor at detecting deceit. This is perhaps not surprising given the difficulties lie detectors face. However, there are several ways to improve lie detection, which could be taught to professional lie catchers. Teaching them these methods would probably not be easy, as they might be received with disbelief. For example, police officers hold strong stereotypical views that liars fidget and look away (Vrij, 2000; Vrij and Graham, 1997; Vrij and Semin, 1996), and it would not be easy to convince them that such views are often incorrect. Perhaps a compelling way to convince professional lie detectors that their beliefs are often incorrect is by asking them to lie, to videotape this lie and subsequently show them how they themselves behaved while lying (Vrij et al., 2001a). This would indicate to them that their own behaviour often does not match with their expectations about behaviour during actual deception. To our knowledge, such an intervention has never been carried out but seems worth while to develop.

SPEECH CONTENT AND DECEPTION

Criteria-Based Content Analysis

The first part of this chapter made transparent the difficulties that lie detectors face and the limited success they usually have in detecting deceit by observing someone's behaviour. Therefore, unsurprisingly, analyses of non-verbal behaviour are never formally used as evidence in criminal courts. Verbal assessments, however, sometimes are. This part of the chapter discusses the most popular verbal detection technique used in court to date: *Statement Validity Assessment* (SVA). SVA assessments are used as evidence in criminal courts in several European countries (such as Germany and the Netherlands) and in several States in the USA (Ruby and Brigham, 1998). (But they are not accepted as evidence in criminal courts in the United Kingdom.) SVA is a technique to measure the veracity of verbal statements. The technique was developed in Germany to determine the credibility of *child* witnesses' testimonies in trials for *sexual offences*. That may not be surprising. It is often difficult to determine the facts of a sexual abuse case. Often there is no medical or physical evidence. Frequently the alleged victim and the defendant give contradictory testimonies and there are often no other witnesses to say what has happened. This means that the perceived credibility of the defendant and alleged victim are important. The alleged victims are in a disadvantageous position if they are children, as adults have a tendency to mistrust statements made by children (Ceci and Bruck, 1995). Tully (1999) pointed out that, at the beginning of last century, European and American psychologists regarded child witnesses as 'dangerous' and likely to give unreliable and misleading eyewitness accounts. In the beginning of the 1950s the forensic psychologist Udo Undeutsch insisted that it is not the reputation of witnesses which matters, but rather the truthfulness of the particular statements (Tully, 1999). According to Undeutsch (1967), a child's statement, derived from memory of an actual experience, differs in content and quality from a statement based on invention or fantasy. This is known as the *Undeutsch hypothesis* (Steller, 1989). Undeutsch (and others) have developed various content criteria which could be used to check the veracity of statements (Undeutsch, 1967, 1982). Based on their work, Steller and Köhnken (1989) compiled a list of 19 criteria to be used in credibility assessment. SVA consists of three phases (Vrij, 2000): (i) in order to extract a statement, children are interviewed following a 'structured interview' procedure, designed to obtain as much information as possible from interviewees in a free narrative style (see Bull, 1992, 1995, 1998 for further details). These interviews are audiotaped and then transcribed. (ii) Subsequently, a systematic assessment takes place of the credibility of the statement given during the interview. For this assessment the written transcripts are used. This assessment, which is called 'Criteria-Based Content Analysis' (CBCA), is based on the list of 19 criteria compiled by Steller and Köhnken (1989). (iii) Finally, an evaluation of the CBCA outcome takes place via a set of questions (so-called validity checklist). The use of transcripts excludes the opportunity to take interviewees' non-verbal behaviour into account when judging the veracity of their statements. Some people believe this to be a disadvantage (Landry and Brigham, 1992). On the other hand, the non-verbal information available on a videotape concerning the interview may distract the SVA rater. As mentioned earlier, many observers have incorrect, stereotyped beliefs about deceptive behaviour and often make incorrect judgements when they detect deceit on the basis of someone's behaviour. This perhaps makes the use of videotapes less advantageous.

The core of the SVA procedure is the systematic assessment of a statement (CBCA, phase 2). Trained evaluators examine the statement and judge the presence or absence of each of the 19 criteria. The presence of each criterion in the statement enhances the quality of the statement and strengthens the (Undeutsch) hypothesis that the account is based on genuine personal experience. CBCA is not a 'verbal lie detector', as it is not searching for 'lie symptoms'. The absence of a criterion does not necessarily mean that the statement is fabricated. Vrij (2000) gives a detailed overview of the 19 criteria used in the assessment. First, observers are looking for 'unstructured production'. Liars tend to tell their stories in a more chronological manner (this happened first, and then this, and then that, and so on), whereas truth tellers tend to give their account in unstructured and incoherent ways, particularly when they talk about emotional events. A second criterion is the number of details mentioned in a statement. It is hypothesised that liars include fewer details in their accounts than truth tellers do. The type of details CBCA evaluators are looking for include: 'contextual embedding' (does the statement contain details about times ('It lasted three hours') and locations ('We were in the living room')), 'description of interactions' ('I said go away, but he didn't and smiled, and then I started crying'), 'reproduction of speech' (did the interviewee recall literally what has been said during the event), and 'unusual details' (are there any details mentioned which are 'odd' but not unrealistic). All the above mentioned criteria are thought to differ between truth tellers and liars because it is believed to be too difficult for people to fabricate them (Steller, 1989). This is similar to the cognitive complexity approach described earlier. Other criteria are less likely to occur for motivational reasons (Steller, 1989). This is related to the attempted control approach described earlier. Liars will try to construct a report which they believe will make a credible impression on others, and will leave out information which, in their view, will damage their image of being a sincere person (Köhnken, 1999). Motivated-based criteria include: 'spontaneous corrections' (when the person spontaneously admits that the previous description was incorrect and modifies that description), and 'admitting lack of memory' (spontaneous admitting not to remember some (crucial) details).

Some authors still describe CBCA as a technique solely to evaluate statements of *children* who are alleged *victims* in *sexual abuse cases* (Honts, 1994; Raskin and Esplin, 1991), while others have advocated the additional use of the technique to evaluate the testimonies of suspects or adult witnesses who talk about issues other than sexual abuse (Köhnken et al., 1995; Ruby and Brigham, 1997; Steller and Köhnken, 1989). This latter group of authors has pointed out that the underlying Undeutsch hypothesis is neither restricted to children, witnesses and victims nor to sexual abuse.

Does CBCA Differentiate between Liars and Truth Tellers?

In order to test whether CBCA actually works and does discriminate between truthful and fabricated accounts, field studies and laboratory studies have been conducted. In field studies, CBCA assessments in real sexual abuse cases are examined. The advantage of a field study is that it is realistic, as it examines actual cases. However, the disadvantage is that in most criminal cases it is virtually impossible to check the 'basic reality', that is, to know for sure which statements were truthful and which were fabricated. Basic reality (also called ground truth) is often based on confessions. That is, whether or not the person accused by the child of sexual abuse confessed to have committed the crime. To base the ground truth on confessions generates problems. As Steller and Köhnken (1989) pointed out, CBCA statements are usually obtained if no other evidence is available. If under such conditions a statement is judged as truthful, the chances for the defendant to obtain an acquittal are decreased. If there is a reduced chance for the defendant to avoid a guilty verdict, it may be a beneficial strategy for the defendant to falsely confess to the crime as this may result in a considerably lower punishment. On the other hand, there is no reason for the guilty defendant to confess to the crime if the CBCA suggests that the witness's statement is not about a genuinely experienced event. As a result, the defendant's decision to confess may be influenced by the outcome of the CBCA assessment. An attempt to validate CBCA assessments by confessions may therefore be at least partly circular.

In laboratory studies, either people have lied or told the truth about a film they have just seen (Vrij et al., in press-a and c), or they have lied or told the truth about having a cat and described daily activities of the cat (Winkel and Vrij, 1995), or they had or had not committed a 'theft' and were interviewed about this (Porter and Yuille, 1996), or they gave truthful or fabricated reports of a blood donation episode (Köhnken et al., 1995). Laboratory studies have problems concerning ecological validity. In real life, CBCA assessments are made solely on statements given by alleged child victims of sexual abuse. In other words, this typically involves statements describing highly emotional events. Obviously, laboratory studies can never simulate those type of experiences. Because of this lack of ecological validity, many CBCA experts believe that laboratory studies are of little use in testing the accuracy of CBCA assessments (Vrij, 2000). Although I am sympathetic towards this point of view, it also creates a problem. It means that it is virtually impossible to test the accuracy of CBCA, which I think is unacceptable, as such assessments are used as evidence in some criminal courts. Because of the significance given to those assessments both criminal justice investigators and criminal justice participants (suspects, victims and witnesses) have the right to know (in fact, should know) how accurate these assessments are. That is why testing the accuracy of CBCA assessments in controlled laboratory studies is essential (although the outcomes should be interpreted with caution).

Vrij (2000) reviewed 17 studies related to CBCA, most of them (12) were laboratory studies, and in most laboratory studies (9) the statements which were assessed were given by adults. These studies showed general support for the *Undeutsch hypothesis*: the criteria occur more often in truthful than in fabricated statements. However, the support for some criteria was stronger than for others (the criteria mentioned above, except admitting lack of memory, all received strong support). Interestingly, when no support for the Undeutsch hypothesis was found, this almost always was because one or more criteria did not differentiate between liars and truth tellers. Findings contradicting the Undeutsch hypothesis (i.e. criterion occurs more often in fabricated accounts than in truthful accounts) are very exceptional (Vrij, 2000). In this respect, findings concerning CBCA scores are more consistent than findings regarding behavioural cues to deceit, as in the latter case contradictory findings are common place (Vrij, 2000).

Some of the laboratory researchers reported accuracy rates, that is the correct classifications of truth tellers and liars on the basis of CBCA assessments. Unfortunately, in none of the field studies were accuracy rates reported, so the accuracy scores below are based solely on laboratory studies.[3] Vrij (2000) calculated the average accuracy rate in CBCA studies. This was around 70%, with slightly higher scores for detecting accounts of genuinely experienced events (76%) than for detecting accounts not relating to genuinely experienced events (68%). Although these accuracy rates are higher than the accuracy rates in non-verbal lie detection, they are simply too low to justify CBCA assessments to be used as the main piece of evidence in criminal courts. Especially the substantial number of incorrect classifications of accounts not relating to genuinely experienced events is worrying. The incorrect decision falsely to believe stories made by alleged victims would have serious consequences. Such an error could result in somebody who is actually innocent being falsely accused of a crime and may lead to an unjustified conviction if a court (either jury or judges) bases its decision on the opinion of a CBCA expert. False convictions of innocent suspects are seen as serious mistakes in Western legal systems which are founded on the principle that it is better to acquit 10 guilty people than to convict one person who is innocent.

Some people are highly critical of CBCA assessments and would like such evaluations not to be used as evidence in criminal courts (Rassin, in press; Ruby and Brigham, 1997). Indeed, it is possible to identify several problems concerning CBCA evaluations (Vrij, 2000), and I will discuss two of them: 'How to determine that a statement is truthful?', and 'What is the truth?'.

A major advantage of laboratory research is that comparisons can be made between lies and 'comparable truths'. In such studies, the situation for the participant in the truth and lie conditions are identical, apart from the fact that they have to lie or not. Hence, the rule 'the higher the CBCA score, the more likely it is that the statement is truthful' can easily be applied. However, in real life there is often no comparable truth. The statement of the child is often the sole piece of information that is available. How then to decide that a statement is truthful or fabricated? Some experts seem to apply decision rules ('at least five criteria should be present in order to judge a statement as truthful'), others even seem to use very detailed decision rules ('the first five criteria should be present plus two more'). (See Vrij, 2000, for a review of decision rules.) The use of decision rules in CBCA assessments is fundamentally wrong as it implies that CBCA is a standardised test, which is not the case. A standardised test has clear norms

---

[3] In a recent field study accuracy rates were reported which were actually very high (Parker and Brown, 2000). However, I have some concerns about how the ground truth was established. For example, cases were classified as 'true' on presence of 'suspect being identified or charged'. These criteria might not be valid criteria, as they might not be independent case criteria. For example, why has the suspect been charged? Perhaps the alleged victim gave a statement which sounded convincingly enough to the prosecution to press charges. This is, however, no guarantee that the statement was actually truthful.

which give the test psychological meaning and make interpretation possible (Kline, 1993). An intelligence test is a standardised test. If a person obtains a score of 130, then we know that they are very intelligent and also that they are more intelligent than someone who obtains a score of 70. This is not the case for CBCA assessments. A child with a low CBCA score is not necessarily fabricating. Other factors (for example, low mental capability of the child) may have influenced the CBCA outcome. Similarly, a child with a high CBCA score is not necessarily telling the truth (for example, the child might have been well coached by a parent, especially one who knows about CBCA). Without any norms at all the meaning of a test score is impossible to gauge. Therefore, standardisation of a test is essential. In an effort to standardise CBCA assessments, the validity checklist has been developed (Steller, 1989). This contains a set of topics which SVA experts address (such as 'cognitive abilities of the child', 'susceptibility to suggestion', 'indication of coaching'). By systematically addressing each topic, the evaluator can explore and consider alternative interpretations of the CBCA outcomes. Given the existence of the validity checklist, the fact that some experts use decision rules is remarkable. It suggests that assessments about the veracity of statements can be made on the basis of CBCA outcomes only, whereas the same experts argue that this is impossible, as external factors may influence the richness of statements (covered by the validity checklist) and therefore may influence the CBCA scores. Numerous external factors may affect the quality of a statement. The problem is to identify such factors and to estimate the effect of those factors on the quality of the statement (Vrij, 2000). Take, for example, susceptibility to suggestion. Some witnesses are more prone to suggestions made by interviewers than others, and might provide information which confirms the interviewer's expectations but which is, in fact, inaccurate. Yuille (1988) and Landry and Brigham (1992) therefore recommend asking the witness at the end of the structured interview (phase 1 of the SVA procedure) a few leading questions in order to assess the witness's susceptibility to suggestion. They recommended asking questions about peripheral information (e.g. 'When you were with your sister, which friend was there as well, Claire or Sarah?' when the interviewer knows that there was no friend present). Obviously, it is not allowed to ask any questions about central information as this may distort the interviewee's memory. Questions may influence somebody's memory of an event, and people may remember events which never took place only because the interviewer suggested to them that these events did happen. The fact that questions can only be asked about peripheral information causes a problem, as children show more resistance to suggestibility for central parts than peripheral parts of the event (Goodman et al., 1990). Moreover, they are more resistant to suggestibility for stressful events (likely to be central events) than for events which are less stressful (likely to be peripheral events) (Davies, 1991). Hence, if an interviewee yields to a leading question about a peripheral part of the event this does not imply that the interviewee was unable to resist suggestion when more important aspects were discussed. Also, this seems to assume that suggestion is more the result of individual differences than of circumstances. This may not be a valid assumption (Milne and Bull, 1999). If two experts disagree about the truthfulness of a statement in German criminal cases, they often disagree about the likely impact of some external factors on that statement (Köhnken, 1997, personal communication).

Second, SVA is a truth-verifying rather than a lie detection method, which raises the question: 'What is the truth?' It is possible that witnesses believe that they have witnessed a particular event, and have detailed memories of this event, although the event never took place. Such false beliefs may occur spontaneously or as the result of suggestive interviewing, which is not uncommon in legal settings (Milne and Bull, 1999; Vrij, in press). In Porter, Yuille and Lehman's (1999) study, 77 students were interviewed. During these interviews, they were presented with events. They were told that, according to their parents, these events had occurred in their childhood. The interviewer gave further details about the events supposedly given by the parents. Unknowingly to the interviewees, the events were false. They were invented by the researchers and had never happened to the participants (according to their parents). Guided imagery instructions were given to the participants to help them generate images for the false event ('Visualise what it might have been like and the memory will probably come back to you'). Results indicated that 26% of participants 'recovered' a complete memory for the false event. Such false, but detailed beliefs, although untrue, might well achieve high CBCA scores.

The problems for CBCA evaluators trying to distinguish between memories of real events and false beliefs might be caused by the fact that, in the development of SVA, psychological theories about memory were not taken into account (Sporer, 1997; Tully, 1999). In that respect, Reality Monitoring might be a useful additional tool in making truth assessments on the basis of verbal statements. The core of Reality Monitoring is that memories of experienced events differ in quality from memories of imagined events (Johnson and Raye, 1981). These authors argue that memories of real experiences are obtained through perceptual processes and are therefore likely to contain *perceptual information* (visual details, sounds, smells and tastes), *contextual information* (details about where and when the event took place), and *affective infor-mation* (details about how someone felt during the event). These memories are usually clear, sharp and vivid. Memories about imagined events are derived from an internal source and are therefore likely to contain *cognitive operations*, such as thoughts and reasonings ('I can only remember my thinking of what my friend would like to have for a present'). They are usually more vague and less concrete. (See Johnson, Hashtroudi and Lindsay, 1993, and Johnson and Raye, 1998, for more recent reviews of Reality Monitoring.) Johnson and her colleagues have developed a questionnaire to measure the quality of someone's memory for a certain event (Johnson et al., 1988). Research has repeatedly shown that this questionnaire can be successfully used to dis-tinguish between genuinely experienced events and imagined events which the person incorrectly believed to have experienced (Henkel, Johnson and De Leonardis, 1998; Johnson, 1988; Johnson et al., 1988; Ost et al., 2002; Suengas and Johnson, 1988). It might be a good idea for SVA experts to add the Reality Monitoring assessment to their SVA procedure. Indeed, Porter and his colleagues (Porter and Yuille, 1996; Porter et al., 1999) already use a combination of the Reality Monitoring and CBCA procedures in their research. However, they use abridged versions of both methods.

Compared to truth tellers, do liars include less perceptual, contextual and affective information and more cognitive operations into their accounts? The answer to this question cannot be derived from Johnson's research. First, her research deals with the question of how people determine whether or not they imagine things. This is not relevant for deception, as liars know that their stories are fabricated. Second, Johnson's work primarily deals with how people *remember* events, not how they *describe* them. She believes that how people describe their memories of events differ from how they actually remember these events. People have a tendency to make their stories sound interesting and coherent. If necessary, they will fill gaps in their memory by including some information that they do not actually remember but that they think makes sense and is probably true (for example, when you know that someone always wears a scarf you might include in the description of a particular event that the person was wearing a scarf, although, in fact, you cannot actually remember this detail anymore). This tendency to fill gaps will particularly happen with imagined events, as they are less clear and vivid. As a result, differences between perceived and imagined events become smaller when people are asked to put their memories into words (Johnson, 1988). It seems plausible that the desire to make stories interesting and cohesive will be even stronger when people tell lies, making it unclear whether differences between truth tellers and liars will actually occur on Reality Monitoring criteria. Recently, researchers have investigated whether Reality Monitoring could be used in lie detection (Alonso-Quecuty, 1992, 1996; Höfer, Akehurst and Metzger, 1996; Sporer, 1997; Vrij et al., 2001a, c; Vrij et al., 2000). Höfer et al. (1996), Sporer (1997) and Vrij et al. (2000) all found accuracy rates of approximately 70% (for both detecting lies and detecting truths) by applying the Reality Monitoring method. These accuracy rates were all above the level of chance (i.e. 50%), and comparable to the accuracy rates found for CBCA assessments. These findings are promising. Reality Monitoring analyses are much easier to carry out than Criteria Based Content Analyses, that is, they are less time consuming to conduct and the inter-rater agreement rates (i.e. to what extent two evaluators obtain the same outcome if they evaluate the same statement independently) are usually higher (Sporer, 1997; Vrij et al., 2000).

As soon as liars realise that evaluators use CBCA to assess the credibility of their statements, it is possible that they will gain knowledge of CBCA and try to 'improve' their statements in order to obtain a truthful assessment from CBCA judges. Our ongoing research investigates to what extent liars are capable of doing this (Vrij, Kneller and Mann, 2000; Vrij et al., 2002b). Results indicate that adults (Vrij, in submission; Vrij et al., 2000), but also children as young as ten (Vrij et al., 2002) can be successfully coached to include CBCA criteria in their fabricated reports. This is a serious drawback for CBCA assessments as tests the outcomes of which can be influenced are of little value in legal settings. At present, we are investigating whether 5- and 6-year-olds can be coached. However, see Vrij (2002a) for ethical concerns and practical difficulties concerning the coaching of very young children.

In summary, truth tellers' and liars' speech content does systematically differ on a variety of CBCA criteria, and evaluators who look for those criteria are able to detect truths and lies well above the level of chance. However, these evaluators are not accurate enough to present such assessments as (the sole) evidence in criminal courts. One possible way to improve SVA assessments is by adding Reality Monitoring analyses to the present procedure. One possible serious drawback of SVA assessments is that people can be coached to obtain higher CBCA scores (increasing the likelihood that their statements will be assessed as truthful).

Implications of the Findings for Lie Detection in Legal Settings

The research findings presented in this chapter reveal that people are not good enough in verbal and non-verbal truth and lie detection to justify their assessments being used as evidence in criminal courts where the standard of proof is 'beyond reasonable doubt'. Experts who currently present such assessments in court will probably challenge this conclusion and will point out that the research on which this conclusion has been based lacks ecological validity. In other words, they will say: 'We simply do not know how accurate these assessments are.' Although I agree to some extent with their point of view, I believe that the uncertainty about their accuracy does not justify the use of such truth and lie detection methods in courts. If experts nevertheless present their outcomes in criminal courts, then they should at least point out the limitations of the method they use, and the uncertainty about its accuracy. However, it is not all pessimistic. First, several promising suggestions have been made to improve lie and truth detection accuracy. More research is needed to further develop these new methods and to test their effectiveness. Second, research has convincingly demonstrated that people are able to detect truths and lies *above the level of chance* by utilising lie detection methods (especially verbal lie detection methods). It means that those methods could be used in the criminal justice system, for example, as an additional piece of evidence in criminal courts (as long as more substantial evidence is presented as well), or as a tool in police investigations to eliminate potential suspects, to check the truthfulness of informants, or to examine contradictory statements of victims, witnesses and suspects in the same case. It might also be used as a piece of evidence in civil courts where the standard of proof is 'on a balance of probabilities'.

REFERENCES

Akehurst, L., Köhnken, G., Vrij, A. and Bull, R. (1996). Lay persons' and police officers' beliefs regarding deceptive behaviour. *Applied Cognitive Psychology*, *10*, 461–471.

Allwood, C.M. and Granhag, P.A. (1997). Feelings of confidence and the realism of confidence judgments in everyday life. In P. Juslin and H. Montgomery (eds), *Judgment and decision making: Neo-Brunswikian and process-tracing approaches* (pp. 123–146). Mahwah, NJ: Lawrence Erlbaum.

Alonso-Quecuty, M.L. (1992). Deception detection and reality monitoring: A new answer to an old question? In F. Lösel, D. Bender and T. Bliesener (eds), *Psychology and law: International perspectives* (pp. 328–332). Berlin, Germany: Walter de Gruyter.

Alonso-Quecuty, M.L. (1996). Detecting fact from fallacy in child and adult witness accounts. In G. Davies, S. Lloyd-Bostock, M. McMurran and C. Wilson (eds), *Psychology, law, and criminal justice: International developments in research and practice* (pp. 74–80). Berlin, Germany: Walter de Gruyter.

Anderson, D.E., DePaulo, B.M. and Ansfield (2002). *The development of deception detection skill: A longitudinal study of same sex friends. Personality and Social Psychology Bulletin*, *28*, 536–545.

Bagley, J. & Manelis, L. (1979). Effect of awareness of an indicator of cognitive load. *Perceptual and Motor Skills*, *49*, 591–594.

Bauer, L.O., Strock, B.D., Goldstein, R., Stern, J.A. and Walrath, L.C. (1985). Auditory discrimination and the eyeblink. *Psychophysiology*, *22*, 629–635.

Bell, K.L. and DePaulo, B.M. (1996). Liking and lying. *Basic and Applied Social Psychology*, *18*, 243–266.

Bond, C.F. and Fahey, W.E. (1987). False suspicion and the misperception of deceit. *British Journal of Social Psychology*, *26*, 41–46.

Bull, R. (1992). Obtaining evidence expertly: The reliability of interviews with child witnesses. *Expert evidence: The international digest of human behaviour science and law*, *1*, 3–36.

Bull, R. (1995). Innovative techniques for the questioning of child witnesses, especially those who are young and those with learning disability. In M. Zaragoza et al. (eds), *Memory and testimony in the child witness* (pp. 179–195). Thousand Oaks, CA: Sage.

Bull, R. (1998). Obtaining information from child witnesses. In A. Memon, A. Vrij and R. Bull (eds), *Psychology and law: Truthfulness, accuracy and credibility* (pp. 188–210). Maidenhead, England: McGraw-Hill.

Buller, D.B., Strzyzewski, K.D. and Hunsaker, F.G. (1991). Interpersonal deception II: The inferiority of conversational participants as deception detectors. *Communication Monographs*, *58*, 25–40.

Burgoon, J.K. and Buller, D.B. (1994). Interpersonal deception: III. Effects of deceit on perceived communication and nonverbal dynamics. *Journal of nonverbal Behavior*, *18*, 155–184.

Burgoon, J.K., Buller, D.B., White, C.H., Afifi, W. and Buslig, A.L.S. (1999). The role of conversational involvement in deceptive interpersonal interactions. *Personality and Social Psychology Bulletin*, *25*, 669–685.

Burgoon, J.K., Kelly, D.L., Newton, D.A. and Keely-Dyreson, M.P. (1989). The nature of arousal and nonverbal indices. *Human Communication Research*, *16*, 217–255.

Burgoon, J.K. and White, C.H. (1997). Researching nonverbal message production: A view from interaction adaptation theory. In J.O. Greene (ed.), *Message production: Advances in communication theory* (pp. 279–312). Mahwah, NJ: Lawrence Erlbaum.

Ceci, S.J. and Bruck, M. (1995). *Jeopardy in the courtroom*. Washington, DC: American Psychological Association.

Davies, G. (1991). Research on children's testimony: Implications for interviewing practice. In C.R. Hollin and K. Howells (eds), *Clinical approaches to sex offenders and their victims*. New York: John Wiley & Sons.

Davis, M. and Hadiks, D. (1995). Demeanor and credibility. *Semiotica*, *106*, 5–54.

DePaulo, B.M. (1988). nonverbal aspects of deception. *Journal of nonverbal Behavior*, *12*, 153–162.

DePaulo, B.M. (1992). nonverbal behavior and self-presentation. *Psychological Bulletin*, *111*, 203–243.

DePaulo, B.M. (1994). Spotting lies: Can humans learn to do better? *Current Directions in Psychological Science*, *3*, 83–86.

DePaulo, B.M., Jordan, A., Irvine, A. and Laser, P.S. (1982a). Age changes in the detection of deception. *Child Development*, *53*, 701–709.

DePaulo, B.M. and Kirkendol, S.E. (1989). The motivational impairment effect in the communication of deception. In J.C. Yuille (ed.), *Credibility assessment* (pp. 51–70). Dordrecht, The Netherlands: Kluwer.

DePaulo, B.M., Lanier, K. and Davis, T. (1983). Detecting the deceit of the motivated liar. *Journal of Personality and Social Psychology*, *45*, 1096–1103.

DePaulo, B.M., LeMay, C.S. and Epstein, J.A. (1991). Effects of importance of success and expectations for success on effectiveness at deceiving. *Personality and Social Psychology Bulletin*, *17*, 14–24.

DePaulo, B.M., Lindsay, J.L., Malone, B.E., Muhlenbruck, L., Charlton, K. and Cooper, H. (2000). *Cues to deception*. Manuscript submitted for publication.

DePaulo, B.M. and Pfeifer, R.L. (1986). On-the-job experience and skill at detecting deception. *Journal of Applied Social Psychology*, *16*, 249–267.

DePaulo, B.M. and Rosenthal, R. (1979). Telling lies. *Journal of Personality and Social Psychology*, *37*, 1713–1722.

DePaulo, B.M., Rosenthal, R., Green, C.R. and Rosenkrantz, J. (1982b). Diagnosing deceptive and mixed messages from verbal and nonverbal cues. *Journal of Experimental Social Psychology*, *18*, 433–466.

DePaulo, B.M., Stone, J.L. and Lassiter, G.D. (1985a). Deceiving and detecting deceit. In B.R. Schenkler (Ed.), *The self and social life* (pp. 323–370). New York: McGraw-Hill.

DePaulo, B.M., Stone, J.I. and Lassiter, G.D. (1985b). Telling ingratiating lies: Effects of target sex and target attractiveness on verbal and nonverbal deceptive success. *Journal of Personality and Social Psychology*, *48*, 1191–1203.

deTurck, M.A. and Miller, G.R. (1985). Deception and arousal: Isolating the behavioral correlates of deception. *Human Communication Research*, *16*, 603–620.

Ekman, P. (1989). Why lies fail and what behaviors betray a lie. In J.C. Yuille (ed.), *Credibility assessment* (pp. 71–82). Dordrecht, The Netherlands: Kluwer.

Ekman, P. (1992). *Telling lies: Clues to deceit in the marketplace, politics and marriage*. New York: W.W. Norton.

Ekman, P. and Friesen, W.V. (1972). Hand movements. *Journal of Communication*, *22*, 353–374.

Ekman, P. and Friesen, W.V. (1974). Detecting deception from the body or face. *Journal of Personality and Social Psychology*, *29*, 288–298.

Ekman, P., Friesen, W.V. and Scherer, K.R. (1976). Body movement and voice pitch in deceptive interaction. *Semiotica*, *16*, 23–27.

Ekman, P. and O'Sullivan, M. (1991). Who can catch a liar? *American Psychologist*, *46*, 913–920.

Ekman, P., O'Sullivan, M. and Frank, M.G. (1999). A few can catch a liar. *Psychological Science*, *10*, 263–266.

Feeley, T.H. and deTurck, M.A. (1997). *Perceptions of communication as seen by the actor and as seen by the observer: The case of lie detection*. Paper presented at the International Communication Association Annual Conference. Montreal, Canada.

Frank, M.G. and Ekman, P. (1997). The ability to detect deceit generalizes across different types of high-stake lies. *Journal of Personality and Social Psychology*, *72*, 1429–1439.

Freud, S. (1959). *Collected papers*. New York: Basic Books.

Goldman-Eisler, F. (1968). *Psycholinguistics: experiments in spontaneous speech*. New York: Doubleday.

Goodman, G.S., Rudy, L., Bottoms, B. and Aman, C. (1990). Children's concerns and memory: Issues of ecological validity in the study of children's eyewitness testimony. In R. Fivush and J. Hudson (eds), *Knowing and remembering in young children* (pp. 249–284). New York: Cambridge University Press.

Granhag, P.A. and Strömwall, L.A. (2001). Detection deception based on repeated interrogations. *Legal and Criminological Psychology*, *6*, 85–101.

Granhag, P.A. and Strömwall, L.A. (in press). Deception detection: Interrogators' and observers decoding of consecutive statements. *Journal of Psychology: Interdisciplinary and Applied*.

Harrigan, J.A. and O'Connell, D.M. (1996). Facial movements during anxiety states. *Personality and Individual Differences*, *21*, 205–212.

Henkel, L.A., Johnson, M.K. and De Leonardis, D.M. (1998). Aging and source monitoring: Cognitive processes and neuropsychological correlates. *Journal of Experimental Psychology: General*, *127*, 251–268.

Hocking, J.E. and Leathers, D.G. (1980). nonverbal indicators of deception: A new theoretical perspective. *Communication Monographs*, *47*, 119–131.

Höfer, E., Akehurst, L. and Metzger, G. (1996, August). *Reality monitoring: A chance for further development of CBCA?* Paper presented at the Annual meeting of the European Association on Psychology and Law in Siena, Italy.

Honts, C.R. (1994). Assessing children's credibility: Scientific and legal issues in 1994. *North Dakota Law Review*, *70*, 879–903.

Hurd, K. and Noller, P. (1988). Decoding deception: A look at the process. *Journal of nonverbal Behavior*, *12*, 217–233.

Johnson, M.K. (1988). Reality monitoring: An experimental phenomenological approach. *Journal of Experimental Psychology: General, 117*, 390–394.

Johnson, M.K. (1993). Reality monitoring: An experimental phenomenological approach. *Journal of Experimental Psychology: General, 117*, 390–394.

Johnson, M.K., Foley, M.A., Suengas, A.G. and Raye, C.L. (1988). Phenomenal characteristics of memories for perceived and imagined autobiographical events. *Journal of Experimental Psychology: General, 117*, 371–376.

Johnson, M.K., Hashtroudi, S. and Lindsay, D.S. (1993). Source monitoring. *Psychological Bulletin, 114*, 3–29.

Johnson, M.K. and Raye, C.L. (1981). Reality monitoring. *Psychological Review, 88*, 67–85.

Johnson, M.K. and Raye, C.L. (1998). False memories and confabulation. *Trends in Cognitive Sciences, 2*, 137–145.

Kline, P. (1993). *The handbook of psychological testing.* New York: Routledge.

Knapp, M.L., Hart, R.P. and Dennis, H.S. (1974). An exploration of deception as a communication construct. *Human Communication Research, 1*, 15–29.

Köhnken, G. (1989). Behavioral correlates of statement credibility: Theories, paradigms and results. In H. Wegener, F. Lösel and J. Haisch (eds), *Criminal behavior and the justice system: Psychological perspectives* (pp. 271–289). New York: Springer-Verlag.

Köhnken, G. (1990). *Glaubwürdigkeit: Untersuchungen zu einem psychologischen Konstrukt.* München, Germany: Psychologie Verlags Union.

Köhnken, G. (1999, July). *Statement Validity Assessment.* Paper presented at the pre-conference programme of applied courses 'Assessing credibility' organised by the European Association of Psychology and Law. Dublin, Ireland.

Köhnken, G., Schimossek, E., Aschermann, E. and Höfer, E. (1995). The cognitive interview and the assessment of the credibility of adult's statements. *Journal of Applied Psychology, 80*, 671–684.

Landry, K. and Brigham, J.C. (1992). The effect of training in criteria-based content analysis on the ability to detect deception in adults. *Law and Human Behavior, 16*, 663–675.

Mann, S., Vrij, A. and Bull, R. (2002). Suspects, lies and videotape: An analysis of authentic high-stake liars. *Law and Human Behavior, 26*, 365–376.

Miller, G.R. and Stiff, J.B. (1993). *Deceptive communication.* Newbury Park, CA: Sage.

Milne, R. and Bull, R. (1999). *Investigative interviewing: Psychology and practice.* Chichester, England: John Wiley & Sons.

Moston, S.J. and Engelberg, T. (1993). Police questioning techniques in tape recorded interviews with criminal suspects. *Policing and Society, 3*, 223–237.

Ost, J., Vrij, A., Costall, A. and Bull, R. (2002). Crashing memories and reality monitoring: Distinguishing between perceptions, imaginings and false memories. *Applied Cognitive Psychology, 16*, 125–134.

Parker, A.D. and Brown, J. (2000). Detection of deception: Statement validity analysis as a means of determining truthfulness or falsity of rape allegations. *Legal and Criminological Psychology, 5*, 237–259.

Porter, S. and Yuille, J.C. (1996). The language of deceit: An investigation of the verbal clues to deception in the interrogation context. *Law and Human Behavior, 20*, 443–459.

Porter, S., Yuille, J.C. and Lehman, D.R. (1999). The nature of real, implanted and fabricated memories for emotional childhood events: Implications for the recovered memory debate. *Law and Human Behavior, 23*, 517–537.

Raskin, D.C. and Esplin, P.W. (1991). Statement Validity Assessment: Interview procedures and content analysis of children's statements of sexual abuse. *Behavioral Assessment, 13*, 265–291.

Rassin, E. (in press). Criteria-based content analysis: The less scientific road to truth. *Expert Evidence.*

Riggio, R.E. and Friedman, H.S. (1983). Individual differences and cues to deception. *Journal of Personality and Social Psychology, 45*, 899–915.

Riggio, R.E., Tucker, J. and Throckmorton, B. (1988). Social skills and deception ability. *Personality and Social Psychology Bulletin, 13*, 568–577.

Ruby, C.L. and Brigham, J.C. (1997). The usefulness of the criteria-based content analysis technique in distinguishing between truthful and fabricated allegations. *Psychology, Public Policy, and Law, 3*, 705–737.

Ruby, C.L. and Brigham, J.C. (1998). Can criteria-based content analysis distinguish between true and false statements of African-American speakers? *Law and Human Behavior, 22*, 369–388.

Seiter, J. (1997). Honest or truthful? A study of persons' mental models for judging veracity. *Human Communication Research, 24*, 216–259.

Sporer, S.L. (1997). The less travelled road to truth: Verbal cues in deception detection in accounts of fabricated and self-experienced events. *Applied Cognitive Psychology, 11*, 373–397.

Steller, M. (1989). Recent developments in statement analysis. In J.C. Yuille (ed.), *Credibility assessment* (pp. 135–154). Deventer, The Netherlands: Kluwer.

Steller, M. and Köhnken, G. (1989). Criteria-based content analysis. In D.C. Raskin (ed.), *Psychological methods in criminal investigation and evidence* (pp. 217–245). New York: Springer-Verlag.

Suengas, A.G. and Johnson, M.K. (1988). Qualitative effects of rehearsal on memories for perceived and imagined complex events. *Journal of Experimental Psychology: General, 117*, 377–389.

Tecce, J.J. (1992). Psychology, physiology and experimental. In *McGraw-Hill yearbook of science and technology* (pp. 375–377). New York: McGraw-Hill.

Tully, B. (1999). Statement Validation. In D. Canter and L. Alison (eds), *Interviewing and deception* (pp. 83–104). Darmouth: Ashgate.

Undeutsch, U. (1967). Beurteilung der Glaubhaftigkeit von Aussagen. In U. Undeutsch (ed.), *Handbuch der Psychologie Vol. 11: Forensische Psychologie* (pp. 26–181). Göttingen, Germany: Hogrefe.

Undeutsch, U. (1982). Statement reality analysis. In A. Trankell (ed.), *Reconstructing the past: The role of psychologists in criminal trials* (pp. 27–56). Deventer, The Netherlands: Kluwer.

Vrij, A. (1994). The impact of information and setting on detection of deception by police detectives. *Journal of nonverbal Behavior, 18*, 117–137.

Vrij, A. (1995). Behavioral correlates of deception in a simulated police interview. *Journal of Psychology: Interdisciplinary and Applied, 129*, 15–29.

Vrij, A. (1998). To lie or not to lie. *Psychologie, 17*, 22–25.

Vrij, A. (2000). *Detecting lies and deceit: The psychology of lying and the implications for professional practice*. Chichester: John Wiley & Sons.

Vrij, A. (2002a). Deception in children: A literature review and implications for children's testimony. In H. Westcott, G. Davies and R. Bull (Eds), *Children's testimony* (pp. 175–194). Chichester: John Wiley & Sons.

Vrij, A. (2002b). *Telling and detecting lies*. In N. Brace and H.L. Westcott (eds), *Applying Psychology* (pp. 179–241). Milton Keynes: Open University.

Vrij, A. (in press). We will protect your wife and child, but only if you confess: Police interrogations in England and the Netherlands. In P.J. van Koppen and S.D. Penrod (eds), *Adversarial versus inquisitorial justice: Psychological perspectives on criminal justice systems*. New York: Plenum.

Vrij, A., Akehurst, L. and Morris, P. (1997). Individual differences in hand movements during deception. *Journal of Nonverbal Behavior, 21*, 87–103.

Vrij, A., Akehurst, L., Soukara, R. and Bull, R. (2002). Will the truth come out? The effect of deception, age, status, coaching and social skills on CBCA scores. *Law and Human Behavior, 26*, 261–283.

Vrij, A., Edward, K. and Bull, R. (2001a). People's insight into their behaviour and speech content while lying. *British Journal of Psychology, 92*, 373–389.

Vrij, A., Edward, K. and Bull, R. (2001b). Police officers ability to detect deceit: The benefit of indirect deception detection measures. *Legal and Criminological Psychology*, *6*, 185–197.

Vrij, A., Edward, K. and Bull, R. (2001c). Stereotypical verbal and nonverbal responses while deceiving others. *Personality and Social Psychology Bulletin*, *27*, 899–909.

Vrij, A., Edward, K., Roberts, K. and Bull, R. (2000). Detecting deceit via analyses of verbal and nonverbal behaviour. *Journal of nonverbal Behavior*, *24*, 239–263.

Vrij, A. and Graham, S. (1997). Individual differences between liars and the ability to detect lies. *Expert Evidence*, *5*, 144–148.

Vrij, A. and Heaven, S. (1999). Vocal and verbal indicators of deception as a function of lie complexity. *Psychology, Crime and Law*, *5*, 203–215.

Vrij, A. and Holland, M. (1998). Individual differences in persistence in lying and experiences while deceiving. *Communication Research Reports*, *15*, 299–308.

Vrij, A., Kneller, W. and Mann, S. (2000). The effect of informing liars about criteria-based content analysis on their ability to deceive CBCA-raters. *Legal and Criminological Psychology*, *5*, 57–70.

Vrij, A. and Mann, S. (2001a). Lying when the stakes are high: Deceptive behavior of a murderer during his police interview. *Applied Cognitive Psychology*, *15*, 187–203.

Vrij, A. and Mann, S. (2001b). Who killed my relative? Police officers' ability to detect real-life high-stake lies. *Psychology, Crime and Law*, *7*, 119–132.

Vrij, A. and Semin, G.R. (1996). Lie experts' beliefs about nonverbal indicators of deception. *Journal of Nonverbal Behavior*, *20*, 65–80.

Wallbott, H.G. and Scherer, K.R. (1991). Stress specificities: Differential effects of coping style, gender, and type of stressor on automatic arousal, facial expression, and subjective feeling. *Journal of Personality and Social Psychology*, *61*, 147–156.

Winkel, F.W. and Vrij, A. (1995). Verklaringen van kinderen in interviews: Een experimenteel onderzoek naar de diagnostische waarde van Criteria Based Content Analysis. *Tijdschrift voor Ontwikkelingspsychologie*, *22*, 61–74.

Yuille, J.C. (1988). The systematic assessment of children's testimony. *Canadian Psychology*, *29*, 247–262.

Zuckerman, M., DePaulo, B.M. and Rosenthal, R. (1981). Verbal and nonverbal communication of deception. In L. Berkowitz (ed.), *Advances in experimental social psychology, Volume 1* (pp. 1–57). New York: Academic Press.

Chapter 1.3

Assessing Individuals for Compensation

Richard A. Bryant
University of New South Wales, Australia

INTRODUCTION

There is increasing demand for psychologists to provide assessments and reports for claims of compensation arising from psychological injury. Claims for damages secondary to the psychological effects of chronic pain, brain injury, and posttraumatic stress disorder (PTSD) are commonplace in courts in most jurisdictions. The increasing scrutiny that psychological testimony is subjected to during legal proceedings highlights the need for strong empirical support for both the methods that psychologists use and the inferences that they draw from their assessments. This chapter reviews the major issues involved in psychological assessments of compensation claims, and highlights many of the areas addressed by psychologists in compensation in which there is scant empirical knowledge.

ROLE OF DAUBERT

Before addressing the core issues of assessing for compensation, it is important to consider the standards that should guide psychological assessments in forensic settings. In the US Supreme Court's 1993 decision in *Daubert* v. *Merrell Dow Pharmaceuticals, Inc.*, it was ruled that admissible evidence needed to satisfy specific scientific standards. Implicit in this ruling was that courts would serve a gate-keeping function by admitting only testimony that was grounded in scientific research. Many people expected that this decision would result in a greater emphasis on scientific justification for psychological evidence in compensation matters. Many features of psychological injury are not amenable to observable or objective assessment. For example, claims of psychological injury involving pain or nightmares rely on claimants' self-reports. This reliance on subjective reports renders many of the alleged damages in psychological

Handbook of Psychology in Legal Contexts, Second Edition
Edited by D. Carson and R. Bull. © 2003 John Wiley & Sons, Ltd.

injury vulnerable to ambiguous interpretation. Ensuring that expert testimony adheres to strict scientific standards was seen by many as a crucial step forward in maintaining psychological testimony as a credible form of evidence that would be acceptable in courtrooms.

It appears that the *Daubert* decision has not influenced how expert evidence is judged as much as was initially expected (for reviews, see Mark, 1999; Shuman and Sales, 1999). Despite the slow change stimulated by the *Daubert* decision, increasing numbers of jurisdictions are adopting the *Daubert* decision in evaluating psychological evidence (Goodman-Delahunty, 1997). One of the major contributions that psychologists make in compensation settings is their expertise in synthesising and interpreting scientific data pertaining to psychological injury. Psychologists need to capitalize on this strength by ensuring that their assessments are integrated into current evidence relating to the psychological injury. The probability that one's psychological assessment will be subjected to rigorous scrutiny in the courtroom highlights the need for the assessment to be fully supported by sound empirical findings. This situation raises questions concerning the quality and quantity of relevant evidence to support the psychologist's assessment strategies and conclusions that are drawn from these strategies.

POSTTRAUMATIC STRESS DISORDER

Although there are many forms of psychological injury that can be the focus of a compensation claim (including chronic pain, cognitive impairment, postconcussive syndrome, depression), this review will focus on posttraumatic stress disorder (PTSD). This condition is diagnosed when the individual has (a) suffered a traumatic experience, and subsequently suffers (b) re-experiencing (e.g. flashbacks, nightmares), (c) avoidance (e.g. effortful avoidance of trauma-related thoughts, emotional numbing), and (d) hyperarousal (e.g. insomnia, irritability) symptoms. According to the *Diagnostic and Statistical Manual of Mental Disorders, Fourth Edition* (DSM-IV; American Psychiatric Association, 1994), PTSD has the distinctive feature of including a precipitating stressor as part of the disorder's definition. This establishes a straightforward connection between a triggering traumatic event and a variety of observed symptoms (Freckelton, 1997). Such a relationship enables PTSD to be susceptible to both compensation and criminal claims (Bryant, 1996; Erlinder, 1983; McFarlane, 1995). This amenability to compensation claims resulted in the introduction of PTSD in 1980 (DSM-III; APA, 1980) causing considerable concern about potential increases in PTSD-related claims (Lees-Haley and Dunn, 1994; Liljequist, Kinder and Schinka, 1998). These concerns have increased in recent years because claims for psychological injury following trauma have risen dramatically (Neal, 1994). Referring to the North American context, Stone (1993, p. 23) noted that, 'No diagnosis in the history of American psychiatry has had a more dramatic and pervasive impact on law and social justice than posttraumatic stress disorder'. PTSD is an excellent example to discuss many of the major issues that need to be considered in assessing psychological states in the context of compensation claims.

Although these issues are to be addressed in terms of PTSD, they are equally applicable in assessments of many forms of psychological injury that present for compensation.

DIAGNOSIS OR DISABILITY

Compensation is only awarded if damage can actually be demonstrated (Epstein, 1995). Compensation is usually awarded on the basis of the degree of impairment that impedes the claimant's capacity to function in a range of domains. A common mistake, in compensation-related assessments, involves the distinction between diagnosis and impairment. It is important that the assessment of psychological injury goes beyond the simple level of diagnostic definitions and addresses how psychological injury is adversely affecting the individual. For example, an individual may not suffer sufficient symptoms to meet a particular diagnostic threshold but may, nonetheless, display marked impairment as a result of the psychological injury. Alternatively, although an individual may suffer a range of PTSD symptoms, the individual may be able to function very ably.

Establishing the level of damage secondary to psychological injury is not simple. In defining damages, different jurisdictions distinguish between compensation for direct results of the injury (e.g. lost wages, medical bills), losses that can be estimated in financial terms (e.g. financial remuneration for physical injury), and future damages (e.g. future loss of wages, medical wages). Whereas the loss of a limb can be quantified objectively, the quantification of damages secondary to psychological injury is difficult. Many jurisdictions refer to pain and suffering as a non-pecuniary damage in recognition of its unquantifiable nature (Douglas et al., 1999). A major issue confronting the field of compensation assessment is the development of reliable means to index psychological suffering. Whereas one can assess functioning, in terms of ability to work, perform family duties, and engage in leisure activities, measuring suffering as a result of PTSD or other psychiatric condition can be difficult. To achieve a defensible conclusion regarding impairment, one should use the claimant's prior level of functioning in occupational, academic, interpersonal, leisure and other domains as the baseline against which any impairment is to be judged. The evaluation of prior and current functioning should rely, to a large extent, on objective and documented evidence (e.g. work record, academic performance, etc.). It would be difficult to argue that marked suffering is occurring in the absence of any objective indices reflecting increased suffering since the injury.

One of the major changes associated with the influence of the *Daubert* decision was that courts were not limited to the general acceptance of prevailing views, as defined by *Frye* v. *United States* (1923, *US S.Ct*). Long-held opinions about matters can be challenged if appropriate scientific evidence is presented to the court. This is a critical development in the domain of PTSD, where many traditional views can be effectively challenged by recent evidence. For example, it has often been argued that PTSD cannot develop where the individual sustained a traumatic brain injury and lost consciousness. This position has been argued on the grounds that the loss of consciousness precludes encoding of the traumatic experience, and this precludes development of PTSD (Sbordone and Liter, 1995). In contrast, recent studies have demonstrated that PTSD symptoms can develop despite impaired consciousness as a result of brain injury (Bryant, 2001; Bryant et al., 2000). Through integration of one's assessment of the claimant with relevant research findings, the psychologist can effectively counter established views by mounting a strong case that is based in sound empirical research. When courts are weighing the evidence of different experts, the psychologist who offers their opinion on the basis of their professional experience will typically be regarded with less credibility than the psychologist who provides substantive research findings to support the opinion.

ISSUE OF CAUSALITY

Once impairment has been established, the issue of causality needs to be determined. In typical compensation matters, there is an argument that a specific (or sometimes cumulative) event has caused or contributed to the resulting psychological injury. This claim results in the psychological assessment being required to make causal inferences about the observed psychological injury.

Nature of the Alleged Event

Identifying the nature of the event that allegedly caused the injury also needs to recognize recent research developments. Whereas DSM-III-R described the stressor as 'a psychologically distressing event that is outside the range of usual human experience' (APA, 1987), DSM-IV (APA, 1994) deleted this constraint. These changes have allowed a wider range of events to be claimed as possible causes of the disorder. Prior to the definition of PTSD in DSM-IV, there was much concern from legal representatives that broadening the definition to the point of not specifically defining the stressor would create excessive opportunity for people to claim damages based on a PTSD presentation. Most jurisdictions adhere to the principle of foreseeability, in which one would expect the injury to occur following the relevant event (Spaulding, 1988). There is much research that informs us about the likelihood of PTSD developing after a specific event. There is largely a direct relationship between the severity of the stressor and the likelihood of PTSD developing (March, 1993). Although there are reports of PTSD occurring after less threatening events (e.g. Burstein, 1985), claims of PTSD developing following minor incidents that do not typically lead to PTSD should be questioned because they are inconsistent with the scientific knowledge of the precipitants of PTSD.

Recent research in the field of PTSD has also indicated the importance of obtaining independent verification of the claimant's accounts of the event. Police, insurance, medical, or military records may be available to verify the reported details about the event, and the claimant's reaction to the event. People's recall of traumatic events can change over time (Wagenaar and Groeneweg, 1990). More importantly, how the event is re-called can be influenced by their current psychological state (Southwick et al., 1997). Prospective studies have reported that people's recall of psychological states, including pain (Bryant, 1993) and PTSD symptoms (Harvey and Bryant, 2000), is influenced by their mood at the time of recall. In a recent study of motor vehicle accident survivors who lost consciousness in the accident as a result of brain injury, 40% reported two years after the accident that they had fully recovered their memories of the incident (Harvey and Bryant, 2001). This pattern highlights the possibility that retrospective reports of a traumatic incident can be reconstructed in ways that are not consistent with historical accuracy. Documentation that can independently verify the nature of the event, and the claimant's response, allows the psychologist to make stronger infer-ences about the relationship between the event and the reported psychological injury.

In determining causation, courts typically focus on the constructs of proximity, re-moteness, and foreseeability (Douglas et al., 1999). These constructs typically result in courts deciding causation in terms of the injury being proximally related to the event. If it cannot be established that the psychological injury commenced in proxim-ity to the alleged causal event, then serious doubts are held about the role of the alleged event. In the case of PTSD, DSM-IV permits 'delayed onset PTSD' to be diagnosed when the symptoms commence more than six months after the event. There are case studies of delayed onset PTSD commencing 30 years after the precipitating event (van Dyke, Zilberg and McKinnon, 1985). This possibility raises marked problems for the psychological assessment because one needs to determine the causal link be-tween currently reported symptoms and an event that may have occurred many years earlier. Negligence laws in both Canada (*Athey* v. *Leonati*, 1996, SCC) and the USA (*Chaney* v. *Smithkline Beckman Corp.*, 1985; US 8th Circuit Ct) have rested on the 'but for' test. This test requires that for causation to be determined, it must be proved that an injury would not have occurred had it not been for a negligent act. Deter-mining this issue can be complex. For example, in 1964 Australia suffered its worse naval disaster when an aircraft carrier collided with a destroyer that subsequently sunk and 81 sailors drowned. More than 35 years later there have been hundreds of claims for PTSD by personnel who were on the aircraft carrier at the time, and a significant proportion of these have involved delayed onset PTSD. Delineating the influence of the collision on a sailor's psychological state is difficult when the psychol-ogist needs to determine the individual's functioning immediately after the collision, during the many years following the event, and identifying other stressors that may have been associated with the delayed onset of the reported PTSD symptoms. This scenario highlights the importance of integrating research findings into the psycholog-ical assessment because, whereas there are many case reports of delayed onset PTSD, properly conducted prospective studies suggest that so-called delayed onset PTSD probably reflects people who have been symptomatic since the time of the trauma but have not met full diagnostic criteria until more recent times (Bryant and Harvey, in press-b; Buckley, Blanchard and Hickling, 1996; Ehlers, Mayou and Bryant, 1998). The psychologist needs to interpret claims of delayed onset PTSD in relation to the scientific data that describe the current knowledge about the relationship between the event and the onset of psychological injury.

Pre-existing Conditions

In general, most jurisdictions will take injury victims as they find them (*Athey* v. *Leonati*, 1996). That is, if the claimant had a pre-existing vulnerability but did not display symptoms prior to the injury, they would be evaluated in terms of their current condition. In reality, different jurisdictions adopt distinctive approaches to people with 'thin skulls' or 'eggshell psyches'. In the USA, for example, whereas some states will be reluctant to compensate an individual who has evidence of vulnerability to a psychological condition (*Theriault* v. *Swan*, 1989; Maine Sup. Jud. Ct), others tend to make awards despite evidence of vulnerability (*Padget* v. *Gray*, 1987; Tex. Ct App.). Complicating this issue further is the scenario of a pre-existing condition being aggravated by an injury. In this case, the 'crumbling skull' doctrine dictates that awards can be made but are typically reduced in acknowledgement of the pre-existing condition (Douglas et al., 1999).

The empirical literature on PTSD highlights the importance of considering the potential contributing role of pre-existing conditions. The possibility that an individual claiming for a psychological injury has suffered a psychological condition prior to the precipitating event, or had a vulnerability to the psychological injury, is significant in all compensation claims for PTSD. Considering that 9% of the population will suffer PTSD at some time in their lives (Breslau et al., 1991), there is a significant proportion of claimants of PTSD who will have suffered PTSD prior to the alleged event. Further, the National Comorbidity Survey in the USA found that 61% of men and 51% of women reported having at least one traumatic event in their life (Kessler et al., 1995), and most of these people reported multiple traumatic experiences. It is likely that most claimants will have had a traumatic event occur prior to the one that is the focus of the claim, and the effects of the earlier events need to be disentangled from the recent event. Further, there is much evidence that the likelihood of PTSD developing after a stressor is increased by a history of childhood abuse, prior psychiatric history, previous trauma, genetic tendencies, and education level (Yehuda, 1999). Determining the causative influence of the recent event requires consideration of the possible influences of these vulnerability factors. The empirical evidence for vulnerability factors for PTSD is limited, however, by the predominantly cross-sectional nature of much of this research in which correlational analyses have been conducted with traumatised populations, or even worse, retrospective data collected after trauma exposure (Friedman, 1999; Harvey and Yehuda, 1999). Inferring vulnerability from evidence other than longitudinal studies is flawed and is susceptible to justified criticism from legal scrutiny.

The Influence of Litigation

A very common issue in litigation proceedings is the extent to which the litigation procedure influences symptoms or symptom reporting. In the case of PTSD, there is a long tradition of attributing reported symptoms to 'compensation neurosis'. After World War I, authorities perceived that compensation for shell shock contributed to the persistence of symptoms after the war (Bonhoeffer, 1926). As a result, The National

Health Insurance Act in 1926 precluding traumatic neurosis as a compensable disorder in Germany (van der Kolk, Weisaeth and van der Hart, 1996). This view is still commonly held today, especially among many legal authorities.

The evidence pertaining to symptom reporting decreasing after litigation resolution is very mixed. There is increasing research that PTSD symptoms persist after compensation has been settled (Brooks and McKinlay, 1992; Bryant and Harvey, in press-a; Mayou, Bryant and Duthie, 1993; McFarlane, 1995), and this pattern of findings reflects evidence from studies of back injury and chronic pain (Evans, 1984; Mendelson, 1995a). There is also evidence that symptom exaggeration is particularly prevalent in compensation-seeking individuals (Frueh, Smith and Barker, in press). There are insufficient prospective studies available that informs us about the modification of symptoms and impairment prior to and following resolution of compensation claims. The studies that are available are from very diverse jurisdictions with distinct compensation systems and provide little information concerning the mechanisms of change in any observed symptom change. The possibility that the stress associated with repeated medico-legal assessments and the experience of cross-examination in court exacerbates symptoms has not been sufficiently addressed in studies of the relationship between PTSD symptom reporting and litigation. Moreover, many of the prospective studies that have been conducted have focused on consecutive hospital admissions or treatment-seeking samples (e.g. Bryant and Harvey, in press-a; Mayou et al., 1993). The observed patterns in these samples may be distinct from other populations, such as exclusively litigation-based samples or those involved in class actions. At this time, we have a limited knowledge base about the exact influence of litigation on reported psychological injury, and particularly on the mechanisms that may mediate symptom change of maintenance during and following the compensation process.

ISSUE OF MALINGERING

A central question within compensation assessments is the extent to which the presentation is genuine, malingered, or exaggerated (Lipton, 1994; McGuire, 1999; Resnick, 1984). The concern over the genuineness of reported posttraumatic symptoms necessitates the development of an objective and accurate evaluation process to ascertain whether or not a client has exaggerated or malingered psychological symptoms (Grillo et al., 1994). The accurate assessment of psychological symptoms following a traumatic event is difficult because PTSD symptoms rely heavily on the self-report of subjective symptoms (Raifman, 1983; Resnick, 1984; Rosen, 1995; Sparr and Pankratz, 1983; Zisken, 1995). Obtaining objective measurement or verification of reported symptoms is often difficult (Freckelton, 1997). Further, growing awareness of symptoms allows many individuals to feign PTSD with a reasonable knowledge base about expected symptoms (Fear, 1996; Gerardi, Blanchard and Kolb, 1989; Lees-Haley, 1992; Mendelson, 1995b; Morel, 1998). Research indicates that attorney 'coaching' of clients is common (Lees-Haley, 1997). Cases have been reported in which attorneys have specifically advised clients on PTSD symptoms (Rosen, 1995; Wetter and

Corrigan, 1995). Wetter and Corrigan (1995) found in a survey of attorneys and law students that the majority of respondents believed they have a responsibility to discuss with their client what is involved in psychological tests before referring them for testing. Importantly, a significant percentage believed this should include specific information about validity scales. Whereas some evidence suggests that preparation enhances successful malingering, other data points to marginal influences (Berry et al., 1994; Lamb et. al., 1994; Rogers, Bagby and Chakraborty, 1993a). These factors make it difficult to accurately discriminate between genuine and feigned PTSD.

Resnick (1997) notes the distinction between pure malingering (i.e. feigning a disorder that does not exist), partial malingering (i.e. the conscious exaggeration of symptoms that do actually exist or falsely claiming that prior genuine symptoms are still present), and false imputation (i.e. ascribing of actual symptoms to a cause that is recognised to have no relationship to the symptoms). In the context of *Daubert*, it is critical that the psychologist is able to support decisions about malingering with scientific research that justifies the methods used to detect malingering. Of significant concern is that in relation to the many guidelines that are available in the literature for detecting malingered PTSD, there is little empirical evidence to strongly support many of these suggested techniques.

PSYCHOMETRIC TECHNIQUES

Instruments that directly index posttraumatic symptoms are successfully faked by naïve and coached simulators, partly because they lack validity scales to detect malingering (Frueh et al., 2000; Liljequist et al., 1998; Morel, 1998). Accordingly, a number of psychological tests have been proposed to assist in detecting the feigning of psychological symptoms, including the Morel Emotional Numbing Test (MENT; Morel, 1998), Millon Clinical Multiaxial Inventory (MCMI; Grillo et al., 1994; Lees-Haley, 1992; Zisken, 1995), Minnesota Multiphasic Personality Inventory (MMPI/MMPI-2; Fairbank, McCaffrey and Keane, 1985; Lees-Haley, 1992, 1997; Lyons and Wheeler-Cox, 1999; McCaffrey and Bellamy-Campbell, 1989; Perconte and Goreczeny, 1990; Rogers et al., 1993a; Zisken, 1995), and the Personality Assessment Inventory (PAI; Liljequist et al., 1998; Rogers, Ornduff and Sewell, 1993b; Rogers et al., 1996, 1998; Rogers, Ustad and Salekin, 1998a; Wang et al., 1997).

The most studied measure to index genuineness of clinical presentation is the MMPI/MMPI-2 (Hathoway and McKinley, 1991). The MMPI-2 has an array of validity scales designed to index motivation underlying responses to items about psychopathology, including the F, Fb, L, K, Gough Dissimulation Index, Fp, S and Mp (for reviews, see Butcher and Miller, 1999; Greene, 1997; Pope, Butcher and Seelen, 2000). The ability of the MMPI-2 to discriminate between genuine and malingered presentations has been studied in a range of populations, including chronic pain, brain injury, and PTSD (Butcher and Miller, 1999). A number of studies have indicated the utility of the MMPI-2 to distinguish genuine from malingered PTSD (Fairbank et al., 1985). Even when malingerers are given information about PTSD, the MMPI-2's F, Fb, Dissimulation Index, and Ds validity scales can distinguish ma-lingerers from genuine presentations (Wetter et al., 1993). In addition, malingerers have also been distinguished by their scores on O-S, OT and FBS (Elhai et al., 2000, 2001).

The PAI (Morey, 1991) is another self-report personality inventory designed to assess response styles, clinical disorders, treatment planning and screen for psychopathology. The PAI was developed to overcome a number of psychometric limitations associated with the MMPI-2 (see Boyle and Lennon, 1994; Helmes and Reddon, 1993; Liljequist et al., 1998). The PAI also has the advantage of item responses that reflect four gradations of endorsement (i.e. 'not at all true', 'slightly true', 'mainly true', and 'very true'), and using non-overlapping scales to maximize discriminant validity (Rogers et al., 1998a). The PAI contains a number of Validity scales, including the Negative Impression scale (NIM), Positive Impression scale (PIM), Malingering Index, and Critical Items scale. Morey (1991) reported very high scores on the NIM for college students who were instructed to feign mental disorders and also found empirical support for the use of the NIM in classifying simulators and genuine patients. In terms of PTSD, Liljequist et al. (1998) administered the PAI to students instructed to feign PTSD, and substance abuse veterans with or without PTSD. Malingerers produced higher scores on the NIM and Malingering Index. In a study of civilians, Bowen and Bryant (2001) compared treatment-seeking patients with posttraumatic stress, naïve simulators who were provided with no information about posttraumatic stress, and sophisticated simulators who were provided with information about posttraumatic stress symptoms. Both naïve and sophisticated malingerers produced PAI profiles that over-endorsed the majority of clinical scales relative to genuine respondents, and also endorsed more items on the NIM validity scale, Malingering Index and Critical items list. The initial evidence points to the utility of the PAI as a measure of feigning PTSD.

Although the MMPI-2 and the PAI have significant potential to index attitudinal and motivational factors in the presentation of an individual, the evidence supporting the use of any particular scales with particular claimants can be effectively challenged. Although the MMPI-2 is widely used as a means to detect malingering, the recom-mended cut-off scores for malingering varies markedly across studies (e.g. Lyons and Wheeler-Cox, 1999; Perconte and Goreczeny, 1990). There is also evidence that using the PAI's NIM scale as an index of malingering can result in a proportion of genuine PTSD cases being misclassified as malingerers (Calhoun et al., 2000). There has also been doubts raised about the cross-validation of MMPI-2 profiles in litigation settings with specific populations, such as adolescents (Archer, 1989). Questions about the accuracy of profiles generated by multiscale inventories are reflected in legal chal-lenges to the admissibility of the MMPI-2. For example, *Byrd* v. *State*, 593 NE 2d (Ind. 1992) noted the limitations of the MMPI, stating that its utility is 'not as a primary source of information, but instead as a means of confirming or challenging clinical impressions previously gained through direct contact with the patient' (460). Courts have also challenged the admissibility of computer-scored MMPI-2 profiles on the grounds that there is uncertainty about the expertise of the programmer, recording procedures, and accuracy of computer-scored profiles (*Sullivan* v. *Fairmont Homes, Inc.*, 543 NE 2d 1130 (Ind. App. 1 Dist. 1989)). Despite these limitations, it has been argued that the best defence of the MMPI-2 is the extensive data attesting to its reliability, which is the cornerstone of many jurisdictions' decision to accept expert testimony (see Pope et al., 2000).

PHYSIOLOGICAL ASSESSMENT

Some commentators have suggested that more sensitive assessment of psychological injury, including PTSD, can be achieved with psychophysiological measurement (Friedman, 1991; Pitman and Orr, 1993). This notion is based on the premise that malingerers may be less able to mimic biological markers of PTSD than self-reported symptoms. The basis for this perspective is the considerable evidence that people with PTSD can be distinguished from those without PTSD on a range of autonomic responses to cues that are specific to their trauma (for a review, see Orr and Kaloupek, 1997). For example, heart rate, skin conductance response, and eyeblink startle have been repeatedly found to be elevated in PTSD individuals when presented with trauma reminders. Further, there is recent evidence that functional magnetic resonance imaging (fMRI) can effectively distinguish the neural networks activated in PTSD and control participants when subliminally presented with threatening stimuli (Rauch et al., 2000). The extent to which these biological indicators can effectively discriminate between people with PTSD and those intentionally feigning PTSD has been rarely studied. Most reports that attempt to justify the use of psychophysiological assessment in psychological assessments tend to rely on a substantive literature that distinguishes the psychophysiological responses of people with and without a psychological injury (e.g. Neal et al., 1999). The utility of these measures in compensation matters relies, however, on their ability to differentiate between genuine claimants and those who are malingering. In one study, veterans without PTSD were able to increase their reactivity to a level that was comparable to veterans with PTSD (Gerardi et al., 1989). Orr and Pitman (1993) found that whereas veterans instructed to respond as if they had PTSD were able to mimic heart rate responses of veterans with PTSD, they could not mimic skin conductance and electromyogram patterns. Overall, psychophysiological measures cannot be regarded as reliable indicators of genuine or malingered PTSD. Although psychohysiological data can be used to present the claimant's physiological responses in the context of current knowledge about the psychophysiology of the disorder, reliance on current scientific knowledge precludes definitive comments being made about malingering on the basis of this type of evidence.

SELF-REPORT

There is evidence that individuals can fake posttraumatic stress symptoms in clinical interviews and self-report symptom inventories with considerable proficiency

(Liljequist et al., 1998; Morel, 1998; Sparr and Pankratz, 1983). On the basis of clinical skills alone, practitioners are considered quite poor in detecting fabricated symptoms (Lees-Haley and Dunn, 1994; Rosen 1995). Clinical experience almost inevitably provides more instances of seeming confirmation than is genuinely the case, fostering inflated confidence for the interviewer (Faust, 1995). Additionally, the extent of a practitioner's experience and the range of their credentials have little or no relation to the outcome of malingering detection (Faust et al., 1988). This pattern seems to be attributable, in part, to the tendency of practitioners to underestimate the knowledge, preparation, and skills of some malingerers (Faust, 1995).

In response to the problems in identifying malingering during interview, there are numerous guidelines available to identify malingered presentations (e.g. Resnick, 1995; Rogers, 1997a). Some of the suggested signs of possible malingering include unvarying and repetitive dreams, over-idealised functioning before the trauma, evasiveness, reporting of rare symptoms, global symptom endorsement, over-endorsement of obvious symptoms, atypical combinations of symptoms, excessive severity of reported symptoms, and reporting of symptoms that are inconsistent with the expected profile (Resnick, 1995; Rogers, 1997a). In addition, other commentators have suggested that malingering during an interview can be detected by resistance or avoidance to questioning (Pankratz, 1988), frequent hesitations in response to questions (Iverson, 1995), idealising prior functioning (Powell, 1991), and vagueness in the respondent's answers (Pitman et al., 1996). It should be noted, however, that there has been very little empirical study of these proposed guidelines, and the available evidence provides mixed support for these alleged indicators of malingering.

Many commentators have suggested that it is useful to draw a distinction between salient symptoms that may be more susceptible to successful malingering and subtle symptoms that malingerers are less likely to report (Rogers, 1997a). Bryant and Harvey (1998) required treatment-seeking PTSD participants and malingerers to listen to a sound effect of a crashing car, and then report their cognitive and affective responses to this stimulus. Their responses were audiorecorded and subsequently rated on a range of domains by independent psychologists. This study found that simulators and PTSD participants could not be distinguished in terms of their levels of imagery, intrusiveness of the reported memories, belief in the reality of the memory, affect, or movement of imagery. Simulators only differed from PTSD participants in that the latter reported trying to distract themselves from their memories to a greater extent than simulators. This study highlights that whereas it is difficult to identify malingerers on the basis of their reported re-experiencing symptoms, they have relative difficulty in mimicking how genuinely distressed people respond to symptoms. McBride and Bryant (2000) asked treatment-seeking PTSD patients and individuals instructed to malinger PTSD to provide information about their symptoms during an open-ended interview. Malingerers were less likely to report subtle symptoms, such as emotional numbing, than genuine patients. In contrast, when all participants were then asked to respond to directive questions about PTSD, malingerers reported emotional numbing more than the genuine patients. These findings indicate that whereas malingerers may be distinguished by an inferior ability to mimic subtle reactions to trauma during uncued interviewing, this difference may be reduced or reversed when the malingerer is provided with cues about expected PTSD symptoms.

There is increasing attention given to the influence of coaching on malingerers' ability to mimic psychological injury (Rogers, 1997a). In a comparison of naïve and coached simulators and genuine PTSD patients, one study found that coached simulators scored higher on a range of psychopathology measures than naïve simulators (Hickling et al., 1999). Freitag and Bryant (2001) found that both naïve and coached malingerers reported dissociative amnesia, emotional numbing, and a sense of a foreshortened future less often than treatment-seeking PTSD patients. Moreover, coached malingerers reported a sense of a foreshortened future more than naïve malingerers. These patterns point to the important differences between reports provided in response to open-ended interviews and those made in response to directive questioning about PTSD symptoms.

Attempts have also been made to identify speech patterns of people trying to malinger. Deceptive comments (not pertaining to psychological disorders) tend to be shorter, more general, contain a smaller number of specific references to people and places, and contain over-generalising words (Miller and Stiff, 1993). Deception is also associated with more pauses (Alonso-Quecuty, 1992), slower responses and slower speech rate (Ekman and O'Sullivan, 1991). In terms of PTSD, Carr-Walker and Bryant (2001) found that treatment-seeking patients with posttraumatic stress displayed less hesitation, less exaggeration, and less vagueness than malingerers.

Overall, there is little evidence to support definitive claims about the means of identifying malingering. Although there is some evidence to suggest that exaggeration of symptom reporting, hesitant responses, over-endorsement of obvious symptoms, positive responding to cued questioning, and over-generalising terms are associated with simulated responses, there is a need to recognise that these findings are based on few studies. In the context of defending decisions about malingered presentations in a legal context, it should be conceded that these findings have typically been found in small sample sizes and with non-clinical populations following simulation instructions. More importantly, it should be recognised that many of the other proposed guidelines for detecting malingered PTSD (e.g. unvarying dreams, inconsistent presentations between assessments) have no justification from controlled studies.

Available evidence would suggest that interviews should commence with open-ended interview that does not cue the respondent to desired responses, and then proceed to more directive questioning about the problems that comprise the compensation claim. This procedure has empirical support from evidence that simulators will tend to under-report symptoms (especially subtle symptoms) during open-ended questioning and over-report symptoms during cued questioning (McBride and Bryant, 2001). Interviewers should be cautious in interpreting claimants' responses, however, because many genuine cases may also under-report for genuine reasons. For example, people with PTSD may avoid reporting symptoms because talking about them elicits distress (Schwarz and Kowalski, 1992) or they fail to perceive that some symptoms are related to a stressful event (Solomon and Canino, 1990). This situation points to the simplicity of decision rules that employ dichotomous categories or cut-off scores because there may be numerous reasons why an individual may report a symptom in a particular way (Rogers, 1997b). Until there is a substantive increase in cross-validation studies, there is little evidence to guide interpretation of reporting patterns and one should be careful about placing excessive emphasis on detection strategies based on single studies.

METHODOLOGICAL ISSUES

The current evidence pertaining to malingered PTSD highlights that an underlying is-sue for malingering assessments is the level of sophistication of malingering research. Defending the use of any technique to detect malingered PTSD requires awareness of and confidence in the methods used to develop that technique. Simulation studies vary enormously in terms of the extent to which they use actual disordered populations, en-gage in coaching of simulators, use empirically derived and standardised simulation instructions, and provide sufficient incentives to motivate simulators. These issues raises serious concerns about generalisability of these findings to forensic settings where one needs to make decisions about a potentially malingered presentation. For example, the Carr-Walker and Bryant (2001) study instructed college students to feign PTSD after being given a summary description of PTSD symptoms. This method-ology, which is common among simulation studies, can be criticised on the grounds that (a) college students' lack of awareness of psychological impairment or a trau-matic experience may limit their ability to simulate effectively, (b) students may not be motivated to simulate to the same extent as those who are involved in litigation, (c) students may not have rehearsed their simulation to the same extent as malin-gerers presenting for compensation assessment, and (d) the demand characteristics associated with experimental testing may be distinct from those evident in a forensic assessment. There are also problems in using clinical populations who are told to simu-late. Apart from uncertainty about the potential overlap between psychopathology and malingered presentation, there is evidence that clinical populations do not necessarily follow simulation instructions (Rogers, 1988). Rogers (1997b) argues that whereas the current simulation research methods are a major advance upon the earlier case studies, there is a significant need for cross-validation across different groups. The distinctive characteristics of particular samples, research settings, instructional sets, and incentives point to the need for substantive replication of findings before it can be concluded that there is an evidence base to support generalised use of malingering guidelines.

Related to the issue of malingering is the difficult distinction between malingering, exaggeration, and misattribution of symptoms to a specific event. These are major issues in compensation assessments that are yet to be specifically addressed by re-searchers. Whereas most research has focused on different profiles of simulators and genuine respondents on various measures, common issues in civil litigation involve psychologically impaired individuals exaggerating their impairment or mistakenly attributing impairment to a particular cause. For example, it is common for trauma survivors to have residual symptoms of PTSD that do actually meet criteria for PTSD and do not cause marked impairment (Kessler et al., 1995). It is difficult to discriminate between one who is genuinely impaired and one who is exaggerating mild impairment in terms of empirically derived methods. Similarly, an individual may present with genuine PTSD but may attribute it to the event that is the focus of litigation rather than to an earlier or subsequent event. At this point in time, there are no accurate means to disentangle the causative agent of PTSD in terms of an individual's presentation. For example, although individuals with PTSD respond with marked hyper-reactivity to trauma reminders (Blanchard et al., 1996; Pitman et al., 1987), individuals can also respond to threat stimuli that are not directly related to the precipitating event (Shalev et al., 2000). Future research will need to extend beyond malingering and address the distinguishing features of exaggeration and misattribution of symptoms.

CONCLUSION

The increasing reliance in courtrooms on scientific support for both the method of acquiring data and the interpretation of results in matters of psychological injury points to the need for a substantive expansion of research activity in this domain. As attorneys become more aware of the relative strengths and weaknesses of different methods of psychological inquiry, psychological assessments for compensation are going to be more rigorously challenged. Considering the enormous amount of activity occurring in compensation assessments, it is surprising that the evidence base for much of this activity is limited. There is no doubt, however, that the challenges put forward by courtrooms about the rigor of psychological assessments will stimulate relevant research that is both relevant and defensible.

REFERENCES

Alonso-Quecuty, M.L. (1992). Deception detection and reality monitoring: A new answer to an old question? In F. Lösel, D. Bender and T. Bliesener (eds), *Psychology and law.* Berlin: Walter de Gruyter.

APA (1980). *Diagnostic and statistical manual of mental disorders* (3rd edn). Washington, DC: American Psychiatric Association.

APA (1987). *Diagnostic and statistical manual of mental disorders* (3rd edn revised). Washington, DC: American Psychiatric Association.

APA (1994). *Diagnostic and statistical manual of mental disorders* (4th edn). Washington, DC: American Psychiatric Association.

Applebaum, P.S. (1997). A theory of ethics for forensic psychiatry. *Journal of the American Academy of Psychiatry and the Law, 25,* 233–247.

Archer, R.P. (1989). Use of the MMPI with adolescents in forensic settings. *Forensic Reports, 2,* 65–87.

Berry, D.T., Lamb, D.G., Wetter, M.W., Baer, R.A. and Widiger, T.A. (1994). Ethical considerations in research on coached malingering. *Psychological Assessment, 6,* 16–17.

Blanchard, E.B., Hickling, E.J., Buckley, T.C., Taylor, A.E., Vollmer, A. and Loos, W.R. (1996). Psychophysiology of posttraumatic stress disorder related to motor vehicle accidents: Replication and extension. *Journal of Consulting and Clinical Psychology*, *64*, 742–751.

Bonhoeffer, M. (1926). Beurteilung, Begutachtung und Rechtsprechung bei den sogenannten Unfallsneurosen. *Deutsche Medizinische Wochenschrift*, *52*, 179–182.

Bowen, C. and Bryant, R.A. (2001). *Feigning posttraumatic stress on the Personality Assessment Inventory*. Manuscript submitted for publication.

Boyle, G.J. and Lennon, T.J. (1994). Examination of the reliability and validity of the Personality Assessment Inventory. *Journal of Psychopathology and Behavioral Assessment*, *16*, 173–187.

Breslau, N., Davis, G.C., Andreski, P. and Peterson, E. (1991). Traumatic events and post traumatic stress disorder in an urban population of young adults. *Archives of General Psychiatry*, *48*, 216–222.

Brooks, N. and McKinlay, W. (1992). Mental health consequences of the Lockerbie disaster. *Journal of Traumatic Stress*, *5*, 527–543.

Bryant, R.A. (1993). Memory for pain and affect in chronic pain patients. *Pain*, *52*, 379–386.

Bryant, R.A. (1996). Atomic testing and posttraumatic stress disorder: Legally defining a stressor. *Australian Psychologist*, *31*, 34–37.

Bryant, R.A. (2001). Posttraumatic stress disorder and traumatic brain injury: Can they co-exist? *Clinical Psychology Review*, *21*, 931–948.

Bryant, R.A. and Harvey, A.G. (1998). A comparison of traumatic memories and pseudomemories in posttraumatic stress disorder. *Applied Cognitive Psychology*, *12*, 81–88.

Bryant, R.A. and Harvey, A.G. (in press-a). The influence of litigation on maintenance of posttraumatic stress disorder. *Journal of Nervous and Mental Disease*.

Bryant, R.A. and Harvey, A.G. (in press-b). Delayed-onset posttraumatic stress disorder: A prospective study. *Australian and New Zealand Journal of Psychiatry*.

Bryant, R.A., Marosszeky, J.E., Crooks, J. and Gurka, J.A. (2000). Posttraumatic stress disorder following severe traumatic brain injury. *American Journal of Psychiatry*, *157*, 629–631.

Buckley, T.C., Blanchard, E.B. and Hickling, E.J. (1996). A prospective examination of delayed onset PTSD secondary to motor vehicle accidents. *Journal of Abnormal Psychology*, *105*, 617–625.

Burstein, A. (1985). Post-traumatic stress disorder. *Journal of Clinical Psychiatry*, *46*, 554–556.

Butcher, J.N. and Miller, K.B. (1999). Personality assessment in personal injury litigation. In A.K. Hess and I.B. Weiner (eds), *The Handbook of Forensic Psychology* (2nd edn; pp. 104–126). New York: John Wiley & Sons.

Calhoun, P.S., Earnst, K.S., Tucker, D.D., Kirby, A.C. and Beckham, J.C. (2000). Feigning combat-related posttraumatic stress disorder on the Personality Assessment Inventory. *Journal of Personality Assessment*, *75*, 338–350.

Carr-Walker, P. and Bryant, R.A. (2001). *Feigning posttraumatic stress: A study of malingerers' reporting styles*. Manuscript submitted for publication.

Douglas, K.S., Huss, M.T., Murdoch, L.L., Washington, D.O. and Koch, W.J. (1999). Posttraumatic stress disorder stemming from motor vehicle accidents' legal issues in Canada and the United States. In E.B. Blanchard and E. Hickling (eds), *International handbook of road traffic accidents and psychological trauma: Theory, treatment and law* (pp. 271–289). Oxford: Elsevier.

Ehlers, A., Mayou, R.A. and Bryant, B. (1998). Psychological predictors of chronic posttraumatic stress disorder after motor vehicle accidents. *Journal of Abnormal Psychology*, *107*, 508–519.

Ekman, P. and O'Sullivan, M. (1991). Who can catch a liar? *American Psychologist*, *46*, 913–920.

Elhai, J.D., Gold, P.B., Frueh, B.C. and Gold, S.N. (2000). Cross-validation of the MMPI-2 in detecting malingered posttraumatic stress disorder. *Journal of Personality Assessment*, *75*, 449–463.

Elhai, J.D., Gold, S.N., Sellers, A.H. and Dorfman, W.I. (2001). The detection of malingered posttraumatic stress disorder with MMPI-2 Fake Bad Indices. *Assessment*, *8*, 221–236.

Epstein, R.A. (1995). *Cases and materials on torts*. New York: Little, Brown & Company.

Erlinder, C.P. (1983). Post-traumatic stress disorder. Vietnam veterans and the law: A challenge to effective representation. *Behavioral Sciences and the Law, 1* (3), 25–50.

Evans, R.W. (1984). The effects of litigation on treatment outcome with personal injury patients. *American journal of Forensic Psychology, 12,* 19–34.

Fairbank, J.A., McCaffrey, R.J. and Keane, T.M. (1985). Psychometric detection of fabricated symptoms of posttraumatic stress disorder. *American Journal of Psychiatry, 142,* 501–503.

Faust, D. (1995). The detection of deception. *Neurologic Clinics, 13* (2), 255–265.

Faust, D., Hart, K., Guilmette, T.J. and Arkes, H.R. (1988). Neuropsychologists' capacity to detect adolescent malingerers. *Professional Psychology: Research and Practice, 19,* 508–545.

Fear, C. (1996). Factitious post-traumatic stress disorder revisited. *Irish Journal of Psychological Medicine, 13* (3), 116–118.

Freckelton, I. (1997). Post-traumatic stress disorder and the law: The need for expert witness and accountability. *Post traumatic stress disorder. Where to now?* Seminar Papers Leo Cussen Institute: Melbourne.

Freitag, R. and Bryant, R.A. (2001). *Feigning posttraumatic stress: The influence of coaching.* Manuscript submitted for publication.

Friedman, M.J. (1991). Biological approaches to the diagnosis and treatment of posttraumatic stress disorder. *Journal of Traumatic Stress, 4,* 67–91.

Friedman, M.J. (1999). Risk factors for PTSD: Reflections and recommendations. In R. Yehuda, R. (ed.), *Risk factors for posttraumatic stress disorder* (pp. 223–231). Washington, DC: American Psychiatric Press.

Frueh, B.C., Hammer, M.B., Cahill, S.P., Gold, P.B. and Hamlin, K.L. (2000). Apparent symptom overreporting in combat veterans evaluated for PTSD. *Clinical Psychology Review, 20,* 853–885.

Frueh, B.C., Smith, D.W. and Barker, S.E. (in press). Compensation seeking status and psychometric assessment of combat veterans seeking treatment for PTSD. *Journal of Traumatic Stress.*

Gerardi, R., Blanchard, E. and Kolb, L. (1989). Ability of Vietnam veterans to dissimulate a psychophysiological assessment for post-traumatic stress disorder. *Behavior Therapy, 20,* 229–243.

Goodman-Delahunty, J. (1997). Forensic psychological expertise in the wake of Daubert. *Law and Human Behavior, 21,* 121–140.

Greene, R.L. (1997). Assessment of malingering and defensiveness by multiscale personality inventories. In R. Rogers (ed.), *Clinical assessment of malingering and deception* (pp. 169–207). New York: Guilford Press.

Grillo, J., Brown, R.S., Hilsabeck, R., Price, J.R. and Lees-Haley, P.R. (1994). Raising doubt about claims of malingering; Implications of relationship between MCMI-II and MMPI performances. *Journal of Clinical Psychology, 50,* 651–655.

Harvey, A.G. and Bryant, R.A. (2000). Memory for acute stress disorder symptoms: A two-year prospective study. *Journal of Nervous and Mental Disease, 188,* 602–607.

Harvey, A.G. and Bryant, R.A. (2001). Reconstructing trauma memories: A prospective study of amnesic trauma survivors. *Journal of Traumatic Stress, 14,* 277–282.

Harvey, P.D. and Yehuda, R. (1999). Strategies to study risk for the development of PTSD. In R. Yehuda (ed.), *Risk factors for posttraumatic stress disorder* (pp. 1–22). Washington, DC: American Psychiatric Press.

Hathoway, S.R. and McKinley, J.C. (1991). *MMPI-2: Minnesota Multiphasic Personality Inventory.* Minnesota: University of Minnesota Press.

Helmes, E. and Reddon, J.R. (1993). A perspective on developments in assessing psychopathology: A critical review of the MMPI and MPI-2. *Psychological Bulletin, 113,* 453–471.

Hickling, E.J., Taylor, A.E., Blanchard, E.B. and Devineni, T. (1999). Simulation of motor vehicle accident-related PTSD: Effects of coaching with DSM-IV criteria. In E.B. Blanchard and E. Hickling (eds) *International handbook of road traffic accidents and psychological trauma: Theory, treatment and law* (pp. 305–320). Oxford: Elsevier.

Iverson, G.L. (1995). Qualitative aspects of malingered memory deficits. *Brain Injury, 9,* 35–40.

Kessler, R.C., Sonnega, A., Bromet, E., Hughes, M. and Nelson, C.B. (1995). Posttraumatic stress disorder in the National Comorbidity Survey. *Archives of General Psychiatry, 52,* 1048–1060.

Lamb, D.G., Berry, D.T.R., Wetter, M.W. and Baer, R.A. (1994). Effects of two types of information on malingering of closed head injury on the MMPI-2: An analog investigation. *Psychological Assessment, 6,* 8–13.

Lees-Haley, P.R. (1992). Efficacy of MMPI-2 validity scales and MCMI-II modifier scales for detecting spurious PTSD claims: F, F-K, Fake bad scale, Ego strength, Subtle-obvious subscales, DIS and DEB. *Journal of Clinical Psychology, 48,* 681–689.

Lees-Haley, P.R. (1997). MMPI-2 base rates for 492 personal injury plaintiffs: Implication and challenges for forensic assessment. *Journal of Clinical Psychology, 53,* 745–755.

Lees-Haley, P.R. and Dunn, J.T. (1994). The ability of naïve subjects to report symptoms of mild brain injury, posttraumatic stress disorder, major depression and generalised anxiety disorder. *Journal of Clinical Psychology, 50,* 252–256.

Liljequist, L., Kinder, B.N. and Schinka, J.A. (1998). An investigation of malingering Posttraumatic stress disorder on the Personality Assessment Inventory. *Journal of Personality Assessment, 71,* 322–336.

Lipton, M.I. (1994). *Posttraumatic stress disorder: Additional perspectives.* Springfield, Illinois: Charles C. Thomas.

Lyons, J.A. and Wheeler-Cox, T. (1999). MMPI, MMPI-2 and PTSD: Overview of scores, scales and profiles. *Journal of Traumatic Stress, 12,* 175–183.

March, J.S. (1993). The stressor criterion in DSM-IV posttraumatic stress disorder. In J.R. Davidson and E.B. Foa (eds), *Posttraumatic stress disorder in review: Recent research and future developments* (pp. 37–54). Washington, DC: American Psychiatric Press.

Mark, M.M. (1999). Social science evidence in the courtroom: *Daubert* and beyond? *Psychology, Public Policy and Law, 5,* 175–193.

Mayou, R., Bryant, B. and Duthie, R. (1993). Psychiatric consequences of road accidents. *British Medical Journal, 307,* 647–651.

McBride, R. and Bryant, R.A. (2001). *Malingering posttraumatic stress disorder: The influence of open-ended and directive questioning.* Manuscript submitted for publication.

McCaffrey, R.J. and Bellamy-Campbell, R. (1989). Psychometric detection of fabricated symptoms of combat-related PTSD: A systematic replication. *Journal of Clinical Psychology, 45,* 76–79.

McFarlane, A.C. (1995). PTSD in the medico-legal setting: Current status and ongoing controversies. *Psychiatry, Psychology and Law, 2,* 25–35.

McGuire, B.E. (1999). The assessment of malingering in traumatic stress claimants. *Psychiatry, Psychology and Law, 6,* 163–173.

Mendelson, G. (1995a). Compensation neurosis revisited: Outcome studies of the effects of litigation. *Journal of Psychosomatic Research, 39,* 695–706.

Mendelson, G. (1995b). Posttraumatic stress disorder as psychiatric injury in civil litigation. *Psychiatry, Psychology and Law, 2,* 53–64.

Miller, G.R. and Stiff, J.B. (1993). *Deceptive communication.* Newbury Park: Sage Publications.

Morel, K.R. (1998). Development and preliminary validation of a forced-choice test of response bias for posttraumatic stress disorder. *Journal of Personality Assessment, 70,* 299–314.

Morey, L.C. (1991). *Personality Assessment Inventory: Professional manual.* Odessa, Florida: Psychological Assessment Resources.

Neal, L.A. (1994). The pitfalls of making a categorical diagnosis of post traumatic stress disorder in personal injury litigation. *Medicine, Science and the Law, 34,* 117–122.

Neal, L., Hill, N., Fox, C. and Watson, D. (1999). The forensic value of psychophysiological measures of post-traumatic stress disorder. In E.B. Blanchard and E. Hickling (eds), *International handbook of road traffic accidents and psychological trauma: Theory, treatment and law* (pp. 291–304). Oxford: Elsevier.

Orr, S.P. and Kaloupek, D.G. (1997). Psychophysiological assessment of posttraumatic stress disorder. In J.P. Wilson and T.M. Keane (eds), *Assessing psychological trauma and PTSD* (pp. 69–97). New York: Guilford Press.

Orr, S.P. and Pitman, R.K. (1993). Psychophysiologic assessment of attempts to simulate posttraumatic stress disorder. *Biological Psychiatry*, *33*, 127–9.

Pankratz, L. (1988). Malingering on intellectual and neuropsychological measures. In R. Rogers (ed.), *Clinical assessment of malingering and deception*. New York: Guilford Press.

Perconte, S.T. and Goreczeny, A.J. (1990). Failure to detect fabricated posttraumatic stress disorder with the use of the MMPI in a clinical population. *American Journal of Psychiatry*, *147*, 1057–1060.

Pitman, R.K. and Orr, S.P. (1993). Psychophysiologic testing for post-traumatic stress disorder: Forensic psychiatric application. *Bulletin of the American Academy of Psychiatry and the Law*, *21*, 37–52.

Pitman, R.K., Orr, S.P., Forgue, D.F., de Jong, J.B. and Claiborn, J.M. (1987). Psychophysiologic assessment of post-traumatic stress disorder imagery in Vietnam combat veterans. *Archives of General Psychiatry*, *44*, 970–975.

Pitman, R.K., Sparr, L.F., Saunders, L.S. and McFarlane, A.C. (1996). Legal issues in posttraumatic stress disorder. In B.A. van der Kolk, A.C. McFarlane and L. Weisaeth (eds), *Traumatic stress: The effects of overwhelming experience on mind, body, and society* (pp. 378–397). New York: Guilford.

Pope, K.S., Butcher, J.N. and Seelen, J. (2000). *The MMPI, MMPI-2, & MMPI-A in court: A practical guide for expert witnesses and attorneys* (2nd edn). Washington, DC: American Psychological Association.

Powell, K.H. (1991). *The malingering of schizophrenia*. Unpublished doctoral dissertation. University of Carolina, Columbia.

Raifman, L.J. (1983). Problems of diagnosis and legal causation in courtroom use of posttraumatic stress disorder. *Behavioral Sciences and the Law*, *1*, 115–130.

Rauch, S.L., Whalen, P.J; Shin, L.M., McInerney, S.C., Macklin, M.L., Lasko, N.B., Orr, S.P. and Pitman, R.K. (2000). Exaggerated amygdala response to masked facial stimuli in posttraumatic stress disorder: A functional MRI study. *Biological Psychiatry*, *47*, 769–776.

Resnick, P.J. (1984). The detection of malingered mental illness. *Behavioral Sciences and the Law*, *2*, 21–38.

Resnick, P.J. (1995). Guidelines for the evaluation of malingering in posttraumatic stress disorder. In R.I. Simon (ed.), *Posttraumatic stress disorder in litigation: Guidelines for forensic assessment*. Washington, DC: American Psychiatric Press.

Rogers, R. (1988). Structured interviews and dissimulation. In R. Rogers (ed.), *Clinical assessment of malingering and deception* (1st edn; pp. 250–268). New York: Guilford.

Rogers, R. (1997a). Malingering of posttraumatic disorders. In R. Rogers (ed.), *Clinical assessment of malingering and deception* (2nd edn; pp. 130–152). New York: Guilford.

Rogers, R. (1997b). Researching dissimulation. In R. Rogers (ed.), *Clinical assessment of malingering and deception* (2nd edn; pp. 398–426). New York: Guilford.

Rogers, R., Bagby, R.M. and Chakraborty, D. (1993a). Feigning schizophrenic disorders on the MMPI-2: Detection of coached simulators. *Journal of Personality Assessment*, *60*, 215–226.

Rogers, R., Ornduff, S.R. and Sewell, K.W. (1993b). Feigning specific disorders: A study of the Personality Assessment Inventory (PAI). *Journal of Personality Assessment*, *60*, 554–560.

Rogers, R., Sewell, K.W., Cruise, K.R., Wang, E.W. and Ustad, K.L. (1998a). The PAI and feigning: A cautionary note on its use in forensic-correctional settings. *Assessment*, *5*, 399–405.

Rogers, R., Sewell, K.W., Morey, L.C. and Ustad, K.L. (1996). Detection of feigned mental disorders on the Personality Assessment Inventory: A descriminant analysis. *Journal of Personality Assessment*, *67*, 629–640.

Rogers, R., Ustad, K.L. and Salekin, R.T. (1998b). Convergent validity of the Personality Assessment Inventory: A study of emergency referrals in a correctional setting. *Assessment*, *5*, 3–12.

Rosen, G.M. (1995). The Aleutian Enterprise Sinking and posttraumatic stress disorder: Misdiagnosis in clinical and forensic settings. *Professional Psychology: Research and Practice*, *26*, 82–87.

Sbordone, R.J. and Liter, J.C. (1995). Mild traumatic brain injury does not produce post traumatic stress disorder. *Brain Injury*, *9*, 405–412.

Schwarz, E.D. and Kowalski, J.M. (1992). Malignant memories: Reluctance to utilize health services after a disaster. *Journal of Nervous and Mental Disease*, *180*, 767–772.

Shalev, A.Y., Peri, T., Brandes, D. and Freedman, S. (2000). Auditory startle response in trauma survivors with posttraumatic stress disorder: A prospective study. *American Journal of Psychiatry*, *157*, 255–261.

Shuman, D.W. and Sales, B.D. (1999). The impact of *Daubert* and its progeny on the admissibility of behavioural and social science evidence. *Psychology, Public Policy, and Law*, *5*, 3–15.

Solomon, S.D. and Canino, G.J. (1990). Appropriateness of DSM-III-R criteria for posttraumatic stress disorder. *Comprehensive Psychiatry*, *31*, 227–237.

Southwick, S.M., Morgan, C.A., Nicolaou, A.L. and Charney, D.S. (1997). Consistency of memory for combat-related traumatic events in veterans of Operation Desert Storm. *American Journal of Psychiatry*, *154*, 173–177.

Sparr, L. and Pankratz, L.D. (1983). Factitious posttraumatic stress disorder. *American Journal of Psychiatry*, *140*, 1016–1018.

Spaulding, W.J. (1988). Compensation for mental disability. In R. Michels (ed.), *Psychiatry* (vol. 3; pp. 1–27). Philadelphia: J.B. Lippincott.

Stone, A.A. (1993). Post-traumatic stress disorder and the law: Critical review of the new frontier. *Bulletin of the American Academy of Psychiatry and the Law*, *15*, 23–36.

van der Kolk, B.A., Weisaeth, L. and van der Hart, O. (1996). History of trauma in psychiatry. In B.A. van der Kolk, A.C. McFarlane and L. Weisaeth (eds), *Traumatic stress: The effects of overwhelming experience on mind, body, and society* (pp. 47–74). New York: Guilford.

van Dyke, C., Zilberg, N.J. and McKinnon, J.A. (1985). Posttraumatic stress disorder: A thirty-year delay in a World War II veteran. *American Journal of Psychiatry*, *142*, 1070–1073.

Wagenaar, W.A. and Groeneweg, J. (1990). The memory of concentration camp survivors. *Applied Cognitive Psychology*, *4*, 77–87.

Wang, E.W., Rogers, R., Giles, C.L., Diamond, P.M., Herrington-Wang, L.E. and Taylor, E.R. (1997). A pilot study of the Personality Assessment Inventory of malingering, suicide risk and aggression in male inmates. *Behavioral Sciences and the Law*, *15*, 469–482.

Wetter, M.W., Baer, D.T.R., Berry, D., Robinson, L.H. and Sumpter, J. (1993). MMPI-2 profiles of motivated fakers given specific symptom information: a comparison to matched patients. *Psychological Assessment*, *5*, 317–323.

Wetter, M.W. and Corrigan, S.K. (1995). Providing information to clients about psychological tests: A survey of attorneys' and law students' attitudes. *Professional Psychology: Research and Practice*, *26*, 474–477.

Yehuda, R. (ed.) (1999). *Risk factors for posttraumatic stress disorder*. Washington, DC: American Psychiatric Press.

Zisken, J. (1995). *Coping with psychiatric and psychological testimony*. California: Law and Psychology Press.

Cases

Athey v. *Leonati*, 3 SCR 458 (1996).

Byrd v. *State*, 593 N.E. 2d (Ind. 1992).

Chaney v. *Smithkline Beckman Corp.*, 764 F. 2d 527 (8th Cir. 1985).

Daubert v. *Merrell Dow Pharmaceuticals, Inc.*, 509 US 579 (1993).

Frye v. *United States*, 293 F. Supp. 1013 (DC Cir. 1923).

Padget v. *Gray*, 727 S.W.2d. 706 (Tex. Ct App. 1987).

Sullivan v. *Fairmont Homes*, Inc., 543 N.E. 2d 1130 (Ind. App. 1 Dist. 1989).

Theriault v. *Swan*, 558 A.2d 369 (Me. 1989).

Part 2

Perspectives on Systems: Psychology in Action

Chapter 2.1

Interviewing by the Police

Rebecca Milne and Ray Bull
University of Portsmouth, UK

INTRODUCTION

Appropriate investigative interviewing is essential across the entire legal arena in every country in the world which professes to seek justice. It is imperative to obtain accurate and comprehensive accounts that are rich in detail from all those involved within the criminal justice process; including witnesses, victims, suspects and colleagues (e.g. first officer at the crime scene). From the initial queries with potential witnesses up to the discovery interviews conducted by legal advisers before court hearings, the manner in which the interviewee is questioned may determine the outcome of a case. This is so whether it be a civil or a criminal case, and across a whole range of professional groups concerned with justice (e.g. police officers, social workers, fraud investigators, lawyers, judges, clinical psychologists, to name but a few).

This chapter aims to describe the most recent initiatives and psychological research concerning the context of investigative interviewing. At the outset the chapter will examine the interviewing of witnesses and victims. Consideration will first be given to recent research (Clarke and Milne, 2001), which examined whether the training package based on PEACE (an acronym describing an interview procedure, see below), has improved police interviewing in Britain. In addition, the applicability of the cognitive interview will be discussed in light of the work conducted by the authors of this chapter both in the UK and abroad. Various practical issues, which were gleaned from these fruitful experiences, will be highlighted. The second area to be approached concerns the 'brave new' legislation adopted in England and Wales which aims to create greater access to the criminal justice system for vulnerable groups (e.g. people with learning disabilities). A number of the issues surrounding its implementation (as they relate to interviewing) and also the guidelines given as to how to interview vulnerable witnesses/victims will be discussed. The major focus of this chapter will be on the interviewing of adults. Readers with an interest in this topic with reference to children can consult the relevant chapter in Milne and Bull (1999).

Handbook of Psychology in Legal Contexts, Second Edition
Edited by D. Carson and R. Bull. © 2003 John Wiley & Sons, Ltd.

This chapter will next turn to the interviewing of those suspected of committing crime. This section will again commence by examining whether training (e.g. in the PEACE package) can improve this aspect of police interviewing. This will be followed by a discussion concerning the use of tactics in interviews (appropriate and inappropriate) and the nature of confessions. Finally the chapter hopes to give some answers and possible solutions on how to improve police interviewing and will refer to the issues of supervision within the workplace and training.

INTERVIEWING WITNESSES/VICTIMS

> The bedrock of [the] adversarial process is the evidence of witnesses for the prosecution, not the confession of the accused. (Wolchover and Heaton-Armstrong, 1997, p. 855)

This hard-hitting quote, by two highly experienced lawyers, sums up the view of many working within the world of criminal justice. Professionals increasingly acknowledge that the investigative interviewing of witnesses/victims has equal, if not more, importance than the interviewing of suspects (e.g. Milne and Shaw, 1999). If the first initial interview with an event-relevant witness (i.e. someone who has been present at the crime) is not conducted appropriately then the entire investigation can fail. It is from that first interview that the whole make-up of a case evolves; defining the nature of the offence itself, outlining the possible suspects, creating the avenues for investigation, and so on (Milne and Bull, 1999). However, it still seems that the focus of many investigator training initiatives (police and others, e.g. fraud investigators) concern the interviewing of suspects. Indeed, it is usually (only) these interviews with suspects which are bound by legislation. And thus are more often open to public scrutiny than witnesses' accounts by being formally recorded. Nevertheless, if the investigation has not been adequately conducted, including appropriate interviews with witnesses/victims, then the evidence to be put before the suspect at interview may not be complete and/or accurate.

The Advent of PEACE

In response to research which highlighted severe shortcomings in police interviewing (Baldwin, 1993), and to public outcry concerning highly publicised miscarriages of justice (e.g. Guildford 4) in the UK, the Home Office (HO—which is the central government department responsible for the criminal justice system) and Association of Chief Police Officers (ACPO) developed the 'investigative interviewing' ethos and PEACE training course in the 1990s (see below). In essence the replacement of the term 'interrogation' by 'investigative interviewing' attempted to change the mind-sets of investigators from a blinkered approach that merely sought a confession to a search for the truth, examining all avenues of possible evidence (including interviews with witnesses/victims). This change of perception is an essential first step to changing the interviewing behaviour of investigators from an oppressive, suggestive, closed questioning manner that tends to be associated with assumptions of guilt to a more open-minded, open-questioning search for the truth.

In conjunction with the change in ethos concerning the nature of interviewing in the UK (which included seven primary principles of ethical investigative interviewing—see Milne and Bull, 1999), a week-long course was developed entitled PEACE, which incorporates elements of two interviewing models: (i) the cognitive interview which is aimed to enhance memory of cooperative interviewees (Fisher and Geiselman, 1992) and (ii) conversation management which is aimed to help interviewers to overcome resistance in interviews (Shepherd, 1988). PEACE is an acronym for the elements of the interview: *p*lanning and preparation, *e*ngage and explain, *a*ccount, *c*losure, and *e*valuate. The course is aimed at training police officers in the most appropriate and ethical methods of interviewing witnesses/victims and suspects of crime (see Milne and Bull, 1999; National Crime Faculty, 2000, for a description of PEACE). Indeed, since its development, the police in many countries seem now to be adopting the PEACE training approach. Furthermore, PEACE can be, and has been, tailored for those other than the police. For example, the government and public sector bodies in the UK decided to give standard training to its fraud investigators (e.g. in the Benefits Agency, Department of Health, Local Authorities, Inland Revenue, and Immigration Service) and PEACE was incorporated into that training (McKeever, 1999).

Although the PEACE package was specifically developed for interviewing relating to the investigation of crime, it is believed (since PEACE training was developed from conversation management, the cognitive interview, and research examining good interviewing practice *per se*) that the basic skills can be applied to a whole host of interview settings from personal selection, debriefing exercises, developmental interviews, etc. One problem with PEACE training seems to be that it tends to be pigeon-holed by the police in the UK as training for interviewing suspects and witnesses/victims only and is not therefore applied throughout the ranks. It is not used flexibly in different settings, for example, with informants, although research is currently underway examining the use of the cognitive interview in this highly specialised area of police work.

Public sector bodies must be accountable for the monies spent, and as training consumes vast sums of money it must be continually evaluated to ensure that value for money is being obtained (O'Mahony, 2000). However, it has only been recently in policing that research has started examining the impact of training. Typically performance measures have concerned numbers trained (i.e. quantity measure) rather than examining whether the training has resulted in the learning outcomes (i.e. quality measure). (For an exception to this see Bull and Horncastle's (1994) police probationer training study.) Nevertheless there has been limited widescale research examining the impact of this expensive, both in terms of time and resources, week-long PEACE course on investigators' interviewing abilities. There have been numerous quality (but unpublished) in-house studies conducted by various police forces regarding their own interviewing of suspects (which by law are audiotaped in England and

Wales), but few have examined the impact of the training on the interviewing of witnesses/victims (see Clarke and Milne, 2001, for a review of these unpublished studies).

Does PEACE Work?

The first author of this chapter was awarded a Home Office grant (in conjunction with Colin Clarke of the Metropolitan Police) to conduct an extensive national research project examining the impact of PEACE training on interviewing ability (Clarke and Milne, 2001). It was deemed necessary to examine real-life interviews of trained (in PEACE) and untrained officers when interviewing witnesses/victims and suspects of crime (see below for research examining the interviews of suspects). Drawing upon past research (pre-PEACE) it was found that there are few published research articles examining the investigative interviewing of adult witnesses/victims. This is primarily because these interviews are generally not recorded in any country (audio or video) and thus are very difficult to examine.

There is a wealth of evidence that the cognitive interview (CI) considerably assists people to recall much more information in respect of quality and quantity (see Köhnken et al., 1999, for a meta-analysis). In addition, research has demonstrated that the CI substantially enhances the recall of 'real' life witnesses/victims (e.g. Clifford and George, 1996). However, these studies used selected officers trained by the researchers. They did not examine the use of the CI as a result of police training programmes administered by police trainers (Clarke and Milne, 2001). It is now necessary to determine whether the police will use the 'special' CI memory-enhancing techniques in the real world after they have gained insight into these as part of a standard training package and not as part of a research study.

Two small-scale studies do exist which examine police interviewing skills of real-life witnesses/victims. McLean (1995) examined 16 interviews with witnesses/victims conducted before PEACE training and found that the majority of questions asked of the interviewees were counterproductive. He concluded, 'the treatment of witnesses appears far worse (than that of suspects)' (p. 48). This is a remarkable finding when it is added that this senior officer asked his team to conduct these interviews for this research and they therefore knew that he would assess their abilities. PEACE training should address these issues and, at least, increase the importance attributed to the interviewing of witnesses/victims of crime in the minds of the investigators. In addition, recent guidance to investigators in the UK suggests that interviews with witnesses/victims to serious crime should be recorded (National Crime Faculty, 1999). However, Daniell (1999) examined seven such interviews and, again, found poor-quality interviewing. She concluded that these interviews were 'a quest to prove what the officer knows to be true . . . officers are liable to bending the truth in accordance with other accounts to this end . . . the resulting statements still remain a far cry from the whole truth as presented by the witness' (p. 60). Mortimer and Shepherd (1999) also found this in police role-plays.

What was needed was a larger sample with which to examine witness/victim interviewing. This is especially important in the UK due to the expected increase in the tape-recording of witness/victim interviews with adults in light of ACPO guidance in the Murder Investigation Manual (National Crime Faculty, 1999) and the implications of the Youth Justice and Criminal Evidence Act 1999 (see below). Clarke and Milne (2001) gained, from across England and Wales, 75 tape-recorded interviews (43 witnesses and 32 victims). The interviews concerned what is termed volume crime (e.g. assault and theft) and serious crime (e.g. murder).

Clarke and Milne (2001) found that witnesses/victims are not actually 'interviewed'. This could be due to the practice in the UK (as in many other countries) of taking a statement (i.e. writing down the information elicited from the interviewee) from adult witnesses/victims, rather than of mandatory tape-recording such interviews. On average only a quarter of the time was spent fully concentrating on what the interviewee had to say, the majority of efforts concerned writing down the information. It was found that the actual statement-taking process lends itself to a question–answer style of interview, as opposed to the more effective, both in terms of quality and quantity of information, open-ended style of interview. It is impossible to conduct an appropriate interview, concentrating on the verbal and non-verbal behaviour of the interviewee, listening to what the interviewee has to say, structuring the next question and so on, whilst simultaneously writing down all that the interviewee has said. Something has to give, and it seems to be that both the interviewing and the record of the interviewee's account that adversely suffer. Indeed, statements are often *missing* approximately a third of what the interviewee actually said (including evidentially significant detail—McLean, 1995) and can be gross distortions of what was said (Daniell, 1999). Additionally, aspects of what the witness said (or, sometimes, did not say) are put into police jargon and are thus not in their own words/language. The information reported by the interviewee is put into a chronological order and thus does not represent their own emphasis. As a result the statement becomes the interviewer's representation of events and not the interviewee's (Milne and Bull, 1999). This renders statements as having limited investigative value (see Milne and Shaw, 1999, for more on this).

It must be noted that there is now considerable agreement from many (e.g. lawyers, police officers, judges, psychologists) that statements are unreliable and do not represent the best evidence possible (Milne and Shaw, 1999). Such statements are also regarded as one of the primary reasons for wrongful acquittals as the credibility of the witness is often questioned if at court the witness now mentions something which was not in their statement (i.e. recorded by the interviewer), especially if the witness claims to have mentioned this at interview (see Wolchover and Heaton-Armstrong, 1997).

Clarke and Milne (2001) found that even after PEACE training the interviewing of witnesses/victims was rather poor, with limited use of either the CI or conversation management. The majority of interviewers used a closed-questioning style in line with the idea of statement-taking. This is indicative of interviewer driven interviews with a confirmatory bias, seeking information to confirm pre-existing views concerning what has happened, rather than an information gathering approach (see Shepherd and Milne, 1999, for more on this). Though the interviews of witnesses to serious crime were better, there was still great room for improvement. The interviews with witnesses/victims were poorer than those with suspects (see below). It was found that, compared to interviews with suspects, the interviews with witnesses/victims had 'far more leading questions asked, most of the interviewers did not allow the witnesses to tell their account, and the interviews were mainly police led' (Clarke and Milne, 2001, p. 77–78). Thus, PEACE training seemed not to have had much of an effect on interviewers' skills when interviewing witnesses to, and victims of, crime. (See below for possible reasons for this lack of improvement.)

Use of the CI in the Field

There was little evidence of the CI in the interviews Clarke and Milne (2001) examined; indeed, no evidence in 83% of interviews. This is not surprising since applying the CI in police investigations can be more difficult than at first thought. It takes longer to conduct, which can be an issue when time is of the essence (Kebbell, Milne and Wagstaff, 1999). Research is, however, examining modified/shorter versions of the CI for use in such situations (e.g. Milne and Bull, 2002). Trained officers also note that they are more likely to use CI techniques in more serious cases, when there is more time and resources available (Kebbell et al., 1999). However, Clarke and Milne (2001) found no difference in use of the CI techniques in interviews of serious compared to volume crime witnesses/victims. One police force in the UK, has attempted to formalise the use of the CI in the investigation of serious crime. It has developed a specific interview policy, a strategy for the interviewing of witnesses and victims of serious crime, and a team of expert interviewers specifically trained in the CI for this task. Each interview is video-recorded, which not only preserves the integrity of the evidence, as well as the nature and skill of the interviewing, but it also allows the assessment of further training needs. The team meets on a regular basis, with a psychologist, the trainer(s), and a senior officer to evaluate the recorded interviews. The authors of this chapter are amazed at how infrequently, if at all, interviewers examine their own interviews. Interviewing is the bread and butter of investigation and self-evaluation (see the section on supervision below) is imperative to effective learning and improvement.

Officers have also noted that the perceived capability of the witness/victim was an additional determining factor of their CI use (Gasson, 2001). However, capability seemed determined by observation and opinion rather than set criteria: 'They (witness/victim) did not look the sort that could handle it' (Gasson, 2001, p. 44). Indeed the CI is sometimes inappropriate, but when this is the case interviewers tend to resort to a Question–Answer (Q-A) style of interviewing rather than using the CI flexibly. A lack of flexibility is one of the main problems the authors find when providing training on it. Investigators seem to think that use of the CI is an all or nothing affair, that is they have to use all the techniques or none at all. Actually, it would be preferable to see one of its techniques used well rather than all techniques used poorly. If you take away all the CI mnemonics from the structure of the CI (see Milne and Bull, 1999) you are left with the 'structured interview' which is similar to the 'phased interview' recommended in the Government's *Memorandum of Good Practice* (Home Office and Department of Health, 1992), for interviewing child witnesses/victims (Bull, 1996) and the more recent *Achieving Best Evidence in Criminal Proceedings: Guidance for Vulnerable or Intimidated Witnesses, including Children* (Home Office and Department of Health, 2002), for interviewing all vulnerable groups. So rather than it being a decision to cognitively interview or not to cognitively interview, the question should be: 'Which CI technique should I use?', 'When should I use it?' and 'How should I present it?'

Many other criminal justice professionals are seeing the benefits of the CI and tailoring it for use in their particular discipline (e.g. clinical psychologists, psychiatrists, fraud investigators, and marine surveyors). Surprisingly, however, lawyers have limited knowledge of it (Williams, 2000). Lawyers ought to be very aware of the CI for two primary reasons. First, when they represent clients at police stations, lawyers need to be aware of current police interviewing practices, so that they can advise their clients appropriately and ensure that interviewers are using ethical interviewing techniques. Second, the CI may be useful as a tool in itself when interviewing their own clients. Thus it is surprising that the CI is not part of the training lawyers receive.

The CI has also been researched for use with a variety of interviewees including vulnerable groups to whom we now turn.

INTERVIEWING VULNERABLE WITNESSES/VICTIMS

A few years ago we made the point (Milne and Bull, 1999) that criminal justice systems around the world seemed unable to accommodate to the needs of special witnesses/victims—for example, those with learning disability (which used to be called mental handicap or mental retardation) or those with physical and/or communicative disabilities. One reason for this was the belief, at least in legal circles, that such people were not competent to testify (Milne and Bull, 2001). Given this, police forces decided, in light of their other priorities, not to focus on improving their interviewing skill in this regard. Nevertheless a number of police forces were becoming ever more aware that certain types of vulnerable adults could well be witnessing crime or being targeted as crime victims (e.g. of abuse). If crimes are committed in private (e.g. sexual assault) and the witness is not regarded as credible in court, perpetrators will soon learn how to offend with impunity.

In Milne and Bull (1999) we gave an account of how one police force sought to improve the interviewing skills of its officers, who were investigating alleged abuse of adults with learning disabilities in residential homes. In the advice we offered to the officers we mentioned the possible use of the CI because we had found it to improve the event recall of such witnesses (Milne, Clare and Bull, 1999). In fact, we had found that use of the CI increased correct recall up to the level of some of our participants from the general population. This finding, and a similar one relating to vulnerable children (Milne and Bull, 1996), is very important because it suggested that, with appropriate interviewing, many witnesses/victims previously ignored by criminal justice systems and by the police could produce worthwhile information.

Though the amount of published research on the investigative interviewing of vulnerable witnesses is very limited, it probably played a role in helping to persuade the Government in England and Wales to introduce the Youth Justice and Criminal Evidence Act 1999 which is due to come into effect in 2002. This pioneering legislation, which has very few parallels around the world (see Milne and Bull, 1999), is designed to assist vulnerable witnesses (who may be victims) to play a worthwhile role within the criminal justice system and therefore in police investigations. Cooke and Davies (2001) provide a concise account of the aims of this legislation. A main feature of the Act involves 'special measures' which may improve the quality of witnesses' evidence in terms of its accuracy. Vulnerable witnesses are deemed to include those with impairment of intelligence and social functioning, and/or mental disorder. The special measures include live television links, screens, video-recorded interviews, the use of intermediaries, and of aids to communication. The Act makes it very clear (e.g. in section 54) that in deciding whether a witness is competent to give evidence (i.e. to understand the questions put and to give answers which can be understood) courts should only assess competence when the witness has the benefit of relevant special measures. This means that not only courts but all those who may interview vulnerable witnesses, including the police, have themselves to be competent in the use of the 'special measures'.

The aids to communication (i.e. special measures) can be defined as anything which enables successful communication with the witness. Such aids include not only physical devices (e.g. communication boards) and electrical devices (e.g. computers) but also good interviewing. To assist the interviewing of vulnerable witnesses the Government commissioned a small team of specialists to draft a document entitled *Achieving Best Evidence in Criminal Proceedings: Guidance for Vulnerable or Intimidated Witnesses, including Children* (Home Office, 2002). The second author of the present chapter was responsible for drafting the section on interviewing vulnerable people. This section, as do many previous documents on investigative interviewing, emphasises the importance of the four phases of (1) rapport, (2) seek free narrative recall, (3) questions, and (4) closure. It emphasises the special importance of establishing rapport with vulnerable people (Milne and Bull, 2001), of going at their pace, and of questioning them appropriately (Bull, 1995; Bull and Cullen, 1993; Cooke and Davies, 2001; Milne, Clare and Bull, 2002). However, it goes beyond this by including concepts from social psychology. These include compliance and the effects of authority figures, acquiescence, empowerment, and the effects of the interviewer's behaviour. While interviewers may intentionally try to act in a friendly and helpful way to vulnerable witnesses, they may at the same time unwittingly be giving off contradictory signals of unease, embarrassment, anxiety, and feelings about their own incompetence. This is why it is so important for interviewers to evaluate their own interviews. Given that legislation is now in place it is crucial that police forces train enough of their personnel for this most challenging aspect of investigative interviewing.

So far we have examined the issues surrounding the interviewing of witnesses and victims of crime. Now the discussion will turn to the interviewing of those suspected of crime.

INTERVIEWING THOSE SUSPECTED OF CRIME

Criticisms of police interviewing of suspects have been well versed (see Milne and Bull, 1999, for a review), especially suspects who may be vulnerable (see Gudjonsson, 2002). One major concern has been interviewing to gain a confession rather than interviewing to gain the facts. In 1997 Plimmer, a senior police officer in England, reported his research demonstrating a belief among police officers that the main aim of an interview with a suspect was still to obtain a confession. Leo and Ofshe (1998) and Ofshe and Leo (1997) provide arresting accounts of several real-life confessions in the USA. (See also Shuy, 1998.)

The effect of an interview containing a confession/admission has been demonstrated (Bull and Cherryman, 1995). As part of a research project for the Home Office a number of forensic psychologists with expertise on the topic of investigative interviewing were asked to listen to a relatively large sample of police audio-taped interviews with suspects (Bull and Cherryman, 1995). These psychologists independently agreed with each other on which interviews were the more skilled overall and on the level of 28 particular interviewing skills demonstrated in the interviews. However, it was found that the evaluations of a sample of these tapes by police officers, who regularly conduct interviews with suspects, did not agree with the forensic psychologists. Instead, their skill evaluations were strongly influenced by whether or not a confession occurred (Cherryman, Bull and Vrij, 1998a). Evaluation of the same interviews by more experienced police officers, who supervised and/or trained interviewers, were not affected by whether a confession occurred. However, these officers' evaluations did not concur with each other (Cherryman, Bull and Vrij, 1998b).

After the introduction of legislation in England and Wales, mandating (since 1986) that all police interviews with suspects in England and Wales be audio-taped, Baldwin (1992) examined 400 interviews of suspects and concluded that 'interviewing was a hit and miss affair' (p. 14). PEACE was designed to rectify this in Britain. Does PEACE result in better interviewing of suspects? In Clarke and Milne's (2001) evaluation, 177 interviews, with suspects were examined, two-thirds being conducted by PEACE trained officers and a third untrained officers. Although these interviews with suspects of crime were deemed better than when officers interviewed witnesses and victims, there was still little difference between trained and untrained officers, and some major skills gaps were found. Nevertheless there was some evidence of the transference of PEACE interviewing skills into these interviews. However, this happened more in areas that concerned the legal requirements, rather than the communication aspects, of the interview or the structured development of the interviewee's account. Interviewers are therefore learning from the course, but are being rigid in the manner in which they interview. A more flexible approach is now required.

It must be borne in mind that those classed as 'untrained' in this sample were not completely naive to the nature of PEACE and, due to frequent practice of interviewing in pairs, were not completely ignorant as to how to conduct PEACE interviews (i.e. could have learned through observation or through osmosis). Perhaps a better comparison is to compare practices to those interviews conducted prior to the introduction of PEACE training (i.e. compare skills to those found in research conducted prior to the advent of PEACE; e.g. Baldwin, 1992). In this light there has been a clear improvement in the ethos and ethical approach to interviewing since the inception of PEACE. This is important. As noted before, a necessary first step to changing behaviour is changing mind sets. It seems that perhaps, at last, in the UK (at least) we may now be more than half way there.

Clarke and Milne (2001) found that in only 17% of interviews with suspects was a comprehensive account given by an interviewee, in 23% a confession was obtained, in 25% a partial admission was elicited, in 29% the suspect denied involvement, and in only 6% the suspect merely said 'no comment'. Research therefore needs to start examining ways to help interviewers to gain truthful accounts from uncooperative suspects (e.g. using 'tactics'). The word 'tactics' seems to have a negative connotation attached to it. This has been fuelled by research which has tended to focus upon psychological tactics which can result in negative outcomes (e.g. false confessions) as opposed to seeing which tactics can be used in an ethical and effective manner (i.e. encouraging the guilty to give a comprehensive account). For example, Pearse and Gudjonsson (1999) report on 18 cases in which the suspects initially denied the allegations against them but, in the police interview, changed their mind and made a confession. The courts subsequently ruled one-third of these audio-taped interviews inadmissible largely in relation to the nature of the interviewers' tactics.

Gudjonsson (2002) is one of the few researchers who has successfully contended, in court cases, that interviewees have been adversely affected by tactics. However, almost no research has gathered information about this from suspects themselves. Holmberg and Christianson (in press) recently conducted a pioneering study involving a questionnaire completed by men who were in prison for murder or for serious sexual offences. This postal questionnaire involved the prisoners rating, on seven-point scales, their judgements/perceptions of the behaviour/manner/attitudes of the police officers who had interviewed them during the (relevant) investigation. The questionnaire also asked the prisoners to rate their emotional reactions to the interviewers' behaviour. The data revealed that only a few 'perceived their interviewers as having shown a great personal interest and having tried to create a personal conversation' or 'perceived their interviewers as highly sympathetic and empathetic' (p. 10). Thus, 'In both groups, few experienced their interviewers as having shown a very positive attitude towards them as human beings' (p. 11). However, 'few participants saw their interviewers as aggressive and explicitly confrontational' (p. 11). With regard to the self-ratings, the sexual offenders rated themselves as experiencing a higher degree of anxiety and as becoming more confrontational during the interviews than did the murderers.

Most of the respondents indicated that they experienced the police interviewers to display impatience, condemning attitudes, and a lack of empathy. 'Half of the sexual offenders and nearly one third of the murderers felt insulted as human beings' (p. 17). Two main interviewing styles emerged from the questionnaire data: one characterised by 'dominance' and one by 'humanity'. The dominating style involved 'a superficial case-oriented approach, characterised by impatience, aggression, a brusque and obstinate condemning approach, presumably aiming to extort a confession' (p. 19). This is what was typically found in research of interviews in the UK pre-PEACE (e.g. Moston, Stephenson and Williamson, 1992). One very interesting aspect of the data concerns the relationships between admission or denial and the suspects' ratings of the police behaviour. It was found that 'participants who perceive humanitarian attitudes from their interviewers were more likely to admit crime' (p. 15). Similarly, for those whose ratings indicated that they felt respected 'the odds of admission are 5.92 times greater' (p. 16) than those who did not feel respected. Holmburg and Christianson noted that their findings suggest that confrontational interviews result in negative outcomes. The dominating interviewer style was associated with suspects denying the crime. Although suspects' denials may cause police interviewers to become dominating, this simple explanation does not seem to account for the data.

One understandable weakness in Holmberg and Christianson's important study is that what people recall months or years later about an event (e.g. an interview with the police) may not be accurate. Analysis of the actual interviews (e.g. if they are recorded and access to the tapes is granted) would greatly increase our knowledge of behaviour, including admission or denial. Since research suggests (at least in England; Baldwin 1992, 1993; Moston et al., 1992) that few suspects change from initially denying the offence to later admitting it *during* a police interview, a large sample of such recorded interviews would seem necessary. Gaining access to such tapes has been rare for those outside the police service and for those not conducting a government-funded research project. Fortunately one of our doctoral students has been granted access, by a large UK police force, to a substantial sample of such tapes. She is currently analysing for the effect of interviewer style on suspects changing from denial to admission. She has also gathered information, from investigative interviewers in the same force, statements regarding what they see as the main aims of interviews with suspects. It was found (Soukara, Bull and Vrij, in press) that they report the main aims of interviews with suspects to be the gathering of information from the suspect and the disclosing of evidence to the suspect. These experienced officers reported that since the 1986 introduction of the Police and Criminal Evidence Act 1984 (PACE) regarding audio-taping interviews with suspects, police interviews have become better planned, more structured, and the use of trickery and deceit has all but vanished. Interestingly 40% of the officers commented that PACE has reduced the pressure on the police to obtain confessions. Preliminary analysis of the interviews recently provided to us by this police force found little sign of the use of 'negative' tactics. Rather, where the interviewers could be criticised this seems to be for a general lack of skill, as found by Clarke and Milne (2001).

It is not only 'outsiders' (i.e. non-police officers) who have outlined the weaknesses and strengths of police interviewing. Cherryman and Bull (2001) analysed information provided by a large sample of police officers experienced in investigative interviewing. This was done to determine which skills they believed to be important in investigative interviews and which were present or absent in police interviews and in themselves as interviewers. They considered 'listening' to be the most important skill, followed by 'preparation' and 'questioning'. Generally the officers indicted that many skill levels could be improved and believed that the skills most often missing in other officers, but not in themselves, were 'preparation', 'open-mindedness' and 'flexibility'. While there was consensus on most issues, officers who were assigned to child protection units ranked 'questioning' higher in importance than did other investigative interviewers who, in turn, ranked 'flexibility' as more important than did child protection officers.

Baldwin (1992) noted that skilled interviewers seemed to demonstrate more compassion but they also sometimes failed to challenge interviewees when they said things that did not 'square' with the available evidence. Bull and Cherryman (1995) also found compassion/empathy to be one of the factors judged to be significantly more present in skilled compared to less-skilled interviews of suspects. However, in a pioneering study Sear and Stephenson (1997) found very little relationship between officers' personality and their interviewing behaviour. Cherryman (2000) investigated whether some personality aspects of officers highly experienced with supervising and/or training investigative interviewing would affect their evaluations of audio-taped interviews with suspects conducted by other officers. In particular she examined the relationship between (i) empathy, (ii) authoritarianism and (iii) the evaluations. While little evidence was found of an effect of authoritarianism, empathy was found to affect some of the skill evaluations. For example, officers with higher empathy scores evaluated interviews as containing more 'undue use of pressure' and more 'inappropriate interruptions' than did officers with lower empathy scores evaluating the same interviews. Such novel findings as this have, of course, many implications, including some for supervision and training.

TRAINING AND SUPERVISION

One way to improve standards in interviewing is to have appropriate training, both in terms of quality and quantity. One of the reasons that Clarke and Milne (2001) offered for the lack of transference of PEACE was that the trainees were being taught too much, too early, before the basic skills had been grasped. Thus one of their 19 recommendations was that a tiered approach to interview training be developed alongside an interviewer's career. This is not a new concept (e.g. see Shepherd, 1988). It was proposed that Tier 1 would be recruit training and concern only basic communication skills. Tier 2 would start a programme of proactive refresher training (identified in part by supervision assessment—see below) and develop on what the interviewer has already learned in practice. One of the problems found with the content of the PEACE training course was that it could easily become legislation-based, as much new legislation concerns interviewing rather than a skills-based course on how to interview. As new legislation is introduced this is incorporated into the time available for PEACE training, and learning the art of interviewing was being sidelined. Rather, as is being done in other public sector agencies in the UK (e.g. Inland Revenue, Benefits Agency and Department of Health), the legislation ought to be taught, say, as a distance learning module. *The Practical Guide to Investigative Interviewing* (National Crime Faculty, 2000) is being sent to trainees in advance of the course, and an entrance test is given based on these materials. Trainers can then base their skills training and development upon the materials rather than start from scratch. Research, involving the first author, is at present examining this method of training.

Tier 2 would also involve training of supervisors and managers (as is also being conducted in public sector training in the UK), demonstrating how the PEACE framework is a method for conducting all types of interviews. Tier 3 concerns specialist training for a variety of different roles (e.g. enhanced CI, child protection, vulnerable groups, etc.). Interviewers entering this tier would be required to undertake some form of skills assessment. This happens in some areas of the UK (e.g. Kent County Constabulary Advanced Interview Course and Sussex Police Advanced Interview Course). The final tier (Tier 4) is for interview advisers who are skilled interviewers and investigators. Their role is to advise and plan interview strategies at a local level and during the investigation of major incidents (Clarke and Milne, 2001). In addition, there also needs to be effective training for the trainers of these courses.

Even with good training not everyone will become a good interviewer (Baldwin, 1992). It seems that some people bring an ability to interview to policing and some definitely do not. We are beginning now to examine who these people are and also how to target them in the future. In addition, good quality and an appropriate level of interview training is not enough on its own. This has to be accompanied by good support in the workplace (Stockdale, 1993). Clarke and Milne (2001) found that the interviews were of a better quality where there was an interview supervision policy in the workplace.

CONCLUSION

Police interviewing in the UK has changed and developed beyond what anyone could have imagined, however there is still a long way to go. Other countries and areas of the criminal justice system need to learn from our steps forward and our mistakes.

REFERENCES

Baldwin, J. (1992). *Video-taping of police interviews with suspects—An evaluation*. Police Research Series Paper No 1. London: Home Office.
Baldwin, J. (1993). Police interview techniques. Establishing truth or proof? *British Journal of Criminology*, *33*, 325–352.

Bull, R. (1995). Interviewing people with communication disabilities. In R. Bull and D. Carson (eds), *Handbook of psychology in legal contexts*. Chichester: John Wiley & Sons.

Bull, R. (1996). Good practice for video recorded interviews with child witnesses for use in criminal proceedings. In G. Davies, S. Lloyd-Bostock, M. McMurran and C. Wilson (eds), *Psychology, law and criminal justice*. Berlin: de Gruyter.

Bull, R. and Cherryman, J. (1995). *Helping to identify skills gaps in specialist investigative interviewing*. London: Home Office Police Department.

Bull, R. and Cullen, C. (1993). Interviewing the mentally handicapped. *Policing, 9*, 88–100.

Bull, R. and Horncastle, P. (1994). Evaluation of police recruit training involving psychology. *Psychology, Crime and Law, 1*, 157–163.

Cherryman, J. (2000). *Police investigative interviewing: Skill analysis and concordance of evaluations*. Unpublished doctoral thesis, University of Portsmouth.

Cherryman, J. and Bull, R. (2001). Police officers' perceptions of specialist investigative interviewing skills. *International Journal of Police Science and Management, 3*, 199–212.

Cherryman, J., Bull., R. and Vrij, A. (1998a). *British police officers' evaluations of investigative interviews with suspects*. Poster presentation at the 24th International Congress of Applied Psychology, San Francisco.

Cherryman, J., Bull, R. and Vrij, A. (1998b). *Investigative interviewing: British police officers' evaluations of real life interviews with suspects*. Paper presented at the Annual Conference of the European Association of Psychology and Law, Krakow.

Clarke, C. and Milne, R. (2001). *National evaluation of the PEACE investigative interviewing course*. Police Research Award Scheme. London: Home Office.

Clifford, B.R. and George, R. (1996). A field investigation of training in three methods of witness/victim investigative interviewing. *Psychology, Crime and Law, 2*, 231–248.

Cooke, P. and Davies, G. (2001). Achieving best evidence from witnesses with learning disabilities: New guidance. *British Journal of Learning Disabilities, 29*, 84–87.

Daniell, C. (1999). *The truth—The whole truth and nothing but the truth? An analysis of witness interviews and statements*. Unpublished undergraduate dissertation. University of Plymouth.

Fisher, R.P. and Geiselman, R.E. (1992). *Memory-enhancing techniques for investigative interviewing*. Springfield, Illinois: Charles C. Thomas.

Gasson, T. (2001). *Cognitive interviewing: Getting the best from memory recall and witness capability. But are we? The acceptance and application of cognitive interviewing within investigations conducted by the police service*. Unpublished undergraduate dissertation. Bradford and Ilkley College.

Gudjonsson, G. (2003). *The psychology of interrogations and confessions*: A handbook. Chichester: John Wiley & Sons.

Holmberg, U. and Christianson, S. (in press). Murderers' and sexual offenders' experiences of police interviews and their inclination to admit or deny crimes. *Behavioral Sciences and the Law*.

Home Office and Department of Health (1992). *Memorandum of good practice for video recorded interviews with child witnesses for criminal proceedings*. London: HMSO.

Home Office and Department of Health (2002). *Achieving best evidence in criminal proceedings: Guidance for vulnerable or intimidated witnesses, including children*. London: HMSO.

Kebbell, M., Milne, R. and Wagstaff, G. (1999). The cognitive interview: A survey of its forensic effectiveness. *Psychology, Crime and Law, 5*, 101–116.

Köhnken, G., Milne, R., Memon, A. and Bull, R. (1999). The cognitive interview: A meta-analysis. *Psychology, Crime and Law, 39*, 127–138.

Leo, R. and Ofshe, R. (1998). The consequences of false confessions: Deprivations of liberty and miscarriages of justice in the age of psychological interrogation. *Journal of Criminal Law and Criminology, 88*, 429–496.

McKeever, G. (1999). Detecting, prosecuting and punishing benefit fraud: The Social Security Administration (Fraud) Act 1997. *Modern Law Review, 62*, 261–270.

McLean, M. (1995). Quality investigation? Police interviewing of witnesses. *Medicine, Science and the Law, 35*, 116–122.

Milne, R. and Bull, R. (1996). Interviewing children with mild learning disability with the cognitive interview. In N. Clark and G. Stephenson (eds), *Investigative and forensic decision making*. Leicester: British Psychological Society.

Milne, R. and Bull, R. (1999). *Investigative interviewing: Psychology and practice.* Chichester: John Wiley & Sons.

Milne, R. and Bull, R. (2001). Interviewing witnesses with learning disabilities for legal purposes: A review. *British Journal of Learning Disabilities, 29*, 93–97.

Milne, R. and Bull, R. (2002). Back to basics: A componential analysis of the original cognitive interview mnemonics with three age groups. *Applied Cognitive Psychology, 16*, 1–11.

Milne, R., Clare, I.C.H. and Bull, R. (1999). Interviewing adults with learning disability with the cognitive interview. *Psychology, Crime and Law, 5*, 81–100.

Milne, R., Clare, I.C.H. and Bull, R. (2002). Interrogative suggestibility among witnesses with mild intellectual disabilities: The use of an adaptation of the GSS. *Journal of Applied Research in Intellectual Disabilities, 15*, 1–10.

Milne, R. and Shaw, G. (1999). Obtaining witness statements: Best practice and proposals for innovation. *Medicine, Science and the Law, 39*, 127–138.

Mortimer, A. and Shepherd, E. (1999). Frames of mind: Schemata guiding cognition and conduct in the interviewing of suspected offenders. In A. Memon and R. Bull (eds), *Handbook of the psychology of interviewing*. Chichester: John Wiley & Sons.

Moston, S., Stephenson, G.M. and Williamson, T. (1992). The effects of case characteristics on suspect behaviour during police questioning. *British Journal of Criminology, 32*, 23–40.

National Crime Faculty (1999). *Murder investigation manual*. Bramshill: National Crime Faculty and National Police Training.

National Crime Faculty (2000). *A practical guide to investigative interviewing*. Bramshill: National Crime Faculty and National Police Training.

Ofshe, R. and Leo, R. (1997). The decision to confers falsely: Rational choice and irrational action. *Denver University Law Review, 74*, 979–1122.

O'Mahony, B. (2000). *How effective is the standard PEACE course in equipping police officers to conduct an investigative interview.* Unpublished Masters dissertation. University of Leicester.

Pearse, J. and Gudjonsson, G. (1999). Measuring influential police tactics: A factor analytic approach. *Legal and Criminological Psychology, 4*, 221–238.

Plimmer, J. (1997). Confession rate. *Police Review*, 7 February, pp. 16–18.

Sear, L. and Stephenson, G. (1997). Interviewing skills and individual characteristics of police interrogations. In G. Stephenson and N. Clark (eds), *Procedures in criminal justice: Contemporary issues*. Leicester: British Psychological Society.

Shepherd, E. (1988). Developing interview skills. In P. Southgate (ed.), *New directions in police training*. London: HMSO.

Shepherd, E. and Milne, R. (1999). Full and faithful: Ensuring quality practice and integrity of outcome in witness interviews. In A. Heaton-Armstrong, D. Wolchover and E. Shepherd (eds), *Analysing witness testimony*. Blackstone Press.

Shuy, R. (1998). *The language of confession, interrogation and deception.* Thousand Oaks, CA: Sage.

Soukara, S., Bull, R. and Vrij, A. (in press). Police detectives' aims regarding their interviews with suspects: Any changes at the turn of the millennium? *International Journal of Police Science and Management*.

Stockdale, J.E. (1993). *Management and supervision of police interviews*. Police Research Group Paper No. 5. London: Home Office.

Williams, E. (2000). *The cognitive interview: Can it be a useful tool for lawyers?* Unpublished Masters dissertation. University of Portsmouth.

Wolchover, D. and Heaton-Armstrong, A. (1997). Tape recording witness statements. *New Law Journal* (6 June), 855–857.

Chapter 2.2

Violence Risk: From Prediction to Management

Kirk Heilbrun
Drexel University, USA

INTRODUCTION

There has been enormous progress in violence risk assessment during the last decade. Much of this progress has been seen in the improved capacity to accurately identify individuals at high risk for future violent behavior, in populations including adults with severe mental illness (Monahan et al., 2001; Steadman et al., 1998), correctional populations (Douglas and Webster, 1999; Andrews and Bonta, 1995), mentally disordered offenders (Webster et al., 1997; Quinsey et al., 1998), and sexual offenders (Hanson, 1998). Associated with these advances have been both conceptual changes (Monahan and Steadman, 1994a; Steadman et al., 1994) and implications for improved practice (Dvoskin and Heilbrun, 2001).

The term 'risk assessment' may be construed narrowly, to describe the process of identifying risk of future violence and enhancing the accuracy of predictions of such future violence. It may also be considered more broadly, to include the areas of *risk management* (identifying and delivering interventions to reduce the risk of future violent behavior), *decision-making* (drawing conclusions and determining consequences in light of the information obtained in the two previous steps), and *risk communication* (describing the process and outcome of the entire assessment process). Whether 'risk assessment' is considered broadly or narrowly, however, it is important to consider the interrelationship of these four areas.

The great majority of work in risk assessment during the last decade has been focused on prediction and risk level classification. However, there has been an increasing recognition during recent years of the importance of risk management, both as a frequent priority of legal decision-makers, clinicians, and policy-makers, and an important consequence of the larger assessment process (Carson, 1994; Heilbrun, 1997).

Handbook of Psychology in Legal Contexts, Second Edition
Edited by D. Carson and R. Bull. © 2003 John Wiley & Sons, Ltd.

The present chapter will focus on risk management, and has two major purposes. First, we will describe recent conceptual, empirical, and practice advances in risk management. Second, we will discuss the implications of the changes in each of these areas, and describe strategies that might yield important further advances.

THEORETICAL ADVANCES IN RISK MANAGEMENT

One of the most important conceptual advances in both prediction/classification and risk management occurred with the disaggregation of the term 'dangerousness', which even today often appears in law, policy, and practice. This term was divided into three components—*risk factors* (influences associated with the probability that violence will occur, as contrasted with protective factors, which are influences that reduce the likelihood that violence will occur), *harm* (the nature and severity of the results of the violent behavior), and *risk level* (the probability that violence will occur)— by the National Research Council (1989). This separation facilitated the specific consideration of each of these areas in theory and research.

This distinction subsequently provided an important influence on the risk assessment project conducted by the MacArthur Research Network on Mental Health and Law (Steadman et al., 1998). The MacArthur Network reconceptualized the research task from dangerousness (the legal construct) to violence risk, a decision that was to greatly facilitate their subsequent research in the area of violence (Steadman et al., 1993). This reconceptualization included the following changes: (1) predicted harm should be scaled in terms of seriousness rather than treated dichotomously (e.g. harm vs no harm), (2) risk should be treated as a continuous variable (e.g. probability of harm) rather than in dichotomous fashion (e.g. risk vs no risk), and (3) risk should be assessed in ongoing fashion rather than on a single occasion, since risk levels may fluctuate over time and with interventions (Monahan and Steadman, 1994b).

The latter point, concerning risk assessment as an ongoing process, was also emphasized by Carson (1994) in his discussion of the elements of dangerousness. He noted that most of the focus in the literature on dangerousness had been in the area of individual and situational risk factors for violence. However, the components of decision-making and the multiple instances in which risk decisions are often made were also described as important considerations in the process of risk assessment. The concept of multiple assessments over time was considered as well in a discussion of the 'prediction vs management' distinction in risk assessment—multiple assessments across time are characteristic of risk management, while predictions made in legal contexts are typically made on a one-time-only basis (Heilbrun, 1997).

During the last five years, three books have been published that are particularly relevant to violence risk reduction in mentally disordered offenders. The first (*Treatment of Offenders with Mental Disorders*; Wettstein, 1998) offers administrative and legal perspectives on the treatment of mentally disordered offenders. It also provides chapters on treatment offered in a variety of settings (inpatient, jail and prison, community) and to specialized populations (sexual offenders, juveniles, offenders with mental retardation). These chapters typically involve an integration of the author's experience with relevant practice literature, accompanied by some empirical studies, yielding guidelines and principles on a given topic. However, a number of contributing authors stressed the relative absence of empirical research on violence risk management that was available through the mid-1990s.

The second book (*Violence Among the Mentally Ill: Effective Treatments and Management Strategies*; Hodgins, 2000a) describes the proceedings of a NATO Conference on risk management in mentally disordered offenders. This conference brought together researchers and practitioners from Europe, Canada, and the United States to focus on what was known about treatment and rehabilitation of mentally disordered offenders, and the relationship of such interventions to violence and crime risk. Some of the empirical studies cited in this conference will be described in the next section of this chapter. Broadly, however, the results of the conference reflected significant cultural differences with important implications for risk management. Researchers describing European cohorts observed a fairly strong, stable relationship between severe mental illness and violent offending (e.g. Tiihonen and Swartz, 2000; see also Volavka and Krakowski, 1989), while Canadian and US researchers noted a much weaker relationship between these variables (e.g. Monahan and Appelbaum, 2000). It may be that different base rates of violent offending and the differential presence of other risk factors (e.g. poverty, substance abuse, weapon access) in these countries can account, in part, for this phenomenon. This does suggest, however, that risk management research findings are somewhat culture-specific; effective risk reduction strategies for Sweden or Germany might be less effective in the United States. Certainly this pattern seemed to explain differences among conference participants in their respective orientations to risk management. Western European researchers and practitioners argued that effectively treating clinical symptoms would necessarily reduce the risk of patients' future violent offending. Canadian and US participants suggested with equal vigor that effective risk reduction must encompass a host of quasi-clinical and non-clinical risk factors (e.g. housing, social support, weapon access). Interestingly, both groups may have been accurate—regarding their respective countries.

The third book (*Violence, Crime, and Mentally Disordered Offenders: Concepts and Methods for Effective Treatment and Prevention*; Hodgins and Müller-Isberner, 2000) provides a perspective somewhat similar to that offered by Wettstein, although dividing offenders by diagnosis and intervention modality rather than setting. The chapters also reflect greater cultural diversity and international perspectives, with contributors from Europe, Canada, and the United States. One of the assumptions underlying the organization of this book involves the nature of the link between clinical diagnosis/symptoms and violent behavior. With 5 of the 10 chapters devoted to describing violence treatment and prevention strategies for individuals in particular diagnostic categories, Hodgins and Müller-Isberner apparently used the 'European perspective' (described in the previous paragraph) to organize much of the material about violence risk reduction with mentally disordered offenders.

Some recent promising developments in risk management have occurred through a particular focus on dynamic (potentially changeable through planned intervention) violence risk factors. Hanson (1998) distinguished between *stable* and *acute* dynamic risk factors, with the former having more stability over time and across situations (e.g. substance dependence) and the latter inclined to shift more rapidly (e.g. intoxication). This distinction has implications for the selection of dynamic risk factors as treatment targets (Hanson and Harris, 2000), as the measurement frequency and monitoring efforts should be adjusted according to the stability of the risk factor.

A more structured approach to describing and rating dynamic risk factors has recently been adopted with the revision of the HCR-20 (cite) manual, with detailed descriptions of potential treatment strategies for the C (Clinical) and R (Risk Management) factors that are elevated (Douglas and colleagues, in press). This manual offers strategies for those involved in delivering risk-reduction interventions; it also provides important clues for researchers investigating the impact of such interventions. The revision may facilitate the expanded use of the increasingly popular HCR-20 by allowing the clinician to plan interventions more systematically. It may also facilitate the validation research of the C and R sections, which is greatly needed.

EMPIRICAL ADVANCES IN RISK MANAGEMENT

This section will focus on studies describing risk-reduction interventions. Measuring the frequency of violence as an outcome is an essential part of such research. One reasonable strategy in selecting outcome measures involves focusing on dynamic risk factors; however, the most basic element of violence risk research—the *sine qua non* of outcomes—involves the measurement of violence and aggression. Of course, the proper measurement of violence as an outcome presents enormous practical problems. Ideally, such an outcome would be measured prospectively, using information from multiple sources (including self-report, collateral observer report, and official records of arrest and hospitalization). Few studies meet this standard (see Lidz, Mulvey and Gardner, 1993; Steadman et al., 1998; Swartz et al., 1998a, 1998b, for noteworthy exceptions). More often, investigators have used outcome sources such as official records of arrest or rehospitalization for a violent act. Limiting the measurement of violence outcome by employing only official records can present very significant problems in countries such as the United States, in which violent behavior among the mentally disordered in the community may occur at six to seven times the rate reflected in official records (Steadman et al., 1998). Using records as a sole source of violence outcome is less problematic in countries where such records more accurately reflect the violence that has actually occurred. However, scholars still need to provide a description of why such records should be considered an accurate reflection of the base rate of violence in the population being studied.

Research on risk management can be conceptualized on three levels. First, there are studies that measure the impact of a *single intervention* on subsequent violence.

An example might involve problem-solving therapy, with manualized administration in an efficacy design, compared with a control group receiving standard treatment. Second, a study may consider the impact of a *programmatic intervention*, involving multiple components. An example of this level of intervention might involve a hospital unit designed following a careful investigation of patient risk-reduction treatment needs, or the impact of a community intervention with multiple components, such as intensive case management. As the nature of the intervention being investigated becomes broader, it becomes much more difficult to conduct an efficacy study; it is also very difficult in violence research to meet such efficacy criteria as random assignment of participants to condition. Consequently, most studies in this area are effectiveness studies. (Efficacy studies employ controlled designs such as clinical trials to assess outcomes under ideal conditions, and tend to have high internal validity that results from the carefully controlled conditions. Effectiveness studies focus on the outcomes of interventions made under 'usual practice' conditions; they are weaker in internal validity but stronger in external validity considerations such as generalizability (see Wells, 1999). Finally, a risk management study at the broadest level may investigate a *policy intervention*. For example, a change in the law pertaining to conditional release of insanity acquittees, or outpatient commitment, can provide an opportunity for research on the impact of such an intervention.

There have been a number of relevant and potentially important empirical studies conducted in the area of violence risk management during the last decade. These studies will be described in the remainder of this section. In the interest of conceptual clarity, they will also be considered on *individual*, *programmatic*, and *policy* levels whenever feasible. Hodgins (2000b) has addressed the etiology and development of offending by persons with mental disorders by citing her own programmatic research and that of other investigators in hypothesizing two broad groups of offenders: early start and late start. Within 'early start' offenders, she further suggested that there are subgroups consisting of those with primary conduct disorder and those with primary substance use problems. Such focus on etiology and development of offending, she noted, has two major advantages: (1) it identifies historical influences more accurately, and yields clues about the mechanisms involved in influencing the disorder and the offending, and (2) it provides some indication of the extent to which certain characteristics may be modifiable risk factors for offending. The latter advantage has implications for both individual and programmatic risk reduction interventions, as the accurate identification of such subtypes would allow either single or multiple forms of a certain intervention that could work reasonably well for one type of offender but not for another. For example, there is some evidence to suggest that interventions delivered in a therapeutic community have an offense risk-reducing effect on individuals who are not psychopaths, but no impact (or possibly even a risk *exacerbating* effect) on psychopaths (Rice, Harris and Cormier, 1992).

The impact of situational variables on violence risk has received less attention than it should. Poverty, for example, is a potent risk factor for violence among individuals with mental disorders who have been discharged from inpatient treatment into the community (Silver, Mulvey and Monahan, 1999). A careful examination of the circumstances surrounding violent acts, including the setting and target of the acts and the use of drugs, alcohol, and/or medication by the individual who is behaving violently, can yield important clues about interventions that would reduce the risk of such violence—particularly when contrasted with occasions on which violence could have occurred, but did not (Steadman and Silver, 2000). Situational influences can be particularly important in risk-reduction interventions delivered on an individual level (e.g. treatment and monitoring for substance abuse; the administration of psychotropic medication via injection rather than orally for an individual who has been non-compliant with taking prescribed medication). Considering situational influences carefully can also help to disaggregate the impact of policy-level interventions.

Rates and risk factors for violence among individuals with mental disorder in the community, described in the MacArthur Risk Assessment study (Steadman et al., 1998), yielded several important clues for violence risk reduction (Monahan and Appelbaum, 2000). Differential diagnosis may be more important in risk reduction than risk assessment, as diagnostic categories may constitute one kind of relevant subtype of individuals who are potentially violent (Rice and Harris, 1997). Consistent with this, the following 'MacArthur clues' to risk reduction may be particularly useful for planning interventions: (1) substance abuse, (2) anger control, and (3) social support (Monahan and Appelbaum, 2000). Interventions that effectively reduce problems in any of these areas may have an associated impact on reducing violence risk. The impact of substance abuse, in particular, has also been cited in a number of other recent studies that include schizophrenia as well as depression among the disorders at risk for violence (e.g. Eronen, Hakola and Tiihonen, 1996; Hodgins et al., 1996; Swartz et al., 1998a, 1998b).

There is some evidence that when 'violence' is defined as conviction for a violent criminal offense, individuals with mental disorder generally are at greater risk than those without mental disorder. Describing a Danish birth cohort over a 43-year outcome period, Hodgins and colleagues (1996) observed that individuals with a history of psychiatric hospitalization were more likely to have been convicted of a criminal offense. In a related vein, the diagnoses of substance abuse and/or antisocial personality disorder, particularly when they co-occur with schizophrenia, may result in an elevated risk for violence among those with such disorders (Bloom, Muesser and Müller-Isberner, 2000). Bloom and colleagues (2000) also addressed the impact of several promising interventions with this population that may have violence risk-reducing impact resulting from general improvement in clinical and social functioning: (1) psychosocial treatment for severe mental illness, (2) assertive community treatment, (3) family intervention, (4) supported employment, (5) social skills training, (6) integrated dual diagnosis treatment, (7) cognitive therapy for psychosis, and (8) medication.

The intervention of medication more specifically for this population is addressed in two NATO Conference chapters (Hodgins, 2000a). In the first, the authors discussed the use of medication in preventing violence among the mentally ill with secondary substance use disorders (Tiihonen and Swartz, 2000). After summarizing evidence suggesting that major mental disorders and substance abuse are associated with increased risk of violent offending, they noted an unfortunate gap in the empirical literature. Although some pharmacological interventions have demonstrated symptom-reducing efficacy among those with major mental disorder, and others have shown such efficacy in those with substance abuse, there are no published controlled studies on the efficacy of medication in reducing the risk of violence among those with such disorders, or among those with co-occurring disorders. There *is* evidence that poor compliance with prescribed medication, combined with substance abuse, significantly *elevates* the risk for violent behavior in patients with major mental disorder (see, e.g. Swartz et al., 1998a, 1998b). However, in the area of co-occurring major mental disorders and personality disorders, there is limited available evidence accompanied by a proposed research agenda to address this deficit (Volavka and Citrome, 2000).

The data suggesting that a certain kind of personality disorder—psychopathy—is a risk factor for violence and violent crime continue to be impressive (Douglas et al., 1999; Douglas and Webster, 1999; Hare, 1991; Hare et al., 2000; Harris, Rice and Quinsey, 1993; Monahan et al., 2001; Salekin, Rogers and Sewell, 1996; Serin, 1996; Steadman et al., 1998). However, evidence for the role of personality disorder more broadly is much less clear (Burke and Hart, 2000). This pattern has important implications for risk-reduction interventions, in the following sense. Psychopathy appears to be a strong static risk factor for violence; although violence risk diminishes with age, no planned interventions have yet been shown to be effective in reducing violence risk for psychopaths. This may be less true for other kinds of personality disorders—such disorders may be more amenable to risk-reducing interventions—but we do not have the empirical evidence to determine whether this is so. Because of the weak state of available scientific knowledge, Burke and Hart (2000) invoke the correctional rehabilitative principles of *risk* (treat and monitor high risk individuals more intensively), *need* (target interventions to criminogenic need), and *responsivity* (determine who is most likely to respond to such interventions) in offering guidance for risk reduction with individuals with personality disorders.

Particular strategies for reducing the risk of violence in the community were addressed in two articles (Heilbrun and Peters, 2000a, 2000b) and related commentary (McGuire, 2000) on this topic. The relative lack of programmatic research on either effectiveness or efficacy of single interventions, programs, or policies was observed (although programs typically do not offer violence risk reduction as a first priority; see Høyer, 2000). However, Heilbrun and Peters (2000a, 2000b) did cite some empirical support for certain community interventions to reduce violence and criminality:

(1) identification and prioritization of violence risk reduction among program goals (allowing the program to be evaluated on its performance in this area),

(2) conditional release,

(3) intensive case management,

(4)   skills-based training delivered by those experienced with forensic populations,

(5)   a range of services including housing support, vocational assistance, and clinical treatment, and

(6)   a particular focus on rehabilitating and preventing substance abuse.

The design of community treatment programs and policies should consider the range of risk factors identified through meta-analysis with mentally disordered offenders (Bonta, Law and Hanson, 1998) and target dynamic risk factors among those identified in this study; this conceptually links risk-reduction strategies in correctional and community forensic settings (McGuire, 2000).

Two particular policy-level aspects of risk-reduction intervention in England and Wales are the restriction order and the community treatment order (Ferris, 2000). The former involves a judge's order for an individual to be hospitalized rather than imprisoned following conviction for a serious criminal offense; conditional discharge (comparable to 'conditional release' in North America; see previous paragraph) is made when the patient is ready to leave the hospital, but the discharged patient must usually accept psychiatric and social supervision. The latter is comparable to the North American policy of outpatient commitment, which has received recent support as a mechanism for reducing arrests in a one-year randomized trial of outpatient commitment of 262 participants with severe mental illness (Swanson et al., 2001). Outpatient commitment is a controversial and much-debated policy in the United States, currently also in use in Australia and New Zealand, and debated but not presently operative in the United Kingdom. Evidence from recent studies suggests that despite its potential impingement upon autonomy and civil liberties, however, outpatient commitment has the potential to significantly reduce violent and criminal behavior among the severely mentally ill in the community.

ADVANCES IN THE PRACTICE OF RISK MANAGEMENT

The advances in risk-reduction planning and implementation have not kept pace with the significant improvements in the prediction of violent behavior and classification of risk. It is worth noting, however, that the area of risk management is approximately at the stage of risk assessment 10–15 years ago. There is growing awareness of the importance of conducting programmatic research to identify interventions—single, programmatic, and policy-level—that have demonstrated efficacy and effectiveness in reducing the likelihood of future violent behavior. It is possible to identify research that is fragmented, conducted with small samples, or performed at single sites that yields promising possibilities. This will be addressed in this section. What has not occurred, however, is the identification of risk management in the severely mentally ill as a research priority by a group such as the MacArthur Research Network on Mental Health and Law—followed by conceptual reconsideration and a multi-site, large-scale empirical study. Such an occurrence would provide a tremendous boost to the area of risk management, as it has previously for risk assessment.

Nonetheless, it is possible to identify important advances in the practice of risk management. Developments in four areas will be discussed:

(1) the use of the individualized principles of risk, need, and responsiveness, and the use of anamnestic assessment (deriving individualized risk factors from the individual's history of violent behavior) to designate specific interventions for individuals with severe mental illness,

(2) the use of structured tools with risk management components, such as the HCR-20 (Webster et al., 1997) and the LSI-R (Andrews and Bonta, 1995), to guide the selection of risk-reducing interventions,

(3) the empirical identification of prominent, risk-relevant treatment needs, perhaps accompanied by empirically defined 'clusters' of patients who have different patterns of needs, to develop specialized programs, and

(4) the application of emerging standards of practice, influenced by research, in designing programs and policies with risk reduction among their highest priorities.

Using the principles of risk, need, and responsiveness can make the linkage between risk level classification and risk reduction more meaningful. When tools such as the HCR-20 (Webster et al., 1997) or the VRAG (Harris, Rice and Quinsey, 1993) are used to assign an actuarial risk level to an individual, this level gives no direct guidance on what should be done to manage or reduce this risk (particularly since actuarial scales tend to be composed primarily of demographic and historical variables that are static risk factors). 'High risk' individuals may be high risk because of intensive treatment needs, which would suggest the need for a longer period of rehabilitation and more conservative release decision-making, and requiring the demonstration of non-aggressive, responsible behavior at each of a series of graduated levels. Alternatively, such individuals may be high risk for reasons (e.g. psychopathy) that apparently cannot be altered through planned interventions, at least presently. Making this distinction for a given individual can be difficult. The anamnestic approach (Melton et al., 1997) involves using an individual's history to identify patterns of behavior to yield a number of dynamic risk factors *associated with that individual's previous violent acts* that may be described as applicable risk factors that can then guide the selection of intervention strategies.

With the development of tools such as the HCR-20 and the LSI-R, it has become possible to assess risk-relevant needs in a systematic, semi-structured fashion. Both tools have a number of items that represent common risk factors for the mentally ill and correctional populations, respectively, to which they primarily apply. When deficits on these items are endorsed, it allows the treatment team or rehabilitative staff to develop an intervention plan that explicitly includes these particular risk-relevant deficits.

The HCR-20 has recently been expanded to provide more guidance for interventions that are targeted toward each of the C (Clinical) and R (Risk Management) items that are problematic (Douglas et al., in press), making it easier to apply toward risk management.

Rather than identifying risk factors through individualized history or structured tools, Quinsey and colleagues (1998) have proposed a different approach to planning and delivering risk-reduction services. They describe a project that began with a series of studies assessing the interpersonal, psychiatric, and criminal problems in a cross-section of mentally disordered offenders in Canada (Quinsey, Cyr and Lavalee, 1988; Rice and Harris, 1988; Rice et al., 1990) by surveying staff familiar with the offenders. Individual problems were factor analyzed to yield Clinical Problem Scales (Life Skills Deficits, Aggression, Health Problems, Management Problems, Family Problems, Social Withdrawal, Active Psychotic Symptoms, and Depression). These scales were then cluster analyzed to identify relatively homogeneous subgroups of mentally disordered offenders with comparable patterns of scores. Paired with risk levels obtained from the VRAG, a total of eight clusters could be identified:

(1) *'low risk, low need'* individuals (30%),

(2) *'low risk, moderate need'* individuals with needs often associated with chronic psychiatric problems, such as social withdrawal, life skills deficits, depression, family problems, and active psychotic symptoms (17%),

(3) *'high risk, low need'* individuals, described as 'model patients but dangerous' (16%),

(4) *'high risk, moderate need'* individuals with needs in the areas of management and aggression (11%),

(5) *'low risk, high need'* individuals with clinical problems in the areas of Aggression, Management, and Active Psychotic Symptoms (6%),

(6) *'low–moderate risk, high need'* individuals with problems in the areas of Life Skills Deficits, Active Psychotic Symptoms, and Social Withdrawal (9%),

(7) *'high risk, high need'* individuals with problems in Aggression and Management (4%), and

(8) *'moderate risk, high need'* individuals with significant problems in every area (Quinsey et al., 1998).

A treatment facility could use this approach to identify clusters specific to its jurisdictions, then consider each cluster in assigning ward or planning programming. This approach has considerable promise in the effective delivery of risk-reducing interventions, although it apparently has not been empirically studied to date.

All three of the advances reviewed thus far in this section are concerned with the planning and allocation of risk-reducing interventions. We will suggest 10 kinds of interventions that have received some combination of empirical and conceptual support as risk factors for violent behavior among mentally disordered offenders, as described earlier in this chapter. While each of these appears 'promising', a clearer verdict on the risk-reducing potential of each will await the results of programmatic research on the delivery of such interventions, under somewhat controlled conditions, to different groups of mentally disordered offenders, in different contexts and sometimes in different combinations, with results gauged by using sensitive outcome measures of violence that include self- and collateral report in addition to official records. These interventions will be described at the individual, program, and policy levels. First, there are seven individual-level interventions that appear promising: (1) substance abuse treatment, particularly when designed for individuals with co-occurring disorders, (2) anger control training, (3) family interventions and social support, (4) employment assistance and vocational training, (5) psychotropic medication, (6) housing support, and (7) other clinical services to address symptoms such as violent fantasies. Second, two interventions could be described at the programmatic level. They are psychosocial rehabilitation/skills-based training in a broad range of skills important in vocational and interpersonal functioning, and specialized case management (Assertive Community Treatment and intensive case management are two of the best examples). Finally, at the broadest policy level, the supervised treatment and management that occurs in the community under policies such as conditional release and outpatient commitment have demonstrated value in reducing violence risk.

DISCUSSION

One of the challenging aspects of writing a review chapter on the current status of violence risk reduction for individuals with mental illness is to be appropriately critical of what has been accomplished—but to acknowledge that risk reduction is an enormously important endeavor that is being practiced (and must be practiced) whatever the state of the science. There is no question that the field of risk assessment has made tremendous progress during the last decade (Borum, 1996; Otto, 2000). Likewise, it seems clear that the field has increasingly acknowledged the importance of risk management (Carson, 1994; Heilbrun, 1997; Hodgins, 2000a; Monahan and Steadman, 1994a), and perhaps is ready to embark upon its systematic study during the next decade.

It will not be easy. Even promising interventions, in order to be studied appropriately, must be considered using designs that control the nature and level of intervention, and the assignment of recipient, in ways that are difficult or impossible in criminal justice or civilly committed populations. Persuading a human subjects committee, hospital administrator, or chief judge to approve a study in which 'experimental' and 'violence' both appear in the title can be a task of Herculean proportion. Yet it can be done (see, e.g. the programmatic work of North Carolina researchers on outpatient commitment—Swanson et al., 2001; Swartz et al., 1998a, 1998b). Table 2.2.1 provides

Table 2.2.1 Studies that would assess the impact of violence risk-reduction interventions

Study	Control/comparison group	Experimental group	Outcome 1	Outcome 2
Impact of intensive, specialized substance abuse treatment	Usual practice	Practice + intensive Substance abuse treatment for dually diagnosed	Substance abuse variables	Violent behavior measured by self-report, collateral report, and official records
Impact of manualized anger control training	Usual practice	Practice + manualized anger control training	Anger experience and control variables	Same
Impact of programmatic interventions to 'risk/need' clusters	Usual practice	Clusters receiving interventions designed to address needs and consider risk	Specific needs targeted by interventions	Same
Impact of intensive release planning/intensive case management	Usual practice	Practice + intensive release planning/ intensive case management	Adjustment perceived support access to services compliance with plan	Same
Impact of outpatient commitment	Usual practice	Practice + release on outpatient commitment	Adjustment compliance	Same

a brief description of five studies that could be performed to address the impact of various kinds (and levels) of risk-reducing interventions. One of the practical aspects of implementing any of these studies involves assuring those who approve such research that there already exists a fairly significant body of evidence suggesting that this kind of intervention will enhance the risk-reducing effectiveness of the standard practice intervention already received. Violence levels of participants should decrease, but they will not (given that participants are receiving everything they would usually receive without the research project) increase.

It is likely that hospitals, agencies, or systems that adopt the systematic use of one of the three kinds of risk-reduction intervention planning described in this chapter—anamnestic, tool-based, or cluster-based—will receive some immediate benefits (e.g. comprehensiveness, consistency) resulting from the systematic application of this approach. To effectively assess the impact of these different approaches to risk management planning, however, will require the collection of process and outcome data like those described in Table 2.2.1. Partnerships between practitioners and researchers will be crucial in determining how well this can be accomplished in the next decade.

One of the least discussed aspects of risk reduction involves the role of protective factors. In a public health sense, an outcome such as violent behavior is affected both by risk factors and protective factors, yet there is apparently no research and relatively little discussion (see Rogers, 2000, for a noteworthy exception) of the role of protective factors in preventing or minimizing violence, and the possibility of reducing violence risk through interventions that identify and strengthen protective factors. This is an area that needs both theoretical and empirical attention.

In the largest sense, risk assessment should be linked with risk management; both should inform decision-making, and be communicated in a way that is understandable and minimizes distortion (Edens and Otto, 2001; Heilbrun et al., 1999). When decision-makers can consider an individual's risk of future violence, the extent to which such risk has been reduced through intervention, and the degree to which it can be managed following release, then the goal of legally informed decision-making is achieved—and assessment and intervention can work as complementary pieces of a larger puzzle (Dvoskin and Heilbrun, 2001). If this is to occur, however, the advances in risk management described in this chapter must be expanded significantly over the next decade.

REFERENCES

Andrews, D. and Bonta, J. (1995). *The level of service inventory—Revised: User's manual.* Toronto, Ontario: Multi-Health Systems, Inc.

Bloom, J.D., Muesser, K.T. and Müller-Isberner, R. (2000). Treatment implications of the antecedents of criminality and violence in schizophrenia and major affective disorders. In S. Hodgins (ed.), *Violence among the mentally ill: Effective treatments and management strategies* (pp. 145–169). Boston: Kluwer Academic Publishers.

Bonta, J., Law, M. and Hanson, K. (1998). The prediction of criminal and violent recidivism among mentally disordered offenders: A meta-analysis. *Psychological Bulletin*, *123*, 123–142.

Borum, R. (1996). Improving the clinical practice of violence risk assessment: Technology, guidelines, and training. *American Psychologist*, *51*, 945–956.

Burke, H. and Hart, S.D. (2000). Personality disordered offenders: Conceptualization, assessment and diagnosis of personality disorder. In S. Hodgins and R. Müller-Isberner (eds), *Violence, crime, and mentally disordered offenders: Concepts and methods for effective treatment and prevention* (pp. 63–85). New York: John Wiley & Sons.

Carson, D. (1994). Dangerous people: Through a broader conception of risk and danger to better decisions. *Expert Evidence*, *3*, 51–69.

Douglas, K., Ogloff, J., Nicholls, T. and Grant, I. (1999). Assessing risk for violence among psychiatric patients: The HCR-20 violence risk assessment scheme and the Psychopathy Checklist: Screening Version. *Journal of Consulting and Clinical Psychology*, *67*, 917–930.

Douglas, K. and Webster, C. (1999). The HCR-20 violence risk assessment scheme: Concurrent validity in a sample of incarcerated offenders. *Criminal Justice and Behavior*, *26*, 3–19.

Douglas, K., Webster, C., Hart, S., Eaves, D. and Ogloff, J. (in press). *HCR-20 violence risk management companion guide*. Burnaby, British Columbia: Mental Health, Law, and Policy Institute, Simon Fraser University.

Dvoskin, J. and Heilbrun, K. (2001). Risk assessment and release decision-making: Toward resolving the great debate. *Journal of the American Academy of Psychiatry and the Law*, *29*, 6–10.

Edens, J.F. and Otto, R.K. (2001). Release decision making and planning. In J.B. Ashford, B.D. Sales and W.H. Reid (eds), *Treating adult and juvenile offenders with special needs* (pp. 335–371). Washington, DC: American Psychological Association.

Eronen, M., Hakola, P. and Tiihonen, J. (1996). Factors associated with homicide recidivism in a 13-year sample of homicide offenders in Finland. *Psychiatric Services*, *47*, 403–406.

Ferris, R. (2000). Community treatment programmes in Europe and the United Kingdom that have proven effective in preventing violence by the mentally ill in the community: Administrative, organizational, legal, and clinical aspects. In S. Hodgins (ed.), *Violence among the mentally ill: Effective treatments and management strategies* (pp. 389–408). Boston: Kluwer Academic Publishers.

Hanson, R.K. (1998). What do we know about sex offender risk assessment? *Psychology, Public Policy, and Law*, *4*, 50–72.

Hanson, R.K. and Harris, A.J.R. (2000). Where should we intervene? Dynamic predictors of sexual offense recidivism. *Criminal Justice and Behavior*, *27*, 6–35.

Hare, R. (1991). *The Hare psychopathy checklist—Revised*. Toronto, Ontario, Canada: Multi-Health Systems.

Hare, R., Clark, D., Grann, M. and Thornton, D. (2000). Psychopathy and the predictive validity of the PCL-R: An international perspective. *Behavioral Sciences and the Law*, *18*, 623–645.

Harris, G.T., Rice, M.E. and Quinsey, V.L. (1993). Violent recidivism of mentally disordered offenders: The development of a statistical prediction instrument. *Criminal Justice and Behavior*, *20*, 315–335.

Heilbrun, K. (1997). Prediction vs management models relevant to risk assessment: The importance of legal decision-making context. *Law and Human Behavior*, *21*, 347–359.

Heilbrun, K., Dvoskin, J., Hart, S. and McNeil, D. (1999). Violence risk communication: Implications for research, policy, and practice. *Health, Risk and Society*, *1*, 91–106.

Heilbrun, K. and Peters, L. (2000a). The efficacy and effectiveness of community treatment programmes in preventing crime and violence among those with severe mental illness in the community. In S. Hodgins (ed.), *Violence among the mentally ill: Effective treatments and management strategies* (pp. 341–357). Boston: Kluwer Academic Publishers.

Heilbrun, K. and Peters, L. (2000b). Community-based treatment programmes. In S. Hodgins and R. Müller-Isberner (eds), *Violence, crime, and mentally disordered offenders: Concepts and methods for effective treatment and prevention* (pp. 193–215). New York: John Wiley & Sons.

Hodgins, S. (ed.) (2000a). *Violence among the mentally ill: Effective treatments and management strategies*. Boston: Kluwer Academic Publishers.

Hodgins, S. (2000b). The etiology and development of offending among persons with major mental disorders: Conceptual and methodological issues and some preliminary findings. In S. Hodgins (ed.), *Violence among the mentally ill: Effective treatments and management strategies* (pp. 89–116). Boston: Kluwer Academic Publishers.

Hodgins, S., Mednick, S.A., Brennan, P.A., Schulsinger, F. and Engberg, M. (1996). Mental disorder and crime: Evidence from a Danish birth cohort. *Archives of General Psychiatry*, *53*, 489–496.

Hodgins, S. and Müller-Isberner, R. (eds) (2000). *Violence, crime and mentally disordered offenders: Concepts and methods for effective treatment and prevention*. New York: John Wiley & Sons.

Høyer, G. (2000). Social services necessary for community treatment programmes designed to prevent crime and violence among persons with major mental disorders. In S. Hodgins (ed.), *Violence among the mentally ill: Effective treatments and management strategies* (pp. 267–382). Boston: Kluwer Academic Publishers.

Lidz, C.W., Mulvey, E.P. and Gardner, W. (1993). The accuracy of predictions of violence to others. *Journal of the American Medical Association*, *269*, 1007–1011.

McGuire, J. (2000). Commentary: Heilbrun and Peters, 'The efficacy and effectiveness of community treatment programmes in preventing crime and violence among those with severe mental illness in the community'. In S. Hodgins (ed.), *Violence among the mentally ill: Effective treatments and management strategies* (pp. 359–366). Boston: Kluwer Academic Publishers.

Melton, G.B., Petrila, J., Poythress, N.G. and Slobogin, C. (1997). *Psychological evaluations for the courts: A handbook for mental health professionals and lawyers* (2nd edn). New York: The Guilford Press.

Monahan, J. and Appelbaum, P.S. (2000). Reducing violence risk: Diagnostically based clues from the MacArthur violence risk assessment study. In S. Hodgins (ed.), *Violence among the mentally ill: Effective treatments and management strategies* (pp. 19–34). Boston: Kluwer Academic Publishers.

Monahan, J. and Steadman, H.J. (eds) (1994a). *Violence and mental disorder: Developments in risk assessment*. Chicago: University of Chicago Press.

Monahan, J. and Steadman, H.J. (1994b). Toward a rejuvenation of risk assessment research. In Monahan, J. and Steadman, H.J. (eds), *Violence and mental disorder: Developments in risk assessment* (pp. 1–17). Chicago: University of Chicago Press.

Monahan, J., Steadman, H., Silver, E., Appelbaum, P., Robbins, P.C., Mulvey, E., Roth, L., Grisso, T. and Banks, S. (2001). *Rethinking risk assessment: The MacArthur study of mental disorder and violence*. New York: Oxford University Press.

National Research Council (1989). *Improving risk communication*. Washington, DC: National Academy Press.

Otto, R. (2000). Assessing and managing violence risk in outpatient settings. *Journal of Clinical Psychology*, *56*, 1239–1262.

Quinsey, V., Cyr, M. and Lavalee, Y. (1988). Treatment opportunities in a maximum security psychiatric hospital: A problem survey. *International Journal of Law and Psychiatry*, *11*, 179–194.

Quinsey, V., Harris, G., Rice, M. and Cormier, C. (1998). *Violent offenders: Appraising and managing risk*. Washington, DC: American Psychological Association.

Rice, M. and Harris, G. (1988). An empirical approach to the classification and treatment of maximum security psychiatric patients. *Behavioral Sciences and the Law*, *6*, 497–514.

Rice, M. and Harris, G. (1997). Cross-validation and extension of the *Violence Risk Appraisal Guide* for child molesters and rapists. *Law and Human Behavior*, *21*, 231–241.

Rice, M., Harris, G. and Cormier, C. (1992). Evaluation of a maximum security therapeutic community for psychopaths and other mentally disordered offenders. *Law and Human Behavior*, *16*, 399–412.

Rice, M.. Harris, G., Quinsey, V. and Cyr, M. (1990). Planning treatment programs in secure psychiatric facilities. In D.N. Weisstub (ed.), *Law and mental health: International perspectives* (Vol. 5; pp. 162–230). New York: Pergamon Press.

Rogers, R. (2000). The uncritical acceptance of risk assessment in forensic practice. *Law and Human Behavior*, *24*, 595–605.

Salekin, R.T., Rogers, R. and Sewell, K.W. (1996). A review and meta-analysis of the Psychopathy Checklist and Psychopathy Checklist-Revised: Predictive validity of dangerousness. *Clinical Psychology: Science and Practice*, *3*, 203–215.

Serin, R.C. (1996). Violent recidivism in criminal psychopaths. *Law and Human Behavior*, *20*, 207–217.

Silver, E., Mulvey, E. and Monahan, J. (1999). Assessing violence risk among discharged psychiatric patients: Toward an ecological approach. *Law and Human Behavior*, *23*, 235–253.

Steadman, H.J., Monahan, J., Appelbaum, P.S., Grisso, T., Mulvey, E.P., Roth, L.H., Robbins, P.C. and Klassen, D. (1994). Designing a new generation of risk assessment research. In J. Monahan and H. Steadman (eds), *Violence and mental disorder: Developments in risk assessment* (pp. 297–318). Chicago: University of Chicago Press.

Steadman, H.J., Monahan, J., Robbins, P.C., Appelbaum, P.S., Grisso, T., Klassen, D., Mulvey, E.P. and Roth, L.H. (1993). From dangerousness to risk assessment: Implications for appropriate risk strategies. In S. Hodgins (ed.), *Crime and mental disorder* (pp. 39–62). Newbury Park, California: Sage Publications.

Steadman, H.J., Mulvey, E., Monahan, J., Robbins, P., Appelbaum, P., Grisso, T., Roth, L. and Silver, E. (1998). Violence by people discharged from acute psychiatric inpatient facilities and by others in the same neighborhoods. *Archives of General Psychiatry*, *55*, 1–9.

Steadman, H.J. and Silver, E. (2000). Immediate precursors of violence among persons with mental illness: A return to a situational perspective. In S. Hodgins (ed.), *Violence among the mentally ill: Effective treatments and management strategies* (pp. 35–48). Boston: Kluwer Academic Publishers.

Swanson, J., Borum, R. Swartz, M., Hiday, V., Wagner, H. and Burns, B. (2001). Can involuntary outpatient commitment reduce arrests among persons with severe mental illness? *Criminal Justice and Behavior*, *28*, 156–189.

Swartz, M., Swanson, J., Hiday, V., Borum, R., Wagner, H. and Burns, B. (1998a). Taking the wrong drugs: Substance abuse, medication nonadherence, and violence in severely mentally ill individuals. *Social Psychiatry and Psychiatric Epidemiology*, *33*, 75–80.

Swartz, M., Swanson, J., Hiday, V., Borum, R., Wagner, H. and Burns, B. (1998b). Violence and severe mental illness: The effects of substance abuse and nonadherence to medication. *American Journal of Psychiatry*, *155*, 226–231.

Tiihonen, J. and Swartz, M. (2000). Pharmacological intervention for preventing violence among the mentally ill with secondary alcohol- and drug-use disorders. In S. Hodgins (ed.), *Violence among the mentally ill: Effective treatments and management strategies* (pp. 171–191). Boston: Kluwer Academic Publishers.

Volavka, J. and Citrome, L. (2000). Pharmacological interventions for preventing violence among the mentally ill with co-occurring personality disorders. In S. Hodgins (ed.), *Violence among the mentally ill: Effective treatments and management strategies* (pp. 193–209). Boston: Kluwer Academic Publishers.

Volavka, J. and Krakowski, M. (1989). Schizophrenia and violence. *Psychological Medicine*, *19*, 559–562.

Webster, C., Douglas, K., Eaves, D. and Hart, S. (1997). *HCR-20: Assessing risk for violence* (Version 2). Burnaby, British Columbia: Mental Health, Law, and Policy Institute, Simon Fraser University.

Wells, K. (1999). Treatment research at the crossroads: The scientific interface of clinical trials and effectiveness research. *American Journal of Psychiatry*, *156*, 5–10.

Wettstein, R. (ed.) (1998). *Treatment of offenders with mental disorders*. New York: Guilford Press.

Chapter 2.3

Risk: The Need for and Benefits of an Interdisciplinary Perspective

David Carson
University of Southampton, UK

> *The revolutionary idea that defines the boundary between modern times and the past is the mastery of risk: the notion that the future is more than a whim of the gods and that men and women are not passive before nature.*
>
> (Bernstein, 1996, p. 1)

Risk is ubiquitous in our lives. From slipping in the shower in the morning to taking too much medicine at night. Technological, medical and other developments have given us more control over lives. 'Fate', associated with determinism and Shakespeare's preferred expression, has given way to 'risk' as more events become more controllable or, at least, more predictable. 'Risk' has also become a ubiquitous expression. We are said to be living in a 'risk society' where the key issue, it is argued, is no longer the distribution of wealth but the distribution of risks (Beck, 1992). 'Risk' is also argued to be the new paradigm for the analysis of social policy—for example, child protection and the delivery of mental health services (Kemshall, 2002). It is central to the analytical and advisory roles of many practising psychologists, not just those in forensic roles. And, in recent years, risk has been the focus for much research within the psychology and law tradition (certainly much more than implied by the sparse references to this chapter).

Law is also intrinsically concerned with risk. The word 'judgement' may be preferred, in practice, but every trial involves several risks. The judge might give custody of the child to the 'wrong' parent. The jury may wrongly convict—or acquit—the defendant. A lying witness may be thought to be telling the truth. And the law has interests in research on risk: how the research is used by others. Are practitioners, for example psychologists advising a parole board about the release of an offender, correctly using the proper research? How might the research be applied to themselves? For example, how might courts and tribunals adopt and apply what has been learnt to reduce the risky nature of their work?

So 'psychology' and 'law' have a common interest in risk. But, it is submitted, there is limited practical interchange between psychology and law, either as disciplines or occupations, towards developing a richer understanding of, and collaborative approach towards, risk. The disciplines are working and developing their concepts of risk, and methods of analysing it, in relative isolation from each other. Despite it ubiquity, 'risk' is not a 'term of art' for lawyers, not a concept which receives detailed analytical attention in jurisprudence, and this chapter will suggest reasons for this relative failure to collaborate. It will propose some models that could aid understanding and collaborative working. And it will be argued that, because of the practical reality of the law's power and authority, which is re-enforced by the courts, psychologists should adapt their perspectives and approaches to risk. It will not be argued that they are somehow 'wrong', and therefore should change. It is simply a pragmatic argument. Risk inevitably involves uncertainty and value judgements. Whilst it is only an exceptionally small—atypical—proportion of this risk decisions that will lead to litigation, the reality is that courts will pronounce upon those decisions and thereby can influence them all. So an adoption of a common perspective on risk will actually help practising psychologists, and others, to avoid unnecessary and unproductive confrontations in court proceedings. It will also facilitate a more common approach in other venues.

Behavioural scientists' work on risk, and risk-taking, has demonstrated the fallibility of humans' risk assessments, and other decisions (e.g. see Janis and Mann, 1977). Unless there is urgent, practical, action to tackle or minimise the consequences of that fallibility then lawyers will find (see below) it exceptionally easy to criticise psychologists' and others' professional work with clients. The time has passed for simply demonstrating that risk and risk-taking are more difficult than is often thought, and that we cannot make very good predictions of the future behaviour of individuals, despite the recent research. The law and lawyers will, and should, ask more searching questions and require more rigorous analysis. Expert and professional witnesses, giving evidence about risk, whether directly or indirectly, must expect more thorough and rigorous cross-examination in the future. Just as soon as lawyers learn a little more about risk, and decision-making based on risk predictions, they will find it very easy to make life difficult for witnesses. Their questions will often be inappropriate, in the sense that they arise from misconceptions about the nature of risk either generally or in particular contexts of professional practice, but that will not stop them being asked. Ironically, however, this criticism could be to the benefit of psychology as it will help to move the focus away from unrealistically narrow conceptions and practice of risk and risk-taking.

'RISK' AND 'RISK-TAKING'

Is it, or should it be, 'risk' or 'risk-taking'? This highlights a key problem for collaboration between psychology and law. The emphasis, in recent research within the psychology and law discipline (e.g. Monahan et al., 2001; Quinsey et al., 1998; Lyon, Hart and Webster, 2001, and references therein), has been on informing risk prediction rather than risk-taking, in the sense of the total process. The paradigm research has involved seeking more powerfully predictive knowledge, usually in the form of risk factors, of different outcomes. It has been valuable for practitioners who, because they need to take a decision, want to know how likely it is that a particular child, for example, will be injured. Indeed it is common for people to refer to 'the risk', assuming it is proper to reify and objectify it. But there is much more to taking a risk decision, or risk-taking, than an assessment of likelihood. If harm results from a risk decision, a court or other form of inquiry is not limited to examining whether the likelihood of the harm occurring was assessed competently. Much more can, and arguably should, be examined. (If and when lawyers are educated about these points they must be expected to ask more penetrating and appropriate questions about these other aspects of risk-taking.) Even if his or her prediction of the harm was competent a psychologist, or other professional, may be criticised and sued for poor practice in other parts of the decision-making process. Many of the problems, it is submitted, for interdisciplinary collaboration arise from the distinction between analysing a risk, per se, and making decisions about the risk in a particular context, or for a particular purpose. In part it is the distinction between 'risk assessment' and 'risk management'. Unfortunately the two are often conflated or the importance of the latter ignored or downgraded.

Dowie (1999) argues passionately against use of 'risk'. He believes it confuses rather than elucidates. It is too narrow. He would prefer that the focus was on decision-making.

> A decision—a choice between available options/strategies/policies—will be better to the extent it incorporates:
>
> - better structured modelling of the scenarios which follow from adoption of each option;
>
> - better assessments of the chances (probabilities) of the events and outcomes which are contained in those scenarios;
>
> - better assessment of the un/desirability (utilities, preferences, valuations) for the outcomes, including, very importantly, intertemporal preferences;
>
> - better ways of integrating the probabilities and utilities into an overall evaluation of each option. (pp. 45–46)

Hopefully the following, necessarily summary, analysis is consistent with the thrust of Dowie's arguments. However, it continues to use the terminology of 'risk' on the grounds that it is so embedded in the literature and practice.

Risk: Elements and Dimensions, Assessment and Management

It is submitted that 'risk' involves two 'elements'. These are likelihood and consequences, and both are variable. There is a chance or possibility that something will occur, for example that a child will be abused. What will occur, for example the nature and degree of that abuse, is also variable. It may be severe or it may be trivial. That possibility may range from low to high. (It will still be a risk if the outcomes are known to be certain or impossible, provided there is some uncertainty such as the degree of harm or benefit.) So the 'elements' of a risk are (a) the possible outcomes and (b) their likelihood. Risk assessment involves collecting information about these two variable elements. What is the likelihood that prisoner X will commit certain degrees of harm if released from prison? We need a risk assessment.

But risks have a context. It is highly unlikely, certainly in a competently run service, that life sentence prisoner X will simply be awarded early release from prison. There will, or should be, a plan for his or her reintegration into society. He or she may be required to see a probation officer at prescribed intervals, to live in a particular house, to avoid certain people or areas. A risk decision, to grant parole, may be taken but attempts can and should be made to control that risk. So 'risk' also involves certain 'dimensions'. They too are variable. These dimensions include resources, such as facilities (hostels, halfway houses), services (treatment programmes, supervision), people (preferably with special skills and, perhaps, legal powers). The dimensions also include time. Risk decisions are, or should be, taken for a period of time. A patient is allowed to leave a hospital. Harm may result. So it is common, and good, practice for the patient to be followed up. In acute medicine the patient will be told to return to hospital for a check-up and/or the patient's general practitioner will be advised so that he or she can decide to check the patient. Knowledge is also a dimension. We have more, and/or better, knowledge about some risks than about others. For example, whilst it still involves a risk, we have better quality and more knowledge about the risks associated with medicines than we have with, say, suicide. And it may be appropriate to think of 'motivation' as being a dimension of risk. Some offenders, parents, patients, etc., will be more motivated to work with those professionals who are prepared to take a risk than with others.

The elements of a risk, outcome and likelihood, are relevant to risk assessment. The dimensions of a risk, resources, time, knowledge, control and 'motivation', are relevant to risk management. Recent psychological research has tended to focus on risk assessment. They have discovered, and improved the predictive power of, risk factors for different outcomes (e.g. Monahan et al., 2001). But practitioner psychologists, such as those making or advising others about decisions to detain or discharge patients or prisoners), must, or should, consider both risk management and risk assessment. They cannot just consider 'the risk' as a reified abstraction but must consider how the risk might be managed and controlled (Heilbrun et al., 1977). To judge the quality of a risk decision, or to justify taking a risk, we need to know about both the elements and the dimensions of a risk. We need both risk assessment and risk management.

There is an iterative relationship between risk assessment and management. A particular case, say about possible child neglect, might have involved high-quality risk assessment. Quality data was collected and examined in a rigorous manner. But when it came to taking the decision it was managed poorly, for example key people were not informed of the decision taken and no arrangements were made for intervention if and when things began to go wrong and/or did not succeed as had been planned. It does not matter, in terms of outcome and legal liability, than there was a good risk assessment because the poor risk management that followed ruined it. That would be sufficient ground for criticising the risk-taking. However, it may appear that good risk management can prevent harm arising from poor risk assessment. For example, the risk posed by giving a prisoner early parole may have been badly assessed. However, when released, the prisoner may have been supervised and managed in an exemplary fashion so that harm, which ought to have been predicted and acted upon, did not occur. In that case harm was avoided. If anyone were to sue for negligence they would fail because there was no loss or causation. But there would still have been poor practice and grounds for criticism by an inquiry and disciplinary action by employers or professional associations! Because risk management comes after risk assessment, it can prevent harm from occurring whether the assessment was good or bad. Poor risk assessors may get lucky, because of good risk management. Risk managers may, indeed should, be helped by good risk assessors but they cannot 'get lucky' in the same way. However, it does not follow that, because there was no loss, there was good risk assessment. To properly assess risk-taking the quality of both the elements and the dimensions of a risk, both the assessment and the management of the decision need to be examined.

It is appropriate for researchers to concentrate upon risk assessment. They are trying to produce better knowledge of the elements of risk, particularly likelihood. But when practitioners have to take a risk decision, they need to know more than the information necessary for risk assessment. So it is inappropriate for lawyers to ask, and for expert witnesses to answer, questions that are posed exclusively in terms of risk assessment. For example, a lawyer might ask: How likely is it that this offender will be violent again? Professional witnesses should refuse to answer in the terms expected. To do so will, at best, misinform the court. It would, for example, be better to reply:

> With respect, Your Honour, I cannot, in good conscience or in good professional practice, answer that question. I cannot predict risk in a contextual vacuum. In order to make a prediction of future behaviour I need to know, as a minimum, how long my prediction is to last for. I also need to know the conditions under which the person in question will be living and behaving. For example will he or she continue to take the prescribed medication? And I need to know whether the individual will be motivated to work with services, for example keep appointments?

Risk assessment should, no longer, be regarded as divisible from risk management whenever it is a question of risk-taking, rather than just risk. Heilbrun and colleagues (1999) discuss these issues in terms of risk communication. They provide 12 guidance points for how risk assessors should communicate with others, such as judges. These points may come to represent good practice. They provide other possible answers to lawyers' questions. The common point is that providing risk assessments, without reference to context and management—even if that is what the lawyers ask for—is no longer good enough. Lawyers need to know more about risk; witnesses may have to teach them by explaining why they should have asked different questions.

Dimensions May be Managed

Is this distinction, between the 'elements' and the 'dimensions' of risk, artificial or unnecessary? Some (e.g. MacCrimmon and Wehrung, 1986) argue that time is, or in the terms of this analysis would be, an element rather than a dimension. Every risk decision involves a period of time, the argument runs. A child will be at a greater risk if he or she is placed with an adult, who is thought to be dangerous, for a week than for a day. Therefore time is an element, not just a dimension. That is true, so far as it goes. But this emphasises the essential integrative, or iterative, character of the elements and the dimensions of risk, risk assessment and risk management. Risk-taking will always involve both elements and dimensions, even if this is not explicit. A decision to refuse someone a service, say to admit to hospital, may appear to lack a time dimension. It is a risk decision because harm may result; it may have been a bad decision because the individual should have been assessed as needing a service. But the decision-maker has not decided that the individual concerned will never, ever, require a service, say admission to hospital. Another request for services may be made in due course—next week, next month—leading to a fresh risk decision, say to admit into hospital. Time may not be an explicit dimension in all risk decisions, although it is submitted that it ought to be. Those who declare that someone is not a danger to others are not claiming that the individual will never, ever, be a danger. They are implicitly declaring that he or she will not be a danger for a reasonably foreseeable period. (They would do themselves, and everyone else, a considerable favour by being more explicit about how long their prediction is to last for.) No, the rationale for considering time to be a dimension, rather than an element, is that it is, to an extent, controllable and open to 'manipulation'. Further, risk assessment focuses on knowledge gained from the past. Risk management relates to how future time may be shaped.

At least to an extent the 'dimensions' of a risk are open to manipulation, to management. More or less, better quality or worse, resources can be made available to support the risk decision. For example more, or better-trained, staff might be allocated. More or fewer opportunities for feedback, on how the risk decision is being implemented, may be made. For example a community nurse might visit more frequently. More or less money and skill may be made available. Specialist services might be involved. For example forensic psychiatric services usually have smaller case loads and, thereby, can spend longer in undertaking risk assessments. More knowledge, whether general about a particular type of risk or its application to a particular client, may be sought—provided it is not an emergency or dilemma (see discussion below). For example someone might undertake a literature search to firm up the team's understanding of the risk, inform them about the quality of their knowledge, what aspects they can rely upon and which parts they should not act upon. And negotiation with the client might make him or her more motivated to work with service providers. So the dimensions of a risk can, within limits, be affected by the risk decision-makers. The elements of the risk, the outcome and its likelihood, cannot be affected over and beyond what is possible by changing the dimensions. Certainly a risk assessment will change between situation A, when it is accepted that the client will continue to abuse illicit drugs, and situation B when, somehow, circumstances have changed so that it is now accepted that the same person will not abuse drugs. But that is because the dimensions have changed.

It is a truism that every risk is different. The risks in letting a patient, perceived to be a danger, leave a ward for an hour on Tuesday will be different from those involved in letting him or her leave the ward for an hour on Wednesday. Acceptance of this truism seems to imply that experience has no place in risk assessment. Just because the patient did not abuse the permission granted on Tuesday, it does not follow that he or she will not abuse it on Wednesday. But experience is relevant to risk management. The apparently successful risk, taken on Tuesday, provides information or knowledge, albeit not overwhelmingly important, for Wednesday. If allowing the patient to leave the ward on Tuesday involved trusting him or her, then the staff have some cause to respect that judgement. Experience relates to the knowledge dimension.

Assessment and Management: Actuarial and Clinical

This distinction, between the elements and the dimensions of risk, also relates to the debate between the actuarial and clinical prediction of risk. (Here 'clinical' does not necessarily refer to a medically qualified individual but rather to any person professing or practising the skill of making risk predictions about other people, for example probation officers, through studying the individual.) The actuarial approach stresses the importance of background variables, such as age (for a recent exposition of this position see Hare, 2002). The clinical approach stresses knowledge and experience of the individual (for a recent exposition of this position see Maden, 2002). Actuarial approaches claim greater predictive accuracy and power (Quinsey et al., 1998). Clinical approaches claim that actuarial information is impersonal, that at best it informs risk decision-makers about a class of people and not the specific individual in question. Clinicians have a poor record, or reputation, in risk prediction (see Limandri and Sheridan, 1995 and sources cited therein). But that, at least substantially, is a consequence of their predicting risk over long periods. Predicting another person's behaviour over several years, for example, is inviting error, unless you can be sure you will have that person under your close custody during that period! Those who predict risk will seldom have control over the individual in question during the period between prediction and the outcome contemplated occurring, or not occurring. Lawyers, and others, may and should be criticised for seeking inappropriate predictions of risk. (Unfortunately adversarial trial systems allow them the excuse of doing the best for their client.) But clinicians should accept responsibility for inappropriately answering. Questions about risk assessment should never be answered without reference to risk management. There is an urgent need for professional organisations to declare and to explain in public documents, which the courts can recognise are authoritative, the questions it would be professionally inappropriate for their members to answer in court.

The MacArthur Research Network on Law and Mental Health conducted a highly regarded empirical study into the prediction of violence by people with a mental disorder. Their iterative classification tree methodology permits the identification of groups of patients with an increased likelihood of violence (Monahan et al., 2001). This actuarial methodology permits a level of accuracy that exceeds best clinical predictions. But the authors do not, in marked contrast with Quinsey and colleagues

(1998), recommend that their approach, or actuarial approaches in general, should replace or exclude clinical assessments of risk. In particular they note (pp. 130–135) that their research population involved groups of civilly detained white, African American or Hispanic adults between 18 and 40 years old. So a patient whose risk has to be predicted may not fall within, or be represented by, those groups. Or there may be some special factor, for example the patient has broken both arms or has declared a desire to be violent, which makes him or her distinctively different and therefore less or more likely to be violent. They conclude that actuarial tools, such as their own, 'are best viewed as 'tools' for clinical assessment . . . —tools that support, rather than replace, the exercise of clinical judgment' (Monahan et al., 2001, p. 134, reference deleted). They believe that clinical judgement, aided by actuarial assessment, reflects current good professional practice. But they seek research, which might cause them to review their judgement, on how often, by how much and why, clinicians revise actuarial assessments. Litwack (2001), in a review of the debate, concludes that actuarial methods have not been conclusively proved superior to clinical. One of his points is that clinical decisions, for example about dangerousness, are not always predictions. So comparison is not always proper. In the terms of the model proposed here the clinician's decision may concern management rather than assessment.

But the problem with clinical assessments of risk is not just their comparative lack of predictive power. There are, also, several serious process problems. These relate to how clinical risk decisions are made and communicated. For example a key problem is the misuse, in practical decision-making, of base rates. They are undervalued (Tversky and Kahneman, 1973, 1980). Information may be available about how likely a particular outcome is, after an actuarial risk assessment has been conducted, but that information is liable to be ignored or under-used.

> There is no question that subjects in psychology experiments tend to ignore base rates (just as physicians do) even when the base rates are clearly indicated. (Rachlin, 1989, p. 54)

A high-quality actuarial risk assessment may have been undertaken. A clinician may appreciate the value of such information but decide that other information about the particular patient, obtained in a clinical examination, should be taken into account and should be allowed to vary the importance attached to the actuarial assessment. For example the actuarial research, based on a large population, might indicate that men are six times more likely to, whatever, than women. But the decision-maker might fail to give that information its due, and/or he or she might rate clinical information, for example the patient had been taking his drugs without problems for a month, as more important.

The clinician does not, with the current state of research, know how much emphasis to give, or not to give, to that clinical information. That must wait, at the very least, upon the research recommended by the MacArthur team. As they note:

> . . . the principal use of violence risk assessments . . . is as an indicator of the need for violence *risk management*. (Monahan et al., 2001, p. 135; italics in original)

Perhaps we could and should go further, using the model of risk being developed here. Actuarial methods could/should be required, where they are available, for risk assessment. But clinical concerns about that assessment, plus additional case-specific information, should (only) be utilised in the risk management plan adopted.

Risk assessment relates to the elements of risk, which is what the empirical research has concentrated upon. Risk management relates to the dimensions of the risk in the particular case context. Special knowledge, about a particular patient, would justify different controls, more or less, on how the decision is implemented. It should not, it is suggested, be allowed to alter a competent actuarial risk assessment. ('Competent', here, is intended to refer to minimum professionally agreed standards rather than to create a definitional argument.) Lawyers should be encouraged to appreciate the distinction between risk assessment and risk management and only to ask questions appropriate to the particular category. It is appropriate for them to challenge the quality of particular risk assessments, for example to ensure that appropriate actuarial approaches were properly used and communicated. Then it is appropriate for them to enquire into how that risk assessment informed the clinicians' (or other risk-takers') plans for action. Such an approach, emphasising the iterative and integrative roles of risk assessment and risk management, has considerable potential for practitioners, both lawyers and risk-takers. It will help to clarify, improve and justify decision-making.

RISK AND RISK JUSTIFICATION

Lawyers have a proper interest in the quality of risk decisions. Was it proper to discharge that patient then? Should the social workers have returned the child to its abusive parents? These familiar examples require a retrospective analysis. We know what happened, the patient suffered loss, the child was abused, but we want to know whether appropriate decisions, which involved risk, were taken. But legal practice is not (*contra* Aubert, 1963; Campbell, 1974) necessarily retrospective. A lawyer can argue that a risk should be taken, that a detained patient should be discharged, that a prisoner should be granted parole, that the father—rather than the mother—should be granted custody of the child. The common features are decision-making and the potential for justification.

A key problem, making collaboration between law and psychology, research and practice, unnecessarily difficult, is the tendency to associate, even to define, risk exclusively in terms of the possibility of harm (e.g. Yates, 1992). Risk is regularly associated or defined as the possibility of harm (e.g. Royal Society, 1992). But that makes it difficult to justify taking a risk. A patient with a mental disorder wishes to be discharged from hospital. But he or she is thought to be a risk for suicide. So a risk assessment is undertaken. The likelihood that patients with this individual's characteristics will self-injure is examined. A practical plan is developed for managing the risk of self-harm, if the patient were to be discharged. This is amended in the light of the risk assessment. A decision is taken. The risk of suicide is, or is not, too high.

But should a decision be taken, on this information? Has not risk assessment been misused?

Risk practitioners have to balance and to take into account the case for as well as the case against. The question—ethically, professionally or legally—is not whether the risk of harm is sufficiently low. It is not just that we do not have a test for what would constitute 'sufficiently low'. It is a moral or value judgement rather than a scientific test. The question is whether the case against this particular patient being discharged is outweighed by the case in favour. This is so even in cases of terminal care, or services for elderly mentally ill people where practice has to focus on slowing and reducing, rather than preventing, decline and disability. The question involves balance and choice between alternatives. It is perfectly understandable that researchers should seek to provide us with more and better information, and tools for, predicting harm and loss. That is what we want to understand, in order to avoid. But that does not prevent us from acknowledging that risk decision-making necessarily involves comparing the possibility of benefits with the possibility of harm. We can act to minimise the likelihood and the seriousness of the harms. We can act to maximise the likelihood and the value of the benefits. That is the role of risk management. But the eventual risk decision, perhaps after several alternative risk management plans have been investigated, will require a balancing operation—a valuing of the options.

Lawyers, at least in the United Kingdom, also tend to associate or define risk exclusively in terms of harms. Knowing that there is a risk of injury to another person, and yet acting, has been deemed to constitute 'recklessness' sufficient for a conviction for manslaughter (*Adamako* [1995] 1 AC 171). It is submitted that this cannot, and it is hoped that this will not, stand when a case arises where it is appropriate to balance potential benefits against potential harms. (We should not be guilty of manslaughter just because we foresaw that someone might be injured when we got in our car to go to work and, without more fault, we happened to kill someone in an accident.) The need to balance has been recognised for civil cases of negligence. In *Bolitho* v. *City and Hackney Health Authority* ([1997] 3 WLR 1151) the House of Lords, the most senior court in the UK, was invited to change the standard of care by which professionals' decisions, including risk decisions, are measured for the law of negligence. They decided to retain the existing law whereby risk decisions do not break the standard of care if a responsible body of professional opinion would support them. They stated:

> In particular in cases involving, as they so often do, the weighing of risks against benefits, the judge before accepting a body of opinion as being responsible, reasonable or respectable, will need to be satisfied that, in forming their views, the experts have directed their minds to the question of comparative risks and benefits and have reached a defensible conclusion on the matter. (p. 1159)

Whilst this demonstrates that the judges consider 'risk' to be limited to possibilities of harm—for otherwise there would be no need to weigh benefits against them—it also emphasises the propriety, indeed the critical role, of balancing.

Although it would simplify matters, and as such it is recommended, it does not really matter whether we define 'risk' as including or excluding reference to the possibility of benefit. What matters is that we acknowledge the necessary role of balancing when it comes to making risk decisions. Those who make risk decisions are entitled to take into account the possibility that each of their reasons (objectives and goals), for taking the proposed risk, may be fulfilled or achieved. The potential value of those benefits may be placed in the balance against the potential seriousness of the harms feared. Indeed, if they fail to consider potential benefits they are not making a proper decision! They are laying themselves open to criticism. Imagine that someone is called upon to justify taking a risk, which led to harm. He or she could list and elaborate upon the value of the potential benefits that were being sought, as well as the potential harms feared. Or he or she could explain simply that the likelihood and/or seriousness of the harms was not considered to be bad enough for them not to take the risk. The first approach is more likely to be successful, not least before judges. It is also perfectly proper practice.

But reconsider the role of risk factors and risk assessment. Because of the tendency to associate risk exclusively with the chance of harm, risk factors and risk assessment schemes invariably only inform us about the chances of harm. They provide us with reasons, or excuses, for not taking a risk. They are inherently conservative, biased towards not taking a risk. A few lists include factors, such as availability and skills of supervising staff (e.g. Gunn, 1990), but they are a minority.

> Indeed it is surprising that we have little or no research about the 'protective factors' . . . in individuals' lives which serve to reduce risk, whether than be to self or to others. (Langan, 1999, p. 172, reference omitted)

But even when protective factors exist they are not the same thing as risk factors for success. They may tell us features of people less likely to experience harm; but that is not the same as identifying people who are likely to experience benefits. We can examine risk factors for male violence (e.g. Webster et al., 1994) or spouse assault (Campbell, 1995; Kropp et al., 1995). They will help us to predict the likelihood of suicide or spouse assault. But they will not help us to predict the likelihood that the patient will be motivated or retain his or her job if discharged from hospital. One spouse might hit the other. For that reason we contemplate separating them, amongst other tactics. But there are many other things to be considered when deciding whether to support an order excluding one spouse from the matrimonial home. Remaining in the same house could do good, as well as ill. The factors which make it less likely that a person will commit suicide, for example, are not necessarily the same as will make it likely that he or she will get pleasure and motivation from living in familiar rooms with more self-control and responsibility. And yet the person making a risk decision needs to consider potential benefits, as well as the potential harms and rights involved. It is not just that risk assessment tools, which concentrate on the chance of failure and loss, incompletely serve practitioners but measures, which could identify the likelihood of success, would help them contemplate alternative risk management strategies.

Lawyers could, and it is submitted should, investigate the use of risk assessment tools, say in negligence claims or inquiries into untoward incidents. They should not just include questions about whether the measure chosen was appropriate for the decision in question, or whether it was properly used. They should examine the process, the balancing exercise. For example, was a proper attempt made to identify the possible benefits of taking the risk, and their likelihood? It is normal practice for an assessment tool to list a range of risk factors. But does the tool imply that the different factors are of equal importance? If so that is almost certainly going to involve an error. Some factors are much more important, more predictive, than others are. For example age, gender and number of prior offences are more predictive of violence than nature of delusions (Monahan et al., 2001). The tool may not tell its users, one way or the other, about the relative importance of the different items. The author may not be satisfied that the science is sufficiently developed to allow for such differential rating (Hagell, 1998), but he or she is likely to know that—explicitly or implicitly—treating each item as of equal importance is improper, and thereby unprofessional.

Are the risk factors mutually exclusive? For example one question, in a list designed to identify risk factors, might ask about past violence whilst another asks about past crimes. But past violence is a past crime! The same cause for concern, past violence, is being 'double counted'. That is likely to be inappropriate. The authors of the tool might have done it deliberately, as a means of weighting the importance of that topic. But that may not be the case. Either way unsophisticated or mechanistic users of such a tool are liable to be caught out by a knowing lawyer alive to the possibility of such a problem.

Intuitively it would seem proper to conclude that a more detailed list of risk factors is going to be better, more predictive, than a short list. It will appear better, more thorough. But that simply does not follow. A long list of risk factors may have more to do with demonstrating the author's imagination than identifying the things that, according to research or clinical experience, are the important predictors. A few key risk factors may be sufficient, or get decision-makers as close as they are ever going to get (with current levels of knowledge) to an appropriate risk assessment. More information may add little additional predictive power (McNeil and Binder, 1994). Generally, more information will help risk-takers, but they must not make the basic mistakes of assuming that it is of equal value or quality. If it is a risk decision then, by definition, it is going to have to be made on the basis of incomplete information. Knowledge of, or insight into, the predictive power and accuracy of what is known will regularly be more important than sheer quantity of information.

Risk assessment is the start, rather than the end, of risk-taking. By definition it is an imperfect science. Imagine there is little, or only poor quality, information available for a risk assessment. Unless it is clear that any possible harms will be trivial, and/or exceptionally unlikely, it will difficult to justify taking that decision. But that is where risk management comes into the 'equation'. Because there is only poor quality information available for a risk assessment, it is more important that a high-quality risk management plan is devised. High-quality risk management, for example the employment of more resources and control, can justify action on a risk assessment necessarily based upon poor-quality information. Assessment and management have an iterative relationship.

Risk Procedures

A risk procedure should, amongst other things, minimise the opportunities for the mis-use and misunderstanding of risk factors. For example, it might be more appropriate to adopt the image of a 'filter', rather than a checklist, when using risk factors. Only those pieces of information, identified by risk factors as being relevant to the feared (or sought) outcomes, should be allowed into the risk assessment. If the information is purely repetitive, for example it reminds the decision-maker to consider any criminal history but he or she had already done that, then it should not alter the assessment any further. And, when extra information is added to the risk assessment, its significance should be appreciated. We need to emphasise the quality of the information in the risk assessment, not simple the quantity.

Imagine that a risk decision has been taken, say, to grant an offender parole. No harm has resulted. Therefore it must have been a good decision. No, that does not follow! A poor decision may have been made but, fortunately, no harm has resulted. That is an example of good fortune rather than good decision-making! If we are going to justify risk-taking then we need to examine the process of decision-making, not just the product. A decision may have been made well, even when examined in retrospect with additional time and resources, but nevertheless led to harm. Without more, that appears to have been a justifiable decision. (However those involved may have been criticised because of the harmful outcome, before a proper assessment of the decision and decision-making process was undertaken.) By way of contrast a decision may have been made poorly but, nevertheless, not resulted in harm. Because no harm has resulted nobody is likely to complain. Indeed nobody may notice that it was a poor decision; that it was not a good, justifiable, decision.

Unfortunately legal practice does not help here. Nobody can sue for negligence if no one has suffered loss which can be compensated. Thus poor risk-taking practice may be overlooked. Indeed very many people will make the erroneous assumption that 'no loss' means 'no negligence' means 'good decision'. And risk-taking practice can be corrupted as people work to outcomes rather than processes, to the avoidance of harm rather than to the use of good processes.

But employers and professional bodies are entitled to take action against their em-ployees and members, respectively, for poor professional practice. But, once again, they can only do this if somebody noticed that there was a poor process. So if we are to improve the quality of risk-taking decisions then we need to develop procedures that encourage good practice. And that must involve some system of feedback. We need systematic knowledge about how decisions are being taken, not just about the outcome of some decisions. This is another area for potentially productive collaboration between psychologists and lawyers. It may appear, certainly in harried practice, superfluous given the pressures of work. But such procedures should quickly come to constitute standards of professional practice. Thus, if they are followed—provision always being made for regular improvement as we learn more—they will help to prevent litigation because the professional standards will be clearer.

The quality of the information relied upon is relevant to risk management as well as risk assessment. For example risk assessors may conclude that they have poor quality information, or may not know how significant a particular piece of information, say gender, is in this particular case. They may have to accept that they cannot obtain, or it is inappropriate to spend more time or other resources in obtaining, more or better information. Thus they have to take a decision. But they can, and should, take their relative ignorance (no pejorative associations intended) into account when they devise and implement a risk management plan. If they know that they lack key information then they should account for that in how they implement the decision. A risk assessment based upon poor quality information, which may be an unavoidable feature of the case, rather than imply anything critical about the quality of the risk assessment, should lead to a more tightly controlled risk management plan. Risk assessment and risk management should be related. Good risk management can justify taking a risk decision, even when the risk assessment, on its own, suggested it should not have been taken.

Extensive studies have repeatedly shown that humans are poor decision-makers, in many circumstances (e.g. Janis and Mann, 1977; Rachlin, 1989; Slovic, 2000). Such research is particularly pertinent to risk decisions. Key reasons for poor performance have been identified. These include problems in perception (e.g. Slovic and Monahan, 1995). For example we tend to overestimate the likelihood of rare events. Thus we overestimate the likelihood of homicides, but underestimate suicides, committed by people with mental disorders. Also when we know that something has happened, say someone has been killed, we overestimate what we would have predicted was the likelihood of that, the homicide, occurring before we knew that it had. This is known as the hindsight error (for a discussion of some legal implications see Wexler and Schopp, 1989). This is very important because our courts, and tribunals of inquiry, work retrospectively and use hindsight. They may be aware of the problem. They may declare the importance of not relying on the benefits of hindsight but do we, do they, know what allowance should be made for it? A risk procedure could reduce the likelihood of, and/or the seriousness of, such errors of perception. For example, a risk procedure should require that decision-makers are familiar with base rate likelihood. At the very least should not those concerned about the dangerousness of a person with a mental disorder know, or have easy access to, data on the base rate for homicides and suicides by people with and without mental disorders? Experience suggests that if lawyers were to ask such people such questions, when they are acting as expert or professional witnesses, then the court should, currently, expect an embarrassed silence and/or erroneous answer.

And we make poor decisions when we have too much information. We cannot, simultaneously think about each piece of the information we have, its relative importance and accuracy. Think of all the pieces of information relevant to a decision whether to risk buying a particular bottle of wine. There is colour, grape variety, country of origin, area of production, alcoholic content, price, age (if relevant), and more, plus the relative importance of each of those points to us, and to anyone else we contemplate enjoying the bottle. Compare that risk with having to decide whether to release an offender on parole. The importance of the decision is so very much greater. Either we make decisions on only some of the information, for example the price and alcoholic content of the wine, or we develop procedures to cope with more complexity. The latter will involve reducing at least some of the information to paper (or equivalent) and concentrating on part of the problem at a time. It will often be possible to break a decision down into smaller parts, for example benefits and harms. Provided that both the analysis and the synthesis are appropriate, the information may be worked on sequentially rather than attempting to do it all simultaneously. Here is another area for urgent inter-disciplinary collaboration. Otherwise, in order to undermine or mock an expert witness, all that a cross-examining lawyer needs to do is demonstrate that the witness has claimed a super-human feat in working on lots of different pieces of information at the same time.

Another feature of risk-taking, which a risk procedure needs to address, is the arrangements for communicating effectively. Risk involves variables, degrees of outcomes and likelihood. The words we use to describe these variables are vague and ambiguous. With reference to outcomes how serious is 'serious'; how important is 'important'? It is often easier to make the point by reference to likelihood. In terms of percentages we may agree that 'certain' means 100% and 'impossible' means 0%. But what do the other words, which refer to degrees of likelihood, mean? Is, for example, something described as 'likely' expected to occur more or less often than half of the time? There is no rule, other than courtesy and the desirability of communication, that obliges us to use words in particular ways. Opinions differ. But a nurse might advise a doctor that something about a patient is 'likely,' implicitly meaning 75% likely, whilst the doctor 'hears' the word as only meaning 25% likely. Neither nurse nor doctor needs to be mistaken or acting in bad faith for the patient to be injured by a subsequent decision based on that information. And yet such professionals regularly communicate about risk in such terms.

Is there a point to spending time and money on quality risk assessments if the conclusions are going to be communicated in such a manner? Once again it will prove very easy for a lawyer to point out, even dramatically, that two 'professionals' apparently communicating about risk in fact did not do so. Even a simple failure to check roughly how each person used and understood such vague expressions is going to appear incompetent, and negligent. The House of Lords, in *Bolitho* v. *City and Hackney Health Authority* ([1997] 3 WLR 1151) noted that courts concerned with questions of professional negligence would usually adopt and apply the standards of the profession concerned. But it reserved a right to impose its own standards if it considered the profession's standards were 'illogical'.

> In the vast majority of cases the fact that distinguished experts in the field are of a particular opinion will demonstrate the reasonableness of that opinion. In particular, where there are questions of the assessment of the relative risks and benefits of adopting a particular medical practice, a reasonable decision necessarily presupposes that the relative risks and benefits have been weighed by the experts in forming their opinions. But if, in a rare case, it can be demonstrated that the professional opinion is not capable of withstanding logical analysis, the judge is entitled to hold that the body of opinion is not reasonable or responsible. (p. 1160)

Whilst 'logical' might be an unfortunate choice of expression, it is submitted that a failure to ensure effective communication about likelihood could, and should, fit within this category. It is not an answer for the experts to say that they do not know, or cannot be sure about the particular likelihood. That is understandable. The complaint is not that risk inevitably involves degrees of uncertainty. The complaint is that one may be thinking: 'My best estimate of likelihood is 75%, however I am sure it will fall within 65% to 85%', whilst the other professional hears 'About 25%'. Being unsure of your knowledge may be inevitable given the state of the science, and therefore be understandable. Failing to communicate what you mean, even if you mean to be vague, is not justifiable. People can communicate about risk in better ways (e.g. Heilbrun et al., 1999). Particularly in the future, when lawyers are better educated about risk and how decisions can be taken well or poorly, it will be negligent to fail to do so.

Risk and Inaction

When we think about a risk we tend to assume that a decision was taken. We think of action. The patient was given an injection even though there was a risk of harmful side effects. The risk may be justified because the likelihood and/or degree of harm was assessed as low, particularly in comparison with the likelihood and/or degree of benefits. Additionally, and/or alternatively, the quantity and quality of resources that were available to manage the risks, once the decision to act was taken, was suitable. But what if the decision was not to give the injection? Was that a risk decision? Or what if no decision was taken at all; the clinical team had, at least in effect, passed by the patient's bed without beginning to thing about taking a risk?

Surely a decision not to act is just as much a risk decision as the converse. Presumably the question, whether an injection should be provided, only arose because it was perceived to be a possibly appropriate means of tackling at least some of the patient's problems. A risk assessment, of possible benefits compared with possible harms, in the light of the possibilities for managing the risk, was completed. But it was decided that the likely benefits did not, at least sufficiently, outweigh the likely harms, and/or the risk could not be sufficiently controlled. So no action was taken. But it was, nevertheless, a risk decision. It can be analysed in the same manner as a decision for action. It could have been a good or a bad decision. But we know very little about these risk decisions in favour of inaction. In reality these may be so common that they constitute the rule rather than the exception.

Decisions in favour of inaction are much less visible. We notice being injected rather than not being injected, an offender being given parole rather than refused. We notice, and tend to register the fact of change, more than we do continuity. But harm can arise from inaction, just as readily as from action. And, at least in theory, there can be legal liability for inaction as readily as for action. The patient, who does not receive medication because the decision was not to take the risk, may experience loss. If that decision, not to risk, was professionally improper then the patient is entitled to complain and receive compensation. But people do not notice negligent omissions as readily as they do negligent commissions. And we do not recognise, as readily, the decisions that were not even mooted, as we do those that were discussed even though not acted upon. I know what my doctor did last time I had an appointment with him. I recall a decision about cholesterol levels. But I do not know what, if any, other decisions he made, let alone could have made, during that appointment. I would have to undertake extensive research, or consult another doctor, in order to begin to have an idea about what other decisions were taken, or should have been taken.

It will be objected that this involves giving 'risk-taking' too wide a meaning. It could become difficult to discover any incident or occasion that could not be properly analysed in terms of risk. First, the focus is on decision-making rather than risk. Second, the key point, it is submitted, is the potential that this extended analysis gives for preventive and proper professional practice.

It is not—or, only exceptionally, rarely—a simple question of should the patient be given the medication. Medication is proposed, for example, to combat symptoms of schizophrenia. But the medication might cause side effects. A risk judgement that that medication is not appropriate, at that time, for that patient, does not, however correct and properly reached a decision, justify inaction evermore thereafter. The patient still has distressing symptoms. An alternative decision, likely to involve a risk, should be considered, until an active risk can be taken. Even then, usually, that is not the end of it. Most likely another risk decision should be considered from the new state of affairs achieved by the last risk. Yes, risk-taking involves individual decisions. But the image of risk-taking as single, one-off, decisions is very unrepresentative, distorting and inaccurate. Invariably risk-taking is an active process. One decision does, and should, lead to another. A sequence of decisions is taken towards what were, initially, immediate, then short-term, then medium-term and finally long-term, goals. The legal system, when it comes to analyse, as it invariably does, one particular decision amongst a series, misrepresents reality.

Here is another area where lawyers and psychologists could productively collaborate. Lawyers are employed to protect and promote the interests of their clients. Thus, for example, they act when there is a risk that their client will be confined or released. But can and should they only protect their client's interests at those times? We, it is submitted, artificially inflate the importance of some of those occasions for legal intervention. For example the decision, as to whether the patient should be detained in or released from hospital, is highlighted as a major occasion for protecting civil liberties. But moving from hospital living to community living, especially when clinicians are positioned into opposition to patients in the legal hearings, is a major, very difficult to manage, jump. It is regularly made into a bigger risk of harm than it needs to be.

We should think of risk-taking as a process, as including decisions for action, inaction and non-decisions. Services should not be allowed to avoid the responsibility to take risks, to tackle clients' problems, to move them on step by step (Elbogen and Tomkins, 2000). Perhaps the patient cannot, realistically, expect discharge from the maximum-security hospital for several years. But that does not justify hospital staff in failing to take a sequence of risk decisions to allow him or her to live with less restriction (and at less cost) albeit within very secure walls. It does not justify failing to take a sequence of risk decisions which could ensure that the individual is better able to make a success of eventual discharge. Lawyers should not be interested exclusively in risk-taking at the 'formal' legal stages such as detention, compulsory treatment, discharge, guardianship. They could do more good for their clients, by advocates in the richer sense of that word, by checking and ensuring that a sequence of risk decisions, appropriate to the client, is taken.

Risk-taking is normal, not abnormal, behaviour. Indeed the failure to take risks ought to be the cause for comment, rather than the converse! A service which does not take risks, or only a few, is as likely, or even more likely, to be a poor service than one that takes several. Risk-taking cannot be avoided; it should be embraced. Imagine that a prison governor is anxious about the number of prisoners who do not return from day release at the correct time. He or she has made risk decisions which have allowed the prisoners out of prison in order to prepare themselves for release, such as by arranging accommodation and employment. On discovering that the risk-taking is 'failing'—because all, some or a few, are not returning to prison when they should—the prison governor has to make a decision. He can stop day release. That will be effective. Fewer prisoners will fail to return on time. This appears to be a successful strategy. No! This approach may appeal to politicians and the popular media but a wider perspective should be adopted. If risks are not taken, in this example, to enable prisoners to develop connections with the community so that it is more likely that their release from prison will be successful, then the eventual release risk decision is more likely to fail. If that release of the offender fails then he or she will have to be detained again, at considerably greater loss and expense than that involved in late return to prison. Lawyers, psychologists, and so many others, have a common interest in ensuring that proactive sequences of risk decisions are taken.

The analysis must be taken a little further. If a service is associated with no, or very few, 'risk failures' then it is likely to be commended, congratulated and regarded as being a good service. Take, for example, a medium secure forensic hospital. One of its many sets of risk-taking jobs is to decide when its patients should be allowed trial leave. It will allow some patients, after a risk assessment, to leave the hospital grounds with an obligation to return by a certain time. If no patients fail to return by the specified time then it will appear to be a wonderful service that ought to be praised and replicated around the country. But it could be a rotten service! That service might, whenever there is any perceived risk of failure, decide not to take a risk. (Its practice is likely to be 'informed' by fear of litigation, or inquiry, should any 'failures' occur.) That service will be making a number of false positive decisions. It will be making erroneous assessments that a patient is liable not to return whenever he or she would do so. Patients will not be getting an opportunity to benefit from day release. They will not get opportunities to practise living in the community again, or to maintain and reinforce social contacts. And that will cause harm. Those patients will not be as well equipped for discharge. They will stay in hospital longer, creating problems for other patients. They will lose motivation. And it will waste money.

We simply cannot avoid it! Not discharging patients who no longer need to be detained is wrong, and is causing harm. In their concern not to make false negative assessments (that is, wrongly deciding that someone is not dangerous) many risk decision-makers make false positive assessments (that is, erroneous assessments that someone is dangerous). Both false negative and false positive decisions are wrong. We 'see' the consequences of false negative decisions more dramatically than we do the consequences of false positive assessments. Both kinds of error need to be addressed. We cannot avoid errors by failing to take risks. To produce an apparently 'excellent' record a hospital, or other risk taker, could adopt a very conservative policy. It could decide that nobody, or hardly anyone, is to be allowed day release. In that way they greatly reduce the likelihood of false negatives, failure to prevent harm. But they increase the likelihood of false positives, failure to identify safety. A unit's absence, absolute or even relative, of 'risk errors' (false positive) implies risk decision-making that is too conservative. The awkward truth is that risk-takers need 'errors'. That some assessments were, apparently, wrong—for example, patients did not return after day release—can be useful information that the service is not being too conservative. Of course the 'errors' should be as minimal as possible; they should be in assessing rather than in managing the risk. Opportunities need to be created whereby 'safe risks', those with low seriousness outcomes, can be taken. And if the idea is still too shocking it can be approached in a different manner. The child unnecessarily removed from parents, the patient unnecessarily (improperly) detained in a high-security hospital, is experiencing harm. It is not a neutral state of affairs! Risk-taking involves balancing. Failure to take a risk can impose as much, or more, harm as can taking a risk! Hopefully lawyers will increasingly identify these losses so that we can develop a more rigorous analysis and practice of risk-taking. And, hopefully, the psychologists and others involved will be prepared for them.

Risk and Dilemma

Confronting a dilemma evokes more sympathy than does taking a risk. And yet there are many common features between them. They both involve decisions and the potential for benefit or harm. They both involve uncertainty and absence of complete control. The difference appears to be in the need to make a decision. You do not have to risk breaking the speed limit on a particular road, or going mountain climbing. You can decide not to take the risk, and drive at the proper speed. But if you are an ambulance driver with a critically ill patient or a member of a mountain rescue team seeking a lost climber, you have a dilemma. If you stick to the speed limits your patient may die. If you break the speed limits you may be prosecuted for speeding and/or you may be involved in a car accident. You have to decide, and one way or the other.

We have more sympathy for the person who confronts a dilemma because he or she was put into a difficult position. He or she did not have the time to collect information and make a considered risk assessment. Delay, in confronting a dilemma, involves imposing more harm. And the law recognises the distinction. The person who acts in an emergency, the legal equivalent to a dilemma, does not have to satisfy as demanding a standard of care in order to avoid a finding of negligence. So an important stage, when seeking to justify a decision, is to examine whether it was a risk or a dilemma. If it is the latter then any judge should be advised and asked to apply an appropriately lower standard.

But many decisions, regularly considered to be risks, would fall to be treated as dilemmas under this distinction. For example, if a patient is discharged he or she may cause, or be the victim of, harm. But if the patient is not discharged he or she is going to suffer disappointment, loss of social experiences and may lose self-care skills. Because we have tended only to associate risks with potential losses, we have overlooked how so many risks should be considered as dilemmas. Much of what currently passes for risk-taking could, justifiably, be re-presented as facing up to a dilemma.

RESPONSIBILITY FOR RISK-TAKING

Whenever we think of 'risk', particularly in the context of the joint interests of lawyers and psychologists, we tend to assume that the risk is 'in' the client concerned. The offender poses a risk; the child is at risk. But this is only one, albeit the most popular, way or level for thinking about risks. It is submitted that five 'levels' of risk can and should be recognised. Adoption of this model will make it much easier to appreciate how and why different people have a responsibility for improving the quality of risk-taking. It is not contended that only one approach or level is correct, and that the others are wrong. Rather the argument is that it is wrong not to have regard to all five levels.

1. Dangerous People

The traditional approach, almost to the exclusion of alternatives, focuses on an individual or, sometimes, a small social unit like a family. The risk is understood as being 'in' them. We examine and collect information about them in order to make a prediction about the kind of harm or loss they may cause or be victim to. The approach resembles the medical model, wherein the problem is perceived as being in the patient and the task perceived as being to cure the disease. Positivist assumptions—for example, that the risk factors are not affected by the process of observation or the making of value judgements—are regularly made. This approach is apolitical; it does not challenge the status quo. It leads to 'blame', or at least causal responsibility, being attached to the client. It has led to extensive and high-quality empirical research (e.g. Monahan et al., 2001). This approach is associated with research into identifying ever more powerful risk factors.

2. Dangerous Settings

This approach, or 'level' of risk-taking, emphasises the contribution of the setting, the local environment. For example a patient may be at risk of committing suicide. He or she will be at a much greater risk of suicide if unemployed, friendless, experiencing stress and having the means of self-injury readily available. Opportunity is a major explanation for events, for suicide as well as for crime; for example the recent increase in street robberies is a consequence of the invention and popularity of mobile phones. We are at greatest risk of violence from people we know simply because we spend so much more time with them than we do with strangers. It is almost a definitional argument. Monahan (1988) has stressed that situational risk factors are amongst the most predictive but least researched.

It is relatively easy to do high-quality empirical research on risk and dangerousness adopting the first approach to risk. It is relatively easy to control particular variables. It is much more difficult to undertake research into risk from a situational perspective, although some situational factors were included in the MacArthur Project (Monahan et al., 2001, p. 148). It is much more difficult to control variables, such as the quality of housing, neighbourhood facilities, and employment opportunities. And a situational perspective is political. It emphasises that money and social policies matter. This is a social work model. It emphasises that risk of harm can be reduced if money and other resources are invested. Get someone a job so that that person is out of his home much more, and he is, thereby, so much less likely to be a danger to others there, because of reduced opportunity. That job is also likely to affect the likelihood of harm because it will increase his motivation by improving his self-image. We can take more and better risks if we invest resources in them. Risk-taking is made more difficult and dangerous when governments and others fail to allocate appropriate resources.

3. Dangerous Decision-Makers

What is the point of having excellent, powerfully predictive, risk factors if we do not have people who know how to use them appropriately? This level of, or approach to, risk emphasises the responsibility of the decision-makers. They can be one, even the main, cause of risk and danger. If they cannot use the quality information available appropriately then only good fortune is going to prevent harm from resulting. Risk-taking is a skill. It requires the collection and application of knowledge in a proper manner with, preferably, provision for learning from feedback. Knowledge of risk factors is insufficient. They must be used properly. Having a particular status, for example consultant forensic psychiatrist or psychologist, is not enough. Status implies job but it does not ensure that knowledge, competence or experiences in risk decision-making are possessed. There may be plenty of instruction in risk factors, and the research that supports them, but there is very little on the practical skills of risk-taking. Any lawyer wishing to undermine the self-confidence and/or reputation of an expert or professional witness, on risk-taking, should enquire about his or her training in, and learning from, risk-taking. Textbook knowledge, even to a high standard, is insufficient to qualify a surgeon. This is not to suggest that risk-taking is an art! Someone may appear to be a good risk-taker because he or she has rarely, if ever, been associated with a decision that has led to harm. But that could be the result, substantially or entirely, of having taken very few decisions and/or adopting a very conservative approach in a service where the consequences of inaction have not been noted. It is a skill. It requires the application of refined knowledge and experience. Computer programs have out-performed experienced and skilful clinicians in the diagnosis of diseases because human decision-makers often forget when and how to avoid common decision errors (e.g. De Dombal, 1988; Eraker and Politser, 1988).

4.   Dangerous Managers and Supervisors

Risk decision-makers need support, training, and feedback. Their managers, supervisors and employers should provide this. It is commonplace for employers to provide a safety policy. Yellow signs will quickly appear on wet floors. Interviewers, of clients perceived to be dangerous, will be told to sit closest to the door. But where is the training in how to make a risk decision; how, for example, to frame it properly, to avoid being over-influenced by information that is available, and to seek information that might be more predictive? Where are the tools of the decision-maker's trade, the aids, the guides to the assessment of values as well as likelihood?

> [T]raining needs to be acknowledged in research accounts of risk work, rather than as something which is simply tacked on as an afterthought. (Titterton, 1999, p. 217)

Many senior managers, of services where the kinds of risk being discussed here are taken, will have undertaken a business management course. That is likely to have included a course, or module, on decision-making (e.g. Cooke and Slack, 1991). That will have stressed the problems associated with complexity. So what have those managers done, in recognition of these problems, to assist those of their staff who have complex risk decisions to make? For example, decisions are easier if, first, they are split into constituent parts. (See chapter by Murphy and Clare in this volume.) This will permit closer attention to be paid to each part. But how many employers provide such decision aids? It would be hypocrisy and, it is submitted, negligence for a manager to recognise the importance of research on decision-making for his or her job but not for his or her colleagues. Even if we were to accept that senior managers' decisions are more important that their juniors', it does not follow that they are more complex. Complexity is a function, *inter alia*, of amount and quality of information. Those making risk decisions about the likely price of coffee beans, for example, in three years time are richly rewarded for their correct decisions. But they have major advantages in being able to reduce their calculations to likelihood and monetary values, as well as having access to long-range climate and environmental assessments. Those making decisions about the likelihood of one person harming another regularly have poorer quality information to work from and they cannot reduce harms, such as a child seeing a parent killed, to easily manipulated monetary expressions. Training in identifying risk factors needs to be complemented by training in their proper usage.

5.   Dangerous Systems

Risk decision-makers work within organisations, structures and systems. These can make the work more difficult. For example, specialist mental health care may be the responsibility of one organisation, social work and primary health care the responsibility of others. Of course these can be so organised that the patient and lay community do not notice any 'gaps'. However, problems are always likely to arise where there are different financial arrangements and professional rivalries. Compare one mental health service where clinicians relate to one team of social workers, in one office, with one employer, to another service where they relate to different teams of social workers in different areas with different employers, codes, criteria, goals, rules. The organisation of the latter service will have added risk and danger, which is separate from and additional to that provided by the patient, the patient's setting, the decision-makers making the risk decisions, and the behaviour of their managers and supervisors.

The rules, policies and practices can be another source of danger. Consider the rules of confidentiality. They have a desirable goal, but create problems in practice. The author has yet to find an audience of practitioners, medical or social work, which has not had problems in getting information about patients or clients from another profession. The problem has existed for decades, at least, and yet it has not been tackled. A major problem is the 'level' of responsibility involved. It is beyond the power of individual risk-taking practitioners to get the problems sorted. It is even beyond their managers and supervisors, and their employers. It needs to be tackled at governmental and/or professional association level. But these people do not seem to perceive, or understand, their contribution to making risk-taking more dangerous. Another example would be the response to relatively minor offences committed by people with a mental disorder and/or learning disability. Few see much point in initiating a prosecution unless serious harm is caused, which could of course be entirely accidental as when a person who is pushed happens to fall against a sharp stone. Imprisonment is expensive and often unproductive. These individuals are unlikely to have the funds to pay major fines, and the cost in taking criminal proceedings will be excessive in comparison. But if nothing is done the individual is being effectively taught that he or she can get away with minor crimes. The individual is being well taught to continue to be dangerous. Policies can be generated with the best of intentions but, nevertheless, they can make things worse, or at least more risky and dangerous, in their negative senses. A rich literature of studies on how laws can have 'anti-therapeutic' effects has been generated by the Therapeutic Jurisprudence movement (see the chapter by Petrucci, Winick and Wexler, in this volume, and references therein). Action is needed at the system level if these are to be tackled.

SYSTEM ANALYSIS AND ACTION

It is not just a question of organisational arrangements, or ill-considered policies, but also organisational culture. It is now relatively commonplace for an enquiry into harm, for example the abuse of children, to conclude that there were 'system' errors. This can be a means of trying to explain that, yes, things did go wrong but no individual was at fault. In this sense the conclusion is rather strange given that systems are constructed, maintained, and should be audited, by identifiable people. But it can also be interpreted as locating the problem in the amorphous, impersonal, 'system'.

So another major area for collaboration between psychologists and lawyers would be in analysing these 'system errors'. What do we mean when we conclude that 'the system' was in error? What can be done to identify systems that are more likely to lead to loss? What are the risk factors for dangerous systems? Where and how should lawyers examine for negligent systems? For example, Flood and Jackson (1991) have identified five metaphors for analysing 'systems': the machine, an organism, learning, cultural and political. They have related these metaphors to different paradigms or models of organisations, and to ways of analysing them and their self-images. The *machine* metaphor refers to organisations where the focus is on efficiency, on ensuring the effective integration of parts in an overall programme. Everything is carefully pre-planned with the parts organised to function as part of a well-oiled machine. By contrast the *organism* metaphor relates to organisations where the key goal is survival rather than performance of other functions. It adapts and changes to meet new challenges. It emphasises differences from other organisations in order to maintain its own identity and sustain its existence. The *learning* metaphor refers to organisations which depend upon, feed upon, information. They adapt and change as information is gained. Structures, such as buildings, can prove handicaps if they discourage change. Advertising and e-commerce organisations may provide examples. The *culture* metaphor refers to those organisations that associate themselves with key ideas, for example, consumer service or employee motivation, and try to relate their goals and activities to that key idea. And the *political* metaphor focuses on groups within the organisation competing for power and influence (generally see McGrew and Wilson, 1982). This model, based on metaphors, is relevant and important, it is submitted, because it helps to identify why some organisations, or systems, may make risk decision-making more difficult.

Risk-taking is heavily reliant upon information. Indeed, if the above five-level model is adopted, then risk-taking is more dependent upon information than we normally concede. If risk-taking is to be improved, then amongst many other desirable changes it needs to include feedback loops at—at least—individual decision, similar type of decision and decision-making system levels. Some of Flood and Young's types of organisation will be more open to accepting, using and learning from information. But some of those organisational types, particularly those associated with the mechanical and the organic, are not well placed to obtain, use and learn from new information. Social work departments, for example, are often associated with being territorial, very concerned with maintaining a separate identity and professional esteem for their discipline. The legal profession may be regarded as 'mechanical' in its traditional focus upon identifying negligence in instances of departure from normal professional practice leading to harm, when there is so much more that they could and should be considering. The learning model seems to be the most appropriate for developing risk-taking practices, but has its own deficiencies.

CONCLUSION

Psychology, along with the other behavioural sciences, has provided a great deal of research and insight into risk decision-making. It is offering that knowledge in legal contexts. But, this chapter has sought to argue, the models of risk-taking which have been adopted have been too narrow. There is a much bigger picture waiting to be seen. And if it is not examined much of the value of the recent work will be wasted. In particular, litigation lawyers could have a field day in misrepresenting and misusing the advice of psychologists about particular risk decisions.

If we are to improve the quality of risk-taking, and/or to avoid the negative and destructive consequences of litigation, then lawyers and psychologists should collaborate. This should begin with agreed models and terminology. The essential balancing nature of risk-taking should be recognised. This will allow more attention to be paid to the benefits of risk-taking and the harms of inaction. That should be to the medium and long-term benefit of the clients of both psychologists and lawyers. The disciplines should cooperate in the identification and development of risk-taking procedures that are designed to reduce the likelihood and seriousness of poor decision-making. Part of this should include lawyers learning the inappropriateness of some of their current tactics and assumptions about risk. It should lead to the production of decision-making aids. These should tackle common causes of erroneous decision-making. It should recognise how much there is yet to learn about risk-taking. In particular contexts—for example, forensic psychiatry or child protection—psychologists, lawyers and others should get together to produce risk-taking policies, standards, protocols or whatever is the preferred expression. These should identify current professional practice. They should address the reality that risk-taking involves many questions of value, many areas of disagreement, many areas of alternative methods of practice. They should include statements of contemporary professional values and standards to inform courts.

And they should provide for regular review of all procedures, policies and practices as we learn more from research and experience.

There is so much to gain. Risk decisions could be so much better and more highly respected, if only we increased the interdisciplinary collaboration.

REFERENCES

Aubert, V. (1963). The structure of legal thinking. In J. Andenaes (ed.), *Legal essays: A tribute to Fride Castberg on the occasion of his 70th birthday*. Boston: Universitetsforlaget.

Beck, U. (1992). *Risk society: Towards a new modernity*. London: Sage.

Bernstein, P.L. (1996). *Against the gods: The remarkable story of risk*. New York: John Wiley & Sons.

Campbell, C. (1974). Legal thought and juristic values. *British Journal of Law and Society*, *1*, 13–31.

Campbell, J.C. (1995). Predictions of homicide of and by battered women. In J.C. Campbell (ed.), *Assessing dangerousness: Violence by sexual offenders, batterers, and child abusers* (pp. 96–113). Thousand Oaks, CA: Sage.

Cooke, S. and Slack, N. (1991). *Making management decisions* (2nd edn). Hemel Hempstead, UK: Prentice Hall.

De Dombal, F.T. (1988). Computer-aided diagnosis of acute abdominal pain: The British experience. In J. Dowie and A. Elstein (eds), *Professional judgment: A reader in clinical decision-making*. Cambridge: Cambridge University Press.

Dowie, J. (1999). Communication for better decisions: Not about 'risk'. *Health, Risk and Society*, *1* (1), 41–53.

Elbogen, E.B. and Tomkins, A.J. (2000). From the psychiatric hospital to the community: Integrating the conditional release and contingency management. *Behavioral Sciences and the Law*, *18*, 427–444.

Eraker, S.A. and Politser, P. (1988). How decisions are reached: Physician and patient. In J. Dowie and A. Elstein (eds), *Professional judgment: A reader in clinical decision-making*. Cambridge: Cambridge University Press.

Flood, R.L. and Jackson, M.C. (1991). *Creative problem solving: Total system intervention*. Chichester: John Wiley & Sons.

Gunn, J. (1990). Clinical approaches to the assessment of risk. In D. Carson (ed.), *Risk-taking in mental disorder: Analyses, policies and practical strategies*. Chichester: SLE Publications.

Hagell, A. (1998). *Dangerous care: Reviewing the risks to children from their carers*. London: Policy Studies Institute and Bridge Child Care Development Service.

Hare, R.D. (2002). Psychopathy and risk for recidivism and violence. In N. Gray, J. Laing and L. Noakes (eds), *Criminal justice, mental health and the politics of risk*. London: Cavendish.

Heilbrun, K., Dvoskin, J., Hart, S.D. and McNeil, D.E. (1999). Prediction versus management models relevant to risk assessment: The importance of legal decision-making context. *Law and Human Behavior*, *21* (4), 347–359.

Litwack, T.R. (2001). Actuarial versus clinical assessments of dangerousness. *Psychology, Public Policy, and Law*, *7* (2), 409–443.

Janis, I.L. and Mann, L. (1977). *Decision making: A psychological analysis of conflict, choice and commitment*. New York: Free Press.

Kemshall, H. (2002). *Risk, social policy and welfare*. Buckingham: Open University Press.

Kropp, P.R., Hart, S.D., Webster, C.D. and Eaves, D. (1995). *Manual for the Spousal Assault Risk Assessment Guide*. Vancouver: B.C. Institute on Family Violence.

Langan, J. (1999). Assessing risk in mental health. In P. Parsloe (ed.), *Risk assessment in social care and social work*. London: Jessica Kingsley.

Limandri, B.J. and Sheridan, D.J. (1995). Prediction of intentional interpersonal violence: An introduction. In J.C. Campbell (ed.), *Assessing dangerousness: Violence by sexual offenders, batterers, and child abusers*. Thousand Oaks (California): Sage.

Lyon, D.L., Hart S.D. and Webster, C.D. (2001). Violence and risk assessment. In R.A. Schullere and J.R.P. Ogloff (eds.), *Introduction to psychology and law: Canadian perspectives*. Toronto: University of Toronto Press.

MacCrimmon, K.R. and Wehrung, D.A. (1986). *Taking risks: The management of uncertainty*. New York: Free Press.

Maden, A. (2002). Risk management in the real world. In N. Gray, J. Laing and L. Noakes (eds), *Criminal justice, mental health and the politics of risk*. London: Cavendish.

McGrew, A.G. and Wilson, M.J. (eds) (1982). *Decision-making: Approaches and analysis*. Manchester: University Press.

McNeil, D.E. and Binder, R.L. (1994). Screening for risk of inpatient violence. *Law and Human Behavior, 18* (5), 579–586.

Monahan, J. (1988). Risk assessment of violence among the mentally disordered: Generating useful knowledge. *International Journal of Law and Psychiatry*, 249.

Monahan, J., Steadman, H.J., Silver, E., Appelbaum, P.S., Clark Robbins, P., Mulvey, E.P., Roth, L.R., Grisso, T. and Banks, S. (2001). *Rethinking risk assessment: The MacArthur study of mental disorder and violence*. New York: Oxford University Press.

Quinsey, V., Harris, G., Rice, M. and Cormier, C. (1998). *Violent offenders: Appraising and managing risk*. Washington DC: American Psychological Association.

Rachlin, H. (1989). *Judgment, decision, and choice: A cognitive/behavioral synthesis*. New York: W.H. Freeman and Co.

Royal Society (1992). *Risk, analysis, perception, management*. London: Royal Society.

Slovic, P. (ed.) (2000). *The perception of risk*. London: Earthscan.

Slovic, P. and Monahan, J. (1995). Probability, danger and coercion: A study of risk perception and decision making in mental health law. *Law and Human Behavior, 19* (1), 49–65.

Titterton, M. (1999). Training professionals in risk assessment and risk management: What does the research tell us? In P. Parsloe (ed.), *Risk assessment in social care and social work*. London: Jessica Kingsley.

Tversky, A. and Kahneman, D. (1973). Availability: A heuristic for judging frequency and probability. *Cognitive Psychology, 4*, 207–232.

Tversky, A. and Kahneman, D. (1980). Causal schemas in judgments under uncertainty. In M. Fishbein (ed.), *Progress in social psychology*. San Diego: Academic Press.

Webster, C.D., Harris, G.T., Rice, M.E., Cormier, C. and Quinsey, V.L. (1994). *The violence prediction scheme: Assessing dangerousness in high risk men*. Toronto: Centre of Criminology, University of Toronto.

Wexler, D.B. and Schopp, R.F. (1989). How and when to correct for juror hindsight bias in mental health malpractice litigation: Some preliminary observations. *Behavioral Sciences and the Law, 7* (4), 485–504.

Yates, J.F. (ed.) (1992). *Risk-taking behavior*. Chichester: John Wiley & Sons.

Chapter 2.4

Beyond 'Offender Profiling': The Need for an Investigative Psychology

David Canter and Donna Youngs
University of Liverpool, UK

THE 'HOLLYWOOD EFFECT'

Public awareness of the contributions that psychologists can make to the investigation of crimes largely grew out of the general fascination with serial killers. These vile and determined murderers have become the stuff of urban myths. They are the mainstay of fictional crime drama and are guaranteed to steal the headlines if they break into fact. They seem to epitomise the essence of evil and to symbolise the darkest corners of the psyche. With such a load resting on the images of people who kill again and again it is perhaps not surprising that the images have been distorted and that fantasy and invention often hide the true facts about the nature of these nasty killers.

Much of the invention about Serial Killers that passes instead of real knowledge has its origins in the often quoted but under-researched writings of the Behavioral Science Unit of the FBI, based in Quantico, Virginia (e.g. Ressler, Burgess and Douglas 1988). The deficiencies of these reports has been noted by a number of authors (e.g. Coleman and Norris, 2000; Canter and Alison, 1999b; Muller, 2000), who all draw attention to the misrepresentation of established psychological theory within the FBI's ideas, the weaknesses of their methodologies as well as the lack of any convincing empirical evidence for their claims. Yet the fascination that Hollywood has with the FBI gives the musings of its agents a currency that far outweighs their validity. Leading film actors are given lines to quote that repeat confused and misinformed opinions in otherwise worthy films such a *Copycat*, or *Seven* and as a consequence audiences from Alaska to Zanzibar gain the mistaken impression that what is said with such conviction and apparent authority must be the truth.

Handbook of Psychology in Legal Contexts, Second Edition
Edited by D. Carson and R. Bull. © 2003 John Wiley & Sons, Ltd.

Out of this 'Hollywood Effect', of gracing personal opinion with dramatic illustration and thereby giving that opinion apparent authority, have emerged a great range of statements about Serial Killers, not one of which survives close scientific scrutiny. So, for example, Serial Killers are thought to be considerably above average intelligence, they are not thought ever to be of African-American extraction. The phenomenon of Serial Killing is presented as an almost uniquely American one that had virtually no existence until the last quarter of the twentieth century. Serial Killers are claimed only to attack victims of the same ethnicity as themselves and a strongly sexual component is assumed always to be present. Most curiously of all, the complex sets of processes that underlie serial killings are apparently reducible to the simple, if rather ambiguous dichotomy of being 'organised' or 'disorganised' (Hazelwood and Douglas 1980).

As a number of systematic studies are beginning to make clear, all of these claims about Serial Killing are false (Missen; 2000; Canter et al., 2000). The claims fall at the first hurdle of systematic study. Even the most elementary reading of the world's newspapers shows that Serial Killing occurs all over the world in many different forms, committed by many different sorts of people. The claims that emanate from FBI 'research' are false precisely because that research is so flawed. In any other context the results of such badly conducted studies would not have been published. It is only because of the hunger that the mass media and Hollywood have for anything that touches on the evil of Serial Killing that the claims we have outlined, and many others, have been so widely broadcast.

THE NEED FOR AN INVESTIGATIVE PSYCHOLOGY

In order to break away from the erroneous assumptions that are so widely popularised about serial criminals and psychological 'profiling' we need to develop a fully-fledged scientific discipline that will generate processes and theories for contributing to police investigations that have their roots firmly within empirical, scientific psychology. In order to develop such a discipline one important foundation is to guard against a merely prurient fascination with crimes and criminals. Taking fictional accounts as the starting point for the consideration of psychological contributions to police investigations is therefore fraught with the risk of undermining this important foundation of scientific work. Yet most academic accounts of such psychological contributions, under the heading of 'Offender Profiling', start by citing these works of fiction (e.g. Homant and Kennedy, 1998).

The particular problem with such fiction is that it almost invariably deals with the investigation of Serial Killers. These murderers provide such a simple icon of evil and depravity that they easily generate an apparently worthy foil for the hero of the story, the 'detective' who solves the case. But in order to create an appealing fictional hero who will detect and uncover the villain, the hero's wit and virtues have to be emphasised by contrast with the person who kills over and over again. To emphasise the power of the hero (or more recently heroine) the killer has to be shown not only to be callous and cold-blooded but also to be clever and devious. There is little dramatic mileage to be obtained from showing that the difficulty in detecting the serial killer is a product of ineffective record keeping, poor police training and the general anonymity that a free society affords.

Further, any account of Serial Killers, in fact or fiction, always runs the risk of sensationalising its subject and pandering to fiction writers', and readers', search for a plot that has a simple momentum, with individuals who are clear antagonists pitted against each other. Processes and systems play little part in such accounts. In fiction research findings are assigned to the insights of the hero, not to painstaking study.

In contrast, the results of empirical research move any insights or understanding into the public domain of scientific knowledge. This knowledge can be utilised by anyone with the skill to understand it. Science deals with actual people and the criminal actions that the police must examine and it focuses on knowledge that can be applied. It is thus able to feed into many aspects of police training and become integrated into the procedures that police use. Such a set of considerations really is the basis of a new discipline that grows out of applied psychology. Canter (1995b) has called this discipline *Investigative Psychology*. It is much more than the production of 'offender profiles' on serial killers. Rather, Investigative Psychology provides a framework for the integration of many diverse aspects of psychology into all areas of police and related investigations. It is concerned with all the forms of criminality that may be examined by the police. The discipline extends further to cover those areas of activity that require investigation but that may not always be conventionally within the domain of law enforcement, but handled by agencies other than the police, such as insurance fraud, malicious firesetting, terrorism, tax evasion or smuggling.

SYSTEM INTEGRATION VERSUS EXPERT OPINION

The usual model that is assumed for the utilisation of psychological knowledge in a police investigation is that an expert is brought into the enquiry, rather in the way that Sherlock Holmes was, to interact directly with the investigation (see Figure 2.4.1). The one-to-one contact between the 'expert' and the 'detective', so beloved of crime fiction, has found its way into police practice in the use of 'profilers' all over the world. Whilst there are probably some values to these contributions it seems likely that they are very limited (Copson, 1995).

Figure 2.4.1

A rather more productive model (discussed in more detail in Canter, 1985) is the one in which scientific psychology generates principles and procedures out of which processes can be developed which then become part of investigative practice.

This does not have the drama to it that the 'heroic profiler' can portray. It also means that the 'expert' is not likely to be needed once the system is in place. There are therefore personal and commercial pressures that undermine the development of this model, but it is one that is gaining ground as Investigative Psychology takes root. It is gaining this ground in part through the development of 'decision support systems' that encapsulate the processes that the science points towards, integrating those processes into, for example, databases held on crimes or background information on potential offenders.

This comparison between the deductive, 'fictional hero' approach and that of the scientific psychologist is not new to psychology. It has many parallels to the distinction between clinical and actuarial judgements that were explored by Meehl (1954). The clinician uses her or his judgements and experience to form an opinion about the patient. In contrast, actuarial judgements are those based on careful measurements and the resultant statistical relationships. In a series of studies first published in 1954 and followed up over the subsequent decades, it has been found that the actuarial decision processes were far more accurate and valid than those based on clinical judgement. In general the scientific approach proves to be far more effective than that based upon personal opinion, not least, as mentioned, because it is not the private resource of the 'expert' but can be turned into objective processes that others can be trained to use.

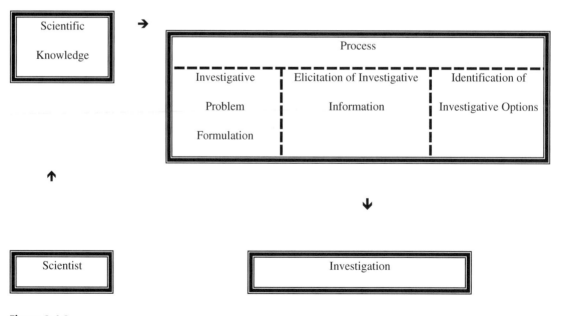

Figure 2.4.2

This raises fundamental questions for psychological offender profiling. These are questions about the extent to which scientific psychology can contribute to the various constituent processes of police investigations and activity (see Figure 2.4.2). They are also questions about the extent to which these contributions will take a form that means they have a practical utility for the police.

In the context of an investigation, the process of information elicitation, for example, is about drawing out those elements of a crime that will guide the detective towards one particular type of suspect rather than other types. Here then, the challenge for psychology is to develop psychological measures of those aspects of criminal activity available to police investigators. These must then be related to those characteristics of the offenders that are useful in the identification and prosecution of the offenders. These are the challenges at the heart of Investigative Psychology.

INVESTIGATIVE PSYCHOLOGY

The domain of *Investigative Psychology* covers all aspects of psychology that are relevant to the conduct of criminal or civil investigations. Its focus is on the ways in which criminal activities may be examined and understood in order for the detection of crime to be effective and legal proceedings to be appropriate. As such *Investigative Psychology* is concerned with psychological input to the full range of issues that relate to the management, investigation and prosecution of crime. These psychological contributions are considered here, in particular, as they relate to the investigation of crime.

Investigation as Decision-Making

The nature of the contributions psychologists can make becomes clear from a recognition that the challenges police face during the course of investigations are readily conceptualised as a series of decision-making tasks. These tasks can be derived from consideration of the sequence of activities that constitute the investigative process, from the point at which a crime is committed through to the bringing of a case to court. As they progress through this sequence of activities, detectives reach choice points, at which they must identify the possibilities for action on the basis of the information they can obtain. For example, when a burglary is committed they may seek to match fingerprints found at the crime scene with known suspects. This is a relatively straightforward process of making inferences about the likely culprit from the information drawn from the fingerprint. The action of arresting and questioning the suspect follows from this inference.

However, in many cases the investigative process is not so straightforward. Detectives may not have such clear-cut information but, for example, suspect that the style of the burglary is typical of one of a number of people they have arrested in the past. Or, in an even more complex example, such as a murder, they may infer from the disorder at the crime scene that the offender was a burglar disturbed in the act. These inferences will either lead them on to seek other information or to select from a possible range of actions, including the arrest and charging of a likely suspect.

Investigative decision-making thus involves the identification and selection of options, such as possible suspects or possible lines of enquiry, which will lead to the eventual narrowing down of the search process. In order to generate possibilities and select from them, detectives and other investigators must draw on some understanding of the actions of the offender(s) involved in the offence they are investigating. They must have some idea of typical ways in which offenders behave that will enable them to make sense of the information obtained. Throughout this process they must amass the appropriate evidence to identify the perpetrator and prove their case in court.

Information Management

It follows that three processes are always present in any investigation that can be improved by psychological study. First, the collection and evaluation of information derived from accounts of the crime. These accounts may include photographs or other recordings derived from the crime scene. There may also be records of other transactions such as bills paid or telephone calls made. Increasingly there are also records available within computer systems used by witnesses, victims or suspects. Often there will be witnesses to the crime or there will be results of the crime available for examination. There will transcripts of interviews or reports from various experts. Further there will be information in police and other records that may be drawn upon to provide indications for action. Once suspects are elicited there is further potential information about them either directly from interviews with them, or indirectly through reports from others. In addition there may be information from various experts that has to be understood and may lead to actions.

The major task of a police investigation is, therefore, typically to collect, assess and utilise a great variety of sources of information that provide accounts of crime. This is a task that can benefit considerably from the scientific study of human memory processes and other psychological studies of the reliability and validity of reports and their assessment. Indeed, much of the information that the police collect is analogous to the 'unobtrusive' or 'non-reactive' measures that social scientists have always utilised (cf. Webb et al., 1966). Therefore, many of the psychometric issues that have been explored to improve the quality and utility of such measures are directly relevant to police investigations. In some circumstance social science approaches may even expand the range of information that detectives may consider.

Effective Decisions

The second set of tasks is the making of decisions and the related actions that will move towards the arrest and conviction of the perpetrator. There is remarkably little study of exactly what decisions are made during an investigation, or how those decisions are made. Yet there is clearly a limited range of actions available to police officers, constrained by practical and financial considerations as well as the legal system within which they operate. From many studies of human decision-making in other contexts it is also apparent that there are likely to be many heuristic biases and other inefficiencies in the decision-making process (see Flin, 1996). Awareness of these can lead to effective ways of overcoming them.

Appropriate Inferences

In order for decisions to be derived from the information available, inferences have to be made about the import of that information. The third set of tasks therefore derives from developing a basis for those inferences at the heart of police investigations. These inferences derive from an understanding of criminal behaviour. For appropriate conclusions to be drawn from the accounts available of the crime it is necessary to have, at least implicitly, models of how various offenders act. Without templates of what is possible within a crime, the investigator cannot know what to look for in an offence, what has occurred, or indeed what has not occurred. These models allow the accounts of crime to be processed in such a way as to generate possibilities for action. This process of model-building and testing is, in effect, a scientific, psychological development of the informal, anecdote-based process often referred to as 'offender profiling' or 'criminal profiling'.

A simple framework for these three sets of tasks that gives rise to the field of Investigative Psychology is shown in Figure 2.4.3. More detailed information about each of these three strands of Investigative Psychology is given below.

Investigation cycle giving rise to field of Investigative Psychology

Information

Action   Inference

More formally, then, *Investigative Psychology* is the systematic, scientific study of:

(a) investigative information, its retrieval, evaluation and utilisation;
(b) police actions and decisions, their improvement and support; and
(c) the inferences that can be made about criminal activity, its development, differentiation and prediction,

The objective is to improve criminal and civil investigations.

Figure 2.4.3   The three strands of Investigative Psychology

INFORMATION RETRIEVAL

Limitations in Information Available

Any serious consideration of the information that is the basis of Investigative Psychology research and practice has to recognise the major limitations of that information, especially when it is directly derived from material which is available during an investigation. This can be quite rich information such as the details of the sexual behaviour of a rapist. It will also include such crucial factors as the time, place and nature of the offence, but it will not include the sorts of material that is the stock in trade of psychologists, such as the mental processes of offenders or their personality characteristics as may be indicated in personality questionnaires. Equally, while the information available does have certain strengths (such as the fact that it may have been given under oath), it does not come from material that has been collected under the careful controls of laboratory research. It is therefore often incomplete, ambiguous and unreliable.

Similarly, in order for the inferences to be of value to investigators they must connect directly with things that police officers can actually act on. Where an offender could be living is a clear example of useful information to an investigator, but more subtle material, such as how others may regard the offender or his/her likely skills and domestic circumstances, may also be of value. However, intensive psychodynamic interpretations of the offender's motivations, which might only become available during in-depth therapeutic interviews, are less likely to be of direct assistance to police investigators. For example, detectives were able to arrest and secure a conviction against Barry George for the murder of Jill Dando in the absence of any clear ideas about why he had committed this crime. As in many crime novels the motivations, or possibly more accurately the reasons, why an offender carried out an offence can be of general interest to investigators but they are only of value if they allow inferences to be made that will facilitate the detective decision-making process. In practice, however, police typically draw on ideas about the possible motive in any direct way only when they have no obvious lines of enquiry.

Any quest for motivation or motive is best seen as an informal attempt to develop some explanatory model that will help to link the crime behaviour to the offender. So, for example, if the motive were thought to be monetary gain then someone who would have a need for such money or who recently seems to have acquired a lot of money would be assumed to be a viable suspect. However, without clear empirical evidence on the particular types of behaviour that are associated with financially motivated crimes, and that the people who carry out these crimes do have a need for such financial gain, the interpretation of the motive and the inference drawn from it are little more than speculation. The weakness of such speculation can be demonstrated by the finding that those who have carried out insurance fraud have usually not been in particularly straightened financial circumstances. Dodd (1998) for example, demonstrated that only 13% of the 209 fraudulent insurance claimants he examined were in financial difficulties, whereas 57% were earning a regular income. In the same way, the commonly expressed view that rape is *not* motivated by the need for sexual gratification (e.g. Godlewski, 1987), again draws attention to the point that one cannot equate the gain derived from a crime with its motivation, or by extension, with a particular type of individual.

What are required scientifically are explanatory frameworks that can lead to hypotheses about the sorts of offender characteristics that are likely to relate to particular offence behaviours. There are very few studies at present that have demonstrated such relationships and even fewer theoretically precise models that provide guidance as to where to search for such relationships. Rather, the stage has been reached at which the various constituents of such models are being explored and the tests of various components of general models are being carried out.

Off-line and On-line Use of Information

It is helpful to distinguish between, on the one hand, information that may be available to a researcher during the course of a scientific study and from which principles may be derived that could be used by investigators. This could include the offender's understanding of what had happened and his/her account of the reasons for the offence. We can think of this as 'off-line' information. Much of it may not be admissible in court, such as hearsay accounts of who said what to whom, and the speculations of various people about the activities of others. But the information can generate trends that are of relevance to later investigations. So, for example, studies of offenders' mental maps (e.g. Canter and Hodge, 2000) have revealed the importance of route-following in structuring the geographical pattern of offending. This is information that could not have been drawn from the simple offence location data held in police crime files. The collection and analysis of such information is not without its problems, but there is a long scientific history of collecting such 'data' and associated knowledge and skills relating to how to improve and evaluate the reliability and validity of such information.

This contrasts, on the other hand, with the 'on-line' information that the police obtain as part of their investigations, on which they base their inferences for a particular case and which is likely to form at least part of the case they bring to court. In addition to forensic evidence such as fibres and the like, this will include behavioural evidence on what the offender did during an offence, where he/she did it and to whom. There is much less known about the quality of such evidence and many psychological questions emerge in relation to its retrieval. Studies have led to the development of procedures to improve the information collected during an investigation. It is this simple task of enhancing the quality of the material with which officers must work that is perhaps the most important contribution psychologists can make to police activities. Some aspects of what those improvements are intended to achieve are therefore worth considering.

Detail

One of the most important aspects of the information obtained during an investigation is that it should have as much relevant detail as possible. Psychologists have therefore helped to develop processes, especially for police interviews, that maximise the information obtained. In doing this, the perspective is taken that there are two issues that need to be as effective as possible. One is based on the assumption that the respondent in an interview is essentially trying to remember what occurred. Therefore anything that can help the memory process should be of value. The second issue is the relationship between the interviewer and the interviewee. If this relationship can be as supportive and as helpful as possible then more effective information is likely to be obtained.

Out of these considerations guidelines for interviews have been developed. The best known of these is referred to as the 'cognitive interview', developed by Fisher and Geiselman (1992). This is based on the assumption that memory is an active reconstructive process rather than a relatively passive act of recall. It draws on the well-established finding that recognition of information is much easier than its recall. Therefore any procedure that can help the interviewee to recreate the events in his/her own mind will be of value. This includes encouraging the respondent to describe the events as they are remembered rather than in strict response to particular questions in a given sequence. Reinstating the circumstances of the offence whenever possible, by returning to the scene or exploring details like sounds and smells, also accord with an understanding of the psychological processes by which memories are reconstructed. Attempts to consider the events from a variety of different perspectives are also considered valuable.

Investigative hypnosis has also been used to improve recall of information. In many respects hypnosis can be seen as a more intensive form of cognitive interview in which the respondent is helped to relax and concentrate (Wagstaff, 1984). There are certainly many anecdotal accounts of its effectiveness. However, the possibilities of leading the respondent to offer information that may be suggested by the interviewing hypnotist are considered much greater than for the interviewer in a cognitive interview. Many jurisdictions therefore have very close controls over the ways in which hypnotic interviews can be conducted.

Accuracy

A number of studies have shown that the cognitive interview generates significantly more detailed information than conventional police interviews (Fisher, Geiselman and Amador, 1989). Some studies show that the information obtained is more accurate and also more relevant. But it is remarkably difficult to measure relevance or accuracy precisely, so the full value of the cognitive interview is likely to vary considerably between situations.

Attempts have also been made to use similar psychological processes to improve the recollection of faces and other details (Koehn, Fisher and Cutler, 1999). This has proved less successful, in part because human recall of faces is so poor. Psychologists have therefore been involved in a variety of studies of how faces are reconstructed from memory and the procedures that can facilitate this. This has led to developments beyond the traditional 'photo-fit' approach. But the training involved in the use of these new systems, and their heavy reliance on effective interviewing, has meant they have not had the uptake that would have been expected from the scientific findings.

Psychological research has also contributed considerably to the improvement in the validity of the traditional 'identity parade'. Various procedures have been introduced by many police forces around the world to ensure that the recognition task set for the witness is appropriate and not open to bias. In particular these take account of the need to protect the suspect against the possibility of the witness's memory being modified by experiences subsequent to the crime, such as meeting the suspect in other circumstances (e.g. Haber and Haber, 2000).

Vulnerable Interviewees

A number of witnesses may be regarded as vulnerable because of their age, emotional state or intellectual ability. Such witnesses may be particularly open to suggestion or may be made especially anxious or confused by the interview process. Special interview procedures have therefore been developed for interviewing such people. They pay particular attention to the relationship established between the interviewee and the interviewer and the need to phrase questions and facilitate answers in ways that make sense to the respondent. An awareness of the vulnerability of some interviewees has also led to the legal requirement that now exists for an appropriate adult to be present at police interviews.

False Confessions

Psychologists, in particular Gudjonsson and MacKeith (e.g. 1988), have drawn attention to the possibility that some individuals may confess to crimes they have not committed. These 'false confessions' may be a consequence of characteristics similar to those that make witnesses vulnerable, such as heightened emotional state and low intellectual ability, making the suspect more willing to accept suggestions from the interviewer (cf. Gudjonsson, 2001). Gudjonsson has developed a measure of a person's 'suggestibility' that has been drawn on by the courts around the world to support claims of a false confession (Gudjonsson, 1984). These may also be a product of cultural processes rather than aspects of personality in which, for example, groups from certain ethnic minorities may deem it essential to agree with whatever a person in authority, such as a police officer, says to them (Gudjonsson, Rutter and Clare, 1995). Investigative psychologists have also considered the ways in which false confessions may be produced in response to various forms of psychological or physical coercion. However, all this work suffers from the practical difficulties of ever being certain that a confession really was false, so the impact of this approach often owes more to the predilections of particular jurisdictions than to the unchallengeable validity of the research on which it is based.

Validity

The lack of objective criteria may also be a reason for questioning allegations. In many circumstances investigators wish to assess the validity of information from witnesses because they consider allegations may be false. If there are no objective criteria for doing this they may use one of a number of validity assessment techniques. Most of these techniques are based on the assumption that honest accounts have identifiable characteristics that are different from fabricated accounts. The most frequently used approach to statement validation is that developed by Undeutsch (1989), known as Statement Validity Assessment which draws upon detailed analysis of the content of a statement referred to as Criteria Based Content Analysis. This procedure has been widely used to evaluate allegations of abuse made by children, especially in Germany where it originated. Attempts have also been made to extend its application to statements from other groups of witnesses with less success.

Authorship

A subset of validity questions relate to whether the words, attributed to a particular author, are actually the words of that person or not. This may occur, for example, when a suspect denies that he made the statement attributed to him, or in cases of forgery or fraud. To deal with these questioned utterances there have been a variety of attempts to use techniques based on the quantitative examination of language. These approaches are sometimes put under the general heading of 'stylistics', or forensic linguistics, or more generally forensic psycholinguistics. Yet although much is claimed for these procedures by their protagonists, the systematic research into them rarely finds any evidence to support even the mildest claims (Aked et al., 1999). Advances in computing techniques may change this.

These procedures are not to be confused with 'graphology', which claims to be able to provide accounts of the personality of an author from the style of his/her handwriting. There is no consistent scientific evidence for these claims (cf. Bar-Hillel and Ben-Shakar, 2000).

Detecting Deception

When the suspect is the source of the information, additional factors are also important beyond those of memory retrieval. These often relate to the need to determine if a person is attempting to deceive the interviewer. Thus although there are many objective, conventional police strategies for detecting deception, most obviously determining if the known facts contradict the suspect's claims, there are a number of situations in which some knowledge of behavioural and psycholinguistic cues to deception would be very helpful. A number of researchers, most notably Ekman (e.g. Ekman and O'Sullivan, 1991), have claimed that such cues are available, but others are more sceptical as to the possibility of any generally available indexes of deception from the actions or words of the suspect during a police interview (Edelman, 1999).

There is much more evidence to indicate that for many people there are psychophysiological responses that may be indicators of false statements (e.g. Kleiner, 1999). The procedure for examining these responses is often referred to as a polygraph or 'lie detector'. In essence this procedure records changes in the autonomic arousal system, i.e. emotional response. Such responses occur whenever a person perceives an emotionally significant stimulus. The most well-established indicator is when the respondent is asked to consider information that only the perpetrator would be aware of, known as the 'guilty knowledge' test.

A more controversial procedure is to ask 'control questions' that many people would find emotionally significant in order to determine if they elicit responses that can be distinguished from those questions relating directly to the crime. However, in both these applications of psychophysiological measures the most important element is the very careful interview procedure before measurements are made and during the process. In general the technique is more productive in supporting a claim of innocence than in providing proof of guilt. For this reason many jurisdictions do not allow 'lie detector' results to be presented as evidence in court.

False Allegations

In recent years there has been growing concern about the various conditions under which people will falsely allege they have suffered at the hands of others. Often, but not always, this is an allegation of sexual abuse or harassment. The various procedures for detecting deception may be relevant in these cases but, because the complainant is not a suspect, the more intrusive processes of lie detection are rarely used. Instead there have been attempts to indicate the circumstances in which such false allegations are made and use those as guidelines for more intensive examination (Mikkelsen, Gutheil and Emens, 1992; Tate, Warren and Hess, 1992). However the validity of these procedures is still highly questionable.

INVESTIGATIVE DECISION-MAKING

The main challenge to investigators is to make important decisions in often ambiguous and sometimes dangerous circumstances. The events surrounding the decisions are likely to carry a great emotional charge and there may be other political and organisational stresses that also make objective judgements very difficult. A lot of information, much of which may be of unknown reliability, needs to be amassed and digested. In decision-making terms the investigative process can be represented as in Figure 2.4.4. In this diagram the lines represent investigative actions by the police while the nodes are the results of that action, i.e. new pieces of information or facts.

Immediately after a crime occurs, detectives often have few leads to follow up. However, as they begin to investigate, information comes to light, opening up lines of enquiry. These produce more information, suggesting further directions for investigative

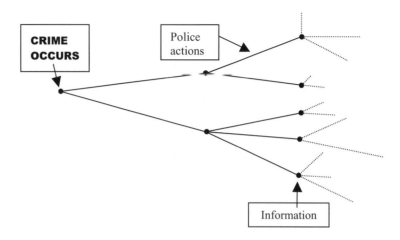

Figure 2.4.4

action. Eventually, detectives will establish facts that close off all but one of these lines of enquiry.

As such, information builds rapidly in the early stages of an investigation, often giving rise to exponential increases in the cognitive load on detectives, reaching some maximum weight, at which point they will often be under considerable stress. As the investigation progresses they will eventually able to start to narrow down their lines of enquiry, reducing the general demands upon them. The general diamond shape in Figure 2.4.5 shows the possible build-up of conditions under which various biases in investigators' thought processes are likely to occur, with consequent inadequacies in the decisions made and the subsequent actions. Recognition of the potential for

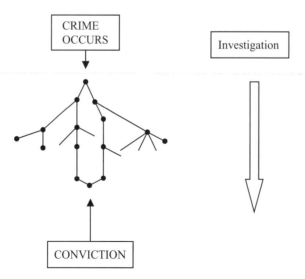

Figure 2.4.5

these problems can lead to the development of procedures to reduce their likelihood, including the management of resources. The challenges of police and other investigations may also be reduced by the development of decision support tools that reduce the complexity of the information that needs to be understood, and assists in the derivation of appropriate inferences from the material that is available to the police. The decision support tools that are emerging for use by police investigators each draw on particular perspectives on the nature of the problem.

Visualisation

Some support tools are based on the fact that human beings can often see patterns, between associations and within activities, if they can be presented in some visual summary. Bar charts of frequencies are one common example of this, but commercially available software will chart networks of contacts and other sequences of associations or actions. A remarkable series of books by Tufte (1999), which explore the wide range of visualisations of data, reveals just what the possibilities are for using visual images to enhance understanding of events and their causes.

Whilst these tools can be productive in summarising a great deal of information and, in association with databases, can improve the search for and access to crucial information, they are very dependent on the skills of the particular user, often referred to in police forces as a Crime Analyst. In the wrong hands these systems can imply a behavioural pattern through the strong visual impact that diagram produces, when in fact the diagram is a biased emphasis of some peripheral aspect of the criminal behaviour being investigated. So, for example, artificially placing an individual at the centre of a visual representation of a criminal network can facilitate an understanding of that particular individual's role in the network. Only with an understanding of how that representation was constructed would the analyst be aware that such apparently powerful visual evidence was not an indication of the individual's central importance in the network.

Description

A further level of support to decisions can be made by identifying the salient characteristics of the offences and offenders and by producing summary accounts of them. One widespread application of this use is in the production of maps that indicate the locations where there are high frequencies of crimes, sometimes called criminal 'hot-spots'. In these cases the salient characteristics are simply where the crimes have occurred and the description consists of some summary or averaging of the crimes over an area in order to indicate where its geographical focus might be. All description requires some selection, distillation or averaging of information and when that is done validly the description is helpful.

However, the decision-making tasks of the police receive most support when descriptions of an offender's actions in a crime are accompanied by information about the relative commonness or rarity of those actions among offenders generally. This base rate information guides the investigator towards those most salient features of an offence that will be most relevant to the process of deriving inferences about that particular offender.

Analysis

A further level of assistance to police decision-makers can be given by carrying out some form of analysis on the crime material, typically looking for patterns of co-occurrences or discriminating non-occurrence. An example of the former would be the recognition that certain acts of vandalism occur shortly after the end of the school day near to schools. Knowledge from descriptive analyses of the age and backgrounds of offenders prosecuted for vandalism and the geographical hot-spot information could be combined to target possible culprits and introduce other forms of crime reduction.

A more advanced analysis of the co-occurrence of criminal behaviours could also be used for classifying offenders and generating different investigative strategies for the different forms of offender. A number of researchers have developed models of the different behaviour patterns within a given type of crime. Merry and Harsent (2000), for example, were able to differentiate between *Intruder*, *Pilferer*, *Raider* and *Invader* styles of burglary, while Canter and Fritzon (1998) identified four stylistic variations of arson relating to Shye's (1985) action systems framework.

Inference

When clear relationships can be established between different aspects of crimes that are of investigative interest, inferences can be made from one to the other. For example, an understanding of the relationships between where offenders offend and where they live can be used to infer residential location from knowledge of offence location. The use of inference for decision support activities is at the core of Investigative Psychology as a scientific discipline and will therefore be elaborated below.

APPROPRIATE INFERENCES

The traditional approach taken by police investigators to making inferences is the one that has always been characterised in crime fiction as *deduction*. This is the process of reasoning from commonly known principles. For example, if a walking stick is found with strong, large teeth marks on it then the it may be reasoned that this was most likely caused by a large dog that carried the stick (as Sherlock Holmes reasons in *The Hound of the Baskervilles*). A subtler piece of reasoning may come from the knowledge that an offender had long nails on his right hand but short ones on his left. This is a pattern favoured by some guitarists and so it may be assumed that the offender was a serious guitar player.

However, as attractive as such deductions are in fiction they are a very poor basis for developing robust inferences in real-life crime. They are vulnerable to the knowledge and reasoning ability of the deducer and the particular features that they notice. Even more importantly, they may be worthless. It turns out that many trades give rise to people having longer nails on one hand than the other and so the inference of a guitarist could be very misleading. A dog may have bitten a walking stick in situations other than carrying, and so may not be directly associated with the owner of the walking stick.

In order to determine what the salient aspects of an offence are and how they may be validly related to useful investigative inferences, it is necessary to collect information across a range of cases and to test hypotheses about the actual co-occurrence of various features. This is the process of *inductive* reasoning that is at the heart of empirical science. Investigative psychologists have consequently been active in conducting a wide range of empirical studies aimed at providing objective bases for investigative inferences. These are studies that have been characterised by Canter (1995b) as attempts to solve the set of equations that link the Actions that occur during the offence, including when and where it happens and to whom, to the Characteristics of the offender, including the offender's criminal history, background and relationships to others. These have become known as the $A \vee C$ equations, or the 'profiling equations', where A are the Actions related to the crime and C are the Characteristics of typical offenders for such crimes.

Studies of these equations have given rise to the identification of a number of aspects of criminal behaviour that are crucial to any models of inference for effective use in investigations. One recurring conceptual basis for these models can be seen as an elaboration of routine activity theory in which it is hypothesised that offenders will show some consistency between the nature of their crimes and other characteristics they exhibit in other situations. This is rather different from the many psychological models that attempt to explain criminality as being a product of psychological deficiencies (Farrington, 1998). The inference models used for profiling are less concerned with the prediction of criminality than with unravelling the structure it takes and how that structure connects with features of the offender that will be of interest during an investigation.

Rather than being concerned with particular individual clues, as would be typical of detective fiction, these inference models operate at the thematic level. This approach recognises that any one criminal action may be unreliably recorded or may not happen because of situational factors. But a group of actions that together indicate some dominant aspect of the offender's style may be strongly related to some important characteristic of the offender. Davies, Wittebrod and Jackson (1997) showed the power of this thematic approach. They demonstrated, from their analysis of 210 rapes, that if the offender took precautions not to leave fingerprints, stole from the victim, forced entry and had imbibed alcohol, then there was a very high probability, above 90%, that the offender had prior convictions for burglary.

Unfortunately Davies et al. (1997) do not provide a detailed structural analysis of the relationships between all the activities that they considered. They used a logistic regression that searches through the data to find the best matches, so that low-level relationships that may add up to provide a stronger picture than any individual indicator, generating an overall picture, may be ignored. Actions brought together by Davies et al. (1997) to predict prior burglary indicate an offender who is determined to commit the crime and get away with it, treating the victim as a resource or 'object' rather than a significant person. When seen in this light other aspects of the assault may be recognised as relevant beyond the limited indicators thrown up by the logistic regression.

Salfati and Canter (1999) examined all the actions together with the offenders' characteristics in their study of 82 stranger homicides. Their analysis did reveal consistency in the themes across actions and characteristics. As with Davies et al.'s (1997) study the clearest associations of criminal actions were with previous offence history. Those murderers who stole non-identifiable property, who were careful not to leave forensic evidence and who hid or transported the victim's body, were more likely to have had a custodial sentence, but interestingly were also more likely to have served in the army.

The most developed exploration of thematic inference hypotheses is Canter and Fritzon's (1998) study of arsonists. They developed scales to measure four themes in the actions of arsonists derived from their action system model. They developed a further four scales to measure themes in the background characteristics of the 175 solved arson cases they studied. Their table, relating measures on all four background scales to all four action scales, showed that the strongest statistically significant correlations were, as predicted, between actions and characteristics that exhibited similar themes, and lowest between those that did not.

These studies of inference are therefore slowly beginning to provide a basis for a more general theory of offender consistency. But they suffer from dealing with the criminal as an individual independently of the social or organisational context in which he or she operates. As Canter and Alison (1999c) have argued, the social processes that underlie groups, teams and networks of criminals, can reveal much about the consistencies in criminal behaviour and the themes that provide their foundation. A clear example of this is the study by Wilson and Donald (1999) looking at the different roles that are taken by teams of 'hit and run' burglars. They demonstrated, for example, that the offender who was given the task of driving the get-away vehicle was most often likely to have a previous conviction for a vehicle-related crime. In contrast, the criminal assigned the task of keeping members of the public at bay, or controlling others who might interfere with their crime, the 'heavy', was most likely to have a previous conviction for some form of violence offence.

These results of consistency between social role and other forms of criminal endeavour are thus in keeping with the general thematic framework that is emerging through the studies of actual actions in a crime. They lend support to a general model of criminal activity that recognises the specific role that criminality plays in the life of the offender. It further supports the perspective that for the sorts of offenders considered in the studies cited, the style of criminality is an integral, natural part of the criminal's general lifestyle, not some special, atypical aspect of it.

As mentioned above when discussing the information at the heart of Investigative Psychology, one important aspect of these models is that the variables on which they can draw are limited to those of utility to police investigations. This implies that the A variables are restricted to those known prior to any suspect being identified. The C variables are limited to those on which the police can act. So an offender's personality characteristics, detailed measures of intelligence, attitudes and fantasies are all of less utility than information about where the person might be living, his or her criminal history or domestic circumstances.

Consistency

In order to generate some form of $A \lor C$ equation it is essential that the two sides of the equation are stable enough for a relationship to be established. Therefore much investigative psychology research is devoted to establishing what the salient features are of an offender's crimes and what it is within those features that is consistent enough to form the basis of their characteristics.

It is from these studies that classification schemes are emerging considering, for example, relevant variations between serial killers (which Hodge (in press) relates to the interpersonal role the offender assigns to the victim) and between stalkers (which Hargreaves and Canter (in press) relate to the nature of the prior relationship between stalker and victim). What is emerging from these studies is that styles of interpersonal transaction may well be consistent enough for some inferential models to be built. A distinct subset of offenders has also been identified that have consistent relationships between their residence and where they commit their crimes, also allowing geographical inference models to be developed.

Differentiation

Although an offender's consistency is one of the starting points for empirically based models of investigative inference, in order to use these models operationally it is also necessary to have some indication of how offenders can be distinguished from each other. If every offender were consistent in the same way then the $A \lor C$ equations would provide characteristics that were the same for every offender. In part this reflects a debate within criminology about whether offenders are typically specialist or versatile in their patterns of offending (Britt, 1996; Klein, 1984). Research tackling this problem has tended to support the contention that the majority of chronic criminals will commit a wide range of crimes and thus cannot be considered specialist, thereby making differentiating inferences extremely difficult. However, current research is suggesting that it is possible to model offender's behaviour in terms of both those aspects that they share with most other criminals and those aspects that are more characteristic of them. It is these rarer, distinguishing, features that may provide a productive basis for differentiating inferences.

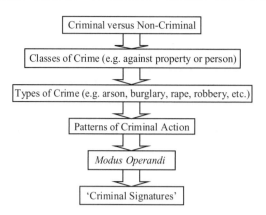

Figure 2.4.6 A hierarchy for the differentiation
of offenders

At a much more specific level there are questions about particular subsets of activities
that occur in a crime, say whether a particular type of weapon was used (Lobato, 2000).
Between the general questions and the particular is a continuum of variations that can
be examined. This would include questions about different subsets of crimes, such
as the comparison of violent offenders and burglars (Farrington and Lambert, 1994);
or at a slightly more specific level, questions about particular patterns of criminal
behaviour, such as the comparison of offenders who prepare carefully in advance of
a crime with those whose actions are impulsive and opportunistic.

Conceptually these different levels in the hierarchy of criminal actions can be represented as in Figure 2.4.6. It seems unlikely, however, that the empirical distinctions
in offenders' behaviour patterns will map on to this hierarchical model. It implies
that the variations at each level are simply subsets of the variations at a higher level.
But, for example, the differences between an offender who came prepared to carry
out his or her crime and one who just grabbed what was available may be more valid
than differences in, say, whether it was a robbery or a burglary. In effect, this makes
the description of crimes multidimensional. The notional hierarchy is better regarded
then as an interrelated set of dimensions for describing crimes.

Such a complex structure is extremely difficult to examine in total. Researchers have
therefore usually focused on one or other of the 'levels' of this hierarchy. For example, there are many studies examining the differences between offenders and non-
offenders. There are fewer comparing the differences between those convicted of one
crime and those convicted of another, and very few considering the differences between people who carry out similar crimes (e.g. rape) in different ways. The results of
all these studies have relevance for 'profiling' although studies that aim to contribute
to 'profiling' tends to focus on the behavioural level. So far, no studies have been
conducted to determine if the value and validity of inferences made on other facets
are greater or less than those based on patterns of behaviour.

The focus on patterns of behaviour in popular, anecdotal, crime publications as well as in the limited research literature is in part due to the many complications and unanswered questions within these multivariate issues. Some relate to the versatility of offenders. These raise questions of just what may be regarded as typical or characteristic of an offender. Other difficulties relate to the problem of defining the subgroup to which an offence should be assigned. Consider, as an illustration, a crime in which a house was burgled and at the same time a fire was set, giving rise to the death of an occupant. Would this crime be best thought of as burglary, arson or murder? The charge made against the accused is usually for the most serious crime, but psychologically that may not be the most significant aspect of the offender's actions.

One central research question, then, is to identify the behaviourally important facets of offences; those facets that are of most use in revealing the salient psychological processes inherent in the offence. These carry great potential for answering questions posed by investigators.

Beyond Types

There is one particularly important implication of this multivariate hierarchy of criminal actions. This is the challenge it presents to the notion of a criminal 'type'. There are some aspects of a criminal's activities that are similar across many offenders. These sit at the most general end of the 'hierarchy'. They involve the actions that define the individual as criminal. But there will be other actions that the criminal engages in that are located further towards the specific end, the activities that identify a particular crime. Furthermore, some of the actions will overlap with those of other offenders, for example whether the criminal carries out their crimes on impulse or plans them carefully. Indeed there will be relatively few aspects of offending, if any, which are unique to one given offender (these are often called, somewhat misleadingly, 'signature'). Even those may not be apparent in all the crimes that a person commits.

The actions of any individual criminal may therefore be thought of as a subset of all the possible activities of all criminals; some of this subset overlaps with the subsets of many other criminals, and some with relatively few. It therefore follows that assigning criminals or crimes to one of a limited number of 'types' will always be a gross oversimplification. It will also often be problematic to determine what 'type' they belong to. If the general characteristics of criminals are used for assigning them to 'types' then most criminals will be very similar and there will be few types. But if more specific features are selected then the same criminals, regarded as similar by general criteria, will be regarded as different when considered in relation to more specific criteria.

This is the same problem that personality psychologists have struggled with throughout the twentieth century. Their research has led to the identification of underlying *dimensions* of personality. This 'dimensional' approach assumed that there were distinct, relatively independent, aspects of personality that could be identified. In recent years rather more complex models have emerged that do not require the simplifying assumption of independent linear dimensions (Plutchik and Conte, 1997).

An analogy that helps in understanding this debate is the problem of classifying colours. Colours come in a virtually infinite variety, but in order to describe them some points of reference are necessary. These points of reference must cover the full spectrum of colours and they must be distinct enough for people to understand the reference. So, for instance, it would be unhelpful to try to discriminate colours merely on the basis of how much grey they contained and how much turquoise. Many differences between colours could not be accommodated in this scheme and many people may be unclear as to what colour turquoise actually is.

Another approach may be classifying colours along dimensions of blueness, redness and greenness. Indeed, many computer colour manipulation systems use just such a dimensional approach. These three hues do account for all colours and they do have very clear meanings to people who are not colour blind. The psychological parallel of personality dimensions of extroversion and neuroticism, or in intelligence of spatial, numerical and verbal ability, also seeks to describe people in their combined position along all the identified dimensions. As with colour naming, a great deal of research has gone into determining what the major dimensions of personality or intelligence are and of specifying how they may be measured as clearly as possible.

But even though the dimensional classification scheme can be very productive it does have a number of limitations. This can be illustrated by considering yellow in our colour example. Most people regard this as a distinctly different colour from red, blue or green. Yet the computer, say, only gives us one of these three dimensions to use. How can yellow be produced? It takes special knowledge of the system and how colour combinations work to realise that red and green will generate yellow. The reason why this difficulty arises is that colours are not perceived along distinct dimensions, but rather as blending into each other. Various oranges sit between red and yellow, browns between yellow and green, turquoises between green and blue, purples between blue and red, and so on. Indeed for some purposes, such as printing, it is more useful to think of the 'between' colours, or 'secondary colours' as they are known, as the defining dimensions, i.e. cyan, magenta, and yellow. This switch from one set of axes to another is only feasible because they all merge into each other in a continuous colour circle (as pointed out by the artist Albert Munsell, 1960).

The existence of a circle of colours does not deny the value of defining the major points of this circle. But rather than treat them as independent dimensions they are dealt with as emphases from which other combinations can be readily derived. The parallels with criminal actions are very strong. In order to describe those actions we need to identify the dominant themes, but it would be unproductive to regard these themes as independent dimensions. It would be even more misleading to regard them as pure types, just as it would be misleading to think that colours can only be pure red, green or blue.

The hierarchy of criminal actions also lends support to a circular ordering of criminal actions as a parallel with the colour circle. At the centre of the colour circle are those aspects of colour that all colours share. This is the degree of greyness. It depends on whether lights or pigments are being considered, but for simplicity it is just necessary to remember that Isaac Newton showed that white light contained all the colours. So if all lights of all colours are combined they produce white. This is the centre of the colour circle. As the colours move out from this central position they become more specific and more distinctly one colour or another. The same mathematical process can be hypothesised for criminal behaviour. At the centre are actions typical of all the criminals being considered. These are the general aspects of the sorts of crimes that are the particular focus. As the actions become more specific to particular styles of offending so they would be expected to be conceptually further from the 'centre' of general criminality and thus more differentiating between criminals.

It can thus be appreciated that this hypothesised model of the variations between criminals has two facets to it. One is the facet of specificity, moving from the general, shared by all offences and therefore conceptually in the middle, to the specific at the periphery (Figure 2.4.7). The other is the thematic facet that distinguishes between the different qualities of the offences, conceptually radiating around the 'core'. This model was recognised by Guttman (1954) as a powerful summary of many forms of differentiation between people and named a *radex*. This is the hypothesised model that a number of researchers are testing as the first step towards answering the psychological and investigative questions introduced above.

The crucial discovery in testing such a hypothesis is the identification of the dominant themes that can be used to classify any set of crimes. In the process it is often possible to give more substance to the meaning of specificity in that criminal context. In other words, the research may allow a determination of what the aspects of crime are that reveal the differences in the thematic emphases. For example, is it the degree of

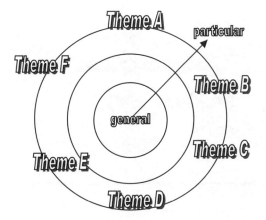

Figure 2.4.7 A general model for a radex as applied to the actions of criminals

planning, or the forms of contact with the victim, or the intensity and legal seriousness of the actions, or some other underlying aspect of the crime, that produces the mixture of salient variations between crimes?

A number of different researchers have explored these possibilities in a variety of ways. Not all of them follow through the details of the radex hypothesis, either because of the weaknesses of the data they have available or the current impoverished levels of conceptualisations of criminal actions. But a growing number of studies are finding the radex model to be a powerful conceptual tool for differentiating criminals (Canter and Alison, 2000).

Behavioural Salience

There are many things that occur in a crime. Therefore the challenge to the police officer, as for the researcher, is to identify those features that are of most relevance to deriving inferences about the offender. The determination of the salient characteristics is an empirical question in the sense that some knowledge of the base rate of behaviours of particular classes of crime is essential before the characteristics that are particularly important in understanding a given offence can be appreciated.

As outlined, the hypothesis is that the hierarchy of criminal differentiation illustrated in Figure 2.4.6 should have an empirical correspondence in the radex structure illustrated in Figure 2.4.7. The more general aspects of a crime, typical of all criminals are hypothesised to be at the centre of the radex with the 'signatures' at the periphery as shown in Figure 2.4.8.

The model of behavioural salience is a refutable hypothesis because it is possible that distinct subgroups of actions could occur in any class of crime that, whilst frequent, were typically associated with distinct sets of rarer actions. In such a case

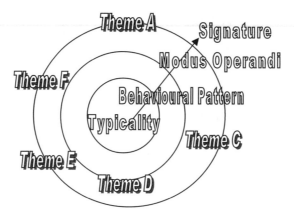

Figure 2.4.8 Representation of behavioural salience in a radex of criminal behaviour

the concentric circles that make up the radex would not be found. In this framework salience is the location of an action at different distances from the centroid of the pattern of actions.

The first published study to demonstrate the existence of such a radial structure for crime was Canter and Heritage's (1990) study of rape. But a more recent study by Canter, Hughes and Kirby (1998) of paedophilia also serves to illustrate the power of the radex model in helping to indicate the salient aspects of a crime. For although in their study the three activities of 'initial force used by offender', 'the offender was recorded to have carried out the offence only once' and 'the offender tried to desensitise the victim to the offence' all occurred in about 40% of the 97 cases they studied, the distribution in the plot (derived from a Multidimensional Scaling Analysis) shows that they tended to occur in very different crimes. Furthermore, they co-occurred with rather different sorts of other actions. For example, initial force was related to a number of other less frequent violent actions carried out by the offender, whereas desensitisation tended to co-occur with rarer actions that implied attempts to develop an intimate relationship with the child victim.

In a number of studies salience has emerged as related to the social psychological context of the offence rather than the focal actions that define the offence. In Canter and Heritage's (1990) study they report that 'the use of the woman as a sexual object is at the core of sexual assault' (p. 198). The salient differentiations therefore are those that relate to *how* this core activity is instantiated in any particular offence. In their study of arson Canter and Fritzon (1998) used Shye's (1985) action systems model to give a more precise definition of the variations in modes of criminal activity that provide the key to understanding differentiation. They demonstrate that differences 'relate to the source of the action and the locus of its desired effects' (p. 80).

This concern with source and locus of the intended effects of crime follows the discussions of the role of emotion in offending that can be traced back to the consideration of instrumental aggression in violent crimes (e.g. Buss, 1961; Fesbach, 1964). Canter and Fritzon (1998) generalised the consideration of whether violent crimes were instrumental or expressive to cover other forms of crime, notably arson. They did this by regarding crimes as aimed at a variety of types of targets. Sometimes the target may be a modification of the feelings of the criminal, and thus essentially expressive, or they may be a search for a particular overt reward, thereby being essentially instrumental. It is this overlay, or elaboration, of the central criminal acts that give those acts their significance and investigative salience. The elaboration is clearest when the acts can be seen in the general context of other actions committed during similar crimes. If they can be modelled in relation to the overall frequency of actions that occur in that class of crimes then a reasonably precise definition of their salience can be determined.

Models of Differentiation

The examination of the salience of offence actions indicates that the consideration of any action in isolation from the others that may co-occur with it can be misleading.

Any single action may be so common across offences or so ambiguous in its significance that its use as a basis for investigative inferences may suggest distinctions between offenders that are unimportant. Models of differentiation therefore need to have foundations in an understanding of the processes that give rise to co-occurring patterns of criminal activity. These studies have tended to explore the hypothesis that these themes reflect the mode of interpersonal transaction that the offender uses to carry out the crime.

One elaboration of this mode of interpersonal transaction is that put forward by Canter (1995a). He takes a more social psychological perspective on what Canter and Fritzon (1998) call the 'locus of desired effects'. The locus here is the role the offender assigns his victim during the crime. This model is a distillation of the findings reported by Canter and Heritage (1990). Rather than the five-fold model they proposed, Canter (1995a) argued that in more general terms the five modes of transaction can be reduced to three general roles to which a victim may be assigned.

1. Where the offender treats the victim as an object (something to be used and controlled only through restraint and threat, often involving alternative gains in the form of other crimes such as theft).

2. Where the offender sees the victim as a vehicle for the offender's own emotional state, e.g. anger and frustration (the victim is subjected to extreme violence and abuse).

3. Where the offender sees the victim as a person (some level of pseudo-intimacy with attempts to create some sort of rapport or relationship).

Canter (1995a) presents some evidence for this model as a basis for differentiating rapists. More recently Canter, Hughes and Kirby (1998) have shown that the model is supported with data from 97 paedophiles. Salfati and Canter (1999) used a somewhat different vocabulary in their study of 82 stranger homicides but still presented an analogous three-fold model. More recently Fritzon, Canter and Wilton (2001) have found support for the model in their study of attempted murder. Hodge (in press) also found the model to be of value in her study of 88 US serial killers. Her particularly detailed argument and MDS results provide one of the clearest examples of this approach.

She hypothesised that for those sexual serial murderers where the role of victim was as an object, the crime scene behaviours would reflect few emotional elements with little interpersonal interaction. The offender would be unlikely to be influenced by the victims' responses, acting out a personal ritualised script, in which the victim plays no part as a human being. She also hypothesised that post-mortem injuries and sexual acts as well as excessive violence and dismemberment would co-occur with these other indicators of the 'victim as object'.

Hodge (in press) took the thematic focus on the role of victim as a vehicle to reflect more overtly emotional reactions. She points out that although the offender may well subject his victim to extreme violence similar to the offender who sees his victim as an object, there will be a difference in the concern the offender has for the sort of people his victims represent to him in his personal life. Therefore, there is likely to be a substantial level of interpersonal interaction between victim and offender. Associated crime scene behaviours may include the use of restraints and there may be evidence that the victim was kept alive for a period of time.

Where the role of the victim is as a person, Hodge (in press) hypothesised that the crime scene behaviour will reflect the importance of the victim as a particular person. She proposes that this will be shown in the co-occurrence of variables that indicate the degree and style of interaction between the two. Excessive violence would be rare, sexual activity would be more likely to be 'normal' ones such as full sexual intercourse prior to death and violence directed at specific areas of the body, especially the facial area.

As the earlier discussion of the radex model makes clear, this three-fold classification is not meant to indicate distinct types of offender but rather themes that will be present in all offences to some degree. The differences between offenders are in the emphases that any particular offender exhibits.

Hodge (in press) tested these hypotheses by carrying out an MDS analysis of 39 crime-related actions of the 88 killers she studied. The resulting two-dimensional configuration is shown in Figure 2.4.9. For full details of this analysis the original

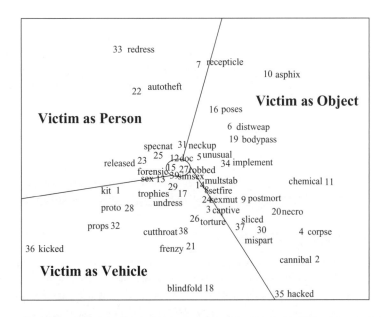

Figure 2.4.9 MDS analysis (Smallest Space Analysis) of the actions of 88 US Serial Killers (from Hodge, in press). (Numbers refer to the variable numbers in the original paper. Brief titles for the variable are given on the plot, the full coding dictionary is given in the original paper.)

paper should be consulted. As Hodge hypothesised, regions of the MDS configuration can be distinguished that indicate the different emphases predicted by the three-fold interpersonal model. To the right of the plot are those variables that suggest that the victim is dealt with as 'an object'. These activities have similarities to those associated with sadistic/lust murderers (Becker and Abel, 1978). Necrophiliac activities, cannibalism, hacking the body, leaving it in a posed position as well as other post-mortem activities all are consistent with the victim being little more than something to use. There is no indication that the victim carries any emotional significance for the offender.

To the bottom left of the plot are those actions that indicate that the victim acts as a vehicle for the offender. The victim being held captive and being involved in the script of the offender elaborate the underlying brutality of the offence. As Hodge (in press) points out, the significance of the victim to the offender can result in the direction of excessive violence to areas of the body that hold importance for the offender. Specific types of victim are selected, and restrained, sometimes using designed crime kits (kit) and restraints (blindfold).

Hodge (in press) points out that at the top left of the plot are those behaviours that indicate that the offender perceives his victim as a person with whom his desire for some degree of interpersonal interaction is fulfilled. This theme may be indicative of the category of rape murder as proposed by Groth, Burgess and Holmstrom (1977). In such cases, the victim's responses are more likely to influence the offender's behaviour. In other words, the interaction is two way rather than from only offender to victim. Here, the victim is not only integral to the offender's script but has a 'speaking part'. The variables of sex (full sexual intercourse) and dressing the victim after the sexual assault (redress) suggest some degree of emotional significance to the victim as a person. The taking of personal documents and belongings from the victim also show an interest in the person rather than just her body.

This study of serial killers illustrates how crime-related actions can be differentiated as a first step towards the development of models that will characterise the dominant themes in criminal behaviour. It is of especial interest because it replicates findings from a number of different studies of criminal behaviour, lending support to the proposition that there may be underlying themes that differentiate all crimes.

Approaches to Making Valid Inferences

The inferences that detectives make in an investigation about the perpetrator's likely characteristics will be valid to the extent that they are based on appropriate ideas about (a) the processes by which the actions in a crime are linked to the characteristics, and (b) *how* the actions and characteristics are linked.

With regard to the linking processes, as outlined there is some indication that processes relating to both the offender's interpersonal style and his or her routine activities may underlie any actions–characteristics link. A number of other potential frameworks for these relationships are also available within social and psychological theory. These include psychodynamic theories and personality theories, as well as frameworks drawing on interpersonal narratives and on socio-economic factors. Any or all of these theories will provide a valid basis for investigative inferences if the differences in individuals they posit correspond to variations in criminal behaviour.

Valid inferences also depend upon an understanding of the way in which a process is operating. Conceptually there are a number of different roles that a theory can play in helping to link an offender's actions and with his or her characteristics. One is to explain how it is that the offender's characteristics are the cause of the particular criminal actions. A different theoretical perspective would be to look for some common set of intervening variables that was produced by the offender's characteristics to cause the particular offending actions. Yet a third possibility is that some other set of variables is the cause of both.

Development and Change

A further complication to establishing the $A \vee C$ equations is that the way a person commits a crime, and indeed the characteristics of a person, will change over time even if there is a background of consistencies. However, if the basis of these changes can be understood then they can be used to enhance the inference process. In essence, the following five forms of change have been identified.

1. *Responsiveness*. One important reason for differences between a criminal's actions on two different occasions may be their reaction to the different circumstances they face. By an understanding of these circumstances, and how the offender has responded to them, some inferences about his or her interpersonal style or situational responsiveness may be made that can have investigative implications.

2. *Maturation*. This is the essentially biological process of change in a person's physiology with age. Knowledge of what is typical of people at certain ages, such as sexual activity, can thus be used to form a view as to the maturity of the person committing the crimes and to the basis for longer-term variations in an individual's criminal activity.

3. *Development*. The unfolding psychological mechanisms that come with age provide a basis for change in cognitive and emotional processes. One reflection of this is increase in expertise in doing a particular task. Evidence of such expertise in a crime can thus be used to help to make inferences about the stages in a criminal's development that he or she has reached and indeed to indicate the way that person's crimes might change in the future.

4. *Learning*. Most offenders will learn from their experiences. They will therefore be expected to alter their actions in the light of the consequences of previous

actions. An inferential implication of this is that it may be possible to link crimes to a common offender by understanding the logic of how behaviour has changed from one offence to the next.

5.   *Careers.* The most general form of change that may be expected from criminals is one that may be seen as having an analogy to a legitimate career. This would imply stages such as apprenticeship, middle management, leadership and retirement. Unfortunately the criminology literature often uses the term criminal career simply to mean the sequence of crimes a person has committed. It is also sometimes confused with the idea of a 'career criminal', someone who makes a living entirely out of crime. As a consequence much less is understood about the utility of the career analogy for criminals than might be expected. There are some indications that the more serious crimes are committed by people who have a history of less serious crimes and that, as a consequence, the more serious a crime the older an offender is likely to be. But commonly held assumptions, such that serious sexual offences are presaged by less serious ones, does not have a lot of empirical evidence in its support.

CONCLUSIONS

Profiling emerged as a response to a hunger from the police for some guidance in those complex cases in which they had no obvious leads, most notably apparently 'motiveless' serial killings. But along the way the homespun rules-of-thumb, and personal opinions derived from prior experience, have made psychologists aware of the necessity and potential for a systematic, empirically based approach to the questions detectives ask. The many different issues of scientific significance that underlie these questions now coalesce under the umbrella term of *Investigative Psychology*. It is therefore appropriate to conclude this brief review of that emerging area by summarising the operational questions that Investigative Psychologists are now carrying out studies to try to answer.

All of these questions relate to what has been distilled above as the $A \vee C$ equations. These equations characterise attempts to demonstrate reliable and robust relationships between aspects of a crime (the A variables) and characteristics of the offender (the C variables). In order to unpack the $\vee$, which indicates the many functional relationships there may be between these two sets of variables, a number of related questions have been identified.

1.   *What are the salient characteristics of the offender that will help investigators to identify and locate him or her?*

So much can happen in a crime and so many different aspects of it can be noted, the aspects of the crime that will most fruitfully act as the predictor variables in the notional equation are not as obvious as they may at first seem. A number of studies have been reported above which reveal the power of multidimensional models of the actions that do occur in a crime. These do offer the prospect of determining what makes any given crime distinct. Future research will need to determine how helpful such distinctions really are, although recent research on arson, in particular, has indicated that, in some contexts at least, salient aspects of criminal actions can be powerfully indicative of characteristics of the offender.

2. *What searches of police records or other sources of information should be carried out to help to identify the offender?*

The question of what are the salient actions is matched by the question of what are the salient aspects of offender characteristics that will lead the police to them. This a challenging set of issues for psychologists because in research terms it suggests that the availability of data should shape what is looked for rather than data collection being driven by prior research questions. This focus gives emphasis to those research results that connect clearly with the sorts of information available to the police, notably previous criminal history. The few studies that have established clear links between actions in a crime and aspects of an offender's criminal background therefore pave the way for powerful operational support in the future. As has been noted above, however, police data management systems and their collection of effective information about offenders can be greatly improved by drawing upon the skills and procedures that social scientists have developed over a century of empirical research.

3. *Where, geographically, should searches for offenders be carried out?*

Another characteristic of an offender of huge significance to the police is where that offender may be living. The geographical focus of a criminal's activities therefore offers considerable potential for police investigations. The emergence of decision support systems that make use of crime locations are a response to this potential and their power is being increased as our understanding grows of how offenders make use of their surroundings.

4. *Which crimes are likely to have been committed by the same offenders?*

The linking of crimes to a common offender has many advantages for police investigations. But such linking requires the determination of what it is about any given offender that is internally consistent enough for that offender, from one crime to the next, to distinguish him or her from the variety of actions that vary across similar offence in general. If most burglars use forced entry, that is not going to help link together two burglaries committed by the same person who also happens to use forced entry. Of course, if a burglar has a mode of operating that is as unique to him as a signature, then that can be used to link his crimes, but it is rare for any criminal to reveal such 'signature' consistently. It therefore follows that issues of salience in the offender's actions are taken to a further level when linking is considered. The salience of the action in distinguishing one offender from another needs to be studied as well as its salience in distinguishing one offence from another.

5. *Where will the offender commit his or her next offence?*

Little work has been done, and virtually none published, on predicting where a serial criminal will offend next. This relates to broader issues in crime mapping such as the hotspots of crime as well as aspects of offender consistency relevant to linking crimes. Broad issues of criminal career are probably relevant too. This is thus an operational question that requires for its solution the bringing together of a number of research questions from different areas of investigative psychology.

6. *What sense can be made of the offence that will help to organise the legal case?*

Psychological models are increasingly finding their way into the conceptual backing for court proceedings. So although they may not be used directly as evidence they are drawn upon by barristers to help to clarify the narrative they present to the jury.

The complexity of deriving inferences to answer these operational questions is considerable. It requires managing issues of consistency and differentiation together with development and change across a range of aspects of crimes that will vary in degree of specialism. As has been noted, dealing with these complexities is being facilitated by collaboration between investigative psychologists and police forces around the world to develop computer-based decision support systems drawing on the ideas indicated above (e.g. Canter et al., 2000). These inductively developed systems are likely to rapidly replace the outmoded methods of police deduction. They will never have the dramatic appeal of the Holmsian hero but they are likely to be considerably more effective and certainly better value for money.

Investigative Psychology provides a holistic perspective on the investigation of crime, showing that all aspects of the detective's work are open to scientific psychological examination. It is helping police forces to recognise that they need to build psychological expertise into their modern computing capability rather than just bring an expert in when an investigation has reached a particularly difficult stage. They are learning to answer the question 'at which point in an investigation should a psychologist be brought in' with 'before the crime is committed!'.

REFERENCES

Aked, J.P., Canter, D., Sanford, A.J. and Smith, N. (1999). Approaches to the scientific attribution of authorship. In D.V. Canter and L.J. Alison (eds), *Profiling in policy and practice, networks*. Offender Profiling Series, Vol II (pp. 157–188). Aldershot: Ashgate.

Bar-Hillel, M. and Ben-Shakar, G. (2000). The a priori case against graphology: Methodological and conceptual bases. In T. Connolly et al. (eds), *Judgement and decision making: An interdisciplinary reader* (2nd edn). New York: Cambridge University Press.

Becker, J.V. and Abel, G.G. (1978). Men and the victimisation of women. In J.R. Chapman and M.R. Gates (eds), *Victimisation of women*. Beverly Hills: Sage.

Britt, C.L. (1996). The measurement of specialisation and escalation in the criminal career: An alternative modeling strategy. *Journal of Quantitative Criminology*, 12 (2), 193–222.

Buss, A.H. (1961). *The psychology of aggression*. New York: John Wiley & Sons.

Canter, D.V. (1985) (ed.). *Facet theory*. New York: Springer-Verlag.

Canter, D.V. (1995a). *Criminal shadows*. London: HarperCollins.

Canter, D.V. (1995b). The psychology of offender profiling. In R. Bull and D. Carson (eds), *Handbook of psychology in legal contexts*. Chichester: John Wiley & Sons.

Canter, D.V. and Alison, L.J. (eds) (1999a). *Interviewing and deception*. Offender Profiling Series, Vol I. Aldershot: Ashgate.

Canter, D.V. and Alison, L.J. (1999b). The social psychology of crime. In D.V. Canter and L.J. Alison (eds), *The social psychology of crime: Teams, groups, networks*. Offender Profiling Series, Vol III. Aldershot: Ashgate.

Canter, D.V. and Alison, L.J. (eds) (1999c). *The social psychology of crime: Teams, groups, networks*. Offender Profiling Series, Vol III. Aldershot: Ashgate.

Canter, D.V. and Alison, L.J. (2000). *Profiling property crimes*. Offender Profiling Series, Vol IV Aldershot: Ashgate.

Canter, D.V., Coffey, T., Huntley, M. and Missen, C. (2000). Predicting serial killers' home base using a decision support system. *Journal of Quantitative Criminology, 16* (4).

Canter, D. and Fritzon, K. (1998). Differentiating arsonists: A model of firesetting actions and characteristics. *Journal of Criminal and Legal Psychology, 3*, 73–96.

Canter, D.V. and Heritage, R. (1990). A multivariate model of sexual offences behaviour: developments in 'offender profiling' I. *Journal of Forensic Psychiatry, 1*, 185–212.

Canter, D. and Hodge, S. (2000). Criminals' mental maps. In L. Turnbull, E. Hallisey and B. Dent (eds), *Atlas of crime: Mapping the criminal landscape*. Phoenix, Arizona: Oryx Press.

Canter, D., Hughes, D. and Kirby, S. (1998). Paedophilia: Pathology, criminality, or both? The development of a multivariate model of offence behaviour in child sexual abuse. *Journal of Forensic Psychiatry, 9* (3), 532–555.

Coleman, C. and Norris, C. (2000). *Introducing criminology*. Cullompton: Willan.

Copson, G. (1995). *Coals to Newcastle? Part 1: A study of offender profiling* (Paper 7). London Police Research Group Special Interest Series. London: Home Office.

Davies, A., Wittebrod, K. and Jackson, J.L. (1997). Predicting the antecedents of a stranger rapist from his offence behaviour. *Science and Justice, 37*, 161–170.

Dodd, N.J. (1998). Applying psychology to the reduction of insurance claim fraud. *Insurance Trends, 18*, 11–16.

Edelman, R. (1999). Non verbal behaviour and deception. In D. Canter and L.J. Alison (eds), *Interviewing and deception*. Offender Profiling Series, Vol I. Aldershot: Ashgate.

Ekman, P. and O'Sullivan, M. (1991). Who can catch a liar? *American Psychologist, 46*, 913–20.

Farrington D. P. (ed.) (1998). *Psychological explanations of crime*. Aldershot: Ashgate.

Farrington, D.P. and Lambert, S. (1994). Differences between burglars and violent offenders. *Psychology, Crime and Law, 1*, 107–116.

Fesbach, S. (1964). The function of aggression and the regulation of aggression drive. *Psychological Review*, 257–272.

Fisher, R. and Geiselman, R. (1992). *Memory-enhancing techniques for investigative interviewing: The cognitive interview*. Springfield: Charles C. Thomas.

Fisher, R., Geiselman, R. and Amador, M. (1989). Field test of the cognitive interview: Enhancing the recollection of actual victims and witnesses of crime. *Journal of Applied Psychology, 74*, 722–727.

Flin, R. (1996). *Sitting in the hot seat*. New York: John Wiley & Sons.

Fritzon, K., Canter, D. and Wilton, Z. (2001). The application of an action systems model to destructive behaviour: The examples of arson and terrorism. *Behavioural Sciences and the Law, 19* (5–6), 657–690.

Godlewski, J. (1987). Typologia zgwalcen/Typology of rapes. *Psychiatria Polska, 21* (4), 296–301.

Groth, A.N., Burgess, A.W. and Holmstrom, L.L. (1977). Rape: Power, anger and sexuality. *American Journal of Psychiatry, 134*, 1239–1243.

Gudjonsson, G. (1984). A new scale of interrogative suggestibility. *Personality and Individual Differences, 5* (3), 303–314.

Gudjonsson, G. (2001). False confession. *Psychologist, 14* (11), 588–591.

Gudjonsson, G. and MacKeith, J. (1988). Retracted confessions: Legal, psychological and psychiatric aspects. *Medical Science Law, 28*, 187–194.

Gudjonsson, G., Rutter, S. and Clare, I. (1995). The relationship between suggestibility and anxiety among suspects detained at police stations. *Psychological Medicine*, *25* (4), 875–878.

Guttman, L. (1954). A new approach to factor analysis: The radex. In P.F. Lazarsfeld (ed.), *Mathematical thinking in the social sciences*. Glencoe, IL: Free Press.

Haber, R. and Haber, L. (2000). Experiencing, remembering and reporting events. *Psychology, Public Policy and Law*, *6* (4), 1057–1097.

Hargreaves, J. and Canter, D. (in press). Stalking behaviour. In D.V. Canter and L.J. Alison (eds), *Profiling rape and murder*. Offender Profiling Series, Vol V. Aldershot: Ashgate.

Hazelwood, R. and Douglas, J. (1980). The last murderer. *FBI Law Enforcement Bulletin*, April 1–5.

Hodge, S. (2000). A multivariate model of serial sexual murder. In D.V. Canter and L.J. Alison (eds), *Profiling rape and murder*. Offender Profiling Series, Vol V. Aldershot: Ashgate.

Homant, R. and Kennedy, D. (1998). Psychological aspects of crime scene profiling. *Criminal Justice and Behavior*, *25* (3), 319–343.

Klein, M. (1984). Offence specialisation and versatility among juveniles. *British Journal of Criminology*, *24*, 185–194.

Kleiner, M. (1999). The Psychophysiology of deception and the orienting response. In D.V. Canter and L.J. Alison (eds), *Interviewing and deception*. Offender Profiling Series, Vol I. Aldershot: Ashgate.

Koehn, C., Fisher, R. and Cutler, B. (1999). Using cognitive interviewing to construct facial composites. In D.V. Canter and L.J. Alison (eds), *Interviewing and deception*. Offender Profiling Series, Vol I. Aldershot: Ashgate.

Lobato, A. (2000). Criminal weapon use in Brazil: A psychological analysis. In D.V. Canter and L.J. Alison (eds), *Profiling property crimes*. Offender Profiling Series, Vol IV. Aldershot: Ashgate.

Meehl, P.E. (1954). *Clinical versus statistical prediction: A theoretical analysis and a review of the evidence*. Minneapolis: University of Minnesota Press.

Merry, S. and Harsent, L. (2000). Intruders, pilferers, raiders and invaders: The interpersonal dimension of burglary. In D.V. Canter and L.J. Alison (eds), *Profiling property crimes*. Offender Profiling Series, Vol IV. Aldershot: Ashgate.

Mikkelsen, E., Gutheil, T. and Emens, M. (1992). False sexual abuse allegations by children and adolescents: Contextual factors and clinical subtypes. *American Journal of Psychotherapy*, *46* (4), 556–570.

Missen, C. (2000). *Taking life: A behavioural approach to the classification of serial killers*. Virgin.

Muller, D.A. (2000). Criminal profiling: Real science or just wishful thinking? *Homicide Studies*, *4*, (3), 234–264.

Munsell, A. (1960). *Munsell book of colour*. Baltimore: Munsell Color Company Inc.

Plutchik, R. and Conte, H.R. (eds) (1997). *Circumplex models of personality and emotions*. Washington DC: American Psychological Association.

Ressler, R.K., Burgess, A.W. and Douglas, J.E. (1988). *Sexual homicide: Patterns and motives*. Lexington, MA: Lexington Books.

Salfati, C.G. and Canter, D. (1999). Differentiating stranger murders: Profiling offender characteristics from behavioral styles. *Journal of Behavioural Sciences and the Law*, *17*, 391–406.

Shye, S. (1985). Nonmetric multivariate models for behavioural action systems. In D.V. Canter (ed.), *Facet theory*. New York: Springer-Verlag.

Stone, M. (1989). Murder. *Psychiatric Clinics of North America*, *12* (3), 643–651.

Tate, C., Warren, A. and Hess, T. (1992). Adults' liability for children's 'lie-ablity': Can adults coach children to lie successfully? In S. Ceci et al. (eds), *Cognitive and social factors in early deception*. Hillsdale, NJ: Lawrence Erlabaum Associates.

Tufte, E. (1997). *Visual explanations*. Cheshire, Connecticut: Graphics Press.

Undeutsch, U. (1989). The development of statement reliability analysis. In J. Yuille (ed.), *Credibility assessment*. Norwell, MA: Kluwer Academic Publishers.

Wagstaff, G. (1984). The enhancement of witness memory by hypnosis: A review and method-ological critique of the experimental literature. *British Journal of Experimental and Clinical Hypnosis*, 2 (1), 3–12.

Webb, E.J., Campbell, D.T., Schwartz, R.D. and Sechrest, L. (1966). *Unobtrusive measures: Non-reactive research in the social sciences*. Chicago: Rand McNally.

Wilson, A. and Donald, I. (1999). Ram raiding: Criminals working in groups. In D.V. Canter and L.J. Alison (eds), *The social psychology of crime: Teams, groups, networks*. Offender Profiling Series, Vol III. Aldershot: Ashgate.

Chapter 2.5

Uses, Misuses and Implications for Crime Data

University of Portsmouth, UK

INTRODUCTION

Imagine if people tried to measure things with rulers made of elastic that could be stretched like a rubber band. Although the inches would be marked out clearly the 'measurement' would be determined by how far the 'ruler' was stretched. There could be no standard measurement. An inch would mean what you wanted it to mean. Comparison and statistical analysis would be meaningless. This is analogous to the situation with crime data. Is it not incredible that we have no standard means of measurement of the extent of crime in our society? What people choose to report to the police combined with wide variations in what the police choose to record as crime means that we are measuring crime with the equivalent of an elastic ruler. Yet instead of providing a government health warning on the unreliability of recorded crime statistics we find that great store is set by them, especially by politicians. The Home Secretary for England and Wales announced a White Paper on 5 December 2001, *Policing A New Century: A Blueprint for Reform*. This comprehensive document sets out as policy objectives a fall in the official crime statistics in recorded crime and an improvement in the percentage of recorded crimes that are detected. A new Standards Unit will be created in the Home Office to drive up these performance standards.

Given the unreliability of recorded crime data it is worrying that a statutory performance management regime has been created, and is now about to be reinforced, that relies on performance indicators based on spurious crime statistics as the main means of measuring the relative effectiveness of police forces and the divisions or basic command units within them. This is exacerbated by importance being placed on small fluctuations in the data when no attempt is made to determine whether such movement has reached a level of statistical significance or is just random

Handbook of Psychology in Legal Contexts, Second Edition
Edited by D. Carson and R. Bull. © 2003 John Wiley & Sons, Ltd.

variation. Our current use of crime statistics can therefore at best only be described as rough-and-ready, crude and lacking in the basic requirements of scientific measurement, namely standardisation and the use of techniques to establish statistical significance.

This paper will therefore seek to examine:

- the reliable measurement of crime

- police recording practices

- the need for 'Quality of Life' indicators for community safety

- more realistic action plans in each District Authority in England and Wales to manage crime and reduce the level of recidivism as required by the Crime and Disorder Act 1998.

POLICE RECORDED CRIME STATISTICS ARE JUST THE TIP OF THE ICEBERG

Historical Context

There are no official statistics for crime in England before 1805. The first statistics related only to those cases that had been committed for trial. In the first half of the nineteenth century, Parliament passed a series of measures to encourage prosecutors. Between 1805 and 1842 the number of trials in higher courts rose seven-fold, while the population increased only by half. After the commencement of the new series of criminal statistics in 1857, the number of higher court trials could be seen to dwindle as much greater use was made of summary hearings; nonetheless, the total number of cases heard both summarily and in the higher courts remained remarkably constant at about 55,000 per year until about 1925. According to historical analysis this stagnation of indictable prosecutions was largely encouraged by the general belief that outputs should not 'exceed the usual average' (Taylor, 1998). Parsimony also had the unintended consequence of shaping the developing police service so that it had increasingly to undertake the role of prosecutor, especially in less serious offences, something which continued until the 1980s and the introduction of the Crown Prosecution Service established by the Prosecution of Offences Act 1985. The preoccupation with prosecution in minor offences was at the expense of the new police in the nineteenth century developing skills required to investigate offences and even the most serious offences, such as murder were unlikely to be properly investigated (Taylor, 1998).

From 1834 the government classified crime statistics according to six crime types:

- Offences against the person (ranging from homicide to assault)

- Offences against property involving violence.

- Offences against property without violence.

- Malicious offences against property (arson, machine-breaking).

- Offences against currency.

- A miscellaneous category (including riot and treason).

In 1856 criminal statistics were further developed to include the following three categories:

- Indictable (the most serious) offences reported to the police.

- Committals for trial (both on indictment and before summary jurisdiction).

- The number of persons convicted and imprisoned.

According to Emsley (1994) there has been considerable debate over the value of these statistics for historians, who have argued that since we cannot be sure why crimes were reported and prosecuted, and because of variations in recording practices across police jurisdictions, the figures are worthless for historical analysis. Even contemporary commentators were sceptical. Whilst the true extent of indictable crime can never be known, Taylor (1998), draws attention to a lawyer in 1860 who suggested that if the criminal statistics were correct when they showed 134,922 criminals at large, and if they each committed one crime a week this would make 'about seven millions' serious crimes each year rather than the 57,868 recorded in the statistics. Taylor points out that this would mean that Victorian levels would have been higher than the levels reported in the 1990s. The gap between real and reported levels of crime in society was reflected in the kind of things the early police did which was to concentrate on minor public order offences such as those contained in the Vagrancy Act of 1824 which dealt with 'rogues', 'vagabonds' and 'suspected persons', the detritus from early urbanisation and the Napoleonic wars. Taylor argues,

> Thus, the legacy of the early years of preventive policing was to create in constables almost a 'zero tolerance' of anyone who looked like he might at some time upset ratepayers. At the same time it created a helpless tolerance of most indictable crimes after they were committed. (Taylor, 1999, pp. 115–116)

Much higher levels of crime than that reflected in the criminal statistics more closely fits with contemporary descriptions and perceptions of offenders. By the 1840s the offender had become a member of the 'dangerous classes' lurking in the urban rookeries and slums; by the 1860s the term 'criminal classes' was rather more in vogue (Stevenson, 1983). Social commentators made forays into the rookeries of the criminal classes and Emsley (1987) argues that those labelled as the criminal classes were often the poorest of the poor. With their poor diet and shabby clothing they looked different from the growing middle classes for whom the poor were categorised and described as if they were members of strange tribes in far-away lands (Emsley, 1987). Criminals might be characterised as those who shunned hard work and enjoyed the vagrant life, but they were also increasingly understood as individuals who turned to crime because of mental and physical, as well as moral degeneracy: defects generally passed on through heredity (Emsley, 1994). The feckless poor was to remain a theme of crime control all the way through to more recent concerns about social exclusion, but the actual criminal activity of offenders was never to be reflected in the government statistics for offences. These have always been kept artificially low in order to manage public perceptions.

An example of the manipulated and misleading nature of criminal statistics is the fact that 'there were 91,671 indictable offences known to the police in 1857 and 50 years later in 1906, despite a trebling of police numbers, a doubling of the population, major changes to criminal law and procedure, rapid urbanisation and industrialisation, and other enormous social upheavals, this had fallen by just *six* crimes to 91,665' (Taylor, 1998, p. 583). From the very beginning of the modern police service we have had police managers, bureaucrats and politicians taking credit for their efficiency in keeping crime statistics low.

Following the 2001 United Kingdom general election the 'New Labour' government signalled its intention to reform the delivery of public services. A key position as far as the police service in England and Wales is concerned is the newly created post in the Home Office of Director, Police Standards Unit. According to the advertisement for the post, the post-holder will 'implement new approaches, based on what works on the ground and will engage with the police at every level, to support their work in building a safer community' (*Economist*, 1 September 2001). According to the recruitment brief (Pricewaterhousecoopers, 2001) the new Director will be expected to produce significant and measurable improvements over a range of areas and the first of these is in:

- *Variations in tackling crime—in clear-up and detection rates and in recent success in reducing different categories of crime:*

This, of course, begs the question of how reliable will the crime data be on which these improvements in performance are to be measured? The evidence from successive British Crime Surveys conducted since 1982 shows that the masking of the true crime rate in official criminal statistics is not confined to the Victorians. Nearly two hundred years preoccupation with bogus numbers has also militated against identifying and addressing the true causes of crime and diverted resources away from successful intervention. Psychological and criminological researchers therefore need to apply great caution to the use made of crime statistics by way of explanation for phenomena being investigated.

EVIDENCE FROM SUCCESSIVE BRITISH CRIME SURVEYS SINCE 1982

Perhaps the most significant recent observation on the subject of crime data is the divergence between crime statistics published by the government, produced from information supplied by forces, and those, which are published by the government from the results obtained in the British Crime Survey (BCS). The BCS measures crimes against people living in private households in England and Wales and has been conducted eight times since 1982. According to the BCS there were 11,297,000 crimes in 1999 as against 2,573,000 for a comparable subset of crimes recorded by the police. This means that only 23% of crimes against private individuals and their households ended up as crimes recorded by the police. There is therefore a dark figure which represents 77% of all crime which respondents say they experienced that does not feature in the published police statistics. The difference between the extent of crime according to police and BCS figures has been known since the first survey in 1982. Despite this the public debate on the prevalence of crime invariably takes place on the basis of statistics published by the relevant government departments including the Home Office or Audit Commission, which have been supplied by the police themselves. It is particularly worrying that the knowledge that the police statistics are a very distorted data set has been in the public domain for nearly two decades and yet it rarely informs the media, public debate or policy formulation. This chapter will address the shortcomings of crime data derived from police forces in England and Wales. Furthermore concerns about the accuracy of statistics produced by the police apply in other countries makes international comparison problematic, for example similar concerns have been raised about the very low official recorded crime rate in Japan (Finch, 1999, 2001).

BCS Methodology

The BCS measures are based on estimates from a sample of the population. The estimates are therefore subject to sampling error. The sample is more complete than police crime statistics because it covers unreported and unrecorded crime. It should give a reliable indication of the trends in many of the crimes in which a member of the public is a victim because the survey is always conducted in the same way. It is therefore unaffected by changes in the level of reporting to police or changes in police recording practice, including changes to the guidance issued by the Home Office specifying precisely what can be classified as a crime, the so-called 'counting rules' (Home Office, 1998; see also Povey and Prime, 1999). Allowing for sampling error it is estimated that the BCS findings lay within a range where there is a 90% chance that the true value lies (Kershaw et al., 2000). For the 2000 survey face-to-face interviews were conducted mainly between January and April 2000. The nationally representative sample consisted of 19,411 people aged 16 and above, together with a further ethnic sample of 3874. The Home Office has decided that, from 2001, the survey will be conducted annually and the sample size will be increased to 40,000.

Comparisons can only be made between the BCS data and a subset of the recorded crime statistics. This is because the BCS does not include crimes where the victim is less than 16 years, where the offence was committed in commercial or public sector premises and where the victim is in an institution or homeless. The BCS does not measure victimless crime, crimes where the victim is not available for interview, fraud or sexual offences. It does, however, collect information on the effects of crime and the variance in the level of risk of crime for different groups. The 2001 BCS shows that there has been a 21% fall in overall crime since 1977 and a 12% reduction in the year from 1999 to 2000. The BCS estimates indicate that the chance of becoming a victim of crime has fallen to its lowest since the introduction of the BCS 20 years ago (Kershaw et al., 2001).

In contrast the police recorded crime data are concerned with number of arrests, the total number of crimes reported and the number of crimes detected and by what method. This provides a 'clear-up' rate that is considered to be the most important measure of effectiveness, despite being easily manipulated. It can only ever be a measure of failure because no account is taken in these statistics of the number of people or premises within a particular area who were not victimised. The figures do not take account of how many victims in the official crime statistics have been victimised more than once. This inflates the number of apparent victims and masks the fact that the majority of crime is concentrated in particular geographic areas and that a proportion of victims are offended against repeatedly (Everson and Pease, 2001).

UNREPORTED VOLUME CRIME

For the comparable subset of crimes the BCS found that only 41% were said by victims to have been reported to the police. Reporting varies according to the type of crime. Theft of a vehicle was reported on 95% of occasions, whereas theft of property from a motor vehicle was only reported on 47% of instances. Similarly, burglary with loss was reported on 81% of occasions whereas attempted burglary and those with no loss were only reported on 49% of instances. Common assault was the least reported crime in the subset at 29%.

In 46% of incidents respondents said that they did not report to the police because they did not consider the offence to be serious enough or they considered the loss to be too trivial. In 30% of cases they did not consider the police could do much about it. In 22% of cases the victim considered that it was a private matter. This was particularly true of violent crime, including domestic violence. The BCS does not seem to have identified fear of reprisal by the offender as a factor in victims not reporting a crime to the police.

UNREPORTED SERIOUS CRIME

Unlike the police statistics, the BCS includes a measure to assess the seriousness of crime on a scale where 0 represents a minor offence and 20 represents murder. The surveys have shown that there is a consensus between people in judgements about seriousness. However, there is much variation within crime categories, with large standard deviations in ratings of seriousness. This may reflect that not only does the impact vary between victims but also that large variations are perceived in seriousness within an offence category. Seriousness ratings appeared to be influenced by financial loss and degree of injury. Those crimes considered to be serious were more likely to get reported. Nevertheless the 2000 Survey found that nearly 6.5 million crimes went unreported to the police, of which nearly 3 million were considered to be serious. The recording shortfall is larger for common assault, no-loss burglaries and theft from the person.

THE SHORTFALL IN RECORDING CRIME REPORTED TO THE POLICE

Another reason for the gap between the BCS and police statistics is the attrition between reporting a crime to the police and it becoming recorded by the police. Calculations, using the BCS sample, indicate that there may have been a 13% shortfall in recording the theft of a motor vehicle reported to the police and a 23% shortfall in recording a burglary with loss. In attempted burglaries and those with no loss the shortfall was 67% next to common assault at 72%. Only 8% of all common assaults get into the police statistics and only 18% of robberies.

REASONS FOR THE GAP BETWEEN SURVEY DATA AND CRIMES RECORDED BY THE POLICE

There may be limitations to accuracy imposed by the current sample size of the BCS and increasing the sampling size will reduce these. Although error variance could be a factor it appears probable that it must surely only be a small one. A more likely explanation, for the gap between the amount of crime reported to the police according to the BCS and the amount that is ultimately recorded by the police in the Criminal Statistics is the difficulty in comparing crimes recorded in two incompatible classification systems. The strength of the BCS data is that the coding system has remained the same since the first survey in 1982. However there have been variations to the Home Office counting rules for crimes recorded by the police which has affected recording practices making comparisons over time difficult, if not impossible.

It could be the case that the unreported crimes, that are being identified in the BCS, did not happen and respondents are either wittingly or unwittingly providing corrupt data. Or respondents could simply be mistaken about what action was taken to report the matter to the police. Because of the difference in the dataset the police could on investigation have recorded the crime in a classification outside the comparable subset. This would mean that although reported and recorded, this was not picked up by the BCS thus inflating the unrecorded findings. However by far and away the biggest factor is police discretion about what to record as a crime.

POLICE DISCRETION IN RECORDING REPORTED CRIME

Burrows and colleagues (2000) assessed the recording policies and practices in 10 police forces. They then went on to investigate, in more depth is five of those forces, what happened when calls involving crime allegations were made to the police by members of the public, and whether they were recorded as crimes and, if not, why not. They found that there was no standard practice and that the way that a crime report originates varies between forces. Forces have different arrangements for dealing with telephone calls from the public, a crucial distinction being between forces which operate 'single tier' and 'two-tier' control rooms, i.e. whether all calls go to one central point or to a number of local points usually at the basic command unit level. Methods of creating crime reports varied, some forces have officers telephoning the details to a central in-putting bureau, others have the officer entering the details themselves on the force computerized crime-recording system. Burrows and colleagues found, however, that most forces still rely on officers preparing hand-written reports, which are subsequently put onto the crime-recording system by others, usually civilian in-puters.

In some forces the police officer is able to assign a crime classification. In others this is restricted to a small number of people in a crime management unit. In two forces they found that it took days for a crime report to materialise, providing opportunities for data manipulation and consequences for crime analysis based on incomplete data. The guidance on the criteria to be applied to recording incidents as crimes is contained in the government's 'Counting Rules' published by the Home Office (Home Office, 1998). This is a massive and arcane document that defies comprehension by all except those individuals steeped in its usage. Most forces do not provide further guidance on what is to be recorded as a crime (HMIC, 2000).

Two models of crime recording were identified by Burrows that were described as '*prima facie*' and '*evidential*'. Forces adopting the *prima facie* model recorded details of the allegation without scrutiny. Forces adopting the *evidential* model require the details to be substantiated before a crime is accepted and recorded in their statistics, creating spurious significant improvements in these force's clear-up rates. When the evidential model is used, alternative crime recording systems can co-exist along with the one used for statistical purposes. Such systems are used to track the journey of an 'incident' being recorded to it subsequently being accepted and recorded as a crime if it passes the evidential test.

The Home Office requirements for the counting of recorded crime are set out in *Criminal Statistics Volume 1, Counting Rules for Recordable Offences (1998)*. In addition, there is a set of rules for counting 'Offences Recorded as Cleared Up' contained within '*Home Office Criminal Statistics, Volume iv. Annual Miscellaneous Returns (1998)*' which contains 12 rules. As long as one rule has been satisfied, any crime which the police are required to notify to the Home Office may be counted as 'detected' or cleared-up.

When Burrows tracked calls made to the police they found that only 47% of crime allegations, made by a member of the public, were eventually recorded as crimes. They also noted that changes to the counting rules, made in 1998, meant that a series of crimes against one victim would be recorded as only one offence, whereas the BCS would count this as a number of occurrences.

Previous research by Bottomley and Coleman (1981) had identified police practices used to reduce the number of crimes recorded. The practice is known as 'cuffing' of crimes. An example would be where a victim alleges that her purse was stolen but the police record the allegation of theft as lost property. The disparity in the recording practices between forces was examined by Farrington and Dowds (1985). They found that, in Nottinghamshire, there was a higher 'true' crime rate as indicated by the BCS than in two neighbouring forces. They found the main reasons for this was the greater number of crimes originating from interviews with offenders who make a number of 'coughs' or admissions, including those to offences of stealing property of very little value.

Manipulating the Clear-up Rate

Success within a performance culture is demonstrated by falling levels of recorded crime and improved clear-up rates, based on the number of admissions (or 'clear-ups') to offences divided by the total number of recorded crimes. Both measures are easily manipulated. Through practices that encourage the 'cuffing' of crime, illustrated above, the true level of victimisation can be minimised. Similarly, as shown above, the number of admissions can be increased. This can happen within the Home Office counting rules when forces obtain admissions for trivial offences, often from juvenile offenders. 'Coughing' also occurs when sentenced prisoners are visited in prison and encouraged to admit to offences that were not dealt with by the court. Her Majesty's Inspector of Constabulary conducted a survey (HMIC, 1996) which showed that crimes which were classified as 'no crime' or 'criminal damage' in one force would be classified as 'burglary' in another. The clear-up rate is therefore not a robust and standardised measurement and cannot be an accurate proxy for comparing performance through league tables of recorded crime or clear-up rates.

When the HMIC revisited this subject in 2000 they found that the average non-recording rate in forces was 24%. Most forces did not have a structured programme for training staff in crime recording. They found that most forces were employing an evidential test of 'beyond reasonable doubt' to record a crime but that officers also went beyond challenging and validating a crime. The officers took into consideration factors such as whether the victim had been cooperative, could the victim be contacted, could the offence be detected and would the Crown Prosecution be likely to prosecute.

These factors are irrelevant to the decision about whether a crime should have been recorded. New guidance from the Association of Chief Police Officers has introduced, from 2001, a new test for determining whether an incident is recorded as a crime which is to be based on the 'balance of probabilities' that a crime occurred. It is difficult to see how this guidance will change a culture where key performance information is routinely manipulated.

FEW QUALITY ASSURANCES PROCESSES FOR POLICE DATA

The HMIC Report (2000) went on to identify that there is a problem with the accuracy of police data in other systems such as the Police National Computer which deals with convicted and wanted persons and the related (Phoenix) intelligence system. The nub of the problem seems to be the quality of police data with few quality assurance processes coupled with a longstanding culture which militates against accurate data being recorded. This has serious implications under Data Protection legislation requiring accurate and relevant data.

THE IMPLICATIONS OF MISLEADING CRIME DATA: RUBBISH IN, RUBBISH OUT

Incompatible Technology

At a time when commercial organisations are making use of enterprise-wide resource planning systems, which integrate the various databases required for managing the business, police information technology is still in functional silos. One consequence of this is that information that first comes to the attention of the police and is logged as an incident on a Command and Control system may never be transferred to the crime-reporting system. The attrition rate from this alone could amount to between 7% and 22% of all incidents that should have become recorded as crimes (HMIC, 2000). Any analysis based purely on crime data is therefore unlikely to portray a clear picture of actual police workload which consists of a wide range of non-crime activities such as tracing missing people and recording traffic accidents.

Different Social Consequences between Responding to a Survey and Reporting a Crime to the Police

The social consequences of reporting an incident some time after the crime, to a researcher on behalf of the BCS, are completely different from the consequences of reporting it to the police. For this reason there will always be a deficit between BCS and recorded crime data that will reflect the decision-making of victims and the exercise of their discretion. One partner in a domestic violence situation may be willing to confide in a researcher, appreciating the anonymity of the survey, but wish the matter to remain private. At the other end of the scale a victim may be too terrified of making a formal complaint to the police for fear of the consequences from non-familial offenders who live in the same neighbourhood. The ease with which the public can contact the police may have a bearing on overall reporting rates, especially for the very poor who may not have access to telephones or cannot afford the cost of travel to report in person to a police station.

NO WEIGHTING OF RECORDED CRIME

It is unfortunate that the debate about crime is taking place on the basis of ordinal data within categories with no account taken of the nature of the crime. For example, in the overall crime statistics, one murder has the same value as one case of shoplifting. The seriousness scale adopted for the BCS (see above) is a step in the right direction, but it is too simplistic. When assessing the seriousness of a crime will the criteria to determine seriousness be objective (e.g. this kind of crime merits this score) or will it be subjective (e.g. this albeit minor crime had a serious negative impact on the quality of my life), in which case seriousness will simply become a matter of opinion. Although an offence may appear trivial, for example verbal abuse, does it become serious if there are aggravating factors such as racism?

There is a growing academic interest in Quality of Life indicators covering life in general, social, environment, health and crime (Sirgy, 1998). It should be possible, on the basis of analysis of the available data, to develop a similar methodology that would give an indication of the level of risk that applies to a particular neighbourhood. Not surprisingly the BCS shows high levels of correlation between crime and other indices of urban deprivation. Similarly, profiles could be provided from the BCS data of the surveyed as against the perceived level of risk based upon victim profiles. According to the BCS, levels of worry are higher among those living in high crime areas, recent victims, those who consider it likely they will become victimised, and those who are socially or economically vulnerable. The survey found that 6% of respondents said that fear of crime greatly affects their quality of life. About 20% were 'very worried' about burglary, car crime, mugging, physical attack by a stranger, and rape. This kind of analysis would allow for a sensible dialogue about the perceived risk of victimisation as compared with the surveyed level of risk.

CRIME DATA AS A PERFORMANCE MEASURE

Any rise in crime recorded by police forces is interpreted as evidence of failure, with much humiliation when the data are published in the national and local media. Is it not unjust to penalise the police for rises in recorded crime when the BCS has revealed that perhaps as much as three-quarters of crime is actually hidden? Should not the police be encouraged to close the gap further between the two datasets although they will never close the gap completely since a proportion of crime is not reported to either of them? Rises in recorded crime happen, for example, when forces introduce policies that create an environment that gives confidence to victims to come forward and report 'hidden' crime such as sexual assaults, child abuse, racial and domestic violence. Can it be right that this is then construed as a 'failure'? Perhaps the BCS alone should be used as the measure of crime for the purpose of social policy and that police-generated statistics be used entirely for police operational and tactical purposes. This shift is particularly important since governments increasingly articulate a multi-agency approach and stress the role that the public and other agencies can play in the prevention of crime.

The government's 'Best Value' regime, as set out in the Local Government Act 1999, contains a range of Key Performance Indicators for the police. Many are based on recorded crime statistics. There is therefore a perverse incentive for forces to find ways of minimising the number of reports of crime that actually make it to the recorded crime statistics. Forces now have too much vested interest in the consequences of recorded crime data for them to be allowed to continue to have the responsibility for collecting the information, which will be used for key performance indicator measurement, and benchmarking against other forces. In July 2000 the United Kingdom Prime Minister, Tony Blair, called a meeting with a group of Chief Constables apparently because the crime rate was rising for the first time in six years. This was not helpful for a government, heading towards an election, that had pledged to be 'tough on crime, tough on the causes of crime' (*Independent*, 4 December 1993). Much was apparently made of the gap between the 'best' and 'worst' force clear-up rates, indicating little understanding of the misleading and crude nature of the statistics about which the Prime Minister was exercised. This was despite the existence of government reports providing abundant evidence that the figures being discussed were unreliable.

Williamson responded to an article in *The Economist* (1 July 2000) analysing the rise in the crime rate by drawing attention to the different recording practices used by forces and argued that:

> As individual forces have such a vested interest in crime rates, it might be better to eschew the current practice and extend the use of the British Crime Survey. Though costly, it would provide independence, integrity and allow for meaningful comparison. To be 'tough on crime, tough on the causes of crime' is good, but Tony Blair needs to be tough on crime statistics too. (Williamson, 2000)

The UK government's White Paper on Police Reform acknowledges the problem of the lack of accuracy of the crime data that will be used for performance measurement. The paper states that 'it will not be nationally proclaimed statistics, but change on the ground, a recognition that something substantial is happening to secure confidence and provide reassurance which will be the measure of success' (para. 1.14). The White Paper addresses the decline in detection and conviction rates. England and Wales have one of the highest victimisation rates within Europe although crime levels have been falling in all European countries over the last five years (para. 1.34) and it is stated in the White Paper that 'Part of the decline in conviction rates undoubtedly reflects better ethical standards in recording crime' (para. 1.35). The desired step change in overall police effectiveness is to come from 'Catching persistent and serious criminals and deterring future crimes' and 'not pursuing prosecutions for the most trivial matters merely to boost conviction rates' (para. 1.36).

Smith (1995) drawing on experience from a range of performance indicator schemes in the public sector identifies eight consequences of publishing performance data that are not necessarily intended, and which are likely to be dysfunctional. The phenomena identified are as follows:

- Tunnel vision

- Suboptimisation

- Myopia

- Measure fixation

- Misrepresentation

- Misinterpretation

- Gaming

- Ossification.

Smith argues that performance indicator schemes will fail unless serious consideration is given to the unintended behavioural consequences of publishing performance data, and he describes the following 10 strategies for minimising the risks:

- Involve staff at all levels.

- Retain flexibility in the use of PIs.

- Quantify every objective.

- Keep the system under constant review.

- Measure client satisfaction.

- Seek expert interpretation of PIs.

- Maintain a careful audit of the data.

- Nurture a long-term career perspective.

- Keep the number of indicators small.

- Develop independent benchmarks.

It remains to be seen whether the new Standards Unit in the Home Office will adopt a narrow view of performance management with all the attendant risks identified by Smith or a broader view that seeks to identify and minimise the risks and encourage a learning culture.

Discussions of police performance usually takes place without acknowledging either the environmental context or the resources being made available. Any discussion of relative efficiency and effectiveness must take these factors into consideration. Carr-Hill (2000) argues that current police resource allocation models are flawed because variations between Police Authorities funding is likely to be a reflection of historical variations in policies and practices than the real 'need for policing'. He argues that multi-level modelling can be developed which shows the relationship between a number of socio-economic variables which affect reported fear of crime. This holds out the prospect that formulae could be developed that better describe relative police efficiency and effectiveness taking into account resources and environment. Such formulae would provide a better link between resources and policy objective outputs described in the White Paper than the narrow focus on crime detection rates.

'PROBLEM SOLVING POLICING' AND ANALYSIS HAMPERED BY UNRECORDED CRIME

More Extensive Use of Surveys using the BCS Methodology

If we do not know about, perhaps, three-quarters of the crime which members of the public are prepared to make known to the British Crime Survey, any analysis of crime data, based purely on reported crime, is going to be inadequate. The Crime and Disorder Act 1998 places a statutory duty on all the 'relevant authorities' to conduct a crime audit in their area and from that develop a 'crime reduction action plan'. Performance against the action plan will then be audited. Because of the current size of the BCS sample it may not be possible to provide data for each Crime and Disorder partnership. However, as such partnerships are required to conduct another audit by 2002, it would be possible for these audits to be conducted under the aegis of the BCS with each partnership buying into the 2002 survey. Instead, it seems likely that most surveys will be superficial and will not use the BCS methodology to benefit from the rich picture it provides. The information gained is unlikely to provide the evidential basis for a true problem-solving approach to crime reduction. The reliance on unreliable recorded crime data will continue.

'Intelligence led Policing' and Geographic Profiling Limited by Lack of Data

Any form of analysis including geographic profiling is going to be limited by the lack of complete, timely and accurate data. This in turn will limit 'intelligence led policing' which is an integral part of the current 'problem-solving' policing philosophy (Read and Tilley, 2000). It is ironic that the adoption of these two major policing theories has not generated any widespread concern about the poor-quality data that are relied on for strategic and tactical analysis. Lack of timeliness and missing data must pose a serious question about the value of the information created by analytic activity.

Special Problems with Analysis of Serious Crimes of Violence

Violent crime accounts for approximately 7% of recorded crime statistics, and of this only a very small number of crimes fall into the category of being very serious, such as extreme violence or rape. This means that in the BCS sweeps there are insufficient serious cases for any meaningful analysis at this stage, although the larger samples sizes in future years may assist in collecting sufficient cases for analysis.

The available data on serious violent crimes have been of a poor quality. A number of factors compromise the quality of such data, including:

- the accuracy of recall from victim statements, especially if they have been the victim of a particularly traumatic crime (e.g. Grubin, Kelly and Bransdon, 2000);

- the reliability of eyewitness statements (e.g. Kebbell and Wagstaff, 1999);

- variations in both interviewing techniques and statement-taking across police forces will affect the amount and quality of information obtained concerning a crime (Clarke and Milne, 2001);

- the loss of the primary data source in homicides as there is no victim available to question;

- identifying what data should be collected has proved problematic as there are often conflicting requirements and low levels of compliance by forces in providing the data;

- variation can also come from the large numbers of people required in data collection and coding;

- inconsistent coding;

- missing information;

- updating and maintaining the data collected.

This problem is particularly acute in relation to homicide. In the United Kingdom most of what we know about the characteristics of homicide is taken from the Home Office Homicide Index (HI). A similar dataset on homicides, in Scotland, is maintained by the Scottish Executive. The Homicide Index is primarily an administrative database that collects details of incidents initially recorded as homicide by the police. The Index was started in 1967, with modifications made to the scope of the information in both 1977 and 1995 and is maintained by the Home Office's Research, Development and Statistics Department.

The Homicide Index may offer an important contribution to assisting the investigation of hard-to-solve homicides by allowing investigators to consider the characteristics of an individual case against detected cases with similar characteristics. The use of national datasets is not new. The database known as CATCHEM, which is maintained by the Derbyshire Constabulary, contains the records of child homicide victims from 1960 to date (Aitken et al., 1995). The database known as BADMAN, which is maintained by the Surrey Constabulary, provides support in respect of child homicide offenders and stranger rapists. The National Crime Faculty has been established at Bramshill, the United Kingdom's national police college, to provide an analytical capability to deal with serious violent crimes but these data are not published. The Serious Crime Analysis Section (SCAS) conducts comparative case analysis on murder, rape and abduction cases that fall within certain criteria. It is based on the Violent Crime Analysis System (ViCLAS) developed by the Canadian government and stores details of relevant offences covering 126 variables. Use of these databases can assist in identifying lines of enquiry and reduce the time taken to investigate serious crime. Empirical data sets have an important role to play in the investigation and analysis of serious crime but they are dependent on police forces supplying the relevant information and this has required the creation of rigorous quality control processes. Serious crime databases can identify the likely geographical relationship between an offence and an offender (Davies and Dale, 1996), the relationship between an offence and the conviction history of an offender (Davies, Wittebrod and Jackson, 1998) and the probable characteristics of the offender for given crime types (Aitken et al., 1995). These databases provide a good example of the use that can be made of crime data if there are sufficient controls over the quality of the data. See the chapter, in this *Handbook*, by Canter for illustration of the importance of quality crime data, including geographic, for effective crime investigation.

THE WAY FORWARD

In addition to improving the quality and timeliness of the recorded crime data a more effective way forward would make greater use of the BCS methodology to provide a richer picture of crime in a particular locality. It would also make better use of findings from criminological research to reduce recidivism.

Increase the Use of BCS Methodology at the Local Level

A Crime and Disorder Partnership audit that was based on BCS methodology would provide a richer picture of the actual crime experienced by people in a particular community. Unlike police recorded crime statistics, where all offences carry the same weight, it would be possible to provide an index of seriousness of the offences committed. A profile of the victims would show the level of risk of becoming a victim for specific categories of crime. The level of risk would vary by geographic areas across the partnership and by time of day. For example, the level of risk in a busy conurbation shopping area at two o'clock in the afternoon would be very different from that at two o'clock in the morning, when clubs and pubs are closing. By using the BCS methodology an action plan could be prepared which was truly evidence based. Then performance on the action plan could be monitored by external bodies including the Crime Directors attached to the Government Offices in the Regions of England and Wales. The crime audits are intended to be conducted on a three-year cycle. The intention would be for all the relevant partners to have achieved a genuine reduction in the level of crimes over that period, as measured by the surveys.

More Effective Use of Criminological Research

Farrington (2001) traces the antecedents of the new philosophies reflected in the Crime and Disorder Act 1998. He classifies major methods of crime prevention into categories with reference to papers that best sum up one of four particular approaches.

1. Developmental prevention, which is designed to inhibit criminal potential by targeting those people at highest risk and using protective factors discovered in studies of human development (Tremblay and Craig, 1995).

2. Community prevention, which is designed to change the social conditions such as families, peers, social norms and organisations that influence offending in communities (Hope, 1995).

3. Situational prevention, which targets the physical environment in order to reduce opportunities for crime (Clarke, 1995).

4. Criminal justice prevention, which refers to traditional deterrence, incapacitation and rehabilitation strategies operated by criminal justice agencies (Tonry and Farrington, 1995).

Farrington argues that, over the last 25 years, successive Home Secretaries for England and Wales have emphasised situational and criminal justice prevention rather than tackling the root causes of crime, which can be addressed in developmental and community prevention approaches.

Criminological research has shown that key risk factors for offending can be identified at an early age. Farrington (1996) includes impulsiveness, low school attainment, poor parental supervision, and harsh or erratic parental discipline. Experimental studies have shown that these can be successfully tackled in early intervention programmes and later offending can be reduced.

The intervention programmes operated by Youth Offending Teams are targeted at detected offenders who are already recidivists. Farrington (2001) submits that

'Nationally and locally, there is no agency whose primary mandate is the early prevention of offending' (p. 183).

The government's White Paper on Police Reform in England and Wales (Blunkett, 2001) estimates that there are approximately one million active offenders in the general population at any one time and that, of these, 100,000 will accumulate more than three convictions during their criminal careers. Tackling persistent offenders is therefore a public policy priority. The White Paper acknowledges that persistent offenders share a common profile:

> Half are under 21 and nearly three quarters started offending between 13 sand 15. The peak age for persistent offenders is 24. Nearly two thirds of them are hard drug users. More than a third were in care as children. Half have no qualifications at all and nearly half have been excluded from school. Three quarters have no work and little or no legal income.

The government announces in the White Paper that it has established a Persistent Offender Task Force with the police to determine how best to deliver their manifesto goal of, within 10 years, doubling the chance of a persistent offender being caught and punished. The paper does not indicate what form the strategy will take, other than being 'hands-on' and that there will be a persistent offender strategy to be implemented in each of the criminal justice agencies at local level.

The Crime and Disorder Partnership Action Plan could specifically address the issue of recidivism. Successful early intervention programmes would reduce the level of offending and some American schemes have shown a seven to one return on the investment (Schweinhart, Barnes and Weikart, 1993). Some of the most disturbed offenders, from the most disadvantaged backgrounds, will need to go through the worthwhile intervention programmes operated by the Youth Offending teams. Such an approach would open up new ways of preventing early offending, for example, through Restorative Justice policies with the police having a much wider social inclusion role rather than a narrow, sterile focus on recorded crime. Restorative Justice has the support of the Association of Chief Police Officers (ACPO) who consider Restorative Justice to be a process which 'seeks to balance the concerns of the victim and the community with the need to reintegrate the offender into society. It seeks to assist the recovery of the victim and enable all parties with a stake in the justice process to participate fully in it' (Standards for Restorative Justice; ACPO, 2001). Participation in education and restorative justice approaches holds out the prospect of genuine reduction in levels of crime. (See the chapter, in this *Handbook*, by Drogin and colleagues, discussing Restorative Justice.)

The government has also established The Youth Justice Board that is tasked with delivering the target of halving the time it takes from arrest to sentence of persistent young offenders from 142 days to 71 by May 2002. The figures as of June 2001 showed that the average time from arrest to sentence had fallen to 69 days (Youth Justice Board, 2001). The Board monitors the operation of the youth justice system, promotes good practice and oversees a range of initiatives designed to prevent offending by children and young persons and works with those who are, or are at risk of, becoming offenders.

At the highest level of organised crime there is a small group in most communities who are career criminals and rarely feature in the official crime statistics, yet they can be responsible, for example through the drugs trade, for much of the low-level crime which does get into the official crime statistics. There are no key performance indicators for tackling this kind of criminal. The government White Paper on Police Reform estimates (para. 3.53) that in 2000 there were about 800 organised criminal groups known to be active in the UK, not necessarily confined to any one particular area or serious criminal activity, but often involved in several. Some 400 major criminals were believed to be in possession of assets of around £440 million that were the proceeds of crime. An estimated 30 tonnes of heroin and 40 tonnes of cocaine are trafficked annually to the UK for consumption there. This level of consumption translates directly into the high level of repeat offenders (nearly two-thirds) who are hard drug users. The White Paper states that the new Standards Unit in the Home Office will be tasked to advise on measures of effectiveness that police forces should work to in fighting organised crime (para. 3.58). The White paper therefore holds out the prospect of better links between agencies to reduce local and organised crime. It is, however, difficult to see how this aspiration can be achieved within the existing structure of 43 independent police forces with considerable discontinuity of scale in size of forces from the very small to extremely large metropolitan forces, where size will clearly be a limiting factor in the ability to effectively tackle organised crime.

CONCLUSION

There is unequivocal evidence that the official recorded crime statistics are unreliable. This has major implications for their use in measuring the performance of police forces. The continued use of league tables, of relative performance of forces, based on problematic data and the use of the crime clear-up rate is nothing short of being knowingly stupid. The over-reliance on the crime clear-up rate also encourages unethical behaviour by the police. Nor is it a fair measure of performance. Worst of all it does nothing to inform the public. Instead it is counterproductive in that it exacerbates the fear of crime in all our communities, very often to way beyond the level of real risk. It skews performance away from policies that address the real causes of crime in our communities. It concentrates scarce police resources on the trivial whilst totally ignoring the effects of serious and organised crime. The clear-up rate encourages unethical recording by the police to minimise the amount of crime recorded, 'cuffing', and artificially inflate the number of crimes 'cleared-up'. Multi-level modelling techniques can be developed that can better describe relative police performance taking into consideration resources and socio-demographic variables. Databases for serious crime show that good-quality crime data can be very useful in solving crime and doing so more quickly. The misuses of crime data will have to be recognized and addressed before we can move on to more effective interventions in tackling crime.

The Crime and Disorder Act 1998 in England and Wales was predicated on the fact that the police alone cannot stop crime and the Act required a partnership approach. It is therefore perverse that the psychological and criminological research which points the way for more effective interventions has been largely ignored, particularly with regard to the early prevention of offending. The White Paper on Police Reform in England and Wales contains commitments to address the prevention of offending by children and young persons and to work with those who are at risk of becoming offenders. Good government should have evidence based policies and practices and government's ignore the available evidence at their peril when they appear to concentrate on minimising the number of offences that get into the official statistics. When this becomes the focus of government policy they end up managing an illusion and not the reality of crime, with interventions that become increasingly dysfunctional.

The time has come for the crime clear-up rate to be consigned to the rubbish bin, for criminological and psychological research to be taken seriously by politicians, policy-makers and practitioners, and for researchers to take a more critical approach to their use of crime data. The present arrangements represent a very significant waste of resources and opportunities. There is an opportunity to develop a set of 'Quality of Life' indicators for community safety that better describes a set of preferred policy outcomes that more realistically reflect people's experience of crime. Meanwhile, all of us, and researchers in particular, should treat official criminal statistics with great caution. The Latin maxim, *caveat emptor*, applies.

ACKNOWLEDGEMENTS

I would like to acknowledge the valuable assistance which I have received from Dr Howard Taylor, Gonville and Gais College, University of Cambridge, regarding nineteenth- and twentieth-century criminal statistics and also Dr Nicky Smith, National Crime Faculty, National Police College, Bramshill, Hamsphire, England, for her assistance regarding the use of crime data in analysing serious crime.

REFERENCES

ACPO (2001). *Restorative justice investigated.* London: Association of Chief Police Officers.

Aitken, C., Connolly, T., Gammerman, A., Zhang, G. and Oldfield, R. (1995). *Predicting an offender's characteristics: An evaluation of statistical modeling.* Police Research Group Special Interest Series, Paper Number 4. London: Home Office.

Blunkett, D. (2001). *Policing a new century: A blueprint for reform.* Cm 5236. London: Home Office.

Bottomley, A.K. and Coleman, C.A. (1981). *Understanding crime rates.* Farnborough: Gower.

Burrows, J.M., Tarling, R., Mackie, A. and Taylor, G. (2000). *Review of police forces' crime recording practices.* Home Office Research Study No 204. London: Home Office.

Carr-Hill, R. (2000). Developing a robust resource allocation formulae for police. *Policing and Society, 10,* 235–261.

Clarke, R.V. (1995). Situational crime prevention. In R.E. Tonry and D.P. Farrington (eds), *Building a safer society: Strategic approaches to crime prevention*. Chicago: Chicago University Press.

Clarke, C. and Milne, R. (2001). National evaluation of the PEACE investigative interviewing course. Home Office Police Research Award Scheme. London: Home Office.

Davies, A. and Dale, A. (1996). *Locating the stranger rapist.* Police Research Group Special Interest Series, Paper Number 3. London: Home Office.

Davies, A., Wittebrod, K. and Jackson, J. (1998). *Predicting the criminal record of a stranger rapist.* Police Research Group Special Interest Series, Paper Number 12. London: Home Office.

Everson, S. and Pease, K. (2001). Crime against the same person and place: detection opportunity and offender targeting. In R.V. Clarke, G. Farrell and K. Pease (eds), *Repeat victimisation.* Crime Prevention Studies, Vol. 12. New York: Criminal Justice Press.

Emsley, C. (1987). *Crime and society in England, 1750–1900.* London: Longman.

Emsley, C. (1994). The history of crime and crime control institutions, c1770–c.1945. In M. Maguire, R. Morgan and R. Reiner (eds), *The Oxford handbook of criminology.* Oxford: Oxford University Press.

Farrington, D. (2001), Crime prevention action plan. *The Psychologist, 14* (4).

Farrington, D. and Dowds, E. (1985). Disentangling criminal behaviour and police reaction. In D. Farrington and J. Gunn (eds), *Reactions to crime: The public, the police, courts and prisons.* Chichester: John Wiley & Sons.

Farrington, D.P. (1996). *Understanding and preventing youth crime.* York: Joseph Rowntree Foundation.

Finch, A.J. (1999). The Japanese police's claim to efficiency: A critical view. *Modern Asian Studies, 33,* (2), 483–511.

Finch, A.J. (2001). Homicide in contemporary Japan. *British Journal of Criminology, 41,* 219–235.

Grubin, G., Kelly, P. and Brunsdon, C. (2001). *Linking serious sexual assaults through behaviour.* Home Office Research Study 214. London: Home Office.

Her Majesty's Inspectorate of Constabulary (1996). *A review of crime recording practices.* London: Home Office.

Her Majesty's Inspectorate of Constabulary (2000). *On the Record. Thematic Inspection on Police Crime Recording. The Police National Computer and Phoenix Intelligence System Data Quality.* Home Office. London.

Home Office (1998). *Counting rules for recorded crime.* Vol. 1: *Counting rules for recordable offences.* Vol. IV: *Annual miscellaneous returns.* Instructions for Police Forces. Home Office. London.

Hope, T. (1995). Community crime prevention. In R.E. Tonry and D.P. Farrington (eds), *Building a safer society: Strategic approaches to crime prevention.* Chicago: Chicago University Press.

Kebbel, M. and Wagstaff, G. (1999). *Face value: Evaluating the accuracy of eyewitness information.* Police Research Series Paper 102. London: Home Office.

Kershaw, C., Budd, T., Kinshott, G., Mattinson, J., Mayhew, P. and Myhill, A. (2000). *The 2000 British crime survey England and Wales.* Home Office National Statistical Bulletin 18/00. London: Home Office.

Kershaw, C., Chivite-Mathews, N., Thomas, R. and Aust, R. (2001). *The British crime survey, first results, England and Wales.* Home Office Statistical Bulletin 18/01. London: Home Office.

Povey, D. and Prime, J. (1999). *Recorded crime statistics: England and Wales.* April 1998 to March 1999. Home Office Statistical Bulletin 18/99. London: Home Office.

Pricewaterhousecoopers (2001). *Recruitment brief for Director of Police Standards Unit.*

Read, T. and Tilley, N. (2000). *Not rocket science? Problem-solving and crime reduction.* Crime Reduction Research Series Paper 6. London: Home Office.

Schweinhart, L.J., Barnes, H.V. and Weikart, D.P. (1993). *Significant benefits: The High/Scope Perry pre-school study through age 27.* Ypsilanti, MI: High/Scope Press.

Sirgy, M.J. (1998). *QOL Research: Classic articles, books, reviews, and other important works*. Blacksburg, Virginia: The International Society for Quality-of-Life Studies.

Smith, P. (1995). On the unintended consequences of publishing performance data in the public sector. *International Journal of Public Administration*, *18* (2 and 3), 277–310.

Stevenson, S.J. (1983). *The criminal class in the mid-Victorian city: A study of policy conducted with special reference to those made subject to the provisions of 34 and 35 Vict.c. 112 (1871) in Birmingham and East London in the early years of registration and supervision*. D.Phil. Thesis, University of Oxford.

Taylor, H. (1998). Rationing crime: the political economy of criminal statistics since the 1850's. *Economic History Review*, *LI 3*, 569–590.

Taylor, H. (1999). Forging the job: A crisis of 'modernization' or redundancy for the police in England and Wales, 1900–39. *British Journal of Criminology*, *39* (1). *The Economist* (2000, July 1). Crime looms larger. London: The Economist.

Tonry, R.E. and Farrington D.P. (1995). Strategic approaches to crime prevention. In R.E. Tonry and D.P. Farrington (eds), *Building a safer society: Strategic approaches to crime prevention*. Chicago: Chicago University Press.

Tremblay, R.E. and Craig, W.M. (1995). Developmental crime prevention. In R.E. Tonry and D.P. Farrington (eds), *Building a safer society: Strategic approaches to crime prevention*. Chicago: Chicago University Press.

Williamson, T.M. (2000). Letter to *The Economist* 22 July 2000 'Police Evidence' London: The Economist.

Youth Justice Board (2001). Annual report for 2001. Home Office.

Chapter 2.6

Crime Prevention

Katarina Fritzon
University of Surrey, UK
and
Andrea Watts
National Crime Faculty, UK

> *The basic mission for which the Police exist is to prevent Crime and Disorder as an alternative to the repression of crime and disorder by military force and severity of punishment.*
>
> (Sir Robert Peel, 1829; cited in Home Office, 1987)

In the UK, the recognition of crime as a political as well as a social problem dates back to the mid-nineteenth century when the Prime Minister, Sir Robert Peel, introduced the Police Service as a crime prevention measure. At that stage the approach of the police was essentially reactive, with 'bobbies on the beat' representing one of the earliest forms of what has become known as *situational* crime prevention.

Over the years, shifting government agendas have influenced the approach taken to crime prevention, with academic debate often reflecting the socio-political *zeitgeist*. For example, prior to the First World War, early positivist perspectives that saw crime as a product of individual dispositions, were more acceptable to the Establishment than focusing on the social and environmental conditions that could give rise to crime (Blackburn, 1993). Later, in the United States, the identification of so-called 'delinquency areas' characterised by poverty and decay (e.g. Shaw and McKay, 1931) led to a presumption that targeting school drop-outs, disadvantaged youth, minority group members, etc., would ameliorate the increasing crime rates (Kobrin, 1959). This 'social positivism' was in turn criticised for focusing on conditions that could not easily be altered. In an important paradigm shift, criminologists such as James Q. Wilson (e.g. Wilson and Herrnstein, 1985) advocated the implementation of policies aiming to alter 'objective conditions', for example the reduction of opportunities for offending. This led to the formulation of the 'routine activities' (Cohen and Felson, 1979) and 'rational choice' perspectives (Cornish and Clarke, 1986) which were influential in the development of situational crime prevention measures. In recent

Handbook of Psychology in Legal Contexts, Second Edition
Edited by D. Carson and R. Bull. © 2003 John Wiley & Sons, Ltd.

years, however, government thinking appears to have come full circle, with the funding of research to identify 'risk factors' for future offending, and the recognition that intervention at the individual level can be seen as 'doing good *now* rather than waiting for long-term and uncertain outcomes' (Hope, 2000, p. xxi).

This chapter outlines the major theoretical approaches to crime prevention, citing examples of successful intervention measures, and concludes by offering the possibility of a framework through which the apparent polarisation of the individual versus situational crime prevention perspectives can be integrated. The implications for the criminal justice system of such an approach to crime prevention are also discussed.

PREVENTION OF DELINQUENCY

Home Office (the British government department responsible for the criminal justice system) research shows that one in two males and one in three females admit to having committed an offence (Audit Commission, 1999). More strikingly in self-report studies, only 2–4% of juveniles claim *never* to have committed an offence (cited in Baldry and Winkel, 2001, p. 35). Given the growing rate at which juveniles appear to be committing crime of an increasingly serious nature, a substantial body of literature has begun to focus on the possibility of early intervention to prevent future criminality (Graham, 1998). Thus the emphasis of this work is on identifying those who are at risk of offending at an early stage. Among the most influential in this field is the pioneering work of David Farrington who found evidence for the continuity of antisocial behaviour (e.g. Farrington, 1994). Mirroring the early thinking of criminologists such as Lombroso (1911) and Burt (1925), research such as the Cambridge Study on Delinquent Development ('the Cambridge study') achieved predictive power through long-term follow-up, allowing for the identification of individual factors at specific stages of development. By tracking a group of boys from 8 years old until they were 32, this research showed, for example, that teacher ratings of problem behaviour in young children were strongly related to criminal behaviour in later years (Farrington, 1989). This consistency in behaviour implied that, to an extent, certain individuals have a disposition to commit crime and that by intervening at an early stage these *pre*-dispositions could be altered. Such an intervention, it is argued, is more likely to be successful the earlier it is implemented (Le Blanc and Loeber, 1993). In fact, Farrington (1994) advocates prenatal and perinatal interventions, such as the prevention of substance abuse, leading to concomitant reductions in the problems associated with low birth weight and pregnancy complications.

So, what are the main factors that have been found to characterise young delinquents or potential delinquents? One consistent finding is of problems in relation to moral development, connected specifically with an inability to take the perspective of another (Baldry and Winkel, 2001). The inability to empathise appropriately with another's psychological state forms the basis for most treatment programmes for sex offenders

(Hills, 2001) and is therefore implicated in the development of at least certain forms of criminal behaviour. This has contributed to the formulation of the method of 'restorative justice' (e.g. Wright, 1996) which has the double aim of allowing victims the opportunity for confrontation, as well as forcing the offender to face up to the psychological and/or physical effects of their actions.

In addition to personality characteristics, there are other factors that have been found to increase the risk of offending, including low intelligence, high impulsivity and hyperactivity, poor parenting, poverty and the influence of a delinquent social environment, including family members, friends, school or neighbourhood (Farrington, 2001). These lead to the possibility of intervention at both the individual, family and community level, which is the aim of the current UK government's policies on community safety partnerships and multi-agency working. There have been a number of attempts to address factors operating at the level of the individual and his or her immediate social environment, leading to both successful and unsuccessful crime prevention initiatives. Some of these are outlined below, but for more comprehensive reviews, see Graham (1998) and Hope (2000).

CRIME PREVENTION AND THE INDIVIDUAL

An early attempt to prevent delinquency was the Cambridge–Somerville Youth Study of the 1940s. Boys aged 5 to 13, who were 'difficult' or 'average' in their social behaviour, received personal and social counselling for an average of five years. However, at follow-up after 30 years there were no differences between this group and those who had not received the intervention in terms of adult criminal history, with many of the experimental group having committed two or more crimes (McCord, 1978). Where this particular venture failed, perhaps, was in not being clear about the specific focus of the intervention. It seems that subsequently more successful programmes have had more targeted goals, for example, in relation to improving academic performance (Bry, 1982; Schweinhart and Weikart, 1980) or cognitive skills (Ross, Fabiano and Ewles, 1988).

The importance of effecting positive change has also been highlighted by the failure of punitive interventions such as corporal punishment, suspension from school, and fear arousal (Gottfredson, 1986). Such approaches seek to prohibit the unwanted behaviour but leave the individual without the skills to achieve viable alternative solutions.

Crime prevention initiatives at the individual level have been classified as family-based, school-based and peer group-based (Graham, 1998). Successful interventions from the former category include the famous Perry pre-school programme (Schweinhart and Weikart, 1980) which targeted both children and their parents from low socio-economic families. Providing training in parenting skills is another form of family intervention, with successful examples including Patterson (1982) in the USA, and Utting (1996; unpublished study cited in Graham, 1998) in the UK. Both have achieved improvements in children's behaviour by showing the parents how to enforce discipline without physical punishments or threats.

School-based interventions include the 'Effective Schools Project' (Gottfredson, 1987) which was aimed at changing the organisation and ethos of the schools, including improving the clarity of rules and the consistency with which they were enforced. This parallels the implication of harsh and inconsistent parenting in the development of delinquency (Farrington, 1996) and highlights the importance of providing safe and predictable boundaries for children. Anti-bullying initiatives are based on the premise that school bullies often become serious violent offenders, and also often raise children who subsequently become bullies themselves (Farrington, 1993). In the UK a number of initiatives have decreased the incidence of bullying in schools (e.g. Pitts and Smith, 1995) and in Norway reductions in anti-social behaviour outside of school have also been achieved (Olweus, 1990).

The difficulty of influencing the association with criminal peer groups is highlighted by the lack of successful initiatives that have attempted this (Graham, 1998). However, one example is the South Baltimore Youth Centre project where young people at risk form an extended family with youth workers. The success of this scheme was evaluated by Baker and colleagues (1995) who found that serious delinquent behaviour among those on the programme decreased by a third, over a period of 19 months, compared to the control group.

Proponents of the dispositional approach to crime prevention have argued for its cost-effectiveness, not only in terms of reducing offending, but also in relation to other social problems linked with criminality, such as substance abuse, family violence, school failure and unemployment (Farrington, 1994). However, because the long-term effects of such interventions are not always known, coupled with the recognition that crime, like any behaviour, is a product of the interaction between a person and a situation, it is also inevitably important to also consider crime prevention initiatives targeted at the reduction of the opportunities to commit crime.

OPPORTUNITY THEORIES OF CRIME

While preventative attempts have traditionally directed an influence at the individual level, situational approaches aim to reduce the opportunities for criminality by altering the relationship between the victim, the offender and the environment (Nietzel and Heimlein, 1986).

This group of theories address the ways in which the opportunity to commit crime contributes to criminality. They became popular in the 1960s and 1970s as a result of an increase in the crime rate, particularly in the USA, which was attributed to changes in the *routine activities* of the population (Cohen and Felson, 1979). These changes were argued to be creating more opportunities for crime to occur.

From a practical perspective, opportunity theories provide a framework to assist crime prevention practitioners in developing workable solutions to prevent specific crime problems. Understanding the influence that opportunity plays in criminal behaviour has important implications for the routine crime prevention work undertaken by police and other agencies and for crime policy and practice.

The fundamental principle underlying opportunity theories is that behaviour is a product of an interaction between the individual and context/setting, emphasising the importance of situational 'cues' which act as a catalyst to translate criminal inclinations into action. Research from the field of environmental criminology such as Newman's (1972) concept of 'defensible space' and 'crime prevention through environmental design' (CPTED) (Jeffery, 1971) focuses on the criminal opportunities provided by the environment. Newman, Jeffery and their followers generated important knowledge regarding the application of the principles of designing out crime in the environment. This broadened the responsibility for crime prevention to include housing planners, architects and manufacturers, so that better designs were implemented for the way people use space. The existence of both environmental opportunities and personal opportunities are thus argued to create more favourable conditions for crime to occur.

To test the theory that opportunities can cause crime, the famous 'Character Education Enquiry' in America in the 1920s included an experiment where children were given the opportunity to cheat on tests, to lie about cheating and to steal coins from puzzles used. The study found that most of the children behaved dishonestly at least some of the time (Hartshorne and May, 1928). In adults, a more recent experiment conducted by Farrington and Knight (1980) showed that letters which were 'found' by participants were less likely to be posted if they contained money. Interestingly, the participants were also less likely to post letters addressed to females rather than males. This was interpreted as providing evidence for the process of making a considered decision as to whether to respond to temptation.

The importance of opportunity in predicting criminality is also highlighted by several examples of policy implementation that reduced crime by removing opportunities. The best known of these was the introduction of mandatory steering locks for all cars in Germany in the 1960s. This had the immediate effect of reducing car thefts. In the UK, however, the requirement for steering locks was made only for new cars. It resulted in a reduction in theft of new cars, but older cars were more frequently stolen (Mayhew, Clarke and Hough, 1980). Similarly, in Sweden the introduction in 1971 of photographic proof of identity when paying with cheques, and later by credit card, brought a dramatic reduction in the theft of these items. (cited in Knutsson, 1998).

Crime Pattern Theory

Research from the field of Environmental Criminology considers the way in which criminals use their environment and move around both spatially and temporally. The concept behind crime pattern theory is that local crime patterns reveal how people interact with their physical environment to produce criminal opportunities (Brantingham and Brantingham, 1984).

Offenders search for crime targets around personal activity *nodes* (points travelled to and from) and the *paths* among them. These nodes and paths are also the locations where people fall victim to crime. Crime pattern theory focuses on the geographical distribution of crime and the daily rhythm of activity, generating crime maps for various times of day and days of the week, for example, linking crime to commuter flows, school closing times and night life.

Some crimes have been shown to be more likely to occur at the *edges* of activity due to the merging of people from different neighbourhoods; these include racial attacks, robbery and shoplifting. Although criminals generally commit crimes close to home, others find it safer to operate at the boundaries of their activity space. This distinction between 'insiders' and 'outsiders' highlights the importance of *edges* in allowing offenders to maintain anonymity whilst having an awareness of escape routes.

Crime pattern theory and environmental criminology generally, have shown that the design and management of areas can produce major shifts in crime rates. This is reflected in the Home Office Secured by Design (SBD) initiative, which is an award scheme run buy the Association of Chief Police Officers (ACPO). The emphasis is on domestic burglary, where in order to achieve SBD status a housing development must incorporate certain design and management features as well as meeting standards of physical security. These features are based upon the principles of crime pattern theory and include: the creation of 'defensible space', 'informal social control', 'territoriality', the removal of 'offender anonymity' as well as maximising surveillance and minimising access/egress routes.

Secured by Design has been evaluated within West Yorkshire by the Home Office Research, Development and Statistics Directorate (Armitage, 2000) with the main findings being that both fear of crime and recorded crime was significantly lower on both new build and refurbished SBD housing estates (26% fewer crime events per dwelling).

Routine Activity Theory

Observing that crime rates in the United States in the 1960s increased despite the amelioration of adverse social and economic conditions, Cohen and Felson (1979) provided an alternative explanation for these trends. They argued that changes in the *routine activities* of Americans, specifically decreases in household and family activities and increases in activities occurring away from home, led to increases in criminal opportunities.

Routine activity theory (RAT) argues that 'the convergence in time and space of suitable targets and the absence of capable guardians can lead to large increases in crime rates without any increase or change in the structural conditions that motivate individuals to engage in crime' (Cohen and Felson, 1979, p. 589). This theory does not so much ignore the disposition of an individual to commit crime, as take the existence of criminal inclination for granted. For example, the recent increase in mobile telephone theft in the UK is regarded as being due to the number of users displaying their telephones in public places, together with the absence of safety features. It follows from the assumptions made by RAT, that crime can increase without there necessarily being an increase in the numbers of criminals. Fluctuations in the overall crime rate can be due to an increase of suitable targets, or a decrease in suitable guardians, without any increase in criminal motivation.

The level of explanation for routine activity theory is thus at the societal level in that predictions about general trends in crime rates can be made from the three basic assumptions about the way in which the legal activities of everyday life provide an opportunity structure for criminal activities. In this way, RAT differs from the third major opportunity theory, the *rational choice* perspective, in which the individual considerations of criminals are examined in relation to the specific opportunities for crime that are acted upon.

The Rational Choice Perspective

The point of departure of this approach from traditional dispositional theories of criminality was their tendency to 'over-pathologise' offending and discount its rational components (Clarke, 1980). This in effect hindered attempts to devise improved crime control strategies, due to a lack of specific focus towards particular subgroups of offence and offender.

Instead, the rational choice perspective advocates that crime be considered as the outcome of decisions made by the offender. Subjective states and thought processes will be influenced by immediate situational variables as well as by the personal circumstances of the individual, and this, it is argued, renders unproductive the notion of a generalised disposition to offend. Due to this change of emphasis on understanding criminal behaviour, the rational choice perspective highlights the need to conduct more crime-specific analysis of criminal behaviour, looking at the criminal event itself and the situational factors influencing its commission.

Cornish and Clarke (1986) discuss the emergence of the rational choice perspective and the development of policy-relevant research. In the 1970s and 1980s they, and other researchers at the Home Office, conducted research examining institutional treatments for delinquents. Their findings supported the importance of the influence of immediate environmental variables including social inducements and opportunities in determining delinquency. This approach therefore focuses on offenders' decision-making processes, while recognising that 'rationality' will vary between offenders and offences. The main assumption, however, is that offending is purposive behaviour designed to benefit the offender.

The rational choice theory itself does not commit to a particular model of decision-making. However, recent studies have tended to support a view of *limited rationality* (e.g. Carroll, 1982) suggesting that criminals do not take account of all the information about a potential crime before making a decision as to whether or not to commit the crime. There can be a number of situational and psychological constraints which limit their rationality.

Proponents of this approach argue that various crime choices are driven by a particular motive within a specific setting, which offers the opportunity to satisfy that motive. For each offence category a different calculus has to made. If we look at categories of vehicle crime for example, the rationality of 'joy riders' will be affected by whether a car is fun to drive and has good acceleration, whereas 'choppers' will choose a car with parts that are valuable for resale (Felson and Clarke, 1998).

This is similar to the principles of routine activity theory in which various dimensions are considered when making a decision that a target is suitable. Rational choice argues that criminal decision-making is largely based on that which is most evident and immediate, failing to consider the more remote costs and benefits of crime or its avoidance. This is reflected in the commonly held belief that a large percentage of crime is considered to be opportunistic, and criminals impulsive. For example, drug users who commit theft are not so concerned with the long-term impact of drug use or the possibility of being caught and punished for stealing, so much as with the immediate gratification offered by obtaining money to buy more drugs (Felson and Clarke, 1998).

The two models of routine activities and rational choice differ in scope but are mutually supportive regarding the preventative measures that they suggest. Both assume that the situation is an important determining factor in criminal activity and this has led to a variety of measures designed to reduce the opportunities offered.

SITUATIONAL CRIME PREVENTION

Clarke (1992) defines situational crime prevention as, '. . . a preventative approach that relies, not upon improving society or its institutions, but simply upon reducing opportunities for crime' (p. 5).

This reduction of opportunities is essentially achieved via the manipulation or modification of the environment as exemplified in ACPO's Secured by Design (SBD) award scheme (see Armitage, 2000). Situational crime prevention measures are founded on four fundamental mechanisms: increasing the perceived effort, increasing the perceived risks, reducing the anticipated rewards, and removing excuses (Knutsson, 1998). The fourth of these involves increasing the moral costs of the illegal act. This can be achieved by stimulating feelings of either guilt or shame by employing internal or external mechanisms respectively (Wortley, 1996).

The most common form of situational prevention is target-hardening through reducing anonymity, maximising surveillance and reducing number of alternative escape routes. These measures change the cost–benefit balance of a crime by increasing the perceived effort involved in perpetrating it. In order to achieve Secured by Design status, necessary standards of door and window security, lighting levels and the design and layout of a development must be achieved. These provide improved opportunities for natural surveillance, decrease the number of possible escape routes, and promote territoriality. Offender anonymity is reduced, and thereby the perceived cost to the offender, in terms of potential capture, is increased.

One of the main criticisms of such forms of situational crime prevention measures is that they can lead to the *displacement* of crime. This was seen in the previously cited example of the introduction of steering locks for new cars in the UK (Mayhew et al., 1980). In his consideration of the issue of displacement, Clarke (1980) argues that the category of offences classed as 'opportunistic' (e.g. some forms of shoplifting and vandalism) are those least likely to be displaced onto alternative targets by increases in the perceived costs associated with a more immediate target. On the other hand those offenders who are both determined and skilled in their approach to crime—'career criminals'—are less likely to be thwarted by localised target-hardening measures, as they will simply seek alternative opportunities elsewhere.

The existence of such highly motivated offenders, as well as psychological states such as emotional arousal and/or impulsivity, represent an important weakness in situational crime prevention measures. Clarke (1980) recognises that some crime will be beyond the scope of this approach, referring to both determination and heightened emotion. Similarly, Blackburn (1993) suggests that deterrence is more likely to be achieved in relation to *instrumental* crimes, as opposed to *expressive* ones, that do not have a material end.

The existence of categories of offender and offence that are potentially 'immune' represents a problem for crime prevention initiatives and suggests the need for further attention to be paid to the specific interactions between individuals and situations. It is this interaction effect that has not been fully explored in previous models, and provides the possible basis for a unified model of crime prevention.

THE NEED FOR AN INTEGRATED FRAMEWORK

The importance of different motives for crime has not been specifically addressed in the crime prevention literature. Routine activities theory admits that the existence of criminal inclination is taken 'as given', while the rational choice perspective recognises that crime is functional, without examining variations in the form of those functions. The implications for crime prevention of more specific motivational functions for crime have only recently come to light. For example, the offence of burglary was traditionally thought of as a primarily acquisitive crime (e.g. Bennett and Wright,

1984). However, recent research (Merry and Harsent, 2000) has shown that in fact much more complex motives exist for this offence, and that what might superficially appear to be an opportunistic burglary often involves premeditation at some psychological level.

Similarly, research into criminogenic factors operating at the individual level fail to account for the reasons why certain sorts of individuals commit certain sorts of crimes, and why particular targets appear to be more attractive to the 'opportunistic' thief. The failure to consider individual differences may lie at the heart of unsuccessful crime prevention initiatives. Repeat victimisation and displacement of criminal activities in response to target-hardening are other crime prevention issues which appear to call for a more comprehensive understanding of the interaction effect between the motivated offender, the victim and the environment.

The effects of crime prevention initiatives on the motives of offenders are considered by Wortley (1998) who argues that certain measures can actually provoke the behaviour that they are designed to inhibit. For example, the creation of physical barriers to reduce attacks on property or on people (such as in prisons) also leads to psychological barriers and the 'dehumanisation' of victims, rendering them psychologically more acceptable targets (Wortley, 1996). This approach recognises the possibility that the situation itself may precipitate criminal motivations rather than simply presenting an opportunity to enact them. The need for an explanatory framework to understand the interaction between the individual and the environment is thus suggested as an important 'next step' in crime prevention research.

A potentially useful model is derived from the work of Shye (1985) who drew on systemic ideas originally developed from the field of artificial intelligence (Parsons, 1953). The action systems framework establishes a set of 'laws' for understanding the way that social systems interact with their environment. It draws attention to both the sources of these interactions, and the role of the target at which the behaviour is directed. It therefore seems relevant in the present context, described by Ekblom (1999) as an 'evolutionary struggle . . . to keep up with changing opportunities for crime and adaptable offenders' (p. 27).

AN ACTION SYSTEMS APPROACH TO CRIME PREVENTION

In various fields of psychology, action systems models have been applied to studies of quality of life, organisational effectiveness, and the individual as a social unit (Shye, 1985). In general, Shye's work has been concerned with effective system functioning, or 'well designed' action systems. The destructive behaviour of criminals can be seen as modes of dysfunctioning, in other words 'badly designed' or deviant action systems. However, parallel processes between functional and dysfunctional action systems can be hypothesised. Recently, a number of studies by Fritzon and colleagues

Table 2.6.1 Summary of action system modes of functioning

Source of action	Locus of effect	Mode
External	External	Adaptive
External	Internal	Conservative
Internal	External	Expressive
Internal	Internal	Integrative

(e.g. Fritzon, Canter and Wilton, 2001; Fritzon and Garbutt, 2001; Brun and Fritzon, 2002) have identified patterns of criminal activity within particular crime types that correspond to the predictions offered by the model.

When applied to criminal behaviour, this framework provides a unified basis for understanding the way in which an offender's actions are aimed at modifying some aspect of his or her internal or external world. Shye (1985) points out that in order to model action systems it is necessary to consider (a) the sources of the action and (b) the effect or desired target of the action. Both these aspects of the action system can be located internally or externally. Thus the source can be within or outside the acting agent, in this case the criminal. The impact or target can be within the environment or the individual. If we consider crime to be a 'rational choice' on the part of the criminal, therefore, this leads to the proposal that the dominant goal is either to change the state of feeling and experience of the criminal or to modify some external state of the world.

Shye (1985) argues that the combination of (a) the internal and external sources of action with (b) agent or environment as the targets of the action gives rise to four basic modes of functioning of action systems labelled *Adaptive*, *Expressive*, *Integrative* and *Conservative*. The four modes of acting, derived from their two primary facets can be summarised as shown in Table 2.6.1. These can be seen as providing hypotheses for distinguishable forms of interactions between a criminal and his or her environment, as well as specific implications for crime prevention.

Adaptive Mode

This is the mode of action to which Ekblom (1999) refers in relation to the problem of *displacement*. Within this mode, the offender takes his or her cue from the environment as to which opportunities present the best target for criminal activity. At the localised level situational crime prevention measures are effective as they reduce the attractiveness of the environmental target. Offenders within this mode are operating on a principle of 'least effort' (Cornish and Clarke, 1986) and may be the easiest to dissuade from carrying out criminal activities if the costs are perceived to outweigh the benefits. However, displacement occurs when alternative suitable targets exist within their awareness space.

Conservative Mode

The conservative mode is also one in which the environment acts as the source of criminal activity, but here changes to the internal state of the offender are sought. This operational style might give rise to crimes that are motivated by a desire for a sense of power or control. Individuals who commit burglary and/or theft to fund a drug habit can also be seen to be operating in this mode, as can creators of computer viruses who derive no financial benefit from their crimes. Within other crimes it is also possible to find examples of criminals who derive psychological, as well as instrumental, gain from their illegal activities. Crime prevention measures directed at these forms of activity will need to recognise the psychological benefits perceived by the offender, and should seek to modify the target so as to deny these benefits. Alternatively, crime prevention measures operating at the individual level must attempt to reduce the perception of crime as a legitimate means to obtain these benefits. Examples of such interventions include anger-management courses for violent offenders, assertiveness training for arsonists, and attempts to increase victim empathy in domestic violence and sexual offenders.

Criminal actions within this mode will tend to be planned, and have an anticipated impact on a specific person or group of persons that the offender wishes to hurt or remove (Canter and Fritzon, 1998). Therefore, the conservative mode involves directed forms of revenge or retaliation. Often a triggering event can be identified, and again psychological interventions aimed at decreasing impulsiveness and promoting planning and problem-solving skills are designed to be effective against this form of 'reactive' crime.

Expressive Mode

The expressive mode reflects an emotional acting out in which the target is not significant, although it must be suitable for its purpose as a vehicle for the offender's displaced emotion. This form of activity can serve as a form of communication. The targeting that occurs in this mode is of an objectified, symbolic orientation. In previous research (Fritzon et al., 2001) the expressive mode was typical of serial offences. More commonly found in crimes of an interpersonal nature, within this mode we can also account for repeat victimisation, where a suitable target is revisited due to its desirable properties. Again, because of the psychological aspect to this form of offending, situational crime prevention measures that focus on the environment are less likely to be effective, whereas increasing perceived risks and/or the moral costs of crime may dissuade the offender from 'acting out' in this way.

Integrative Mode

This is the hardest mode of functioning to impact by external measures as both the source and target are internal to the agent. In the context of crime, therefore, this represents the small minority of offenders who may be mentally disturbed and who commit crimes driven by impulses with no obvious direct relationship to the targets that they are acted upon. If we accept that this reflects a psychological disintegration of the individual, then crime prevention measures may be effective in early intervention, such as those suggested by Farrington and others (Baldry and Winkel, 2001; Farrington, 1993, 1996). While it is recognised that offences committed by the mentally ill are relatively rare, they seem to nevertheless occupy a disproportionate significance in the public fear of crime, and the media are always quick to highlight 'failures' in the system. Therefore a number of political agendas could be served by directing resources towards interventions that diffuse the burden for affecting psychological change to include the support services, not just the criminal justice system.

SUMMARY AND CONCLUSIONS

This chapter has reviewed existing knowledge relating to models of crime and implications for intervention and prevention. By applying the action systems framework to the area of crime prevention, it has been shown that previous models have tended to emphasise only one aspect of the interaction between an individual who is motivated to commit crime, and the target that is acted upon. Even the rational choice model (Cornish and Clarke, 1986), which does explicitly recognise this interaction, does not fully explore the variations in criminal motivation that seek out targets with psychologically meaningful qualities that may go beyond any conscious decision-making on the part of the offender.

As suggested by Van Dijk (1994), the ultimate implications of this model are that the onus for crime prevention measures must to some extent also be borne by the victims of crime. He advocates government subsidies for private individuals and companies to equip themselves with basic security measures. However, this would still appear to be tackling only particular forms of crime, offences which confer instrumental gain. Certainly 'front-line' measures, such as car and residential security features, can be effective against crimes where the primary source is external to the offender. Equally, however, there may be other aspects of victim behaviour that act as triggers or cues for criminal behaviour in offenders who have internal sources for crime. These are the crimes that can only realistically be prevented at the psychological level, with education programmes aimed at both early intervention, and recognition of the roles of victims in criminal interactions. Indeed, Wortley (1998) makes a similar point in drawing the distinction between precipitation-control for crimes with triggers within the environment, and opportunity-reduction strategies for offenders who enter situations already determined to commit offences.

Finally, many of the previous perspectives on crime prevention were recognisably limited to 'crime' as defined by legal, rather than moral, sanctions. However, the perspective offered by the action systems approach provides principles that can take account of individual interactions within broader socio-moral contexts.

REFERENCES

Armitage, R. (2000). *An evaluation of secured by design housing within West Yorkshire.* Home Office Policing and Reducing Crime Unit, Police Research Series, Briefing Note 7/00.

Audit Commission (1999). *Safety in numbers: Promoting community safety.* London: Audit Commission.

Baker, K. et al. (1995). Violence prevention through informal socialisation: An evaluation of the South Baltimore Youth Centre. *Studies on Crime and Crime Prevention, 4* (1), 61–85.

Baldry, A.C. and Winkel, F.W. (2001). Early prevention of delinquency. In G.B. Traverso and L.Bagnoli (eds), *Psychology and law in a changing world: New trends in theory, practice and research* (pp. 35–49). London: Routledge.

Bennett, T. and Wright, R. (1984). *Burglars and burglary: Prevention and the offender.* Aldershot: Gower Publishing Company.

Blackburn, R. (1993). *The psychology of criminal conduct: Theory, research and practice.* Chichester. John Wiley & Sons.

Brantingham, P.J. and Brantingham, P.L. (1984). *Patterns in crime .* New York: Macmillan.

Brun, A. and Fritzon, K. (2002). Violent deaths in schools: An action systems model. Submitted to *Annals of the American Academy of Political and Social Science* (submitted).

Bry, B.H. (1982). Reducing the incidence of adolescent problems through preventive intervention: One- and five-year follow-up. *American Journal of Community Psychology, 10,* 265–276.

Burt, C. (1925). *The young delinquent.* London: University of London Press.

Canter, D. and Fritzon, K. (1998). Differentiating arsonists: A model of firesetting actions and characteristics. *Legal and Criminological Psychology, 3,* 73–96.

Carroll, J.S. (1982). Committing a crime: the offender's decision. In V.J. Konecni and E. Ebbeson (eds), *The criminal justice system: A socio-psychological analysis.* San Francisco: Freeman.

Clarke, R.V. (1980). Situational crime prevention: Theory and practice. *British Journal of Criminology, 20,* 136–147.

Clarke, R.V. (1992). Introduction. In R.V. Clarke (ed.), *Situational crime prevention: Successful case studies.* Albany, New York: Harrow & Heston.

Cohen, L.E. and Felson, M. (1979). Social change and crime rate trends: A routine activity approach. *American Sociological Review, 44,* 588–608.

Cornish, D.B. and Clarke, R.V. (eds) (1986). *The reasoning criminal. Rational choice perspectives on offending.* New York: Springer-Verlag.

Van Dijk, J.J.M. (1994). Understanding crime rates. *British Journal of Criminology, 34* (2), 105–121.

Ekblom, P. (1999). Can we make crime prevention adaptive by learning from other evolutionary struggles? *Studies on Crime and Crime Prevention, 8* (1), 27–51.

Farrington, D. and Knight, B.J. (1980). Stealing from a 'lost' letter. *Criminal Justice and Behaviour, 7,* 423–436.

Farrington, D. (1989). Early predictors of adolescent aggression and adult violence. *Violence and Victims, 4,* 79–100.

Farrington, D. (1993). Understanding and preventing bullying. In M. Tonry (ed.), *Crime and Justice,* vol. 17 (pp. 381–458). Chicago: University of Chicago Press.

Farrington, D. (1994). Early developmental prevention of juvenile delinquency. *Criminal Behaviour and Mental Health, 4,* 209–227.

Farrington, D. (1996). *Understanding and preventing youth crime.* York: Joseph Rowntree Foundation.

Farrington, D. (2001). The need for a co-ordinated program of cross-national longitudinal research. In G.B. Traverso and L. Bagnoli (eds), *Psychology and law in a changing world: New trends in theory, practice and research* (pp. 19–34). London: Routledge.

Felson, M. and Clarke, R.V. (1998). *Opportunity makes the thief: Practical theory for crime prevention.* In B. Webb (ed.), Home Office Policing and Reducing Crime Unit, Police Research Series, Paper 98.

Fritzon, K., Canter, D. and Wilton, Z. (2001). The application of an actions systems model to destructive behaviour: The examples of arson and terrorism. *Behavioral Science and the Law.*

Fritzon, K. and Garbutt, R. (2001). A fatal interaction: The role of the victim and function of aggression in intrafamilial homicide. *Psychology, Crime and Law*, 7 (4), 309–331.

Gottfredson, D. (1986). An empirical test of school-based environmental and individual interventions to reduce the risk of delinquent behaviour. *Criminology*, 24, 705–731.

Gottfredson, D. (1987). An evaluation of an organisation development approach to reducing school disorder. *Evaluation review*, 11, 739–763.

Graham, J. (1998). What works in preventing criminality. In P. Goldblatt and C. Lewis (eds), *Reducing offending: An assessment of research evidence on ways of dealing with offending behaviour*. Home Office Research Study, 187. London: Home Office, pp. 7–22.

Hartshorne, H. and May, M.A. (1928). *Studies in deceit*. New York: Macmillan.

Hills, A.M. (2001). Empathy and offender behaviour: The motivational context. In G.B. Traverso and L. Bagnoli (eds), *Psychology and law in a changing world: New trends in theory, practice and research* (pp. 51–63). London: Routledge.

Home Office (1987). *The story of our police*. London: HMSO.

Hope, T. (2000). Introduction. In T. Hope (ed.), *Perspectives on crime reduction*. Aldershot: Ashgate Dartmouth.

Jeffery, C.R. (1971). *Crime prevention through environmental design*. Beverly Hills, CA: Sage.

Knutsson, J. (1998). The Swedish experience of situational crime prevention. *Studies on Crime and Crime Prevention*, 7 (2), 189–212.

Kobrin, S. (1959). The Chicago area project—A 25 year assessment. *Annals of the American Academy of Political and Social Science*, 322, 19–29.

Le Blanc, M. and Loeber, R. (1993). Precursors, causes and the development of criminal offending. In: D.F. Hay and A. Angold (eds), *Precursors and causes in development and psychopathology* (pp. 233–265). New York: John Wiley & Sons.

Lombroso, C. (1911). *Crime: Its causes and remedies*. Boston: Little, Brown.

Mayhew, P., Clarke, R.V.G. and Hough, J.M. (1980). Steering column locks and car theft. In R.V.G. Clarke and P. Mayhew (eds), *Designing out crime*. London: HMSO.

McCord, J. (1978). A thirty-year follow-up of treatment effects. *American Psychologist*, 33, 284–289.

Merry, S. and Harsent. L. (2000). Intruders, pilferers, raiders and invaders: The interpersonal dimensions of house burglary. In L. Alison and D. Canter (eds), *Profiling property crimes. Offender profiling series volume IV*, (pp. 31–56). Aldershot: Dartmouth.

Nietzel, M.T. and Heimlein, M.J. (1986). Prevention of crime and delinquency. In B.A. Edelstein and L. Michelson (eds), *Handbook of prevention*. New York: Plenum Press.

Newman, O. (1972). *Defensible space: Crime prevention through urban design*. New York: Macmillan

Olweus, D. (1990). Bullying among school children. In K. Hurrelmann and F. Loesel (eds), *Heath hazards in adolescence. Prevention and intervention in childhood, adolescence*, (pp. 259–297). Berlin: Walter De Gruyter.

Parsons, T. (1953). A revised analytical approach to the theory of social stratification. In R. Bendix and S.M. Lipset (eds), *Class status and power: A reader in social stratification*. Glencoe, Illinois: Free Press.

Patterson, G.R. (1982). *Coercive family process*. Eugene, OR: Castalia.

Pitts, J. and Smith, P. (1995). *Preventing school bullying*. London: Home Office.

Ross, R.R., Fabiano, E.A. and Ewles, C.D. (1988). Reasoning and rehabilitation. *International Journal of Offender Therapy and Comparative Criminology*, 20, 29–35.

Schweinhart, L.J. and Weikart, D.P. (1980). *Young children grow up*. Ypsilanti, MI: High/Scope.

Shaw, C.R. and McKay, D. (1931). *Social factors in juvenile delinquency*. Washington, DC: Government Printing Office.

Shye, S. (1985). Nonmetric multivariate models for behavioural action systems. In D. Canter (ed.), *Facet theory approaches to social reserach*. New York: Springer-Verlag.

Wilson, J.Q. and Herrnstein, R.S. (1985). *Crime and human nature*. New York: Simon & Schuster.

Wortley, R. (1996). Guilt, shame and situational crime prevention. In R. Homel (ed.), *The politics and practice of situational crime prevention. Crime prevention studies vol.5*. Monsey, NY. Criminal Justice Press.

Wortley, R. (1998). A two-stage model of situational crime prevention. *Studies on Crime and Crime Prevention*, 7 (2), 173–188.

Wright, M. (1996). *Justice for victims and offender. A restorative response to crime* (2nd edn). Winchester: Waterside Press.

Chapter 2.7

The Development of Delinquent Behaviour

Friedrich Lösel
University of Erlangen-Nuremberg, Germany

There are numerous theories that explain the origins of delinquent behaviour. Depending on their background, from biology, psychology, sociology, economy, or other disciplines, these theories emphasize different core constructs, hypotheses, and levels of explanation. Here, with leading exponents of the explanations associated, are some examples:

1. Social disadvantage and strain (Merton)

2. Subcultural orientation and normative conflict (Cohen)

3. Social disadvantage and normative conflict (Cloward and Ohlin)

4. Differential association with deviant persons (Sutherland)

5. Social learning (Bandura)

6. Emotional deprivation (Healy and Bronner)

7. Moral orientation (Tapp and Kohlberg)

8. Cognitive neutralization of norms and norm breaking (Sykes and Matza)

9. Social bonding and informal social control (Hirschi)

10. Self-control (Gottfredson and Hirschi)

11. Social information processing (Dodge)

Handbook of Psychology in Legal Contexts, Second Edition
Edited by D. Carson and R. Bull. © 2003 John Wiley & Sons, Ltd.

12. Social attitudes and values (Jessor)

13. Personality factors (Eysenck)

14. Prefrontal brain functioning (Raine)

15. Cognitive deficits (Wilson and Herrnstein)

16. Rational choice (Cornish and Clarke)

17. Situational opportunity and criminal routine activity (Clarke and Felson)

18. Social disorganization (James)

19. Labelling and social segregation (Lemert)

20. Distribution of power in societies (Taylor, Walton and Young).

Many of these explanations are not mutually exclusive but overlap and complement each other. For their integration, a developmental, bio-psycho-social learning perspective seems to be particularly promising (e.g. Farrington, 2000; Gottfredson and Hirschi, 1990; Lösel and Bender, in press; Moffitt, 1993; Sampson and Laub, 1993). This should contain the following issues .

(a) Delinquency is not a static behavioural category but may vary over time and situations.

(b) In explaining delinquent behaviour we must differentiate between various forms and developmental pathways.

(c) Delinquent behaviour is rarely due to a single explanatory variable but results from multiple bio-psycho-social influences.

(d) Even well-designed studies cannot always demonstrate clear causal relationships but only risk factors that enhance the probability of delinquent behaviour.

(e) The development of delinquency depends not only on risk factors but also their interplay with protective factors and mechanisms.

(f) Specific behavioural outcomes can result from different risks (equifinality) and the same risk factors may lead to different outcomes (multifinality).

(g) Factors that are relevant for the onset of delinquent behaviour may differ from those that influence persistence or aggravation.

(h) Delinquent individuals are not only a more or less passive object of biosocial influences but also active constructors of their own development.

(i) Whether an individual exhibits delinquent behaviour depends not only on long-term influences and dispositions but also on situational factors.

(j) The situational risks of delinquent behaviour derive both from objective characteristics and subjective interpretations of the situation and related interactions.

Based on these principles, the present chapter gives a brief overview on developmental pathways of delinquency, their origins and risk factors, the influence of protective mechanisms, the impact of prevention and intervention measures, and situational conditions of offending.

PATHWAYS OF DELINQUENT DEVELOPMENT

One of the best-proven criminological results is the 'age curve' of delinquent behaviour (Blumstein, Farrington and Moitra, 1985; Loeber, Farrington and Waschbusch, 1998). In relation to the population as a whole, young people show a disproportionately much greater level of delinquency. The incidence and prevalence rates of offending rise strongly in early adolescence and peak between ages 16 and 20 (depending on the respective kind of crimes). From early adulthood onwards, the rates of delinquency decreases. This characteristic age curve is not only found in official crime statistics (e.g. police data) but also in self-reports. Although males show much more delinquent behaviour, and in particular more violent crime, the age curve is similar for both sexes. In accordance with earlier maturation, however, female delinquency seems to increase and decrease a little earlier than male delinquency (Stattin and Magnusson, 1996).

The increase of offending in early adolescence is primarily due to youngsters who are registered only once (Farrington, 1992; Wolfgang, Figlio and Sellin, 1972). These are supplemented by a group that offend repeatedly but desist soon from delinquency. Both groups represent an adolescence-limited pathway of delinquent development (Moffitt, 1993). Approximately one-third of all young males become officially registered as having committed a crime. And that must be an underestimate, because many other crimes and individuals are not detected. So this kind of delinquency can be interpreted as a more or less normal transition of youth. Most typical offences are shoplifting, bicycle theft, and other petty property offences. Even cases of violent crime are often not very serious (e.g. robbery of baseball caps from other youngsters; fighting among rival groups).

In contrast to this adolescence-limited delinquency, a small group of 5–8% of young males continue offending into adulthood. It has been found that many of these offenders already exhibited aggression, delinquency, and other conduct problems during childhood (e.g. Farrington and Loeber, 2001; Patterson et al., 1998). Youngsters who follow this early starting, and relatively persistent, pathway of delinquent development are clearly over-represented among serious and violent offenders (Snyder, 2001). In late adolescence and young adulthood, more than half of the offences in each age cohort are due to this group (Loeber et al., 1998; Wolfgang et al., 1972).

Naturally, Moffitt's (1993) differentiation between adolescence-limited and life-course persistent antisocial behaviour does not cover the whole range of delinquent developments in real life. For example, Nagin and Land (1993) found three subgroups in the Cambridge Study on Delinquent Development.

1. *Adolescence-limited.* These have a maximum of delinquency around the age of 16 and mostly no convictions after age 21.

2. *Low-level chronics.* These demonstrate a slowly increasing registration until age 18 and relatively constant recidivism on a low level.

3. *High-level chronics.* These individuals develop a steep increase until age 18 and only a slow decrease in adulthood.

Other models of antisocial development differentiate between specific kinds of problem behavior (Loeber and Stouthamer-Loeber, 1998; Nagin and Tremblay, 1999). Loeber and Hay (1994), for example, suggest three developmental pathways from childhood through adolescence (see Figure 2.7.1).

1. Direct aggressive behaviour, such as bullying, hitting, fighting, cruelty to animals and later assault or rape (*overt antisociality*).

2. More indirect forms of antisocial behaviour such as shoplifting, frequent lying, vandalism, fire setting and later burglary, fraud, or serious theft (*covert antisociality*).

3. Stubborn behaviour, defiance, disobedience, and later truancy, running away, or staying out late (*authority conflict*).

In all three pathways, the proportion of youngsters exhibiting such problem behaviour decreases with age, whereas the severity increases. There are young people who exhibit problem behaviour in all three areas (versatile antisociality). In cases of early starting, this group is equivalent to Moffitt's (1993) description of life-course persistent antisociality. Similarly, Patterson et al. (1998) describe a regular sequence of strong disobedience, anger outbursts, fighting, and stealing in adolescents that became 'chronic offenders' at age 18 years.

Although there is strong empirical support for the early-starting and long-term persistent pathway of delinquent development, one should not overestimate the continuity

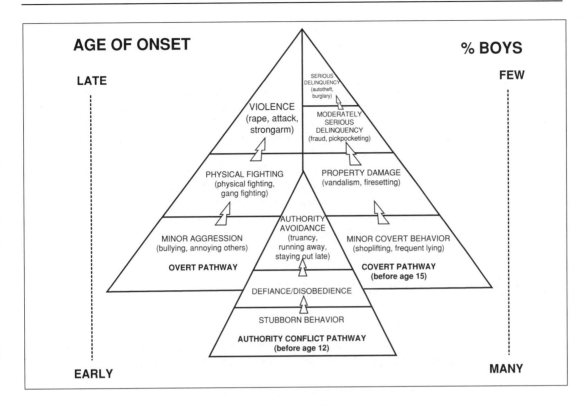

Figure 2.7.1 Developmental pathways in disruptive/delinquent behavior
Source: Loeber et al., 1999

of deviant behaviour. For example, Lahey et al. (1995) report that approximately 50% of boys with a diagnosis of conduct disorder did not remain in this category continuously over four years. This is a typical degree of problem stability from pre-school to school age (Campbell, 1995; Lavigne et al., 1998). Similarly, about one half of children with conduct disorders or extreme antisocial behaviour in childhood did not go on to serious criminal behaviour in adolescence (e.g. Moffitt et al., 1996; Robins, 1978). Although, as mentioned, Patterson and colleagues (1998) found a clearly persistent pathway, approximately half of the children who ranked high in antisocial behaviour at age 9 or 10 did not progress to early arrest and chronic offending by age 18. In the more specific area of aggression, there is also a large part of children whose problem behaviour is not stable over time (e.g. Haapasalo and Tremblay, 1994; Nagin and Tremblay, 1999).

At first glance, this seems to contradict the relatively high stability coefficients for aggressiveness as found in meta-analyses (Olweus, 1979, 1994; Zumkley, 1994). Whereas average correlations are approximately 0.70 after one year, they decline as a function of the time interval between two measurement times. One should also bear in mind that such correlations only indicate the similarity of ranking orders between individuals and not the stability of the behaviour itself (Farrington, 1990,

2002; Loeber and Stouthamer-Loeber, 1998). Furthermore, assessors' biases in single informants also seem to contribute to high stability coefficients (Lösel and Schmucker, in press).

Such arguments do not devaluate the theoretical and practical fruitfulness of a relatively persistent pathway of delinquent development from childhood through adolescence. However, emphasizing both continuity *and* change as basic principles of human development sets a realistic framework for the accuracy of long-term predictions in delinquent development. On the one hand, with more than 80% correct predictions such prognoses can be highly relevant for practice (e.g. Hawkins et al., 1998; Lipsey and Derzon, 1998; Lösel, 2002). On the other hand, depending on the respective base rates and selection rates, there remain substantial proportions of false positives and negatives that must be addressed by differentiated explanations of the natural history of delinquent development (Lösel, 2002).

ORIGINS OF DELINQUENT DEVELOPMENT

Adolescence-Limited Delinquency

Compared to relatively persistent and serious delinquency, the origins of the adolescence-limited form have less to do with the youngsters' social background and personality. Adolescence-limited delinquent behaviour is mainly an expression of developmental transitions and status passages. According to Moffitt (1993), adolescents go through a temporary phase of delinquent behaviour because of its benefits in terms of subjective cost and utility. Deviant behaviour has a positive function when, for example, it contributes to the process of separation from parents and other authorities, helps to confirm self-esteem, and supports the attainment of youth-typical goals. Moffitt considers that modern industrialized nations reveal a major discrepancy between the biological maturity of adolescents and their social status or responsibility. Associating with peer groups helps to close this maturity gap. During a limited phase, the behaviour of delinquent youngsters is imitated because it seems to fulfil needs for autonomy, adventure and status symbols. For most adolescents, however, antisocial behaviour becomes less attractive as reinforcement opportunities for conformity increase (e.g. successful termination of school, professional career, steady partners, regular income). In addition, criminal sanctions exert a learning effect. This is more easily the case because these youngsters show less severe risks in their developmental background and personality.

Although adolescence-limited delinquency is relatively frequent, a large proportion of each cohort exhibit no, or only very little, problem behaviour. In these cases we may expect, for example, delayed puberty, roles that are already recognized by adults, few models for learning delinquency in the social environment, or personal characteristics that hinder gang contacts. Furthermore, there may be protective mechanisms and fewer situational opportunities for offending.

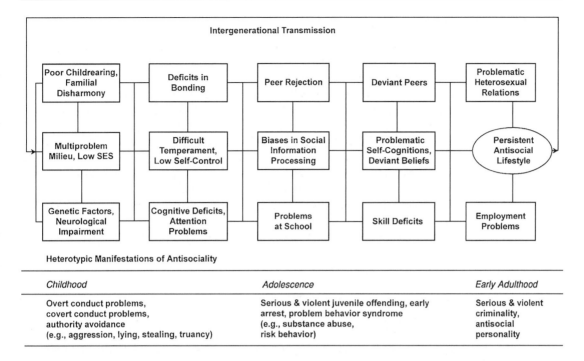

Figure 2.7.2   A model of cumulating risks in the development of persistent antisocial behavior.

Serious and Long-Term Antisocial Behaviour

In contrast to the adolescence-limited form, juveniles exhibiting serious and relatively permanent delinquency have developmental problems that are much more serious. Figure 2.7.2 presents a model summarizing important risk factors of this pathway. Some of these factors also play a role in adolescence-limited delinquency. However, they are much less accumulated than in cases of persistent and serious delinquency (Lösel, 2002; Tremblay and Craig, 1995; Yoshikawa, 1994).

The model in Figure 2.7.2 integrates constructs and variables that are particularly relevant from a social-learning perspective. Most of the single variables have only low correlations with later delinquency (Hawkins et al., 1998; Lipsey and Derzon, 1998). Nonetheless, each of these variables may double or even quadruple the risk of delinquent development. However, the odds for delinquency are much higher when there is an accumulation of risk factors from different areas. Beyond mere statistical relationships, an accumulation indicates learning processes during which dispositions towards delinquent behaviour are successively shaped, reinforced, and consolidated. At the same time this process reduces opportunities for non-deviant behaviour and the chances for a 'normal' development (see Caspi and Moffitt, 1995). Findings on the various risk factors are briefly described in the following sections.

Family Climate and Parenting

Although the impact of family factors is sometimes a matter of controversy, they are still among the best-confirmed risks for serious delinquency (Farrington, 2002; Loeber and Farrington, 1998, Lösel and Bliesener, 2002). The families often lack harmony, emotional warmth, and mutual acceptance. Parents treat the child insensitively and aggressively, are sometimes overly strict but also sometimes too permissive and thus are inconsistent. Frequently there is child abuse and serious neglect. Through such experiences the child learns aggressive behaviour via modelling and reinforcement, and develops cognitive schemata that enhance similar reactions in the future (Bandura, 1973; Crick and Dodge, 1994; Huesmann, 1997). However, although there is a clear relation between domestic violence and aggression in the children affected (Maxfield and Widom, 1996), the 'cycle of violence' is not closed. Many children growing up in such a milieu will not become deviant and even highly aggressive adolescents may come from relatively normal families. Family influences should not be seen as a one-way process. Multiply stressed parents, with little competence in child-rearing, react to difficult children in an impatient, aggressive or inconsistent manner (Rutter, 1990). Similar reactions of the child contribute to a cycle of forced interactions (Patterson, Reid and Dishion, 1992). In such circumstances, there is also an enhanced risk of developing insecure, avoiding, anxious or disorganized modes of emotional attachment (Fagot and Pears, 1996). This is, in turn, a risk for later difficulties with social relations and successful coping (Cassidy et al., 1996; Egeland, Carlson and Stroufe, 1993).

Multi-problem Milieu

Problems in the family climate and parenting behaviour interact with more objective and demographic family risks. These are, for example, poverty, lower socio-economic class, early and single motherhood, parental divorce, alcoholism, and criminal record. Taken individually none of these factors explains much variance (Hawkins et al., 1998; Lipsey and Derzon, 1998). However, their accumulation and interaction with other risks constitutes a multi-problem milieu of high risk for delinquency (Rutter, Giller and Hagell, 1998). Such accumulations are found outside the family as well. For example, deprived, disintegrated and violent neighbourhoods represent a delinquency risk (Catalano et al., 1998; Gorman-Smith and Tolan, 1998). Such a milieu contains social models for delinquency, violence, truancy, drug use, and so forth. However, the influence of the wider social context must be seen in interaction with family and individual factors. Wikström and Loeber (2000), for example, found that a deprived neighbourhood did not generally increase the risk of serious delinquency but only for late-starting youngsters from otherwise low-risk backgrounds. Intact families can also buffer the negative impact of a violent neighbourhood (Richters and Martinez, 1993) and positive neighbourhoods may have a protective effect for children from disadvantaged families (Kupersmidt et al., 1995). One should also bear in mind that most studies on community effects come from the United States, where neighbourhood segregation and growth of slums is more advanced than in Europe.

Biological Factors

Biological and biosocial risks are also involved in persistently delinquent and particularly aggressive adolescents (Raine, 1997; Rowe, 1994). Genetic factors play a significant role in differences in temperament and cognitive functions (Plomin, 1994). Biological dispositions for criminal behaviour can also emerge prenatally through alcohol abuse and smoking during pregnancy, perinatally through birth complications or post-natally through deprivations in emotional care, stimulation, and nutrition during infancy (Hodgins, Kratzer and McNeil, 2002; Moffitt, 1993; Raine, 1993). However, biological risks should not be viewed in too isolated a manner. For example, prenatal and perinatal complications seem to become only significant for specific forms of delinquency when they are accompanied by social risks such as lower-class milieu, parental rejection, or family instability (Brennan, Mednick and Raine, 1997; Hodgins et al., 2002). A deprived relationship with the primary caregiver can impair brain development and attachment behaviour in infancy (Kraemer, 1997). Biological predispositions also influence how far children react impulsively and are less able to learn from negative experiences. Aggressive youngsters exhibit, for example, lower pulse rates, less electrodermal reactivity, and slower waves in the EEG (Raine, 1997). Such dispositions may manifest themselves in a heightened need for stimulation (sensation-seeking), less fear of punishment and less successful avoidance learning (Eysenck, 1977). These biological dispositions seem to be particularly significant when delinquent adolescents come from an otherwise intact milieu (Lösel, Bender and Bliesener, 1998; Raine, 1997). The hypothesis of prefrontal deficits in specific groups of chronic offenders has been supported by direct analyses of CNS functioning via brain imaging (Hare, 2001; Raine, 2001). Some studies also report low serotonin levels and high testosterone levels in aggressive individuals (see Brain and Susman, 1997; Berman, Kavoussi and Cocccaro, 1997). However, more replications and differentiated analyses are needed to provide a clearer picture of the biosocial relations between brain functioning, neurotransmitters, hormones and delinquent development.

Personality Factors

The social and biological influences contribute to risks involving the child's temperament and cognitive competence. These include, for example, impulsiveness, hyperactivity, attention deficits, emotional lability, verbal problems and below-average intelligence (Farrington, 1998; Hawkins et al., 1998; Lipsey and Derzon, 1998). Deficits in executive brain functions impact on abstract thinking, planning, goal-directed behaviour and self-control (Moffitt and Henry, 1991). Again, one should not overemphasize one single risk factor. For example, even the attention-deficit-hyperactivity-disorder syndrome shows only a moderate correlation with later criminality (Loeber and Stouthamer-Loeber, 1998). The personality dispositions may also have a different impact on various delinquent pathways. Frick (1998), for example, distinguishes between two causal pathways of antisocial development. The first results primarily from poor parental socialization and low intelligence. The second is mainly due to callous, unemotional, and other traits of psychopathy (see Hare, 2001). It should also not be forgotten that some aggressive offenders are not impulsive and hyperactive, but more inhibited. Such over-controlled hostile individuals (Megargee, 1996;

White and Heilbrun, 1995) often exhibit other psychological problems and act violently when conflicts escalate under strong affects.

School Factors

The school is both a place of antisocial behaviour and a context of further risks for general delinquency. In contrast to popular opinions, neither class size, school size, nor architecture exert any strong significance on school bullying (Olweus, 1994). More important are features of the school and classroom climate. For example, committed, empathic and consistent teachers and an emphasis on school values have a positive effect (Gottfredson, 2001; Mortimore, 1995; Rutter et al., 1979). The concentration of aggressive youngsters provides role models and reinforcement for antisocial behaviour (Kellam et al., 1998). With regard to the students, deficits in school achievement and school bonding (e.g. truancy, having to repeat the school year, dropping out of school, bad relationships with teachers, low school interests in parents and student) are important predictors of delinquent development (Farrington, 2002; Farrington and Loeber, 2001; Hawkins et al., 1998). Only a small number of cases involve a real inability to cope with academic demands, negative attitudes and motivations towards the school seem to be more crucial (Jessor, Donovan and Costa, 1991). Obviously, such school factors are not independent origins of delinquency but risks that are already proximal and interacting with a delinquent development.

Peer Group

The peer group has a highly significant impact on both adolescence-limited and persistent delinquency (Bender and Lösel, 1997; Elliott, Huizinga and Menard, 1989; Thornberry, 1998). Many offences are committed in groups (Reiss and Farrington, 1991; Kaiser, 1997). Most aggressive and delinquent adolescents belong to groups in which deviant activities are common practice (e.g. Lösel and Bliesener, 1998). Peers function as models and simultaneously reinforce delinquency, alcohol and drug use, and a lifestyle directed towards satisfying immediate needs (Jessor et al., 1991; Lösel and Bliesener, 1998). Delinquent cliques or gangs take on a special role. Adolescents affiliate more readily with such gangs when they come from families with multiple risks and child-rearing deficits, have problems at school, exhibit early antisocial behaviour, are rejected by other peers, live in socially disorganized residential areas, and have contacts with other adolescents with similar difficulties (Thornberry, 1998). Insofar, the gang effects are both due to processes of selective mating and to social influences from the group (Thornberry, 1998; Tremblay et al., 1995). This is a particularly important area of interactive processes in delinquent development.

Social Information Processing

Experiences of aggression in the family, the peer group, the mass media, and other social contexts enhance the development of schemes of social information processing that encourage antisocial behaviour (Crick and Dodge, 1994; Huesmann, 1997; Lösel, Bliesener and Bender, in press). According to Crick and Dodge (1994), aggressive youngsters show specific tendencies in the (a) encoding of cues, (b) interpretation of cues, (c) clarification of goals, (d) response access and construction, (e) response decision and evaluation and (e) behavioural enactment. For example, they perceive more aggressive stimuli in social situations, interpret the intentions of others more frequently as being hostile, set more egocentric goals for actions, retrieve more aggressive reaction patterns from their memory, evaluate the consequences of aggressive actions more positively, and possess fewer non-aggressive interaction skills. Such modes of information processing make aggression a subjectively adequate reaction in social interactions. They are important mediators between long-term social influences, personality factors, and situational conditions of delinquent behaviour. However, more research on the relations between the various phases of information processing, social experiences and antisocial behaviour is necessary (Lösel et al., in press). There are also not only unidirectional influences but more complex interactions in the chain reaction towards chronic delinquency. For example, in spite of methodological problems, the majority of research supports a significant effect of media violence consumption on the aggressive behaviour of youngsters (Huesmann and Miller, 1994; Huesmann, Moise and Podolski, 1997). However, the media effects interact with an already existing aggressiveness and other consumer characteristics (Paik and Comstock, 1994). Because aggressive youngsters consume more violent films than others, they face the risk of consolidating aggression-prone schemes of information processing and related affective patterns (Lösel et al., in press).

Attitudes and Self-cognitions

Through the interaction with group influences, delinquent adolescents develop attitudes, values and self-related cognitions that encourage deviant behaviour. According to Jessor and colleagues (1991), they tolerate, for example, more deviance than other adolescents, place greater value on autonomy, and have less interest in traditional achievement norms. They also have more negative attitudes towards conformist institutions (Hirschi, 1969). At moderate levels, such dispositions may contribute to the mastering of developmental tasks (see adolescence-typical delinquency). However, critical thresholds are passed when adolescents identify exclusively with deviant groups and subcultures. Personal problems are often blamed on the environment, making it harder for self-critical insights to evolve (Averbeck and Lösel, 1994). To some extent, this pattern relates to a low self-esteem. However, there is also a subgroup of aggressive youngsters in which the self-concept is not negative but unrealistically positive, fragile, and thus easily challenged (Baumeister, Smart and Boden, 1996; Bushman and Baumeister, 1998).

Work and Vocational Factors

As delinquency progresses, it elicits sanctions and processes of exclusion. These may reduce social opportunities in the sense of social stigmatization, strengthen a deviant identity, and contribute to recidivism (Herrmann and Kerner, 1988). At the same time many such adolescents have difficulties with their jobs and careers. They more frequently do not commence occupational training or drop out of apprenticeships (e.g. Sampson and Laub, 1993). Their lack of qualifications impacts negatively on opportunities on the labour market. Delinquency follows unemployment in some cases; other cases tend to exhibit the opposite causal direction (Farrington, 2000). Therefore, unemployment should not be emphasized as an isolated risk factor. This is also indicated by relatively poor effects of employment programmes for young delinquents (Lipsey and Wilson, 1998). In addition to getting a job, it seems critical that delinquents are able to hold it down and develop a less deviant motivation and lifestyle.

Partnership and Adult Lifestyle

If the delinquent behaviour persists into adulthood, this may indicate an antisocial personality disorder or the more narrowly defined psychopathy (Hare, 1995, 2001). In these cases, deviant behaviour is very hard to modify (Lösel, 1998). Such chronic delinquents often have difficulties in forming stable intimate relations or they chose partners that have similar problems (Quinton et al., 1993). Although most criminal careers fade out after the age of 40, other difficulties such as alcoholism, chronic unemployment, psychiatric problems and violence in the family often continue (Farrington, 1989). Such lifestyles, and the inheritance of genetic information create, in turn, developmental risks for the next generation. But, again, this is not necessarily a closed cycle and depends on interactions with protective factors and mechanisms.

PROTECTIVE FACTORS AGAINST DELINQUENT DEVELOPMENT

The developmental chain reaction depicted in Figure 2.7.2 is not a necessary sequence but can be interrupted in all phases and areas of risk. Research on prediction has shown that many high-risk youngsters do not get into serious trouble with the law and others desist from a delinquent career (Lösel and Bender, in press). These 'false positives' illustrate how the negative chain reaction can be disrupted, and how turning points enter development. This involves natural protective processes or successful prevention measures. To date far less attention has been paid to protective factors and mechanisms than to risks. Werner and Smith (1992) studied a birth cohort from childhood to adulthood, and compared those who had grown up into socially competent individuals, despite developmental risks, with a group that exhibited the major behaviour problems to be anticipated from their risk exposure. They also examined those factors that contributed to positive turning points in the development of adolescents who had already started delinquent careers. Lösel and Bliesener (1994) compared adolescents from a multi-problem milieu who exhibited a relatively healthy psychosocial development with ones in whom serious behaviour problems had emerged.

These and other studies indicate that the following features may possess a protective function against delinquency (see Lösel and Bender, in press):

(a)   an easy temperament

(b)   above-average intelligence and good planning behaviour

(c)   secure attachment to an important other (in multi-problem families, this may not be a parent but a relative or teacher)

(d)   emotional care accompanied by supervision in child-rearing

(e)   adults who provide positive models under adverse conditions

(f)   social support from non-delinquent persons

(g)   more active rather than avoidant coping behaviour

(h)   academic success and a bonding to school values and norms

(i)   membership of non-delinquent groups or a degree of social isolation

(j)   experiences of self-efficacy in non-delinquent activities (e.g. a hobby)

(k)   a positive but not unrealistically heightened sense of self-esteem

(l)   a sense of meaning and structure in one's life (e.g. a sense of coherence).

Similar to risk factors, protective factors should not be viewed in isolation. Whether they exert a protective effect against delinquent development may depend on specific patterns of various variables (Bender and Lösel, 1997; Lösel and Bender, in press). As with risks, an accumulation of several protective factors seems to be particularly effective (Lösel, Kolip and Bender, 1992; Stattin, Romelsjö and Stenbacka, 1997). However, research on protective factors is confronted with various conceptual and methodological problems (Lösel and Bender, in press; Luthar, Cicchetti and Becker, 2000) and we are just beginning to understand their mechanisms in the development of youngsters who are at high risk for delinquency.

PSYCHOSOCIAL INTERVENTIONS INTO DELINQUENT DEVELOPMENT

Whereas protective factors refer to 'natural' turning points in the development of delinquent behaviour, similar processes can result from systematic psychosocial interventions. Until the 1980s, there was a widespread view that positive effects of offender treatment or rehabilitation programmes could not yet be demonstrated (e.g. Lipton, Martinson and Wilks, 1975). However, during the 1990s this 'nothing works' doctrine was overcome by a more differentiated and constructive perspective of 'what works'. Meta-analyses of hundreds of evaluation studies demonstrated a small but overall positive effect in comparison to untreated control groups (Lösel, 1995, 2001a; McGuire, 2001). There are also significant differences between kinds of treatment (Andrews et al., 1990; Lipsey, 1992; Lipsey and Wilson, 1998; Redondo, Sánchez-Meca and

Garrido, 1999). The largest effects result from theoretically well-founded, multi-modal, cognitive-behavioural and skill-oriented programmes. Also promising are family-oriented programmes in ambulatory treatment for serious juvenile offenders and clearly structured therapeutic communities in institutional treatment of adult offenders.

Successful interventions fit with the level of offenders' risk, address criminogenic needs precisely (instead of vague personality changes), and take into account the specific learning styles of the offenders (the responsivity principle). Such programmes are founded on empirical knowledge about the causes and development of the respective criminal behaviour and not specifically derived from psychotherapeutic 'schools'. They address, for example, motivation for change, self-control, crime-related beliefs and attitudes, social skills, interpersonal problem-solving, self-critical thinking, moral reasoning, anger management, victim awareness, and coping with risk situations for relapse (e.g. Goldstein et al., 1994; Ross and Ross, 1995).

Effect sizes in the most appropriate programs can be twice as high as the average. In contrast unstructured case work, traditional psychodynamic, and non-directive approaches show smaller effects than the overall mean. Relatively low-structured, self-governing, permissive, therapeutic communities and milieu therapy also seem to range at the lower end of effectiveness. The same holds for merely formal variations in punishment or probation, diversion without any educational or psychosocial component, deterrence, boot camps, and other measures of 'smarter' punishment or intermediate sanctions (e.g. Andrews, Dowden and Gendreau, 2002; Lipsey and Wilson, 1998; MacKenzie, Wilson and Kider, 2001). In some studies, effects of inappropriate treatment are even negative. Although there is growing evidence that various programmes lead to a positive change in delinquent development, there is still a lack of methodologically sound evaluations, particularly of complex programmes and multiple services for adult and serious offender groups (Lösel, 2001b). More process data are needed about the content of programme delivery, staff characteristics and dimensions of institutional regime. It is also necessary to tackle the drop-out problem more effectively. Last, but not least, practice-oriented evaluations must put offender treatment programmes in their wider social context.

EARLY PREVENTION OF DELINQUENT DEVELOPMENT

Because the origins of serious and violent offending can often be traced back to childhood, measures of early prevention are particularly promising (Farrington, 2002; Loeber and Farrington, 1998; McCord and Tremblay, 1992; Peters and McMahon, 1996). However, although there is an increasing body of relatively controlled studies on universal, selective, or indicated prevention of antisocial behaviour in children and youth (e.g. Beelmann, 2001; Catalano et al., 1998; Farrington and Welsh, in press; Gottfredson, 2001; Lösel and Beelmann, in press; Wasserman and Miller, 1998), a general conclusion on the efficacy of this approach is difficult. Some studies report substantial long-term effects extending into adulthood (e.g. Schweinhart, Barnes and

Weikhart, 1993). Other long-term evaluations give less grounds for optimism (e.g. McCord, 1978). More typical are studies with much shorter follow-up intervals. Most of these use a broad spectrum of success measures on which findings may vary greatly. For criteria relating to antisocial behaviour in daily life, recent studies on universal or selective prevention have produced small effects (e.g. Conduct Problems Research Group, 1999a, 1999b; Sanders et al., 2000). As in offender treatment, it is not only outcomes that vary considerably but also types of programme, intensity of intervention, and contexts of implementation (e.g. early interventions in the family, pre-school programmes, school-based programmes, special education, child guidance clinics, and community-oriented programmes). Furthermore, it is doubted whether results from research-oriented model projects can be generalized to the everyday practice (Gottfredson, 2001; Weisz et al., 1995).

Overall controlled evaluations of early prevention programmes reveal similar effect sizes as adequate delinquency treatment (Lösel, 2002). This is plausible insofar as most early prevention/intervention studies refer to behavioural, cognitive-behavioural and multi-modal programmes. It should also be noted that this includes not only universal or selective approaches, but also programmes of indicated prevention or child psychotherapy. The use of methodologically stricter inclusion criteria seems to lead to smaller effects (e.g. Lösel and Beelmann in press; Tremblay et al., 1999). The evaluations of early intervention programmes also frequently have relatively short follow-up intervals and include outcome measures that correspond closely to the contents of training or are 'softer' than recidivism data (Beelmann, Pfingsten and Lösel, 1994).

Currently, well-implemented social-cognitive skills training for high-risk children, cognitive-behavioural parent trainings, multi-systemic therapy, and comprehensive programmes that combine clinic-based parent and child training reveal the most promising outcomes (e.g. Farrington and Welsh, 1999, in press; Lösel and Beelmann, in press; Kazdin, 1997; Tremblay, LeMarquand and Vitaro, 1999). In all, it would seem that the basic characteristics of successful early prevention and later treatment programmes are similar. Instead of polarizations between early prevention and offender treatment, we need to develop systematic intervention packages that are suited to different phases of development and levels of delinquency (Farrington, 2002; Lösel, 2002).

SITUATIONAL INFLUENCES ON DELINQUENT BEHAVIOUR

Whether offences are committed does not just depend on long-term influences and dispositions but on situational factors as well. For example, many property offences can be explained as an outcome of spontaneous cost-utility judgements (Cornish and Clarke, 1989). People tend to commit offences when they consider the probability of desired outcomes and their value to be high, but that of undesired consequences and their negative valence to be low. Tempting shop displays, a temporary lack of material resources, as well as needs for adventure and group processes may provide a high incentive to offend. If this is combined with the (realistic) experience that offences often remain undetected, delinquency becomes highly probable. Comparing both parameters, it is not so much a potential punishment that acts as a deterrent but more a high risk of detection and a negative response in the social environment (Albrecht, 1993).

Delinquents often act impulsively without considering possible negative and long-term consequences in a given situation (Gottfredson and Hirschi, 1999; Lösel, 1975). Situational group processes play an important role in this. For example, peers can provide a modelling effect in an offence situation, the diffusion of responsibility in a group can reduce inhibitions, and perceived group pressure can increase the need for status symbols. Offending may also be motivated by a striving for recognition or consolidation of the own position. Such processes may lead groups to commit more serious offences that their members would commit on their own. For example, escalations in aggression, greater injury, and use of weapons are more frequent in attacks between groups than in fights between individuals (Farrington, 1993; Thornberry, 1998).

Information processing contributes to the readiness for antisocial behaviour in a concrete situation (Farrington, 1993; Sampson and Lauritsen, 1994). Perceived provocations, injuries, or hindrance by others may trigger violent offences. These triggers do not have to be real or serious. It may take only the 'wrong look', or the 'wrong words' (e.g. in fights), or the 'wrong' appearances (e.g. in xenophobic offences), or trivial conflicts (e.g. in violence within families) for a predisposition to erupt into actual violence. When apparently trivial causes trigger extreme violence there are often long-term conflicts simmering under the surface. In these cases, there may be an outburst of over-controlled hostility (Blackburn, 1993).

Other situational triggers of delinquent behaviour are, for example, the presence of deviant models, a lack of informal social control, the availability of weapons, or acute alcohol effects on self-control. The situation after an offence is also highly important (Bandura, 1986). Direct positive reinforcement or vicarious reinforcement, escape from punishment, and delayed or inconsistent sanctioning may strengthen delinquent behaviour. However, it is not only the objective consequences but also subjective cognitions that play a role. For example, offenders may minimize their own guilt, blame or dehumanize the victim, attribute responsibility to group members, and use other techniques to neutralize self-critique (Bandura, 1986; Sykes and Matza, 1957; Minor, 1980, 1981). These are further examples for the relation between situational conditions of delinquency and the developmental factors mentioned above.

CONCLUSIONS

International longitudinal research has clearly expanded our knowledge about different pathways of delinquent development. Of particular interest is the small group of early-starting and long-term persistent offenders that is responsible for a large proportion of crime. Their development is due to a successive accumulation of bio-psycho-social risk factors from multiple levels and areas. Both social and personal resources may interrupt this chain reaction of delinquency-prone learning processes. However, we need much more research on the protective mechanisms that enable high-risk individuals to abstain or desist from a delinquent development. This is not only the case for the natural history of delinquency but also for systematic programmes of prevention and intervention. In the latter areas, there are promising guidelines of what works, but more controlled evaluations and implementations into practice are necessary. We need also to improve our knowledge on the linkage between situational conditions of offending and long-term developmental factors.

REFERENCES

Albrecht, H.-J. (1993). Generalprävention. In G. Kaiser, H.-J. Kerner, F. Sack and H.Schellhoss (eds), *Kleines Kriminologisches Wörterbuch* (3rd edn; pp. 157–164). Heidelberg: C.F. Müller.

Andrews, D.A., Zinger, I., Hoge, R.D., Bonta, J., Gendreau, P. and Cullen, F.T. (1990). Does correctional treatment work? A clinically relevant and psychologically informed meta-analysis. *Criminology, 28*, 369–404.

Andrews, D.A, Dowden, C. and Gendreau, P. (2002). *Clinically relevant and psychologically informed approaches to reduce re-offending: A meta-analytic study of human service, risk, need, responsivity, and other concerns in justice contexts.* Manuscript under review.

Averbeck, M. and Lösel, F. (1994). Subjektive theorien über jugendkriminalität. In M. Steller, K.-P. Dahle and M. Basqué (eds), *Straftäterbehandlung* (pp. 213–226). Pfaffenweiler: Centaurus.

Bandura, A. (1973). *Aggression: A social learning analysis.* Englewood Cliffs, NJ: Prentice Hall.

Bandura, A. (1986). *Social foundations of thought and action.* Englewood Cliffs, NJ: Prentice Hall.

Baumeister, R.F., Smart, L. and Boden, J.M. (1996). Relation of threatened egotism to violence and aggression: the dark side of high self-esteem. *Psychological Bulletin, 103*, 5–33.

Beelmann, A. (2001). *Prävention dissozialer Entwicklungen: Psychologische Grundlagen und Evaluation früher kind- und familienbezogener Interventionsmaßnahmen.* Habilitationsschrift. Universität Erlangen-Nürnberg: Philosophische Fakultät I.

Beelmann, A., Pfingsten, U. and Lösel, F. (1994). Effects of training social competence in children: A meta-analysis of recent evaluation studies. *Journal of Clinical Child Psychology, 23*, 260–271.

Bender, D. and Lösel, F. (1997). Protective and risk effects of peer relations and social support on antisocial behaviour in adolescents from multi-problem milieus. *Journal of Adolescence, 20*, 661–678.

Berman, M.E., Kavoussi, R.J. and Coccaro, E.F. (1997). Neurotransmitter correlates of human aggression. In D.M. Stoff, J. Breiling and J.D. Maser (eds), *Handbook of antisocial behavior* (pp. 305–313). New York: John Wiley & Sons.

Blackburn, R. (1993). *The psychology of criminal conduct: Theory, research, and practice.* Chichester: John Wiley & Sons.

Blumstein, A., Farrington, D.P. and Moitra, S. (1985). Delinquency careers: Innocents, amateurs, and persisters. In M. Tonry and N. Morris (eds), *Crime and justice: An annual review of research* (vol. 6; pp. 187–222). Chicago: University of Chicago Press.

Brain, P.F. and Susman, E.J. (1997). Hormonal aspects of aggression and violence. In D.M. Stoff, J. Breiling and J.D. Maser (eds), *Handbook of antisocial behavior* (pp. 314–323). New York: John Wiley & Sons.

Brennan, P.A., Mednick, S.A. and Raine, A. (1997). Biosocial interactions and violence: A focus on perinatal factors. In A. Raine, P.A. Brennan, D.P. Farrington and S.A. Mednick (eds), *Biosocial bases of violence* (pp. 163–174). New York: Plenum Press.

Bushman, B. and Baumeister, R.F. (1998). Threatened egotism, narcissism, self-esteem, and direct displaced aggression: Does self-love or self-hate lead to violence? *Journal of Personality and Social Psychology*, 75, 219–227.

Campbell, S.B. (1995). Behavior problems in preschool children: A review of recent research. *Journal of Child Psychology and Psychiatry*, 36, 113–149.

Caspi, A. and Moffitt, T.E. (1995). The continuity of maladaptive behavior: From description to understanding in the study of antisocial behavior. In D. Cicchetti and D.J. Cohen (eds), *Developmental psychopathology. Vol. 2, Risk, disorder, and adaptation* (pp. 472–511). New York: John Wiley & Sons.

Cassidy, J., Scolton, K.L., Kirsh, S.J. and Parke, R.D. (1996). Attachment and representations of peer relationships. *Developmetal Psychology*, 32, 892–904.

Catalano, R.F., Arthur, M.W., Hawkins, J.D., Berglund, L. and Olson, J.J. (1998). Comprehensive community- and school-based interventions to prevent antisocial behavior. In R. Loeber and D.P. Farrington (eds), *Serious and violent juvenile offenders: Risk factors and successful interventions* (pp. 248–283). Thousand Oaks: Sage.

Conduct Problems Prevention Research Group (1999a). Initial impact of the Fast Track Prevention Trial for Conduct Problems: I. The high-risk sample. *Journal of Consulting and Clinical Psychology*, 67, 631–647.

Conduct Problems Prevention Research group (1999b). Initial impact of the Fast track Prevention trial for conduct problems: II. Classroom effects. *Journal of Consulting and Clinical Psychology*, 67, 648–657.

Cornish, D.B. and Clarke, R.V. (1989). Crime specialisation, crime displacement and rational choice theroy. In H. Wegener, F. Lösel and J. Haisch (eds), *Criminal behavior and the justice system* (pp. 103–117). New York: Springer.

Crick, N.R. and Dodge, K.A. (1994). A review and reformulation of social information-processing mechanisms in children's social adjustment. *Psychological Bulletin*, 115, 74–101.

Egeland, B., Carlson, E. and Stroufe, L.A. (1993). Resilience as a process. *Development and Psychopathology*, 5, 517–528.

Elliott, D.S., Huizinga, D. and Menard, S. (1989). *Multiple youth*. New York: Springer.

Eysenck, H.J. (1977). *Crime and personality*. London: Routledge & Kegan Paul.

Fagot, B.I. and Pears, K.C. (1996). Changes in attachment during the third year: Consequences and predictions. *Development and Psychopathology*, 8, 325–344.

Farrington, D.P. (1989). Later adult life outcomes of offenders and nonoffenders. In M. Brambring, F. Lösel and H. Skowronek (eds), *Children at risk: Assessment, longitudinal research, and intervention* (pp. 220–244). Berlin: de Gruyter.

Farrington, D.P. (1990). Age, period, cohort, and offending. In D.M. Gottfredson and R.V. Clarke (eds), *Policy and theory in criminal justice: Contributions in honour of Leslie T. Wilkins* (pp. 51–75). Aldershot: Avebury.

Farrington, D.P. (1992). Psychological contributions to the explanation, prevention, and treatment of offending. In F. Lösel, D. Bender and T. Bliesener (eds), *Psychology and law: International perspectives* (pp. 35–51). Berlin, New York: De Gruyter.

Farrington, D.P. (1993). Motivations for conduct disorder and delinquency. *Development and Psychopathologie*, 5, 225–241.

Farrington, D.P. (1998). Predictors, causes, and correlates of youth violence. In M. Tonry and M.H. Moore (eds), *Youth violence, crime and justice*. Chicago: University of Chicago Press.

Farrington, D.P. (2000). Explaining and preventing crime: The globalization of knowledge. The American Society of Criminology 1999 presidential Address. *Criminology*, 38, 801–824.

Farrington, D.P. (2002). Key results from the first forty years of the Cambridge Study in Delinquent Development. In T.P. Thornberry and M.D. Krohn (eds), *Taking stock of delinquency: An overview of findings from contemporary longitudinal studies* (pp. 137–183). New York: Kluwer Academic/Plenum Publishers.

Farrington, D.P. and Loeber, R. (2001). Summary of key conclusions. In R. Loeber and D.P. Farrington (eds), *Child delinquents* (pp. 359–384). Thousand Oaks, CA: Sage.

Farrington, D.P. and Welsh, B.C. (1999). Delinquency prevention using family-based interventions. *Children and Society*, *13*, 287–303.

Farrington, D.P. and Welsh, B.C. (in press). Family-based prevention of offending: a meta-analysis. *Australian and New Zealand Journal of Criminology*.

Frick, P.J. (1998). *Conduct disorders and severe antisocial behavior*. New York: Plenum Press.

Goldstein, A.P., Glick, B., Carthan, W. and Blancero, D.A. (1994). *The pro-social gang: Implementing aggression replacement training*. Thousand Oaks, CA: Sage.

Gorman-Smith, D. and Tolan, P. (1998). The role of exposure to community violence and developmental problems among inner-city youth. *Development and Psychopathology*, *10*, 101–116.

Gottfredson, D.C. (2001). *Schools and delinquency*. Cambridge, UK: Cambridge University Press.

Gottfredson, M. and Hirschi, T.M. (1990). A general theory of crime. Stanford, CA: Stanford University Press.

Haapasalo, J. and Tremblay, R.E. (1994). Physically aggressive boys from ages 6 to 12: Family background, parenting behavior, and prediction of delinquency. *Journal of Consulting and Clinical Psychology*, *62*, 1044–1052.

Hare, R.D. (1995). Psychopathy: A clinical construct whose time has come. *Criminal Justice and Behavior*, *23*, 25–54.

Hare, R.D. (2001). Psychopaths and their nature: some implications for understanding human predatory violence. In A. Raine and J. Sanmartin (eds), *Violence and psychopathy* (pp. 5–34). New York: Kluwer Academic/Plenum Publishers.

Hawkins, J.D., Herrenkohl, T., Farrington, D.P., Brewer, D., Catalano, R.F. and Harachi, T.W. (1998). A review of predictors of youth violence. In R. Loeber and D.P. Farrington (eds), *Serious and violent juvenile offenders* (pp. 106–146). Thousand Oaks, CA: Sage.

Herrmann, D. and Kerner, H.J. (1988). Die Eigendynamik der Rückfallkriminalität. *Kölner Zeitschrift für Soziologie und Sozialpsychologie*, *40*, 485–504.

Hirschi, T. (1969). *Causes of delinquency*. Berkeley: University of California Press.

Hodgins, S., Kratzer, L. and McNeil, T.F. (2002). Are pre- and perinatal factors related to the development of criminal offending? In R.R. Corado, R. Roesch, S.D. Hart and J.K. Gierowski (eds), *Multi-problem violent youth* (pp. 58–80). Amsterdam: IOS Press, Nato Science Series.

Huesmann, L.R. (1997). Observational learning of violent behavior: Social and biosocial processes. In A. Raine, P.A. Brennan, D.P. Farrington and S.A. Mednick (eds), *Biosocial bases of violence* (pp. 69–88). New York: Plenum Press.

Huesmann, L.R. and Miller, L.S. (1994). Long-term effects of repeated exposure to media violence in childhood. In L.R. Huesmann (ed.), *Aggressive behavior: Current perspectives* (pp. 153–186). New York: Plenum.

Huesmann, L.R. Moise, J.F. and Podolski, C.-L. (1997). The effects of media violence on the development of antisocial behavior. In D.M. Stoff, J. Breiling and J.D. Maser (eds), *Handbook of antisocial behavior* (pp. 181–193). New York: John Wiley & Sons.

Jessor, R., Donovan, J.E. and Costa, F.M. (1991). *Beyond adolescence: Problem behavior and young adult development*. Cambridge: Cambridge University Press.

Kaiser, G. (1997). *Kriminologie* (10th edn). Heidelberg: C.F. Müller.

Kazdin, A.E. (1997). Parent management training: Evidence, outcomes, and issues. *Journal of the American Academy of Child and Adolescent Psychiatry*, *36*, 1349–1356.

Kellam, S.G., Ling, X., Merisca, R., Brown, C.H. and Ialongo, N. (1998). The effect of the level of aggression in the first grade classroom on the course and malleability of aggressive behavior into middle school. *Development and Psychopathology*, *10*, 165–185.

Kraemer, G.W. (1997). Social attachment, brain function, aggression, and violence. In A. Raine, P.A. Brennan, D.P. Farrington and S.A. Mednick (eds), *Biosocial bases of violence* (pp. 207–229). New York: Plenum Press.

Kupersmidt, J.B., Griesler, P.C., DeRosier, M.E., Patterson, C.J. and Davis, P.W. (1995). Childhood aggression and peer relations in the context of familiy and neighborhood factors. *Child Development*, *66*, 360–375.

Lahey, B.B., Loeber, R., Hart, E. and Frick, P. (1995). Four-year longitudinal study of conduct disorder in boys: Patterns and predictors of persistence. *Journal of Abnormal Psychology*, *104*, 83–93.

Lavigne, J.V., Arend, R., Rosenbaum, D., Binns, H.J., Christoffel, K.K. and Gibbons, R.D. (1998). Psychiatric disorders with onset in the preschool years: I. Stability of diagnosis. *Journal of the American Academy of Child and Adolescent Psychiatry*, *37*, 1246–1254.

Lipsey, M.W. (1992). The effect of treatment on juvenile delinquents: Results from meta-analysis. In F. Lösel, D. Bender and T. Bliesener (eds), *Psychology and law: International perspectives* (pp. 131–143). Berlin, New York: de Gruyter.

Lipsey, M.W. and Derzon, J.H. (1998). Predictors of violent or serious delinquency in adolescence and early adulthood: A synthesis of longitudinal research. In R. Loeber and D.P. Farrington (eds), *Serious and violent juvenile offenders* (pp. 86–105). Thousand Oaks, CA: Sage.

Lipsey, M.W. and Wilson, D.B. (1998). Effective intervention for serious juvenile offenders: A synthesis of research. In R. Loeber and D.P. Farrington (eds), *Serious and violent juvenile offenders* (pp. 313–345). Thousand Oaks, CA: Sage.

Lipton, D.S., Martinson, R. and Wilks, J. (1975). *The effectiveness of correctional treatment. A survey of treatment evaluation studies*. New York: Praeger.

Loeber, R. and Farrington, D.P. (eds) (1998). *Serious and violent juvenile offenders: Risk factors and successful interventions*. Thousand Oaks, CA: Sage.

Loeber, R., Farrington, D.P. and Waschbusch, D.A. (1998). Serious and violent juvenile offenders. In R. Loeber and D.P. Farrington (eds), *Serious and violent juvenile offenders* (pp. 13–29). Thousand Oaks, CA: Sage.

Loeber, R. and Hay, D. (1994). Developmental approaches to aggression and conduct problems. In M. Rutter and D.F. Hay (eds), Development through life: A handbook for clinicians (pp. 488–516). Oxford: Blackwell.

Loeber, R. and Stouthamer-Loeber, M. (1998). Development of juvenile aggression and violence: Some common misconceptions and controversies. *American Psychologist*, *53*, 242–259.

Loeber, R. and Farrington, D.P. (2001). The significance of child delinquency. In R. Loeber and D.P. Farrington (eds), *Child delinquents* (pp. 1–22). Thousand Oaks, CA: Sage.

Loeber, R., Wei, E., Stouthamer-Loeber, M., Huitinga, D. and Thornberry T.P. (1999). Behavioral antecedents to serious and violent juvenile offending: Joint analyses from the Denver Youth Survey, the Pittsburgh Youth Survey and the Rochester Development Study. *Studies in Crime and Crime Prevention*, *8*, 245–263.

Lösel, F. (1975). *Handlungskontrolle und Jugenddelinquenz [Action control and juvenile delinquency]*. Stuttgart: Enke.

Lösel, F. (1995). Increasing consensus in the evaluation of offender rehabilitation? *Psychology, Crime and Law*, *2*, 19–39.

Lösel, F. (1998). Treatment and management of psychopaths. In D.J. Cooke, A.E. Forth and R.B. Hare (eds), *Psychopathy: Theory, research, and implications for society* (pp. 303–354). Dordrecht: Kluwer.

Lösel, F. (2001a). Rehabilitation of the criminal offender. In N.J. Smelser and P.B. Baltes (editors-in-chief), *International encyclopedia of the social and behavioral sciences, vol. 3.12: Clinical and applied psychology*. London: Elsevier.

Lösel, F. (2001b). Evaluating the effectiveness of correctional programs: Bridging the gap between research and practice. In G.A. Bernfeld, D.P. Farrington and A.W. Leschied (eds), *Offender rehabilitation in practice* (pp. 67–92). Chichester: John Wiley & Sons.

Lösel, F. (2002). Risk/need assessment and prevention of antisocial development in young people: Basic issues from a perspective of cautionary optimism. In R.R. Corrado, R. Roesch, S.D. Hart and J.K. Gierowski. *Multi-problem violent youth* (pp. 35–57). Amsterdam: IOS Press, Nato Science Series.

Lösel, F. and Bliesener, A. (2002). *Aggression und Delinquenz unter Jugendlichen*. Neuwied: Luchterhand.

Lösel, F. and Bender, D. (in press). Resilience and protective factors. In D.P. Farrington and J. Coid (eds), *Prevention of adult antisocial behavior* (pp. 130–204). Cambridge: Cambridge University Press.

Lösel, F., Bender, D. and Bliesener, T. (1998). *Biosocial risk and protective factors for antisocial behavior in juveniles: Heart rate and family characteristics.* Paper presented at the XVth Biennial Meetings of the International Society for the Study of Behavioral Development, Berne, Switzerland.

Lösel, F. and Bliesener, T. (1994). Some high-risk adolescents do not develop conduct problems: A study of protective factors. *International Journal of Behavioral Development*, *17*, 753–777.

Lösel, F. and Bliesener, T. (1998). Zum Einfluß des Familienklimas und der Gleichaltrigen-gruppe auf den Zusammenhang zwischen Substanzengebrauch und antisozialem Verhalten von Jugendlichen. *Kindheit und Entwicklung*, *7*, 208–220.

Lösel, F. and Beelmann, A. (in press). Effects of child skills training in preventing antisocial behavior: A systematic review of randomized experiments. *The Annals of the American Academy of Political and Social Science.*

Lösel, F., Bliesener, T. and Bender, D. (in press). Social information processing, experiences of aggression in social contexts, and aggressive behavior in adolescents. *Criminal Justice and Behavior.*

Lösel, F., Kolip, P. and Bender, D. (1992). Stress-Resistenz im Multiproblem-Milieu: Sind seelisch widerstandsfähige Jugendliche 'Superkids'? *Zeitschrift für Klinische Psychologie*, *21*, 48–63.

Lösel, F. and Schmucker, M. (in press). Assessor's biases. In R. Fernandez-Ballesteros (editor-in-chief), *Encyclopedia of psychological assessment*. Thousand Oaks, CA: Sage.

Lösel, F., Bliesener, T. and Bender, D. (in press). Social information processing, experiences in social contexts and aggressive behavior in adolescents. *Criminal Justice and Behavior.*

Luthar, S.S., Cicchetti, D. and Becker, B. (2000). The construct of resilience: A critical evaluation and guidelines for future work. *Child Development*, *71*, 543–562.

MacKenzie, D.L., Wilson, D.B. and Kider, S.B. (2001). Effects of correctional boot camps on offending. *The Annals of the American Academy of Political and Social Sciences*, *578*, 126–143.

Maxfield, M.G. and Widom, C.S. (1996). The cycle of violence: Revisited 6 years later. *Archives of Pediatrics and Adolescent Medicine*, *150*, 390–395.

McCord, J. (1978). A thirty-year follow-up of treatment effects. *American Psychologist*, *33*, 284–289.

McCord, J. and Tremblay, R. (eds) (1992). *Preventing antisocial behavior: Interventions from birth through adolescence.* New York: Guilford Press.

McGuire, J. (2001). What works in correctional intervention? Evidence and practical implications. In G.A. Bernfeld, D.P. Farrington and A.W. Leschied (eds), *Offender rehabilitation in practice* (pp. 25–43). Chichester: John Wiley & Sons.

Megargee, E.I. (1966). Undercontrolled and overcontrolled personality types in extreme antisocial aggression. *Psychological Monographs*, *80*, Whole No. 611.

Minor, W.W. (1980). The neutralization of criminal offense. *Criminology*, *18*, 103–120.

Minor, W.W. (1981). Techniques of neutralization: A reconceptualization and an empirical examination. *Journal of Research in Crime and Delinquency*, *18*, 295–318.

Moffitt, T.E. (1993). Adolescence-limited and life-course-persistent antisocial behavior: A developmental taxonomy. *Psychological Review*, *100*, 674–701.

Moffitt, T.E., Caspi, A., Dickson, N., Silva, P. and Stanton, W. (1996). Childhood-onset versus adolescent-onset antisocial conduct problems in males: Natural history from ages 3 to 18 years. *Development and Psychopathology*, *8*, 399–424.

Moffitt, T.E. and Henry, B. (1991). Neuropsychological studies of juvenile delinquency and juvenile violence. In J.S. Milner (ed.), *Neuropsychology of aggression*. Boston: Kluwer.

Mortimore, P. (1995). The positive effects of schooling. In M. Rutter (ed.), *Psychosocial disturbances in young people: Challenge for prevention* (pp. 333–363). New York: Cambridge University Press.

Nagin, D. and Land, K.C. (1993). Age, criminal careers, and population heterogeneity: Specification and estimation of a nonparametric, mixed Poisson model. *Criminology, 31*, 327–362.

Nagin, D. and Tremblay, R.E. (1999). Trajectories of boys' physical aggression, opposition, and hyperactivity on the path to physically violent and nonviolent juvenile delinquency. *Child Development, 70*, 1181–1196.

Olweus, D. (1979). Stability of aggressive reaction patterns in males: A review. *Psychological Bulletin, 86*, 852–875.

Olweus, D. (1994). *Bullying at school*. Oxford: Blackwell.

Patterson, G.R., Reid, J.B. and Dishion, T.J. (1992). *Antisocial boys*. Eugene, OR: Castalia.

Patterson, G.R., Forgatch, M.S., Yoerger, K.L. and Stoolmiller, M. (1998). Variables that initiate and maintain an early-onset trajectory for juvenile offending. *Development and Psychopathology, 10*, 531–547.

Paik, H. and Comstock, G. (1994). The effects of television violence on antisocial behavior: A meta-analysis. *Communication Research, 21*, 516–546.

Peters, R. DeV. and McMahon, R.J. (eds) (1996). *Childhood disorders, substance abuse and delinquency*. Thousand Oaks, CA. Sage.

Plomin, R. (1994). *Genetics and experience*. Newbury Park, CA: Sage.

Quinton, D., Pickles, A., Maughan, B. and Rutter, M. (1993). Partners, peers and pathways: Assortive pairing, and continuities in conduct disorder. *Development and Psychopathology, 5*, 763–783.

Raine, A. (1993). *The psychopathology of crime*. San Diego: Academic Press.

Raine, A. (1997). Antisocial behavior and psychophysiology: A biosocial perspective and a prefrontal dysfunction hypothesis. In D.M. Stoff, J. Breiling and J.D. Maser (eds), *Handbook of antisocial behavior* (pp. 289–304). New York: John Wiley & Sons.

Raine, A. (2001). Psychopathy, violence and brain imaging. In A. Raine and J. Sanmartin (eds), *Violence and psychopathy* (pp. 35–55). New York: Kluwer Academic/Plenum Publishers.

Redondo, S., Sánchez-Meca, J. and Garrido, V. (1999). The influence of treatment programmes on the recidivism of juvenile and adult offender: An European meta-analytic review. *Psychology, Crime and Law, 5*, 251–278.

Reiss, A.J. and Farrington, D.P. (1991). Advancing knowledge about co-offending: Results from a prospective longitudinal survey of London males. *Journal of Criminal Law and Criminology, 82*, 360–395.

Richters, J.E. and Martinez, P.E. (1993). Violent communities, family choices, and children's chances: An algorithm for improving the odds. *Development and Psychopathology, 5*, 609–627.

Robins, L.N. (1978). Sturdy childhood predictors of adult antisocial behavior: Replications from longitudinal studies. *Psychological Medicine, 8*, 611–622.

Ross, R.R. and Ross, B. (eds) (1995). *Thinking straight*. Ottawa: Cognitive Centre.

Rowe, D.C. (1994). *The limits of family influence: Genes, experience, and behavior*. New York: Guilford.

Rutter, M. (1990). Psychosocial resilience and protective mechanisms. In J. Rolf, A. Masten, D. Cicchetti, K. Nuechterlein and S. Weintraub (eds), *Risk and protective factors in the development of psychopathology* (pp. 181–214). Cambridge: Cambridge University Press.

Rutter, M., Giller, H. and Hagell, A. (1998). *Antisocial behavior by young people*. Cambridge UK: Cambridge University Press.

Rutter, M., Maughan, B., Mortimore, P. and Ouston, J. (1979). *Fifteen thousand hours: Secondary schools and their effects on children*. Cambridge, MA: Harvard University Press.

Sampson, R.J. and Laub, J.H. (1993). *Crime in the making: Pathways and turning points through life*. Cambridge, MA: Harvard University Press.

Sampson, R. and Lauritsen, J. (1994). Violent victimization and offending: Individual-, situational-, and community-level risk factors. In A.J. Reiss and J.A. Roth (eds), *Understanding and preventing violence: Vol. 3. Social influences* (pp. 1–115). Washington, DC: National Academy Press.

Sanders, M.R., Markie-Dadds, C., Tully, L.A. and Bor, W. (2000). The Triple P-Positive Parenting Program: A comparison of enhanced, standard, and self-directed behavioral family interventions for parents of children with early onset conduct problems. *Journal of Consulting and Clinical Psychology*, *68*, 624–640.

Schweinhart, L.L., Barnes, H.V. and Weikhart, D.P. (1993). Significant benefits: The *High/Scope Perry Preschool Study through age 27*. Ypsilanti, MI: High/Scope Press.

Snyder, H.N. (2001). Epidemiology of official offfending. In R. Loeber and D.P. Farrington (eds), *Child delinquents* (pp. 25–46). Thousand Oaks, CA: Sage.

Stattin, H., Romelsjö, A. and Stenbacka, M. (1997). Personal resources as modifiers of the risk for future criminality. *British Journal of Criminology*, *37*, 198–223.

Stattin, H. and Magnusson, D. (1996). Antisocial development: A holistic approach. *Development and Psychopathology*, *8*, 617–645.

Sykes, G.M. and Matza, D. (1957). Techniques of neutralization: A theory of delinquency. *American Sociological Review*, *22*, 664–670.

Thornberry, T.P. (1998). Membership in youth gangs and involvement in serious and violent offending. In R. Loeber and D.P. Farrington (eds), *Serious and violent juvenile offenders: Risk factors and successful interventions* (pp. 147–166). Thousand Oaks, CA: Sage.

Tremblay, R.E. and Craig, W.M. (1995). Developmental crime prevention. In M. Tonry and D. Farrington (eds), *Building a safer society: Strategic approaches to crime prevention. Crime and Justice: An annual review of research* (vol. 19; pp. 151–236). Chicago: University of Chicago Press.

Tremblay, R.E., LeMarquand, D. and Vitaro, F. (1999). The prevention of oppositional defiant disorder and conduct disorder. In H.C.Quay and A.E. Hogan (eds), *Handbook of disruptive behavior disorders* (pp. 525–555). New York: Kluwer Academic Publisher/Plenum Press.

Tremblay, R.E., Masse, L.C., Perron, D., Vitaro, F. and Dobkin, P.L. (1995). The impact of friends' deviant behavior on early onset of delinquency: Longitudinal data from 6 to 13 years of age. *Developmen and Psychopathology*, *7*, 649–667.

Wasserman, G.A. and Miller, L.S. (1998). The prevention of serious and violent juvenile offending. In R. Loeber and D.P. Farrington (eds), *Serious and violent juvenile offenders* (pp. 197–247). Thousand Oaks, CA: Sage.

Weisz, J.R., Donenberg, G.R., Weiss, B. and Han, S.S. (1995). Bridging the gap between laboratory and clinic in child and adolescent psychotherapy. *Journal of Consulting and Clinical Psychology*, *63*, 688–701.

Werner, E.E. and Smith, R.S. (1992). *Overcoming the odds*. Ithaca: Cornell University Press.

White, A.J. and Heilbrun, K. (1995). The classification of overcontrolled hostility: comparison of two diagnostic methods. *Criminal Behaviour and Mental Health*, *5*, 106–123.

Wikström, P.-O and Loeber, R. (2000). Do disadvantaged neighborhoods cause well-adjusted children to become adolescent delinquents? A study of male juvenile serious offending, individual risk and protective factors, and neighborhood context. *Criminology*, *38*, 1109–1142.

Wolfgang, M.E., Figlio, R.M. and Sellin, T. (1972). *Delinquency in a birth cohort*. Chicago: Chicago University Press.

Yoshikawa, H. (1994). Prevention as cumulative protection: Effects of early family support and education on chronic delinquency and its risks. *Psychological Bulletin*, *115*, 28–54.

Zumkley, H. (1994). The stability of aggressive behavior: A meta-analysis. *German Journal of Psychology*, *18*, 273–281.

Chapter 2.8

Children in Disputes

Judith Trowell
Tavistock Clinic, London, UK

INTRODUCTION

Most countries have now ratified the UN Convention on the Rights of the Child 1989. *Working Together to Safeguard Children* (Department of Health, 1999), a guidance Document for England and Wales (1999), summarises this as (Chapter 1, page 1):

All children deserve the opportunity to achieve their full potential. They should be able to:

- be as physically and mentally healthy as possible

- gain the maximum benefits from good quality educational opportunities

- live in a safe environment and be protected from harm

- experience emotional well-being

- feel loved and valued and be supported by a network of reliable and affectionate relationships

- become competent in looking after themselves and coping with everyday living

- have a positive image of themselves, and a secure sense of identity, including cultural and racial identity

- develop good interpersonal skills and confidence in social situations.

The Children Act 1989 of England and Wales (HMSO, 1991), which has been reproduced in many countries around the world, states that where there are disputes and decision-making with regard to children,

the child's welfare shall be the Court's paramount consideration . . . the Court shall have due regard to:

Handbook of Psychology in Legal Contexts, Second Edition
Edited by D. Carson and R. Bull. © 2003 John Wiley & Sons, Ltd.

(a)   the ascertainable wishes and feelings of the child concerned (considered in the light of his age and understanding);

(b)   his physical, emotional and educational needs;

(c)   the likely effect on him of any change in his circumstances.

(The Children Act uses 'he' for he and she and 'his' for his and hers throughout.)

These then are the ground rules or the context within which one is required to consider children in disputes. But it is important to remember—as King (1997, pp. 177–178) points out:

> If we search globally for the causes of the most widespread and most severe suffering to children, we find not deliberate acts by adults to cause children harm, but rather such general calamities as war, disaster, poverty, disease and family breakdown and ... that the most general and far-reaching improvements in children's lives are likely to come about only as the result of amelioration in living conditions, the control of disease, the redistribution of wealth, high levels of employment, and educational provision. These improvements involve complex forces, often today on a global scale, over which both individuals and individual governments can expect to have only limited control. We must therefore try to understand and where appropriate speak for children mindful that any policy and social change will be limited in what it can achieve for children although it may benefit these children.

The disputes to be considered in this chapter are those in the domains of child welfare—reception into care and placement including adoption, loss of liberty in secure accommodation and in matrimonial disputes, divorce, disputes over residence, and contact including domestic violence. Consideration will also be given to the child's capacity to contribute to the decision-making, and the child's rights to express his or her view and have it taken seriously, or his or her right to decide.

THE CHILD

The capacity and competence of a child and the assessment process is considered in the first section of this book. But some comments are required here in this consideration of children and disputes. There has been a growth and spread of the Children's Rights movement, the employment of Children's Rights officers, and serious attempts to implement the *UN Convention on the Rights of the Child* and human rights legislation. These vary between countries but the principles are the same.

But there are problems as yet unresolved. Children are in the process of developing, so when can they grasp fully the implications of any decision, and when can they be held responsible for their actions? The variation in the age of criminal responsibilities between countries confirms that there is uncertainty. Do adults opt out of their responsibility to take painful, tough decisions by allowing the child to decide? And yet where a child totally opposes a change frequently the outcome will be problematic—for example, a child in foster care or boarding school runs home.

There are difficulties in setting age limits, a child of 14 or 15 may be very mature and sensible while a young person of 17 or 18 may be very immature and vulnerable and yet is seen as capable of major decision-making. There is a strong desire in legislators and policy-makers to have clear answers. For example, when does a child know right from wrong, fully understand the implications of his or her actions or decisions? It is unsatisfactory to insist on an individual assessment, in each case, but even broad bands can be unhelpful or harmful to children. In the UK 10 years is seen as the age of criminal responsibility. In France, it is 13 years. In other European countries, it varies from 18 years in Belgium, Romania and Lithuania, to 7 years in Switzerland and Ireland; and in Scandinavian countries it is 15 years.

Children's development of memory is an important component in trying to understand capacity and competence, and recent work has shown that in laboratory settings 70% of children down to as young as 3 years can reasonably accurately recall events but can also be coached to change their story (suggestibility) (Leitchman and Ceci, 1995; Fundudis, 1997). Fundudis has written a helpful review of children's memory where its complexity is explored and the question of suggestibility and the implications for traumatised children and interview techniques are discussed. Noting two memory systems of (i) an unintentional non-conscious form of retention (memory without awareness)—implicit memory; and (ii) a conscious recollection of previous experiences (intentional recall)—explicit memory, is important (Shacter, 1992) since it is shown that they develop independently, and so what a child can remember changes. Fundudis suggests that there are significant developmental milestones in explicit memory that are linked to language skills, acquisition, narrative autobiographical recall, the development of self-awareness, and the early beginning of theory of mind. He also suggests that implicit memory is more robust and less linked to age (Fivush and Shukat, 1995).

It is also important to recognise that the child's comprehension as well as memory has to be considered. The case of *Gillick* reminds us that competence must be borne in mind when a child is deemed of sound mind, reasonable intelligence and capable of informed consent. A court decision, such as *Gillick* (1986), where the House of Lords (the Senior Appeal Court in the UK) decided that children under 16 years could consent to treatment where they were able to understand the particular decision and its implications even when their parents disagreed, was important. In addition to memory and comprehension, there is moral development and the individual's intelligence and context. This means the family and attachments, the emotional, interpersonal setting in which the child has developed so far that have helped to develop empathy and reflection, and the capacity to anticipate consequences for self and other.

So capacity and competence involve intelligence, memory, moral development, thought, feelings and significant relationships and are based on learning from experience. Capacity in children evolves but is not directly linked to age. However, children's views and wishes must be heard and taken seriously and due consideration given to race, gender and cultural issues. Children with disabilities merit sufficient time to ensure that they can participate in the process of decision-making in situations where there are disputes.

CHILD WELFARE, CHILDREN INVOLVED IN PUBLIC LAW DISPUTES

This involves three areas. First, there are children who are received into care. They may be accommodated, that is, in the care of the state at the request of the parent; or they may be in care on an interim or full care order as the result of a court hearing. Disputes often occur with these arrangements particularly when and if they should end, that is, should the child be rehabilitated home or not? Second, when or if it has been decided that the child cannot return to live at home, there is then a further dispute when consideration is given to placement, should it be long-term fostering or adoption? Third, there are decisions which can detain some children in secure accommodation if their behaviour is such that they or others are at risk.

The implications of these decisions matter greatly. The outcomes for the children are now known to be poor if they remain in the care system. National Children's Bureau research in 1995 shows that:

- 10,000 young people leave care each year

- 75% leave with *no* qualification, compared with 11% nationally

- 3% get 5 GCSE passes, compared to 64% nationally

- 0.4% qualifiy for college or university, 44.7% nationally

- 80% of care leavers are jobless at 18–24 years, compared to 16% nationally

- 55% of single homeless people have been in care

- 60% have serious health issues

- 80% experience destitution

- 38% of the young prison population (18–25) have been in care

- 22% have identified themselves as experiencing abuse.

However, Minty (1999) has undertaken a comprehensive review of the outcomes of long-term foster family care. He concludes that, despite adverse comments and perceptions, long-term fostering can provide good care and good outcomes for children and that the pressure only to have short placements may be unhelpful. He is, however, clear that for there to be good outcomes, there must be good support for the carers and a reservoir of good foster placements. He also stresses the need for much more emphasis on the education of the children (Stevenson, 1998).

This would suggest that where the original family cannot or will not provide adequate care, removal is a viable option. However, the size of this problem, although not vast, does demand considerable resources. The document *Child Protection—Messages from Research* (HMSO, 1995) records that there were, in 1992, 11 million children in England of whom 160,000 were referred to the child protection process. There were 40,000 child protection conferences of which 11,000 had no further involvement and 21,500 children were placed on the Child Protection Register. Approximately 3000 children were accommodated and about another 3000 children entered the care system. This is not a large number of children, despite the number of professionals that are involved. But the impression given is that it is an enormous problem. It also needs to be recognised that the disputes these children are caught up in are often the ones that attract high profile media attention so that children, parents and professionals feel exposed and judged.

The child's voice is essential in this process but the child's best interest is also vital and needs equal weight. How can a child know that life can be different, that 'sexual abuse' is not what happens in all families, that physical abuse is not the usual mode of disciplining children or for adults to relate to each other, that adequate food, warmth and clothing is usual, that not all parents use alcohol or drugs so much that there are periods when they cannot function, or that all parents do not see the world as their parents do when the parent is suffering with a mental illness or severe personality disorder (Cleaver, Unell and Aldgate, 1999).

Steven, aged 11 years, went into care on an interim order and was desperate to return home to his mother and younger sister. He had bruising and had stopped functioning at school. Mother, a paranoid schizophrenic, had episodes when she saw Steven as the informer, controlled by the enemy relaying orders from outside forces, the surveillance police, social security or her ex-partner. Steven knew he had to care for his mother and sister during his mother's episodes, buying food, taking his sister to school, opening tins and packets for them to eat.

How then do we think about these cases, think about the children where there is a dispute between the statutory services and their parents, which leaves them caught in the crossfire or more usually desperately clinging to their parent(s)?

ASSESSMENT OF THESE CHILDREN

The *Framework for the Assessment of children in need and their families* (Department of Health, 2000) advocates a multi-agency assessment. Their figures suggest that, in 1999, of 11 million children, 4 million were vulnerable of which 300,000–400,000 were 'in need'; 53,000 were children looked after, which included those coming into care that year and those in long-term care.

As outlined in the *Framework*, the assessment needs to include:

1. A full social, medical, educational and mental health history for each parent and each child.

2. An individual assessment of each parent and each child, which should include a physical examination of each child, a mental state assessment, an educational and psychological assessment, and a clinical interview with each.

3. A family assessment looking at family interaction and functioning.

4. Parental couple assessment and parent–child assessment.

5. Police screening for the adults may be useful.

6. Frequently an assessment of treatability is needed to see if changes are likely and a series of interviews over time may indicate whether behaviour and attitudes can alter and evolve or not.

Children in public and private law disputes deserve a careful and thorough assessment. Each discipline contributes a different perspective and can undertake an aspect of the assessment. A professionals' meeting is then essential to pull the ideas together to achieve the maximum understanding possible of the family and the individuals in it. Families have many forms and structures and there are also racial, cultural and religious differences as well as members with disabilities and different sexual orientations. The professionals' meetings often therefore need to include advisers.

An Asian family consisted of a parent and step-parent with a daughter who had learning difficulties and had possibly been sexually abused. Mother was deaf and they spoke Muslim Gujarati. There needed to be a signer, an interpreter and a religious adviser. Often, in such a case, the family will be seen for assessment because a crisis has arisen. Unemployment may have occurred or physical or mental illness or domestic violence. The assessment tries to clarify how troubled and damaged the children are and whether the situation will ameliorate once the crisis is past or whether this was a chronically unacceptable situation that the crisis has brought into the open. In this case, could the girl remain living at home?

The attachments, or significant relationships, need to be paid particular attention. A securely attached child is likely to be resilient and cope with a disruption and is also likely to reattach if this is essential. An anxious or avoidently attached child will be less resilient, do less well at school and generally demonstrate his or her insecurity. A small number of children have no attachment figure, and no significant relationship. They may be indiscriminately too friendly and too close to others, or they may be withdrawn and detached, not relating. Some children have a disorganised attachment where there has been a loss—bereavement—or a past history of abuse. Assessing attachment involves observing interaction, play and exploring behaviours, and observing separations and reunions. In adults it involves listening to and observing the description of their early life and significant relationships. While any trained professional can consider attachments, other aspects of the assessment are better done by specific professionals.

Families can become very persecuted and distressed during an assessment. Others seem to find it a relief that they are finally being listened to and their problems considered. Most are aware that all is far from well. It is important to stress that dealing with the dispute in a formal process alters the family functioning. Parents who were at war can, with a shared external enemy, come together in a powerful alliance. Others fragment under stress and the care of other children disintegrates. A family, where the daughter's allegation of sexual abuse has led to an investigation, is not helped by the uncle, the alleged abuser, who is resident in the household, committing suicide. Supporting all family members alongside the assessment is therefore essential; any assessment is trying to capture a kaleidoscope, a picture that is shifting.

Once completed the assessment leads to decision-making and court. Children are rarely involved in this process but may well be aware of the power of the judge. Children will frequently express surprise that the judge makes decisions for them without ever speaking to them. They may instruct their own solicitor if they realise this is possible; and this applies to adolescents in particular.

More and more guidelines, books and proposals are put forward to structure these assessments. They can be helpful and certainly writing reports has a well-recognised structure. But clinical judgement, the multidisciplinary perspective, and the best interest of the child need to come together in a rationally objective and thoughtful way with adequate time for reflection and discussion if sound decision-making is to follow (Thorpe and Clarke, 1998).

DISPUTES ABOUT RECEPTION INTO CARE

Most children do not want to enter the care system, though a small number do. Most children are desperate to remain with their families, the familiar people, continuity and routine. Most disputes are resolved by agencies working in partnership with the parent(s), finding ways to offer support and to bring about change without the child(ren) needing to be received into care. Many children can enter care for short periods while the main carer is unable to look after them, such as when there is illness or hospital admission.

But adversarial disputes are damaging to children and create the impression that the system is 'out to remove' children from their homes. The parents generally do not understand why they are seen as inadequate (Cleaver and Freeman 1995). A number have grown up in care themselves and do not want this for their children. Others may have mild to moderate learning difficulties or mental health problems. A small number are self-absorbed and either preoccupied in their own need or see the child as a means for their own gratification. The children, whatever the family difficulties, are usually very frightened, may be psychologically frozen and paralysed or may become depressed or angry and defiant. Once in care, they may blossom physically but many may miss their parents and be distressed and preoccupied, or for a period they may switch off and become detached. Many of these children have diagnosable psychopathology as well as poor physical health (McCann et al., 1996).

Parents need to fight for their children to be able to live with them and professionals need to intervene where there is significant harm. The Court hearing is therefore frequently cruel to parents as they hear how their parenting was perceived. Professionals need to do this to make the best case they can to remove the child if this is felt to be the better option. If parents can be helped to understand, and the children also to understand even if they do not agree, the long-term distress can be ameliorated (Farmer and Owen, 1995).

A single mother had two children, who had probably been sexually abused by her cohabitee. He had disappeared but the children were very troubled and it was the third abusive relationship she had had. The children, with her reluctant agreement, were placed in foster care, offered treatment and attended school regularly. Mother initially was distraught and took to drink but in time sought help and was able to have beneficial contact with her children. These children were on full care orders and were in long-term foster care with regular contact.

Disputes where the Child Remains in Long-Term Care or is made Available for Adoption

If the situation with the parent(s) does not improve, children are thought to need stability and permanence. This may involve long-term fostering on a full care order, or a move towards adoption. Permanent placement is a major decision and a full care order is often fought over painfully. A care plan must be drawn up so that parents realise the implications. Children may, by this time, have formed attachments to their current carers and be distressed at the prospect of moving from these short-term carers (up to two years) to long-term carers, particularly if this may involve a change of location, schools and friends. If the children have seen their parents regularly, or if the situation at home seems to have improved, the children may be keen to return home (Newman, 1995; Dagoo, 1995).

Where parents are desperate to have their child home and the child knows this and wishes to return home, the professionals have a distressing task if, in their view, the child should not return. This may be because of the child's problems and difficulties or those of the parents. But, since giving evidence of these often feels like a personal attack, the parent or child inevitably becomes very distressed, and the situation can often be very damaging with little or no possibility of improvement until after the final decision has been made and the child and his or her parents can be offered support and some reflective discussion perhaps with another professional.

ADOPTION DISPUTES

In National Children's Home (a UK children's charity) Action for Children Fact/File (Dunn and McCluskey, 1997), 4427 care orders were made, and 579 care orders were discharged. There were 1100 children freed for adoption. Of the 51,200 children being looked after, 29,000 were on care orders, so most children were not on orders but were subject to voluntary agreement; 33,200 of these children were in foster placements and the remainder were in residential constitutional placements. The NCH document suggests that most children freed for adoption have been cared for by incompetent, neglectful and abusive or indifferent and rejecting parents. So the majority of these children have been in foster care or residential care and subject to disputes about their future. Howe (1997) has studied the outcome for a sample of adoptive children. He showed that children adopted late (mean age 8.7 years), but who had had relatively good care in their first two years, managed reasonably well in adolescence, whereas children who had a poor start and were then placed (mean age 4.4 years) had a greater risk of behavioural and psychiatric problems. It is known that adopted children are over-represented in referrals to Child and Adolescent Mental Health services (Hersov, 1990). Although the good start/late placed children have experienced adversity, the good early start seems to be protective and to have led to some resilience. Attempts to try to explain the problems for adoptive children involve discussion of genetic inherited factors and psychosocial factors and their interplay (Hersov, 1990).

Placing a child for adoption involves freeing the child, which is a legal process, and the biological parent may or may not consent. If the child is having contact with the parent then he or she is very aware of the dispute.

Janice, aged 6 years, was seeing her mother fortnightly. Mother and her partner had wanted Janice returned but sexual abuse of Janice by mother's previous partner and mother's inability to believe or accept what had happened, mother's lifestyle, and her very limited capacity to change did not make rehabilitation possible. Janice consistently said she wanted to live with her mother and, if she could not, then she wanted to stay with her foster mother and see mother regularly. A permanent placement in a new family with adoption seemed the better outcome but Janice's distress and rejection of the prospective adoptive parents were not easy to handle. If the parent(s) can work with Social Services, and can concede they cannot care for the child, then they can help the child to separate and move on to a new family. Within extended families adoptions can sometimes involve much less conflict but grandparent or aunt or uncle adoption may also lead to disputes when there are disagreements about how to bring up the children. Where the parent continues to fight it is very difficult for the child, parents and professionals.

Considerable emphasis is being placed on speeding up the process. Many children, where no parent is involved and Social Services are stretched drift into care; but where the adoption is disputed, time does allow the parent and child to explore whether rehabilitation or regular good contact is possible or not. An attempt to make adoption less contentious has involved the possibility of open adoption, but its implementation depends on the adoptive parents. Anna's mother had learning difficulties and schizo-affective disorder. Anna was in and out of care whenever mother needed admission. Two years later this 5-year-old had been back and forth to one foster family and had had more time with them than with her mother. Open adoption was proposed; mother was distressed. But with further contact with her social worker, prospective adoptive parents and Anna, mother decided that it was better for Anna to be adopted if she could continue to see her. The prospective adopters recognised it would be helpful to Anna to see her mother when mother was well.

All these public law cases will involve the Child and Family Court Advisory and Support Service (CAFCASS) specialist workers (ex Guardian ad Litem, the Official Solicitors, Children's Officers and the Court Welfare Service). Their task is to repre-sent the best interests of the child. Some try to find ways to resolve the dispute for the sake of the children and to find solutions acceptable to all parties while safeguarding the safety and best interest of the child. This is certainly preferable given the distress and damage caused by these disputes when they continue over many years. Public Law dispute resolution, where possible, has much to recommend it. Most children placed for adoption have been fostered for 1 to 5 years (76% of adoptions). If the con-flicts and disputes could be resolved sooner and adoption services improved, children would benefit.

SECURE ACCOMMODATION

A secure order can be applied for if the child needs his or her liberty restricted:

(a)   if he/she absconds, he/she is likely to suffer significant harm, or

(b)   if he/she is likely to injure himself/herself or other persons.

Sadly, some adolescents on full care orders are in such a disturbed state that they need this provision. Those who have major mental health problems are dealt with under the Mental Health Act 1983. Young people on secure orders are often traumatised from abuse but desperate to return to their families, or have disorders such as conduct disorder, oppositional defiant disorder, and a personality disorder often with self-harming behaviour. These orders are for a few weeks and need renewal; very rarely they can be extended to six months.

These young people cause great concern. Often parents or carers are desperate and the young person is outraged. Once in secure accommodation, the young person should have a future plan arranged and receive intensive input and education. Young people can be independently represented since the restriction of liberty is very serious and failure to do so might be a human rights law infringement. Evidence for the need for secure accommodation must be very clearly and powerfully put. The treatment alliance with the young person can be threatened or damaged by this process.

Secure orders are only sought in extreme cases, but currently the dilemma is what happens to the young people next. Where can they go? Many young people are aware of this. Living much or most of the time on the streets, these young people are aware of the system. So often the dispute with them is 'What is the point?', 'Where will I go next?'.

MATRIMONIAL DISPUTES

How do we understand the impact of divorce upon children? Wallerstein, Corbin and Lewis (1988, p. 197) state:

> For divorce, as we have fully recognised, is not a single circumscribed event, but a multistage process of radically changing family relationships. This process begins in the failing marriage, sometimes many years prior to the marital breakdown, may include one or more separations within the marriage, and extend over years following the decisive separation and the legal divorce.

They go on to suggest that the phenomenon of divorce itself has had a profound effect on society as a whole, changing patterns of relationships and attitudes to family, raising anxiety between men and women, and between children and their parents.

They studied children of different ages to consider the developmental impact. Their view was that overall the main hazard to psychological health for the children was the disrupted parenting, ongoing parental conflicts, the flawed or tragic role models of parents who are subsequently unable to stablise their lives, the diminished quality of life for the children, the economic deprivation, and the curtailed educational and social opportunities.

One area that is particular cause for concern is the effect of divorce on antisocial behaviour in boys. Forgatch, Patterson and Skinner (1988) suggest that where there is a single mother under stress, post divorce there may be inept discipline (that is inconsistent mothering and then explosive discipline) and that this inept discipline leads to the child's antisocial behaviour that involves aggressive, defiant and destructive problems. O'Connor and colleagues (2001) have shown that behavioural and emotional problems were increased in children, in step-mother/complex step-families and single-parent families, but not in simple step-father families. The psychopathology was associated with family type and was explained by the compromised quality of the parent–child relationship, parental depression and socio-economic adversity.

Children, post divorce, growing up in step-families, are also known to show more developmental difficulties than those with both biological parents, particularly behavioural and emotional adjustment. However, they have fewer learning problems and show better physical health than those in single-parent families (Zill, 1988).

There seems to be general agreement that children under 5, when a parent leaves, particularly if it was the main carer, are those most at risk of long-term effects (Smith, 1999). Primary and secondary school children can be troubled long term, with anger, distress and poor concentration at school. Older children can react with risk-taking behaviour, staying out, cutting themselves, and eating disorders. The conflicting feelings about themselves, their identity and self-esteem is linked to their conflicting feelings about their parents (Zimmerman et al., 1997). Harter (1999) suggests self-esteem depends on the competence and the adequacy of the young person, and approval from significant others particularly where there is a long-term supportive relationship. Where there has been domestic violence there is considerably more trauma to the child (Hemmings et al., 1997).

Rodgers and Pryor (1998) estimate that 19% of children born to married couples will experience parental divorce by the age of 10 and 28% by age 16. Haskey (1993, 1994) states that in the early 1990s in England and Wales 160 000 families with children under 16 went through the experience of parental divorce. Of these children one in three was under 5, and a further 7000 were between 5 and 10 years. Dunn, Deater-Deckard, Pickering, O'Connor, Golding and Avon Longitudinal Study of Pregnancy and Childhood (ALSPAC) Team (1998) have looked at a community sample to examine the implications for children. The risk factors are socio-economic, parental mental health and well-being (such as depression), patterns of family relations with a high level of conflict and a lack of coherence or joint activities, poor educational achievement, transitions in family settings, and finally subsequent cohabitations. They studied these in the ALSPAC, which looked at 7219 4-year-olds and 4071 older siblings and compared those in this sample who were in intact families and those in single- and step-parent families post divorce. The children who were reported to be more hyperactive were also likely to have peer problems and conduct disorder and the boys' levels of problems in this study were higher than the girls. However, the differences were not great and the difficulties seemed to be significantly linked to negativity in the mother–child relationship, for example, where there was a battle of wills and/or where the children were seen as irritating, and as making excessive noise and mess. They also concluded that the direct impact on older children of transitions was important in their adjustment, but not for the 4-year-olds.

The recognition of domestic violence and intractable hostility in matrimonial disputes has lead to increasing use of mental health services both to assess the degree of disturbance of the child caught in the crossfire and to advise on residence, contact, and the need for support or treatment for the children.

A mother had stopped her two daughters' contact with father. She insisted they were reluctant to go and that they returned very distressed. She described how her elder daughter had told her about kisses and cuddles with dad that made the daughter feel uncomfortable. Mother felt this was quite inappropriate. Dad had been quite distant and uninvolved before the separation and divorce. Mother emerged as very angry, resentful and bitter about her ex-husband. She loathed him and alleged domestic violence and excessive sexual demands. Father saw mother as a vicious, vindictive, destructive person poisoning their children against him. If the parents met there were hostile enraged exchanges. The elder, 9 years old, a sad rather depressed child who was desperate to do well at school and was struggling, declared she did not wish to see father ever again. However, the younger daughter, 6 years old, shyly and warily in front of her sister said she loved her dad and wanted to see him but it was hard as mum and her sister were against it. The suggestion of contact for the younger girl with father and his extended family, and a group meeting for the older girl, did not please either parent but seemed what the children could manage.

A boy, aged 14, was enraged with both his parents as they continued to fight with each other and over him. He had a home visit with each of them and lived part of the week with each. Mother alleged emotional and psychological abuse and domestic violence. Father alleged persecution and complete unreasonableness with impossible demands and expectations as he worked at his new relationship. Their son was right. Both mother and father were preoccupied with their own versions of events. He stopped school, was in a group of young people that drank, roamed the streets and stole what they could find, including from their parents' homes. His contempt, bitterness and lack of remorse were worrying. The parents could stop blaming each other just long enough to hear that their son was in trouble. A boarding school was suggested and greeted by all with horror. The Court ordered joint parental responsibility, with the boy resident with mother in the week and alternate weekends, and one evening with father and alternate weekends. No one was satisfied and the boy left home to stay with a friend.

WHAT DO CHILDREN AND YOUNG PEOPLE NEED?

Now that the whole child welfare field has become increasingly driven by procedures and guidelines and colonised by the law, it is not always easy to keep in the forefront the child or young person who is at the centre of all this activity. The children have to live through the disputes, the assessments and find their placement decided for them and their relationships prescribed.

But alongside this turmoil in the external world, children have to try to make sense of the experience and what it means to them as well as manage the normal developmental processes. Children and young people require their physical needs to be met, but more relevant here is their need for emotional, psychological and social development alongside moral development and spirituality. Any child needs significant relationships, not just attachments, and within these relationships the child needs to be valued and re-spected. The important task for the parent or carer is that of containment. The adult needs to be able to accept the child's hopes, fears, anxiety, longing, omnipotence, arrogance, self-doubt, terror and aggression. These feelings may be communicated verbally, non-verbally or unconsciously. The adult needs to be able to tolerate the feel-ings, reflect on the process, and help the child by reducing the intensity and showing that he or she is bearable and can be understood. The adult has to avoid retaliation or acting out by becoming caught up in the child's emotional state while remaining sensitive and thoughtful. Slowly, children manage to take in this capacity to bear the feeling and reflect, and can then 'contain' themselves, but they can only do this if they have had a relationship with such an adult for sufficient duration. Where parents never had this experience themselves, it may be that a nursery worker, a teacher or a family friend becomes important, or it may be that the children's first experience of containment is once the dispute is resolved and they are with substitute carers or have been offered help (e.g. psychotherapy).

Children also have to learn certain fundamentals, such as that there are male and female people, children and adults, racial differences and, the most universal, that there is life and death. However, 'learn' does not mean only intellectual knowing but knowing from experience about difference and mortality. If children have experienced containment and faced difference, then curiosity and creativity begin to emerge, as does the wish to learn about, to understand and to express themselves.

And all this needs to be in the context of feeling safe, aware of boundaries, and that if told 'no' this is usually adhered to and cannot be manipulated. Children will then slowly develop a sense of identity, a racial identity, a sexual identity, all of which they can be proud of and then develop friendships which grow into intimate satisfying relationships.

An encouraging aspect of development is that if there have been problems in early childhood, there is, in adolescence, the opportunity to re-work many of the issues and conflicts if the emotional environment is more stable and containing.

Understanding oneself and one's history is important and many adopted children and children leaving care seek out their birth parent(s) not only to try to find out about their past but also to find their 'family' even when they have a good enough psychological family. It is important that the substitute carers can support and understand this and not feel too threatened. Children of divorce less often seek out the absent parent, perhaps because they have lived with the angry, resentful, sad parent even if life has moved on. Many of these children and young people can do well, but many need some counselling or therapy to help them find their own perspective on events.

If the children are reasonably attractive physically and do well in one area—academically, sport, the arts such as drama or music—and make friends, then they are likely to move into adulthood satisfactorily even if the adolescent turmoil is fairly stormy. The children who struggle, who opt out, who develop mental or physical health problems, are the ones where there is cause for concern. Their despair may be unbearable and their situation appear so bleak that they either become suicidal, or they become indifferent and cut off, living just for the moment for what gratification is available now. There is increasing evidence that one important factor in the outcome is the father (Phares, 1996, 1997; Burgess, 1997; Trowell and Etchegoyen, 2001).

If the father (or step-father or adoptive or foster father) has a relationship directly with the child or young person, both in the internal and external world, there seem to be benefits. If there is no actual father then the father in the mother's mind or a benign male figure can assist the child to develop the space they need in their mind to think to learn to reflect and to manage their feelings.

What then do children and young people need? They need a parent or substitute carer who can:

- Anticipate difficulties.

- Empathise.

- Protect.

- Stimulate.

- Imagine what it is like to be a child.

- Make commitments.

- Show love and approval.

- Let them go and relinquish the central emotional position.

Then if they have experienced containment, have attachments, self-worth and paternal as well as maternal awareness, they should be able to manage adversity, develop, learn and love.

CONCLUSION

Separation and divorce is always a distressing dispute for children but it is known that after the initial crisis, if the parents manage themselves and the situation well enough, many children recover and can get on with their lives reasonably well. This is in contrast to public law disputes, reception into care, long-term fostering or adoption (except perhaps that of babies below six months who are adopted) where there are particular adjustment problems. These are the children who have more conflicts, are disrupted, are often moved and regularly lack even one parent to provide continuity.

But all the children in divorce, residence and contact disputes, and in care and adoption proceedings, want to be heard and want to be told what is happening but usually do not want the burden of choosing where to live and with whom. The exceptions to this are many adolescents who do need to be involved in the decision-making. All these children and young people want to be valued and respected, and want to understand.

Some of these children will have transient difficulties; others will have more extensive emotional, behavioural and educational difficulties. They will need a range of inputs, such as individual work, group work, family work, and support from substitute carers, teachers and the extended family to try to prevent long-term problems.

REFERENCES

Burgess, A. (1997). *Fatherhood reclaimed: The making of the modern father*. London: Vermillon.

Cleaver, H. and Freeman, P. (1995). Parental perspectives in cases of suspected child abuse. In *Child protection—messages from research*. London: HMSO.

Cleaver, H., Unell, I. and Aldgate, J. (1999). *Children's needs—parental capacity: The impact of parental mental illness, problem of alcohol and drug use and domestic violence on children's development*. London: HMSO.

Dagoo, R. (1995). The significance and meaning of contact for black families. In H. Argent (ed.), *See you soon*. London: British Agencies for Adoption and Fostering.

Department of Health (1999). *Working together to safeguard children*. London: HMSO.

Department of Health (2000). *Framework for the assessment of children in need and their family*. London: HMSO.

Dunn, M. and McCluskey, J. (1997). *NCH fact file*. Rochester: Chapel Press.

Dunn, J., Deater-Deckard, K., Pickering, K., O'Conner, T. C., Golding, J. and ALSPAC Team (1998). Children's adjustment and pro-social behaviour in step, single parent and non-step family settings: Findings from a community study. *Journal of Clinical Psychology and Psychiatry*, *39*, 1083–1095.

Farmer, E. and Owen, M. (1995). Child protection practice: Private risks and public remedies. Decision-making intervention and outcome in child protection work. In *Child protection—messages from research*. London: HMSO.

Fivush, R. and Shukat, J. R. (1995). Content, consistency and coherence of early autobiographical recall. In M. Zaragoza, J. Graham, G. Hall, R. Hirschma and Y. Ben-Horath (eds), *Memory and testimony in the child witness* (p. 5–23). Thousand Oaks: CA. Sage.

Forgatch, M., Patterson, G. and Skinner, M. (1988). A mediational model for the effect of divorce on antisocial behaviour in boys. In E. Hetherington and J. Arasteh (eds), *The impact of divorce, single parenting and step-parenting on children*. London: Erlbaum.

Fundudis, T. (1997). Young children's memory: How good is it? How much do we know about it? *Child Psychology and Psychiatry Review*, *II*, 150–158.

Gabarino, J., Guttman, E. and Seeley J. W. (1986). *The psychologically battered child*. San Francisco: Jossey Bass.

Gillick v. *West Norfolk and Wisbech AHA* [1986] AC 112.

Harter, S. (1999). The construction of the self. London: Guilford.

Haskey, J. (1993). Divorce in England and Wales. *Population trends, OPCS, vol. 74*. London: HMSO.

Haskey, J. (1994). Step-families and step children in Great Britain. *Population Trends OPCS*, vol. 76. London: HMSO.

Hemmings, K., Leitenberg, H., Coffey, P., Bennet, T. and Jankowski, M. (1997). Long-term psychological adjustment to witnessing inter-parental physical conflict during childhood. *Child Abuse and Neglect*, *21*, 501–516.

Hersov, L. (1990). The seventh Jack Tizard memorial lecture: Aspects of adoption. *Journal of Clinical Psychology and Psychiatry*, *31*, 493–510.

HMSO (1991). *Children Act (1989)*. London: HMSO.

HMSO (1995). *Child protection—messages from research*. London: HMSO.

Howe, D. (1997). Parent reported problems in 211 adopted children: Some risk and protective factors. *Journal of Clinical Psychology and Psychiatry*, *38*, 401–411

King, M. (1997). *A better world for children*. London: Routledge.

Leitchman, M.D. and Ceci, S.J. (1995). The effects of stereotypes and suggestions on preschoolers. *Developmental Psychology*, *31*, 568–578.

McCann, J., James, A., Wilson S. and Dunn, G. (1996). Prevalence of psychiatric disorder in young people in the care system. *British Medical Journal*, *313*, 1529–1530.

Minty, B. (1999). Annotation: Outcome in long term foster family care. *Journal of Clinical Psychology and Psychiatry*, *40*, 991–999.

Newman, R. (1995). From access to contact on a local authority setting. In H. Argent (ed.), *See you soon*. London: British Agencies for Adoption and Fostering.

O'Connor, T., Dunn, J., Jenkins, J., Pickering, K. and Rasbash, J. (2001). Family settings and children's adjustment: differential adjustment within and across families. *British Journal of Psychiatry*, *179*, 110–115.

Phares, V. (1996). *Fathers and developmental psychopathology*. Chichester: John Wiley & Sons.

Phares, V. (1997). Psychological adjustment, maladjustment and father–child relationships. In M. Lamb (ed.), *The role of the father in child development*. Chichester: John Wiley & Sons.

Rodgers, B. and Pryor J. (1998). *Divorce and separation: The outcomes for children*. York: Joseph Rowntree Foundation.

Shacter, D. L. (1992). Understanding implicit memory: A cognitive neuroscience of approach. *American Psychologist*, *47*, 559–569.

Smith, H. (1999). *Children, feelings and divorce: Finding the best outcome*. London: Free Association.

Stevenson, O. (1998). *Neglected children: Issues and dilemmas*. Oxford: Blackwell.

Thorpe, M. and Clarke, E. (eds) (1998). *Divided duties—family law*. Jordan Publishing.

Trowell, J. and Etchegoyen, A. (2001). *The importance of fathers*. London: Psychology Press.

Wallerstein, J., Corbin, S. and Lewis, J. (1988). Children of divorce: A 10 year study. In E. Hetherington and J. Arasteh (eds), *The impact of divorce, single parenting and step-parenting on children*. London: Erlbaum.

Zill, N. (1988). Behaviour, achievement and health problems among children in step families: Findings from a national survey of child health. In E. Hetherington and J. Arasteh (eds), *The impact of divorce, single parenting and step-parenting on children*. London: Erlbaum.

Zimmerman, M., Copeland, L., Shape, J. and Dielman, T. (1997). A longitudinal study of the self-esteem: Implications for adolescent development. *Journal of Youth and Adolescence*, *26*, 117–142.

Child Defendants
and the Law

Peter Yates
Stamford House, London, UK
and
Eileen Vizard
The Peckwater Centre, London, UK

INTRODUCTION

The legal context of child defendants is complicated and there is uncertainty about how to deal with the welfare needs of children charged with serious offences. Civil and criminal legislation has sought to address the dual status of many young defendants who are both children in need and young delinquents.

This chapter will address this difficult area by looking at the age of criminal responsibility, the human rights and the welfare needs of young offenders before looking more specifically, and in detail, at psychological and mental health issues in relation to the age of criminal responsibility. The chapter concludes with a discussion of alternative legal provisions and implications for practice.

AGE OF CRIMINAL RESPONSIBILITY

Every criminal jurisdiction should have a minimum age below which children will be presumed not to have the capacity to infringe the penal law (United Nations Convention on the Rights of the Child, Article 40(3)(a)) and this age 'shall not be fixed at too low an age level, bearing in mind the facts of emotional, mental and intellectual maturity' (United Nations Standard Minimum Rules for the Administration of Justice; UN, 1986).

In England and Wales the age of criminal responsibility is set at 10 years (Children and Young Persons Act 1933). In the eyes of the law, a child under that age is incapable

Handbook of Psychology in Legal Contexts, Second Edition
Edited by D. Carson and R. Bull. © 2003 John Wiley & Sons, Ltd.

of committing a crime. It follows that prior to his or her tenth birthday he or she can neither be arrested nor prosecuted in the criminal courts for any act considered to be criminal. However, after a child has attained the age of 10 years, he or she is subject to the full rigours of the criminal law.

In England and Wales, until 1998, there was a presumption that a child under the age of 14 years was incapable of forming the necessary criminal intent. This presumption—known by the Latin phrase *doli incapax*—could be rebutted if the prosecuting authorities could prove that the child knew that the criminal act was seriously wrong as opposed to merely naughty. However, judges felt that the presumption was inappropriate and unnecessary. So it was abolished. Now there is no longer any assessment of the child's moral understanding before attributing criminal culpability. Now childhood provides scant protection from the full rigours of the substantive law, although there are procedural differences, or from a penal philosophy of retribution which underlies its application to adults.

The age of 10 years is not remarkable in comparison with other jurisdictions in the British Isles (in Scotland the age of criminal responsibility is 8 years while in the Republic of Ireland it is 7 years) but it is low in comparison with other countries within the European Union where the median age is 14 or 15 years. It is noteworthy, too, that the trend in Europe has been to raise the age: for example, from 14 to 15 in Norway, and from 14 to 18 in Romania.

Article 6 of the European Convention on Human Rights guarantees to all defendants the right to a fair hearing. It states that 'it is essential that a child charged with an offence is dealt with in a manner which takes full account of his age, level of maturity and intellectual and emotional capacities, and that steps are taken to promote his ability to understand and participate in the proceedings' (paragraph 85). Bearing in mind these Human Rights considerations, therefore, the trial of children and young people within a full adult court context is inappropriate in relation to his or her developmental immaturity and cognitive limitations and a more appropriate youth court context should be sought in all cases to ensure that the child's human rights are not contravened and that he or she is able to participate effectively in the trial process. A recent Practice Direction (*Practice Direction: Trial of Children and Young Persons in the Crown Court*, 2000) suggests ways in which the trial procedure may be modified for a child defendant to promote understanding and participation. Suggestions include allowing the child to sit with his or her family and legal advisers; removal of wigs and gowns; simplification of the language used in court; and regular breaks.

Local authorities in England and Wales have a duty to safeguard and promote the welfare of children who are in need (Children Act 1989). The main agency that carries out this duty is the Social Services department. Where a child is considered to have suffered, or to be at risk of suffering significant harm and that harm is attributable to the care received from his or her parents, the local authority may institute care proceedings.

Many of the children charged with a criminal offence, whose backgrounds include experiencing very high levels of abuse, trauma and psychiatric disturbance, fulfil the threshold criteria for the making of a full care order under the Children Act 1989. In addition there is an argument, applicable to some cases at least, that offending behaviour on the part of the child represents a breakdown in parenting on the part of the parent(s). The reality is that while some of the children charged with criminal offences may be known to Social Services, very few are the subjects of interim or full care orders.

PSYCHOLOGICAL AND MENTAL HEALTH ISSUES IN RELATION TO THE AGE OF CRIMINAL RESPONSIBILITY

This section considers intelligence and cognitive abilities, assessment of fitness to plead, the role of the psychological assessment and mental health issues in relation to the age of criminal responsibility.

Intelligence and Cognitive Abilities

Intelligence is a concept that is difficult to define. A useful definition is that it is the sum of those aspects of mental life which relate to general cognitive abilities necessary for appraising and adapting to the environment. It is often perceived as a unitary entity but research is increasingly demonstrating different components. Many of these are clearly relevant when considering child defendants.

Vocabulary and Comprehension

Young people may present as being relatively articulate but in fact may have poor comprehension of spoken language. Limited reading and listening comprehension may imply that the young people cannot understand and make use of information presented to them when being interviewed by the police, their solicitors or in the court room.

Attention and Concentration

Attention allows absorption of information and adaptation to the environment and an increasing span of attention is a characteristic feature of normal development. Any impairment in the ability to maintain attention and concentration may therefore impinge on a young person's ability to accurately assess situations and make informed judgements.

Problem-Solving Ability

Another facet of intelligence is an ability to solve problems, especially social problems, and an ability to plan. When assessing these facets one should examine whether a young person is able to identify existing problems and formulate an effective plan of action so as to solve the problem. In terms of risk assessment the question to answer might be 'Does this person plan their actions or do they usually act impulsively?'

Guilt, Shame and Empathy

Empathy, morality and guilt are abstract concepts that demand a certain level of cognitive development. Only once a series of cognitive developmental stages are achieved can an individual take on the perspective of others and then include this perspective in one's moral decision-making. This stage of cognitive development was described by Piaget (1932) as the Stage of Formal Operations that begins around the age of 12 years. It follows that young people with low intelligence or other cognitive deficits may have deficits in terms of their ability to experience empathy or guilt. This is then a result of their inability in taking on the perspective of others.

Other Important Cognitive Processes

In addition to the more traditional cognitive abilities mentioned above there are other important cognitive processes including 'theory of mind', moral development, emotional development and development of self-control. These should not be seen as unrelated processes but rather as different interdependent parts of a complex cognitive network.

- *Theory of mind*. The most likely basic deficits in Autism (and Asperger's Syndrome) appear to be cognitive, in particular involving the ability to appreciate the point of view of others, and that this will differ from one's own (Baron-Cowen, 1989). This has been variously described as a deficit in the 'theory of mind' and these disorders are also known as disorders of social communication. Very few offenders suffer from Autism or Asperger's Syndrome, but for those who do, deficits in their 'theory of mind' capacity may help to explain the lack of empathy for their victims often shown by these offenders.

- *Moral development*. Much of the research in this area has built on the work of Piaget (1932) and Kolhberg (1974). Generally speaking, it is felt that moral development continues into adulthood. However, between 12 and 14 years most adolescents have achieved Kolhberg's 'Conventional' level of moral development. That is to say, they have developed an understanding of the rules of society in which they live and the consequences for themselves and for others, should they break the law.

- *Emotional development*. Emotional development is dependent on several factors including cognitive development and one's experience of parenting. Alongside and interwoven with young people's cognitive development is their emotional development. This includes emotional introspection and the ability to consider the consequences of their actions for themselves and others in emotional terms.

- *Self-control*. Self-control and the ability to resist impulses increases gradually from an early age. The capacity to inhibit irrelevant stimuli comprises the ability to attend selectively to certain stimuli. It involves central attentional processes, which are

Table 2.9.1 Classification of learning disability by IQ

Category	ICD-10	DSM-IV	Educational category
Mild	50–70	50–55 to approx. 70	Moderate learning difficulties
Moderate	35–49	35–40 to 50–55	
Severe	20–34	20–25 to 35–40	Severe learning difficulties
Profound	Below 20	Below 20 or 25	

developmentally determined, and much of this function is carried out in the frontal lobes of the brain. This part of the central nervous system plays an important role in managing the large amount of information entering consciousness from many sources, in changing behaviour, in using acquired information, in planning actions and in controlling impulsivity. Generally the frontal lobes are felt to mature at approximately 14 years. The ability of self-control will overlap with other abilities. For example, a young person who has developed self-control appropriate to his or her developmental status, will be able to reflect on the consequences of his or her actions in the longer term and will also have the capacity to delay gratification of impulses, if reflection confirms to him or her that these impulses are inappropriate.

Children with learning disabilities deserve additional consideration. Abnormal intellectual development may be due to slowness in development (delay) or to distortions in development (deviation) or a combination of both. One major functional consequence of intellectual impairment is learning disability, a term used in the United Kingdom for the problems experienced by people who previously would have been labelled as having mental handicap or mental retardation. Learning disability may take the form of specific learning disabilities (such as dyslexia) as well as more general learning disabilities (mental retardation).

For a diagnosis of mental retardation or generalised learning disability the developmental impairment should be global and long term. In addition, the child's Intelligence Quotient (IQ) should be less than 70 and the child should be functionally impaired in everyday life skills. ICD-10 (*International Classification of Diseases*; WHO, 1992) and DSM-IV (*Diagnostic and Statistical Manual*; APA, 1994) classifications differ to some degree and, as their educational terminology is also different and some older terms persist, it is not surprising that confusion commonly occurs.

The child with general learning disabilities (mental retardation) functions overall at a lower mental age. However, there are difficulties from the psychological perspective in the use of the term 'mental age', even although this can be a useful legal concept. Whatever the cause of the child's disability, its effect is usually to give uneven superimposed selective deficits. The result may be to leave the child with a range of capacities, some of which may be misleadingly competent and may engender false optimism in the interviewer or the child's carer. Any psychological assessment therefore has to cover a wide range of issues, and discrepancies are particularly likely between the following.

- Educational achievement, adaptive skills and social/emotional development. A child's ability often is gauged on the former and given as being equivalent to that of a certain age, for example a 15-year-old child might have the everyday living skills of a 7-year-old. However, while he or she might be unable to cope with money or public transport, he or she may well have had the emotional and social experiences of an older child and the drives of an adolescent. Any figure, whether IQ or age-equivalent, must be recognised as specific to the particular area of development from which it was derived.

- Language reception and expression. The child may sound articulate, perhaps even using legal phrases. But it does not necessarily follow that he or she understands. Even when there is adequate understanding, comprehension will depend on the child's ability to pay attention.

Assessment of Fitness to Plead

Ashford (2000) describes the test of whether a defendant is fit to plead as having been set out by Alderson, B in *R* v. *Pritchard* ((1836) 173 ER 135) over 150 years ago as follows:

> Whether he is of sufficient intellect to comprehend the course of proceedings of the trial so as to make a proper defence—to know that he might challenge (any jurors) to whom he may object—and to comprehend the details of the evidence . . . if you think that there is no certain mode of communicating the details of the trial to the prisoner so that he can clearly understand them, and be able properly to make his defence to the charge; you ought to find that he is not of sane mind. It is not enough that he may have a general capacity of communicating on ordinary matters.

Translated into the clinical assessment of fitness to plead, the following questions may form part of the psychiatrist's assessment:

- Do you know what the police say you have done?

- Can you tell your solicitor your side of things?

- Do you know the difference between saying 'guilty' and 'not guilty'?

- Do you know what will happen to you if you are found guilty or not guilty?

- If you think a witness in court is not right in what he or she says, who would you tell?

- Do you know what it means if they say you can object to some of the people on the jury in your case?

Ashford points out that the above fitness to plead test is still 'firmly embodied in our law' and whereas it may have been designed originally to deal with adults, at the present moment the assessing psychiatrist should presumably apply these principles to the mental state of children from age 10 upwards.

Bearing in mind the issues described above in relation to the cognitive abilities of child defendants, the general developmental immaturity of young children and the lack of sophisticated reasoning abilities in such children, it is worth considering whether a 'normal' (i.e. non-disturbed and non-learning disabled) child between 10 and 14 years old would be fit to plead in criminal proceedings, let alone a seriously psychiatrically disturbed and developmentally delayed child of the type most frequently described in the literature as appearing before the Courts for serious offences.

Nevertheless, under the current legal system in England and Wales, the task for the assessing forensic child psychiatrist is to undertake a full mental state examination of the child. This should exclude the possibility of serious mental illness in terms of the Mental Health Act 1983. It should describe the most significant features of the child or young person's mental state and gather these features together into a clear formulation of the child's presentation. It should express a diagnostic opinion in terms of ICD-10 or DSM-IV diagnostic categories and make clear recommendations to the court about disposal and treatment.

Given the correlation between psychiatric disturbance and learning disability, it is essential that a concurrent cognitive assessment by an experienced clinical psychologist is undertaken on all child defendants. Furthermore, it would clearly be of assistance to the assessing forensic child psychiatrist to be able to see the forensic clinical psychology report on the child defendant before undertaking any assessment of fitness to plead. The forensic clinical psychology report should describe any cognitive factors that could impair a defendant's ability to understand the proceedings and participate effectively in the trial process. Ideally, liaison between the psychologist and psychiatrist on this issue would be most helpful to the court, the Crown Prosecution Service and the defence solicitors.

It is important to note that, if a child or young person is psychologically assessed as learning disabled, this does *not* automatically preclude that person from standing trial for crimes. Depending on the specific deficits identified in psychological assessment, a learning disabled young child or young person may still be able to participate effectively in the trial process and may be fit to plead, and if this is the case there is no reason on psychological grounds why the trial should not proceed.

The Role of the Psychological Assessment

Ashford and Chard (2000) argues that the defence lawyer must be alert to the possibility that his or her client may be unable to participate effectively in the trial process. This is particularly important when the client is under the age of 14, has learning problems or a history of absence from school. Ashford describes the issues that a clinical psychologist with experience of assessing adolescents should be asked to address. He or she should assess the client's intelligence and identify any developmental or cognitive defects. He or she should then assess how any such deficits are likely to affect the client's ability to:

- understand the charges;

- understand the possible consequences of guilty and not guilty pleas;

- make rational decisions relevant to the legal process;

- remember relevant facts;

- communicate in a coherent manner;

- understand testimony in court; and

- behave appropriately in the court room.

Depending on the outcome of such an assessment by a clinical psychologist, Ashford suggests that the defence lawyer may then have to consider raising the question of fitness to plead.

Recent research from the USA (Grisso, 2000) has suggested worrying variations in the cognitive capacities of youths as trial defendants when learning disability is confirmed. Grisso has made the point, in relation to youths' adjudicative capacities, that there must be competence in four areas of functioning. They must be able to:

- understand the legal process;

- appreciate the significance of the legal circumstances;

- communicate information; and

- reason.

The point is made that 'even when adolescents' cognitive abilities are similar to adult capacities, theory suggests that they will deploy those abilities with less dependability in new, ambiguous, or stressful situations, because the abilities have been acquired more recently and are less well established'. And it should be added that there is always a considerable variation in the level of competence achieved by different children at any one age.

Mental Health Issues

In order for someone to be 'guilty' of a crime there must be both of the following:

- a voluntary act, the *actus reus*

- a mental element, the *mens rea*.

However, even if the *actus reus* and *mens rea* are established, there are reasons for not blaming a person for a crime. One such reason is young age. This arises from consideration of the distinction between blame, guilt and responsibility and whether or not the child has sufficient maturity of mind to understand such issues. Thus, within the criminal legal system, a young person can be found guilty of the commission of a crime but may not be responsible for his or her actions because of one or more of the following:

- limited cognitive development;

- limitations in moral development; and/or

- presence of a psychiatric illness or disorder.

Therefore, the question arises as to what age should children be held responsible for their actions legally and socially? More particularly, in making this decision, what part is played by what is known about child development, and what part is played by the social and cultural context?

The role of child and adolescent forensic psychiatry in the assessment of child defendants is relevant in relation to the child or young person's ability to participate effectively in the trial process and his or her fitness to plead. Psychiatric opinion in relation to the child defendant's mental state will also be highly relevant in relation to sentencing and disposal since evidence of mental illness may require intervention under the Mental Health Act 1983, and serious psychiatric disturbance which does not fulfil the criteria for admission for assessment or treatment under the Mental Health Act 1983 may still affect disposal by the court.

Furthermore, the level of psychiatric disturbance, the capacity to accept responsibility and to develop appropriate remorse, moral understanding, empathy for victims and motivation for personal change will need to be assessed in order to recommend appropriate treatment. An essential component of the psychological and psychiatric assessments of child defendants is the capacity for change inherent in a young person. Can the child or young person be expected to change his or her attitudes and behaviour to some extent, or to any extent? Furthermore, the assessment of the capacity for change should deal with the time scale within which any such change may be expected since this has direct implications both for sentencing and for any treatment recommendations.

Given that research and practice confirm that virtually all children committing extremely serious offences, and many children and young people committing less serious offences, have major emotional, behavioural and social difficulties, it is perhaps surprising that routine requests for psychiatric assessment of child defendants appearing before the courts do not occur very much earlier in the trial process. Studies looking at the characteristics and background of young children committing serious offences have indicated high levels of parental delinquency and psychopathy, childhood abuse and exposure to domestic violence, a higher than expected level of neuro-psychiatric disorders in the offending children, an association with learning disability, academic failure and severe childhood onset conduct disorder (Bailey, 1996; Myers, Burket and Harris, 1995; Myers, Scott, Burgess and Burgess, 1995; Vizard, forthcoming).

Research looking at the outcomes for juvenile offenders in adult life confirms that the earlier the onset of offending behaviour, the more likely this behaviour is to persist into adult life (Moffitt, 1993) and to be associated with heavy use of mental health, criminal justice and welfare systems (West and Farrington, 1973; Office for National Statistics, 2000).

Unlike adolescents in their late teens committing more minor offences—such as car theft or burglary, most of whom can be expected to 'grow out' of this behaviour in adult life—very young children committing more serious offences are usually much more disturbed and have shown signs of worrying antisocial behaviour from early childhood. 'Life course persistent' conduct disorder (Moffitt, 1993) or antisocial behaviour beginning before age 10 has been associated with later adult disturbance, delinquency and poor parenting (Quinton and Rutter, 1988).

ALTERNATIVE LEGAL PROVISION

Any changes to the existing legal system involving child defendants would need to take on board the developmental, psychiatric and ethical issues discussed above and place these within a workable legal system which could in some way bring together the criminal and civil (welfare) considerations around each child.

The recommendations of the Justice (1996) report, in relation to children and homicide, do appear to have relevance also for child defendants facing a wide range of serious and less serious charges. The recommendations include re-examination of the age of criminal responsibility, trying children under 14 years of age in private before a specially convened panel comprising a judge and two magistrates with relevant experience and training, and trying children aged 14 to 18 charged with homicide in a public Crown Court hearing. In addition, therapeutic help should not be deferred for fear of compromising the legal process; a single offence of homicide should replace the distinction between murder and manslaughter for child defendants under the age of 18 years. The mandatory sentence of detention during Her Majesty's pleasure, of 10- to 18-year-olds convicted of murder, should be abolished and the trial judge (or judicial panel) who have heard the evidence should determine the sentence required with full discretionary powers. Also, for children and young people sentenced to indeterminate detention, decisions regarding their release should be taken by an independent panel. Children, who have been detained after conviction, should be appropriately and consistently assessed and treated in order to promote their rehabilitation. Finally the report suggested that a more reasoned public debate was necessary in relation to children who kill.

In addition to these recommendations should be added the need for formal integration between the criminal process involving child defendants and civil justice, particularly where welfare issues are concerned. For instance, a case could be made for the consideration by a local authority of an application for an interim care order on any child under 14 years of age charged with a very serious offence. For these purposes, a serious offence can be defined as murder, manslaughter, abduction, rape, grievous bodily harm, etc. Application for a care order could be made on the basis that the threshold criteria for a care order have been met, that significant harm has already been experienced by the child, as demonstrated by the commission of such offences, and that there has been a major failure to protect the child from the consequences of his or her actions by those with parental responsibility at the time of the offence. Such an approach would be unnecessary with children whose offending is rather less serious, but for the reasons described above, younger children facing very serious offences are almost inevitably children in need, in terms of the Children Act 1989, whose welfare needs have not been addressed to date.

However, there are important ethical issues to consider before arguing for care orders on children accused of very serious offences. First, because research shows that a group of such children have many characteristics of serious disturbance, it cannot therefore be said that any one child will share these features, hence meriting an automatic care order. Second, even when such serious disturbance is shown to be present, good practice demands that an individual care plan approach is taken in every case since the welfare needs of each child will be different and may or may not include a full care order.

The recommendations of a recent conference of experts (Vizard, 2001) on the needs of child defendants included the suggestion that a government led consultation process on the age of criminal responsibility should occur. Clearly, in the light of continued professional concerns about the competence of young child defendants, and the research evidence indicating serious levels of psychiatric disturbance in young child defendants, a review of the current age of criminal responsibility seems appropriate.

Another possibility in terms of alternative legal provisions for child defendants would be the appointment of a *Guardian ad Litem* for the child to assess issues of significant harm, child protection issues in relation to the child defendant and to coordinate the provision of pre-trial psychiatric and psychological assessments. Finally, any integration of the criminal and civil justice elements of cases involving child defendants needs to be agreed between all relevant government departments. Furthermore, on an individual case basis, a multi-agency care plan for each child defendant needs to be agreed and should include all relevant criminal justice and welfare components.

CONCLUSIONS AND IMPLICATIONS FOR PRACTICE

There should be a government led process of consultation to review the current age of criminal responsibility in the light of clinical and research evidence about the developmental immaturity and psychiatric disturbance of many young child defendants. All child defendants facing serious criminal charges (murder, manslaughter, abduction, rape or grievous bodily harm) should be assessed by a clinical psychologist and by a child psychiatrist. There should be agreement between clinical psychologists and child psychiatrists as to the principles of such psychological and psychiatric assessments. If appropriate, pre-trial therapy should be provided for all child defendants suffering from identifiable and treatable psychiatric disorders. A child defendant's pack should be made available to inform children facing criminal charges about their rights and the legal process. Relevant training covering the areas of child development, psychiatric and psychological issues, the relevant forensic and welfare issues, child protection and The Children Act 1989, within a multidisciplinary context, should be developed and made available to all legal professionals, child care professionals and child psychiatrists and clinical psychologists working with child defendants. Where children face very serious charges, such as murder, manslaughter, rape, abduction, etc., consideration should be given to the appointment of a *Guardian ad Litem* to protect the welfare needs of the child and to coordinate any necessary assessments.

ACKNOWLEDGEMENTS

The main issues outlined in this chapter are taken from a more detailed discussion of these topics in a forthcoming publication on *Child Defendants* from the Royal College of Psychiatrists.

REFERENCES

APA (1994). *Diagnostic and statistical manual* (4th edn). Washington, DC: American Psychiatric Association.

Ashford, N. and Chard, A. (2000). *Defending young people in the criminal justice system.* London: Legal Action Group.

Bailey, S. (1996). Adolescents who murder. *Journal of Adolescence, 19,* 19–39.

Baron-Cowen, S. (1989). The autistic child's theory of mind: A case of specific developmental delay. *Journal of Child Psychology and Psychiatry, 30,* 285–297.

Grisso, T. (2000). What we know about youth's capacities as trial defendants. Chapter 5 in T. Grisso (ed.), *Youth on trial.* Chicago: Chicago University Press.

Justice (1996). *Children and homicide: Appropriate procedures for juveniles and murder and manslaughter cases.* London: Justice.

Kohlberg, L. (1974). Discussion: Development gains in moral judgement. *American Journal of Mental Deficiency*, *79* (2), 142–146.

Moffitt, T.E. (1993). Adolescence—limited and life-course-persistent anti-social behaviour: A developmental taxonomy. *Psychological Review*, *100*, 674–701.

Myers, W.C., Burket, R.C. and Harris, H.E. (1995). Adolescent psychopathy in relation to delinquent behaviours, conduct disorders and personality disorders. *Journal of Forensic Science*, *40* (3), 436–440.

Myers, W.C., Scott, K., Burgess, A.W. and Burgess, A.G. (1995). Psychopathology, biopsychosocial factors, crime characteristics, and classification of 25 homicidal youths. *Journal of the American Academy of Child and Adolescent Psychiatry*, *34* (11), 1483–1489.

Office for National Statistics (2000). *Psychiatric morbidity among young offenders in England and Wales*. London: National Statistics.

Piaget, J. (1932). *The moral judgement of the child*. New York: Harcourt, Brace & World.

Quinton, D. and Rutter, M. (1988). *Parenting breakdown: The making and breaking of intergenerational links*. Aldershot: Avebury.

Royal College of Psychiatrists (forthcoming). *The needs of child defendants*. London: Gaskell.

UN (1986). *United Nations Standard Minimum Rules for the Administration of Justice*.

Vizard, E. (ed.) (2001). *The needs of offending children*. London: Sieff Foundation.

Vizard, E. (forthcoming). *Sexual offending in adolescence*. In S. Bailey and M. Dolan (eds), *A textbook of adolescent forensic psychiatry*.

West, D.J. and Farrington, D.P. (1973). *Who becomes delinquent?* London: Heinemann Educational.

WHO (1992). *International classification of diseases* (10th edn). World Health Organisation.

Part 3

Perspectives on Courts: Trials and Decision Making

Chapter 3.1

Juror Decision-Making in the Twenty-First Century: Confronting Science and Technology in Court

Bradley D. McAuliff
University of Nebraska-Lincoln, USA
Robert J. Nemeth
Louisiana State University, USA
Brian H. Bornstein
University of Nebraska-Lincoln, USA
and
Steven D. Penrod
The City University of New York, USA

> *In this age of science we must build legal foundations that are sound in science as well as in law. Scientists have offered their help. We in the legal community should accept that offer.*
> (Stephen Breyer,
> Associate Justice of the United States Supreme Court)

In his introduction to the *Reference Manual on Scientific Evidence* (2000), Justice Breyer described a symbiotic relationship between science and the law in which valid scientific principles and tools inform the effective resolution of legal disputes. Today, we are witnessing a piecemeal realization of Justice Breyer's vision as law has begun to embrace science and technology in court. Although forensic experts routinely have testified about fingerprint and blood-type evidence for many decades, other forms of scientific evidence are gaining rapid acceptance in the United States. For example, nearly two-thirds (65%) of state court judges responding to a national survey indicated that they had some experience with DNA evidence in their courtroom (Gatowski

Handbook of Psychology in Legal Contexts, Second Edition
Edited by D. Carson and R. Bull. © 2003 John Wiley & Sons, Ltd.

et al., 2001). The role of psychological science in the legal system has burgeoned recently as well. Although courts historically have embraced testimony from clinical psychologists on matters such as insanity and competency to stand trial, now increasing numbers of social and cognitive psychologists use their empirical research to educate jurors about a wide range of issues, including eyewitness identification and witness suggestibility. Social or behavioral scientists constituted nearly one-quarter of all scientists testifying in US criminal appellate cases involving expert testimony from 1988 to 1998 (Groscup et al., in press). Finally, in addition to scientific evidence involving forensic and psychological issues, trial attorneys often rely on state-of-the-art technology such as videotape and computer animation to recreate a wide range of physical and behavioral events including murders, automobile collisions, medical procedures, and elaborate mechanical systems (Kassin and Dunn, 1997). Despite the increasing prominence of science and technology in court, little is known of how legal decision-makers reason about scientific and technologically advanced evidence.

Concern in the United States regarding the ability of judges and jurors to reason about scientific evidence has increased in the wake of several recent Supreme Court rulings on the admissibility of expert evidence (*Daubert v. Merrell Dow Pharmaceuticals, Inc.*, 1993; *General Electric Co. v. Joiner*, 1997; *Kumho Tire Co. v. Carmichael*, 1999). The *Daubert* decision and its progeny have entrusted judges with a gatekeeping role in which they should base their admissibility decisions on the relevance and reliability of the proffered expert evidence. According to the Court, judges should consider certain nonexclusive factors (e.g. falsifiability, known or potential rate of error, peer-review, and general acceptance) when determining evidentiary reliability. In *Kumho*, the Court clarified that judges' gatekeeping role applies to all expert evidence covered under Federal Rule of Evidence 702 (i.e. scientific, technical, or other specialized knowledge) and not just expert scientific evidence. Judges' reliance on the *Daubert* criteria has increased in both federal and state criminal cases in which the admissibility of expert testimony was appealed, particularly in those cases containing scientific experts (e.g. chemists, social scientists) and to a lesser degree in cases involving technical, medical/mental health, and business experts (Groscup et al., in press).

Recent research suggests that the US Supreme Court was premature in placing its confidence in judges' ability to fulfill their gatekeeping role. Many judges lack the requisite scientific literacy necessary for a *Daubert* analysis (Gatowski et al., 2001) and have difficulty identifying methodologically flawed expert testimony (Kovera and McAuliff, 2000). When asked to describe how they would apply the *Daubert* factors in determining the admissibility of expert testimony, only 5% of responding state court judges demonstrated a clear understanding of falsifiability and only 4% sufficiently understood the concept of error rate in a national survey by Gatowski et al. Another study found that variations in the internal validity of an expert's research did not influence judges' simulated admissibility decisions (Kovera and McAuliff, 2000). Judges in that study read a brief fact pattern of a hostile work environment case and a description of the expert's testimony that the plaintiff wished to present. When asked whether they would admit the expert testimony, judges were no more likely to admit a valid study than they were to admit a study that lacked a control group, contained a confound, or included the potential for experimenter bias. However, notwithstanding the threats to internal validity present in some versions of the research, 17% of judges admitted the expert testimony.

Despite research calling into question judges' scientific literacy and their ability to evaluate scientific evidence effectively, judges overwhelmingly support their role as gatekeepers (Gatowski et al., 2001) and appear confident in their gatekeeping abilities (Shuman, Whitaker and Champagne, 1994). Nearly 80% of judges responding to a three-state survey by Shuman et al. indicated that expert testimony was rarely too technical for them to understand. Moreover, even though the vast majority of judges in the Gatowski et al. study were unable to demonstrate a clear understanding of the falsifiability and error rate concepts, only a small percentage asked interviewers for a definition or for further explanation. When judges fail to recognize or acknowledge their limited scientific literacy and admit invalid expert scientific testimony, jurors must rely on their own determinations of the quality of expert scientific testimony to make decisions at trial.

Recent technological advances in demonstrative evidence have generated controversy within the legal system as well. The Sixth Amendment to the US Constitution (with similar provisions in other jurisdictions) guarantees criminal defendants the right to a fair and impartial trial. However, innovations in video and computer-animation technology are leading the American justice system to a new crossroads, one in which the prejudicial nature of certain forms of demonstrative evidence may overshadow defendants' right to a fair trial (Bornstein and Nemeth, 1999). At the heart of this controversy lies the question of whether the vivid qualities of videotape and computer-animated displays substantially impair the ability of triers of fact to make impartial decisions regarding a defendant's guilt or liability.

Thus, the evolution of science, technology, and the law presents a host of new challenges for legal decision-makers in the twenty-first century. Are judges and jurors able to evaluate statistical, probabilistic, and methodological issues accurately when confronted with scientific evidence? What other factors might influence jurors' evaluations of scientific evidence in addition to its quality? Is the probative value of certain forms of demonstrative evidence outweighed by its prejudicial impact? We will address questions such as these in this chapter by reviewing empirical research on jurors' scientific reasoning ability and the effects of technologically sophisticated demonstrative evidence on their judgments.

Because experts are the conduits of science from the laboratory to the courtroom, the first half of this chapter focuses on expert scientific evidence. By 'expert scientific evidence', we mean statistical, probabilistic, or experimental findings presented by an expert in legal proceedings. Such evidence by nature is often quite complex; however, one should note that our emphasis differs from that of other researchers who have conceptualized trial complexity as the amount of testimony or legal jargon contained therein (e.g. Horowitz, ForsterLee and Brolly, 1996). With regard to technology, space limitations preclude an exhaustive discussion of all forms of technology currently used by courts (for a more thorough review, see Lederer, 1994). Consequently, the second half of this chapter focuses exclusively on the use of videotape and computer-animated displays as demonstrative evidence and considers whether those forms of technology might improve or hinder jurors' ability to make impartial decisions.

SCIENCE IN THE TWENTY-FIRST CENTURY

Jurors' Ability to Reason About Expert Scientific Evidence

Previous psychological research raises doubt regarding jurors' ability to reason about statistical, probabilistic, and methodological issues effectively. When judging the probability of certain outcomes, lay people prefer anecdotal information and underutilize base-rate information (Bar-Hillel, 1980; Kahneman and Tversky, 1973; Simonson and Nye, 1992; Stanovich and West, 1998; see also Clifford, this volume). People often are insensitive to sample bias (Hamill, Wilson and Nisbett, 1980) and fail to recognize the unreliability of results obtained from small samples (Kahneman and Tversky, 1972; Fong, Krantz and Nisbett, 1986). Participants in one study who completed a series of inductive reasoning problems varied considerably in their use of certain statistical reasoning skills (e.g. the law of large numbers, regression, and base-rate principles; Jepson, Krantz and Nisbett, 1983). Participants in other studies have failed to recognize missing comparative or control-group information when evaluating certain scientific claims, such as the relation between fluoride use and tooth decay (Gray and Mill, 1990; Mill, Gray and Mandel, 1994).

Lay people may be unable to reason about scientific issues in legal contexts as well. Mock jurors underutilize expert probabilistic testimony compared to Bayesian norms (Faigman and Baglioni, 1988; Goodman, 1992; Kaye and Koehler, 1991; Schklar and Diamond, 1999; Thompson and Schumann, 1987) and are reluctant to base verdicts on statistical evidence alone (Niedermeier, Kerr and Messé, 1999; Wells, 1992). Mock jurors in one study underweighed expert testimony about probabilistic incidence rates in favor of highly salient, individuating information such as an eyewitness identification (Loftus, 1980). Similarly, clinical opinion expert testimony exerted a greater influence on mock jurors' judgments in a simulated capital sentencing hearing than did actuarial expert testimony (i.e. testimony based on empirically established risk factors; Krauss and Sales, 2001). Mock jurors also had difficulty comprehending expert testimony on statistical matters (Faigman and Baglioni, 1988). Only 14% of mock jurors in that study correctly answered two questions designed to assess their understanding of a statistical expert's testimony, and 43% provided incorrect answers to both questions.

Jurors in actual trials have exhibited similar deficits in their ability to understand statistical and probabilistic evidence (Selvin and Picus, 1987). One field experiment involving real jurors in civil and criminal cases found that as evidence complexity increased, jurors were more likely to report that they were well informed by the trial, but also that it was more difficult for them to render a verdict (Heuer and Penrod, 1994). Those findings suggest that jurors, although satisfied with the information presented in trials containing complex evidence, may have difficulty using that information to decide cases.

Previous research indicates that lay people may experience difficulty when serving as jurors in trials containing expert scientific evidence. Despite this conclusion, it would be misleading to suggest that mock jurors altogether lack the ability to reason about scientific evidence. Certain studies paint a more optimistic picture of jurors' reasoning skills (Goodman, 1992; Smith et al., 1996). In one study, a forensic serologist provided crucial blood- and enzyme-type evidence within the context of a videotaped simulation of a rape trial (Smith et al., 1996). Mock jurors who learned that 20% of the population had an enzyme type that was shared by the assailant and the defendant judged the defendant as more guilty than did mock jurors who learned that 80% of the population had the same enzyme type. Although the mock jurors underutilized the statistical evidence compared to Bayesian norms, they nonetheless gave it the proper relative weight depending on its probative value. Similarly, mock jurors' guilty verdicts in another trial simulation decreased as the blood-type frequency shared between the defendant and the population increased (Goodman, 1992). Once again, however, a Bayesian analysis revealed that jurors underutilized the probabilistic scientific evidence by failing to accord that evidence sufficient weight when rendering their verdicts.

In conclusion, researchers have garnered somewhat mixed findings regarding jurors' ability to reason about scientific evidence. Lay people consistently underutilize certain probabilistic information and fail to understand a wide array of statistical principles. Similar shortcomings in scientific reasoning ability have emerged in simulated and real legal settings as well, even though people sometimes appear to be sensitive to the scientific content of expert testimony. These findings raise an intriguing question: If jurors have difficulty reasoning about scientific evidence, what information actually does influence their decision making in trials containing complex expert testimony? Information-processing models from the social-cognitive psychological literature on persuasion provide a much needed theoretical framework to predict how jurors make decisions when confronting scientific evidence.

Dual-Process Models of Persuasion and Juror Decision-Making

Persuasion plays a critical role in every trial. In essence, judges and jurors must evaluate persuasive arguments from multiple sources (e.g. attorneys, plaintiffs, defendants, and witnesses) to decide a variety of legal questions that arise in each case (e.g. What are the facts? What is the applicable law? Is particular evidence admissible? Which side should the verdict favor?). These trial attributes have led several applied researchers (Cooper, Bennett and Sukel, 1996; Kovera, McAuliff and Hebert, 1999;

Leippe and Romanczyk, 1989) to adopt information-processing models from the persuasion literature to examine decision making in legal contexts. Two models that have proven particularly useful are the heuristic-systematic model (HSM; Chaiken, 1980) and the elaboration likelihood model (ELM; Petty and Cacioppo, 1986).

According to the HSM and ELM, people use two cognitive processes to evaluate persuasive messages. People who engage in systematic (HSM) or central (ELM) processing expend a great deal of cognitive effort scrutinizing the content of a persuasive message. Systematic processors attend to argument quality and are more likely to adopt the position advocated in the persuasive message if it contains valid, high-quality arguments than if it does not (Petty and Cacioppo, 1984; Petty, Cacioppo and Goldman, 1981). Heuristic (HSM) or peripheral (ELM) processors, in contrast, rely on mental shortcuts or decision rules when evaluating a persuasive message and focus less on its content and quality. Various cues associated with a persuasive message (e.g. the length or number of arguments; Petty and Cacioppo, 1984), its source (e.g. expertise, likeability, or physical attractiveness; Chaiken and Maheswaran; 1994), and the audience (e.g. positive or negative audience reactions; Axsom, Yates and Chaiken; 1987) may affect message evaluation for people processing heuristically.

Ability and motivation are two factors that moderate the extent to which people engage in systematic or heuristic processing according to the HSM (Chaiken, 1980) and ELM (Petty and Cacioppo, 1986). A person must be able and motivated to process a persuasive message systematically before such processing can occur. If either ability or motivation is low, an individual is more likely to engage in heuristic processing when evaluating the persuasive message compared to someone who is able and motivated to process systematically.

Systematic Processing of Expert Scientific Evidence

Various forms of scientific training can improve the ability of lay people to reason about statistical and methodological issues related to everyday problems (see Nisbett, 1993, for a review). Statistical training involving the law of large numbers improved both the frequency and quality of participants' statistical reasoning skills in a study by Fong et al. (1986). Undergraduates majoring in the social sciences (e.g. psychology) showed greater improvement in their ability to apply statistical and methodological skills to a wide variety of problems compared to students majoring in the natural sciences (e.g. chemistry) and humanities (e.g. history; Lehman and Nisbett, 1990). Similar findings emerged when researchers tested the reasoning skills of graduate students who were majoring in law, medicine, psychology, and chemistry (Lehman, Lempert and Nisbett, 1988). However, specialized tutoring in addition to statistics and research methodology coursework may be necessary to increase students' ability to identify certain methodological flaws, such as a missing control group (Mill et al., 1994).

The ability to scrutinize the content and quality of a message, although important, is not the sole requirement for systematic processing according to persuasion theory (Chaiken, 1980; Petty and Cacioppo, 1986). Motivation also plays a key role. One individual difference variable that might affect jurors' motivation to reason about expert evidence effectively is the need for cognition (NFC). Cacioppo and Petty (1982) proposed that certain stable individual differences exist in the degree to which people engage in and enjoy effortful cognitive endeavors. High-NFC individuals tend to seek, acquire, and think about information in order to better understand the world around them, whereas low-NFC individuals tend to rely on other methods of acquiring information that are less cognitively taxing (e.g. adopting the opinions of others, using cognitive heuristics, engaging in social comparison processes; Cacioppo et al., 1996). High- versus low-NFC individuals differ in the degree to which they embrace and derive pleasure from a wide array of cognitively oriented tasks. Compared to low-NFC individuals, those high in NFC report greater satisfaction after completing complex versus simple number tasks (Cacioppo and Petty, 1982), expend more cognitive effort when evaluating arguments, and recall a higher number of message-relevant arguments (Cacioppo, Petty and Morris, 1983).

NFC is relevant to the systematic processing and elaboration of persuasive messages. Using meta-analytic techniques, Cacioppo et al. (1996) combined the results from 11 relevant studies and found that argument quality exerted more influence on the attitudes of high-NFC individuals than it did on low-NFC individuals' attitudes (Cohen's $d = 0.31$). Moreover, in 5 of the 11 studies, researchers directly had asked participants to evaluate the quality of the persuasive messages. Meta-analysis of those five studies revealed that argument quality influenced the evaluations of high-NFC individuals more than those of low-NFC individuals (Cohen's $d = 0.54$). Based on these results, it seems reasonable to predict that high-NFC jurors will be more likely to process expert scientific evidence systematically than low-NFC jurors.

Only a handful of studies have assessed the relation between NFC and jurors' decisions. One study found that NFC was related to the amount and type of reasoning that mock jurors reported when rendering verdicts in a case involving the unlawful transportation of a stolen car across state lines (Graziano, Panter and Tanaka, 1990). However, NFC did not predict mock jurors' ultimate verdicts. Researchers in another study observed that high-NFC participants judged a criminal suspect who made a questionable confession as having a greater likelihood of guilt than did low-NFC participants (Lassiter et al., 1992). A third study demonstrated that NFC interacted with the order in which ambiguous evidence was introduced and rebutted in a criminal trial simulation (Kassin, Reddy and Tulloch, 1990). Rebuttal arguments that preceded the ambiguous evidence influenced high-NFC jurors' judgments more than rebuttal arguments that followed the evidence, whereas the exact opposite was true for low-NFC jurors.

Thus, NFC appears to be related to jurors' judgments in at least some trial simulations containing different types of evidence. However, those studies may underestimate the relation between NFC and juror judgments in two regards. First, all three studies included evidence that was relatively low in cognitive complexity. The NFC literature predicts that differences in NFC should be particularly salient in cases involving complex evidence, such as expert scientific testimony. Second, the NFC studies reviewed thus far did not manipulate evidence quality; therefore, it is impossible to determine whether jurors were more or less likely to discriminate between sound and questionable evidence based on NFC.

Two recent studies specifically addressed the relation between NFC and jurors' judgments in cases involving expert scientific evidence. McAuliff and Kovera (2003, Study 2) presented a trial simulation to citizens awaiting jury duty in which an expert testified about the effects of viewing sexualized materials on men's behavior toward women. In addition to manipulating the publication status and ecological validity of the expert's study, those researchers varied its internal validity by describing the study as either including or lacking an appropriate control group. High-NFC jurors found the defendant liable more often and evaluated the quality of the expert's study more favorably when it contained an appropriate control group than when it did not. Low-NFC jurors did not differentiate between the internally valid and invalid study. Thus, high-NFC jurors in at least one study recognized variations in the quality of expert scientific evidence and used that information when rendering verdicts. Findings from another study (Bornstein, 2003), however, raise some concern as to whether those results generalize to all types of expert scientific testimony.

Bornstein (2003, Study 2) presented mock jurors with a simulated personal injury case involving different types of expert testimony. He predicted that participants' NFC and their preference for numerical information (PNI; Viswanathan, 1993) would be related to their verdicts and other trial-relevant judgments (e.g. expert credibility). Although PNI and NFC are positively correlated, PNI is a more specific construct in that it taps individuals' tendency to enjoy thinking about a certain type of information (i.e. numbers) rather than thinking in general (Viswanathan, 1993). Results revealed that mock jurors' NFC and PNI scores did not differ for those who did or did not find the defendant liable. Moreover, with the exception of one negative correlation between NFC and the perceived credibility of the plaintiff's expert, NFC and PNI were unrelated to jurors' judgments.

One way to reconcile the conflicting results of McAuliff and Kovera (2003) and Bornstein (2003) is to suggest that the effect of NFC on jurors' judgments may be moderated by the nature of the expert scientific testimony presented. McAuliff and Kovera's expert testimony consisted of social scientific research findings from a study involving the effects of sexual priming, whereas Bornstein's consisted of statistical, experimental, or anecdotal findings on the relation between lead exposure and illness. Another possibility is that the variations in the quality of expert evidence were more serious (i.e. a missing control group) or salient in the former study compared with the latter one. Whatever the explanation may be, it is clear that additional research is necessary to inform our understanding of what role (if any) NFC plays in juror decision-making in cases involving expert scientific testimony.

Heuristic Processing of Expert Scientific Evidence

Jurors who lack the ability or motivation to engage in systematic processing may rely on information other than argument quality to process expert evidence in a heuristic manner (Kovera et al., 1999; Saks and Kidd, 1980). Source-related cues are one type of information that might influence jurors' judgments about scientific evidence when they are unable to process information systematically. Cooper et al. (1996) investigated this possibility by varying an expert's credentials (his educational pedigree, employer, and publication record) and the complexity of his testimony (the amount of technical and specialized terminology it contained) in a products liability case. Those researchers believed that jurors would be more likely to rely on source-related heuristic cues (i.e. expertise) when their ability to evaluate the expert's testimony was low rather than high due to evidence complexity. As predicted, mock jurors in the complex testimony condition were more likely to find for the plaintiff, to believe that the product caused the plaintiff's illness, and to be confident in their verdict when they viewed the expert with high versus moderate credentials. However, the expert's credentials did not influence mock jurors' decisions when the testimony was relatively easy to understand.

Other source-related cues may influence juror decision-making in cases involving complex expert testimony as well. In a second series of studies, Cooper and Neuhaus (2000) varied cues associated with the expert (e.g. credentials, rate of pay, frequency of testimony) and discovered that jurors evaluated the well-paid, highly-credentialed expert and the well-paid, high frequency of testimony expert negatively on several trial-related dimensions. Cooper and Neuhaus reasoned that jurors might rely on a 'hired gun' heuristic when the expert's testimony is complex. Because the expert's testimony remained highly complex across all experimental conditions in the first two studies, Cooper and Neuhaus factorially crossed the complexity (moderate versus high) of the expert's testimony with the amount he was paid for testifying (small versus large sum) in a third study. They informed all participants that the expert witness frequently provided testimony in similar cases. Mock jurors found the highly paid expert witness to be less likable, less believable, and less influential when they viewed the highly complex testimony compared to the moderately complex testimony. Thus, consistent with predictions from the HSM and ELM, research by Cooper and colleagues has demonstrated that certain source-related cues affect jurors' judgments when they are confronted with highly complex evidence.

Message-related cues are a second type of information that could influence decision making when jurors are unable to process information systematically (Kovera et al., 1999). For example, jurors might use a 'consensus implies correctness' heuristic when evaluating the research on which an expert's testimony is based. People often rely on others' judgments of message quality (Axsom et al., 1987) and consensus information when evaluating persuasive messages under conditions that produce heuristic processing (Giner-Sorolla and Chaiken, 1997; Maheswaran, Mackie and Chaiken, 1992). Extrapolating those findings to the legal domain, jurors may rely on the general acceptance status of a study when evaluating its quality. Jurors may reason that research published in a peer-reviewed journal is methodologically sound because qualified members of the scientific community have evaluated the research favorably. Conversely, jurors may undervalue research that has not been published or generally accepted.

Jurors may use a second message cue when evaluating expert evidence: the representativeness of the research. When people generate probabilities about the relation between two variables, they often consider the degree to which those variables are similar to or representative of one another (Kahneman and Tversky, 1973). Participants in that study assessed the probability that a hypothetical person held various occupations based on certain described characteristics of that person. Participants provided higher probability estimates when they viewed the person's characteristics (e.g. shy, withdrawn, structured, and helpful) as representative of people who typically hold a particular occupation (e.g. librarian). When evaluating an expert's research, jurors may rely on a similar representativeness heuristic involving the study's ecological validity. Jurors may judge a study more favorably when it contains a sample of participants who are similar to the population to which the expert wishes to generalize his or her research findings than when it does not.

A recent study by Kovera et al. (1999) investigated the effects of general acceptance (consensus information) and ecological validity (representativeness) on mock jurors' evaluations of expert testimony. College undergraduates in that study viewed a video-taped simulation of a hostile work environment case in which an expert testified about a study she had conducted. The study's general acceptance status (a heuristic cue), ecological validity (a heuristic cue), construct validity (evidence quality), and whether jurors viewed a scientifically-informed or scientifically-naïve cross-examination (reasoning ability) varied across conditions. Mock jurors relied on the heuristic cues when evaluating the trustworthiness and credibility of certain witnesses; however, the validity of the expert's study and the scientific nature of the defense attorney's cross-examination did not affect jurors' judgments.

In addition to general acceptance and ecological validity, jurors evaluating research may rely on a 'quantity heuristic' involving the sample size of a study. According to the law of large numbers, larger samples better approximate the characteristics of the population from which they were drawn than do smaller samples. People are sometimes sensitive to the law of large numbers when making predictions about specific behavioral domains, such as athletic or academic performance (Fong et al., 1986; Kunda and Nisbett, 1986). Highly motivated students in one study relied more heavily on information presented in an opinion poll that contained a large versus small sample when forming their attitudes (Darke et al., 1998). Jurors may make heuristic judgments involving the number of participants in an expert's study when they are unable to engage in systematic processing. Consistent with this quantity heuristic, jurors should evaluate studies with larger samples more favorably than those with smaller samples (i.e. 'bigger is better').

Two studies have examined jurors' sensitivity to variations in the sample size of an expert's study (Bornstein, 2003, Study 1; McAuliff and Kovera, 2003, Study 1). Recall that Bornstein investigated the influence of different types of expert testimony on jurors' decisions in a personal injury case involving a plaintiff with arthritis. A statistician testified on the plaintiff's behalf about the arthritis incidence rates for a city with or without lead-polluted water, and a defense expert summarized either experimental or anecdotal findings on the relation between lead and certain health problems. Bornstein varied the number of citizens included in the statistician's study as well as the arthritis incidence rate for the citizens exposed to lead-contaminated water. He found that those variables interacted to influence jurors' perceptions of the defense expert's credibility, such that variations in the arthritis incidence rate mattered only when the sample size was large. In other words, mock jurors found the defense expert to be more credible when the statistician's study reported a low arthritis incidence rate compared to a high one, but only when the sample size of that study was large. However, sample size did not influence jurors' verdicts, the amount of compensation they awarded to the plaintiff, or their perceptions of the plaintiff expert's credibility. Similarly, a second study by McAuliff and Kovera observed that variations in the sample size of an expert's study did not influence jurors' judgments on any of the dependent measures (e.g. verdict, evidence quality, expert and plaintiff credibility) included in that study.

Based on the findings of Bornstein (2003) and McAuliff and Kovera (2003), it appears that mock jurors generally neglect to account for sample size when evaluating scientific research. However, future studies should orthogonally manipulate additional variables that may moderate jurors' sensitivity to sample size, such as the salience of the study's sample size information or an explanation of statistical power as it relates to the study's conclusions. Moreover, novel manipulations of sample size may yield different results from those used by Bornstein (200 versus 50,000) and McAuliff and Kovera (20 versus 300).

Simultaneous Systematic and Heuristic Processing of Expert Scientific Evidence

Both the HSM (Chaiken, Liberman and Eagly, 1989) and ELM (Petty, et al., 1987) propose that systematic and heuristic processing may co-occur, and research has supported that proposition (Chaiken and Maheswaran, 1994; Chaiken et al., 1989; Petty and Cacioppo, 1984). However, predictions as to whether jurors engage in systematic and heuristic processing simultaneously when evaluating the quality of expert scientific evidence are difficult to evaluate on the basis of extant research. First, Cooper's studies (Cooper et al., 1996; Cooper and Neuhaus, 2000) did not include an evidence quality manipulation. Manipulating evidence quality is necessary when examining jurors' information processing using the HSM or ELM because systematic (or central) processing is defined in the literature as attention to argument quality (Chaiken, 1980; Petty and Cacioppo, 1986). Studies that lack an evidence quality manipulation can only assess the degree to which jurors rely on heuristics when evaluating expert evidence and not whether they systematically evaluated that evidence. Second, even though Kovera et al. (1999) included an evidence quality manipulation, they failed to observe any evidence of systematic processing in their study. That is, Kovera et al.'s reasoning ability manipulation (i.e. a scientifically informed or naïve cross-examination of the expert) did not influence jurors' judgments. As a result, those researchers were unable to examine the extent to which the two types of information processing co-occurred. Finally, McAuliff and Kovera (2003) made predictions regarding the interaction between NFC, internal validity (evidence quality), and various heuristic cues associated with that evidence (e.g. ecological validity, general acceptance, sample size), but did not observe the predicted effects. Thus, additional research is necessary to determine whether jurors simultaneously can process expert scientific testimony in a systematic and heuristic manner as predicted by the HSM and ELM.

Summary of Jurors' Ability to Reason About Scientific Evidence

Research has shown that people consistently underutilize certain probabilistic information and fail to understand a wide array of statistical principles. Similar shortcomings in scientific reasoning ability have emerged in simulated and real legal settings as well. Even though jurors sometimes appear to be sensitive to the scientific content of expert testimony, they often fail to accord that evidence sufficient weight according to Bayesian norms. Scientific training and NFC appear to play an important role in jurors' systematic evaluation of expert scientific evidence. Certain source-related cues, such as an expert's credentials, rate of pay, and frequency of testimony, can influence jurors' judgments when they confront complex scientific evidence at trial. Jurors viewing expert scientific testimony also may rely on certain message-related cues, such as a study's general acceptance and its ecological validity, when evaluating the trustworthiness and credibility of certain witnesses. To date, research on legal decision-making has not provided support for the theory-based prediction that jurors simultaneously may engage in systematic and heuristic processing when evaluating expert scientific evidence.

Additional research investigating jurors' ability to reason about different types of scientific evidence within the context of different types of cases is needed to advance our understanding of how jurors evaluate expert evidence presented at trial. Assuming that jurors continue to have difficulty identifying flawed expert scientific evidence, studies investigating the effectiveness of the legal safeguards delineated by the Supreme Court in *Daubert* (i.e. cross-examination, opposing experts, judicial instructions on the burden of proof) could prove beneficial. Does a cross-examination that focuses on internal validity issues, such as a missing control group, increase jurors' sensitivity to flawed scientific evidence? Future research addressing these questions may help courts better accommodate jurors' reasoning skills in trials containing expert scientific evidence. Finally, future research based on other theoretical frameworks not discussed in this chapter undoubtedly will contribute to our understanding of how jurors process scientific evidence. For example, a series of three studies by Koehler (2001) demonstrated that exemplar cueing theory (ECT) is a useful tool for predicting how jurors will react to DNA match statistics. Koehler showed that jurors are more persuaded by presentations of mathematically equivalent DNA match statistics that target the suspect and are framed as probabilities (e.g. 'The probability that the suspect would match the blood drops if he were not their source is 0.1%') than those that target a broader reference group and that are framed as frequencies (e.g. 'One in 1000 people in Houston would also match the blood drops'). Future research based on ECT and other theoretical models should help maximize jurors' use of expert scientific evidence at trial.

TECHNOLOGY IN THE TWENTY-FIRST CENTURY

Videotape and Computer-Animated Demonstrative Evidence

Success at trial often hinges on an attorney's ability to present evidence to triers of fact in a clear and persuasive manner. Today that task may be more challenging than ever in light of marked increases in the complexity of trials and the evidence contained therein. Recent advances in videotape and computer animation technology may aid attorneys by allowing them to enhance or substitute traditional oral testimony with visually captivating presentations (Bornstein and Nemeth, 1999). One of the most controversial applications of videotape and computer animation is when they take the form of demonstrative evidence at trial. Whereas physical evidence involves the production of some tangible object (e.g. drugs, weapons, articles of clothing), demonstrative evidence is more speculative in nature and portrays one side's version of the facts. For example, attorneys may use a computer-animated recreation of an automobile accident to present their theory of what occurred and to demonstrate certain principles of physics to jurors. Even though demonstrative evidence generally is based on known facts, videotape and computer animation provide attorneys with malleable media to illustrate the facts in a way that most benefits their client. Those characteristics raise the possibility that videotape and computer-animated demonstrative evidence may unduly influence jurors compared to traditional oral testimony. In other words, the traditional legal question governing the admissibility of evidence under Rule 403 of the Federal Rules of Evidence arises: is the probative value of technologically advanced demonstrative evidence outweighed by its potential for prejudicing the jury?

Research to Inform the Probative/Prejudicial Debate

Cognitive and social psychological research suggests that videotape and computer-animated demonstrative evidence may influence jurors' judgments more than oral testimony. One line of relevant research is the picture-superiority effect of memory (Paivio and Csapo, 1969, 1973; Paivio, Philipchalk and Rowe, 1975). In general, people's memory for pictures is superior to that of verbal stimuli (words presented either visually or auditorily) in free recall and recognition memory tests. According to the picture-superiority effect, demonstrative evidence may be more influential than other evidence simply because it is more memorable. However, studies demonstrating the picture-superiority effect have compared static pictures (i.e. line drawings) to verbal stimuli, which may limit the generalizabilty of those findings to situations in which jurors view dynamic demonstrative evidence or oral testimony. Other researchers have argued that people differentially weigh evidence presented in a vivid versus pallid manner (Bell and Loftus, 1985). Vivid information is emotionally engaging, concrete and imagery-provoking, and proximate in a sensory, temporal, or spatial way (Nisbett and Ross, 1980). Vivid information attracts and maintains people's attention and excites their imaginations. Several properties of videotape and computer-animated demonstrative evidence (e.g. the visual depiction of emotionally arousing events such as an accident or murder) may make it more vivid than corresponding oral testimony.

Why might we expect people to weigh vivid information more heavily than pallid information? To the extent that vivid information draws attention, memory may be enhanced due to the increased probability of encoding and subsequent elaboration. However, certain forms of oral testimony may be just as likely to draw attention and concomitantly enhance memory. The fact that people retrieve vivid information more easily from memory than pallid information also may help to explain people's preference for vivid information. Participants in one study recalled vivid prosecution arguments better than pallid prosecution arguments after a two-day delay (Reyes, Thompson and Bower, 1980). Both types of arguments expressed the same basic evidentiary idea, but did so using differing levels of specificity and elaboration. For example, one argument that implied the defendant was drunk was phrased 'On his way out the door, Sanders staggered against a serving table, knocking a bowl to the floor' (p. 4) in the pallid argument condition and 'On his way out the door, Sanders staggered against a serving table, knocking a bowl of guacamole dip to the floor and splattering guacamole on the white shag carpet' (p. 4) in the vivid argument condition. Reyes et al. argued that the vivid information was more available in memory relative to the pallid information. Others have suggested that vivid information may be more highly associated with other information and thus is more likely to be remembered (Bell and Loftus, 1985).

Vivid information may be more influential than pallid information because it evokes more emotional responses due to its greater ability to excite the imagination (Bell and Loftus, 1985). Those emotional responses may lead to subsequent biases in memory. For example, jurors in a civil case often take pain and suffering into account when determining damages. Compared to pallid testimony, vivid testimony may include more details about injury severity, which may increase the vividness of the evidence without changing its probative value. As a result, jurors may remember and use the details more than if they had not considered the vivid, emotion-provoking testimony. Two studies that investigated the impact of crime-scene photographs (Douglas, Lyon and Ogloff, 1997) and videotape re-enactments (Fishfader et al., 1996) found that mock jurors had a stronger emotional reaction to the demonstrative evidence than they did to oral testimony. Again, jurors' increased emotional reaction to vivid demonstrative evidence may enhance their memory more than when hearing pallid oral testimony.

Vividness may provide a reasonable theoretical basis for expecting videotape or computer-animated demonstrative evidence to affect jurors' decisions differently than oral testimony; however, a previous review of that literature revealed few consistent effects of vividness on people's judgments (Taylor and Thompson, 1982). For example, those researchers observed only a modest effect of presentation medium (videotape, written, or audiotape) on people's judgments. The videotaped information was more influential than its written or audio counterparts in approximately half of the studies reviewed. Taylor and Thompson also examined studies that compared the effects of direct presentations (i.e. face-to-face interactions) with print or audio presentations. Only two of the nine studies found that face-to-face interactions had a greater persuasive impact than did the other presentation forms, and in one study face-to-face interaction had the unintended effect of producing attitudes opposite to those proposed in the message.

At first glance, Taylor and Thompson's (1982) review seems to suggest that vivid demonstrative evidence might not influence jurors' judgments any more than pallid oral testimony. However, certain caveats govern the interpretation of those findings as they apply to videotape and computer-animated demonstrative evidence. For example, the studies that Taylor and Thompson reviewed concerning presentation medium compared static images of speakers reading information to written or audio presentations. Technologically advanced demonstrative evidence undoubtedly will contain more dynamic, sensory-rich imagery compared with the relatively simplistic format of videotape presentations used in earlier research. Taylor and Thompson also observed great variability in the types of judgment tasks included in vividness studies and speculated that this feature may have contributed to the lack of consistent effects across studies. In contrast, judgments made within real or simulated legal settings are much more homogeneous in nature (e.g. verdict, witness credibility, evidence quality) and therefore should be less likely to mask any differences arising from the presentation of vivid versus pallid information. Indeed, at least three trial simulation studies have observed vividness effects on mock jurors' judgments (Bell and Loftus, 1988, 1989; Reyes et al., 1980).

Another methodologically-oriented explanation for the lack of consistent vividness effects that Taylor and Thompson posed was that researchers have failed to covary information vividness and participants' attention level. As a result, vividness may have exerted little or no effect on judgments in those studies because the information was encoded and recalled regardless of its vividness. At least one relevant trial simulation has manipulated both variables and observed the predicted Vividness X Attention Level interaction (Wilson, Northcraft and Neale, 1989). Participants in that study rendered more verdicts and gave larger damage awards in favor of the side that presented arguments in a vivid versus pallid manner, but only when participants' information load was high. For these reasons, Taylor and Thompson's review may underestimate the impact of vividness on jurors' decisions when viewing videotape and computer-animated testimony versus traditional oral testimony.

Based on the corpus of research reviewed thus far, it seems reasonable to expect that the pictorial nature and vivid qualities of technologically advanced demonstrative evidence may influence jurors' judgments more than traditional oral testimony. People are better able to remember information presented pictorially rather than auditorily. The vivid qualities of videotape and computer animation may enhance people's memory by requiring more attentional resources and evoking more emotional responses from jurors than oral testimony. However, when considering the relevance of those findings to the probative/prejudicial debate, it is important to distinguish between 'enhanced' influence and 'undue' influence. Although certain forms of demonstrative evidence may exert more influence on jurors' decisions than oral testimony, that enhanced influence is not necessarily undue and prejudicial in a legal sense. In fact, just the opposite may be true—oral testimony that is less influential than videotape or computer-animated demonstrative evidence may actually be more prejudicial insofar as it fails to alert jurors to probative evidence that ought to be given additional weight. In other words, a showing of undue influence requires more than a showing of enhanced influence. It requires a demonstration that the enhanced influence of videotape or computer-animated demonstrative evidence led to erroneous verdicts or that jurors weighted it inappropriately compared to oral testimony. Thus, applied research examining the effects of technologically advanced demonstrative evidence on jurors' decisions may be better suited to determine whether that evidence is more probative than prejudicial compared to oral testimony.

Applied Research on Videotape and Computer-Animated Demonstrative Evidence

We have focused primarily on basic cognitive and social research to inform our understanding of what impact videotape and computer-animated evidence may have on juror decision-making relative to oral testimony. We now shift our focus to empirical studies that have directly investigated demonstrative evidence. Although demonstrative evidence research is still in its infancy, several studies have examined the effects of computer animation on mock jurors' judgments. Other research has compared computer animation to oral testimony or static demonstrative evidence (i.e. charts and graphs). Collectively, those studies fail to reveal a decisive answer to the question of whether demonstrative evidence is more probative than it is prejudicial. However, our goal is to familiarize readers with the current state of social scientific research on demonstrative evidence so that future studies can better illuminate its effect on juror decision-making.

One of the earliest demonstrative evidence studies examined the effects of video recreations on jurors' decisions in a wrongful death case (Fishfader et al., 1996). In that case, the parents of a 12-year-old girl claimed that their daughter had drowned as a result of her hair becoming entangled in the suction cover of their spa. Participants viewed either a print transcript only, live testimony, or live testimony and video recreation. The trial content was identical across conditions, except that participants in the third condition viewed an additional video recreation of the girl's drowning and the unsuccessful attempts to resuscitate her. Fishfader et al. hypothesized that the video recreation would provoke a stronger emotional reaction than the other two conditions. Results failed to indicate any effects of trial presentation on mock jurors' liability estimates, damage awards, or factual retention of the evidence. The only statistically significant effect was that participants who either viewed the live testimony or live testimony plus video recreation had a stronger emotional reaction to the evidence than did participants who read the trial transcript.

Like videotape evidence, computer animation is a medium in which attorneys can recreate certain events in question. However, unlike videotape evidence, computer animation offers unlimited possibilities for manipulating the presentation of facts because it frees the creator from any of the physical limitations of the real world. As people in general are poor intuitive physicists (McCloskey and Kohl, 1983; McCloskey, Washburn and Felch, 1983), they may not identify attorneys' efforts to stretch the truth by manipulating certain physical properties of the disputed events. Two recent studies investigated the impact of computer-animated displays on mock jurors' decisions within the context of a civil trial simulation (Kassin and Dunn, 1997).

The first study sought to determine whether computer animation facilitates jurors' understanding of physical evidence. Participants viewed a trial in which a widow sued an insurance company for allegedly failing to honor her husband's life insurance policy after he fell from a building in a job-related accident. The wife claimed her husband slipped on an I-beam while working, whereas the insurance company argued the death was a suicide that rendered the policy void. Kassin and Dunn (1997) varied the nature of the physical evidence (pro-plaintiff or pro-defendant) and the presence of computer animation. Experts testified on behalf of both parties about the critical issue of where the victim's body landed relative to the building and certain factors (e.g. wind resistance, forward momentum) that may have contributed to that distance. In addition to the standard testimony, participants in the computer animation condition watched a short animation depicting the victim's fall and the distance from the building where the body landed. A stick figure was used to represent the victim and the distance of the fall was marked with red dash lines either 5–10 feet (pro-plaintiff) or 20–25 feet (pro-defendant) from the building. Counsel introduced the computer animation as a theory of what they believed took place and showed it to jurors three times. In the animation conditions, 75% of participants in the pro-plaintiff condition found for the plaintiff, whereas only 8% of participants in the pro-defendant condition found for the plaintiff. The percentage of pro-plaintiff and pro-defendant participants who found for the plaintiff in the no computer animation condition did not differ (42% and 25%, respectively). A similar interaction between computer animation and physical evidence emerged on two other dependent measures (ratings of liability and whether the death was an accident or suicide). Interestingly, participants who viewed the computer animation rated it as the least influential of any of the evidence (e.g. the victim's mental/emotional state, the body's distance from the building, the victim's familial history of suicide).

Kassin and Dunn (1997) designed a second experiment to determine whether computer animation might have prejudicial effects on juror decision-making. Unlike the first experiment in which the computer animation depicted the stick figure simply dropping to the ground, the animation conditions in the second experiment depicted either a fall or a jump. Once again, the researchers manipulated the pro-plaintiff versus pro-defendant nature of the physical evidence by varying the distance between the victim's body and the building (5–10 feet in the pro-plaintiff condition versus 20–25 feet in the pro-defendant condition). They also included a 'no animation' control condition. The nature of the physical evidence affected participants in the 'jump' animation and control conditions, but not in the 'fall' animation condition. That is, participants in the fall animation condition who heard the pro-defense case judged the death to be an accident and favored the plaintiff just as much as did those who heard the pro-plaintiff version, even though the weight of the physical evidence clearly favored the defense. As in the first experiment, participants who viewed the computer animation believed it was less important than other evidence in determining their verdicts.

These studies by Kassin and Dunn (1997) demonstrate that computer-animated displays can be more persuasive than oral testimony, either facilitating the comprehension of physical evidence or biasing jurors in the direction of a particular litigant's theory. Mock jurors in the first experiment who heard only the testimony failed to render verdicts and judgments consistent with the physical evidence. However, when mock jurors viewed a short computer animation, their verdicts and judgments were more consistent with the physical evidence. In the second experiment, mock jurors who viewed the fall animation believed the death was an accident, even when the body landed 20–25 feet away from the building. Thus, computer animation may cause jurors to disregard diagnostic physical evidence in some cases.

A related experiment by Bennett, Leibman and Fetter (1999) further explored the potential impact of computer animation on juror decision-making by comparing that form of evidence to a more static display (i.e. charts and photograph). Two experiments presented mock jurors with a trial involving a car accident between a restaurant delivery boy and a teenage student. The plaintiffs argued that the delivery boy was driving in excess of the posted speed limit and lost control of his vehicle as a result. An accident reconstruction expert argued on the plaintiffs' behalf that the delivery boy was speeding. As part of the expert testimony, half of the participants saw a computer animation of the accident and half saw some charts and an aerial photograph of the intersection. In both experiments, Bennett et al. observed no differences between participants who viewed the computer-animated evidence and those who viewed the static displays. Irrespective of condition, mock jurors provided similar damage awards and attributions of fault between the plaintiff and defendant.

Other social scientists also have compared the effects of computer-animated displays and static diagrams on jurors' decisions (Dunn, 2000). Dunn conducted two different experiments using different cases. The first study used an automobile collision case in which a car turning left crossed two lanes of traffic and was hit by an oncoming truck. Dunn manipulated the format of the plaintiff's and defendant's presentation (animation versus diagram) and did not observe any effect of computer animation on verdicts. Computer animation did not influence mock jurors' verdicts even though jurors who saw the animation believed that evidence was more important in deciding the case than did those who saw the diagram. In addition, mock jurors who saw the computer animations found them to be more vivid and easier to visualize than did those who saw the diagrams.

A second study involving a plane crash aimed to replicate the results of the first study (Dunn, 2000). Unlike the automobile collision case, the results from the second study revealed that computer animation influenced mock jurors' verdicts. The overall verdicts were skewed toward the defendant; however, when the plaintiff presented animation and the defendant presented diagrams, 68% of the participants found for the plaintiff. In contrast, when both the plaintiff and the defendant presented diagrams, only 26% found for the plaintiff. Once again, mock jurors who viewed the computer animations found them to be more vivid and easier to imagine than did jurors who viewed the diagrams. However, unlike jurors in the first study, they did not believe that the animated displays were the most important factor in deciding their verdicts. Instead, mock jurors believed that the expert testimony itself was most important. One potential explanation for the inconsistent findings of Study 1 and 2 is that jurors rely more heavily on computer animation in cases involving subject matter with which they are less familiar or have less direct experience (Dunn, 2000). For example, although some jurors undoubtedly have experienced automobile accidents, it is highly unlikely that they have direct experience or increased familiarity with plane crashes.

Overall, previous research examining the effects of computer animations on jurors' decisions has yielded somewhat mixed findings. Some studies have failed to observe that technologically advanced demonstrative evidence influences jurors' decisions any differently than other forms of evidence, such as charts, diagrams, or pictures. Although mock jurors in one study had a stronger emotional reaction to a videotape recreation of a drowning accident, that emotion did not translate into any detectable differences in jurors' decisions on a variety of measures (Fishfader et al., 1996). However, other studies comparing the presence or absence of demonstrative evidence have observed that computer animations do influence jurors' judgments and that they may be unaware when this occurs. Finally, mock jurors in at least two of the studies we reviewed found computer animations to be more vivid and easier to visualize than the diagrams (Dunn, 2000).

Summary of the Probative/Prejudicial Impact of Videotape and Computer-Animated Demonstrative Evidence

Returning now to our original question of whether the probative value of videotape and computer-animated demonstrative evidence is outweighed by its prejudicial impact, we believe it is too early to provide a definitive answer. Clearly, research has shown that demonstrative evidence has the potential both to inform and prejudice jurors. In at least one study, mock jurors made better decisions when they viewed physical evidence that was accompanied by computer-animated demonstrative evidence than when it was not (Kassin and Dunn, 1997). That is, computer animation helped mock jurors to make decisions that were more consistent with the physical evidence of the case. However, demonstrative evidence that is inconsistent with physical evidence could negate or even reverse any potential beneficial effects of demonstrative evidence. For example, participants in one study who viewed a computer animation depicting a victim's 'fall' ignored contradictory testimony and physical evidence indicating that the body landed 20–25 feet away from the building (Kassin and Dunn, 1997).

The Kassin and Dunn (1997) findings have important implications for the role of judges and attorneys in trials in which videotape or computer-animated testimony is proffered. First, judges must carefully scrutinize the content and nature of demonstrative evidence to ensure its reliability. Are the essential ingredients of the videotape simulation or computer animation supported by other known facts or credible evidence?

Does the demonstrative evidence represent a reasonable depiction of the alleged event? If the videotape or computer animation incorporates physics theorems or mathematical models, is that information accurately portrayed? Second, attorneys must attend to the reliability of proffered videotape and computer-animated demonstrative evidence as well. If opposing counsel fails to raise and substantiate a valid objection to the admission of unreliable demonstrative evidence (e.g. inconsistency between the physical facts and the videotaped or computer-animated simulation), judges most likely will admit the evidence without question. Moreover, if inconsistent or exaggerated demonstrative evidence is admitted, opposing counsel must discover these defects in order to bring them to the jurors' attention through rigorous cross-examination (assuming that expert testimony accompanies the demonstrative evidence) or in closing arguments. Thus, it behooves both judges and attorneys to scrutinize videotape and computer-animated demonstrative evidence to ensure that these media are consistent with any known physical evidence in the case.

Assuming that attorneys object to unreliable demonstrative evidence and judges refuse to admit it, one question that remains is whether reliable videotape and computer animations are more probative than prejudicial relative to oral testimony in cases involving evidence more ambiguous than that included in Kassin and Dunn (1997). In those cases, we can expect attorneys zealously advocating for their clients to present theories or versions of the evidence in a manner that benefits their clients the most. Do judges need to be more concerned about technologically advanced methods of depicting theories than they are about traditional methods, such as oral arguments and testimony? Future research should better address this question by covarying the evidence presentation format (demonstrative evidence versus oral testimony) and the nature of that evidence (ambiguous versus concrete). It also will be important to discover the effects of videotape and computer-animated demonstrative evidence presented at different points during the trial (opening statements versus closing arguments) by different sources (attorney versus expert). Moreover, studies should investigate judges' and jurors' thresholds for taking demonstrative evidence into account. At what point do judges and jurors perceive that demonstrative evidence is too suggestive or too speculative and thus disregard it? Do judicial instructions clarifying the nature of demonstrative evidence (i.e. to present one side's theory or version of the facts) help sensitize jurors to unreliable or extremely suggestive demonstrative evidence? Finally, should jurors be allowed to take videotape and computer-animated demonstrative evidence with them into the deliberation room for additional viewing? In the interim, it appears that at least one form of technologically sophisticated demonstrative evidence (computer animations) can both enhance and bias juror decision-making in certain circumstances.

SCIENCE AND TECHNOLOGY IN THE TWENTY-FIRST CENTURY

Final Thoughts and Future Directions

We structured the organization of our chapter to address separately the roles of science and technology in legal proceedings. Clearly, however, science and technology are interdependent. As both fields continue to evolve both outside and within the law, we can expect jurors to confront new hybrids of science and technology in court. For example, in 1996 a chief judge in the US District Court of Northern Alabama appointed a neutral panel of four scientists (later referred to as the National Science Panel) to evaluate the scientific merit of claims that silicon breast implants cause chronic disease (Judson, 1999). The National Science Panel reported its findings in 1998 and submitted lengthy videotape depositions for use in subsequent breast implant litigation in federal courts (Breyer, 2000).

The fusion of science, technology, and the law illustrated here raises a variety of new questions worthy of empirical and legal attention. Does videotaped expert testimony increase or decrease jurors' comprehension of scientific evidence compared to live expert testimony? If either form of expert scientific testimony is easier for jurors to comprehend, do those differences affect jurors' verdicts and, if so, how? Legal questions include whether courts will rule that videotaped summaries and evaluations of large bodies of research (such as those provided by the National Science Panel) 'fit' the facts of subsequent litigation and therefore are admissible if reliable. If courtroom testimony is required to supplement the videotaped depositions, will one panel member be allowed to testify on the panel's behalf or will all members be required to appear in court? Answers to questions such as these should help courts to use science and technology in a manner that best enhances jury decision-making without compromising defendants' rights.

ACKNOWLEDGMENT

The first author extracted large portions of this manuscript from his doctoral dissertation, which he conducted under the direction of committee chair Margaret Bull Kovera and committee members Brian Cutler, Ronald Fisher, and Howard Frank at Florida International University. The first author would like to acknowledge their contributions, for without their helpful input and constructive feedback, that work would not have been possible.

Correspondence concerning this chapter should be addressed to the first or second author at the Department of Psychology, University of Nebraska-Lincoln, 238 Burnett Hall, Lincoln, NE 68588-0308. Electronic mail may be sent via Internet to bmcaulif@unlserve.unl.edu or rnemeth@unlserve.unl.edu

REFERENCES

Axsom, D., Yates, S. and Chaiken, S. (1987). Audience response as a heuristic cue in persuasion. *Journal of Personality and Social Psychology, 53*, 30–40.
Bar-Hillel, M. (1980). The base-rate fallacy in probability judgments. *Acta Psychologica, 44*, 211–233.
Bell, B.E. and Loftus, E.F. (1985). Vivid persuasion in the courtroom. *Journal of Personality Assessment, 49*, 659–664.

Bell, B.E. and Loftus, E.F. (1988). Degree of detail of eyewitness testimony and mock juror judgments. *Journal of Applied Social Psychology*, *18*, 1171–1192.

Bell, B.E. and Loftus, E.F. (1989). Trivial persuasion in the courtroom: The power of (a few) minor details. *Journal of Personality and Social Psychology*, *56*, 669–679.

Breyer, S. (2000). Introduction. In *Federal Judicial Center reference manual on scientific evidence* (2nd edn, pp. 1–8). New York: Thomson Legal Publishing.

Bennett, R.B., Leibman, J.H. and Fetter, R.E. (1999). Seeing is believing: Or is it? An empirical study of computer simulations as evidence. *Wake Forest Law Review*, *34*, 257–294.

Bornstein, B.H. (2003). The impact of different types of expert scientific testimony on mock jurors' liability verdicts. Manuscript submitted for publication.

Bornstein, B.H. and Nemeth, R.J. (1999). Jurors' perception of violence: A framework for inquiry. *Aggression and Violent Behavior*, *4*, 77–92.

Cacioppo, J.T. and Petty, R.E. (1982). The need for cognition. *Journal of Personality and Social Psychology*, *42*, 116–131.

Cacioppo, J.T., Petty, R.E. and Morris, K.J. (1983). Effects of need for cognition on message evaluation, recall, and persuasion. *Journal of Personality and Social Psychology*, *45*, 805–818.

Cacioppo, J.T., Petty, R.E., Feinstein, J.A. and Jarvis, W.B.G. (1996). Dispositional differences in cognitive motivation: The life and times of individuals varying in the need for cognition. *Psychological Bulletin*, *119*, 197–253.

Chaiken, S. (1980). Heuristic versus systematic information processing and the use of source versus message cues in persuasion. *Journal of Personality and Social Psychology*, *39*, 752–766.

Chaiken, S., Liberman, A. and Eagly, A. (1989). Heuristic and systematic information processing within and beyond the persuasion context. In J.S. Uleman and J.A. Bargh (eds.), *Unintended thought* (pp. 212–251). New York: Guilford Press.

Chaiken, S. and Maheswaran, D. (1994). Heuristic processing can bias systematic processing: Effects of source credibility, argument ambiguity, and task importance on attitude judgment. *Journal of Personality and Social Psychology*, *66*, 460–473.

Cooper, J., Bennett, E.A. and Sukel, H.L. (1996). Complex scientific testimony: How do jurors make decisions? *Law and Human Behavior*, *20*, 379–394.

Cooper, J. and Neuhaus, I.M. (2000). The 'hired gun' effect: Assessing the effect of pay, frequency of testifying, and credentials on the perception of expert testimony. *Law and Human Behavior*, *24*, 149–171.

Darke, P.R., Chaiken, S., Bohner, G., Einwiller, S., Erb, H.P. and Hazlewood, J.D. (1998). Accuracy motivation, consensus information, and the law of large numbers: Effects on attitude judgment in the absence of argumentation. *Personality and Social Psychology Bulletin*, *24*, 1205–1215.

Daubert v. Merrell Dow Pharmaceuticals, Inc., 509 US 579 (1993).

Douglas, K.S., Lyon, D.R. and Ogloff, J.R.P. (1997). The impact of graphic photographic evidence on mock jurors' decisions in a murder trial: Probative or prejudicial? *Law and Human Behavior*, *21*, 485–501.

Dunn, M. (2000, March). The effects of computer animation on juror decision making. Poster presented at the annual meeting of the American Psychology-Law Society, New Orleans, LA.

Faigman, D.L. and Baglioni, A.J. (1988). Bayes' theorem in the trial process: Instructing jurors on the value of statistical evidence. *Law and Human Behavior*, *12*, 1–17.

Fishfader, V.L., Howells, G.N., Katz, R.C. and Teresi, P.S. (1996). Evidential and extralegal factors in juror decisions: Presentation mode, retention, and level of emotionality. *Law and Human Behavior*, *20*, 565–572.

Fong, G.T., Krantz, D.H. and Nisbett, R.E. (1986). The effects of statistical training on thinking about everyday problems. *Cognitive Psychology*, *18*, 253–292.

Gatowski, S.I., Dobbin, S.A., Richardson, J.T., Ginsburg, G.P., Merlino, M.L. and Dahir, V. (2001). Asking the gatekeepers: A national survey of judges on judging expert evidence in a post-*Daubert* World. *Law and Human Behavior*, *25*, 433–458.

General Electric Co., et al. v. Joiner et ux., 522 US 136 (1997).

Giner-Sorolla, R. and Chaiken, S. (1997). Selective use of heuristic and systematic processing under defense motivation. *Personality and Social Psychology Bulletin, 23*, 84–97.

Goodman, J. (1992). Jurors' comprehension and assessment of probabilistic evidence. *American Journal of Trial Advocacy, 16*, 361–389.

Gray, T. and Mill, D. (1990). Critical abilities, graduate education (Biology versus English), and belief in unsubstantiated phenomena. *Canadian Journal of Behavioural Sceince, 22*, 162–172.

Graziano, S.J., Panter, A.T. and Tanaka, J.S. (1990). Individual differences in information processing strategies and their role in juror decision making and selection. *Forensic Reports, 3*, 279–301.

Groscup, J.L., Penrod, S.D., Studebaker, C.A., Huss, M.T. and O'Neil, K.M. (in press). The effects of *Daubert v. Merrell Dow Pharmaceuticals* on the admissibility of expert testimony in state and federal criminal cases. *Psychology, Public Policy, and Law.*

Hamill, R., Wilson, T.D. and Nisbett, R.E. (1980). Insensitivity to sample bias: Generalizing from atypical cases. *Journal of Personality and Social Psychology, 39*, 578–589.

Heuer, L. and Penrod, S. (1994). Trial complexity: A field investigation of its meaning and its effects. *Law and Human Behavior, 18*, 29–51.

Horowitz, I.A., ForsterLee, L. and Brolly, I. (1996). Effects of trial complexity on decision making. *Journal of Applied Psychology, 81*, 757–768.

Jepson, C., Krantz, D.H. and Nisbett, R.E. (1983). Inductive reasoning: Competence or skill? *Behavioral and Brain Sciences, 6*, 494–501.

Judson, O. (1999, October 9). Slide-rule justice. *National Journal*, pp. 2882–2886.

Kahneman, D. and Tversky, A. (1972). Subjective probability: A judgment of representativeness. *Cognitive Psychology, 3*, 430–454.

Kahneman, D. and Tversky, A. (1973). On the psychology of prediction. *Psychological Review, 80*, 237–251.

Kaye, D.H. and Koehler, J.J. (1991). Can jurors understand probabilistic evidence? *Journal of the Royal Statistical Society Series A, 154*, Part 1, 75–81.

Kassin, S.M. and Dunn, M.A. (1997). Computer-animated displays and the jury: Facilitative and prejudicial effects. *Law and Human Behavior, 21*, 269–281.

Kassin, S.M., Reddy, M.E. and Tulloch, W.F. (1990). Juror interpretations of ambiguous evidence: The need for cognition, presentation order, and persuasion. *Law and Human Behavior, 14*, 43–55.

Koehler, J.J. (2001). When are people persuaded by DNA match statistics? *Law and Human Behavior, 25*, 493–513.

Kovera, M.B. and McAuliff, B.D. (2000). The effects of peer review and evidence quality on judge evaluations of psychological science: Are judges effective gatekeepers? *Journal of Applied Psychology, 85*, 574–586.

Kovera, M.B., McAuliff, B.D. and Hebert, K.S. (1999). Reasoning about scientific evidence: Effects of juror gender and evidence quality on juror decisions in a hostile work environment case. *Journal of Applied Psychology, 84*, 362–375.

Kraus, D.A. and Sales, B.D. (2001). The effects of clinical and scientific expert testimony on juror decision making in capital sentencing. *Psychology, Public Policy, and Law, 7*, 267–310.

Kumho Tire Co., Ltd., et al. v. Carmichael et al., 526 US 137 (1999).

Kunda, Z. and Nisbett, R.E. (1986). Prediction and the partial understanding of the law of large numbers. *Journal of Experimental Social Psychology, 22*, 339–354.

Lassiter, G.D., Slaw, R.D., Briggs, M.A. and Scanlan, C.R. (1992). The potential for bias in videotaped confessions. *Journal of Applied Social Psychology, 22*, 1838–1851.

Lederer, F.I. (1994). Technology comes to the courtroom, and... *Emory Law Journal, 43*, 1095–1122.

Leippe, M.R. and Romanczyk, A. (1989). Reactions to child (versus adult) eyewitnesses: The influence of jurors' preconceptions and witness behavior. *Law and Human Behavior, 13*, 103–132.

Lehman, D.R. and Nisbett, R.E. (1990). A longitudinal study of the effects of undergraduate training on reasoning. *Developmental Psychology, 26*, 952–960.

Lehman, D.R., Lempert, R.O. and Nisbett, R.E. (1988). The effects of graduate training on reasoning: Formal discipline and thinking about everyday life events. *American Psychologist, 43*, 431–443.

Loftus, E.F. (1980). Psychological aspects of courtroom testimony. *Annals of the New York Academy of Sciences, 347*, 27–37.

Maheswaran, D., Mackie, D.M. and Chaiken, S. (1992). Brand name as a heuristic cue: The effects of task importance and expectancy confirmation on consumer judgments. *Journal of Consumer Psychology, 1*, 317–336.

McAuliff, B.D. and Kovera, M.B. (2003). Need for cognition and juror sensitivity to methodological flaws in psychological science. Manuscript submitted for publication.

McCloskey, M. and Kohl, D. (1983). Naive physics: The curvilinear impetus principle and its role in interactions with moving objects. *Journal of Experimental Psychology: Learning, Memory, and Cognition, 9*, 146–156.

McCloskey, M., Washburn, A. and Felch, L. (1983). Intuitive physics: The straight-down belief and its origin. *Journal of Experimental Psychology: Learning, Memory, and Cognition, 9*, 636–649.

Mill, D., Gray, T. and Mandel, D.R. (1994). Influence of research methods and statistics courses on everyday reasoning, critical abilities, and belief in unsubstantiated phenomena. *Canadian Journal of Behavioural Science, 26*, 246–258.

Niedermeier, K.E., Kerr, N.L. and Messé, L.A. (1999). Jurors' use of naked statistical evidence: Exploring bases and implications of the Wells effect. *Journal of Personality and Social Psychology, 76*, 533–542.

Nisbett, R.E. (1993). *Rules for reasoning.* Hillsdale, NJ: Lawrence Erlbaum.

Nisbett, R.E. and Ross, L. (1980). Assigning weights to data: The 'vividness criterion'. *Human inference: Strategies and shortcomings of social judgment.* Englewood Cliffs, NJ: Prentice-Hall.

Paivio, A. and Csapo, K. (1969). Concrete image and verbal memory codes. *Journal of Experimental Psychology, 80*, 279–285.

Paivio, A. and Csapo, K. (1973). Picture superiority in free recall: Imagery or dual coding? *Cognitive Psychology, 5*, 176–206.

Paivio, A., Philipchalk, R. and Rowe, E.J. (1975). Free and serial recall of pictures, sounds, and words. *Memory and Cognition, 3*, 586–590.

Petty, R.E. and Cacioppo, J.T. (1984). The effects of involvement on responses to argument quantity and quality: Central and peripheral routes to persuasion. *Journal of Personality and Social Psychology, 46*, 69–81.

Petty, R.E. and Cacioppo, J.T. (1986). The elaboration likelihood model of persuasion. In L. Berkowitz (ed.), *Advances in experimental social psychology*, (Vol. 19; pp. 123–203). New York: Academic Press.

Petty, R.E., Cacioppo, J.T. and Goldman, R. (1981). Personal involvement as a determinant of argument based persuasion. *Journal of Personality and Social Psychology, 41*, 847–855.

Petty, R.E., Kasmer, J.A., Haugtvedt, C.P. and Cacioppo, J.T. (1987). Source and message factors in persuasion: A reply to Stiff's critique of the elaboration likelihood model. *Communication Monographs, 54*, 233–249.

Reyes, R.M., Thompson, W.C. and Bower, G.H. (1980). Judgmental biases resulting from differing availabilities of arguments. *Journal of Personality and Social Psychology, 39*, 2–12.

Saks, M.J. and Kidd, R.F. (1980). Human information processing and adjudication: Trial by heuristics. *Law and Society Review, 15*, 123–160.

Schklar, J. and Diamond, S.S. (1999). Juror reactions to DNA evidence: Errors and expectancies. *Law and Human Behavior, 23*, 159–184.

Selvin, M. and Picus, L. (1987). *The debate over jury performance: Observations from a recent asbestos case.* Santa Monica: CA: The RAND Corporation, R-3479-ICJ.

Sherman, S.J., Cialdini, R.B., Schwartzman, D.F. and Reynolds, K.D. (1985). Imagining can heighten or lower the perceived likelihood of contracting a disease: The mediating effect of ease of imagery. *Personality and Social Psychology Bulletin, 11*, 118–127.

Shuman, D.W., Whitaker, E. and Champagne, A. (1994). An empirical examination of the use of expert witnesses in the courts—Part II: A three city study. *Jurimetrics, 34*, 193–208.

Simonson, I. and Nye, P. (1992). The effect of accountability on susceptibility to decision errors. *Organizational Behavior and Human Decision Processes, 51*, 416–446.

Smith, B.C., Penrod, S.D., Otto, A.L. and Park, R. C. (1996). Jurors' use of probabilistic evidence. *Law and Human Behavior, 20*, 49–82.

Stanovich, K.E. and West, R.F. (1998). Who uses base rates and $P(D/\sim H)$? An analysis of individual differences. *Memory and Cognition, 26*, 161–179.

Taylor, S.E. and Thompson, S.C. (1982). Stalking the elusive 'vividness' effect. *Psychological Review*, 89, 155–181.

Thompson, W.C. and Schumann, E.L. (1987). Interpretation of statistical evidence in criminal trials: The prosecutor's fallacy and the defense attorney's fallacy. *Law and Human Behavior, 11*, 167–187.

Viswanathan, M. (1993). Measurement of individual differences in preference for numerical information. *Journal of Applied Psychology, 78*, 741–752.

Wells, G.L. (1992). Naked statistical evidence of liability: Is subjective probability enough? *Journal of Personality and Social Psychology, 62*, 739–752.

Wilson, M.G., Northcraft, G.B. and Neale, M.A. (1989). Information competition and vividness effects in on-line judgments. *Organizational Behavior and Human Decision Processes, 44*, 132–139.

Chapter 3.2

Assessing Evidence: Proving Facts

Michael J. Saks
Arizona State University, USA
and
William C. Thompson
University of California, Irvine, USA

INTRODUCTION

In this chapter we consider ways in which psychological research and a psychological perspective have contributed (and may contribute in the future) to understanding and enhancing proof of facts and assessment of evidence in a legal context. We focus primarily on the Anglo-American system of trial in which battling lawyers present evidence in an adversarial manner to lay jurors who must evaluate the evidence in accordance with legal standards articulated by the trial judge.

Although the use of lay juries is the cornerstone of Anglo-American trial procedure (Damaska, 1997; Thayer, 1898), jurors are not the only actors in the system who must evaluate evidence. Because advocates (lawyers or barristers) control the presentation of evidence, they must constantly consider both the meaning of the evidence and how the jury is likely to react to various possible presentations. The advocates must also evaluate evidence to decide such important issues as whether to file a claim and whether to settle a case. Less obviously, judges must evaluate evidence in order to determine, in accordance with the rules of evidence, what the jury will be permitted to hear. The rules of evidence require judges to classify evidence as admissible or inadmissible, and thereby to regulate the flow of information to the jury. Lawyers, in turn, must make predictions about how judges will decide admissibility questions in order to evaluate the strength of their cases.

The rules of evidence are designed to promote accurate fact-finding by shielding jurors from evidence that might distract or mislead them. These rules developed through

Handbook of Psychology in Legal Contexts, Second Edition
Edited by D. Carson and R. Bull. © 2003 John Wiley & Sons, Ltd.

common law and, in many jurisdictions, are incorporated into legislation. Common law judges, and rulemakers, have decided that evidence should be filtered to prevent lay jurors from drawing incorrect inferences from it.[1] The filtering is accomplished principally by the exclusion of specific types of evidence, though a secondary way has been by instructing jurors on the proper way to use the evidence. Those who develop rules of evidence are themselves involved in evidence assessment. In order to decide which types of evidence should be excluded, they must evaluate its potential both to enlighten and to mislead a lay jury, and in so doing must think about the abilities and limitations of jurors.

Thus, in order to make important decisions at many stages of the legal process, various actors must evaluate evidence themselves and must make predictions about how others will evaluate evidence. How do they make these judgments? How accurate are their assessments and predictions? Can their decisions be explained and predicted? Can their choices be made better?

FILTERING AND CONTROLLING EVIDENCE

The Rules of Evidence

Though they have evolved over time, and continue to do so, the elaborate set of procedural and evidentiary rules that specify the types of evidence that are and are not admissible have their origins in English common law (Lempert and Saltzburg, 1982). Restrictions on the use of hearsay, for example, can be traced to common law precedent several hundred years old (Landsman and Rakos, 1991), as can restrictions on the use of character evidence (Wydick, 1987). In the United States, evidentiary rules may also arise from constitutional law. The exclusionary rule (*Weeks* v. *United States*, 1914; *Mapp* v. *Ohio*, 1961) restricts the admissibility of evidence gathered in violation of a defendant's rights under the Fourth Amendment. Evidence that violates a defendant's Fifth Amendment privilege against self-incrimination or Sixth Amendment right of confrontation is also excluded.

To further understand the psychology of the evidence rules it is helpful to appreciate some of the purposes judges and rule-makers have had in mind when developing the rules (Lempert, 1977; Lempert and Saltzburg, 1982). One purpose is to screen out evidence that has such limited relevance that it would needlessly prolong the trial

---

[1] In Civil Law systems, including those of most Latin American and continental European nations, there are few exclusionary rules of evidence. Screening of evidence is viewed as unnecessary; the common-sense judgment of fact-finders is viewed as sufficient to afford a reasonable interpretation of the evidence (Damaska, 1997). This confidence in common-sense may rest in part on the use, in most Civil Law systems, of professional or semi-professional fact-finders rather than lay juries. Whether 'trained' fact-finders, such as professional judges, are indeed better than lay jurors at avoiding prejudice and reaching rational conclusions in light of the evidence is an empirical question that has yet to be thoroughly examined.

without contributing to the proper resolution of the matter at hand. Such evidence is ruled inadmissible because it is deemed insufficiently diagnostic to be worth the trouble of hearing.

A second reason for excluding evidence is to screen out material that is prejudicial—that is, evidence that is so likely to bias or mislead the jury that the fact-finding process would be more accurate without it (Kaplan, 1968). One way evidence can be prejudicial is by inflaming the passions of the jury and evoking hostility toward a party without casting much light on the issue at hand. Evidence that a defendant on trial for drunk driving is a pedophile, for example, would likely be judged prejudicial because it is likely to generate more heat than light. Evidence can also be prejudicial if jurors tend to overvalue it, that is, give it more weight than it deserves. Evidence may therefore be excluded because it is thought to be weak or problematic in ways that jurors are unlikely to appreciate. Hearsay evidence, character evidence, and some types of scientific evidence fall into this category.

Finally, some exclusionary rules of evidence are designed to serve specific public policy goals. For example, when a person is sued for negligence after someone has been injured on the defendant's property, evidence that the defendant took subsequent remedial action to prevent future accidents is inadmissible to prove negligence (in the United States, codified in Federal Rule of Evidence 407). This rule is justified in part by 'a fear that if such evidence were admitted, people would be unwilling to take post-accident precautions, to the general detriment of society' (Lempert and Saltzburg, 1977, p. 187). Similarly, evidence that a party offered an out-of-court settlement is inadmissible to prove liability (Federal Rule of Evidence 408) because out-of-court settlements are a favored means of resolving disputes and 'individuals would be reluctant to negotiate compromises if they knew evidence of their offers could be used against them in court' (Lempert and Saltzburg, 1977, p. 191). Rules of privilege also fall into this category. The attorney–client privilege, for example, helps assure that people can communicate freely with their attorneys by preventing disclosure of communications between attorney and client. The marital privilege protects the marital relationship by preventing testimony about communications between spouses. These policy-oriented rules reflect a judgment that accuracy and completeness of fact-finding at trial are less important to society than certain other goals (Lempert and Saltzburg, 1982).

Judges as Amateur Psychologists Making Rules and Rulings

In the process of creating rules of evidence, or making rulings on evidence, judges unavoidably are thinking about the psychology of witnesses, litigants or jurors. For example, to create a rule conditioning testimony on a witness's taking an oath bespeaks an assumption that something about oath-taking will increase the veracity of witnesses. Similarly, to create a rule excluding evidence of subsequent remedial measures requires a theory that litigants will weigh risks and benefits when deciding whether or not to repair a dangerous situation, and perhaps even a theory of what that risk calculus will be. And to create a rule for the exclusion of evidence likely to be overvalued by jurors, judges had to believe that jurors would assess some evidence differently—and incorrectly—compared to what the judges thought was the correct assessment of the evidence. In effect, evidence rule-makers are amateur psychologists theorizing about the psychology of witnesses and jurors and litigants. These theories and the observations, assumptions, and inferences that give rise to them have been memorably referred to as 'fireside inductions' (Meehl, 1989).

Where the focus of the rule-maker is on the people or circumstances that produce more or less reliable testimony, the rule-makers are generally acting as applied cognitive psychologists. This perspective is reflected in the rules concerning the competency of witnesses, oath, cross-examination, leading questions, habit, and some of the exceptions to the rule against hearsay. The rule-maker generally is acting as an applied social psychologist when focusing on the behavior of litigants, reflected in such rules as those excluding evidence on offers of compromise, subsequent remedial measures, pleas, and insurance. But most of the rules reveal the rule-makers to be amateur cognitive social psychologists concerned with the jury, reflected in such rules as those governing hearsay and many of its exceptions, character evidence, and assessment of witness credibility.

The decision-making of these amateur psychologists can, in its turn, be examined. How well are they doing? Part of evaluating their performance as decision-makers could involve evaluating the beliefs on which their decisions are based. How accurate are their beliefs about witness, litigant, and juror psychology? Rules and the rulings might be improved by improving the information base on which they rest—by replacing intuition and guesswork with improved systems of logic (including probability theory) or with empirically based knowledge about the psychology of witnesses and jurors and litigants.

Note that judges are not merely trying to predict how jurors will assess evidence. The mental gymnastics in which these judges are necessarily engaged is far more complicated. They first have to decide what the correct (or a range of correct) inferences are that should be drawn from the evidence. (Query how well judges do that.) Then they must predict how jurors will assess, and what inferences jurors will draw from the same evidence. (Query how well judges do that.) And then they must compare the two sets of inferences and judge whether the gap is so large that something must be done to correct the discrepancy. It is entirely possible that the judges are themselves in error either about the proper inferences to be drawn from the evidence or about the inferences that jurors will draw, or both. What little research exists making direct comparisons between the decisions judges make on evidence and the decisions jurors make, shows them to be far more similar than different (Rakos and Landsman, 1992; Wells, 1992; Kalven and Zeisel, 1966). Such findings suggest that the fundamental assumption that jurors are poorer decision-makers about facts than judges are might itself be in error. From there it is a short step to wondering whether the corrections embodied in the rules of evidence might be over- or under-corrections.

Historical Perspective

The most infamous of the early efforts to improve the law's decisions about what evidence should be admitted and what evidence excluded, or how to weigh the evidence, was that of Hugo Münsterberg, through his book, *On the Witness Stand* (1908) and in a series of articles and commentary in and about specific trials. Münsterberg mixed sensible data-based propositions with arguments based on less sound data, among them such ideas as the suggestion that psychologists should evaluate witnesses for credibility and then the courts should be guided by the psychologists' assessments. (That is a notion that actually is not uncommon today in some Continental legal systems (see van Koppen and Saks, 2002) but which was and remains anathema to Anglo-American courts.) That Münsterberg had little impact on the thinking of Anglo-American judges and legal scholars is even more understandable considering that he was highly critical of them, and locked horns with the giant of early twentieth-century evidence law, John Henry Wigmore (Magner, 1991). Notwithstanding his disdain for Münsterberg's ideas (Münsterberg, 1908), it is worth noting that Wigmore had a considerable interest in the potential contributions of psychological research and theory to issues of evidence and proof. His book, *The Principles of Judicial Proof as Given by Logic, Psychology, and General Experience and Illustrated in Judicial Trials* (1913), contained extensive extracts from the psychological literature, and Wigmore reported his own series of 'Testimonial and Verdict Experiments' (Wigmore, 1931, 2nd edn., pp. 536–540). Wigmore himself was quite skeptical about the psychological assumptions underlying some rules of evidence and thought they could be corrected and refined with help from psychological research.

The most explicit and productive program of research to compare the psychological assumptions of evidence doctrine against the facts of human psychology was undertaken at Yale by legal scholar Robert M. Hutchins and psychologist Donald Slesinger. Their collaboration produced a series of studies of the psychological bases of the rules of evidence, in light of what was then known from psychological research, on such topics as spontaneous exclamations (Hutchins and Slesinger, 1928a), memory (Hutchins and Slesinger, 1928b), witness competency (Hutchins and Slesinger, 1928c), family relations (Hutchins and Slesinger, 1929a), state of mind to prove an act (Hutchins and Slesinger, 1929b), state of mind in issue (Hutchins and Slesinger, 1929c), and consciousness of guilt (Hutchins and Slesinger, 1929d). 'In this series, preliminary to experimental attack, the law of evidence is being analyzed in order to make explicit its psychological assumptions, and criticise them in light of those of modern psychology' (Hutchins and Slesinger, 1929e, note 1, p. 13). Their work grew out of a wider vision of law as amateur applied psychology:

> For centuries the law has been fumbling with what has only recently become the subject matter of psychology. Lawyers, judges, juries, legislators, and governmental officers have always vaguely known that their task was the prediction and control of human conduct.

In performing this task they built up an empirical technique of regulation called the law, in every branch of which, from contracts to crimes, appear assumptions as to why and how people act in given situations. . . . Out of this technique of regulation has grown a rough and ready science of behavior which crystallized unfortunately before the dawn of modern psychology. (Hutchins and Slesinger, 1929c, pp. 13–14)

Despite its lively beginnings, interdisciplinary study of evidence fell dormant in the mid-twentieth century, perhaps due to the general retreat of legal scholarship from social realism toward process models of justice (Monahan and Walker, 1996, ch. 1). By the late 1960s the field was 'moribund' as the few scholars writing about evidence relied on traditional doctrinal analysis with 'no overarching critical theory to give it life' (Lempert, 1986, p. 439). What Richard Lempert has called 'the new evidence scholarship' began to emerge in the 1970s as experts in other fields, particularly statistics, epistemology, and psychology 'discovered' the law of evidence and began using the tools of their disciplines to address important evidentiary issues. Major symposia at Boston University (Symposium, 1986) and Cardozo Law School (Symposium, 1991) brought legal scholars together with experts from other fields to discuss problems of evidence, and the area continues to be active.

Specific Examples of Evidence Doctrine and Psychological Approaches to Illuminating Them

Hearsay is defined as an out-of-court statement made by one individual (the declarant) and presented in court by another individual (the hearsay witness) as proof of the fact asserted. Under rules initially developed through English common law, hearsay is generally inadmissible in Anglo-American courts unless it falls within an established exception to the hearsay rule. The exceptions allow the presentation of hearsay when special circumstances exist that are thought to help assure that it is reliable or where strong practical considerations favor its use (Park, 1987). For example, a statement made while under the 'stress of excitement' caused by the event being described may be admissible under the 'excited utterance' exception to the hearsay rule (Federal Rule of Evidence 803(2)), or a statement made to a physician for purposes of medical diagnosis and treatment may be admissible as another exception (Federal Rule of Evidence 803(4)).

Courts have long viewed hearsay with skepticism due to fears that it will be overvalued by jurors and therefore will be prejudicial. These fears arise in part from historic cases in which miscarriages of justice were seen to arise from the use of hearsay evidence, such as the trial of Sir Walter Raleigh (Landsman and Rakos, 1991). But these fears are primarily grounded in a psychological intuition: courts have traditionally assumed, without empirical verification, that jurors fail to adequately appreciate the unreliability of hearsay testimony (Park, 1987).

Hearsay is considered difficult for jurors to evaluate because it entails at least two levels of uncertainty. There is the possibility that the declarant (i.e. the person making the out-of-court statement) was lying or mistaken about what he or she perceived and the possibility the hearsay witness is lying or mistaken about what the declarant said (Tillers and Schum, 1992; Schum, 1992). Moreover, it may be difficult to expose biases or errors of the declarant, who is not present in court and cannot be cross-examined.

Hearsay has recently attracted the attention of a number of psychological researchers. For example, a 'special theme' issue of *Psychology, Public Policy and Law* was recently devoted to the issue of hearsay testimony in trials involving child witnesses (Special Theme, 1999).

Thompson and Pathak (1999) identified two major approaches to studying jurors' reactions to hearsay, which they labeled the analogue approach and the decomposition approach. The analogue approach requires elaborate simulations in which the researcher stages an event that is seen by an observer (e.g. Kovera, Park and Penrod, 1992; Pathak and Thompson, 1999). The observer (who is analogous to a hearsay declarant) makes statements about the event to a witness who, in turn, recounts those hearsay statements to mock jurors. This design allows the mock jurors' conclusions about the reported event to be compared with what really happened. More importantly, it allows for tests of the mock jurors' sensitivity to factors that affect the accuracy of hearsay testimony, such as the length of time that passes between when the witness hears and reports what the declarant said (Kovera et al., 1992) or the use of suggestive questions to elicit information from the declarant (Pathak and Thompson, 1999).

The decomposition approach is suggested by the work of David Schum and Peter Tillers (Schum, 1992; Tillers and Schum, 1992), who have used 'cascaded inference' models to describe the judgments required to evaluate hearsay evidence. Their models show how a 'global' judgment regarding the overall value of a piece of hearsay evidence can be decomposed into a series of more 'local' judgments about such matters as the observational sensitivity, objectivity and veracity of the declarant and hearsay witness. These models are potentially useful to psychologists because they provide a means for testing the logical consistency of 'global' and 'local' judgments about hearsay (Thompson and Pathak, 1999). A psychologist who is interested in whether information about the reliability of a declarant is correctly integrated into people's global judgments about the value of hearsay, for example, can test to see whether global and local judgments are equally sensitive to that variable.

The global–local comparison can also yield helpful information about the reasons for people's insensitivity to important factors. If people are insensitive to a particular factor because they fail to appreciate its importance, then both local and global judgments should be insensitive. On the other hand, if people appreciate the factor but are insensitive due to a failure to correctly integrate information about it into their judgments, then the local judgments should be more sensitive to the factor than global judgments.

Next, consider an exception to the rule against hearsay that we mentioned above: the excited utterance exception to the rule against hearsay. Wigmore strongly advanced the notion that people in an agitated state were unlikely to lie because they lacked sufficient time in which to fabricate (Wigmore, 1974, vol. 6, sec. 1747, p. 135). This is based on the patently psychological theory that the stress of an arousing event consumes so much of a person's available cognitive resources that they lack sufficient residual capacity with which to do the cognitive work needed to invent falsehoods. If Wigmore, judges, and rule-makers believed that humans had greater cognitive capacities, or could process thoughts in parallel (so that while part of the mind was taken up with reacting to the stimulus of the incident, another part could separately analyze the possibilities for lying), this exception would have been viewed with far less favor. While Wigmore's theory certainly is plausible, it was advanced without data. The alternative, against which the Wigmore's cognitive capacity theory needed to be tested, is that stressful arousal impairs the ability to perceive and store information accurately. Determining whether excited utterances lead to more honesty or less accuracy, and therefore whether making it a hearsay exception is a perspicacious or a misguided choice, requires testing. Today, it is a commonplace of research on cognition and memory that stressful arousal degrades accuracy (in other words, 'stress makes you stupid'), a finding consistent with the Yerkes–Dodson law, and which can be found in almost any introductory psychology textbook. Indeed, Hutchins and Slesinger (1928a) reviewed the available psychological literature and concluded even then that arousal sufficient to trigger the excited utterance exception is arousal that is also sufficient to make the statements untrustworthy.

The law's speculations have fared better in the area of character evidence. Under a rule initially established in English common law, evidence of a defendant's previous bad behavior is inadmissible when its sole purpose is to prove that he has a 'bad character' or criminal propensity and therefore is likely to be guilty (Wydick, 1987; Uviller, 1982). The standard rationale for this restriction was set forth by the United States Supreme Court in *Michaelson* v. *United States* (1948):

> The state may not show defendant's prior trouble with the law, specific criminal acts, or ill name among his neighbors, even though such facts might logically be persuasive that he is by propensity a probable perpetrator of the crime. The inquiry is not rejected because character is irrelevant; on the contrary, it is said to weigh too much with the jury and to so overpersuade them as to prejudge one with a bad general record and deny him a fair opportunity to defend against a particular charge. The overriding policy of excluding such evidence, despite its admitted probative value, is the practical experience that its disallowance tends to prevent confusion of issues, unfair surprise and undue prejudice.

Clearly the rationale rests in large part on psychological assumptions concerning the consistency of human behavior across situations and people's ability to correctly assess the character of others. To be sure, the psychological assumptions are not beyond controversy (Mischel, 1968; Funder, 1997, 1999). Among psychologists there has been considerable debate about whether accurate predictions of behavior in a given instance can be made on the basis of previous instances of behavior in other settings, or on the basis of intuitive personality assessments. But the weight of the research evidence suggests that unless special methodological steps (unavailable in the trials context) are taken, our confidence in character-based predictions (or post-dictions) exceeds our accuracy (see Ross and Nisbett, 1991).

Analysis of character evidence is difficult due to the complexity of the applicable rules. Although the government cannot introduce evidence solely to show the defendant's criminal propensities, evidence that reflects negatively on a defendant's character may nevertheless be admissible if it has some other purpose. If the defendant chooses to testify in his own behalf, for example, evidence of prior crimes can be admitted to impeach his credibility. Additionally, evidence of prior bad acts may be admissible as proof of motive, opportunity, intent, preparation, plan, knowledge, identity, or absence of mistake or accident (Federal Rule of Evidence 404(b)). Thus, for example, evidence that the defendant previously assaulted the victim of the present crime might be admissible to show his animosity toward the victim and hence his motive to commit the present crime. Evidence that a defendant committed a previous crime might be admissible to prove his identity if it was a 'signature crime' sufficiently similar to the current charge to support an inference that the same person committed both. Evidence that the defendant committed a previous crime might be admissible to show his knowledge if both crimes required similar knowledge, such as knowing how to crack a safe or make a bomb. Whether such evidence is actually admitted or not is decided on a case-by-case basis by the trial judge, who is required to weigh the probative value of the evidence against its potential for prejudice. In other words, the judge considers whether the evidence is sufficiently important with respect to permissible inferences (e.g. motive, identity, knowledge, etc.) to justify the risk that the jury will use it to draw impermissible inferences (e.g. the defendant's criminal propensities).

When such evidence is admitted, the judge often gives the jury 'limiting instructions', which tell the jury to use the evidence only for specified permissible purposes, and not to use the evidence to draw impermissible inferences. Several studies have tested the ability of mock jurors to follow such instructions (Wissler and Saks, 1985; Tanford and Cox, 1987; Tanford and Penrod, 1984). These studies suggest that jurors make and use the impermissible inferences, notwithstanding the limiting instructions.

THE BAYESIAN PERSPECTIVE

The use of probability analysis, and especially Bayesian analysis, to evaluate evidence and the inferences to which the evidence leads, has been discussed sporadically for decades (Kaplan, 1968; Finkelstein and Fairley, 1970; Lempert, 1977; Kaye, 1988a; Robertson and Vignaux, 1995), and has become one of the centerpieces of the new evidence scholarship. Bayes' theorem is a basic principle of logic that indicates how a rational evaluator should adjust a subjective probability assessment in light of new evidence. The process of reassessment in the light of new information can begin with the first piece of evidence and continue in iterative fashion through to the last. Or it can describe the effect that any given piece of evidence should have on a factfinder's belief in alternative hypotheses. Bayes' theorem is best understood as a statement regarding the logical consistency of beliefs. It is useful for identifying inconsistencies among the various beliefs a fact-finder might hold and for demonstrating the logical implications of one set of beliefs for another. Fact-finders must place a value on the evidence (how believable it is), see how it fits into the puzzle of the entire case, and judge how each piece of evidence fits into and affects the rest of the evidence in the case, leading to a verdict. Bayesian analysis can provide a model of that process.

A key issue for psychologists is whether Bayesian models accurately describe the inferences of human decision-makers. There is strong evidence that they do not. When updating judgments based on single pieces of evidence, people tend to be 'conservative' relative to Bayesian norms—that is, they revise their beliefs about the likelihood of alternative hypotheses less than Bayesian models say they should given their beliefs in the probability of the new evidence arising under the alternative hypotheses (Edwards, 1968; Slovic and Lichtenstein, 1971). However, when the evaluation of evidence requires people to consider multiple sources of uncertainty, they sometimes make more extreme judgments than Bayesian models dictate (Gettys, Kelly and Peterson, 1973). Furthermore, research on mock jurors' evaluations of statistical evidence has revealed a number of distinct errors in assessing conditional probabilities that lead people to deviate from Bayesian norms (Thompson, 1989; Kaye and Koehler, 1991). For example, when evaluating evidence that the suspect in a criminal case has the same blood type as the perpetrator, and that this blood type is found in $X\%$ of the population, people sometimes conclude that the probability the suspect is the perpetrator, given the evidence, is necessarily equal to $1/X$, an error that Thompson and Schumann (1987) labeled 'the prosecutor's fallacy'. On other occasions people commit the 'defense attorney's fallacy' of giving such evidence no weight at all (Thompson, 1989). And people perform poorly, relative to Bayesian norms, when combining information on the frequency of a matching characteristic (such as a blood group) with information on the error rate of the test showing the match (Koehler, Chia and Lindsey, 1995; Schklar and Diamond, 1999). Courts are becoming sensitive to the potential for such errors. In the United Kingdom, two criminal convictions have been reversed in cases in which prosecutors and the government's expert witnesses made arguments consistent with the prosecutor's fallacy when characterizing the value of DNA evidence for the jury (*Regina* v. *Deen*, 1994; Balding and Donnelly, 1994).

Bayesian models also fail to capture the process of human decision-making. Jurors appear to evaluate evidence in a trial not by sequential updating (as posited by a Bayesian model) but by constructing plausible narratives that might account for the evidence (Hastie and Pennington, 1992; Pennington and Hastie, 1991a,b). According to the 'story model', proposed by Pennington and Hastie, various narratives (including those explicitly advanced by the parties) are evaluated according to how coherently and comprehensively they can account for the facts. The most plausible narrative is then assessed *vis-à-vis* relevant legal standards to determine the verdict. Forensic identification evidence, such as evidence that the suspect and perpetrator share a rare blood type, may also be evaluated in non-Bayesian fashion. Koehler (2001) has recently suggested that jurors evaluate such evidence according to the ease with which they can imagine other individuals who might match and has shown that mock jurors' judgments are affected in ways inconsistent with Bayesian norms by factors that influence the availability of 'coincidental match exemplars'.

If Bayesian models fail to describe human judgment, then of what use are they? Defenders of Bayesianism argue that the principal value of these models is normative rather than descriptive. They claim that their models show how evidence *should* be evaluated and thus serve as a framework for understanding evidence and as a standard of rationality against which actual human judgment can be compared (Robertson and Vignaux, 1995; Schum, 1994; Kaye, 1988; Lempert, 1977). However, these claims have been controversial. An anti-Bayesian group consisting of philosophers (most notably Cohen, 1981, 1977) and legal scholars (Cullison, 1979; Callan, 1982; Brilmeyer, 1986; Allen, 1986) has questioned the fundamental value of a Bayesian perspective as a framework for understanding legal evidence. They point to apparent paradoxes that arise from applying a Bayesian perspective to legal decision-making (Cohen, 1981; Brilmayer and Kornhauser, 1978) and argue, contrary to Bayesian assumptions, that base rates are inherently inferior to more particularized evidence (Cohen, 1981). Bayesians dispute the existence and/or relevance of the purported paradoxes (Lempert, 1986; Kaye, 1979) and defend reliance on base rates (Koehler, 1993).

Despite challenge, the Bayesian perspective is alive and well in evidence scholarship. Scholars have relied on Bayesian models to analyze such diverse evidentiary issues as the meaning of the concept of relevance (Lempert, 1977), the value of forensic identification evidence (Robertson and Vignaux, 1995), the proper interpretation of DNA evidence (Evett and Weir, 1998), the value of expert testimony in child abuse cases (Lyon and Koehler, 1996), the value of hearsay (Tillers and Schum, 1992), and the appropriateness of questioning children in a suggestive manner (Lyon, 1999; Ceci and Friedman, 2000).

Bayesian Decision Aids for Juries?

If Bayesian models provide a standard for appropriate judgment, and if actual human judgment deviates from those models, then perhaps jurors need some assistance in drawing proper conclusions from evidence. This line of thinking has led to a number of proposals for the use of Bayesian decision aids, generally to help jurors to draw conclusions from forensic identification evidence, such as evidence of matching blood types or matching DNA profiles. Most proposals entail the use of likelihood ratios to characterize the value of the identification evidence, along with instructions to the jurors on how to use the likelihood ratio to update their prior subjective assessments of the probability of a relevant proposition. An early proposal of this nature (Finkelstein and Fairley, 1970) drew a famously eloquent response from constitutional scholar Laurence Tribe (1971), who acknowledged the appeal of a Bayesian perspective as a way for scholars to think about evidence, but lambasted the idea of providing Bayesian decision aids to jurors on doctrinal, constitutional and practical grounds. Tribe's analysis was in turn challenged as psychologically naïve and anti-empirical (Saks and Kidd, 1980). Other psychologists (Faigman and Baglioni, 1988), statisticians (Friedman, 1997), philosophers (Cohen, 1977), and legal scholars (Kaye, 1979; Koehler and Shaviro, 1990) have joined the debate, which gained currency with the growing use of scientific evidence in the courtroom. Proponents of decision aids have made some progress. In paternity cases, for example, some courts provide jurors charts showing how a prior probability of paternity should be revised in light of the paternity index (likelihood ratio) associated with a genetic test (Kaye, 1988b). The National Research Council has suggested that experts might compute posterior probabilities to show jurors the power of DNA evidence for establishing identity (National Research Council, 1996, pp. 201–202), although this proposal remains controversial (see Thompson, 1997).

Inference and Decision-Making in Litigation

One current thrust of 'the new evidence scholarship' is concerned less with the rules of evidence and more with the problem of processing evidence and drawing inferences from it in order to prepare for trial, try, and decide cases. It seeks to develop theories of inference in the litigation context (Schum and Tillers, 1991a, b; Twining, 1991).

Lawyers confront masses of evidence that they must organize in a meaningful and effective way if they want to support the conclusions they would wish to urge on a fact-finder. Legal education is devoted to teaching legal analysis, not fact analysis and not the organizing of facts in preparation for trial. In modern times, the sheer volume of evidence confronted by lawyers has become daunting and computer assistance in managing that evidence is not unusual. But how are lawyers to sort through the maze of evidence to determine which propositions that need to be proved are supported by what evidence, in a complex interconnected hierarchy of raw facts, intermediate inferences, and ultimate conclusions? Wigmore (1913, 1931, 1937) developed the first system for organizing and assessing evidence for litigation by employing careful logic to trace the factual support for inferences. 'Wigmorian analysis is an attempt to capture the way we think when we think at our best' (Robertson and Vignaux, 1993, p. 1447).

Wigmorean charting was a major milestone in lawyerly thinking about facts, particularly when one considers that few legal theorists paid any attention to facts, but it still was somewhat crude. Anderson and Twining (1991) not only resurrected Wigmorean charting, but improved upon it, such as by enabling it to take into account the applicable substantive law and by expanding it beyond requiring the chartist to have a single 'ultimate probandum' in mind before starting. Instead, the chartist is able to explore alternative conclusions to which the evidence might lead.

Although Wigmore's system involved no probability analysis and Twining and Anderson are ambivalent about the connection between quantitative analysis and charting, Robertson and Vignaux (1993, 1995) have argued that the two complement each other quite well. Probability theory is a relatively accessible form of quantified logic. Wigmorean and related kinds of charting clarify the elements of evidence and their interrelationships. The addition of an element to the chart is an implicit probability statement, at least of the chartist's subjective probability judgment of the element's importance. It is a small step to add quantified probability statements either of the objective (empirical, relative frequency) probability of each element or the chartist's subjective probability of the element. Robertson and Vignaux (1993, p. 1456) state:

> Once this is done, one's view of the evidence is changed. Rather than seeing particular pieces of evidence as supporting particular hypotheses, one sees more clearly that the role of each item of evidence is to discriminate among the alternatives. One considers the probability of the evidence given each hypothesis, which means that one is starting with arrows downward from the hypothesis to the evidence rather than upward as the arrows in a Wigmore Chart normally flow. This leads to calculating likelihood ratios to assess how well the evidence succeeds in discriminating between pairs of hypotheses. Bayesian analysis and Wigmorian analysis have then been combined.

Wigmorean charting sets the stage for probability analysis, and probability analysis adds to the power of charting. Probability analysis is facilitated even more by the improvements in Wigmorean charting offered by Twining and Anderson (1991), and by such devices as decision trees, influence diagrams, and Bayes networks (Robertson and Vignaux, 1995).

FUTURE CONTRIBUTIONS OF PSYCHOLOGY TO EVIDENCE EVALUATION

We can, of course, expect future contributions of psychologists (and other social and behavioral scientists and statisticians) to include a variety of continuations and extensions of recent past work. Prominent among these will be research that tests the assumptions about human perception, memory, and other behavior that rule-makers rely upon when they make evidence doctrine, with the research often focused on and making contributions to controversies surrounding particular evidence doctrines that are ripe for reform. Also prominent will be continued explorations into how lawyers can better organize and present evidence, and how judges and jurors can more effectively and accurately comprehend and evaluate the evidence presented to them. These efforts will build on the Wigmorean, Bayesian, and story model methods that have been of much recent interest. A continuing general contribution of psychologists (in particular) will be to subject various ideas about evidence doctrine and trial practice to empirical testing.

Emerging issues to which we can expect psychological research and theory to be addressed will center around the growing use of scientific evidence in court. Good science can lead judges and jurors closer to correct verdicts only if the judges and jurors properly understand and apply the evidence. We can expect research to uncover where the most serious problems are in fact-finders' processing of evidence, especially scientific and quantitative evidence, and then to develop and test ways of improving how fact-finders process and use such evidence. For example, a continuing problem has been enabling judges and jurors to understand and properly evaluate statistical and other quantitative evidence presented in trials. Some psychologists, in effect operating as educational psychologists, are working on ways to more efficiently and effectively teach judges to understand statistics.

But not all that is offered to judges and jurors as science is valid. Recent data suggest that errors by forensic scientists rival errors by eyewitnesses as the foremost causes of erroneous convictions (Saks et al., 2001). Research by psychologists will contribute: to the evaluation of the underlying validity of a number of these sciences and of new offerings by new sciences, to the procedures employed in performing their tests (such as to reduce observer bias effects; see Risinger et al., in press), to evaluation of the applications of sound principles to case-specific data, and (as already stated) to the proper presentation of such research by the expert witnesses and proper interpretation of such evidence by the fact-finders.

REFERENCES

Allen, R. (1986). A reconceptualization of civil trials. *Boston University Law Review, 66,* 401–438.

Anderson, T. and Twining, W. (1991). *Analysis of evidence: How to do things with facts based on Wigmore's Science of Judicial Proof.* Boston: Little, Brown and Co. (Republished 1998, Evanston, IL: Northwestern University Press.)

Balding, D.J. and Donnelly, P. (1994). The prosecutor's fallacy and DNA evidence. *Criminal Law Review,* 711–721.

Brilmayer, L. and Kornhauser, L. (1978). Review: Quantitative methods and legal decision. *University of Chicago Law Review, 46,* 116–153.

Brilmayer, L. (1986). Second-order evidence and Bayesian logic. *Boston University Law Review, 66,* 673–691.

Callan, C.R. (1982). Notes on a grand illusion: some limits on the use of Bayesian theory in evidence law. *Indiana Law Journal, 57,* 1–44.

Ceci, S.J. and Friedman, R.D. (2000). The suggestibility of children: Scientific research and legal implications. *Cornell Law Review, 86,* 33–108.

Cohen, L.J. (1977). *The probable and the provable.* Cambridge: Cambridge University Press.

Cohen, L.J. (1981). Can human irrationality be experimentally demonstrated? *Behavioral and Brain Sciences, 4,* 317–370.

Cullison, A.D. (1979). Identification by probabilities and trial by mathematics (a lesson for beginners in how to be wrong with greater precision). *Houston Law Review, 6,* 471–518.

Damaska, M.R. (1997). *Evidence law adrift.* New Haven: Yale University Press.

Edwards, W. (1968). Conservatism in human information processing. In B. Kleinmuntz (ed.), *Formal representation of human judgment.* New York: John Wiley & Sons.

Evett, I.W. and Weir, B.S. (1998). *Interpreting DNA Evidence: Statistical Genetics for Forensic Scientists.* Sunderland, Mass.: Sinauer.

Faigman, D. and Baglioni. (1988). Bayes' theorem in the trial process. *Law and Human Behavior, 12,* 1–22.

Finkelstein, M.O. and Fairley, W.B. (1970). A Bayesian approach to identification evidence. *Harvard Law Review, 83,* 489–517.

Friedman, R.D. (1997). Answering the Bayesioskeptical challenge. *International Journal of Evidence and Proof, 1,* 276–278.

Funder, D.C. (1997). *The personality puzzle.* New York: W.W. Norton.

Funder, D.C. (1999). *Personality judgment: A realistic approach to person perception.* San Diego: Academic Press.

Gettys, C.F., Kelly, C. and Peterson, C.R. (1973). The best-guess hypothesis in multistage inference. *Organizational Behavior and Human Performance, 10,* 364–373.

Hutchins, R.M. and Slesinger, D. (1928a). Some observations on the law of evidence—Spontaneous exclamations. *Columbia Law Review*, *28*, 432–440.

Hutchins, R.M. and Slesinger, D. (1928b). Some observations on the law of evidence—Memory. *Harvard Law Review*, *41*, 860–873.

Hutchins, R.M. and Slesinger, D. (1928c). Some observations on the law of evidence—The competency of witnesses. *Yale Law Journal*, *37*, 1017–1028.

Hutchins, R.M. and Slesinger, D. (1929a). Some observations on the law of evidence—Family relations. *Minnesota Law Review*, *13*, 675–686.

Hutchins, R.M. and Slesinger, D. (1929b). Some observations on the law of evidence—State of mind to prove an act. *Yale Law Journal*, *38*, 283–298.

Hutchins, R.M. and Slesinger, D. (1929c). Some observations on the law of evidence—State of mind in issue. *Columbia Law Review*, *29*, 147–157.

Hutchins, R.M. and Slesinger, D. (1929d). Some observations on the law of evidence—Consciousness of guilt. *Pennsylvania Law Review*, *6*, 725–740.

Hutchins, R.M. and Slesinger, D. (1929e). Legal psychology. *Psychological Review*, *36*, 13–26.

Kalven, H. and Zeisel, H. (1966). *The American jury*. Chicago: University of Chicago Press.

Kaplan, J. (1968). Decision theory and the factfinding process. *Stanford Law Review*, *20*, 1065–1106.

Kaye, D. (1979). The Paradox of the Gatecrasher and other stories. *Arizona State Law Journal*, 101–134.

Kaye, D. (1988a). Introduction: What is Bayesianism? In P. Tillers and E. Green (eds), *Probability and inference in the law of evidence: The uses and limits of Bayesianism* (pp. 1–19). Dordrecht, Netherlands: Kluwer Academic Press.

Kaye, D. (1988b). Plemel as a primer on proving paternity. *Willamette Law Journal*, *24*, 867–883.

Kaye, D. and Koehler, J.J. (1991). Can jurors understand probabilistic evidence? *Journal of the Royal Statistical Society*, *154* (1), 75–81.

Koehler, J.J. and Shaviro, D. (1990). Veridical verdicts: Increasing verdict accuracy through the use of overtly probabilistic evidence and methods. *Cornell Law Review*, *75*, 247–279.

Koehler, J.J. (1993). The Normative Status of Base Rates at Trial. In N. J. Castellan (ed.), *Individual and group decision making* (pp. 137–149). Hillsdale, NJ: Lawrence Erlbaum Associates.

Koehler, J.J., Chia, A. and Lindsey, J.S. (1995). The random match probability (RMP) in DNA evidence: Irrelevant and prejudicial? *Jurimetrics*, *35*, 201–219.

Koehler, J.J. (2001). When are people impressed by DNA match statistics? *Law and Human Behavior*.

Kovera, M., Park, R.C. and Penrod, S.D. (1992). Jurors' perceptions of eyewitness and hearsay evidence. *Minnesota Law Review*, *76*, 703–722.

Landsman, S. and Rakos, R.F. (1991). Research essay: A preliminary empirical enquiry concerning the prohibition of hearsay evidence in American courts. *Law and Psychology Review*, *15*, 65–85.

Lempert, R.O. (1977). Modeling relevance. *Michigan Law Review*, *75*, 1021–1101.

Lempert, R. (1986). *The new evidence scholarship: Analyzing the process of proof*. Boston University Law Review, *66*, 439–477.

Lempert, R. and Saltzburg, S. (1977). *A modern approach to evidence* (1st edn.). St Paul, MN: West Publishing.

Lempert, R. and Saltzburg, S. (1982). *A modern approach to evidence* (2nd edn.). St Paul, MN: West Publishing.

Lyon, T.D. and Koehler, J.J. (1996). The relevance ratio: Evaluating the probative value of expert testimony in child sexual abuse cases. *Cornell Law Review*, *82*, 43–78.

Lyon, T.D. (1999). The new wave in children's suggestibility research: A critique. *Cornell Law Review*, *84*, 1004–1087.

Magner, E. (1991). Wigmore confronts Münsterberg: Present relevance of a classic debate. *Sydney Law Review*, *13*, 121–137.

Meehl, P. (1989). Law and the fireside inductions (with postscript): Some reflections of a clinical psychologist. *Behavioral Sciences and the Law*, 7, 521–550.

Mischel, W. (1968). *Personality and assessment*. New York: John Wiley & Sons.

Monahan, J. and Walker, L. (1998). *Social science in law: Cases and materials* (4th edn). Westbury, NY: Foundation Press.

Münsterberg, H. (1908). *On the witness stand*. Garden City, NY: Doubleday.

National Research Council (1996). *The evaluation of forensic DNA evidence*. Washington, DC: National Academy Press.

Park, R.C. (1987). A subject matter approach to hearsay reform. *Michigan Law Review*, 86, 51–122.

Pathak, M.K. and Thompson, W.C. (1999). From child to witness to jury: Effects of suggestion on the transmission and evaluation of hearsay. *Psychology, Public Policy, and Law*, 5, 372–387.

Pennington, N. and Hastie, R. (1991a). A cognitive theory of juror decision making: The Story Model. *Cardozo Law Review*, 13, 519.

Pennington, N. and Hastie, R. (1991b). Explaining the evidence: Tests of the Story Model for juror decision making. *Journal of Personality and Social Psychology*, 62, 189–206.

Rakos, R.F. and Landsman, S. (1992). Researching the hearsay rule: Emerging findings, general issues, and future directions. *Minnesota Law Review*, 76, 655–682.

Risinger, D.M., Saks, M.J., Thompson, W.C. and Rosenthal, R. (in press). The Daubert/Kumho implications of observer effects in forensic science: Hidden problems of expectation and suggestion. *California Law Review*.

Robertson, B. and Vignaux, G.A. (1993). Taking fact analysis seriously. *Michigan Law Review*, 91, 1442–1464.

Robertson, B. and Vignaux, G.A. (1995). *Interpreting evidence. Evaluating forensic science in the courtroom*. Chichester: John Wiley & Sons.

Ross, L. and Nisbett, R.E. (1991). *The person and the situation: Perspectives on social psychology*. Boston: McGraw-Hill.

Saks, M.J. and Kidd, R.F. (1980). Human information procesing and adjudication: Trial by heuristics. *Law and Society Review*, 15, 123–160.

Saks, M.J. et al. (2001). Toward a model act for the prevention of erroneous convictions. *New England Law Review*, 35, 669–683.

Schklar, J. and Diamond, S.S. (1999). Juror reactions to DNA evidence: Errors and expectancies. *Law and Human Behavior*, 23 (2), 159–184.

Schum, D. and Tillers, P. (1991a). Marshalling evidence for adversary litigation. *Cardozo Law Review*, 13, 657.

Schum, D. and Tillers, P. (1991b). A theory of preliminary fact investigation. *University of California Davis Law Review*, 24, 931.

Schum, D.A. (1992). Hearsay from a layperson. *Cardozo Law Review*, 14, 1–77.

Schum, D.A. (1994). *Evidential foundations of probabilistic reasoning*. New York: John Wiley & Sons.

Schum, D. (1999). Marshalling thoughts and evidence during fact investigation. *South Texas Law Review*, 40, 401–454.

Slovic, P. and Lichtenstein, S. (1971). Comparison of Bayesian and regression approaches to the study of information processing in judgment. *Organizational Behavior and Human Performance*, 6, 649–744.

Special Theme. (1999). Hearsay testimony in trials involving child witnesses. *Psychology, Public Policy and Law*, 5 (2), 251–498.

Symposium (1986). Probability and inference in the law of evidence: The uses and limits of Bayesianism. *Boston University Law Review*, 66 (3 and 4), 377–952.

Symposium (1991). Decision and inference in litigation. *Cardozo Law Review*, 13 (2 and 3), 253–1079.

Tanford, S. and Cox, M. (1987). Decision processes in civil cases: The impact of impeachment evidence on liability and credibility judgments. *Social Behavior*, 2, 165–182.

Tanford, S. and Penrod, S. (1984). Social inference processes in juror judgments of multiple-offense trials. *Journal of Personality and Social Psychology, 47*, 749–765.

Thayer, J. B. (1898). *A Preliminary Treatise on Evidence at Common Law*. Boston.

Thompson, W.C. and Schumann, E.L. (1987). Interpretation of statistical evidence in criminal trials: The prosecutor's fallacy and the defense attorney's fallacy. *Law and Human Behavior, 11*, 167–187.

Thompson, W.C. (1989). Are juries competent to evaluate statistical evidence? *Law and Contemporary Problems, 52*, 9–41.

Thompson, W.C. (1997). Accepting lower standards: The National Research Council's second report on forensic DNA evidence. *Jurimetrics, 37* (4), 405–424.

Thompson, W.C. and Pathak, M.K. (1999). Empirical study of hearsay rules: Bridging the gap between psychology and law. *Psychology, Public Policy, and Law, 5*, 456–472.

Tillers, P. and Schum, D.A. (1992). Hearsay logic. *Minnesota Law Review, 76*, 813–858.

Tribe, L. (1971). Trial by mathematics: Precision and ritual in the legal process. *Harvard Law Review, 84*, 1329–1393.

Twining, W. (1991). The new evidence scholarship. *Cardozo Law Review, 13*, 295–302.

Uviller, H.R. (1982). Evidence of character to prove conduct: Illusion illogic and injustice in the courtroom. *University of Pennsylvania Law Review*, 845–913.

van Koppen, P. and Saks, M.J. (2002). Preventing bad psychological scientific evidence in the Netherlands and the United States. In P. van Koppen and S. Penrod (eds), *Adversarial versus inquisitorial justice: Psychological perspectives on criminal justice systems*. New York: Plenum.

Wells, G. (1992). Naked statistical evidence of liability: Is subjective probability enough? *Journal of Personality and Social Psychology, 62*, 739–752.

Wigmore, J. (1913). *The science of proof: As given by logic, psychology, and general experience and illustrated in judicial trials*. Boston: Little, Brown.

Wigmore, J. (1931). *The science of proof: As given by logic, psychology, and general experience and illustrated in judicial trials* (2nd edn). Boston: Little, Brown.

Wigmore, J. (1937). *The science of proof: As given by logic, psychology, and general experience and illustrated in judicial trials* (3rd edn). Boston: Little, Brown.

Wigmore, J. (1974). *Evidence in trials at Common Law* (Chadbourne rev.). Boston: Little, Brown.

Wissler, R.L. and Saks, M.J. (1985). On the inefficacy of limiting instructions: When jurors use prior conviction evidence to decide guilt. *Law and Human Behavior, 9*, 37–48.

Wydick, R.C. (1987). Character evidence: A guided tour of the grotesque structure. *University of California Davis Law Review, 21*, 123–195.

Cases

Mapp v. *Ohio*, 367 US 643 (1961).
Michaelson v. *United States*, 335 US 439 (1948).
Regina v. *Deen*, Court of Appeals (Criminal Division), London, Jan. 10, 1994.
Weeks v. *United States*, 232 US 383 (1914).

Statutes

Federal Rule of Evidence 404(b).
Federal Rule of Evidence 407.
Federal Rule of Evidence 408.
Federal Rule of Evidence 803(2).
Federal Rule of Evidence 803(4).

Chapter 3.3

Advocacy: Getting the Answers You Want

David Carson
University of Southampton, UK
and
Francis Pakes
University of Portsmouth, UK

'Police chiefs attack criminal justice "game".'

Such was a headline in *The Guardian*, a national broadsheet newspaper circulating in the United Kingdom, on 11 January 2002. Four chief constables, or equivalent, were complaining about criminal trial procedures. The president of the Association of Chief Police Officers (ACPO) submitted that 'current regulations permitted solicitors and barristers to play a game in which they were encouraged to "exaggerate and obfuscate".' ACPO had submitted a number of criticisms to the Criminal Courts Review, undertaken by Lord Justice Auld. His report was published in 2001. As it was put in the report:

> the adversarial procedure relegates the court to a reactive role when it should have far greater direction and control of the way in which the issues and the evidence are put before it; fact-finders are wrongly denied access to material relevant to their findings of fact; procedural law—'due process'—dominates substantive law to the extent of creating, rather than preventing, injustice, resulting in a loss of public confidence in the courts' contribution to the control of crime; the 'adversarial dialectic' and the 'principle of orality' have been elevated to ends in themselves rather than means to get at the truth and also, as a result, discourage modern and more efficient ways of putting evidence before the courts. (Auld, 2001, ch. 11, para. 9)

Lawyers and civil liberty organisations responded forcefully. A vice-president of the Law Society, which represents solicitors, argued that defence lawyers were not exploiting loopholes in the law. 'It is the system which needs to change, not the lawyers,' she argued. The journalist writing the report noted that the context of this

Handbook of Psychology in Legal Contexts, Second Edition
Edited by D. Carson and R. Bull. © 2003 John Wiley & Sons, Ltd.

dispute was a debate over proposals to change the criminal justice system in England and Wales (Auld, 2001). Changes have been proposed which would further remove the defendant's right to choose trial by judge or by jury and would increase the occasions when juries might be told about a defendant's prior convictions

Is there any substance to the chief constables' claims? Are criminal trials too much like a game? Noting that there was some measure of agreement among those quoted in the article, does the system need to change? These are some of the questions that this chapter will address. It will seek to achieve this by examining what is possible within the current rules and practices of advocacy in the adversarial courts of England and Wales. It will not choose 'easy targets,' for example rude or badgering questions. Rather it will focus on methods of asking questions that are accepted as right and proper in and by courts. Indeed these techniques are often described and advocated in books written to train practising lawyers, who wish to know how better to cross-examine witnesses and represent their clients (for example: Evans, 1983, 1993; Hyam, 1990; Stone, 1995). It will demonstrate that there are a number of ways in which courtroom questioning can misrepresent the evidence and the witnesses. This, however, is not an empirical study. We are not describing how often these techniques are used. Experience of the courts suggests some are commonplace. The techniques are also likely to be used regularly in other trial systems, particularly in the United States of America, and in Canada and other countries in the Commonwealth, because they are, substantially, a product of the adversarial system. We will see that the same effects are achieved, in rather different ways, in inquisitorial systems. A concluding discussion will consider some of the implications.

At the start, however, it is important to note that, even if there is substance to the police chiefs' criticisms, it does not follow that lawyers are misbehaving or acting improperly. They may simply be taking advantage of the rules of a system that permits them, for example, to misrepresent a witness's evidence. If it is concluded that the techniques are inappropriate then, as was suggested in the newspaper article, the system should be criticised. But, even if the system can be criticised it does not follow that it ought to be replaced. It may be the best, or almost the best, that can, in practice rather than in theory, be achieved. Part of the problem, it will be argued, is that we, as a society, are not entirely sure what the proper or main purpose of trials is. Because of that it is difficult to be prescriptive about the conduct of counsel. This chapter will, however, proceed with an examination of advocacy skills and their effect on witnesses.

CAN LAWYERS PUT WORDS INTO A WITNESS' MOUTH?

Leading Questions

A key rule, regularly adopted in adversarial trial systems (McEwan, 1998) is that the lawyers who call a witness may not ask leading questions. A question is leading if the terms of the question suggest the answer. 'Did you see anything?' is not a leading question. It does not suggest what, if anything, was to be seen. If the witness replies to the effect that something was seen then the lawyer could continue by asking: 'What did you see?' That is not a leading question. But to ask 'Did you see a man with a limp?' would be to put ideas, images and words into the witness's mind and therefore, possibly, into his or her mouth. That would involve leading the witness and is, in initial examination (examination-in-chief), considered to be improper. However, it is considered proper in cross-examination.

The rule against leading questions is long-standing one. Years ago, prior to published research on the topic, lawyers seem to have predicted, or assumed, that leading questions will or may affect the witness and lead to incorrect evidence being given. It seems that they were correct. Leading questions have indeed been shown to have a profound effect in distorting the reporting of an incident. Loftus and Palmer's (1974) seminal work, for example, has demonstrated the power of word 'colouring'. Although all the research participants had observed the same vehicle accident on a film, their estimates of the speed of one of the vehicles varied considerably depending upon whether the question included the word 'collided', 'bumped', 'hit', 'smashed' or 'contacted'. Participants' estimates were 9 miles per hour (25%) higher when the word 'smashed' was used instead of 'contacted'. The latter participants were also more likely to report having seen broken glass when in fact that was no broken glass to be seen. Leading questions can misrepresent the witness's evidence by planting ideas, associations and giving him or her words to use, in reply, which he or she might not have chosen if they had not been used in the question (Loftus, 1979). (See also: Gorden, 1975; Gudjonsson 1984; Moston, 1990; Richardson, Dohrenwend and Klein, 1965.) Gudjonsson (1992) has identified their potential for affecting accurate recall of memory and in affecting witnesses' suggestibility.

There is ample evidence that leading questions are prone to produce inaccurate evidence. This constitutes good grounds for prohibiting them during examination-in-chief when the witness answers questions from the lawyer who called him or her. During cross-examination, however, leading questions can be deployed. Arguably there are equally good grounds for controlling their use during this phase of trial proceedings. Restrictions on their use, in pre-trial investigations, are already developing. For example a key feature of the *Memorandum of Good Practice for Video Recorded Interviews with Child Witnesses for Criminal* Proceedings (Home Office and Department of Health, 1992) is avoidance of leading questions, at least until the end of the interview when they may be thought necessary to ensure that the witness considers certain topics. This has become standard practice in England and Wales. If it is not followed lawyers may make adverse comments during the trial, including the suggestion that a child's evidence is not reliable because the interviewer suggested the answers. There is a certain irony in lawyers criticising others' use of leading questions when put to children but not being prevented from using them themselves in cross-examination with adults.

The increasing use of the cognitive or investigative interview, by police officers, is another example of developments seeking to enhance the quality of information obtained at the front end of the criminal justice system (Fisher and Geiselman, 1992; Milne and Bull, 1999). Cognitive interviews are credited with increasing the amount of information that a witness can recall without increasing errors. Its beneficial effect in terms of the quality of information obtained is unquestionable (Köhnken et al, 1999). They involve a very gentle form of interviewing which stresses how much the interviewee is valued and in control. The witness is encouraged to recall all that he or she can, in his or her own words. The approach emphasises completeness and the witness's own words. Police officers have, at least in England and Wales, been extensively trained in the use of cognitive interview under the title of the 'investigative interview' (Bull, 1998).

Directed Questions

With a directed question the lawyer points the witness in the direction of the answer without actually supplying it. 'What colour was the car?' is a directed question. It points, or directs, the witness to a particular kind of information. The lawyer is not asking about the make, model or age of the car, nor is he or she suggesting a particular colour. (We will assume that prior evidence has established that there was a car.) The witness is in charge of selecting whichever word or words that he or she considers most appropriate. There appears to be nothing objectionable about this kind of question. We can however, compare the use of directed questions to painting by numbers. Painters are invited to fill in sections of a pre-sketched drawing with the colour prescribed for the number in the space provided. The lawyer is only asking for a part of the total picture or story to be described, to be coloured in. That does not necessarily mean that a complete picture will be provided. Rather this type of question is liable to provide a partial perspective.

The key problem with directed questions is one of selectivity. A witness may be asked about the injuries to the child's left leg, but not to the right. The witness may have important evidence to give about the child's right leg, but not be given a question to answer about it. The witness may assume, reasonably it is suggested, that the lawyer will, to continue the example, move from the left to the right leg in due course. The lawyer is in charge of which questions are asked and in which order. So the witness may not be asked for information which might, on an impartial reading of the case, be critical. Without that information only part of the picture will have been presented to the jury. Of course the witness may be assertive enough to insist on giving that evidence, although the lawyer may object. Witnesses are often told, directly and indirectly, to answer the question, and only the question. The lawyer for the other side may provide the witness with an opportunity for the whole picture to emerge but that does not necessarily happen. Directed questions provide a means whereby a partial picture is provided. And as it is provided through the witness's mouth it appears uncontroversial, which only enhances the danger.

Another feature of directed questions, which makes them more dangerous, is that they regularly appear to be gentle and helpful. Anxious and verbose witnesses may appear to be being helped, rather than controlled, by this type of question. So witnesses are liable to let down their guard and not appreciate the significance of their sequence of answers. Instead of utilising an open question, such as 'What did he look like?' which does not tell the witness where to start, what to cover in, or when to end the answer, a lawyer could begin, 'How tall was he?' or 'What colour of hair did he have?' This will avoid a witness's tendencies to wander, to be prolix or verbose. A sequence of directed questions ensures that the interaction between lawyer and witness does not lose focus. That may come as a relief to judges and courts anxious that time means money, and to jurors who may lose interest with long unfocused answers. However, competent lawyers will only ask questions which produce answers that colour in the part of the picture they want painted. In that sense a witness is a means to an end; directed questions are a useful tool.

Directed Choices

Directed questions are more obvious when the lawyer offers alternatives for the witness to choose between. This involves mixing directed with leading questions. 'Would you describe the car's colour as "brown" or "fawn"?' 'Were the injuries "serious" or "life-threatening"?' The witness has a choice. He or she is given a choice. It is not, technically, a forced choice. He or she might prefer to opt for, and insist upon citing, any other colour or description. But most witnesses are likely to be anxious and ready to adopt one of the offered answers. After all, because of the way in which the question is phrased, the lawyer has communicated that at least one of the expressions is acceptable. The witness may defy this and tender an alternative description. But if that happens more than once or twice he or she is going to appear awkward or pedantic. It would seem un-cooperative, perhaps even unreasonable, to repeatedly object to the terms of the choices offered by the lawyer. Only the witness and the lawyer can know whether the alternative expressions offered are indeed suitable. The witness has provided the information that the lawyer is working upon, in a statement made before the trial, and the lawyer is aware of that.

Often the choice offered to witnesses will not be between two equally appropriate expressions. Rather the lawyer will offer one choice knowing it to be inappropriate, for example 'life threatening', in the hope that the other, 'serious', is adopted by the witness. Both the lawyer and the witness may know that the injuries were not life threatening, but were very serious and extensive. But the lawyer may not want the witness to tell the court that the injuries were 'very serious' or 'extensive'. So the expression offered was 'serious', rather than 'very serious'. By this technique the skilful lawyer can obtain some degree of control over what the witness says. Even if the witness insists upon emphasising '*very* serious' the lawyer should be able, by tone and gesture, to suggest that such a qualification was not necessary.

The witness who qualifies too often is liable to be portrayed as being awkward and unnecessarily quibbling. O'Barr (1982) studied how witnesses are perceived in court.

He noted that witnesses who were perceived to equivocate too often were seen as being awkward, and rated as having less authority than others. The equivocating witness, insisting on different expressions or descriptions, is perceived as wasting time. The judge or jury is liable to think that such distinctions are unimportant, and is liable to think that a fuss is being made about nothing. The judge and jury do not know what the witness and questioning lawyers know. The witness knows why it is important to equivocate but, without that extra knowledge, neither the judge nor the jury does. And if the lawyer is skilful and prepared then his or her questions will be asked so that the information, which would explain the witness's concern, is either never revealed or only after the awkward questions are answered.

A reason for the finding that witnesses who equivocate are rated as relatively poor witnesses, is likely to be the apologetic tone in which this is commonly performed. Having to equivocate makes us feel that we are in the wrong, as if it is our fault that we are not able to give a 'simple' answer. An alternative would be to get angry and cross with the questioner for asking inappropriate questions or for phrasing them in a particular way. But witnesses are, at least initially, likely to be diffident and nervous. The lawyer is in a much better position to respond in a manner suggestive that any objection to the question was petty. It is possible to equivocate assertively, such as by turning to the judge and explaining to him or her that answering the question, in the terms suggested by the lawyer, will lead to false evidence being given. But few witnesses will know that they can do that, or have the presence of mind to do so. If the witness answers the question in the terms the lawyer has offered, he or she 'loses' because the information will be presented less than optimally. If the witness equivocates about the question then, in terms of credit with the court, he or she 'loses' and the evidence given may be given less than appropriate weight.

Short Questions

Lawyers are encouraged, in the books teaching them their court craft, to ask short questions (e.g. Evans, 1983). This will make it easier for the judge and jury to understand the evidence as well as make it easier for witnesses to answer. So we might expect that lawyers, when cross-examining, would ask longer questions to confuse their witnesses. But this is not the case, for reasons to do with control. The reasoning, and experience, is that short questions give the questioning lawyer more, not less, control over the information provided by the witness. A long question, with several parts and/or qualifications, will encourage the witness to give a long, convoluted and possibly confusing answer. There is more leeway and implicit permission for a witness to go beyond the question. The witness who is given a short question is constrained into only answering about that topic. It is much easier to control or influence the witness's answer by a short question. If it fails, and the witness insists upon giving a long answer to a short question, then he or she is liable to lose credit with the judge and jury, particularly if it happens on a regular basis. There is an implicit association that shortness of question equates with simplicity of question; if it is short it must be easy. Hence equivocating with a short question is particularly dangerous.

The classic 'directed short choice' question is '[statement of fact], yes or no?' This type of question comes naturally to lawyers who are used to dichotomising. Categories are a key tool for lawyers. Their job is substantially about fitting evidence into categories. For example, the evidence either supports a finding of 'similar facts', which will authorise the introduction of evidence of the defendant's prior convictions for crimes committed in a similar manner, or it does not (Tapper, 1999). The legal consequence depends upon whether the evidence submitted falls into the category, or not: 'Is there a serious risk? Yes or no? It is a simple question.' Sometimes it is a simple enough question but frequently it is not. It is regularly artificial and inappropriate to simply divide situations into 'reasonable' and 'unreasonable', or posing 'a risk' or 'no risk'.

Casting Doubt

In a criminal case, the prosecution must prove its case beyond reasonable doubt. Thus, if the defence can lead the judge or the jury to believe that there is a doubt, which is a reasonable doubt, then that will count as a success. The defence, as their lawyers and the judge will reiterate, does not have to prove that the defendant is innocent. In a civil case the party bringing the case must, usually, prove his or her case on a balance of probabilities. That does not have to be a strong case as there is no minimum threshold. It only has to be better than the case produced by the other side. Invariably litigation is about persuasion rather than proof (Hart, 1963). Even if one part of a case can be demonstrated to such a standard that it is apt to speak in terms of 'proof', the rest of the case is liable to remain at the level of persuasion. After all, if a case can be decisively proven it is unlikely ever to get to trial. On realising the strength of the evidence, and arguments against them, the other parties are likely to appreciate that there is little point in continuing the case. Their interests will usually best be served by conceding the case. These facts help to explain the importance of words like 'possible' and 'reasonable' in litigation. There are other comparable words, such as 'likely', but these are the key ones.

Defence counsel, in a criminal case, does not need to get prosecution witnesses to admit that they are liars, or that they were wrong or incompetent. He or she only needs, first, to get a witness to accept that he or she might have been mistaken or wrong. Then, second, he or she only needs to suggest that this *possible* mistake or error, on its own or with others, is enough to constitute a reasonable doubt. Defence counsel may try to get the witness, who has just conceded a possible error, to label it as constituting a 'reasonable' doubt. If a defence lawyer can get a prosecution witness to concede a reasonable doubt then that counts as a success. But even if that is not achieved the lawyer may be able to use the witness's admission of a mistake in order to suggest a 'reasonable doubt' to the judge and jury. That may be done by arguing about the evidence or by making suggestions on the basis of the demeanour and behaviour of the witness when giving evidence.

A key tool for the lawyer, and problem for the witness, is the word 'possible.' It appears to be an innocuous word, and that is a major part of the problem. It is of almost universal application. After all, many a thing is possible, at least in theory.

> 'In the light of the incredible strides that have been made in bio-engineering recently, is it not possible, remember I am only asking about possibility, not certainty or likelihood that, in the near or even far future, pigs may fly?'

Indeed to deny that something may be possible can sound anti-scientific. It is almost a declaration of a closed mind, an unwillingness to concede and to be of assistance.

Once the witness has conceded that there is the possibility of a mistake, the door has been opened.

> 'Yes, it is possible that I made a mistake.'
> 'I may have been confused.'
> 'I may have forgotten, after all it was a long time ago.'

The lawyer appears to have won a major concession. The witness is beginning to undermine his or her own evidence, and/or credibility. In the context of a public trial it is relatively dramatic, even if unaccompanied by raised voices. The lawyer has gained ground, and the witness has lost some credibility. But what could the witness have said instead? If the question was 'Did you make a mistake?' then a simple, straightforward and effective answer of 'No' could have been given. But the question uses the word 'possible'. 'Is it possible that you made a mistake?' An answer of, 'No, it is not possible for me to have made a mistake' will, at best, sound arrogant. And a simple answer of 'No' is not too dissimilar in effect. The word 'possible' is inserted into the question in order to get an affirmative answer from the witness or, if that fails, to undermine his or her credibility. If it works, the witness has said what the lawyer wanted him or her to say. And if it does not work, the witness is less credible. The witness is in a 'no win' situation.

Of course a witness might respond:

> 'Your Honour it is, of course, possible that I made a mistake. I make no claims to perfection. But, given that I studied the subject-matter very closely, carefully, in excellent conditions, and confirmed my conclusion in writing immediately it is highly unlikely that I made a mistake.'

Few witnesses will be sufficiently assertive, prepared and competent to make such a response. Indeed, if the lawyer suspected that the witness was that competent then he or she will avoid asking such a question. The lawyer will have 'sized up' the witness in advance. And the witness, who does answer with such an assertive response, is liable to be accused of having been coached. While telling a witness what to say in a particular case, with reference to particular evidence, is objectionable, general training to be a skilful witness is not.

Once the possibility of error has been created the lawyer will work on making it more significant and 'reasonable'. The mere possibility of error in a criminal trial, a doubt, is not sufficient to constitute reasonable doubt. But the process of gaining these admissions, of possible error, can be powerful. In this context 'possible' is being used both as a dichotomous and a relative category. First the witness is asked whether the topic could fit within the category of 'possible'. The answer almost has to be affirmative, given that it is such a large category. But, once the category is acknowledged the relative characteristics of the category come into play. That something is 'possible' tells us nothing about how likely, how possible. But magnitude can be suggested. Once 'possibility' is conceded 'probability' will be suggested. Other problematic words can be called in aid to help in this suggestion process. Key examples among these are 'reasonable', 'fair' and 'sensible'.

> 'Now, in retrospect, do you really think it was reasonable to come to that conclusion?'
> 'Is not the only fair and sensible conclusion that it was not, in fact, possible?'

The witness wishes to be associated with the positive features of words like, 'reasonable', 'fair' and 'sensible'. But the lawyer has appropriated them for his or her own use. To get them back, to be considered reasonable, fair or sensible, the witness is pressurised into an affirmative answer. To disagree, to reply that it is not reasonable, fair or sensible, is not only to challenge the lawyer but also to risk association with the converse qualities. No witness wants to be seen as unreasonable, unfair or foolish.

FACTS AND OPINIONS

Asking a witness whether something is 'reasonable', 'sensible', or 'fair' is asking for an opinion. In many jurisdictions only expert witnesses are allowed to express an opinion, and then only on their specialist topic (Tapper, 1999). But objection may not be made to their use in the almost rhetorical manner discussed in the last paragraph. It is 'almost rhetorical' because the implication is that there is only one possible answer to the question. The problem is the slide from permitting the words to be used as a means of making a question more interesting, to the words being understood as a judgement on the evidence. The objection to a non-expert stating an opinion is that it usurps the role of the judge or jury. But when a witness admits, 'it is only reasonable to conclude', then that opinion, being of someone who ought to know as a witness, takes on qualities of a fact.

Lawyers treat the distinction between facts and opinions as if it was dichotomous. A statement is either statement of a fact or an opinion. This is false. Rules of evidence to develop this distinction, are promoting error. When a witness reports to a court, 'I saw a horse' he or she would have been more correct and complete had he or she said:

> 'I believe I correctly recall that what I saw was, and is correctly understood by others to be, a horse.'

It however would obviously be absurd to require a witness to give such an answer. Arguably, factual evidence is actually stating an opinion that what he or she recalls is (a) accurately and (b) sufficiently described by the words given in the answer (Smith and Wynne, 1989). Particularly where the item being described is ambiguous, or it is not readily distinguishable from similar 'facts', the lawyer is going to be able to suggest that alternative words are appropriate. 'Distressed' could be 'upset', 'confused,' 'animated' even 'drunk'. 'Cut' might be 'stab', 'laceration', or 'injury'. The lawyer can re-present facts, by drawing upon alternative words, to place them in, or at least suggest that they ought to be in, different categories. Because words are ambiguous, and because evidence is based first upon perception, second upon interpretation, and third upon memory of an event, the lawyer can legitimately expect witnesses to change their choice of descriptive words. A witness cannot expect to reply 'It was a stab, not a cut, not anything else', and retain the confidence of a court. Some other words will be suitable, even if the witness thinks that the original word(s) he or she gave was the most appropriate. But by accepting alternative words the quality of the evidence gets changed, the picture takes on a different hue. By accepting alternative words the witness appears to change his or her evidence, or allow it to be altered. And that affects credibility.

Given the association between opinions, experts and expertise, it might be expected that witnesses who state opinions gain greater credit with the court. But this appears not to be the case. Napley (1991), giving advice to lawyers seeking advocacy skills, argued that it is easier to cross-examine opinion-stating expert witnesses, even high status doctors, than lay people who are restricted to factual evidence.

> The fact remains, however, that expert witness in general and medical witnesses in particular, provide, if the advocate is properly prepared, the most useful and easily assailable material for successful cross-examination. Witnesses as to facts speak to matters of positive recollection within their own experience. Medical experts, by comparison, are dealing within the realm of informed opinion, with the subject matter of an art, which is neither exact or necessarily scientific. (Napley, 1991, pp. 28–29)

The difference appears similar to that between an assertion and an argument. An argument, unlike an assertion, provides a reason for accepting it. Those reasons may be good or bad, strong or weak. By stating a 'fact' the witness refers to something concrete, something which the judge or jury can imagine or envisage. It is likely to fit within the judge's or jury's experience of the world. But an opinion, as understood here, is a naked statement of viewpoint. Unless the witness adds reasons for believing it to be correct, it will remain an opinion which the judge or jury is being asked to take on faith or to rely upon the reputation of the witness.

Evidence, which is conceived of as being 'factual' appears to be trusted more than that which is purely 'opinion' based. The judge or jury can test 'factual' evidence by comparing it to their own experience. They can imagine the facts being acted out before their eyes to examine the extent to which they fit together, are consistent. But they cannot act on, intellectually role-play, opinion evidence. It becomes a case of assessing the witness rather than the evidence. It may boil down to choosing between two expert witnesses, on the basis of the way they present their evidence rather than the evidence itself.

The lawyer can utilise this ambiguity of 'fact' and 'opinions'. The reality, philosophically, is that facts and opinions are not dichotomous categories but points on a continuum. Evidence which is considered to be a fact can be made more factual by describing it in more concrete and empirical terms. Indeed some 'fact' evidence is so factual that it can be put in a box, brought to court and displayed. Whether a bone is broken may appear to be a matter of opinion. But someone may take an x-ray of it and bring that to court. He or she will have to give evidence linking the individual to his or her x-ray and it may require some interpretation, but judges and juries can see with their own eyes a gap or compare an alignment. Indeed, sometimes evidence can be made so factual that it appears impossible to dispute and remain rational. Similarly, something which may appear to be a fact may nevertheless be pushed along the fact to opinion continuum in order to gain the appearance of being an opinion, and thereby less credible. For example the lawyer may choose to emphasise that the fact being described is subject to interpretation and opinion.

> 'You tell this court that the person you observed, that day, is my client, the
>   defendant?'
> 'Yes.'
> 'That you saw him across a road?'
> 'Yes.'
> 'Along with several other people?'
> 'Yes.'
> 'In conditions which were not, by your admission, perfect?'
> 'Yes.'
> 'And that was almost a year ago?'
> 'Yes.'
> 'But you remembered him to this day?'
> 'Yes.'
> 'Even though the police only asked you about him a fortnight after you had
>   seen him?'
> 'Yes.'
> 'But you believe the defendant is the same person?'
> 'Yes.'
> 'You think that the police have apprehended the correct person?'
> 'Yes.'
> 'That is your opinion?'
> 'Yes.'
> 'Thank you.'

The witness might be able to give reasons for his or her conclusion, to turn the assertion into an argument, to make the facts more factual. Perhaps the person in question is the witness's neighbour. But the witness will not be asked for that information if the lawyer would prefer that the court did not hear it. The lawyer can play with the fact–opinion continuum. Inexperienced witnesses can be persuaded into using terms which maximise or minimise the credibility of their evidence.

INTERCHANGES

Evidence is provided by a sequence of questions and answers. The naïve assumption is that the witness provides the evidence while the lawyer simply chooses the topics to be covered and in which order. But consider an exchange such as that in the last paragraph. The lawyer is not only selecting the information but, effectively, also providing it. The witness is only there to confirm it. Certainly the witness could rebel, could disagree with the suggestion in the question. But a competent lawyer will ensure that the terms of each question are sufficiently acceptable for the answer sought. If the last question had been asked first it is highly unlikely that it would have received the answer it eventually did. The intervening sequence of questions produces or aids the last answer, which was the lawyer's goal for that sequence.

Such interchanges can be a powerful way of encouraging the witness to say what you want said. The power and simple rhythmic effect of an interchange should not be overlooked. It might induce a witness to, at some point, acknowledge something seemingly trivial. That may come back to haunt him or her at a later stage. Asking a witness 'You've made a mistake, haven't you?' is liable to receive a flat denial. It is more likely to be successful if the lawyer uses a sequence of questions. During the sequence the lawyer will take the witness through a number of points. He or she will be able to predict the witness's answer. Individually the questions will be uncontroversial. But each one builds on the last. Then, when the lawyer has sufficiently prepared the ground, he or she points out that the witness has made a mistake or gets any other answer he or she wants. For example, the lawyer may have noticed a discrepancy between a description given in oral evidence in court and how it was described in a written statement given to the police. That discrepancy may, in itself, be trivial. However to make that discrepancy more dramatic the lawyer can ask the witness a number of questions that accentuate its importance.

> 'Do you recall taking an oath to tell the truth?'
> 'The whole truth?'
> 'Have you told the truth?'
> 'Have you given this court false evidence?'
> 'Have you given it mistaken evidence?'
> 'Have you lied to this court?'
> 'Then how can you explain how you told the police, in your statement, that
>   it was X but, not five minutes ago, you told me it was Y?'

This is known as pinning out. The witness is effectively pinned to an archery target by the initial answers. The lawyer knows what the witness's answers will be: 'Yes', 'Yes', 'Yes', 'No', 'No', 'No'. Indeed could they, realistically, be anything different? Then the denouement comes. And the witness cannot dodge it. The earlier questions and answer have pinned the witness into a position where he or she cannot avoid the damage caused by the final question. A variation on it, with expert witnesses, involves a sequence of questions about their specialist topic. The witness answers with aplomb, possibly relishing the opportunity to display his or her knowledge. But then there is a question to which the witness does not know the answer because it is just outside the expertise of the witness. The witness cannot answer the question. For example a psychiatrist might be asked a lot of questions about the clinical use of a drug. This will imply that the psychiatrist knows a great deal about it. But then he or she is asked a question about the chemical composition of the drug. The lawyer will know that the witness cannot answer the question, indeed should not be able or willing to answer the question because it is outside the witness's expertise. The witness falters, cannot answer the question. This is dramatic. The expert appears to be a charlatan. How does this happen? The earlier questions led the judge and jury to think that the question was well within the witness's competence. But, apparently, it is not.

Another effective sequence involves taking advantage of common misunderstandings about memory. Ask a witness a question about a central aspect of his or her evidence and the lawyer should expect a clear, correct, answer. So, if you want to make a witness make a mistake then do not ask those kind of questions but rather head for the peripheral, the relatively unimportant, topics (Hyam, 1990). The witness will not have thought about these topics so rigorously. He or she will not have exercised his or her memory so much on these issues because he or she does not expect questions on them. Thus errors are much more likely. But an error is an error. Getting a witness to admit that he or she has, or may have, made an error is a success.

> Approach the witness on the areas peripheral to the client's account, testing the witness on the areas peripheral to the essential facts first. If doubt can be sown, either in his mind or the mind of the court, as to the accuracy of his recollection of peripheral facts, it will make more effective the suggestion that his account of the central issue may also be mistaken. (Clitheroe, 1980)

Sequencing

Dramatic media representations of trials, naturally enough, emphasise a few relatively short interchanges between the lawyer and witness. The impression given is that there are key questions and answers. Of course that is sometimes the case. But, unfortunately, that downplays the importance of sequencing and 'picture-building'. A competent lawyer will be thinking about both the particular question and the sequence within which it arises. For example, it would be a courageous or foolhardy lawyer who would ask, straightaway: 'Was he drunk?' (The foolhardy lawyer, who does this frequently but with success, is liable to jump to an exalted status.) The witness may simply, and assertively, answer: 'No'. It would be much safer, although take longer, to ask, in order to receive a sequence of affirmative answers:

'Was his tie loose?'
'Was his top shirt button undone?'
'Was he laughing?'
'Did he begin singing?'
'Was he loud?'
'Was he walking slowly?'
'Was his route indirect?'
'Was his gait unsteady?'

The witness may still answer, in the negative, the final (dichotomous) question: 'Was he drunk, yes or no?' But at this stage it matters little. The picture painted, by the affirmative answers, produces a sufficient—albeit ambiguous if the jury cared to think about it closely—picture of a drunken man. Indeed a 'No' answer to the final question whether he was drunk could be turned into an advantage. It would appear to contradict the earlier answers and so discredit the witness.

The skilful lawyer asks questions in a particular sequence. The object of the sequence only becomes evident at the end. By the time that the final question is reached it is very difficult for the witness to resist the inferences of his or her previous answers.

> Professional cross-examination proceeds by indirect approaches, by a series of questions on apparently peripheral matters, with a crucial issue dropped in en route, by a series of questions leading the witness to an accusation which the witness cannot logically deny without discrediting his previous answers. (McBarnett, 1981)

The 'rhythm' of the sequence becomes clear with the denouement. Listeners can identify when a sequence of questions has ended. If the witness has said what the lawyer was working towards then the lawyer can make a comment, or use emphasis, to indicate that fact. But if, instead, the witness has not 'cooperated', as was planned, the lawyer can quietly move to another topic making it appear that he or she was simply seeking information.

Emphasis

It is difficult to pay attention and distinguish the important points when evidence is provided in court. One person asks questions while the other answers them. Both may have different agendas and objectives. (Contrast it with a lecture that is, or should be, planned to develop in a comprehensible and memorable manner over a limited period, possibly with visual aids.) If it is a cross-examination then the lawyer wants the witness to say some things that the witness and/or his or her counsel would rather he or she did not. If the witness had already said, in suitable terms, all that the cross-examining lawyer wanted the court to hear, then there would be no need to ask a single question. To get the witness to say what he or she wants said the lawyer must be subtle. A direct challenge is liable to be met with a direct contradiction. A safer approach is to help the witness to say what you want him or to say, and then draw the judge or jury's attention to that. For example, it is not very wise to warn the witness:

> 'The next question will be critical. I am going to invite you to say something that, if you do, will seriously compromise your credibility before this court. Now, what . . . ?'

Rather the lawyer can ask the question, using sequencing and, if and when the witness does say what was wanted, draw attention to it.

> 'Ah, thank you!'
> 'Umm, that is interesting.'

That is all the lawyer needs to do. He or she is drawing the jury's attention to what has just been said. And he or she is being polite and generous, so it cannot be seen as a bad thing. The judge and jury are working hard to distinguish the important from the unimportant evidence, and to remember the former. The lawyer should not, at the stage of asking questions, be commenting on the evidence. But if it is so short, and as apparently innocuous as such brief responses, who is to complain? The lawyer is helping the judge or jury to remember key words and answers from that witness. Selection is an important skill for the advocate.

Another method, allowing the lawyer to choose which of the witness's words are to be emphasised and thereby become more memorable, involves the use of summaries. A witness could be asked:

> 'Would you agree that the three key points from your evidence are: one . . . , two . . . , three . . . ?'

Of course the witness may not, and certainly does not have to, accept those three points. However, in such circumstances it would be reasonable, and human, for an anxious witness to accept the lawyer's suggestion. Of course the lawyer will have carefully chosen the points in the question, and the language used to describe them. And the judge and jury are likely to be grateful, as a lot of evidence has been summarised into manageable chunks for them. The summary points should be relatively easy to remember. And, as the witness has agreed them, the judge and jury do not have to worry about those points being controversial. But the lawyer has selected words perhaps, but not necessarily, used by the witness earlier in his or her evidence, and used them to represent the witness's evidence.

RE-EXAMINATION

A number of techniques, for lawyers to seduce witnesses into saying what the lawyer wants said, have been identified. The clear implication has been that this is wrong. The reader may know and have been thinking that the lawyer for the other side may do the same or similar things in order to neutralise the effects. The lawyer, who called the witness in the first place, is entitled to re-examine the witness. In doing so he or she may counteract the effects of the other side's lawyer's questions. That is a critical safeguard of the adversarial system. The implicit assumptions are that the best ways of getting to the truth of a disputed issue, and of assessing the evidence in the process, is to allow each side to pursue its version of the truth through questions. This counter-argument assumes equality of skill and opportunity, that it is equally easy to counter a case, as it is to propose one, and that the lawyers are equally skilled. But lawyers have different skills, can demand differential payments. However such arguments will not be considered in this chapter since it is concentrating upon points relating to question and answer form.

The lawyer who calls a witness is entitled to re-examine him or her after he or she has been cross-examined. While that lawyer is not entitled to lead the witness, as the cross-examiner is, he or she can utilise many of the techniques identified here. But it is unlikely to have the same effect. It is not a simple exercise of inviting the witness to undo the harm that he or she may have created in cross-examination. If the lawyer decides to tackle that topic then he or she is drawing the attention of the judge or jury to it, telling them that the exchange with the cross-examining lawyer was important and significant enough to deserve rebuttal. If the lawyer ignored the topic then the judge and jury might have forgotten it or, if they had remembered it, not regarded it as being significant and important. Addressing a topic presupposes its importance. And there can be no guarantee that the witness will 'cooperate' in being extracted from the problems he or she created during cross-examination. The witness may have, for example, used key words that are unhelpful to the lawyer's argument. The lawyer can invite the witness to change those words. But the witness may stick with the words used in cross-examination. Indeed he or she may insist upon digging an even bigger hole! So the lawyer may prefer to take a risk and not re-examine the witness.

TRYING TRIALS

This conclusion, that lawyers can affect witnesses' evidence, may shock some. But should it? Provided that the lawyer is not breaching a rule of law, evidence or professional etiquette, he or she should not be criticised. Lawyers are operating a system, not just in the manner that they are entitled to do, but as they should if they are to do the best for their clients. Perhaps they ought to be more critical and questioning of the system they operate and the rules that they abide by. But how many occupations are keen to undertake a radical review of how they operate, particularly one that is beloved of and regularly reinforced by media examples which draw upon its potential for excitement and truth finding? Lawyers would stress that they do not make the decisions. They present—better understood as 're-present'—the evidence to the courts. It is the court, the judge or jury, which makes the decision. They, the lawyers, must do their job as well as they can if they are to help the judge or jury to do their job best.

We might think that the key criteria for judging a trial system are obvious. For a criminal trial they are to ensure that the guilty are convicted and the innocent acquitted. But that is not entirely correct (Walker, 2001). It is a desirable by-product rather than system goal. First, trials can be decided upon the burden and onus of proof rather than determination of guilt or innocence. A finding of 'not guilty' is not a finding of innocence, although that may appear appropriate and is often interpreted as such. All a judge or jury may be deciding is that there is insufficient proof, that there is a reasonable doubt. They may have believed the defendant to be guilty, but have had to accept that there is a reasonable doubt in the evidence. That is perfectly proper, under our system. Second, the focus is on individual cases and there is nobody, no agency, charged with developing a system perspective. Third, even if there was we have no—perfect—system for judging trials. They are self-validating. Who tries trials?

A court may find and declare someone to be guilty, or not guilty. For legal and practical purposes they are now, guilty or not guilty. There is, or is not, authority for punishing him or her. And, in practice, most of us believe, or assume, that the individual is, or (less frequently) is not, guilty. But we do not know, and cannot know for certain, that the court's conclusion is correct. Action may be taken, for example fresh evidence found, leading to a review of a conviction, although not of an acquittal. In England and Wales the Criminal Cases Review Commission may undertake a review of a case and refer it to the Court of Appeal for reconsideration. That may lead to a reversal of that conviction. Such a reversal does not prove innocence, although that conclusion often seems to be the obvious inference. It only suggests that the defendant should not have been convicted, or should no longer be regarded as guilty on the requirement of proof of guilt beyond reasonable doubt. A finding of not guilty is not a finding of innocence. We cannot say that a finding of wrongful conviction provides data about false positive (incorrect guilty) decisions, unless we qualify it as 'not guilty according to legal standard of proof'. By definition, because we have chosen trials as our fact-finding system, we do not have another system to test, or to try, them by.

Examination in court, by questions, is part of a bigger system. It would be inappropriate to hurl opprobrium at just this part whenever it may be a necessary consequence of other parts of the system. For example, we allow lawyers a great deal of latitude in what questions, and how they may ask them in court. We can then begin to believe that, if we were on trial, our lawyer could do his or her best for us. We would have a champion unconstrained by petty restrictions. We can also begin to believe that everything thought to be relevant would get aired in our case, and by extension, is aired in other cases. There is something reassuring, as well as exciting and dramatic, about the notion of courts as contests. That that may conflict with their fact and truth-finding roles, and certainly does not fit the daily monotony of most courts, is overlooked. When we think of trials we focus on the atypical which is the contested trial. When we review the criminal justice system we again tend to focus on the atypical case, the expensive, long, jury trial (Auld, 2001).

It would be unrealistic to assume that in inquisitorial justice systems witnesses' words would reach the ears of decision makers, usually judges, in any purer state. Their statements have been paraphrased by officials into written statements to enter in a case file (Pakes and McKenzie, forthcoming). Police officers or investigative judges often write down their statements in summary, and in doing so they translate it into 'proper terms' so as to facilitate its process through the system. In the Netherlands, for instance, the rule is that such summary statements are to be recorded in the suspect's or witness's own words. The practice, however, is quite different. Information undergoes what Den Boer (1990) calls 'narrative transformations', so as to fit the legal purpose of the official recording the information.

A typical inquisitorial ploy would be to record the following in such a statement.

> 'I tell you that I was not in the pub when the fight broke out. You however tell me that you have obtained various witness statements to the effect that I was present in said pub kicking person X several times, or least once or at least attempting to kick person X. I do not know why those people would say that. I have no enemies and cannot imagine people lying about me.'

In this way, the recorder clearly communicates the degree of credibility he or she wants the subsequent decision-makers to assign to this statement.

The Auld report proposes changes to trial proceedings, although these might be regarded as minor adjustments to curtail the impact of persuasion in the courtroom. They include provision for the judge to give to the jury an objective summary of the case and the questions they are there to decide. This is to be supported with a written *aide-memoire*. Counsel for both parties should also submit information to the jury, and judge, in writing. It should identify: the nature of the charges; a brief narrative including the agreed evidence and the admissions of either side, the matters of fact disputed and, with no, or minimal, reference to the law, a list of the likely questions for their decision (Auld, ch. 11, para. 22).

If jurors are better prepared for what is to come, they might be better equipped to pay attention to the evidence and less to persuasion or other 'communication mischief', a term coined by Walker (1993). But the remedies proposed seem to lie in the preparation of those who enter the arena of an adversarial trial. Jurors could be informed better to assist their decision-making as Auld is suggesting. Advocates and judges today receive better training than they have in the past. Information is now often given to vulnerable witness such as children (Plotnikoff and Woolfson, 1995) for whom protective measures such as live links and video-recorded evidence are now in place (see Davies and Noon, 1991: Davies et al., 1995). However the rules of the game, once the trial begins, do not seem to be open for change. What is changing is the preparation and training of those who play in it.

In the absence of a method for being able to know how well trials perform, as determinants of guilt and non-guilt, we should focus upon auditing both the parts as well as their integration into a whole system. We could examine the effectiveness of parts, for example the potential of our current systems of questioning to ensure truthful and accurate evidence. Then we could examine the integration of the parts into the whole. Additionally, and/or alternatively, we might develop ways in which the criminal justice system receives feedback. Without feedback an organisation, or system, cannot learn or develop organically. It does not make provision for automatic adaptation, change and improvement (Flood and Jackson, 1991). Indeed, without this provision, its adherents are liable to perceive criticism and examples of error as challenges from the outside. It increasingly becomes a 'closed' system with regard to, and separate from, the rest of the world. If we were to adopt this perspective then we might begin an audit of the quality of the parts of the system. Although we still have difficult, and basic, decisions to face about what are the goals of our legal system.

REFERENCES

Auld, R. (2001). *A review of the criminal courts of England and Wales*. London: HMSO.

Bull, R. (1998). Police investigative interviewing. In A. Memon and R. Bull (eds), *Handbook of the psychology of interviewing*. Chichester: John Wiley & Sons.

Clitheroe, J. (1980). *A guide to conducting a criminal defence*. Oyez.

Davies, G.M. and Noon, E. (1991). *An evaluation of the live link for child witnesses*. London: Home Office.

Davies, G.M, Wilson, C., Mitchell, R. and Milsom, J. (1995).*Videotaping children's evidence: An evaluation*. London: Home Office.

Den Boer, M.G.W. (1990). *Legal whispers: Narrative transformations in Dutch criminal evidence*. Doctoral dissertation, European University Institute, Florence, Italy.

Evans, K. (1983). *Advocacy at the Bar: A beginner's guide*. London: Financial Training Publications.

Evans, K. (1993). *The golden rules of advocacy*. London: Blackstone Press.

Fisher, R. and Geiselman, R.E. (1992). *Memory-enhancing techniques for investigative interviewing: The cognitive interview*. Springfield, Ill.: Charles C. Thomas.

Flood, R.L. and Jackson, M.C. (1991). *Creative problem solving: Total systems intervention*. Chichester: Wiley.

Gorden, R. (1975). *Interviewing: Strategy, techniques and tactics*. Homewood, Ill.: Dorsey.

Gudjonsson, G.H. (1984). A new scale of interrogative suggestibility. *Personality and Individual Differences*, 5: 303–314.

Gudjonsson, G.H. (1992). *The psychology of interrogations, confessions and testimony*. Chichester: Wiley.

Hart, H. (1963). Preface. In C. Perelman, *The idea of justice and the problem of argument*. London: Routledge & Kegan Paul.

Home Office and Department of Health (1992). *Memorandum of good practice for video recorded interviews with child witnesses for criminal proceedings*. London: HMSO.

Hyam, M. (1990). *Advocacy skills*. London: Blackstone Press.

Köhnken, G., Milne, R., Memon, A. and Bull, R. (1999). The cognitive interview: A meta-analysis. *Psychology, Crime and Law*, 5, 3–27.

Loftus, E.F. and Palmer, J.C. (1974). Reconstruction of automobile destruction: An example of the interaction between language and memory. *Journal of Verbal Learning and Verbal Behaviour*, *13*, 585–589.

Loftus, E.F. (1979). *Eyewitness testimony*. Cambridge, MA: Cambridge University Press.

McEwan (1998). *Evidence and the adversarial process: The modern law*. Oxford: Hart.

McBarnett, D. (1981). Magistrates courts and the ideology of justice. *British Journal of Law and Society*, *8*, 181.

Milne, R. and Bull, R. (1999). *Investigative interviewing: Psychology and practice.* Chichester: John Wiley & Sons.

Moston, S. (1990). How children interpret and respond to questions: Situation sources of suggestibility in eyewitness interviews. *Social Behaviour, 5,* 155–167.

Napley, D. (Sir) (1991). *The technique of persuasion* (4th edn). London: Sweet & Maxwell

O'Barr, W.M. (1982). *Linguistic evidence: language, power and strategy in the courtroom.* New York: Academic Press.

Pakes, F.J. and McKenzie, I.M. (forthcoming). *Law, power and justice in the Netherlands.* Westport, CT: Praeger.

Plotnikoff, J. and Woolfson, R. (1995). *The child witness pack—An evaluation.* Home Office Research and Statistics Department. Research Findings no. 9. London: HMSO.

Richardson, S.A., Dohrenwend, B.S. and Klein, D. (1965). *Interviewing: Its forms and functions.* London: Basic Books.

Smith, R. and Wynne, B. (eds) (1989). *Expert evidence: Interpreting science in the law.* London: Routledge.

Stone, M. (1995). *Cross-examination in criminal trials* (2nd edn). London: Butterworths.

Tapper, C. (1999). *Cross and Tapper on evidence* (9th edn). London: Butterworths.

Walker, A.G. (1993). Questioning young children in court: A linguistic case study. *Law and Human Behaviour, 17,* 59–81.

Walker, N. (2001). What does fairness mean in a criminal trial? *New Law Journal, 151,* 1240–1242.

Chapter 3.4

Expert Evidence: The Rules and the Rationality the Law Applies (or Should Apply) to Psychological Expertise

David L. Faigman
University of California at Hastings, USA

INTRODUCTION

Most evidentiary rules are structured in such a way as to strike a balance between the judge's responsibility to evaluate the admissibility of the evidence and the fact-finder's responsibility to determine what weight the evidence deserves. The factors at stake in this determination change with the evidentiary context. With character evidence, for instance, the rules balance such considerations as fairness to the defendant not to be judged or prejudiced by past deeds and the probative value that such prior conduct offers regarding the specific instance in dispute. Expert testimony similarly presents a broad array of policy considerations that affect where the balance should be struck between judge and fact finder. Expert evidence, however, presents an additional complication. Jurisdictions must not merely decide where the balance should be struck, but how—i.e. what rule of decision—should be employed in making this judgment.

The variability in how jurisdictions treat expert evidence revolves around two basic aspects of the admissibility determination. The first concerns the nature and rigor of the legal test to be applied. Courts differ substantially in the ways they define the judge's role concerning scientific evidence, with some adopting an active role in screening the evidence and others taking little or no responsibility to check the evidence. The second concerns the criteria used to assess the expertise under whatever legal test is adopted. Some courts use criteria that call for deference to the professional opinion of experts from the respective field, whereas others assume the responsibility themselves to evaluate the scientific basis of the proffered opinion.

Handbook of Psychology in Legal Contexts, Second Edition
Edited by D. Carson and R. Bull. © 2003 John Wiley & Sons, Ltd.

Legal standards vary from rigorous to permissive. The more permissive the legal standard, the greater the quantum of expert testimony that will be heard by the trier of fact. A jurisdiction's decision regarding how high the bar should be set for experts typically depends on its resolution of the classic problem of defining the proper roles for judges and juries in the trial process. A high threshold indicates a relatively active judicial role in screening expert opinion for the jury. A low threshold leaves the weighing functions to jurors—a task that might include, of course, according some expert evidence a weight of zero.

The second basic matter involves the manner by which a jurisdiction evaluates the probative value of proffered expertise. Some jurisdictions, for example, are highly deferential to the proffered expert and rely principally on qualifications or credentials. Other jurisdictions also consult the particular field from which the expert comes, requiring it to achieve some consensus regarding the proffered opinion. Finally, some jurisdictions, while considering the expert's qualifications and the field's acceptance of the basis for the opinion, also consider directly the theoretical principles, research methods, and accumulated data behind the expert's opinion.

In this chapter,* I consider the various approaches jurisdictions take to the employment of expert testimony. As a general matter, these approaches vary on at least two dimensions. First, as noted in the introduction, jurisdictions differ in the kinds of factors they use and the amount of deference they give to experts when evaluating proffered expert opinion. These differences concern the nuts and bolts of applying evidence rules in the trial process. To a large degree, however, these differences reflect a more substantial theoretical issue. Specifically, expert evidence rules raise the issue, as do most evidentiary rules, of how to draw the division of responsibility between the judge and trier of fact for evaluating the expertise. This suggests the second important dimension, how adversarial should the trial process be? Courts in the United States, especially federal courts, appear to be increasingly amenable to court appointed experts and technical advisers to assist them with complex science. This growing practice, together with admissibility rules that make the judge a relatively active participant in the reception of expert evidence, have made some American courts resemble the more inquisitorial style of adjudication embraced in recent English reforms and which are prevalent in many European countries.

This chapter, therefore, is divided into two sections. The first and main body of the chapter is devoted to the nuts and bolts of expert testimony. This section focuses on the rule set forth in *Daubert* v. *Merrell Dow Pharmaceuticals, Inc.* (1993), a rule further developed in two subsequent cases, *General Electric Co.* v. *Joiner* (1997) and *Kumho Tire Ltd.* v. *Carmichael* (1999) and finally codified in the Federal Rules

---

* This chapter draws heavily on the ideas and text of David L. Faigman, David Kaye, Michael J. Saks and Joseph Sanders, *Modern Scientific Evidence: The Law and Science of Expert Testimony*, Ch. 1, Admissibility of scientific evidence (2nd edn, 2002). Therefore, I am much indebted to the contributions of my colleagues David Kaye, Michael Saks and Joseph Sanders for this chapter. I would also like to thank my research assistants, Alexandria Graham, Cliff Hong, Lucia Sciaraffa, and Faith Wolinsky for their invaluable work.

of Evidence in 2000. The first section also considers the general acceptance test, first stated in *Frye* v. *United States* (1923), which has been partly incorporated into the *Daubert* test. Section two examines the growing trend toward making expert testimony an inquisitorial exercise rather than subject to the adversary process. In this section, I examine the English reforms and the use of court-experts in the United States. The chapter, it should be noted, does not consider expert evidence exclusively from the standpoint of psychological expertise. It is now clear that psychologists and other behavioral scientists are subject to the same rules of admissibility as all experts. Therefore, my main focus is on those general standards, although substantial attention is given to special considerations that might be raised by psychological expertise.

RULE 702 AND THE *DAUBERT* TRILOGY

In *Daubert* v. *Merrell Dow Pharmaceuticals, Inc.* (1993), the United States Supreme Court held that the Federal Rules of Evidence obligate trial courts to be gatekeepers who must evaluate the scientific basis of proffered expert testimony. If *Daubert* is a significant break from the past, the departure lies in the changed focus of the admissibility determination. Under the former predominant test—though still used in many jurisdictions—*Frye* v. *United States* (1923), judges determine the admissibility of scientific expert testimony by deferring to the opinions of scientists in the 'particular field'. If novel scientific evidence is deemed to have achieved general acceptance in the field from which it comes, it is considered admissible under *Frye*. Thus, under *Frye*, judges seemingly do not need to have any facility with scientific methods to make the admissibility decision. They must merely have some basis for knowing what most scientists believe. Under *Daubert*, judges have the specific responsibility of evaluating the scientific validity of the basis for expert testimony. The 'revolution' of *Daubert* lies therein (Faigman, 2000). Judges and lawyers, long insulated from the scientific revolution, are now obligated to become familiar with the methods and culture of science.

The Supreme Court stated in *Daubert* that it was simply interpreting the Federal Rules of Evidence as written (Taslitz, 1995). A reading of even a small sample of the voluminous literature dedicated to explaining *Daubert*, however, suggests that the meaning of Rule 702 in 1993 was not so plain (Faigman et al., 2002). Indeed, the variety of views in the lower courts before *Daubert*, and especially the then prevailing reliance on the general acceptance test of *Frye*, indicate a certain lack of clarity in Rule 702. Ironically, perhaps, the Court's interpretive style betrayed no break with the past (Giannelli, 1994), yet most courts and commentators found *Daubert* to herald a substantial change from past practice (see, e.g. *Polaino* v. *Bayer Corp.* (2000)). The sense that *Daubert* had changed the rules was confirmed when Federal Rules 701, 702 and 703 were amended in 2000 to set forth the new practice. Thus, the Federal Rules were amended in 2000 to state more plainly the plain meaning that the Court had ascribed to them in 1993. Federal courts, of course, are bound to follow this new course, and the States, in increasing numbers, have followed suit (Faigman et al., 2002; Hamilton, 1998).

Rule 702, as of December, 2000, provides as follows:

> If scientific, technical, or other specialized knowledge will assist the trier of fact to understand the evidence or to determine a fact in issue, a witness qualified as an expert by knowledge, skill, experience, training, or education, may testify thereto in the form of an opinion or otherwise, provided that (1) the testimony is sufficiently based upon reliable facts or data, (2) the testimony is the product of reliable principles and methods, and (3) the witness has applied the principles and methods reliably to the facts of the case.

APPLYING *DAUBERT*

Pretrial Considerations

Under *Daubert*, the trial court itself is initially responsible for determining the admissibility of scientific expert testimony by determining that the science supporting that opinion is valid (*Cavallo* v. *Star Enterprise* (1995)). Although courts and commentators initially debated the point, it now appears clear that *Daubert* deepened and expanded the trial judge's responsibilities over scientific evidence. That new obligation was captured colorfully in the Court's use of the gatekeeper metaphor to describe the judge's task.

An important component of the *Daubert* trilogy concerns the trial court's management of the expert testimony before trial. In particular, courts have divided somewhat on just when they should hold preliminary hearings under Rule 104(a) to fulfill their gatekeeping obligations. Rule 104(a) of the Federal Rules provides that preliminary factual questions, such as whether expert testimony has a valid basis, are to be determined by the trial court using the preponderance of the evidence (i.e. more likely than not) standard. Although the decision whether to hold a preliminary hearing appears to be largely within the trial judge's discretion, failure to hold a 104(a) hearing might constitute an abuse of discretion under certain circumstances (see *United States* v. *Smithers* (2000)). In general, most courts considering the matter hold that a separate hearing to determine the validity of the basis for scientific evidence is not required. Very often, however, courts do hold '*Daubert* hearings' or 'Rule 104(a) hearings' in order to assess the validity of the science. Indeed, *Daubert* apparently allows judges to exclude expert testimony as invalid even in the absence of an objection by the opponent of the evidence. At the same time, as many courts have emphasized, a key aspect of the *Daubert* standard is its flexibility. While in one case proper application of *Daubert* might call for a separate hearing, in another no separate hearing might be needed (Faigman et al., 2002).

Appellate courts increasingly insist that even when no *Daubert* hearing is held, the district court must create a sufficient record so that the basis for the admissibility decision can be reviewed. The Tenth Circuit, in *Goebel* v. *Denver Rio Grade Western Railroad Co.* (2000), for instance, emphasized the importance of a detailed record for purposes of appellate review. In *Goebel*, the district court admitted plaintiff's medical doctor who testified that the plaintiff's brain damage was caused by exposure to diesel fumes. The lower court denied the defendant's request for a *Daubert* hearing, but allowed a *voir dire* of the witness at trial. Thereafter, the court overturned the defendant's objection, stating simply that 'I believe there is sufficient foundation here for the jury to hear this testimony' (p. 1087).

The Tenth Circuit reversed, holding that the district court had failed its gatekeeping duties. The court observed that '[t]his gatekeeper function requires the judge to assess the reasoning and methodology underlying the expert's opinion, and determine whether it is scientifically valid and applicable to a particular set of facts' (p. 1087). Whether this gatekeeping function was fulfilled, the court explained, is reviewed on appeal *de novo*. 'While the district court has discretion in the manner in which it conducts its *Daubert* analysis, there is no discretion regarding the actual performance of the gatekeeper function.' Here, the district court never stated its reason for admitting the expert opinion and, thus, it could not be evaluated on appeal. The court then stated that 'we specifically hold that a district court, when faced with a party's objection, must adequately demonstrate by specific findings on the record that it has performed its duty as gatekeeper' (at 1088). Under *Daubert*, therefore, judges must have—and demonstrate on the record—a sufficient appreciation of the scientific method to make this preliminary assessment.

The Requirement of Relevancy

Focusing on the language 'assist the trier of fact' in Rule 702, many courts and commentators characterized this rule as a 'relevancy test'. In the area of scientific evidence, the *Daubert* Court explained, relevance foremost is a question of fit. Specifically, whatever the validity of the science, it must pertain to some disputed issue in the case. As the *Daubert* Court stated succinctly, Rule 702 'requires a valid scientific connection to the pertinent inquiry as a precondition to admissibility' (pp. 591–592). Only when the science pertains to a factual question in the case can expert testimony be helpful to the trier of fact. This helpfulness component is at the core of Rule 702.

The 'helpfulness' standard departs from the more stringent standard that was prevalent before the Federal Rules and is still in use in some jurisdictions today. This more stringent standard requires that the expert testimony provide knowledge that is 'beyond the ken' of an ordinary person. Although some jurisdictions continue to adhere to this more stringent standard, sometimes implicitly, most follow the Rule 702 mandate that permits expert testimony when it will merely assist the trier of fact. In this way, the helpfulness standard incorporates the idea of 'probative value' to be found in Rule 401's definition of relevance.

In addition, Rule 702 contains two other requirements. The first, explicitly stated in the Rule, is the qualifications test. The second, scientific validity, is now an explicit component of Rule 702 and is the central operating tenet of the *Daubert* trilogy.

The Qualifications Test

Courts have always required experts to be 'qualified' in order to testify (see, e.g. *Poust* v. *Hunleigh Healthcare* (1998)). The more controversial issue is whether qualifications are not only a necessary, but also a sufficient condition for expert testimony. Although no modern court has held that qualifications alone suffice, many commentators suspect that, in practice, some courts adhere to this view. In addition, this seemingly straightforward criterion turns out to contain considerable ambiguity. In particular, two issues arise. The first concerns what sorts of qualifications are necessary; for instance, must the expert have an advanced degree? The second concerns whether the expert's credentials must be in the specialty area in which the expert is to testify.

Rule 702 defines expertise broadly. Not just PhDs and MDs are contemplated by the Rule, but a wide assortment of specialists, ranging from nuclear physicists to real estate agents. Because the range is wide, so are the standards for qualifications. Rule 702 requires only that the expert be qualified 'by knowledge, skill, experience, training, or education'. By necessity, therefore, courts approach the issue of what background qualifications are necessary in a flexible manner.

In general, courts interpret the main qualifications requirement in relation to the expert's claimed expertise and the demands of the testimony (see, e.g. *Seatrax* v. *Sonbeck Int'l, Inc.* (2000)). Hence, experts on medical matters are expected to have medical degrees, appropriate certifications, and experience, but auto mechanics might only need years of experience and demonstrable skills. In many contexts, experience alone will be sufficient to qualify a witness, while in others, the lack of experience will disqualify an expert. As a practical matter, this means courts consult the experts' respective fields for guidance regarding what constitutes a 'qualified' expert. Not all fields, however, have well-articulated standards and many subjects of interest to the law are studied by fields with widely varying professional requirements. In psychology, for instance, a proffered expert might have one or more of a variety of degrees, ranging from a BA to a PhD.

The hallmark of late twentieth-century science (and all expertise) is specialization. This trend leaves courts somewhat uncertain as to whether generalists should be permitted to testify about matters that are highly specialized. Once again, courts approach this matter flexibly. Some courts require experts to have demonstrated expertise in the specific areas and topics on which they are to testify (see, e.g. *Gates* v. *The City of Memphis* (2000)). Other courts provide that generalists may testify on specialty areas and that their lack of expertise in those areas is a matter of weight for the trier of fact (see, e.g. *TUF Racing Products, Inc.* v. *American Suzuki Motor Corp.* (2000)). Too often, however, expedience leads courts to allow experts to venture into areas outside of their true expertise.

The evaluation of qualifications is a fact-based preliminary inquiry that will be overturned on appeal only for an abuse of discretion. There seems to be a small trend toward greater scrutiny of expert credentials and qualifications in post-*Daubert* admissibility hearings. A number of recent cases have rejected expert testimony on the basis of a lack of qualifications. Representative of these is *Mancuso* v. *Consolidated Edison Co. of New York* (1997). There, the court concluded that an internist did not have the requisite qualifications to testify that the plaintiff's ailments were caused by exposure to polychlorinated biphenyls (PCB). The internist lacked formal training and credentials in PCB toxicology or in environmental or occupational medicine. The internist was unable to answer basic questions about PCB toxicology and relied upon the plaintiffs' attorney to provide him with the scientific literature with which he formed his opinion.

It is worth noting that the issue of qualifications is intrinsically bound to the Court's holding in *Kumho Tire* that *Daubert*'s gatekeeping requirement extends to non-scientific expert testimony. Of course, if an asserted expertise cannot be shown to be sound, then even the most eminent (most highly qualified) practitioner of that asserted expertise still would not be permitted to testify as an expert. In fact, courts are likely to find that the issues of qualifications, reliability and fit are inextricably entwined and, in practice, cannot easily be disentangled. Qualifications are relative, being more or less useful depending on the expert's familiarity with the subject that fits, or is relevant to, the matter to be decided by the trier of fact. Qualifications, therefore, cannot be evaluated in the abstract. At some point, certainly, the question of qualifications becomes a matter of weight rather than admissibility. But just as with validity assessments, the judge's gatekeeping obligation should extend not merely to qualifications in the abstract, but qualifications to testify about the subject that is relevant to the issues in controversy.

Determining Validity

The validity test is the core component of *Daubert*. Under this test, judges must find by a preponderance of the evidence that the basis for proffered expert testimony is reliable and valid. The Court articulated four *non-exclusive* factors that courts should consider when evaluating the validity of the basis for proffered expert opinion: (1) testability (or falsifiability), (2) error rate, (3) peer review and publication and (4) general acceptance. Other courts and commentators offer additional factors that might be of assistance to the gatekeeping court (see Faigman et al., 2002). Moreover, some disciplines do not lend themselves to assessment by these criteria, and so courts must use other factors instead. This section examines the four *Daubert* factors together with several of the additional factors that might contribute to a judge's evaluation of scientific validity.

At the outset, certain general observations can be made about the approach to validity assessment encompassed by these four factors. Despite the substantial concern raised by many that *Daubert* demands a level of scientific sophistication among judges that would make them 'amateur scientists' (see *Daubert* (1993) (Rehnquist, C.J., concurring), only two of the *Daubert* factors focus on the scientific merit directly. Of the remaining two, one—general acceptance—is very deferential to the field from which the evidence comes. The other, peer review and publication, is somewhat deferential to the opinion of the field and should operate as an aid to courts needing to evaluate the methodology employed by the experts. The Court thus indicated that although judges must become sophisticated consumers of science, and must understand the philosophical and practical considerations raised by the scientific method, they can sometimes employ proxies to help them to decide the issue. Of course, scientists themselves do the same when they evaluate scientific fields that are not their areas of specialty or when time prohibits a more thorough evaluation.

No single list of factors, however, can capture the sundry considerations that go into determining the validity of research results. Indeed, it is somewhat misleading to suggest one, for, as every scientist knows, validity is not a categorical conclusion. Scientists tend to speak of validity in terms of the strength of the evidence and reasoning supporting a conclusion, not in terms of its 'truth'. Similarly, although judges must assess validity in order to make a categorical decision—admitting or excluding the testimony—judges need not have a categorical view of the science. Judges are expected to use the *Daubert* factors (and others) to determine if it is more likely than not that the methods and reasoning validly support the proffered expert testimony.

An issue that arose very soon after *Daubert* was whether the decision would lead to more or less expert testimony. Many courts assumed that *Daubert* set a lower threshold for admissibility than had *Frye* (see, e.g. *United States* v. *Kwong* (1995)). Yet, over time, courts have discovered that the conscientious application of *Daubert* leads them at least to the brink of excluding asserted areas of expertise that under *Frye* had gained admission easily (see, e.g. *United States* v. *Starzecpyzel* (1995)). But the two tests look at different attributes of asserted knowledge. *Frye* inquires into the general acceptance of a proposition among a community thought to understand the matter; *Daubert* inquires directly into a proposition's scientific foundation. These two questions usually lead to the same result. Testimony that has a strong scientific foundation usually will be generally accepted; opinions with a weak scientific foundation usually will not be widely accepted. In those situations, both standards will admit or both will exclude.

Sometimes, however, the two tests will diverge. When asserted knowledge is sound but not generally accepted, *Daubert* permits its admission while *Frye* does not. This is the category of cases that most commentators and courts have in mind when they think that *Daubert* is more liberal than *Frye*. When asserted knowledge has not been shown to be sound, but nevertheless has gained general acceptance in its field, then *Daubert* excludes even though *Frye* would admit. This category contains the asserted areas of expertise that have surprised judges who did not expect to find *Daubert* leading toward exclusion. Put most simply, *Daubert* sets a higher threshold for admissibility under some circumstances and a lower threshold under other circumstances. *Frye* and *Daubert* diverge because of widely varying practices among different scientific communities. Some fields are very rigorous in their evaluation of hypotheses, while others are rather less so. Courts have been surprised at *Daubert's* tendency to bar evidence when applied to fields that for too long rested on uncritical consensus rather than uncompromising empirical investigation.

Testability (Falsifiability)

The problem of identifying uniquely scientific knowledge has occupied countless volumes in the philosophy of science. Of the sundry philosophical choices the Supreme Court could have made, it chose the criterion of falsifiability, which is most closely associated with Sir Karl Popper. Although the Court cited Popper in only a passing reference, it chose as its first factor his falsifiability criterion for distinguishing scientific from non-scientific and, especially, pseudoscientific statements. In short, the criterion of falsifiability provides that 'a statement or theory is ... falsifiable if and only if there exists at least one potential falsifier—at least one possible basic statement that conflicts with it logically' (Popper, 1983, p. xx). As the Court quoted Popper, 'the criterion of the scientific status of a theory is its falsifiability, or reputability, or testability' (*Daubert*, 1993, p. 593). The hallmark of scientific statements is that they are vulnerable to refutation.

Contrary to Popper's original formulation of falsifiability, the Court selected this factor as one of four possible indices of validity. For Popper, however, falsifiability was *the* criterion of scientific status. In fact, courts will find application of *Daubert* difficult if they treat testability as an optional factor. The other three factors all presuppose testability; in science, a non-testable hypothesis cannot have an error rate and is exceedingly unlikely to be published in a peer-reviewed journal and achieve general acceptance. And indeed, since *Daubert*, courts generally appear to treat testability as a prerequisite rather than just another factor. In practice, therefore, the *Daubert* testability criterion is entirely consistent with Popper's philosophy.

The concept of falsifiability is separate from the question of when a scientific theory has been corroborated or falsified by observations. The *status* of a statement as scientific depends on its amenability to test; the *merit* of a scientific statement depends on the degree to which it has survived attempts at falsification. Both the status and the merit of purportedly scientific statements are subjects to be assessed by judges (Faigman, 1989).

Not all empirical tests of a theory are equally valuable. Research methods vary considerably, and some tests amount to no test at all. Judges, therefore, must develop sufficient scientific literacy to recognize research designed to truly test a hypothesis as compared to research designed merely to supply impressive looking graphs and imposing numbers to a researcher's theory. In other words, judges (and lawyers) must be able to distinguish the methods of science from those methods that merely imitate science.

The Methodology–Conclusion Paradox

When applied to scientific research offered in the trial setting, the falsification criterion contains an added complexity. It is not entirely clear which aspects of the science must have been tested to cross the threshold of admissibility, and which aspects are a matter of weight for the trier of fact to determine. The *Daubert* Court wrote that the 'focus, of course, must be solely on principles and methodology, not on the conclusions that they generate' (p. 595).

This statement caused some confusion among courts and in the scholarly literature, because it does not provide as clear a demarcation between the issues for judges and the issues for triers of fact as it implies (see, e.g. Chesebro, 1994). When scientists conduct research, although they clearly demarcate the methods employed from the conclusions they reach, they also well understand that the two are mutually dependent. Some conclusions are permitted by a particular methodology and some are not. Thus, when studying the toxic effects of drugs, using animals rather than humans as subjects restricts the conclusions that might be drawn from the work. The decision to use multiple regression analysis rather than analysis of variance affects what conclusions might be drawn from the data. Failure to include a comparison group in a study of leukemia rates in a particular neighborhood would obviously affect what conclusions could be reached. Research on the carcinogenic character of second-hand smoke conducted on white rats, by subjecting them to the equivalent of ten packs-a-day, might employ exactly the right methodology and reasoning for concluding that such smoke causes cancer in white rats; but if the researcher is interested in generalizing the study to humans, then we must evaluate the methodology and reasoning in light of that purpose. Scientific conclusions are inextricably connected to the methodologies used to reach them.

In *Joiner*, the Court agreed with the above analysis and rejected the suggestion that *Daubert* created a sharp distinction between the validity of scientific methodology and the plausibility of conclusions:

> [C]onclusions and methodology are not entirely distinct from one another. Trained experts commonly extrapolate from existing data. But nothing in either *Daubert* or the Federal Rules of Evidence requires a district court to admit opinion evidence which is connected to existing data only by the *ipse dixit* of the expert. A court may conclude that there is simply too great an analytical gap between the data and the opinion proffered. (p. 519)

Courts have begun to suggest another way to understand Justice Blackmun's distinction between methodology and conclusions, an interpretation that conforms to both the realities of scientific research and the needs of the law. The primary purpose of the methodology–conclusion distinction was to draw a line between the judge's task as gatekeeper and the jury's role as finder and weigher of fact. The line between methodology and conclusions was ill-suited for this purpose, because it did not describe the reality of scientific practice. However, courts have increasingly noted the different levels of abstraction at which science comes to the law. Science comes to courts as an amalgam of general principles or theories and specific applications of those principles. These two basic levels of abstraction offer a solution to the judge/jury problem inherent in all admissibility determinations (Faigman et al., 2002).

Courts have recognized these levels of abstraction most clearly in medical causation cases in which they routinely distinguish between 'general causation' and 'specific causation'. These levels of abstraction are present in virtually all expert testimony, if sometimes only implicitly. General and specific causation are sub-instances of the more general phenomenon, but they nicely illustrate the value in highlighting the distinction between the general and the specific. General causation refers to the proposition that one factor (or more) can produce certain results, and thus the finding transcends any one case. Specific causation refers to those factors having had those results in the specific case at bar. Consider, for example, the complaint in *Daubert* itself. The plaintiffs claimed that Jason Daubert's mother's ingestion of Bendectin during pregnancy caused or contributed to his birth defects. This claim has both general and specific components. As a matter of general causation, the plaintiffs were obligated to show that Bendectin sometimes causes birth defects. This hypothesis transcends the particular dispute, and is as true in California as it is in New York. In addition, the plaintiffs had to show that Jason's birth defects were attributable to his mother's ingestion of Bendectin. This proof might involve showing that she took the drug during the relevant period and that other factors probably did not cause the defects. This is specific causation.

Virtually all scientific evidence shares this basic dichotomy between the general and the specific. The general premises of fingerprinting, for instance, are that every person's fingerprint is unique, and that a known print can be compared to a latent print for purposes of identification. The conclusion regarding the identity of the person who left a particular print at a particular place is specific. Litigation involving asbestos, agent orange, trichlorethelyne, phen-fen, cellular phones, and so on, all have both general premises and specific conclusions. Engineering and the forensic and social sciences also fit this description. In the case of the Battered Woman Syndrome, for example, there is both the theory of the consequences of prolonged familial violence and the specific question whether a particular victim of that violence suffers from the syndrome.

Science provides a method by which relationships or associations can be identified and, typically, quantified. Scientific theories often involve induction from the particular to the general. The law, however, is interested in applying these general lessons to specific cases. It may be said that scientists tend to focus on general propositions, whereas judges and lawyers concentrate primarily on specific applications.

Although not without ambiguities, the distinction between the general and the specific helps to distinguish the admissibility decision for the judge from the weight determination for the jury. The following rule of thumb might be suggested. Judges must find that the general principles and theories underlying an expert's opinion are reliable and valid. This responsibility includes an evaluation of the methodology used to make a specific inference, since the validity of such methodologies (such as clinical assessments, differential diagnosis, polygraph machines, DNA technologies (PCR or RFLP) and so on) depend on general principles and theories. If a body of data supports both valid generalizations and the methods employed to determine specific propositions, the jury should evaluate what weight to accord the testimony.

This reading of Justice Blackmun's distinction between methodology and conclusions is consistent with the traditional roles of these two decision-makers. Judges, by virtue of their education and experience, are well situated to assess the features of science and technology that are general and do not change from case to case. Moreover, courts should be reluctant to allow different juries to decide common issues differently. The effects of second-hand smoke are the same in Iowa and Florida. Giving judges a strong initial role in evaluating scientific findings that transcend particular cases will go a long way toward achieving consistency. In contrast, whether a particular plaintiff's lung cancer is due to second-hand smoke, or possibly has a genetic cause, is unique to the case. If doctors have the theory and technology to make these determinations, then the accuracy of the conclusion that the plaintiff's cancer was caused by the defendant's cigarettes should be for the trier of fact to decide.

In short, judges should evaluate the validity of the general principles or methods by which experts derive their opinions about specific causation. Once the court has determined that such methods exist and that they were applied in the particular case, the trier of fact must assess the weight the result receives. For instance, if research indicates that a method of characterizing DNA is accurate and the expert used that technology in the particular case, it should be for the trier of fact to determine whether the test was employed correctly (Imwinkelried, 1991).

Not all scientific expert testimony, of course, will be able to meet validity requirements, especially at the start. In the usual case, general relationships will be validated before they can be extended to individuals in a reliable fashion. This does not mean juries will be left without guidance, for the general science itself often provides substantial assistance. Moreover, allowing experts to take the next step and apply the science to the case without research supporting their ability to do so invites unfounded speculation. In fact, many scientists refuse to take this step, because of the lack of competence to offer an opinion better than triers of fact could do on their own. For example, experts on the reliability of eyewitness identifications do not testify on case-specific facts. Researchers looking at factors associated with unreliable identifications are able to specify factors that interfere with identifications, such as 'weapons focus', but they cannot state with any confidence whether a particular witness is accurate (Wells, 2002). Their testimony might still be of use to triers of fact, but the science simply does not permit an opinion on case-specific facts. Such humility should be appreciated by the courts. Sometimes, the law asks factual questions that scientists, or any expert, cannot answer any better than laypersons.

Ordinarily, experts should not be allowed to testify to specific conclusions when there is a lack of data on the general proposition sought to be generalized to the specific case. Courts considering the issue have agreed with this proposition. Yet, this proposition has proved difficult to enforce in practice. Many experts reason backward from their conclusions to their premises. For example, a doctor's statement that the plaintiff's exposure to chemical Y caused her respiratory ailment might be premised on both the specifics of the case (e.g. temporal proximity between exposure and onset of illness) and more general experience with this or similar chemicals. The question, then, is what value 'experience' should be accorded in demonstrating general causation. This is an important subject that is considered below in the discussion of *Kumho Tire*. It is safe to say here that with no proof of general causation, an expert should not be permitted to testify about specific causation.

The Question Researched v. The Relevant Legal Query

An extremely important issue on which courts stumble is the matter of translating the 'answers' that respective fields offer into the questions that the law asks. This is a problem of vocabulary and general lack of understanding among lawyers and judges regarding what, exactly, a particular field's interest is in the subject. There are numerous examples. Probably the best two examples of the sometimes lack of understanding between law and science come from the fields of medicine and psychology, professions that occupy a disproportionate amount of courts' attention.

Medical doctors and lawyers both use the term 'differential diagnosis', but the two professions often mean different things by it. The Eighth Circuit's decision in *Turner* v. *Iowa Fire Equipment Co.* (2000) illustrates the different meanings the two professions attribute to the term. In *Turner*, the plaintiff brought suit after the automatic fire extinguisher system at her workplace was accidently activated. It dumped a white powdery substance—mainly baking powder—on her grill. Soon after, plaintiff developed a host of symptoms, including shortness of breath and headaches. At trial, her treating physician testified in support of her claim. He stated, however, that as the treating physician, his task was to determine what the plaintiff suffered from, not what had caused her condition. The district court excluded the expert and the Eighth Circuit affirmed.

The Eighth Circuit explained that there were two meanings of the term 'differential diagnosis'. The medical community defines it as the attempt to identify the ailment in order to determine treatment. This has to be contrasted with the legal community's definition of 'differential diagnosis', which is concerned with the identification of the *cause(s)* of the ailment. For instance, a doctor's ability to employ differential diagnosis to determine that a patient's stomach pain is due to cancer rather than an ulcer does not necessarily mean that the doctor can reliably determine what caused the cancer. Most medical doctors focus on diagnosis for purposes of treatment, whereas lawyers are typically interested in causality. The legal use of the phrase differential diagnosis might be better termed 'differential etiology'. In *Turner*, the court explained, the treating physician had conducted a medical differential diagnosis, but had failed to conduct a legal one.

In psychology, the phenomenon is even more salient. Lawyers and judges routinely consider psychological diagnoses for forensic purposes when, to the extent they have been tested at all, they are deemed valid only for therapeutic purposes. Thus, for example, a lawyer asking a clinical psychologist whether post-traumatic stress disorder (PTSD) is 'generally accepted' or 'has been tested' is likely to get an affirmative response. However, psychologists mean that it has been tested for therapy, not necessarily that it has been tested for forensic use (*United States* v. *Barnette* (2000)). For example, when PTSD is used by a prosecutor in a rape trial, typically as a component of Rape Trauma Syndrome, the rape itself serves as the traumatic stressor that a psychologist relies on to make the diagnosis. Psychologists, however, do not challenge their patients' claims to have been raped. In court, of course, that is the controverted issue. In effect, then, a PTSD diagnosis, which partly rests on the alleged victim's statements that she was raped, is introduced to prove that very contention. Other examples abound. Lawyers and judges, therefore, must consider not only whether the basis for the expertise is valid for some purpose, but whether it is valid for its intended use by courts. This is a matter of 'fit'.

Error Rate

At first glance, the *Daubert* Court's inclusion of error rates as a principal factor for judges to consider would seem obvious. Yet, on closer inspection, employing this important concept might seem perplexing. It appears that 'error' occurs in science in a multitude of ways, not all of which are quantifiable. It is useful once again to distinguish between the general levels of science and the application of that general work to an individual situation.

Error Rates in Stating Features of an Individual

The typical use of the term 'error rate' refers to the number of 'mistakes' a particular technique or method will make in some specific number of trials. In this sense, error rate corresponds primarily to the 'general technology' level of science outlined above. There are two types of mistakes that might be made. A polygraph examiner, for instance, might mistakenly conclude that the subject is telling the truth when he is lying (a 'false negative'), or the examiner might mistakenly conclude that the subject is lying when he is telling the truth (a 'false positive'). A scientist's judgment of the value of a technique will depend on both the amount and kind of error.

Importantly, the Court did not specify what error rates are tolerable. There are good reasons for this omission. The costs of making an error are different in different contexts. For example, the error rate associated with predictions of violence is fairly high (Monahan, 2002). Yet, psychiatric predictions appear to be better than chance and, for some populations, substantially better. The costs of making a mistake, therefore, should guide a court's evaluation of the proffered evidence. Thus, a judge might require a relatively low error rate before admitting predictions of violence in a capital case, but permit higher error rates in a probation matter. This determination, however, cannot simply be an application of Rule 702. Rule 702 queries whether the scientific evidence will 'assist the trier of fact'. Subject to the other qualifications discussed in this chapter, any science that is even slightly better than flipping a coin is likely to meet this test. The Rule 702 error rate factor thus embodies, at least in part, a Rule 403 analysis. Rule 403 balances probative value against possible prejudice and thus permits a more finely tuned assessment (Faigman et al., 2002). But in practice, it would be virtually impossible to disentangle the Rule 702 probative value component of scientific evidence from the matter of error rate. Because scientific knowledge is not known with certainty, its value (i.e. relevance) depends substantially on the costs associated with being wrong.

Error Rates Attributable to Studying Population Features

In scientific investigation, a multitude of limitations affect the methods that are chosen and thus the knowledge that they generate. The sources of error (or limitations) include such matters as sample size, sample studied (college students, registered voters, or white rats?), choice of comparison group (random assignment, self-selection, or none?), and apparatus or materials used (live, video, or written?).

Errors can be random or systematic. Random sampling, for example, entails random error. A random sample of 20 is less likely to represent an underlying population than a random sample of 2000. Unreliable coding of data could produce essentially random error. Researchers might accidently code some people who are exposed to a substance as not exposed and vice versa.

Systematic errors, unlike random errors, tend to work in a single direction and, therefore, introduce bias into the data. For example, if researchers rely on self-reports of exposure to some substance, and if some of the people asked have already become ill, 'recall bias' can arise. Those who are sick will be more likely to have searched through their past and recalled more exposures than those who are well. As a consequence, there will be an artificially high correlation between exposure and illness. Inferential statistics cannot quantify systematic errors. A basic advantage of experimental research is its ability to control for many systematic errors.

Because of the limitations inherent in scientific studies, few scientists would be confident in stating conclusions from one or even a few studies. Only through replications, using various designs and methods, do scientists gain confidence that a hypothesis has been sufficiently corroborated. No magic number or moment determines this point, however; like many areas of the law, science presents a broad spectrum of grays that only over time sharpens into black and white.

Peer Review and Publication

For the average scientist, publication in a peer reviewed journal is the mark of successful completion of a research project. But not all peer-reviewed journals are equal in status. Since scientists view the quality of scholarship, in part, through the lens of the journal name in which it is situated, it should be no surprise that judges too notice this criterion. At the same time, even the highest quality journals sometimes publish work that is later found to be wrong. In addition, mainstream peer-reviewed journals, by definition, are more likely to publish conventional scholarship and might be slow to recognize revolutionary findings or methods. In *Daubert*, the Court considered these costs and benefits and concluded that peer review and publication is a factor to be considered in assessing admissibility, but it is not a prerequisite.

The limitations of peer review and publication are akin to those of using general acceptance, discussed below, as a factor. Both criteria are mere proxies for the determinative factor. The value of peer review depends on the quality of those reviewers. If scientists publish in journals with lax standards, this criterion is not likely to lead to the exclusion of bad science. Thus, judges must consider carefully the range of journals that qualify under this standard. Judges would be well advised to return to the first two factors discussed above, falsifiability and error rate. These two criteria clearly indicate the use of a conventional ('scientific realist') view of the scientific method. Publication in journals that do not share the values reflected in these first two factors, therefore, should warn judges that the studies need to be scrutinized with particular care. To be sure, just as publication is not a prerequisite to admissibility, so too publication in non-rigorous journals should not mean *per se* exclusion. But in both cases, when studies lack placement in mainstream journals or when they have not been published at all, judges should use caution before admitting testimony relying on them.

Many courts and commentators take 'peer review and publication' in isolation, as merely one factor among many for assessing the reliability of scientific evidence. This common interpretation of the *Daubert* decision reflects the organization and emphasis within the paragraph that seeks to explain the factor, rather than the logic of the point being made. 'Peer review and publication' are features of a larger project, a synecdoche for a more important and more fundamental activity of scientific communities, for which the phrase stands. The more important point is found in the middle of the paragraph: 'submission to the scrutiny of the scientific community is a component of "good science"... because it increases the likelihood that substantive flaws in methodology will be detected.' That is the real concern of scientific communities— detecting serious flaws in the design of studies (Saks, 2000). A substantive finding is no better than the methods used to find it. Peer review and publication facilitate that effort. They are not the beginning and the end of the effort.

A scientific community is interested in critically evaluating the research products of its members, as part of the process of deciding whether any given set of findings is good enough to be added to the field's corpus of knowledge. 'Peer review and publication' are a part of, and contribute to, that larger process of critical evaluation. 'Peer review' is not limited to deciding what gets published. Peer review takes place before research is conducted (such as when a funding agency evaluates research proposals). And it takes place after publication. Indeed, most of the 'scrutiny of the scientific community' takes place after publication. Work that is too weak or flawed or unimportant even to be published, it is hoped, does not survive the first, small phase of peer review, is not published, and is thus not set before the relevant scientific community for its larger and ultimately more thorough scrutiny. *Daubert*'s discussion of 'peer review and publication' takes pains to alert the reader to the fact that publication in a peer reviewed journal is no assurance of soundness of a finding, and the lack of publication is no assurance that a study and its findings are not sound. These are merely aids to assessing the soundness of a study's methodology and execution.

The larger purpose of such scrutiny in all its forms is to assess the quality of a study's (or a line of studies') research methodology and, in light of that assessment, the meaning and value of the data generated by the research. The courts, no less than the scientific community, should be concerned not with the mere formal act of submission to the scrutiny of the scientific community, but with what the community concluded following such scrutiny (Saks, 2000). What weaknesses were discovered in the research methods? How do those affect the meaning or weight of the findings? Were there erroneous interpretations of the findings? Or did the study's design and its findings withstand the critical evaluation of a discerning community?

In short, 'peer review and publication' do not themselves establish the 'reliability' of the proffered knowledge. The more sensible reading of this '*Daubert* factor'—if the *Daubert* Court was tracking the common sense of most scientific communities—is that it stands for critical evaluation, with the help of the scientific community, of the research on which the asserted expertise is based.

General Acceptance

Like peer review and publication, general acceptance is only as good as the field that is surveyed. Under *Frye*, of course, general acceptance was the standard by which expert testimony was judged. But general acceptance operates slightly differently under *Daubert*, where it is used in conjunction with other factors and is no longer a necessary or sufficient condition for admission.

Although barely noticed for decades, the '*Frye* Test' eventually became the icon for one of the dominant notions of the proper criterion for the admissibility of scientific evidence—general acceptance within its field. *Frye* may have become the standard of choice for several reasons. Foremost, perhaps, it was easy to apply and required little scientific sophistication on the part of judges. Moreover, the controversial cases were of the subset of scientific evidence cases that *Frye* was designed to deal with: asserted new knowledge that lacked an established clientele. To established fields of endeavor, to old 'knowledge', the courts implicitly applied the old marketplace notions: if one were a card-carrying member of a recognized occupation or profession, one's proffered expert testimony was admitted and the validity of the underlying knowledge was assumed. Finally, by the middle of the twentieth century, the distinction between experts and expertise had grown more apparent. Not only did new fields or new specializations arise, but old fields acquired and offered distinct new knowledge. New knowledge was sometimes put before courts in a form more abstracted and isolated from the people who presented it. *Frye* had been designed to fit just these kinds of situations (Faigman, Porter and Saks, 1994).

Over time, courts and commentators found the general acceptance test to have significant limitations. In particular, the vagueness of the general acceptance test renders it susceptible to manipulation and tends to obscure the relevant inquiry. Indeed, virtually every component of the test has sustained severe criticism.

Frye is often criticized as overly conservative, for it imposes a protracted waiting period that valid scientific evidence and techniques must endure before gaining legal acceptance. This criticism highlights the fact that all significant scientific findings gestate before they are accepted by the general scientific community. During this time period courts and the parties before them are deprived of this work. Moreover, many critics also note the 'nature' of the scientific enterprise which sometimes responds negatively to revolutionary findings, because they might threaten entrenched 'paradigms' and thus entrenched scientists (Horrobin, 1990). Proponents of this view observe that the findings of a scientist heralded today as brilliant, but dismissed in his day as misguided or worse, would be excluded under a general acceptance test. Galileo, for example, or Einstein early in his physics career, would not have been allowed to testify because of the radical nature of their opinions.

Commentators responding to this criticism of *Frye* argue that for every Galileo or Einstein there are hundreds of Lysenkos with 'revolutionary' theories that are eventually proven false by empirical research. They maintain further that judges (and jurors) should not be expected to distinguish 'true' scientific revolutions from 'false' ones. If scientists are unable to recognize an Einstein when they see one, laypersons are unlikely to have this ability (Faigman et al., 2002).

Another asserted weakness of the *Frye* approach concerns the difficulty of ascertaining when a scientific proposition has been generally accepted. The test does not specify what proportion of experts constitute general acceptance. Courts have never required unanimity, and anything less than full consensus in science can quickly resemble substantial disagreement. In fact, the most rigorous fields with the healthiest scientific discourse might fail the *Frye* test with the greatest frequency. In light of the skeptical perspective of good scientific investigation, judges should be cautious when they approach a field in which there is too much agreement.

Moreover, the *Frye* test requires general acceptance in the *particular field*. But there are no standards defining which field to consult. Courts have had considerable difficulty assessing scientific information under this standard because it often extends into more than one academic or professional discipline. Furthermore, each field may contain subspecialties. This difficulty leads to paradoxical results. General acceptance, often criticized for being the most conservative test of admissibility, in practice can produce the most liberal standards of admission. The more narrowly a court defines the pertinent field, the more agreement it is likely to find. The general acceptance test thus degenerates into a process of deciding whose noses to count. The definition of the pertinent field can be over-inclusive or under-inclusive. Because the pertinent field can be so readily manipulated, the test by itself provides courts with little protection against shoddy science.

Even more critically, the particular field of inquiry leaves the law at the mercy of the practitioners of the respective fields. Different fields have widely varying standards. Some fields have a tradition of vigorous debate, data gathering, and hypothesis testing, an ethos consistent with the scientific enterprise. In these fields, an idea does not become generally accepted until it passes a rigorous gauntlet of testing. Other fields lack these traditions and accept ideas with far less scrutiny. The courts have difficulty telling one of these fields from another. Indeed, and especially ironically for courts, they may mistake vigorous research and debate over the meaning of the findings for lack of agreement (rather than the process of reaching trustworthy findings) and the lack of research and debate as a sign of consensus (rather than a sign of an immature or retarded science). Under the *Frye* variant, because the courts have to rely on the standards set within each field, they find themselves accepting more readily the offerings of less rigorous fields and less readily the offerings of more rigorous fields. Fields that set higher thresholds will place a smaller proportion of their knowledge over the threshold.

DAUBERT'S APPLICATION TO 'TECHNICAL, OR OTHER SPECIALIZED KNOWLEDGE': KUMHO TIRE, LTD. V. CARMICHAEL

In *Kumho Tire, Ltd.* v. *Carmichael* (1999), the Supreme Court considered a question that had bedeviled the lower courts, whether *Daubert's* gatekeeping obligation extended to so-called non-scientific expert testimony. The Court declared that it did: 'We conclude that *Daubert*'s general holding—setting forth the trial judge's general "gatekeeping" obligation—applies not only to testimony based on "scientific" knowledge, but also to testimony based on "technical" and "other specialized" knowledge' (p. 141). The plaintiffs had brought suit after their tire blew out causing an accident in which one person was killed and several others were severely injured. Their claim rested largely on the testimony of their expert witness who testified in a deposition that the blowout was caused by a defect in the manufacture or design of the tire. His testimony was based exclusively on his experience in the tire industry. He had conducted no tests on the tire in question or on similarly situated tires. He provided no statistical information linking the factors he identified as being indicative of tire failures to a manufacturing defect. The defendant moved to exclude the expert's testimony and for summary judgment. It claimed that the plaintiff's expert's testimony failed the *Daubert* standard, for it was not based on tested research, had no known error rate, had not been published in peer-reviewed journals, and was not generally accepted among engineers. The trial court agreed that the plaintiff's engineer failed the *Daubert* test. Plaintiffs asked for reconsideration, arguing that the court had applied the *Daubert* factors too inflexibly. The court concluded that, however flexibly it applied the *Daubert* test, the plaintiffs' expert's testimony was not sufficiently reliable to allow.

On appeal, the Eleventh Circuit Court of Appeals reversed. The Circuit Court applied a *de novo* standard to 'the district court's legal decision to apply *Daubert*' (*Carmichael* v. *Samyang Tire, Inc.* (1997)). It then went on to find that the *Daubert* test was limited to 'scientific knowledge', and that since the plaintiffs' expert based his testimony on his 'experience' and not the scientific method, it had to remand for a different admissibility analysis.

The Supreme Court reversed. Justice Breyer, writing for the Court, stated that the *Daubert* gatekeeping function applies to all expert testimony. The Court explained that Rule 702 'makes no relevant distinction between "scientific" knowledge and "technical" or "other specialized" knowledge' (p. 147). The limitation of *Daubert* to 'scientific knowledge' occurred merely because 'that [was] the nature of the expertise at issue' there (p. 148). The plain meaning of Rule 702, therefore, supports extending the gatekeeping function to all experts. Moreover, the policy underlying Rule 702 supports this result. First, experts are granted great leeway in testifying to opinions, a fact that is true for non-scientist experts as well. Second, 'it would prove difficult, if not impossible, for judges to administer evidentiary rules under which a gatekeeping obligation depended upon a distinction between "scientific" knowledge and "technical" or "other specialized" knowledge. There is no clear line that divides the one from the others' (p. 148). The Court concluded 'that *Daubert*'s general principles apply to the expert matters described in Rule 702' (p. 149). This means that, as regards all expert testimony, trial court judges 'must determine whether the testimony has a reliable basis in the knowledge and experience of [the relevant] discipline' (p. 149).

On the more specific question whether a trial court 'may' consider the *Daubert* factors in assessing so-called non-scientific evidence, the Court said it could. Initially, the Court observed, engineering is itself a discipline that relies on scientific principles. It might even be the quintessential 'applied science'. Hence, some of the *Daubert* factors could be helpful in assessing the reliability of an engineering expert. More to the point, however, the Court stated that, '[a]s the Solicitor General points out, there are many different kinds of experts, and many different kinds of expertise' (p. 150). The form of the expertise will dictate what factors might be of assistance in assessing its evidentiary reliability. The Court explained:

> The conclusion, in our view, is that we can neither rule out, nor rule in, for all cases and for all time the applicability of the factors mentioned in *Daubert*, nor can we now do so for subsets of cases categorized by category of expert or by kind of evidence. Too much depends upon the particular circumstances of the particular case at issue. . . . [A] trial court should consider the specific factors identified in *Daubert* where they are reasonable measures of the reliability of the expert testimony. (pp. 150–152)

Whether or not the specific *Daubert* factors apply, the trial court still has gatekeeping responsibilities.

The *Kumho Tire* Court next turned to an issue that is likely to create some difficulty in the years ahead. In *Joiner*, the Court had held that the abuse of discretion standard applied to appellate review of Rule 702 admissibility determinations. In *Kumho Tire*, the Court extended this very deferential standard to the matter of the district court's selection of factors by which it evaluates reliability. '[W]hether *Daubert*'s specific factors are, or are not, reasonable measures of reliability in a particular case is a matter that the law grants the trial judge broad latitude to determine' (p. 153). The Court also pointed out, '[t]he trial court must have the same latitude in deciding how to test an expert's reliability, and to decide whether or when special briefing or other proceedings are needed to investigate reliability, as it enjoys when it decides whether or not that expert's relevant testimony is reliable' (p. 152).

This appellate deference to the factors used to assess the different categories of expertise is a possible Achilles' heel in an otherwise solidly reasoned opinion. If taken literally, it would allow different judges in the same district to apply different factors to similar kinds of expert testimony. It might allow the same judge to apply different factors to similar kinds of experts. For instance, in one case, forensic document examination might be evaluated harshly because it has yet to be tested adequately, and, in another case in the same district, it might be permitted because it is thought to be reliable based on the practitioner's experience with the subject. If trial courts fail to craft consistent guidelines for these cases, parties will engage in forum shopping to obtain judges most sympathetic to their point of view.

This sort of inconsistency, in practice, is unlikely to be too great a problem among trial courts. District court judges are interested in maintaining some consistency and are likely to look to prevailing practices in their circuits as regards particular forms of expert testimony. Moreover, despite the Court's injunction that appellate courts should defer to trial courts about the factors chosen to assess reliability, appellate judges will almost certainly still provide some oversight to maintain consistency. In a concurring opinion, for example, Justice Scalia emphasized that '[t]hough, as the Court makes clear today, the *Daubert* factors are not holy writ, in a particular case the failure to apply one or another of them may be unreasonable, and hence an abuse of discretion' (p. 159). Although some within circuit variation will inevitably occur, the more likely danger is that differences will emerge between circuits. The Supreme Court might yet find the need to revisit this issue.

The task for judges after *Kumho Tire*, therefore, is to select factors that are useful in assessing the evidentiary reliability of the many types of expertise that enters their courtrooms (see Risinger, 2002). Trial courts, of course, do consistently see specific types of expert testimony, from firearms identification experts to clinical medical doctors. Given the press of time, they are likely to seek factor-lists or tests, such as the one *Daubert* offered for traditional scientific evidence, for the myriad of 'subsets of cases categorized by category of expert'.

As scientists well know, different empirical questions require different methods of inquiry. This is true both between and within subject areas. Whether it is physics, biology, engineering, psychology, economics, sociology or anthropology, some questions can be approached experimentally, others require more indirect means, and most require an assortment of research strategies in order to approach an answer. This is why the so-called *Daubert* factors could never have been the test for all expert testimony. Under *Daubert* and *Kumho Tire*, judges are gatekeepers who are responsible for checking the bases for all expert testimony. The tools used to conduct this test might differ depending on the identity of the proposed entrant, but the basic responsibility remains the same. As judges and lawyers become more proficient in the scientific method, this responsibility will increasingly appear less daunting.

Finally, the opinion in *Kumho Tire* is suffused with the recognition that a court should not focus on the dependability of the expertise in some global sense, but its dependability in its application to the 'task at hand'. The question is whether the practitioners of the expertise can be shown to be able to do what they are claiming to do in the particular case. Thus, the existence of data showing that engineers, or physicians, or psychologists, or forensic scientists, can measure or diagnose or predict or correct certain conditions does little if anything to support an inference that they possess the requisite expertise for another task or condition for which there are no data. Put simply, evidence with regard to dependability for one task does not establish dependability for a different task. Courts must identify the nature of the particular problem that an expert is being asked to solve, and then assess whether the available data support a conclusion that the necessary expertise exists to offer a dependable opinion on that problem.

WHEN MUST A FACT BE A MATTER OF SCIENTIFIC INQUIRY?

The other side of the inquiry regarding whether the same legal standards apply to all experts is the following question: 'How much research, and what kinds of research, should we expect?' For instance, a particular cause and effect relationship might be supported by anecdotal experience or case studies, toxicological animal studies (using animals ranging from rats to monkeys) and human epidemiological research. The problem is that standards of admissibility are not static. Whether the basis for a proffered expert opinion is valid depends on what that opinion is, and what consequences follow from it. This is a matter of policy, not science.

Implicit in the admissibility decision, therefore, is a sufficiency analysis. It is not sufficiency in the classic civil procedure sense, but rather a judgment about how much evidence it takes before we believe a certain proposition. For instance, we might be mildly skeptical if told it would rain today because the day dawned with a red sky (i.e. 'red sky at night, sailor's delight; red sky in the morning, sailor take warning'), but typically little turns on this prediction and we might simply accept the opinion and carry an umbrella. However, if the dire predictions of global warming were premised on similar evidence, presumably few would be willing to spend billions of dollars to avoid this predicted fate. We demand opinion premised on sounder grounds. It appears that courts have made similar judgments, albeit implicitly. In civil cases, the more expensive and numerous the litigation, the more science that is expected. In criminal cases, the more likely the jury is to be overwhelmed by the expert opinion, the better the research is expected to be.

The Parameters of 'Science'

Although the *Daubert* Court spoke of the importance of 'scientific' knowledge, the key to the admissibility decision lies in the search for 'facts' that are, without expert assistance, beyond a jury's ability to appreciate fully. The purpose of expert testimony is to 'assist the trier of fact'; and the trier of fact's task is to arrive at the best possible conclusions in light of the evidence before it. Sometimes non-scientific disciplines will have access to facts that might assist jurors. Perhaps the best way to approach admissibility, then, is to understand the judge's task as regulating the supply of facts to the jury in a manner that states a preference for science as the preeminent method for discovering facts.

In explaining, predicting, and controlling the world around us, science is by far the most powerful intellectual technique known. The recognition of the power of science, however, should not lead to blind allegiance to its dictates. Science provides no assistance over broad and profoundly important areas of human concern, most particularly that of values. Moreover, science is slow, even plodding. Often, it requires ideal conditions that rarely exist, or it studies only small numbers of variables, limiting its ability to generalize any findings. Finally, researchers' values guide the questions they ask and can affect the conclusions they reach.

These limitations on science are implicit in most rules' recognition that 'technical or other specialized knowledge' should sometimes be permitted to form the foundation for expert opinion. But given the power of the scientific method, these alternatives should suffice only where science provides too little assistance or so much assistance that it amounts to overkill. In general, two situations limit science's usefulness to the law. The first involves factual questions that do not lend themselves to scientific analysis because they are either inherently not amenable to it or they are so complex that scientists do not have the tools to study them; the second concerns matters so elementary that non-scientists' extensive experience with them should be sufficient for the law's purposes.

Some facts are simply not amenable to the methods of science. Science, as the Supreme Court recognized, operates in the realm of testable hypotheses. For example, an expert might be called upon to validate the authenticity of a painting. The expert's conclusion that the painting was painted by, say, Cezanne, on the basis of the character of the brush strokes, cannot be tested, since it defies replication and does not generate testable hypotheses. This is not to say that the law should not demand the best methods that art experts and other non-scientists have in their arsenal, only that those methods are not 'scientific'. Nonetheless, judges should still be responsible for applying standards of good art evaluation to art evidence just as they are required to apply standards of good science to scientific evidence. Historians would be expected to adhere to valid historical methods, engineers to engineering methods, and so on through the many expertises judges must consider. Just as there are a number of factors by which scientists evaluate the validity of science, there are factors that artists, historians and engineers bring to their work for ensuring the best results possible given the inherent limitations of the subject.

Some facts of relevance to the law involve matters so complex that scientists have not, and perhaps can never, isolate the phenomena sufficiently to study them in depth. Indeed, many of the factual questions the law raises about human behavior are examples of complex phenomena not easily studied. For example, the psychological effects of extreme stress present formidable difficulties for psychologists. To recognize that many reputedly scientific matters remain on the margins of scientific skill, however, should not lead to scientific nihilism. The appropriate response to complexity should not be to call in the witch doctor for a magic spell, but rather to demand the best science available and remain aware of its limitations. For instance, although meteorologists remain some distance from being able to predict accurately as complex a phenomenon as the weather, they far outperform their witch doctor competitors. Similarly, the difficulty inherent in studying, for instance, the Battered Woman Syndrome, should not excuse researchers' failure to use sound research methods. Judges must be sophisticated enough to appreciate the differences in the methodological tools used by meteorologists and those wielded by the authors of the *Farmers Almanac*.

At the other extreme, the law depends on facts that are readily known through extensive study or experience, but with which triers of fact are likely to have little familiarity. A common example of specialized knowledge is that possessed by mechanics. The law permits auto mechanics to testify, as long as they spent enough time studying the matter, because their knowledge is thought to be readily obtainable. But recognizing that some facts can be known without the elaborate methods of science does not refute the relevance of the scientific method; it only indicates that sometimes that level of expertise is not necessary. The workings of a carburetor are no less susceptible to scientific understanding than the workings of an atom. The law merely assumes that an experienced mechanic can accurately describe the former, but only a scientist can accurately describe the latter. In short, admissibility standards should relax—but not entirely omit—the requirement for a scientific demonstration when a less rigorous, less time consuming, and less expensive alternative would provide sufficiently accurate information. When the subject of expert testimony is straightforward, the law dispenses with the requirement of scientific proof because it is excessive, not because it is unavailable.

The 'Same Intellectual Rigor that Characterizes . . . the Relevant Field'

Beginning with *Kumho Tire*, courts have recognized the value of the lesson that experts, whether they are physicists, psychologists, historians, engineers or artists, should employ the best tools their respective fields have to offer. Unfortunately, some courts have used this standard not merely as a necessary condition, but also as a sufficient condition, for admissibility. In *Kumho Tire*, the Supreme Court stated that trial judges should ensure that the proffered expert 'employs in the courtroom the same level of intellectual rigor that characterizes the practice of an expert in the relevant field'. Many courts, however, ask this question but fail to inquire further. This is a dangerous trend and one certainly not endorsed by the *Kumho Tire* Court, much less the operating premises of *Daubert*. As the *Kumho Tire* Court stated in the very same paragraph in which the quoted language appears, 'the objective of [the gatekeeping] requirement is to ensure the reliability and relevancy of expert testimony'. Bringing the same intellectual rigor to the courtroom that is used in the respective field is, like the other *Daubert* factors, merely a factor to consider on the way to making the ultimate determination: 'the reliability and relevancy of expert testimony'. It should not substitute for that determination.

The same intellectual rigor requirement is not a sufficient condition for an obvious reason. If the field itself brings little intellectual rigor to the subject, this factor will provide scant gatekeeping protection against bad science or flimsy expertise. In this way it is similar to the general acceptance standard. If the field is occupied by those who uncritically accept the 'science' or technique, surveying their opinion will provide almost no information about the reliability of the evidence. The *Kumho Tire* Court itself stressed this danger: 'Nor . . . does the presence of *Daubert*'s general acceptance factor help show that an expert's testimony is reliable where the discipline itself lacks reliability.' In the same way, where the discipline lacks intellectual rigor, finding that an expert has applied the same intellectual rigor will not show that that testimony is reliable. Therefore, failing 'the same intellectual rigor' test should usually lead to exclusion, but passing that test should not lead to automatic admission. The courts must still determine whether the amount of rigor employed by the field is rigorous enough.

Is Social Science *Science*?

In principle, the character of social science does not differ substantially from the other sciences, such as forensic science, in regard to its 'scientific' status. Yet, in terms of complexity and difficulty in testing the phenomena of interest, social scientists might have a better excuse than other scientists for having little data to support their opinions (McCord, 1989). Moreover, despite the free use of the science label, the general perception is that social science is soft and non-threatening. With *Kumho Tire*, however, social scientists are expected to demonstrate the validity of the premises that lie behind their testimony. The question now for lower courts concerns how to carry out the gatekeeping duties in this difficult area (*United States* v. *Hall* (1996)).

Social science is, in principle, testable, though it is often advanced before any significant testing has been done. The social sciences differ from many other sciences, however, in two significant respects. The first might support treating it differently than traditional science (see, e.g. *Officer* v. *Teledyne Republic/Sprague* (1994)), while the second counsels against such a move. On the one hand, whereas much of the science that comes to court, such as the forensic sciences of fingerprinting and handwriting identification, are eminently testable, much social science that is legally relevant is very difficult to test. On the other hand, social science, more than most scientific evidence, is likely to convey normative considerations that are outside the jury's charge to decide.

Because social science's subject matter is the human animal, many hypotheses prove quite difficult to test. In particular, experiments on, and direct observations of, certain phenomena can be complicated, both by the complexity of the subject and, often, by ethical considerations. For instance, researchers studying the Battered Woman Syndrome cannot simply record the psychological manifestations of violence between family members without proffering assistance from mental health professionals or reporting the situation to the appropriate authorities. But these limitations on the social sciences should not change the essential legal analysis significantly. In every scientific field, from physics to psychology, there are hypotheses that defy direct observation or straightforward testing. Our inability to 'see' an electron, for example, does not foreclose a rigorous examination of its existence and nature. Similarly, our inability to lace drinking water with PCBs does not foreclose our examination of the effect of the chemical on human health. Our reluctance to blow up the universe does not foreclose our testing of the Big Bang theory of cosmology. Difficult and complex theories sometimes require more imaginative research designs. Certainly, the difficulty of studying certain social phenomena does not excuse sloppy research. One of the basic lessons of *Daubert* should not be lost: *Daubert* exhorts scientists to do good science and expects them to be scientists first and expert witnesses (and advocates) second (see, e.g. *Collier* v. *Bradley University* (2000)).

To the extent that social science is not tested, it contains the potential for a large advocacy component. To be sure, the forensic sciences, too, pose this danger, but they tend to be fairly blunt in specifically favoring the side paying the fees (typically the prosecution). The social science normative component is more complex. In a wide range of contexts, permitting social science expert testimony leads to the admission of information that the jury would not otherwise hear. There are numerous examples. In battered woman self-defense cases, admission of the Battered Woman Syndrome means the jury hears evidence of the abuse the woman endured before the fatal act. In Rape Trauma Syndrome cases, use by defendants can lead to character evidence of the alleged victim that is ordinarily protected by rape shield statutes. Moreover, it might be presented through an eloquent and highly experienced witness. In effect, this form of testimony appears to call upon the jury to nullify the law, either because the defendant is particularly sympathetic or the victim is not.

ADVERSARIAL OR INQUISITORIAL PROCESS?

Although judicial systems are labeled as 'adversarial' or 'inquisitorial', no system is purely one or the other. The most adversarial systems incorporate elements of the inquisitorial model, such as rules of evidence and privileges, that take the process out of the parties' hands. Similarly, the most inquisitorial systems incorporate elements of the adversarial model, such as representation by counsel and presentation of witnesses, that place the process into the parties' hands. Legal systems, therefore, are perhaps best characterized as having either adversarial or inquisitorial orientations, with processes borrowed from the other to correct perceived flaws in the basic model. In regard to expert evidence, the move toward a more inquisitorial style among legal systems previously adversarial in composition can be understood as movement along a spectrum rather than a change in the spectrum itself. Giving judges greater control over experts represents not so much a rejection of the adversarial process as a needed correction of one of its basic flaws. The adversarial process tends to distort the presentation of good science and promote the production of bad science. In somewhat similar ways, recent reforms in both England and the United States have sought to correct this defect in the adversarial process by adopting more inquisitorial processes for expert evidence.

INQUISITORIAL EXPERTISE: THE ENGLISH REFORMS

Unlike in the United States, in which expert evidence reform was largely piecemeal and initiated by the courts, England amended its expert practices as part of extensive reforms to its civil justice process (Slapper and Kelly, 1999). These reforms were considered necessary because of the high costs, extensive delays and great complexity of civil litigation. A core aspect of the pervasive reforms adopted was the greatly altered procedure for hearing expert evidence. The new rules were consciously directed at changing the very culture of the civil process, from one in which the adversarial ethic prevailed to one in which the court took control of key elements of the process. Lord Taylor, then Lord Chief Justice, summarized this change in his statement accompanying the new rules:

> The aim is to try and change the whole culture, the ethos, applying in the field of civil litigation. We have over the years been too ready to allow those who are litigating to dictate the pace at which cases proceed. Time is money, and wasted time in court means higher charges for litigants and for the taxpayer. It also means that everyone else in the queue has to wait longer for justice. (Slapper and Kelly, 1999, p. 211)

The English reforms were the product of a report prepared by Lord Woolf which extensively documented defects in the existing civil process and recommended wholesale changes in an effort to bring order and efficiency to dispute resolution. Basic to the proposed Woolf reforms were his recommendations for the reception of expert evidence. In short, in Chapter 23 of his report, he 'recommended that the calling of expert evidence should be under the complete control of the court' (Woolf, 1996, p. 137).

As was true with the other recommended reforms, the change in expert evidence practice was driven by the objective to make the civil process newly efficient, less costly, and more just. According to Lord Woolf, experts had increasingly become partisans, advocating for one side or the other, and failing to give the court neutral or sound expert advice. Indeed, expert evidence had become big business. Lord Woolf observed as follows:

> A large litigation support industry, generating a multi-million pound fee income, has grown up among professions such as accountants, architects and others, and new professions have developed such as accident reconstruction and care experts. This goes against all principles of proportionality and access to justice. In my view, its most damaging effect is that it has created an ethos of what is acceptable which has in turn filtered down to smaller cases. Many potential litigants do not even start litigation because of the advise they are given about cost, and in my view this is as great a social ill as the actual cost of pursuing litigation. (Woolf, 1996, p. 137)

In order to cure the excessively adversarial quality of expert evidence, Lord Woolf sought to correlate the expert's fidelity with the court itself rather than one of the parties. The expert would be non-aligned and his obligation would be to inform the court regarding scientific opinion. Especially in smaller cases, this would mean that only one expert would testify, thus cutting cost and time, and promoting a more accurate rendition of the state of the art of the expertise. The parties would participate in the selection of this neutral expert, and only if they could not agree on an individual expert would the court assume the task of appointing its own selection.

In cases justifying it, however, the parties might be permitted their own experts to buttress the court's expert, and, in any case, the parties would have the opportunity to cross-examine the neutral expert. Lord Woolf explained, 'The appointment of a neutral expert would not necessarily deprive the parties of the right to cross-examine, or even to call their own experts in addition to the neutral expert if that were justified by the scale of the case' (Woolf, 1996, p. 141). In this way, the reforms did not abolish all adversarial characteristics, they simply attempted to bridle them substantially. Still, ordinarily, only one expert would be needed, and even that one will not be called unless he would substantially assist the court.

The English reforms are directed at much the same objective as the *Daubert* reforms. The adversarial process is perceived as polarizing expert opinion, and turning experts into partisans at the expense of good science. One salutary result expected from the English reforms will be the narrowing of the issues genuinely in dispute. Even when the parties have their own experts, a neutral court expert will do much to keep the parties' experts from straying too widely from mainstream opinion and will help the court identify real differences among the experts. Empowering the court, and giving it the sophistication extant in the field of expertise, rather than the highly practiced versions of the adversarial process, will lead to a narrowing of the issues and a more efficient and valid fact finding process.

Much of the opposition to court experts comes from attorneys who have difficulty imagining a less-adversarial litigation process and who object to their loss of power over the proceedings. Lord Woolf observed that resistance to his proposals was strong, it being 'clear that the idea [of a single expert] is anathema to many members of the legal profession in this country who are reluctant to give up their adversarial weapons' (Woolf, 1996, p. 140). American attorneys are similarly loathe to give up their adversarial weapons. Nonetheless, though more reticent to openly embrace the inquisitorial system, courts in the United States are slowly inching toward a roughly similar approach to that articulated by Lord Woolf. American courts are using the tools at their disposal to increasingly take control of expert evidence by making the experts their own.

THE MOVE TOWARD THE INQUISITORIAL PROCESS IN AMERICA: COURT–APPOINTED EXPERTS

The most striking difference between judges' pre-*Daubert* job responsibilities and those post-*Daubert* is the greater sophistication in science expected from them. Not surprisingly, for judges with little background in the many technical subjects that enter the courtroom today, this new responsibility can be daunting. With increasing frequency, though still a relatively rare occurrence, courts are turning to independent court appointed experts for assistance. For the judge who wants to employ his own expert, two basic models are available to choose from. The first is the traditional one of appointing an independent expert under the rules of evidence who would assist the court—judge and jury—to fulfill its obligations. Under the Federal Rules, Rule 706 provides the blueprint by which this model is governed. A second model, and one that has emerged largely in response to *Daubert*, is the appointment of technical advisers. Unlike traditional court-appointed experts, who primarily assist the jury, technical advisers provide exclusive assistance to the judge. Although Rule 706 experts sometimes help judges make admissibility decisions, their principal role is to help triers of fact to understand the weight expert evidence should be given. Technical advisers, in contrast, serve the more limited function of helping judges decide admissibility. I begin with the more traditional court-appointed expert, and then examine the recent innovation of the appointment of a technical adviser.

Rule 706 Experts

Although rules of evidence have long provided for court-appointed experts, judges have been reluctant to embrace this option. However, the chorus of voices calling for judges to exercise Rule 706 has grown nearly deafening (Berger, 1994; Sanders, 1993). The impetus is obviously *Daubert*'s mandate to judges to act as gatekeepers to keep out invalid science and the concomitant concern that they will have difficulty accomplishing this task. This chorus has now been joined by an influential voice. Concurring in *Joiner*, Justice Breyer wrote specially to emphasize the availability of court appointed experts and other procedural devices that would assist courts to parse difficult scientific and technical subjects.

Justice Breyer wrote separately to underline the importance of the gatekeeping function and the necessity that judges develop an understanding of the methods of science. The gatekeeping requirement, he explained, 'will sometimes ask judges to make subtle and sophisticated determinations about scientific methodology and its relation to the conclusions an expert witness seeks to offer' (*Joiner*, 1997, p. 146). Recognizing that 'judges are not scientists', he asserted that, nonetheless, 'neither the difficulty of the task nor any comparative lack of expertise can excuse the judge from exercising the "gatekeeper" duties that the Federal Rules impose' (p. 146). Accordingly, he urged, to do the assigned task trial judges should be encouraged to seek assistance. He cited the *amicus* brief filed by the *New England Journal of Medicine* which called upon courts to employ non-affiliated experts to assist them when navigating the complex pathways of science:

> [A] judge could better fulfill this gatekeeper function if he or she had help from scientists. Judges should be strongly encouraged to make greater use of their inherent authority . . . to appoint experts. . . . Reputable experts could be recommended to courts by established scientific organizations, such as the National Academy of Sciences or the American Association for the Advancement of Science. (p. 149)

Justice Breyer noted that with the cooperative effort of the scientific community, the gatekeeping task of *Daubert* would 'not prove inordinately difficult to implement'

(p. 149). Faithful accomplishment of this function, Breyer concluded, would 'help secure the basic objectives of the Federal Rules of Evidence; which are ... the ascertainment of truth and the just determination of proceedings' (p. 149).

Researchers at the Federal Judicial Center conducted a survey of federal judges examining the use of court-appointed experts (Cecil and Wilging, 1994). In general, they found that judges relied little on this mechanism. Two factors, in particular, explain judges' failure to seek expert assistance. First, many judges view the appointment of experts as a highly unusual act, only to be done under extraordinary circumstances. Second, a significant number of judges expressed their belief that the adversarial process should be relied upon, and that court-appointed experts would take the matter away from the able hands of the parties.

The second factor leading judges not to seek expert assistance, the adversarial process, is not very compelling under close scrutiny. Two aspects of this complaint must be evaluated. First, Rule 706 experts often play a significant role assisting the judge in making the admissibility decision. On this matter, although the adversarial process remains part of the equation, the adversarial principle contains less force when the fact-finding is part of the gatekeeping responsibility. Judges regularly raise, research, and resolve legal matters *sua sponte*. The 'factfinding' judges do under Rule 104(a) resembles such legal issues, in that these facts are found by judges as a necessary prerequisite to the application of legal rules. Moreover, the task for court-appointed experts will often be to educate the judge on technical matters, so that the judge can make a better informed decision. In fact, over time, the use of court-appointed experts should decline as judges' sophistication with scientific methods increases. Second, even in their role as experts for the jury, Rule 706 experts do not entirely undermine the basic elements of the adversarial process. In most cases, the court-appointed expert will not displace parties' own experts, but will merely add an additional view to the jury's deliberations. Moreover, the court's expert will often pay dividends by helping move the parties to resolve issues not seriously disputed and allow them to concentrate on those that are. The court's expert is likely to influence the parties' experts' testimony, leading them to curtail more extreme statements and have them focus on the more important differences separating the sides.

Technical Advisers Appointed Under the Inherent Authority of the Court

Under *Daubert*, judges must determine whether the basis for proffered expert testimony is valid, or has evidentiary reliability. Under the *Frye* test, this determination depended mainly on the court's surveying a group of experts to find out what they thought about the subject. This task, at least the way most courts practiced it, required little knowledge of the scientific method. *Daubert* demands more. Yet most judges have had little advanced training in science and statistics, subjects central to carrying out their gatekeeping obligations. Therefore, judges have increasingly sought technical assistance to aid them in making the admissibility decision. In effect, technical advisers sit at judges' sides, like law clerks, helping them to maneuver through the labyrinth of scientific evidence.

District courts appoint technical advisers pursuant to their inherent authority under the rules of evidence. This authority is sometimes located in Rule 104(a). Unlike Rule 706 experts, technical advisers are not strictly subject to the adversarial process. They are not subject to cross-examination or the discovery process more generally. Depending on one's point of view, this is either the virtue or the vice of using technical advisers.

In *The Assoc. of Mexican-American Educators* v. *California* (2000), the Ninth Circuit considered the use of technical advisers for the first time. In the underlying case, plaintiffs were a class of Mexican-American, Asian-American and African-American educators who challenged the district court's ruling that the California Basic Education Skills Test (CBEST), which was given to teachers for continuing certification purposes, did not violate Titles VI or VII of the Civil Rights Act of 1964. In reaching this conclusion, the trial court was aided by a technical adviser who assisted it parse the difficult technical and statistical validation methods used by the State. The plaintiffs complained both about the appointment of the adviser and their inability to cross-examine him. The Ninth Circuit, however, dismissed these complaints, noting that 'Rule 706 applies to court-appointed *expert witnesses*, but not to technical advisers' (p. 591). Only if the court had called him to testify, or if he was a 'source of evidence', would he be subject to the provisions of Rule 706 and thus be subject to cross-examination. The court held, therefore, that '[i]n those rare cases in which outside technical expertise would be helpful to a district court, the court may appoint a technical advisor' (p. 590).

The role of a technical adviser is, to be sure, a delicate one. For a process based in fact, and even more so in romantic theory, on the adversarial process, the use of technical advisers might appear inconsonant. However, American courts regularly rely on law clerks for substantial assistance, and technical advisers could be seen as merely part-time, specially trained, law clerks. Of course, advisers must refrain from impermissibly influencing court decisions, and the parties should have ample opportunity to object on grounds of lack of neutrality or qualifications. Ultimately, of course, the decision regarding admissibility is the judge's. Technical advisers, like law clerks, can better enable a court to render an informed decision, but they cannot substitute their judgment for that of the court.

Court-appointed experts are no panacea. They will not free judges from making difficult decisions regarding scientific evidence. Also, scientists, though perhaps not identified with the parties to a matter, possess biases of their own. Inevitably, scientists are more or less conservative concerning their willingness to draw certain inferences or make certain conclusions based on the available data. While these biases cannot be avoided, court-appointed experts should make them explicit so that judges can take them into account to the extent possible in making their decisions.

CONCLUSION

Virtually all courts and commentators agree that some line must be drawn between the judge's responsibility to evaluate the admissibility of expert testimony and the jury's role to assess its weight. It would be radical, indeed, to suggest that the parties decide what evidence to bring to the jury. Thus, astrology, tea leaf reading and alchemy are considered obviously unfit for jury consideration. The issue, then, is relatively easy to define. What principle should determine when expert proof can be admitted and when it must be turned away? In *Daubert*, the United States Supreme Court articulated a validity test, which premises admissibility of expert opinion on the merit of the principles, methods and reasoning behind it. In England, Lord Woolf's reforms accomplish similar results by premising the admission of expert evidence on its power to educate the court, rather than its capacity to serve a party's interests. Both the *Daubert* standard and Lord Woolf's reforms premise the utility of expert evidence on its evidentiary reliability.

In effect, a test of evidentiary reliability is nothing more—or less—than utilization of the scientific method itself. Thomas Huxley said that science is nothing more than 'organized common sense'. Scientific common sense has come to the law. This fact, of course, hardly settles the many difficult debates over the admissibility of the wide assortment of experts and expertises courts see every day. Indeed, it has unsettled matters considerably. But this is a very good thing. The law's embrace of the scientific method, and its adoption in principle of the basic premises of the scientific revolution, were largely inevitable. In fact, it came very late in the day. Now the questions confronting courts are much more interesting, though admittedly of enormous complexity. Courts must now get down to the business of examining the many experts and the myriad of types of expertise before them. In time, they should find this task to be increasingly less daunting and more and more invigorating. They should also find that this task results in a more efficient and more just legal system.

REFERENCES

Berger, M.A. (1994). Novel forensic evidence: The need for court-appointed experts after Daubert. *Shepard's Expert and Scientific Evidence Quarterly*, *1*, 487.
Chesebro, K.J. (1994). Taking Daubert's 'focus' seriously: The methodology/conclusion distinction. *Cardozo Law Review*, *15*, 1745.
Cecil, J.S. and Wilging, T.E. (1994). Accepting Daubert's invitation: Defining a role for court-appointed experts in assessing scientific validity. *Emory Law Journal*, *43*, 995.
Faigman, D.L., Kaye, D.H., Saks, M.J. and Sanders, J. (eds) (2002). *Modern scientific evidence: The law and science of expert testimony* (2nd edn). St. Paul, MN: West Group.

Faigman, D.L. (2000). The law's scientific revolution: Reflections and ruminations on the law's use of experts in year seven of the revolution. *Washington and Lee Law Review, 57*, 661.

Faigman, D.L., Porter, E. and Saks, M.J. (1994). Check your crystal ball at the courthouse door, please: Exploring the past, understanding the present and worrying about the future of scientific evidence. *Cardozo Law Review, 15*, 1799.

Faigman, D.L. (1989). To have and have not: Assessing the value of social science to the law as science and policy. *Emory Law Journal, 38*, 1005.

Giannelli, P.C. (1994). Daubert: Interpreting the federal rules of evidence. *Cardozo Law Review, 15*, 1999.

Hamilton, H.G. (1998). Note, the movement from Frye to Daubert: Where do the states stand? *Jurimetrics, 38*, 201.

Horrobin, D. (1990). The philosophical basis of peer review and the suppression of innovation, *Journal of the American Medical Association, 263*, 1438.

Imwinkelried, E.J. (1991). The debate in the DNA cases over the foundation for the admission of scientific evidence: The importance of human error as a cause of forensic misanalysis. *Washington University Law Quarterly, 69*, 19.

McCord, D. (1989). Syndromes, profiles and other mental exotica: A new approach to the admissibility of nontraditional psychological evidence in criminal cases. *Oregon Law Review, 66*, 19.

Monahan, J. (2002). The scientific status of research on clinical and actuarial predictions of violence. In D.L. Faigman, D.H. Kaye, M.J. Saks and J. Sanders (eds), *Modern scientific evidence: The law and science of expert testimony* (2nd edn). St. Paul, MN: West Group.

Popper, K. (1983). Realism and the aim of science. [From the Postscript to the *Logic of scientific discovery.*]

Risinger, D.M. (2002). Taxonomy of expertise. In D.L. Faigman, D.H. Kaye, M.J. Saks and J. Sanders (eds), *Modern scientific evidence: The law and science of expert testimony* (2nd edn). St. Paul, MN: West Group.

Saks, M.J. (2000). The aftermath of Daubert: An evolving jurisprudence of expert testimony. *Jurimetrics, 40*, 229–241.

Sanders, J. (1993). From science to evidence: The testimony on causation in the Bendectin cases. *Stanford Law Review, 46*, 1.

Slapper, A. and Kelly, D. (1999). *The English legal system* (4th edn). London: Cavendish.

Taslitz, A. (1995). Daubert's guide to the federal rules of evidence: A not-so-plain-meaning jurisprudence. *Harvard Journal on Legislation, 32*, 3.

Wells, G. (2002). The scientific status of research on eyewitness identification. In D.L. Faigman, D.H. Kaye, M.J. Saks and J. Sanders (eds), *Modern scientific evidence: The law and science of expert testimony* (2nd edn). St. Paul, MN: West Group.

Woolf, Rt Hon. Lord (1996). *Access to Justice: Final Report.* London: HMSO.

Case Authority

Carmichael v. *Samyang Tire, Inc.*, 131 F.3d 1433 (11th Cir. 1997).

Cavallo v. *Star Enterprise*, 892 F. Supp. 756, 774 (E.D. Va. 1995), aff'd in part, rev'd in part, 100 F.3d 1150 (4th Cir. 1996).

Collier v. *Bradley University*, 113 F. Supp. 2d 1235 (C.D. Ill. 2000).

Daubert v. *Merrell Dow Pharmaceuticals, Inc.*, 579 US 563 (1993).

Frye v. *United States*, 293 F. 1013 (DC Cir. 1923).

Gates v. *The City of Memphis*, 210 F.3d 371, 2000 WL 377343 (6th Cir. April 6, 2000).

General Electric Co. v. *Joiner*, 522 US 136 (1997).

Kumho Tire, Ltd. v. *Carmichael*, 526 US 137 (1999).

Mancuso v. *Consolidated Edison Co. of New York*, 967 F. Supp. 1437 (SDNY 1997).

Polaino v. *Bayer Corp.*, 122 F.Supp. 63, 66 (D. Mass. 2000).

Poust v. *Hunleigh Healthcare*, 998 F.Supp. 478 (D. NJ 1998).

Seatrax v. *Sonbeck Int'l, Inc.*, 200 F.3d 358 (5th Cir. 2000).

The Assoc. of Mexican-American Educators v. *California*, 231 F.3d 572 (9th Cir. 2000).
TUF Racing Products, Inc. v. *American Suzuki Motor Corp.*, 223 F.3d 585 (7th Cir. 2000).
Turner v. *Iowa Fire Equipment Co.*, 229 F.3d 1202 (8th Cir. 2000).
United States v. *Barnette*, 211 F.3d 803, 815–16 (4th Cir. 2000).
United States v. *Hall*, 93 F.3d 1337 (7th Cir. 1996).
United States v. *Kwong*, 69 F.3d 663 (2d Cir. 1995).
United States v. *Smithers*, 212 F.3d 306 (6th Cir. 2000).
United States v. *Starzecpyzel*, 880 F.Supp. 1027 (SDNY 1995).

Chapter 3.5

Decision Making by Juries and Judges: International Perspectives

Edith Greene
University of Colorado, USA
and
Lawrence Wrightsman
University of Kansas, USA

The vast bulk of research on decision making by juries and judges has been conducted in the United States and has focused on American procedures and traditions.[1] Several recent reviews, including those of Ellsworth and Mauro (1998), Greene and her co-authors (2002), and Nietzel, McCarthy and Kerr (1999) have examined the literature on jury decision making. Wrightsman (1999) provided a review and analysis of the literature on judicial decision making. It is not our intention to re-review that work here. Rather, in the first part of this chapter, we step off American soil and offer a cross-cultural perspective on the role and workings of the jury systems in various countries. In so doing, we borrow heavily from a recent issue of *Law and Contemporary Problems* that offered a comparative panorama of the contemporary jury systems of Australia, Canada, England and Wales, Ireland, New Zealand, Scotland, Spain, Russia, and the United States (Vidmar, 1999a). Because the civil jury has all but disappeared in most jurisdictions, we focus exclusively on the criminal jury systems of these countries and describe various controversies, a few empirical findings, and several suggestions for future research. In the second part of the chapter, we return to the United States and describe what American researchers have discerned regarding decision making

---

[1] The multiple, converging reasons for this situation are detailed in the chapter. In general, the absence of stringent contempt laws in the United States (and their presence in other countries) has allowed for more open discourse and analysis of how juries operate. And, although judicial decision making is historically hidden from view, American scholars have become increasingly interested in understanding how judges make decisions.

Handbook of Psychology in Legal Contexts, Second Edition
Edited by D. Carson and R. Bull. © 2003 John Wiley & Sons, Ltd.

by judges. Unfortunately, we have little insight into the judgment processes of judges in other countries.

JURY DECISION-MAKING

It goes without saying that enormous contextual differences exist among countries that underlie distinctions in the rationale for trial by jury, the manner in which trials are conducted, and the role of the jury in resolving disputes. Indeed, no jury system can be understood or analyzed devoid of its historical, cultural, and political context and origins. Beyond this acknowledgment, we will have little to say about the political or cultural underpinnings of the jury systems that we describe. Rather, we take a more practical, present-minded perspective and analyze how various jury-related issues (e.g. jury selection, the effects of publicity, jurors' use of evidence, the influence of the judge, and verdict determinations) are managed in different countries and how jurors' judgments and juries' decisions are (or may be) influenced by these choices.

To complement this practical, issue-oriented focus, we describe the results of recent research studies on several of these topics, primarily as they apply to American juries. Where possible, we include the work of non-American researchers as well, although less work has been conducted on juries outside of the US because many countries make it a crime to publish or to solicit for publication any information about what happens behind the closed doors of a jury deliberation room (Lloyd-Bostock, 1995).

As a preliminary step toward increased scientific scrutiny of the jury, we offer a variety of suggestions for future research. Because little is known about the workings of the jury in many countries, numerous questions present themselves. Do laws permitting simple majority verdicts (as exist in Scotland) effectively silence the voices of jurors in the minority faction? Do judges' summations of the evidence (as occur in Canada, Australia, and England) have inordinate influence on jurors' sentiments about the case? What use do English jurors make of knowledge that the defendant refused to answer questions asked by the police? Can lay jurors in Canada effectively gauge bias and predisposition in fellow jurors? Although we are not sanguine that answers to these questions will be soon forthcoming, we perceive slowly increasing curiosity about the workings of the jury system in many countries (witness the collection of articles in *Law and Contemporary Problems*), fostered in no small part by enhanced *public* scrutiny of the institution. But regardless of its source, we hope that this interest will spawn a surge in jury-related research conducted on non-American soil. We anticipate its findings.

Jury Selection

Although significant variation in *voir dire* procedures exist within the United States, the practice of selecting juries is more liberal in the US than in other countries. Most American judges allow attorneys to question prospective jurors and many courts grant attorneys considerable leeway to begin to argue their case during the *voir dire* process.

In complex cases and in highly sensitive cases (e.g. involving matters such as domestic violence or child abuse), judges may allow the use of lengthy written questionnaires that serve to supplement in-court questioning and that may probe the prospective jurors' personal experiences and beliefs. At the conclusion of questioning, attorneys for each side may strike an unlimited number of prospective jurors for cause and varying numbers without cause (so-called peremptory challenges). Although some commentators have called for the elimination of peremptory challenges—arguing that they taint the selection process, lead to invidious discrimination against some potential jurors, waste time, and contribute to the public's cynicism regarding jury service (Hoffman, 1997)—a long history of litigant autonomy in the US suggests that peremptory challenges will not soon disappear (King, 1999).

One wonders about the effectiveness of peremptory challenges: Do they enable attorneys to identify prospective jurors who may be biased against their clients? The data are mixed. Olczak, Kaplan and Penrod (1991) asked lawyers to play the role of defense attorneys in a criminal case and, armed with demographic information about 36 prospective jurors, indicate 12 jurors they deemed acceptable and 12 whom they would exclude. The attorneys were more likely to make incorrect decisions (i.e. reject jurors who acquitted the defendant and accept jurors who convicted the defendant) than correct decisions. But analysis of *voir dire* in four felony cases indicated that attorneys excuse those jurors who are most biased against their side (Johnson and Haney, 1994). (Interestingly, though, jurors who survived *voir dire* did not differ from a randomly chosen group of 12 jurors on measures of legal authoritarianism [Johnson and Haney, 1994].)

In contrast to these relatively lengthy procedures in which attorneys are granted considerable freedom to sculpt a jury in their favor, jury selection procedures in other countries are restricted in a variety of ways. For example, Scottish courts have nothing comparable to the *voir dire* procedure and peremptory challenges were abolished completely in 1995 (Duff, 1999). Three rationales accompanied their elimination: that peremptory challenges effectively allowed defendants to 'stack the deck' with jurors who were unlikely to convict, that the practice puzzled, embarrassed, and angered conscientious citizens, and that it inconvenienced the public (Duff, 1999).

In some countries (e.g. Ireland, New Zealand), peremptory challenges are allowed but no provision is made to question prospective jurors during *voir dire*. Thus, the parties must exercise peremptory challenges on the basis of superficial characteristics of prospective jurors such as age and perceived socio-economic status. The extent to which these practices invite decisions based on gender, race, or ethnicity, and the extent to which stereotypes and unfounded assumptions operate, are questions that have gone largely unexamined.

Although English prosecutors are allowed unlimited opportunities to 'stand a juror by' (effectively removing him or her without showing cause), defendants in England have no right to peremptorily challenge a prospective juror. After a juror is stood by, he or she returns to the jury pool and, in theory, may be called again if the pool is exhausted.

Although the government argues that this right is used sparingly, and an appeal court ruled in 1989 that race should not be taken into account in selecting jurors, a serious consequence of the imbalance in jury challenges is the loss of a means to ensure a representative, racially-mixed jury (Lloyd-Bostock and Thomas, 1999). This concern is especially prevalent in cases with racial overtones or in which the defendant is a member of an ethnic or racial minority. Indeed, a system of jury selection—such as the English procedure—that grants vastly disparate opportunities for excusing jurors to the two sides may have an array of anticipated and unexpected consequences that cry out for empirical scrutiny. How representative of their communities are juries that are eventually chosen to try a case? How often are minority jurors asked to stand by? What role does their race or ethnicity play in this decision? Does the resulting racial and ethnic composition of the jury affect the thoroughness of its deliberation? The satisfaction of its members? The predictability of its verdict? Legal commentators in the US have given considerable thought to the issue of racially discriminatory peremptory challenges and to their alternatives (e.g. King, 1994; Ogletree, 1994).

Setting aside the race issue, because many Commonwealth courts make no attempt to understand the attitudes and beliefs of prospective jurors who are selected for trial, certain jurors may be prejudiced against the defendant (or against the government, for that matter), before hearing any of the evidence (Jackson, 1995). Although the American system may be inefficient and fraught with other shortcomings, the pretrial *voir dire* screening can more effectively determine whether a prospective juror is fit to decide the case.

The Canadian method of selecting jurors differs from others in important, practical ways that are also amenable to scientific analysis. In Canada, the impartiality of jurors is deemed a question of fact, not a question of law. Therefore, the decision about whether a juror can be impartial is made by two lay 'triers' selected from the pool of potential jurors, rather than by the judge. At the commencement of *voir dire*, lay triers selected at random from the jury pool listen to a prospective juror's answers to the questions posed and render a verdict on whether that prospective juror is 'impartial between the Queen and the accused'. After the first two jurors are selected, they assume the role of triers and determine the impartiality of juror number three. This rotation occurs until 12 jurors are seated.

There are obvious advantages and disadvantages to this system, as compared to systems in which the judge is actively involved in determining partiality. Canadian jurors undoubtedly have more involvement in the process as the task of assessing impartiality in themselves and others becomes especially salient. The Canadian system obviates concerns about judicial favoritism because the judge has no input in which prospective jurors are dismissed for cause. On the other hand, the triers themselves may be less than neutral with respect to judging partiality and worse, may not be cognizant of their own biases and shortcomings (Greene et al., 2002).

Empirical comparisons of these starkly contrasting methods of selecting jurors might reasonably ask several questions: whether one system is more effective than others at identifying and eliminating biased jurors, whether involvement of potential jurors in the *voir dire* process increases awareness of one's own biases and preconceptions, whether such involvement enhances jurors' perceptions of control and satisfaction with the process (and ultimately, of the outcome), or whether the system makes demands of laypeople that they feel inadequate to meet (Greene et al., 2002).

Publicity and Juries

Many cases tried in the United States pit one constitutional protection (e.g. freedom of the press guaranteed by the First Amendment to the Constitution) against another (e.g. the right to an impartial jury trial guaranteed by the Sixth Amendment). Because the media are not prohibited from disseminating information about the defendant or the crime before, during, or after the trial,

> [a] defendant's inadmissible confession or prior record, the details of the victim's loss, legal pundits' speculation about the trial and sentence, reports of rulings made outside the hearing of the jury, and other inadmissible information may be freely broadcast into the homes and delivered to the doorstep of every juror and potential juror prior to and during the trial. (King, 1999, p. 62)

In cases with extensive media coverage before or during trial, the concern arises that jurors will be prejudiced by exposure to this trial-related information. Indeed, a recent meta-analysis of the effects of pretrial publicity found that across 44 studies, mock jurors who were exposed to negative pretrial publicity were more likely to judge the defendant guilty than were jurors exposed to less or to no negative publicity (Steblay et al., 1999). The analysis also showed that pretrial publicity effects were strongest when multiple points of information about the crime and defendant were publicized, when the pretrial publicity was real as opposed to fabricated, and when the delay between exposure to the pretrial information and jurors' judgments exceeded one week. Interestingly, these are the features that most commonly occur in an actual case. The findings raise concerns about the likelihood that pretrial publicity will prejudice jurors and about how to combat the harmful effects of the pretrial information.

In the US, attempts to control the influence of the media are primarily retroactive. Jury selection is expected to screen out prospective members who have been unalterably tainted by exposure to publicity. Thus, judges rely (perhaps naively) on jurors' promises of fairness and impartiality despite their pretrial knowledge about the case (Moran and Cutler, 1991), and further presume that jurors will refrain from attending to publicity about the case during the trial. In both the US and England, judges typically rely on their 'common sense' to assess the effects of any potentially prejudicial pretrial knowledge (Studebaker and Penrod, 1997; Corker and Levi, 1996). Only rarely will a judge grant a request for a change of venue to a different location. One prominent example—the change of venue in the Oklahoma City bombing trial—has been described by psychologists involved in analysis of the publicity and motion for changing venue (Studebaker and Penrod, 1997).

Other jurisdictions avoid this dilemma by restricting the opportunity of the press to publicize details of ongoing, or even of completed trials. For example, the press in England and Ireland is frequently barred from, and occasionally prosecuted for, publishing prejudicial material before, during, and after a trial (Lloyd-Bostock and Thomas, 1999; Jackson, Quinn and O'Malley, 1999). In Australia, the media may be fined for publishing material which is later found to have prejudiced the fairness of a trial (Chesterman, 1999). Notably, however, courts assume that jurors will critically judge what they see, read, and hear and that they will attempt to focus on the evidence presented in the courtroom rather than information conveyed by the media. Whether this is a reasonable assumption is, of course, an empirical question. In fact, relatively little is known about the effects of exposure to media coverage or of judges' directives to disregard such extralegal information on juries outside of North America. Do these limitations on press coverage of trial-related information effectively render prospective jurors free from pretrial taint? Do they adequately limit jurors' access to information during the course of the trial? Equally important—are there negative ramifications (e.g. less thorough public scrutiny of the courts, decreased confidence in the judiciary, less public awareness about trial procedures and outcomes) to muzzling the media?

Despite their relatively tight regulations on press coverage, European courts have recently acknowledged that some jurors may be prejudiced by pretrial publicity. On occasion, English and Irish judges have halted proceedings or overturned convictions in part because pretrial publicity made or would have made a fair trial impossible (Lloyd-Bostock and Thomas, 1999; Jackson et al., 1999).

Results of a recent survey of 312 New Zealand jurors in 48 trials suggests that media coverage of pretrial information may not be especially problematic, however (Lane, 1999). The study, conducted by Professor Warren Young from Victoria University in Wellington, showed that any lingering effects of sketchy or slanted pretrial media reports were essentially overwhelmed by the evidence actually presented in court.

The Role of Evidence

Hearsay Evidence

Obviously, rules of evidence differ among jurisdictions but all effectively function to control the amount and kind of evidence that can be introduced in court. In American courts, for example, hearsay evidence is not admissible at trial; a witness cannot simply repeat another person's out-of-court statements. An exception to this general rule (and there are many) is made in cases where children are victims. Here, adults to whom the child has disclosed, may speak for that child in court.

What effects do children's out-of-court statements, presented either as hearsay evidence by another person or directly by the child, have on jurors' perceptions of that witness's credibility? This question was addressed by John Myers et al. (1999)—Myers, Redlich, Goodman, Prizmich and Imwinkelried—in a questionnaire study of 248 American jurors (representing 42 juries), all of whom had just served as jurors in child molestation or child exploitation trials. At least one child testified live in court in each of these trials, as did at least one adult who testified about the child's out-of-court disclosure of abuse. Thus, the study allowed for a direct comparison of perceptions of the child witness and the adult-hearsay witness.

Jurors perceived adult-hearsay witnesses as *more* accurate, consistent, and confident than child witnesses. In addition, adult-hearsay witnesses' testimony was judged to be more complete and less likely to have been influenced by the attorneys' questions. One explanation of this finding is that jurors tend not to believe child witnesses who testify about their abuse experiences, favoring instead the testimony of adults to whom the children spoke. Another explanation is that many of the adults were police officers and teachers who may have been afforded more credibility because of their professional status.

Expert Evidence

Evidence from expert witnesses also plays a significant role in US courts. One study of the use of experts in courts in three American cities suggests that this kind of evidence is introduced in 60% of all criminal trials (Shuman and Champagne, 1997). That figure is undoubtedly higher in complex, civil cases.

Expert evidence, particularly related to psychological and psychiatric issues, plays a less prominent role in English courts (Lloyd-Bostock and Thomas, 1999) where, for example, jurors are assumed to have common knowledge of the vagaries of eyewitness testimony. As a result, expert testimony on this issue is not admitted (Gudjonsson, 1996). Suggested Lord Justice Lawton: 'jurors do not need psychiatrists to tell them how ordinary folk who are not suffering from any mental illness are likely to react to the stresses and strains of life' (quoted by Lloyd-Bostock and Thomas).

Empirical research on the effects of expert testimony on eyewitness reliability is relevant here. Can jurors, in fact, be aided by the testimony of an expert on eyewitness identification? Or will the expert render them overly skeptical of eyewitnesses? Cutler, Penrod and Dexter (1989) showed mock jurors a realistic videotaped trial that focused on the accuracy of an eyewitness's identification of an armed robbery defendant. Some participants heard an expert testify about the effects of identification conditions on accuracy, others did not. In addition, some mock jurors heard evidence that the witnessing and identification conditions were good, and others heard that they were bad. Analysis of the verdicts and mock jurors' post-trial sentiments indicated that jurors who were exposed to the expert testimony more carefully evaluated the role of various factors (e.g. weapon focus, line-up procedures) on eyewitness reliability than did jurors who had no such testimony. Those who heard an expert also gave less weight to the expressed confidence of eyewitnesses (a desirable finding in light of evidence that witness confidence and witness accuracy are only weakly related). These findings suggest that the effect of expert testimony was to generally sensitize jurors to the importance of witnessing and identification conditions rather than to make jurors skeptical of the eyewitness.

Prior Record Evidence

The Fifth Amendment to the Constitution guarantees American defendants the right not to 'be compelled in any criminal case to be a witness against himself'. Relying on this constitutional protection, defendants often 'plead the fifth' and opt not to talk to the police or to testify at trial. Any statement obtained in violation of the Fifth Amendment is inadmissible in American courts and jurors are instructed not to draw any inferences from the defendant's refusal to testify on his own behalf.

By contrast, recently-enacted English laws allow juries to be told that a defendant refused to answer questions posed by the police and to be instructed that they may draw inferences (presumably negative) if the defendant opts not to testify in his defense. The practical effects of this knowledge and instruction on jurors' decision-making have not yet been evaluated (Lloyd-Bostock and Thomas, 1999).

Evidence of a defendant's prior record is excluded in most jurisdictions for fear that jurors would be prejudiced by it and judge the current offense in light of past misdeeds. The exclusion of prior record evidence has recently caused much consternation in England, particularly in cases of child abuse (Lloyd-Bostock and Thomas, 1999), where this approach is believed to favor the defense. But empirical work conducted for the Law Commission shows that mock jurors' ratings of the likelihood that a defendant committed the presently charged offense were affected by evidence of a conviction for a similar offense. Evidence that the defendant had previously been convicted of an indecent assault on a child was particularly prejudicial (Law Commission, 1995).

Why does evidence of a prior conviction increase the likelihood of conviction on a subsequent charge? For some jurors, the prior record, in combination with allegations related to the subsequent charge, may show a pattern of criminality; together they point to an individual who is prone to act in an illegal or felonious manner (Greene and Loftus, 1985). Other jurors, upon hearing evidence of a prior conviction, may need less evidence to be convinced of the defendant's guilt beyond a reasonable doubt on the subsequent charge (Wissler and Saks, 1985).

On rare occasions, a jury may hear evidence not of a prior *conviction*, but of a prior *acquittal* (i.e. the defendant was previously tried and found not guilty of charges unrelated to the present case). The US Supreme Court has held that the admission of prior acquittal evidence does *not* unfairly prejudice the defendant (*Dowling* v. *US*, 1990). To test this notion, Greene and Dodge (1995) presented a summary of the facts in the *Dowling* case to three groups of mock jurors who were deciding whether the defendant should be found guilty of armed robbery. One third of the jurors learned that the defendant had been previously tried and *convicted* of charges stemming from a home break-in. Another third was informed that the defendant had been *acquitted* of the home break-in charges and the final group had no information about the defendant's prior record. The results supported the Supreme Court's reasoning: jurors who heard evidence of a prior acquittal were no more likely to convict the defendant than were jurors who had no information about a prior record and both groups were less likely to convict than jurors who had evidence of a prior conviction. These findings suggest that jurors may exercise some restraint in their use of prior acquittal evidence and may indeed not be prejudiced by it.

Influence of the Judge

The criminal jury was reintroduced in Russia in 1993. One of the key provisions of the 1993 Russian Jury Law was to strip judges of their inquisitorial duty to dominate the questioning of defendants and witnesses. Nonetheless, Russian judges are still allowed to intervene with questions after the parties have finished their questioning and judges have apparently maintained a dominant, inquisitorial stance (Thaman, 1999). One wonders what impact this active intervention on the part of judges will have on Russian jurors. No data yet address this issue.

Trial judges play an active role in other countries, as well. In Canada, for example, the judge has limited discretion to call witnesses who were not summoned by either side if he or she deems it necessary (Vidmar, 1999b). More importantly, Canadian judges (as well as their Australian and English counterparts) are obliged to review the case for the jury and are entitled to present their opinions about the strength of various pieces of evidence and about the credibility of various witnesses. The judge is also required to raise any questions about the evidence that favor the defendant, even if they were not brought up by the defense attorney. In England, the judge's summing up may last up to several hours (Lloyd-Bostock and Thomas, 1999). These practices are decidedly different from American trial procedures in which the judge rules on evidentiary issues and instructs the jury on the law, but leaves interpretation of the evidence in the hands of the jury. (In fact, when American juries pose a question to the judge during their deliberations, the judge is typically reluctant to provide assistance and usually refers jurors back to the evidence without comment.)

Although judges must make it clear that jurors are not bound by judicial summation and evaluation (and Australian jurors are instructed to ignore the judge's views if they differ from their own conclusions), one wonders whether a layperson can maintain his or her personal interpretation of the facts in light of a learned judge's appraisal of the evidence. To what extent is jurors' decision-making influenced by the judge's comments? To what extent does the summation assume an aura of legal and factual correctness? To what extent are the deliberations guided by jurors' impressions of the judge's reasoning and opinions?

Some answers come from a 1993 study of 800 cases conducted for the English Crown Court (Zander and Henderson, 1993). Nineteen percent of jurors surveyed in these cases said that they would have had a more difficult task had the judge not summarized the evidence for them. The longer the trial, the more likely they were to find the judges' summations useful. One-third said that the summations were tilted in favor of one side or the other (approximately equally often in each direction).

Were jurors swayed by the judges' hints? Data on this issue are somewhat fuzzy. Although the judges' biases in summing up were closely associated with the results of most cases, jurors' verdicts occasionally did not agree with the judges' apparent inclinations. So, for example, 9% of jurors who believed that the judge favored conviction reported that their jury opted to acquit. Of jurors who perceived a *mild* bias in favor of conviction, 13% decided to acquit. These data suggest that at least some juries are able to resist the influence of the judge's perceptions if those perceptions are counter to their own. However, some juries went against their personal beliefs and convicted or acquitted because the judge favored that particular verdict.

Some recent work in Italy also suggests that judges can have persuasive power over laypeople. In the Italian system, juries are composed of three lay 'judges' and two expert 'judges'. In an examination of the influence of group discussion on individual judgments, 30 mock juries were composed in this manner (i.e. three lay judges and two experts). They viewed the videotape of an alleged rape victim reporting the crime and an interview with the defendant, and were asked to reach a verdict about the defendant's guilt. Participants changed their opinions after deliberation but expert 'judges' were more influential over lay 'judges' than vice versa (Baldy and Manetti, 1999).

Jury Verdicts

Three interesting issues arise in the context of verdict requirements: (1) the availability of various verdict options, (2) the requirement of unanimity, and (3) the confidentiality of the deliberative process after the verdict has been reached. Juries in different countries operate under decidedly different rules on these issues (as do different States in the US, at least in terms of unanimity) thus making for intriguing cross-cultural comparisons.

Neither Russian nor Spanish jury systems subscribe to the Anglo-American verdict options of 'guilty' and 'not guilty'. Rather, like some civil juries in the US that answer 'special verdict' forms, Russian and Spanish juries are presented with a series of discrete questions or propositions about the evidence (Thaman, 1999). Spanish judges prepare a list of propositions at the end of trial, some favorable to the defendant and others favorable to the prosecution. Jurors must decide whether these propositions were proven or not proven during the trial. The jury is also asked to affirm or deny proof of the defendant's guilt, but even if jurors believe that guilt has been proven, they may recommend that the government grant complete or partial amnesty to the defendant.

In the Russian system, jurors answer three questions: (1) whether the substance of the crime has been proven, (2) whether the defendant's identity as the perpetrator has been proven, and (3) whether the defendant is guilty of having committed the crime. These detailed special verdict forms are in place to allow the trial and appellate judges to understand the jury's reasoning processes—certainly a feature of the inquisitorial system in which the judge wields considerable power.

The Scottish jury is offered three verdict options: guilty, not guilty, and not proven (Duff, 1999). Although the intermediate, 'not proven' option counts as an acquittal, it does not function as a positive declaration of innocence. Rather, it conveys the notion that the defendant's guilt has not been conclusively demonstrated. (In the US and many other countries, inconclusive proof of guilt in conjunction with the presumption of innocence would result in outright acquittal.) Scottish juries frequently select this verdict option, as we suspect would be true in many other jurisdictions if juries were given that option. (One wonders whether the 'not proven' verdict option would draw from cases that under a two-verdict system resulted in convictions or from cases that ended in acquittals.) Yet one feature of Scottish law—the requirement that the prosecution's case be corroborated[2]—may make it an especially attractive alternative in this locale. A Scottish Office study showed that the not proven verdict option comprised a slightly higher proportion of acquittals in rape and sexual assault cases, where there is typically only one victim, than in other cases where there are likely to be multiple witnesses or victims (Scottish Office, 1994).

Duff (1999) suggests that the not proven option is sometimes used when the jury is convinced that the accused is guilty but wishes to extend mercy to that particular defendant. In so doing, the jury effectively nullifies the law (Duff, 1999). Evidence of this possibility is purely anecdotal, however; real data are lacking.

On the issue of decision rule (unanimity v. majority), requirements differ considerably among different jury systems. Although non-unanimous verdicts comply with US constitutional interpretation (King, 1999), only two States—Louisiana and Oregon—currently allow non-unanimous verdicts.[3] The situation in Australia is similarly inconsistent: unanimity is required in three jurisdictions (New South Wales, Queensland, and the Australian Capital Territory) but not in five others (Chesterman, 1999). In England and Ireland, a 10–2 majority is required (Lloyd-Bostock and Thomas, 1999) while a mere 8–7 majority will suffice for conviction in Scotland (Duff, 1999).

In response to US Supreme Court rulings of the early 1970s that non-unanimous decisions passed constitutional muster (*Apodaca et al.* v. *Oregon*, 1972; *Johnson* v. *Louisiana*, 1972), psycholegal researchers busily addressed the issue to examine how the decision rule affects the deliberation process. These studies revealed a number of important differences in the nature and quality of the deliberation process as a function of decision rule (unanimity v. majority). For example, juries assigned to a

---

[2] In Scotland, the prosecution's case cannot stand unless there is testimony to corroborate that of the complaining witness, even if that witness is highly believable.

[3] Because of concerns about the increasing incidence of hung juries, the prospect of majority verdicts has recently been discussed in other states, however.

majority rule discuss both the evidence and the law less thoroughly and spend less time deliberating than do juries assigned to a unanimous rule (Hastie, Penrod and Pennington, 1983). Members of minority factions under majority rule are less likely to express themselves and, perhaps as a result, are less satisfied with the result (Hastie et al., 1983). More recent research with Spanish mock juries has shown that half of the groups that operated under a majority rule nonetheless continued their discussion until all individuals agreed with the verdict (Velasco, 1995).

The Scottish requirement of a mere one-vote margin for conviction poses special concerns about the quality of deliberations. Although this system obviates the threat of a hung jury, one wonders about the thoroughness of evidence evaluation, attentiveness to the judge's instructions, and quality of debate when a bare majority is all that is needed to convict. Empirical analysis of this issue is sorely needed.

There are notable differences across legal systems in whether the content of the jury deliberations can be made public. In some Commonwealth jurisdictions (e.g. England, Scotland, New Zealand, and parts of Australia), verdicts are strictly confidential and jurors swear not to reveal the content of their deliberations. In several of these countries, anyone who obtains, discloses, or solicits information about the particulars of the jury deliberations can be held in contempt of court. Although the veil of secrecy that surrounds jury deliberations was meant to enhance faith in the system, it may have the counter result of actually undermining confidence in the institution of the jury (Jackson and Doran, 1997). By contrast, Spanish jurors *must* justify their verdicts publicly. The US adopts an intermediate stance in which jurors are permitted to speak with the media if they desire, but they are not required to present their conclusions or to describe their decision-making processes to the court or to other authorities.

Some of the secrecy surrounding juries in New Zealand has begun to abate recently, as the New Zealand Law Commission has undertaken a study that involves interviewing jurors in 50 trials about the content of their deliberations, among other things (Cameron, Potter and Young, 1999). The Commission is apparently responding to concerns that jurors have difficulty understanding technical or complex evidence, that some jurors excessively dominate the deliberative process, and that jurors with minority opinions are intimidated by those in the majority. The report will apparently serve as a springboard for possible reforms to the jury system in New Zealand.

The most stringent disclosure requirements may be those of Spain: juries in Spain must give the rationale for their verdict, indicate the evidence upon which their verdict was based, and give the reasons why various propositions were either proven or not proven (Thaman, 1999). Apparently, though, many juries provide only stock answers or give minimalist responses like 'witnesses'. Still, these requirements raise provocative questions about whether Spanish juries are truly free to evaluate the evidence and make decisions that seem appropriate to them, and to what extent the specter of judicial oversight influences their deliberative process. (Indeed, Spanish judges must review the jury's verdict for defects before making it public and may request the jury to make any necessary changes.) Does the concern about subsequent publicity of the jury's deliberations impede candid discussion among jurors? Does it discourage jurors from reaching unpopular verdicts (Cameron et al., 1999)? And, in turn, does it decrease the public's willingness to serve as jurors in the first place? These questions beg for answers.

JUDICIAL DECISION-MAKING

Decision making by judges is, in some respects, similar to decision making by juries, but in many respects it is not. Judges, of course, have a wider set of responsibilities in the legal system than do juries, and some of their important decisions go beyond the fact-finding tasks of juries. Yet judges—like jurors—are human beings, despite the image sought through the donning of the priestly robe, and some of the models of judicial decision-making reflect the place of human bias.

Judges' Verdicts versus Jury Verdicts

In comparing the two, we first ask: How similar are their verdicts? Given the same information, would judges presiding at a trial render the same decision that juries, given this responsibility, make? There is an empirical answer to this question, and it is reassuring although it is flawed.

More than fifty years ago, a law professor and a statistician/sociology professor at the University of Chicago, Harry Kalven, Jr, and Hans Zeisel, began a series of studies of the jury system in the United States. One of their challenging tasks was to answer the above question. Each trial judge in the United States (whether a state or federal judge) was sent a questionnaire by mail. The judge was asked to select a recent jury trial over which he or she had presided, and to respond to a number of questions, including the judge's hypothetical verdict as well as the jury's actual verdict. The first wave of questionnaires was distributed in 1954 and 1955; somewhat more structured questionnaires were sent to judges in 1958. A total of 555 judges responded; some judges described only one trial, but others provided a large number. The result was a database of 3576 criminal trials, clearly an impressive number but by no means a random sample of all such trials.

In these criminal trials, the judge's hypothetical verdict agreed with the jury's actual verdict in approximately 75% of the cases (the actual percentage depends on whether one includes the 5 to 6% of trials in which the jury had a hung verdict). When the two disagreed, the jury more often voted for acquittal and the judge more often voted for conviction. (In 19% of the trials the jurors voted not guilty when the judge would have convicted, while in only 3% of the cases was the outcome the opposite.) A similar level of agreement, 78%, was obtained in civil trials; both the jury and the judge ruled in favor of the plaintiff about 58% of the time (Kalven and Zeisel, 1966).

These findings are sometimes interpreted as supporting a conclusion that the jury system in the United States 'works', that juries agree with judges' verdicts to a significant and hence satisfactory degree. Perhaps implicit in such a conclusion is the treatment of the judge's verdict as a criterion, as the correct decision. But such an assumption is too simplistic; first of all, judges possess certain information about the case that jurors may not have; for example, in the United States if a criminal defendant does not testify, the jury will not know whether he or she has a criminal record. Judges have defendants' past records in their files, and Kalven and Zeisel's study was not able to control how many individual judges used such information in determining their hypothetical verdicts.

A second source of uncontrolled variation was the reason or reasons for selecting particular trials by the judge. Did the judge include a particular trial in the survey because the jury's verdict was consistent with the judge's? Or because it was inconsistent? Or simply because it was a recent case? Certainly, different judges had different motivations, but this aspect of the procedure makes interpretation of the results more problematic.

Regardless, Kalven and Zeisel chose to focus on some of the possible reasons that jury verdicts sometimes differed from the judges' hypothetical verdicts. Under a category that they called 'jury sentiments' (which accounted for at least half of the disagreements), they included acquittals by juries based on their feeling that the case was too trivial for formal review, plus acquittals based on a belief that the defendant had already suffered enough, as well as other non-evidentiary reactions to the defendant, the prosecution, and the legal system. In contrast, judges' verdicts were seen as sticking closer to the law and the weight of the evidence. However, they noted that such 'sentiments' were more likely to occur when, according to the judge, the evidence in the case was close and capable of supporting either verdict. Thus they proposed a 'liberation hypothesis,' arguing that the closeness of the evidence freed the jurors to give weight to their own feelings of justice (Kalven and Zeisel, 1966).

The difference in the determinations of verdicts by judges and by juries reflects the expert-novice distinction that achieved some visibility in experimental psychology in the 1980s (Chi, Glaser and Farr, 1988). Experts are better able to discern the 'big picture' and meaningful patterns in their areas of expertise, they can process information faster than can novices, and they see deeper implications of the material in their domain. But a faster processing of information does not necessarily mean a more valid one, and the advantage of the expertise of the judge must be balanced against the motivation to do a good job present in most juries. This is especially true when one considers that judgments of credibility of witnesses are central to the fact-finding in many criminal trials, and judicial 'expertise' is probably not a contributor to accuracy in this regard.

Trial Judges as Decision Makers

Unfortunately, Kalven and Zeisel's monumental study has not been replicated, and changes in the composition of juries in the United States (cf. Hans and Vidmar, 1991) may have lowered the degree of agreement between these two types of decision-makers. Yet the initial *process* of decision-making between trial judges and individual jurors may be similar: the construction of story-like representations of actions by, for example, a defendant and then an assessment of the reasons for these actions. Communication theorists Bennett and Feldman (1981, p. 5) described stories as 'systematic means of storing, bringing up to date, rearranging, comparing, testing, and interpreting available information about social behavior'. When questioning a female defendant in order to establish a motive for running away from the crime scene, for instance, the prosecuting attorney may try to form a story in the mind of the fact finder (whether judge or jury) by saying, 'Isn't it true... the reason you gave your purse to D__[before the crime] was because you wouldn't be burdened down with it when you ran?' (Bennett, 1979, p. 316).

Social psychologists Nancy Pennington, Reid Hastie, and Steven Penrod (Pennington, 1981; Hastie, Penrod and Pennington, 1983; Pennington and Hastie, 1986, 1988) provided a formal delineation of the story model, by showing that fact finders (in their studies, actual jurors) inferred events as well as actors' mental states and motivations in order to fill in gaps in the trial testimony, thus creating a complete story. They found that stories people create do influence their verdict choices rather than the opposite; that is, fact finders are not always 'locked in' to an outcome before hearing the evidence (Pennington and Hastie, 1988).

Trial judges, as human beings, reflect their own past experiences, assumptions, and biases, when 'filling in the gaps' and forming a story to explain a defendant's actions. It is true that trial judges have only rarely been placed in experimental situations as subjects of psychological research. What we do know from a limited number of studies is that judges, like jurors, may have widely differing verdicts in response to identical information. Austin and Williams (1977) asked district court judges (i.e. trial judges) in the state of Virginia to respond to the same hypothetical cases by recommending a verdict and sentence. In the case involving the charge of possession of marijuana by a minor, 29 of the judges concluded the defendant was not guilty and 18 concluded that she was guilty. The sentences given by the latter 18 judges ranged from probation (eight judges) to a fine, to a jail term (three judges).

When there is latitude in the punishments that judges can give, their personal characteristics may influence their decisions. They may have prejudices against certain groups—racial minorities, homosexual persons, war resisters—that affect the way they process evidence as well as the type of punishment they assign. Judges who have been prosecutors may maintain their sympathy with the state's evidence in a criminal trial. In the United States, judges' political philosophy was found, in one study, to be highly related to their sentencing behavior (Nagel, 1962).

Appellate Judges' Decision-Making

Appellate judges face a different task from that of trial judges. Rather than assessing the credibility of certain witnesses and rendering a verdict, their job is to determine if the law has been correctly applied in previous decisions by trial judges and juries, as well as by prosecutors and police. Rather than deciding which piece of evidence is most probative, they must decide which statute, case decision, or constitutional principle (if the country has a constitution) should be applied to the issue at hand. Appellate judges will often claim that they decide cases based on the process of legal reasoning taught in law school. That is, they consider the facts and the issues of the current case and relate them to the aforementioned types of considerations. United States Supreme Court Justice Clarence Thomas, in a public address, said: 'There are right and wrong answers to legal questions' (Thomas, 1996), and Justice Antonin Scalia has often concluded that these can clearly be discerned from a reading of the intent of the authors of the United States Constitution (Scalia, 1997).

These statements reflect what has been called the *legal model* of appellate judicial decision-making, that judges dispassionately consider the relevant statutes, court decisions and constitutional principles and straightforwardly follow the weight of these. There is no place for judicial bias in the legal model. Yet we know that judges, when faced with the same issue, can differ not only in the sentences they give (as noted earlier) but also in their judgment about the applicable legal principle. Each term, the majority of decisions rendered by the United States Supreme Court are split decisions, and about 20% generate the greatest division possible, a 5-to-4 split. Most contemporary political scientists who study judicial decision-making have rejected the legal model and have come to adopt what is called the *attitudinal model*. Here, judges' decisions are viewed as based on the facts of the case 'in light of the ideological attitudes and values of the justices' (Segal and Spaeth, 1993, p. 32). The genesis of the attitudinal model was the legal realist movement that dominated the teaching in some law schools in the United States, beginning in the 1920s. In this view, judicial opinions that referred to legal rules used them as rationalizations for personal preferences (Pritchett, 1948). That is, legal rules expressed social policies, and a judge's conception of such policies reflected his or her social, economic, and political outlook, which usually derived from the judge's education and social environment (Frank, 1949). According to this position, most judges do not recognize the influence coming from their own values. Segal and Spaeth, prime advocates of the attitudinal model, wrote:

> Justices . . . do not admit the validity of [the attitudinal model] as an explanation of their decisions. To do so would give the lie to the mythology that the justices, their lower court colleagues, and the off-the-bench apologists have so insistently and persistently verbalized: that judges . . . do not speak; rather, the Constitution and laws speak through them. (p. 33)

Support for the attitudinal model comes from several types of sources:

1. United States Supreme Court justices tend to vote in predictable ways on cases that reflect basic values (for example, cases involving civil liberties, free speech, defendant's rights, search and seizure, or federalism concerns) (Segal, 1984; Segal and Cover, 1989).

2. On issues related to liberalism or conservatism, decisions by federal judges appointed by US Presidents from the Democratic Party differed from those by

judges appointed by Republican Presidents. For example, on race-discrimination cases, 78% of the decisions by judges appointed by Democratic President Carter were liberal, compared to only 18% for Republican Reagan appointees; for right-to-privacy cases, the difference was 78% to 45% (Rowland and Carp, 1996).

3.   Even though appellate judges are not supposed to be fact-*finders*, as trial judges are, two appellate judges can read the same set of facts from the record and place different interpretations on them, leading to completely divergent rulings (see, for example, the majority and dissenting US Supreme Court opinions in the case of *Ake* v. *Oklahoma*, 1985).

Appellate Judges and Group Decision-Making

In a number of countries, trial judges are the sole arbiters of issues in their courts. But some countries compose fact-finding bodies of judges, or judges as well as lay persons; furthermore, decisions by appellate judges almost always reflect a group, rather than an individual. Therefore, a legitimate consideration in studying appellate decision-making is the effect of group interaction. Scholars have studied the group process in the US Supreme Court more than in any other appellate judicial body, so it will serve as our example.

The nine justices of the US Supreme Court individually read the briefs by each party, plus any supporting briefs, before they hear one-hour-long oral arguments for every appeal they have agreed to consider. A few days after the oral arguments, a judicial conference is scheduled, at which the case is discussed and a tentative vote is taken. If the Chief Justice is in the majority, he assigns a justice from the majority to write the opinion for the Court; otherwise, the senior Associate Justice who is in the majority assigns the opinion. The designated opinion writer then drafts (with significant assistance from law clerks) an opinion that is circulated to the other justices for comment and reaction. Drafting an opinion with just the right tone and breadth is often a challenge; if the tentative vote generated only a slim majority, the draft opinion needs to keep each of those voters on board (and perhaps recruit dissenters). But some who initially voted with the majority may demand changes in the draft that the draft writer cannot accommodate. Sometimes what begins as a majority loses support and the opposite position becomes that of the majority. Justices negotiate and bargain in hopes of achieving a final opinion that reflects their (sometimes-idiosyncratic) goals. An analysis of the docket books and other records of the justices indicated that shifts in votes from the conference to the final opinion were 'commonplace' (Howard, 1968). These vote shifts, or *fluidity* to use the political scientists' term, occur in at least half of the cases, and even more frequently on less important cases (Brenner, 1982).

Consistent findings support a proposition that actual votes reflect an effect from the type and importance of the case. Judges may feel more accountable when they know a decision will be scrutinized by the media and legal scholars, so they may pay more attention to the briefs and the oral arguments, making their initial vote harder to dislodge. Furthermore, the salience of the case is probably related to its ideological relevance; few judges are passionate about taking on tax cases or patent-law controversies, and such issues are rarely salient. In contrast, cases involving affirmative action, abortion, or federalism issues are currently ideologically salient to both conservative and liberal judges in the United States.

Uncertainty about the issue has been offered as an explanation for fluidity. Maltzman and Wahlbeck (1996), in analyzing shifts from conference votes to final votes during the 1969 to 1985 Supreme Court terms, found that 'freshman' justices (defined as those during their first two years on the Court) shifted their votes significantly more often than did their seniors, a finding consistent with the analysis of vote shifts in earlier terms, done by Dorff and Brenner (1992).

Strategic versus Sincere Voting

But it should not be assumed that responses to influence in the courts are always passive responses. Many appellate judges have clear-cut policy goals, and they use their votes as bargaining chips. (By *policy* we mean proposed courses of action or general plans the Court should advance.) They may even switch their votes to achieve decisions consistent with their goals. An analysis of cases over the period when Warren Burger was Chief Justice found that 85% of the requests to the opinion writer for a change in language indicated that the requester's joining the opinion was contingent on the change being made (Wood, 1996). But judges are social beings; they do not make their choices in isolation. They must pay heed to the preferences of others. In summary, their decisions and their votes are not straightforwardly determined, and their votes are not necessarily 'sincere' in the sense of reflecting only what the judge prefers.

The distinction between *sincere* and *strategic voting* was first introduced by political scientist Walter Murphy in 1964; he based his distinction on detailed analyses of a few landmark court decisions. A recent book by Epstein and Knight (1998) has given new support to this perspective through extensive analyses of court dockets. They offer a correction to an extreme application of the attitudinal model; they urge us to view appellate judges *not* '...as unconstrained decision makers who are free to behave in accord with their own ideological attitudes, [but] rather...[as] the sophisticated actors Murphy made them out to be' (1998, p. xii). Specifically, they wrote:

> ...Justices are strategic actors who realize that their ability to achieve their goals depends on a consideration of the preferences of others, of the choices that they expect others to make, and of the institutional context in which they act. In other words, the choices of justices can best be explained as strategic behavior, not solely as responses to either personal ideology or apolitical jurisprudence. (1998, p. xiii)

Political scientist Lawrence Baum, a long-time observer of the Supreme Court and author of several books about it, has concluded that judges employ sincere voting when they support the case outcome that they most prefer 'without considering the impact of their votes on the collective result in their court' (1997, p. 90). Judges who vote strategically consider the effects of their choices on 'collective results'; that is, their motivation to achieve the most desirable results in their own court and the government as a whole. Two well-documented case decisions may reflect strategic voting on the part of some of the justices. In the 1954 *Brown* v. *Board of Education* decision, several of the justices did not *initially* advocate outlawing racially segregated schools, but they came to realize that it was in the best interests of the country to have the unanimous vote sought by Chief Justice Earl Warren (Kluger, 1975). And the final opinion in the *Roe* v. *Wade* (1973) case looked quite different from the initial draft by Justice Harry Blackmun.

POSTSCRIPT

At the start of the millennium, the jury system is being instituted in some countries, revived in others, and scientifically scrutinized (often for the first time) in still others. As a result, we are now able to provide an international picture of what jurors in different countries are likely to experience and how those experiences are likely to influence their decisions. As the courtroom doors begin to open, however slightly, we are optimistic that more scientific analysis of judicial decision-making will follow, providing new insights into the reasoning, judgment, and decision-making processes of people highly educated in the ways of law.

REFERENCES

Austin, W. and Williams, T. (1977). A survey of judges' responses to simulated legal cases: A research note on sentencing disparity. *Journal of Criminal Law and Criminology*, *68*, 306–310.

Baldy, A.C. and Manetti, L. (1999). Mixed jury decision making. Paper presented at the International Conference of the American Psychology-Law Society and European Association of Psychology and Law, Dublin.

Baum, L. (1997). *The puzzle of judicial behavior*. Ann Arbor, MI: University of Michigan Press.

Bennett, W.L. (1979). Rhetorical transformation of evidence in criminal trials: Creating grounds for legal judgment. *Quarterly Journal of Speech*, *65*, 311–323.

Bennett, W.L. and Feldman, M.S. (1981). *Reconstructing reality in the courtroom: Justice and judgment in American culture*. New Brunswick, NJ: Rutgers University Press.

Brenner, S. (1982). Fluidity on the United States Supreme Court: 1956–1967. *American Journal of Political Science*, *26*, 388–390.

Cameron, N., Potter, S. and Young, W. (1999). The New Zealand jury. *Law and Contemporary Problems*, *62*, 103–139.

Chesterman, M. (1999). Criminal trial juries in Australia: From penal colonies to a federal democracy. *Law and Contemporary Problems*, *62*, 69–102.

Chi, M.T.H., Glaser, R. and Farr, M.J. (eds) (1988). *The nature of expertise*. Hillsdale, NJ: Erlbaum.

Corker, D. and Levi, M. (1996). Pretrial publicity and its treatment in the English courts. *Criminal Law Review*, 622–632.

Cutler, B.L., Penrod, S.D. and Dexter, H.R. (1989). The eyewitness, the expert psychologist, and the jury. *Law and Human Behavior*, *13*, 311–322.

Dorff, R.H. and Brenner, S. (1992). Conformity voting on the United States Supreme Court. *Journal of Politics*, *54*, 762–775.

Duff, P. (1999). The Scottish criminal jury: A very peculiar institution. *Law and Contemporary Problems*, *62*, 173–201.

Ellsworth, P.C. and Mauro, R. (1998). Psychology and law. In D.T. Gilbert, S.T. Fiske and G. Lindzey (eds), *The handbook of social psychology* (4th edn; pp. 684–732). Boston: McGraw-Hill.

Epstein, L. and Knight, J. (1998). *The choices justices make*. Washington, DC: Congressional Quarterly Press.

Frank, J. (1949). *Courts on trial*. Princeton, NJ: Princeton University Press.

Greene, E., Chopra, S., Kovera, M.B., Penrod, S., Rose, V.G., Schuller, R. and Studebaker, C. (2002). Jurors and juries: A review of the field. In J. Ogloff (ed.), *Taking psychology and law into the 21st century*. New York: Kluwer/Plenum.

Greene, E. and Dodge, M. (1995). The influence of prior record evidence on juror decision making. *Law and Human Behavior*, *19*, 67–78.

Greene, E. and Loftus, E.F. (1985). When crimes are joined at trial. *Law and Human Behavior*, *9*, 193–207.

Gudjonsson, G. (1996). Psychological evidence in court. *Psychologist*, *9*, 213–217.

Hans, V.P. and Vidmar, N. (1991). The American jury at twenty-five years. *Law and Social Inquiry*, *16*, 323–351.

Hastie, R., Penrod, S.D. and Pennington, N. (1983). *Inside the jury*. Cambridge, MA: Harvard University Press.

Hoffman, M.B. (1997). Peremptory challenges should be abolished: A trial judge's perspective. *University of Chicago Law Review*, *64*, 809–871.

Howard, J.W., Jr (1968). On the fluidity of judicial choice. *American Political Science Review*, *62*, 43–56.

Jackson, J. (1995). Juror decision-making and the trial process. In G. Davies, S. Lloyd-Bostock, M. McMurran and C. Wilson (eds), *Psychology, law and criminal justice: International developments in research and practice* (pp. 327–336). Berlin: Walter de Gruyter & Co.

Jackson, J. and Doran, S. (1997). Juries and judges: A view from across the Atlantic. *Criminal Justice*, *15*, 15–18.

Jackson, J.D., Quinn, K. and O'Malley, T. (1999). The jury system in contemporary Ireland: In the shadow of a troubled past. *Law and Contemporary Problems*, *62*, 203–232.

Johnson, C. and Haney, C. (1994). Felony voir dire: An exploratory study of its content and effect. *Law and Human Behavior*, *18*, 487–506.

Kalven, H., Jr and Zeisel, H. (1966). *The American jury*. Boston: Little, Brown.

King, N.J. (1994). The effects of race-conscious jury selection on public confidence in the fairness of jury proceedings: An empirical puzzle. *American Criminal Law Review*, *31*, 1177–1201.

King, N.J. (1999). The American criminal jury. *Law and Contemporary Problems*, *62*, 41–67.

Kluger, R. (1975). *Simple justice: The history of Brown v. Board of Education and black America's struggle for equality*. New York: Knopf.

Lane, B. (1999). Juries untainted by media reports. *The Australian*, retrieved from the World Wide Web, 12/6/99. (http://www.news.com.au/news_content/national_content/4109736.htm)

Law Commission (1995). Evidence in criminal proceedings: Previous misconduct of a defendant. Consultation Paper No. 141.

Lloyd-Bostock, S. (1995). The jury in the United Kingdom: Juries and jury research in context. In G. Davies, S. Lloyd-Bostock, M. McMurran and C. Wilson (eds), *Psychology, law and criminal justice: International developments in research and practice* (pp. 349–359). Berlin: Walter de Gruyter & Co.

Lloyd-Bostock, S. and Thomas, C. (1999). Decline of the 'little parliament': Juries and jury reform in England and Wales. *Law and Contemporary Problems*, *62*, 7–40.

Maltzman, F. and Wahlbeck, P.J. (1996). Strategic policy considerations and voting fluidity on the Burger Court. *American Political Science Review*, *90*, 581–592.

Moran, G. and Cutler, B.L. (1991). The prejudicial impact of pretrial publicity. *Journal of Applied Social Psychology*, *21*, 345–367.

Murphy, W.F. (1964). *Elements of judicial strategy*. Chicago: University of Chicago Press.

Myers, J., Redlich, A., Goodman, G., Prizmich, L. and Imwinkelried, E. (1999). Jurors' perceptions of hearsay in child sexual abuse cases. *Psychology, Public Policy, and Law*, *4*, 1025–1051.

Nagel, S.S. (1962). Judicial background and criminal cases. *Journal of Criminal Law, Criminology, and Police Science*, *53*, 333–339.

Nietzel, M.T., McCarthy, D.M. and Kerr, M.J. (1999). Juries: The current state of the empirical literature. In R. Roesch, S.D. Hart and J.R.P. Ogloff (eds), *Psychology and law: The state of the discipline* (pp. 23–52). New York: Kluwer Academic/Plenum Publishers.

Ogletree, C.J. (1994). Just say no! A proposal to eliminate racially discriminatory uses of peremptory challenges. *American Criminal Law Review*, *31*, 1099–1051.

Olczak, P.V., Kaplan, M.F. and Penrod, S. (1991). Attorneys lay psychology and its effectiveness in selecting jurors: Three empirical studies. *Journal of Social Behavior and Personality*, *6*, 431–452.

Pennington, N. (1981). *Causal reasoning and decision making: The case for juror decisions*. Unpublished doctoral dissertation, Harvard University.

Pennington, N. and Hastie, R. (1986). Evidence evaluation in complex decision making. *Journal of Personality and Social Psychology*, *51*, 242–258.

Pennington, N. and Hastie, R. (1988). Explanation-based decision making: Effects of memory structure on judgment. *Journal of Experimental Psychology: Learning, Memory, and Cognition*, *14*, 521–533.

Pritchett, C.H. (1948). *The Roosevelt Court: A study in judicial politics and values, 1937–1947*. New York: Macmillan.

Rowland, C.K. and Carp. R.A. (1996). *Politics and judgment in federal district courts*. Lawrence, KS: University Press of Kansas.

Scalia, A. (1997). *A matter of interpretation*. Princeton, NJ: Princeton University Press.

Scottish Office (1994). *Juries and verdicts*. Edinburgh: HMSO.

Segal, J.A. (1984). Predicting Supreme Court cases probabilistically: The search and seizure cases, 1962–1981. *American Political Science Review*, *78*, 891–900.

Segal, J.A. and Cover, A.D. (1989). Ideological values and the votes of US Supreme Court justices. *American Political Science Review*, *83*, 557–565.

Segal, J.A. and Spaeth, H.J. (1993). *The Supreme Court and the attitudinal model*. New York: Cambridge University Press.

Shuman, D. and Champagne, A. (1997). Removing the people from the legal process: The rhetoric and research on judicial selection and juries. *Psychology, Public Policy, and Law*, *3*, 242–258.

Steblay, N.M., Besirevic, J., Fulero, S.M. and Jimenez-Lorente, B. (1999). The effects of pretrial publicity on juror verdicts: A meta-analytic review. *Law and Human Behavior*, *23*, 219–235.

Studebaker, C.A. and Penrod, S.D. (1997). Pretrial publicity: The media, the law, and common sense. *Psychology, Public Policy, and Law*, *3*, 428–460.

Thaman, S.C. (1999). Europe's new jury systems: The cases of Spain and Russia. *Law and Contemporary Problems*, *62*, 233–259.

Thomas, C. (1996, April 8). *Judging*. Invited address, School of Law, University of Kansas, Lawrence, KS.

Velasco, P. (1995). The influence of the size and decision rule in jury decision-making. In G. Davies, S. Lloyd-Bostock, M. McMurran and C. Wilson (eds), *Psychology, law and criminal justice: International developments in research and practice* (pp. 344–348). Berlin: Walter de Gruyter & Co.

Vidmar, N. (1999a). Foreword. *Law and Contemporary Problems*, *62*, 1–15.

Vidmar, N. (1999b). The Canadian criminal jury: Searching for a middle ground. *Law and Contemporary Problems*, *62*, 141–172.

Wissler, R. and Saks, M. (1985). On the inefficacy of limiting instruction: When jurors use prior conviction evidence to decide on guilt. *Law and Human Behavior*, *9*, 37–48.

Wood, S.L. (1996, August). Bargaining and negotiation on the Burger Court. Paper presented at the meetings of the American Political Science Association, San Francisco.

Wrightsman, L.S. (1999). *Judicial decision making: Is psychology relevant?* New York: Kluwer Academic/Plenum Publishers.

Zander, M. and Henderson, P. (1993). *Crown Court study*. Research Study No. 19 for the Royal Commission on Criminal Justice. London: HMSO.

Cases

Ake v. *Oklahoma* (1985), 105 S.Ct. 1087.

Apodaca et al. v. *Oregon* (1972), 32 L.Ed. 2d 184.

Brown v. *Board of Education of Topeka, Kansas* (1954), 347 US 483.

Dowling v. *US* (1990), 110 S.Ct. 668.

Johnson v. *Louisiana* (1972), 406 US 356.

Roe v. *Wade* (1973), 410 US 113.

Chapter 3.6

Restorative Justice: The Influence of Psychology from a Jurisprudent Therapy Perspective

Eric Y. Drogin
Franklin Pierce Law Center, USA
Mark E. Howard
Franklin Pierce Law Center, USA
and
John Williams
University of Wales, Aberystwyth, UK

INTRODUCTION

Restorative Justice seeks to achieve education, empowerment, and personal as well as societal reintegration of both victims and offenders, by means of promoting a collaborative, mediated dialogue between affected parties. This approach reflects a value system similar to that of psychology, which seeks to study and enhance both behavior and perception, not merely for historically utilitarian, 'practical' purposes (Wallerstein, 1952; Wolman, 1973), but ultimately for 'the understanding of social and community change' and the alleviation of 'social inequities that continue to plague our society' (Heller et al., 1984, p. ix). Given this congruence of purpose and perspective, it was inevitable that advocates for Restorative Justice would draw upon psychological principles and techniques in its implementation.

Subsequent to a review of assumptions, foci, objectives, and foundations, we will describe recent Restorative Justice innovations in the United Kingdom, as well as

---

The authors do not imply endorsement of the opinions contained herein by the United States Department of Justice.

Handbook of Psychology in Legal Contexts, Second Edition
Edited by D. Carson and R. Bull. © 2003 John Wiley & Sons, Ltd.

systemic barriers to broader application of such principles in the United States. In keeping with the emphasis of this *Handbook* upon 'psychology in legal contexts', this chapter will conclude with a 'Jurisprudent Therapy' (Drogin, 2000a) analysis of the utilization and effects of psychological science, psychological practice, and psychological roles in the application of Restorative Justice.

ASSUMPTIONS, FOCI, OBJECTIVES, AND FOUNDATIONS OF RESTORATIVE JUSTICE

As defined by the Restorative Justice Consortium (1998), 'Restorative Justice seeks to balance the concerns of the victim and the community with the need to reintegrate the offender into society. It seeks to assist the recovery of the victim and enable all parties with a stake in the justice process to participate fruitfully in it' (p. 2). In support of this endeavor, the following core assumptions have been identified:

- that crime has its origins in social conditions and relationships in the community;

- that crime-prevention is dependent on communities taking some responsibility (along with local and central governments' responsibility for general social policy) for remedying those conditions that cause crime;

- that the aftermath of crime cannot be fully resolved for the parties themselves without facilitating their personal involvement;

- that justice measures must be flexible enough to respond to the particular exigencies, personal needs and potential for action in each case;

- that partnership and common objectives among justice agencies, and between them and the community, are essential to optimal effectiveness and efficiency; and

- that justice consists of a balanced approach in which a single objective is not allowed to dominate the others (Marshall, 1999).

This model stands in stark contrast to elements of the traditional, 'retributive' justice paradigm, characterized by 'an exact scale of punishments for acts without reference to the criminal's circumstances' (Masters and Robertson, 1990, p. 88). Since the inception of 'the first professional police department, created in 1829 by Sir Robert Peel ... [as] a liberal, humanitarian response to the problems of social disorder and crime' (Gilsinan, 1990, p. 85), there have existed forward-thinking attempts to 'understand and interpret information dealing with human behaviors' in a criminal context (Parry and Drogin, 2000, p. 1). It has long been recognized that '[c]rime problems have been dealt with too long with only the aid of common sense. Catch criminals and lock them up; if they hit you, hit them back. This is common sense, but it does not work' (Menninger, 1966, p. 12; Roach, 2000).

Restorative Justice differs from retributive presumptions in several specific aspects. A retribution-based model focuses upon the state as the violated party, emphasizing adversary relationships, the imposition of pain as a deterrent, the offender's past behavior, and a dependence upon professional judgment. By contrast, the concerns of Restorative Justice include victims as violated parties, the primacy of dialogue and negotiation, restitution as a means of restoration, the harmful consequences of offenders' behavior, and direct involvement by participants (Zehr, 1990).

Such assumptions and foci have led proponents of Restorative Justice to a delineation of key objectives, including the following:

- to attend fully to victims' needs—material, financial, emotional and social (including those personally close to the victim who may be similarly affected);

- to prevent re-offending by reintegrating offenders into the community;

- to enable offenders to assume active responsibility for their actions;

- to recreate a working community that supports the rehabilitation of offenders and victims and is active in preventing crime; and

- to provide a means of avoiding escalation of legal justice and the associated costs and delays (Marshall, 1999).

In essence, such objectives embrace a 'problem-solving', preventative model (Bazemore and Schiff, 1996) that promotes a sense of responsibility for the offender's destructive, demeaning, and/or disenfranchising actions (Cather, 1995; Steinfeld, 1998; Walters and White, 1998). This approach further instills an empowering sense of responsibility for the resolution and repair of these situations by those against whom a crime has been committed (Dignan and Cavadino, 1996). Participants are thus freed from the mechanical constraints of a system limiting criminal procedure to a series of rules that are viewed as abstract and impersonal by offenders as well as victims (Apospori and Alpert, 1993; Mitchell, 1998). Instead, they may focus on the specific factors unique to each separate, discrete human interaction, including personal perspectives on loss as well as blame (Mohr and Luscri, 1995; Shepherd, 1990), in addition to the predictable fallout from a combination of distinct, individual personalities (Bradfield and Acquino, 1999; Vaccaro, 1988).

Restorative Justice has roots in 'the traditional justice of the ancient Arab, Greek, Indian and Roman civilizations, and the familial perspective of indigenous peoples of North America and Australasia' (Association of Chief Police Officers of England, Wales, and North Ireland, 2000, p. 4). As such, it exists as a truly international, multicultural phenomenon, rather than an imposition of one legal system's organizing construct upon another. Not confined in its genesis merely to adjudicative concerns, Restorative Justice is grounded in the spiritual underpinnings of most widely espoused faith traditions; for example:

- Christianity's tradition of 'compassion for offenders' and its historical reaction against an inherited Roman notions of 'retributive law' (Allard and Northey, 2001, p. 127; Baier and Wright, 2001; Ellis and Peterson, 1996; Pettersson, 1991);

- Hinduism's overlap between the concepts of penance and punishment, with acknowledgment of a duty to restore victims to health (Neufeldt, 2001; Padayachee and Singh, 1998);

- Islam's focus upon 'forgiveness and minimum punitive measures', with 'participation of the victim, the offender, and the community' (Ammar, 2001, pp. 172–173; Azayem and Hedayat-Diba, 1994);

- Judaism's 'interest in the criminal's repentance, direct confrontation between litigants, and avoidance of punitive incarceration' (Segal, 2001, p. 194; Ben-David and Weller, 1995; Mesch and Fishman, 1998); and

- Sikhism's promotion of 'mutual coexistence and understanding' with 'actual practice that fully restores an offender in the community' (Singh, 2001, p. 214; Cochrane and Bal, 1990; Hans, 1986).

RESTORATIVE JUSTICE: RECENT INNOVATIONS IN THE UNITED KINGDOM

The United Kingdom's first coherent attempt to introduce Restorative Justice has been the Crime and Disorder Act of 1998 (1998, c. 37 (Eng.)—hereinafter the 'Act'). Earlier attempts at similar reforms were not successful (Marshall and Merry, 1990). In the White Paper that led to the Act, the Government (1997) emphasized the need to reshape the criminal justice system 'to produce more constructive outcomes with young offenders' (para. 9.21). The proposed reforms were built upon the following three principles:

- *Restoration*: young offenders apologizing to their victims and making amends for harm done;

- *Reintegration*: young offenders paying their debt to society, putting their crimes behind them, and rejoining the law-abiding community; and

- *Responsibility*: young offenders (and their parents) facing the consequences of offending behavior, and taking responsibility for the prevention of further offending. (Government, 1997, para. 9.21)

Utilizing what have become known at the '3Rs', this approach is designed to involve young people more effectively in decisions taken about them. Youthful offenders will be encouraged to admit their guilt, and to face up to the consequences of their behavior. Victims will also participate more directly in these proceedings, if they consent to do so.

In marked contrast to the exclusionary approach, typified by the 'boot camp' and 'short sharp shock' techniques, once so popular with politicians, the Act (1998) maintains that it is the 'principal aim of the youth justice system to prevent offending by children and young persons', elevating this notion to the level of a statutory duty (s. 37). As recently reported by the National Association for the Care and Resettlement of Offenders, locking up young offenders actually increases the risk of youth crime, as prison time 'stops young people growing out of crime, with three quarters of 18- to 24-year-olds going on to re-offend' (*The Observer*, 2001, p. 6).

The potential effectiveness of the Act cannot be seen in isolation, as it is part of a more comprehensive legislative and societal approach. One complementary measure involves a 'welfare-to-work initiative', guaranteeing work and/or training opportunities to young persons who have been unemployed for at least six months. Youthful offenders leaving custody have direct access to this program. The Government's social exclusion unit has a wide remit in this regard, including educational opportunities, the promotion of health and social housing, and the fostering of local initiatives to create local employment (Scanlan, 1998).

Despite such broad initiatives, the main obstacles to an integrated Restorative Justice approach remain structural. Recent constitutional developments, such as the establishment of a National Assembly for Wales, have resulted in a fragmentation of ultimate strategic responsibility for various components of reform, which may be driven by different—and potentially conflicting—political agendas. Following are examples of innovations that have enhanced the potential for Restorative Justice on a system-wide basis, despite the presence of structural barriers.

Youth Offending Teams

Recognizing the need for interdisciplinary cooperation in order to implement Restorative Justice, the new Labour Government introduced Youth Offending Teams (YOTs) as the primary vehicle for preventing re-offending at the local level (Act 1998, s. 39). The specific duties of the YOTs include coordinating the provision of youth justice services for all requiring them, and carrying out duties assigned under local Youth Justice Plans (Act 1998, s. 39(7)). YOTs must confront young offenders with the consequences of their offending, for themselves and their family, their victims and their community, and help them to develop a sense of personal responsibility (Home Office, 1998). Youth Justice Plans set out each individual authority's plans for how youth justice services are to be provided and funded and how the YOTs will operate within their area (Act 1998, s. 40).

YOTs must include at least one representative from probation, social services, police, health and education agencies. Membership should also include representatives of the voluntary sector—for example, organizations working with young offenders, or providing services for young persons generally. The Home Office (1998) has maintained that Victim Support, and organizations specializing in mediation and parenting, should also be invited participate in YOTs (para. 13).

Reprimands and Warnings

Before the Act, a non-statutory practice had evolved whereby the police would divert young offenders from the courts by issuing 'cautions' or, in more serious cases, 'cautions plus'. The latter were often accompanied by an additional element of counseling or therapy. Such schemes were patchy in operation, with inevitable expressions of concern over their relative informality. Under the Act (1998), formal 'reprimands and warnings' have replaced cautions and cautions plus (s. 65). This new approach is far more systematic, with considerably clearer restorative objectives. A reprimand or warning may be issued where:

- a police officer has evidence that an offence has been committed by a child or young person;

- the evidence is such that the officer believes that there would be a realistic prospect of conviction;

- the offender admits that he or she has committed the offense;

- the offender has not previously been convicted of an offense; and

- the officer is satisfied that it would not be in the public interest for the offender to be prosecuted. (Act 1998, s. 65(1))

If a warning or reprimand is issued, the young person in question must be referred to a YOT, which provides an assessment, and arranges where appropriate for participation in a rehabilitation program, the purpose of which is to 'rehabilitate participants and to prevent them from re-offending'. The Act (1998) has specified that a key objective of such programs is to make the offender understand the effect that his or her behavior has on others, most notably the victim (s. 66).

The Home Office (2000) emphasizes that the delivery of reprimands and warnings should incorporate principles of Restorative Justice wherever possible. Along these lines, a 'restorative conference' may be warranted, if the offense is suitable, and if the young person, his or her parents, and the victim are all willing. This option provides for administration of the warning within an inclusive environment, helping to ensure that the offender fully realizes the impact of his or her behavior. Once every party has had the opportunity to provide input into the discussion, the police officer may issue the warning. The Act (1998) requires that such transactions occur at a police station (s. 65(5)), although, for obvious reasons, this may not be the most conducive setting for meaningful attitudinal and/or behavioral change.

Reparation Orders

Where a child or young person has been convicted of an offense (other than where the penalty is fixed by law), the court may require the offender to make reparation to the victim, or to the community at large. Courts have considerable discretion in deciding the form of this reparation. In some cases, an apology may be adequate. In others, something more tangible is required, such as making good the damage caused by the offense. Before reparation can be made directly to the victim, his or her agreement is required, and it is important that the victim is not overtly or covertly pressured into accepting a particular scheme (Scanlan, 1998).

Unfortunately, early research indicates that such precautions are not always observed, and that some courts may seek to impose offender–victim mediation without appropriate regard for the victim's perspective on this issue (Dignan, 2000). Similarly, in recognition of the corresponding importance of offender consent, Dignan (1999) further notes that, where such input is neither required nor solicited, imposed reparation orders may be seen as insufficiently distinct from traditional punitive measures.

A probation officer, a social worker, or another designated YOT member will be responsible for the effective operation of the reparation order, and the YOT will be charged with coordinating reports to the court on the appropriate form of reparation (Act 1998, s. 68). Pilot studies on reparation orders have identified a particular problem in this regard: the courts are often demanding detailed information on the nature of the proposed order before reaching their decisions. This directly threatens the core assumption underlying such interventions—namely, that the substance of the reparation should be agreed upon by the parties, and not imposed by the courts (Akesher, 2000). This shortcoming disregards the amount of careful work required to devise a reparative plan, and belittles the professionalism of the YOT members charged with that responsibility.

Ultimately, such concerns reflect a more fundamental criticism, relating to the judiciary's willingness to embrace, or ability to comprehend, the idea of Restorative Justice:

> YOT staff who are involved in the delivery of reparative interventions complain that some magistrates and their clerks do not fully grasp the Restorative Justice ethos which underpins the Restorative Justice measures contained within the Act, which frequently result in inappropriate orders being made. (Dignan, 2000, p. 27)

Action Plan Orders

Utilized pursuant to relatively serious offenses, Action Plan Orders enable early intervention in order to prevent future, similar behavior. They are of three-month duration. Before issuing an Action Plan Order, the courts will consider a written report prepared by a YOT member (Act 1998, ss. 69 and 70; Home Office, 2000). By such means, offenders may be required to do any or all of the following:

- participate in specified activities at specified times;

- present themselves to a specified person (e.g. a YOT member);

- present themselves at an attendance center;

- refrain from frequenting a particular location;

- comply with specified educational requirements;

- make reparation to a consenting victim, or to the community; and

- attend any hearing fixed by the court. (Act 1998, s. 69(5))

As far as reparation is concerned, care is taken to emphasize that this activity is not a purely mechanistic or 'eye for an eye' approach. Intended to meet the needs of a victim who is willing to be involved, as well as addressing the young person's offending, reparation may take a number of different forms, including a letter of apology, a restorative or family group conference, or some type of practical work that benefits the victim and perhaps the wider community as well (Akesher, 2000).

Is Current Legislation Sufficiently Comprehensive?

Dignan (1999) notes that, while Restorative Justice has now taken root in England and Wales, the measures described *supra* hardly qualify as a 'revolution', given the Government's continued commitment to a prison-building program, and the use of 'zero tolerance' language in key legislation.

Similarly, Morris and Gelsthorpe (2000) assert that the Restorative Justice theme, found in the Act, is just one in a 'broadly punitive and controlling piece of legislation' (p. 19). It includes such measures as the abolition of *doli incapax* for 10–13-year-olds, local curfew schemes, antisocial behavior orders, and the extension of imprisonment for 'persistent' juvenile offenders. Dignan (1999) concludes that 'it remains to be seen whether the reparative elements that are currently being grafted onto the criminal justice system will be nurtured into a full blown Restorative Justice approach' (p. 60).

Has the Act gone far enough in embedding a Restorative Justice approach into the criminal justice system in England and Wales? These are early days and it is difficult to predict the answer.

RESTORATIVE JUSTICE: SYSTEMIC BARRIERS IN THE UNITED STATES

The development and implementation of Restorative Justice and practices are predictably hampered where institutional obstacles are most firmly entrenched. Particularly prominent among such impediments are 'guideline sentencing constructs', such as those developed in recent years in many American jurisdictions. The most pervasive and illustrative example of these systemic barriers involves the US Sentencing Commission's *Federal Sentencing Guidelines* (2000; hereinafter, the *Guidelines*), enacted by the US Congress to direct federal judges in meting out criminal penalties.

The *Guidelines:* An Overview

In order to gain a full appreciation for the dampening effect of the *Guidelines* upon Restorative Justice, it is necessary not only to acquire an understanding of their functioning and nuances, but also to consider the limited power of a federal court in a criminal case. Taking the latter point first, the federal district courts, which are the criminal trial courts in the federal system, are courts of 'limited' jurisdiction. That is, under Article III of the US Constitution, these courts are created by and derive their power from the US Congress. As such, federal district courts must apply criminal sentences in accordance with the law as defined by Congress. Unlike a court of 'general' jurisdiction functioning in an indeterminate sentencing structure, the federal courts have only such power to impose a sentence, and to impose conditions attendant to that sentence, as Congress may bestow upon them.

The Sentencing Reform Act (1984) was instituted in specific response to perceived disparities in criminal sentences handed down by federal district court judges. Congress subsequently created the US Sentencing Commission, and ordained this body with the task of creating a detailed set of sentencing guidelines. The first such guidelines were issued in 1987 and, with limited exceptions, they have been amended annually to reflect changes in policy, to provide clearer interpretive guidance, and to resolve any interpretive splits among federal appellate courts.

The *Guidelines* establish a standardized analysis for determining, in the first instance, a defendant's appropriate sentencing range. Among other considerations, judges must weigh the nature of the basic offense, specific aggravating or mitigating characteristics, the defendant's criminal history, and the defendant's acceptance of responsibility (i.e. whether the defendant pleaded guilty, was truthful in his or her admission of guilt, and/or accepted responsibility in a timely manner).

Once the applicable baseline guideline sentencing range is determined, it is incumbent upon the court to sentence the defendant within preordained parameters, unless a recognized basis exists to 'depart' to a higher or lower sentencing range. For example, there may be downward departures for 'substantial assistance' to law enforcement, as well as those permitted in recognition of exceptional circumstances inadequately addressed by other portions of the *Guidelines*. Specific offender characteristics may be considered, depending upon whether the Sentencing Commission has deemed them relevant (an 'encouraged' factor for departure), not 'ordinarily' relevant (a 'discouraged' factor), or not relevant at all (a 'prohibited' factor).

Downward Departure

As befits the specific emphasis of this chapter, a particularly illustrative model for exploring the limitations imposed on prospects for Restorative Justice concerns the

Guidelines' treatment of mental health issues, addressing both the offender and the victim of the offense. Tellingly, the *Guidelines* only consider mental health factors in the context of a departure from the applicable guideline range.

Addressing offender mental health issues first, 'diminished capacity' provides an 'encouraged' ground for downward departure. As amended in 1998, this portion of the *Guidelines* indicates that a departure 'may be warranted if the defendant committed the offense while suffering from a significantly reduced mental capacity'. According to the guideline commentary, this requires a 'significantly impaired ability to (A) understand the wrongfulness of the behavior comprising the offense or to exercise the power of reason; or (B) control behavior that the defendant knows is wrongful' (US Sentencing Commission, 2000, s. 5K2.13).

Interestingly, while the Insanity Defense Reform Act (1987) does not recognize behavioral disorders as a form of insanity, the Sentencing Commission included volitional impairments in addition to cognitive disabilities as an appropriate sentencing consideration (*United States* v. *McBroom*, 1997). The federal courts have recognized major depression (*United States* v. *Ribot*, 1999), post-traumatic stress disorder (*United States* v. *Cantu*, 1993), bipolar or manic-depressive disorder (*United States* v. *McMurry*, 1993), and schizophrenic disorder (*United States* v. *Ruklick*, 1990) as acceptable bases for departure pursuant to this provision.

This departure option is not available, however, if 'the significantly reduced mental state was caused by the voluntary use of drugs or other intoxicants'. Departure is also obviated if 'the facts and circumstances of the defendant's offense indicate a need to protect the public because the offense involved actual violence or a serious threat of violence', or if 'the defendant's criminal history indicates a need to incarcerate the defendant to protect the public'. Overall, 'if a departure is warranted, the extent of the departure should reflect the extent to which the reduced mental capacity contributed to the commission of the offense' (US Sentencing Commission, 2000, s. 5K2.13).

In addition to the requirement of significant mental health impairment, downward departure is further predicated upon a finding that this condition contributed to the commission of the offense itself. The court is directed to determine in some fashion the *degree* of this impairment's contribution, and to adjust the offender's sentence downward only to that specific extent (*United States* v. *Lauzon*, 1991). Further limiting to prospects for the application of Restorative Justice, the *Guidelines* forbid application of a 'diminished capacity' adjustment if the offense involved 'actual violence' or the 'serious threat of violence'. Coupled with additional prohibition of departure where the diminished capacity was caused by the voluntary use of intoxicants, this reduces the availability of the departure to primarily 'white collar', regulatory, or status offenses.

The *Guidelines* further mandate that certain 'mental and emotional conditions' (as artificially distinguished from 'significantly reduced mental capacity') are not ordinarily relevant in determining whether a sentence should be outside the guideline range.

As such, they constitute a 'discouraged' departure basis (US Sentencing Commission, 2000, s. 5H1.3).

The courts have labeled the following as 'mental or emotion conditions' ineligible for downward departure: being a 'victim of spousal abuse' (*United States* v. *Desorneaux*, 1991), 'borderline intelligence' (*United States* v. *Lauzon*, 1991), 'suicidal tendencies' (*United States* v. *Harpst*, 1991), 'compulsive gambling' (*United States* v. *Rosen*, 1990), and 'HIV-positive status or AIDS' (*United States* v. *Rabins*, 1995; *United States* v. *Woody*, 1995). One federal court, however, did find 'panic disorder with agoraphobia' (*United States* v. *Garza-Juarez*, 1993) and having suffered 'extraordinary childhood abuse' (*United States* v. *Roe*, 1992) to justify downward departures. Another court even held that an offender's 'potential for victimization' in prison, due to his small size, immature appearance and bisexual orientation, merited a downward departure (*United States* v. *Lara*, 1990).

The *Guidelines* do provide one ray of hope for the application of Restorative Justice, albeit substantially after the fact of formal sentencing, with their acknowledgment that 'mental and emotional conditions may be relevant in determining the conditions of probation or supervised release'. In these circumstances, although it may not reduce the offender's sentence due to an impairment, the court can impose mental health treatment or counseling for the offender as a condition of probation or supervised release (US Sentencing Commission, 2000, ss. 5B1.3(d)(5), 5D1.3(d)(5)). Presumably, a victim–offender mediation component could be crafted to fit this scheme, providing an important reflective and integrative opportunity for all parties.

Upward Departure

The *Guidelines* do take into account the potential mental health effects of crime upon victims, but this is implemented in a fashion distinct from Restorative Justice goals and principles. Courts may apply an *upward* departure from the applicable guideline range 'if a victim ... suffered psychological injury much more serious than that normally resulting from commission of the offense'. Several parameters exist concerning the extent of the injury contemplated under this 'encouraged' upward departure factor. The injury should constitute 'substantial impairment of the intellectual, psychological, emotional, or behavioral functioning of a victim'. The impairment should prove 'likely to be of an extended or continuous duration', manifested by 'physical or psychological symptoms or by changes in behavior patterns'. The court is further directed to consider 'the extent to which such harm was likely, given the nature of the defendant's conduct' (US Sentencing Commission, 2000, s. 5K2.3).

For example, an upward departure was deemed justifiable where the victim had suffered 'particularly degrading and insulting forms' of abuse (*United States* v. *Ellis*, 1991). In another case, an upward departure was affirmed when it was determined that a victim had received nine months of therapy for 'post-traumatic stress disorder' subsequent to the offense (*United States* v. *Chatlin*, 1995). An upward departure was reversed, however, in proceedings where there was no expert opinion to support the assertion of a victim's 'extreme psychological injury' (*United States* v. *Fawbush*, 1991). While such adjustments seek to take into account the victim's experience where appropriately substantiated, they do so specifically at the offender's expense, and limit the victim's role to the satisfaction putatively derived from the imposition of a harsher sentence. Whatever the independent merits of such a system, they promote a judicial environment firmly inhospitable to the application of Restorative Justice.

Future Prospects for Restorative Justice in the Federal System

As the foregoing examples demonstrate, in the arena of interplay between Restorative Justice and mental health issues, guideline sentencing, as found in the American federal scheme, leaves little room for alternative approaches to criminal justice. In such systems, where the courts are of limited jurisdiction or are otherwise tightly controlled by the legislative branch of government, Restorative Justice is unlikely to find a receptive ear in the courts—no matter how eagerly jurists themselves might welcome such developments. Victim and offender focused innovations are more profitably advocated, instead, via elected general assemblies, where the crafting of public policy is a more common pursuit.

PSYCHOLOGICAL SCIENCE, PRACTICE, AND ROLES: THE JURISPRUDENT THERAPY ANALYSIS

The popular 'Therapeutic Jurisprudence' model has served as a mainstay of psycholegal academe for over a decade (Wexler and Winick, 1991), and is described in detail in Chapter 4.6 of this *Handbook*. Therapeutic Jurisprudence involves 'the study of the use of the law to achieve therapeutic objectives' (Wexler, 1990, p. 4).

> An enhanced perspective can be achieved by inverting (or extending) the Therapeutic Jurisprudence model to examine not only the effects of the law on the therapeutic status of the public at large but also the effects of the mental health system on the legal rights of its own constituencies. From this 'Jurisprudent Therapy' point of view, legal scholars can pinpoint desirable developments in the concision and utilization of mental health science, practice, and roles in the service of justice for litigants and for the broader public. (Drogin, 2000b, p. 284)

Here, applications of psychological science, psychological practice, and psychological roles, with reference to Restorative Justice, may be gauged in terms of their just, neutral, or unjust effects upon victims, offenders, and other affected parties (Drogin, 2001a). The context in which this analysis adheres most directly is the employment of mediation, the primary active modality in Restorative Justice. Specifically, what does psychological science tell us about potential barriers to participation in mediation? What can psychological practice offer to identify those individuals capable of participating in mediation, and to suggest how mediation itself may optimally be conducted? How do psychological roles impact upon the practical delivery of related services?

Psychological Science: Barriers to Participation in Mediation

It has been specifically acknowledged that by virtue of various psychological disabilities, not all persons may be capable of participating in mediation. 'In order for the mediation process to work, the parties must be able to understand the process and the options under discussion, and to give voluntary and informed consent to any agreement reached' (ADA Mediation Guidelines Work Group, 2000, p. 7). Psychological science has identified several conditions that may impair (and even obviate) meaningful engagement (Drogin, 2000c). Most prominent among these are depression, substance dependence, schizophrenia, and mental retardation.

Depression

According to American Psychiatric Association's *Diagnostic and Statistical Manual of Mental Disorders* (DSM-IV; APA, 1994) persons suffering from a Major Depressive Episode may display:

(1)   depressed mood;

(2)   diminished interest or pleasure;

(3)   weight loss;

(4)   sleep disturbance;

(5)   agitated or slowed movements;

(6)   fatigue or loss of energy;

(7)   feelings of worthlessness or guilt;

(8)   concentration problems or indecisiveness; and

(9)   thoughts of death or suicide. (APA, 1994, p. 327)

During mediation, depressed individuals may be listless, apathetic, and seemingly disinterested in the details of these proceedings. Often, the depressed individual may dissolve into tears, seemingly incapable of taking an active role in the mediation process. The depressed individual is not merely so 'sad', 'miserable' or 'unhappy' that a preoccupation with these emotions is crowding out the desire to participate in mediation. Rather, clinical depression is characterized cognitively by a 'negative cognitive triad', involving an entrenched negative of one's self, situation, and prospects that interferes *logically* with the desire and/or ability to interact effectively (Beck et al., 1979).

Substance Dependence

Persons who have become dependent on any of a range of substances may share several of the following experiences:

(1)   tolerance (needing more to become intoxicated, or not getting as intoxicated with the same amount);

(2)   withdrawal symptoms;

(3)   consuming more, and for a longer time, than intended;

(4)   failed attempts or persistent desire to minimize consumption;

(5)   increased time spent in obtaining or recovering from the substance in question;

(6)   giving up social, occupational, or recreational activities; and

(7)   continuing to consume despite knowledge that there is a problem. (APA, 1994, p. 181)

'Withdrawal' is likely to be marked by considerable pain and psychological disturbance (Massman and Tipton, 1988; Rosenbloom, 1988). This is distinct from the longer-term process of 'recovery', which involves, among other aspects, the gradual return of the central nervous system to an approximately pre-morbid level of functioning. In the case of long-term alcohol dependence, this component of 'recovery' is generally estimated to take between nine and 15 months (Wright et al., 1993).

These persons often lead chaotic personal lives, are likely confused, and frequently have difficulty with trust issues, in a fashion seemingly similar to persons with paranoid personality disorder (Moring, 1997). Comprehension difficulties are a significant issue in these cases (Schaeffer, Parsons and Errico, 1989). While deficits are typically neither as profound nor as pervasive as those encountered with, for example, developmental or learning disabilities, they may still provide a substantial barrier to collaboration and communication (Kaplan and Sadock, 1998).

The trademark attitude (and primary psychological defense) of the addicted person is *denial* (Duffy, 1995; Ward and Rothaus, 1991; Wiseman, Souder and O'Sullivan, 1996). Mediators should not be surprised when addicted persons resolutely refuse to acknowledge aspects of their cases that would seem readily apparent to anyone else (Drogin and Barrett, 1998).

Schizophrenia

Persons who have received a diagnosis of schizophrenia will often experience some or all of the following:

(1)   delusions;

(2)   hallucinations;

(3) disorganized speech;

(4) disorganized or catatonic behavior; and

(5) social or occupational dysfunction. (APA, 1994, p. 285)

Clearly, an active phase of this disorder will probably render an individual incapable of effective collaboration and communication (Bloom, Williams and Bigelow, 1992; Kaliski, 1995). In those cases where psychotic symptoms are currently inactive, and thus at least temporarily in 'remission', there may be a working basis for participation in mediation. From a classic reference designed for the families of persons with schizophrenia:

> Interpretations of this kind may indeed increase the anxiety of the patient and hasten a new psychotic episode...[h]owever, distance is not desirable either and does not promote rehabilitation...

> Many of these patients were not able to express their emotions. An apparent insensitivity should not be interpreted as imperviousness. Even a catatonic schizophrenic who seems insensitive and immobile like a statue feels very strongly...

> With the recovering schizophrenic we find ourselves in a completely different situation. He is very sensitive...and would not forgive relatives for not telling him the truth. And yet knowing the truth may be detrimental to him when he is still unstable and still struggling to recover fully his mental health. (Arieti, 1979, pp. 156–162).

Developmental and Learning Disabilities

Persons who have received a diagnosis of mental retardation will typically exhibit:

(1) significantly low intellectual functioning; and

(2) impairments in adaptive behavior. (APA, 1994, p. 6)

These difficulties must begin before the person reaches the age of 18 for the diagnosis to apply. The Intelligence Quotient (IQ) range associated with this condition is typically 70 or below, although certain test-specific and other considerations may result in such persons having IQ scores several points higher (APA, 1994, pp. 39–45; Koocher, Norcross and Hill, 1998).

'People with mental retardation tend to think in concrete and literal terms. As a result, they may not understand the meaning of [core legal] concepts' (Keyes, Edwards and Derning, 1998, p. 529). Although mediators may attempt to converse at a level most likely to be understood by the defendant with mental retardation, this should not be taken as advice to speak with such persons as if they are children. According to foundational training resources in the field of psychiatry:

[T]he interviewer should not be guided by the patient's mental age, which cannot fully characterize the person. A mildly retarded adult with a mental age of 10 is not a 10-year-old child. When addressed as if they were children, some retarded people become justifiably insulted, angry, and uncooperative. Passive and dependent people, alternatively, may assume the child's role that they think is expected of them. In both cases, no valid [information] can be obtained. (Kaplan and Sadock, 1998, p. 1148)

Because of the likely presence of suggestibility, mediators must take care not to 'lead' parties with mental retardation into misrepresentative statements about past or present behaviors, feelings, and attitudes. The same dynamics that defense attorneys are concerned will impair an offender's ability to provide a valid waiver (or confession) may also burden mediation participants with bogus information and attributions that will frustrate attempts at meaningful, truly interactive dialogue (Dattilo, Hoge and Malley, 1996; Elias, Sigelman and Danker-Brown, 1980; Sigelman et al., 1981).

These and other conditions may have a considerable impact on the ability of victims, offenders, and other related parties to participate validly in mediation as a function of Restorative Justice. Impairment of the mediation process cannot help but have a deleterious effect upon the overall results of such interventions (Umbreidt, 1994). For this reason, the effects of the diagnostic component of psychological science directly contribute to just outcomes in this regard (Bradford, 1995; Cohen and Dvoskin, 1992; Gurevich, 1991).

Psychological Practice: Determining Individual Capacity to Participate in Mediation

The clinical determination of an individual's capability to participate in the mediation process has received surprisingly minimal attention in the professional literature, reflecting an apparent disregard for this concern even in practical, day-to-day applications. A recent survey of American victim–offender mediation programs attempted to identify what mediators identified as the 'most important mediator tasks'. While such aspects as dialogue facilitation, comfort of the parties, movement toward a written agreement, and comment paraphrasing were cited, the accommodation and/or amelioration of disabilities was not reflected among significantly referenced categories (Umbreidt, 2001). This ranking of emphases is all the more surprising when one considers the commonly acknowledged prevalence of mental illness among persons convicted of a range of criminal offenses (Drogin and Monahan, 2001; Lewis and Pincus, 1986; Lewis et al., 1988; US Department of Justice, 1999).

Recently, one organization has attempted to institute measures to gauge and promote mediation-oriented capacity. The Kukin Program for Conflict Resolution at the Benjamin Cardozo School of Law (USA) has promulgated *ADA (Americans with Disabilities Act) Mediation Guidelines*, providing the following focused direction:

Mediators and provider organizations . . . should determine whether the parties [to] mediation have the capacity to do so. In making such determinations, neither the mediator nor the provider organization should rely solely on a party's medical condition or diagnosis. Instead, they should evaluate a party's capacity to mediate on a case by case basis, if and when a question arises regarding a party's capacity to engage in the mediation process and enter into a contract.

> This evaluation should be based on several factors. The mediator should ascertain that a party understands the nature of the mediation process, who the parties are, the role of the mediator, the parties' relationship to the mediator, and the issues at hand. The mediator should determine whether the party [is qualified to] assess options and make and keep an agreement. An adjudication of legal incapacity is not necessarily determinative of capacity to mediate. However, a mediation agreement signed by a person without legal capacity may require co-signing by a surrogate to ensure its enforceability.

> (ADA Mediation Guidelines Work Group, 2000, pp. 7–8)

The formal assessment of 'communication competence' has received considerable attention in published clinical studies (Colliver et al., 1999; Kretschmer and Kretschmer, 1988; Spano and Zimmerman, 1995).

Part One of this *Handbook* reviews in considerable detail the contributions of psychology to the legal system, describing how clinicians may provide both quantitative and qualitative information about individuals in a range of adjudicative contexts. For the purposes of the present chapter, it suffices to observe that a properly conducted forensic psychological examination of the constructs described *supra* will include not only cognitive and personality assessment via testing (Camara, Nathan and Puente, 2000; Meyer et al., 2001), but also specific attention to several supplementary sources of information. Many of these sources will have been identified in the course of the criminal investigation leading to the offender's current conviction. Relevant data will be produced from review of legal, treatment, military, forensic, and other records; interviews with teachers, family, friends, law enforcement personnel, and other parties; and consultation with legal counsel and other professional colleagues (Drogin and Barrett, 1996).

Several psychological studies have sought to identify factors that contribute to successful mediation in a variety of different contexts. The most prominent among the earliest of these surveys, specifically geared to concerns germane to Restorative Justice, was conducted under the auspices of the State University of New York at Buffalo (USA), reviewing 73 cases for the Neighborhood Justice Project in Elmira, New York. No relationship was found to exist between the objective 'quality' of the agreements reached and long-term success. On the other hand, factors such as the opportunity for joint problem-solving, fairness in adherence to relevant contours of the mediation process, and full visitation of all significant problems were seen as significant contributors to positive long-term outcomes (Pruitt et al., 1993; Zubek et al., 1992).

Similarly, a study conducted by faculty members of the University of Virginia (USA) found that such procedural factors are at least as determinative of participant satisfaction in procedural justice interventions, as whether parties obtained the specific results they had initially sought (Kitzmann and Emery, 1993; Vidmar, 1992). In the United

Kingdom, social scientific research has helped to confirm the hypothesis that supportive interventions employed in family therapy and individual psychotherapy exert a positive influence over the outcome of the mediation process as well (Robinson, 1988). Victims in England, participating in face-to-face mediation with offenders, reported approximately 14% greater satisfaction as a result of this psychological informed modality than with less direct methods of confrontation and/or reintegration (Umbreidt, 2001). Canadian investigators have noted increasing acknowledgment on the part of attorneys that psychological screening is an important pre-mediation function in successful dispute resolution (Girdner, 1990; Lee, Beauregard and Hunsley, 1998; McCoy and Hedeen, 1998).

Overall, studies from around the world have confirmed that parties' perceptions of having been afforded adequate participation contribute to optimal satisfaction with the interactive process (Roberson, Moye and Locke, 1999), and are thus crucial to the success of mediation in a Restorative Justice context. The application of psychological practice—in assessment, research, and the instillation of proven psychotherapeutic techniques—has clearly contributed to just outcomes for participants in Restorative Justice interventions.

Psychological Roles: The Functioning of the Psychologist as Mediator

In recent years, increasing attention has been paid to independent aspects of the psychologist's professional role in legal and other service provision environments. Such analyses are often performed without emphasizing the scientific research providing their context, or the psychotherapeutic and assessment duties performed therein (Drogin, 2001b; Tyler and McCallum, 1998; Watts, 2000). Where mediation is the service in question, '[l]awyers, psychologists, social workers, clergy, students, teachers, homemakers, and a host of others have contributed their own special skills and insights to the negotiation [of] disputes' (Drogin, 2001b). The distinct, role-bound considerations of the psychologist mediator will be reflected in the following issues.

Training

Noted Restorative Justice expert Mark Umbreidt has identified a series of 'basic characteristics' that should be possessed by persons considered to serve as mediators:

> These include good communication skills, particularly deep listening skills, which require patience and a high tolerance for silence; problem-solving and negotiation skills; the ability to exercise appropriate leadership; good organizational skills; commitment to the philosophy of Restorative Justice and techniques of nonviolent conflict resolution; and the ability to understand and work within the criminal justice system. (Umbreidt, 2001, p. 150)

Where psychologists are concerned, 'deep listening skills' (Phillips, 1999) and a 'high tolerance for silence' (Del Monte, 1995; Fuller and Crowther, 1998; Leira, 1995; Sabbadini, 1991) are very much tools of the successful psychotherapist's trade.

This has led those seeking to mold the psychologist *cum* mediator to ensure that such persons are branching out from a profitable practice, rather than fleeing failure as a healer (Thompson et al., 1993; Young, 1991). 'Good organizational skills' will figure prominently in this background. 'Leadership' is at best a nascent emphasis of the contemporary psychologist (Kiesler, 1999; Sullivan et al., 1998a, 1998b). A growing emphasis on forensic practice, however, has provided a steadily increasing number of psychologists with ample skills in this regard (Bersoff et al., 1997; Hafemeister, Ogloff and Small, 1990; Ogloff, 1999; Tomkins and Ogloff, 1990).

Ethics

Irrespective of the particular avocation to which they are applying themselves at a given time, psychologists remain bound to uphold applicable ethical codes and guidelines that govern professional practice across different areas of specialization (Adair, 2001; Figlio, 2000; Robson et al., 2000; Swain, 2000). Given the overt psychotherapeutic orientation of most sources of ethical guidance, psychologists and those employing them must remain alert to the possibility that role conflicts may arise, particularly in the more directive aspects of mediation practice. Key to success in this regard will be admonitions to the psychologist mediator to focus regularly on the particular function being served during each distinct phase of service provision (APA, 1993; Bennett, 1990; Bersoff, 1999; Figlio, 1993).

Participant Regard

No discussion of psychological roles would be complete without consideration of the esteem (or lack thereof) in which patients, clients, colleagues, and the public at large hold psychologists. While there has been considerable debate concerning the reliability and/or validity of methods employed in obtaining such data (Williams and Wilkinson, 1995), results of surveys lead one inexorably to the conclusion that psychologists are in significant need of outreach to the general populace (Obholzer, 1988). This appears to apply not only to problematically divergent values, but also, perhaps ironically, to mutually stigmatizing views of persons with mental illness and related disabilities (Chaplin, 2000; Leong and Zachar, 1999).

Lay perceptions of psychologists *per se* are often clouded by an inability—or disinclination—to distinguish between different types of mental health providers (Farberman, 1997). Studies conducted over the course of the last four decades (Von Sydow and Reimer, 1998), however, have consistently noted public image problems for psychologists, not the least of which has been the recently identified perception that psychotherapy and counseling have been characterized by many respondents as only moderately effective (Richardson and Handal, 1995).

In order to counter any negative (or interferingly positive, even dependent) perceptions on the part of victims, offenders, and other related parties, it remains important to the success of the mediation process—as well as ethically indicated from an informed consent perspective (Beahrs, 2001; Davies, 2001; Hamilton, 1983; Wirshing et al.,

1998)—to identify the specific background of each mediator. At the same time, a vital aspect of the initial engagement process will be a thorough explanation of the distinct functions of each actor in question, irrespective of overarching professional identities, in every mediation exercise.

These considerations lead to the conclusion that psychological roles may have a considerably varied effect upon just outcomes for Restorative Justice participants. Tailored, context-sensitive presentation and boundary construction will considerably influence these results.

CONCLUSION

Current Restorative Justice prospects in the United Kingdom contrast sharply with entrenched barriers found at the Federal level of the American justice system, reflecting what appear to be fundamentally different perspectives on the utility, effectiveness, and overall social desirability of flexibility in criminal sentencing. Whatever the future may hold for jurisdictions world wide, a Jurisprudent Therapy analysis confirms that the positive influence of psychological science, practice, and roles will remain considerable, as long as mediation remains the core modality exercised in the application of Restorative Justice.

REFERENCES

ADA Mediation Guidelines Work Group (2000). *ADA mediation guidelines.* New York: Author.

Adair, J.G. (2001). Ethics of psychological research: New policies, continuing issues, new concerns. *Canadian Psychologist, 42,* 25–37.

Akesher, K. (2000). The changing face of youth justice. *New Law Journal, 150,* 566.

Allard, P. and Northey, W. (2001). Christianity: The rediscovery of restorative justice. In M.L. Hadley (ed.), *The spiritual roots of restorative justice* (pp. 309–390). Albany, NY: State University of New York.

Ammar, N.H. (2001). Restorative justice in Islam: Theory and practice. In M.L. Hadley (ed.), *The spiritual roots of restorative justice* (pp. 161–180). Albany, NY: State University of New York.

APA (1993). *Legal risk management.* Washington, DC: American Psychological Association.

APA (1994). *Diagnostic and statistical manual of mental disorders* (4th edn). Washington, DC: American Psychiatric Association.

Apospori, E. and Alpert, G. (1993). The role of differential experience with the criminal justice system in changes in perceptions of severity of legal sanctions over time. *Crime and Delinquency, 39,* 184–194.

Arieti, S. (1979). *Understanding and helping the schizophrenic.* New York: Simon & Schuster.

Association of Chief Police Officers of England, Wales, and North Ireland (2000). *Restorative justice investigated.* Gloucestershire, England: Author.

Azayem, G.A. and Hedayat-Diba, Z. (1994). The psychological aspects of Islam: Basic principles of Islam and their psychological corollary. *International Journal of Psychology and Religion, 4,* 41–50.

Baier, C.J. and Wright, B.R. (2001). If you love me, keep my commandments: A meta-analysis of the effect of religion on crime. *Current Perspectives on Crime and Delinquency, 38,* 3–21.

Bazemore, G. and Schiff, M. (1996). Community justice/restorative justice: Prospects for a new social ecology for community corrections. *International Journal of Comparative and Applied Criminal Justice*, *20*, 311–335.

Beahrs, J.O. (2001). Informed consent in psychotherapy. *American Journal of Psychiatry*, *158*, 4–10.

Beck, A., Rush, A., Shaw, B. and Emery, G. (1979). *Cognitive therapy of depression*. New York: Guilford.

Ben-David, S. and Weller, L. (1995). Religiosity, criminality and types of offences of Jewish male prisoners. *Medicine and Law*, *14*, 509–519.

Bennett, B. (1990). *Professional liability and risk management*. Washington, DC: American Psychological Association.

Bersoff, D.N., Goodman-Delahunty, J., Grisso, J.T., Hans, V.P., Poythress, N.G. and Roesch, R. (1997). Training in law and psychology. *American Psychologist*, *52*, 1301–1310.

Bersoff, D.N. (1999). *Ethical conflicts in psychology* (2nd edn). Washington, DC: American Psychological Association.

Bloom, J.D., Williams, M.H. and Bigelow, D.A. (1992). The involvement of schizophrenic insanity acquittees in the mental health and criminal justice systems. *Psychiatric Clinics of North America*, *15*, 591–604.

Bradfield, M. and Acquino, K. (1999). The effects of blame attributions and offender likeableness on forgiveness and revenge in the workplace. *Journal of Management*, *25*, 607–631.

Bradford, J.M. (1995). Mentally disordered offenders and the law. *Canadian Journal of Psychiatry*, *40*, 223–224.

Cather, P. (1995). Violence and personal responsibility. *American Journal of Public Health*, *85*, 413–414.

Camara, W.J., Nathan, J.S. and Puente, A.J. (2000). Psychological test usage: Implications in professional psychology. *Professional Psychology: Research and Practice*, *31*, 141–154.

Chaplin, R. (2000). Psychiatrists can cause stigma too. *British Journal of Psychiatry*, *177*, 467.

Cochrane, R. and Bal, S. (1990). The drinking habits of Sikh, Hindu, Muslim and white men in the West Midlands: A community survey. *British Journal of Addiction*, *85*, 759–769.

Cohen, J. and Dvoskin, J. (1992). Inmates with mental disorders: A guide to law and practice. *Mental and Physical Disability Law Reporter*, *16*, 339–346.

Colliver, J.A., Swartz, M.H., Robbs, R. and Cohen, D. (1999). Relationship between clinical competence and interpersonal and communication skills in standardized-patient assessment. *Academic Medicine*, *74*, 271–274.

Crime and Disorder Act 1998, c. 37 (Eng.).

Dattilo, J., Hoge, G. and Malley, S. (1996). Interviewing people with mental retardation: Validity and reliability strategies. *Therapeutic Recreation Journal*, *30*, 163–179.

Davies, T. (2001). Informed consent in psychiatric research. *British Journal of Psychiatry*, *178*, 397–398.

Del Monte, M. (1995). Silence and emptiness in the service of healing: Lessons from meditation. *British Journal of Psychotherapy*, *11*, 368–378.

Dignan J. (1999). The Crime and Disorder Act and the prospects for restorative justice, *Criminal Law Review*, *48*, 48–60.

Dignan, J. (2000). *Youth justice pilots evaluation*. London: Home Office.

Dignan, J. and Cavadino, M. (1996). Towards a framework for conceptualizing and evaluating models of criminal justice from a victim's perspective. *International Review of Victimology*, *4*, 153–182.

Drogin, E.Y. (2000a). From therapeutic jurisprudence . . . to jurisprudent therapy. *Behavioral Sciences and the Law*, *18*, 489–498.

Drogin, E.Y. (2000b). Family law, evidence, and expert mental health witnesses: A jurisprudent therapy perspective. In E. Pierson (ed.), *2000 family law update* (pp. 281–313). New York: Aspen.

Drogin, E.Y. (2000c). Breaking through: Communicating and collaborating with the mentally ill defendant. *The Advocate*, *22*, 27–34.

Drogin E.Y. (2001a). Utilizing forensic psychological consultation: A jurisprudent therapy perspective. *Mental and Physical Disability Law Reporter*, *25*, 17–21.

Drogin, E.Y. (2001b). Jurisprudent therapy, scientific evidence, and the role of the forensic psychologist. *Scientific Evidence Review*, *5*, 129–154.

Drogin, E.Y. and Barrett, C.L. (1996). But doctor, isn't that just your opinion? Contributing to the decision-making process of the forensic psychologist as expert witness. *The Advocate*, *18*, 14–20.

Drogin E.Y. and Barrett, C.L. (1998). Addictions and family law. In E. Pierson (ed.), *1998 family law update* (pp. 61–106). New York: Aspen.

Drogin, E.Y. and Monahan, E.C. (2001). Acknowledging the prevalence of severe mental illness on death row. *The Advocate*, *23*, 56–57.

Duffy, J. (1995). The neurology of alcoholic denial: Implications for assessment and treatment. *Canadian Journal of Psychiatry*, *40*, 257–263.

Elias, S., Sigelman, C. and Danker-Brown, P. (1980). Interview behavior of and impressions made by mentally retarded clients. *American Journal of Mental Deficiency*, *85*, 53–60.

Ellis, L. and Peterson, J. (1996). Crime and religion: An international comparison among thirteen industrial nations. *Personality and Individual Differences*, *20*, 761–768.

Farberman, R.K. (1997). Public attitudes about psychologists and mental health care. *Professional Psychology: Research and Practice*, *28*, 128–136.

Figlio, K. (1993). The field of psychotherapy: Conceptual and ethical definitions. *British Journal of Psychotherapy*, *9*, 324–335.

Figlio, K. (2000). Registration and ethics in psychotherapy. *British Journal of Psychotherapy*, *16*, 327–334.

Fuller, V.G. and Crowther, C. (1998). A dark talent: Silence in analysis. *Journal of Analytical Psychology*, *43*, 523–543.

Gilsinan, J. (1990). *Criminology and public policy*. Englewood Cliffs, NJ: Prentice Hall.

Girdner, L.K. (1990). Mediation triage. *Mediation Quarterly*, *7*, 365–376.

Government (1997). *No more excuses: A new approach to tackling youth crime in England and Wales*. London: HMSO.

Gurevich, K.M. (1991). Psychological diagnostics and the laws of psychology. *Soviet Journal of Psychology*, *12*, 99–109.

Hafemeister, T.L., Ogloff, J.R. and Small, M.A. (1990). Training and careers in law and psychology. *Behavioral Sciences and the Law*, *8*, 263–283.

Hamilton, M. (1983). On informed consent. *British Journal of Psychiatry*, *143*, 416–418.

Hans, S.S. (1986). The psychological substrate of Sikh theology. *Personality Studies and Group Behavior*, *6*, 47–54.

Heller, K., Price, R., Reinharz, S., Riger, S. and Wandersman, A. (1984). *Psychology and community change: Challenges of the future*. Homewood, IL: Dorsey Press.

Home Office (1998). *Interdepartmental circular on establishing youth offending teams*. London: Author.

Home Office (2000). *The Crime and Disorder Act guidance document: Action plan orders*. London: HMSO.

Insanity Defense Reform Act (1987), 18 USC §17.

The Observer (2001). Jailing young causes crime says charity. 15 July, p. 6.

Kaliski, S. (1995). Violence, sensation seeking, and impulsivity in schizophrenics found unfit to stand trial. *Bulletin of the American Academy of Psychiatry and the Law*, *23*, 147–155.

Kaplan, H. and Sadock, B. (1998). *Synopsis of psychiatry* (8th edn). Baltimore: Williams & Wilkins.

Keyes, D., Edwards, W. and Derning, T. (1998). Mitigating mental retardation in capital cases: Finding the 'invisible' defendant. *Mental and Physical Disability Law Reporter*, *22*, 529–539.

Kiesler, C.A. (1999). Psychologists and organizational leadership. *Psychologist-Manager Journal*, *3*, 105–113.

Kitzmann, K. and Emery, R.E. (1993). Procedural justice and parents' satisfaction in a field study of child custody dispute resolution. *Law and Human Behavior*, *17*, 553–567.

Koocher, G., Norcross, J. and Hill, S. (1998). *Psychologist's desk reference*. New York: Oxford University Press.

Kretschmer, R.R. and Kretschmer, L.W. (1998). Communication competence and assessment, *Journal of Academic Rehabilitation Audiology*, *21*, 5–17.

Lee, C.M., Beauregard, C.P. and Hunsley, J. (1998). Lawyers' opinions regarding child custody mediation and assessment services: Implications for psychological practice. *Professional Psychology: Research and Practice*, *29*, 115–120.

Leira, T. (1995). Silence and communication: Nonverbal dialogue and therapeutic action. *Scandinavian Psychoanalytic Review*, *18*, 41–65.

Leong, F.Y. and Zachar, P. (1999). Gender and opinions about mental illness as predictors of attitudes toward seeking professional psychological help. *British Journal of Guidance and Counselling*, *27*, 123–132.

Lewis, D.O. and Pincus, J.H. (1986). Psychiatric, neurological, and psychoeducational characteristics of 15 death row inmates in the United States. *American Journal of Psychiatry*, *143*, 838.

Lewis, D.O., Pincus, J.H., Bard, B., Richardson, E., Prichep, L.S., Feldman, M. and Yeager, C. (1988). Neuropsychiatric, psychoeducational, and family characteristics of 14 juveniles condemned to death in the United States. *American Journal of Psychiatry*, *145*, 584.

Marshall, T. (1999). *Restorative justice: An overview*. London: Home Office.

Marshall T. and Merry, S. (1990). *Crime and accountability: Victim/offender mediation in practice*. London: HMSO.

Massman, J. and Tipton, D. (1988). Signs and symptoms assessment: A guide for the treatment of the alcohol withdrawal syndrome. *Journal of Psychoactive Drugs*, *20*, 443–444.

Masters, R. and Roberson, C. (1990). *Inside criminology*. Englewood Cliffs, NJ: Prentice Hall.

McCoy, P.G. and Hedeen, T.M. (1998). Disabilities and mediation readiness in court-referred cases: developing screening criteria and service networks. *Mediation Quarterly*, *16*, 113–127.

Menninger, K. (1996). *The crime of punishment*. New York: Penguin.

Mesch, G. and Fishman, G. (1998). Fear of crime and individual crime protective actions in Israel. *International Review of Criminology*, *5*, 311–330.

Meyer, G.J., Finn, S.E., Eyde, L.D., Kay, G.G., Moreland, K.L., Dies, R.R. et al. (2001). Psychological testing and psychological assessment: A review of evidence and issues. *American Psychologist*, *56*, 128–165.

Mitchell, B. (1998). Public perceptions of homicide and criminal justice. *British Journal of Criminology*, *38*, 453–472.

Mohr, P.B. and Luscri, G. (1995). Blame and punishment: Attitudes to juvenile and criminal offending. *Psychological Reports*, *77*, 1091–1096.

Moring, P. (1997). Trust, the counselor and containment in counseling the drug-addicted client. *Psychodynamic Counseling*, *3*, 433–446.

Morris, A. and Gelsthorpe, L. (2000). Something old, something borrowed, something blue, but something new? A comment on the prospects for restorative justice under the Crime and Disorder Act of 1998. *Criminal Law Review*, *49*, 18–30.

Neufeldt, R. (2001). Justice in Hinduism. In M. L. Hadley (ed.), *The spiritual roots of restorative justice* (pp. 143–160). Albany, NY: State University of New York.

Obholzer, A. (1988). Fostering a climate for growth. *British Journal of Psychotherapy*, *5*, 186–191.

Ogloff, J.R. (1999). Graduate training in law and psychology at Simon Fraser University. *Professional Psychology: Research and Practice*, *30*, 99–103.

Padayachee, A. and Singh, S.R. (1998). Violence against women: A long history for South African Indian women, with special reference to Hinduism and Hindu law. *Social Science International*, *14*, 1–10.

Parry, J. and Drogin, E. (2000). *Criminal law handbook on psychiatric and psychological evidence and testimony*. Washington, DC: American Bar Association.

Pettersson, T. (1991). Religion and criminality: Structural relationships between church involvement and crime rates in contemporary Sweden. *Journal of the Scientific Study of Religion, 30,* 279–291.

Phillips, B. (1999). Reformulating dispute narratives through active listening. *Mediation Quarterly, 17,* 161 180.

Pruitt, D.G., Peirce, R.S., McGillicuddy, N.B., Welton, G.L. and Castrianno, L.M. (1993). Long-term success in mediation. *Law and Human Behavior, 17,* 313–330.

Restorative Justice Consortium (1998). *Standards in restorative justice.* London: Author.

Richardson, P. and Handal, P. (1995). The public's perception of psychotherapy and counseling: Differential views of the effectiveness of psychologists, psychiatrists, and other providers. *Journal of Contemporary Psychotherapy, 25,* 36–85.

Roach, K. (2000). Changing punishment at the turn of the century: Restorative justice on the rise. *Canadian Journal of Criminology, 42,* 249–280.

Roberson, Q.M., Moye, N.A. and Locke, E.A. (1999). Identifying a missing link between participation and satisfaction: The mediating role of procedural justice perceptions. *Journal of Applied Psychology, 84,* 585–593.

Robinson, M. (1988). Mediation with families in separation and divorce in the United Kingdom: Links with family therapy. *American Journal of Family Therapy, 16,* 60–72.

Robson, M., Cook, P., Hunt, K., Alred, G. and Robson, D. (2000). Towards ethical decision-making in counseling research. *British Journal of Guidance and Counselling, 28,* 533–547.

Rosenbloom, A. (1988). Emerging treatment options in the alcohol withdrawal syndrome, *Journal of Clinical Psychiatry, 49,* 28–31.

Sabbadini, A. (1991). Listening to silence. *British Journal of Psychotherapy, 7,* 406–415.

Schaeffer, K.W., Parsons, O.A. and Errico, A.L. (1989). Performance deficits on tests of problem solving in alcoholics: Cognitive or motivational impairment? *Journal of Substance Abuse, 1,* 381–392.

Segal, E. (2001). Jewish perspectives on restorative justice. In M. L. Hadley (ed.),*The spiritual roots of restorative justice* (pp. 181–197). Albany, NY: State University of New York.

Scanlan, D. (1988). *The Crime and Disorder Act 1998: A guide for practitioners.* London: Callow Publishing.

Sentencing Reform Act (1984), 28 USC §994.

Shepherd, J. (1990). Victims of personal violence: The relevance of Symonds' model of psychological response and loss-theory. *British Journal of Social Work, 20,* 309–332.

Sigelman, C.K., Budd, E.C., Spanhel, C.L. and Schoenrock, C.J. (1981). When in doubt, say yes: Acquiescence in interviews with mentally retarded persons. *Mental Retardation, 19,* 53–58.

Singh, P. (2001). Sikhism and restorative justice: theory and practice. In M.L. Hadley (ed.), *The spiritual roots of restorative justice* (pp. 199–216). Albany, NY: State University of New York.

Spano, S. and Zimmerman, S. (1995). Interpersonal communication competence in context. *Communication Reports, 8,* 18–26.

Steinfeld, G.J. (1998). Personal responsibility in human relationships: A cognitive-constructivist approach. *Transactional Analysis Journal, 28,* 188–201.

Sullivan, M.J., Groveman, A.M., Heldring, M.B., DeLeon, P.H. and Beauchamp, B. (1998). Public policy leadership opportunities for psychologists. *Professional Psychology: Research and Practice, 29,* 322–327.

Sullivan, M.J., Johnson, P.I., Kjellberg, B.J., Williams, J. and Beauchamp, B. (1998). Community leadership opportunities for psychologists. *Professional Psychology: Research and Practice, 29,* 328–331.

Swain, R. (2000). Awareness and decision making in professional ethics: The new Code of the Psychological Society of Ireland. *European Psychology, 5,* 19–27.

Thompson, J.K., Riley, P.M., Staver, N., Steinman, C.Z. and Trust, C. (1993). A successful private practice referral service. *Social Work, 38,* 227–228.

Tomkins, A.J. and Ogloff, J.R. (1990). Training and career options in psychology and law. *Behavioral Sciences and the Law, 8,* 205–216.

Tyler, D. and McCallum, S.R. (1998). Assessing the relationship between competence and job role and identity among direct service counseling psychologists. *Journal of Psychoeducational Assessment, 16*, 135–152.

Umbreidt, M. (1994). *Victim meets offender: The impact of restorative justice and mediation.* Monsey, NY: Criminal Justice Press.

Umbreidt, M. (2001). *The handbook of victim offender mediation.* San Francisco: Jossey-Bass.

US Department of Justice (1999). *Mental health treatment of inmates and probationers.* Washington, DC: Author.

US Sentencing Commission (2000). *Federal sentencing guidelines manual.* Minneapolis, MN: West Group.

Vaccaro, A.J. (1988). Personality clash. *Personnel Administration, 33*, 88–92.

Vidmar, N. (1992). Procedural justice and alternative dispute resolution. *Psychological Science, 3*, 224–228.

Von Sydow, K. and Reimer, C. (1998). Attitudes toward psychotherapists, psychologists, psychiatrists and psychoanalysts: A meta-content analysis of 60 studies published between 1948 and 1995. *American Journal of Psychotherapy, 52*, 463–488.

Ward, C. and Rothaus, P. (1991). The measurement of denial and rationalization in male alcoholics, *Journal of Clinical Psychology, 47*, 465–468.

Wallerstein, H. (1952). *Penguin dictionary of psychology.* New York: Penguin.

Walters, G.D. and White, T.W. (1988). Crime, popular mythology, and personal responsibility. *Federal Probation, 52*, 18–26.

Watts, G.W. (2000). Psychologist-entrepreneurs: Roles, roll-ups and rolodexes. *Psychologist-Manager Journal, 4*, 79–90.

Wexler, D. (1990). *Therapeutic jurisprudence: The law as a therapeutic agent.* Durham, NC: Carolina Academic Press.

Wexler, D. and Winick, B. (1991). Therapeutic jurisprudence as a new approach to mental health law policy analysis and research. *University of Miami Law Review, 45*, 979–1004.

Williams, B. and Wilkinson, G. (1995). Patient satisfaction in mental health care: Evaluating an evaluative method. 166 *British Journal of Psychiatry, 166*, 559–562.

Wirshing, D.A., Wirshing, W.C., Marder, S.R., Liberman, R.P. and Mintz, J. (1998). Informed consent: Assessment of comprehension. *American Journal of Psychiatry, 155*, 1508–1511.

Wiseman, E.J., Souder, E. and O'Sullivan, P. (1996). Age and denial of alcoholism severity. *Clinical Gerontologist, 17*, 55–58.

Wright, J., Thase, M., Beck, A. and Ludgate, J. (1993). *Cognitive therapy with inpatients.* New York: Guilford.

Wolman, B. (1973). *Dictionary of behavioral science.* New York: Van Nostrand Reinhold.

Young, B.A. (1991). Reasons for changing jobs within a career structure. *Leadership and Organizational Development Journal, 12*, 12–16.

Zehr, H. (1990). *Changing lenses: A new focus for crime and justice.* Scottsdale, PA: Herald Press.

Zubek, J.M., Pruitt, D.G., Peirce, R.S., McGillicuddy, N.B. and Syna, H. (1992). Disputant and mediator behaviors affecting short-term success in mediation. *Journal of Conflict Resolution, 36*, 546–572.

Cases

United States v. *Cantu*, 12 F.3d 1506 (9th Cir. 1993).

United States v. *Chatlin*, 51 F.3d 869 (9th Cir. 1995).

United States v. *Desorneaux*, 952 F.2d 182 (8th Cir. 1991).

United States v. *Ellis*, 935 F.2d 385 (1st Cir. 1991).

United States v. *Fawbush*, 946 F.2d 584 (8th Cir. 1991).

United States v. *Garza-Juarez*, 992 F.2d 896 (9th Cir. 1993).

United States v. *Harpst*, 949 F.2d 860 (6th Cir. 1991).

United States v. *Lara*, 905 F.2d 599 (2nd Cir. 1990).

United States v. *Lauzon*, 938 F.2d 326 (1st Cir. 1991).
United States v. *McBroom*, 124 F.3d 533 (3rd Cir. 1997).
United States v. *McMurry*, 833 F.Supp. 1454 (D. Neb. 1993).
United States v. *Rabins*, 63 F.3d 721 (8th Cir. 1995).
United States v. *Ribot*, 97 F.Supp.2d 74 (D. Mass. 1999).
United States v. *Roe*, 976 F.2d 1216 (9th Cir. 1992).
United States v. *Rosen*, 896 F.2d 789 (3rd Cir. 1990).
United States v. *Ruklick*, 919 F.2d 95 (8th Cir. 1990).
United States v. *Woody*, 55 F.3d 1257 (7th Cir. 1995).

Chapter 3.7

Proactive Judges: Solving Problems and Transforming Communities

Leonore M.J. Simon
East Tennessee State University, USA

> *In many of today's cases, the traditional approach yields unsatisfying results. The addict arrested for drug dealing is adjudicated, does time, then goes right back to dealing on the street. The battered wife obtains a protective order, goes home and is beaten again. Every legal right of the litigants is protected, all procedures followed, yet we aren't making a dent in the underlying problem. Not good for the parties involved. Not good for the community. Not good for the courts.*
>
> (Kaye, 1999, p. 13)

New York State Chief Judge, Judith S. Kaye, is not alone in her analysis of the failure of traditional judges and courts to adequately solve many of the problems their cases present. Many United States courts are inundated with particular categories of cases that take up a disproportionate amount of court time. For example, between 1985 and 1997, there was a 65% rise in domestic relations, a 68% increase in juvenile and a 45% increase in criminal court filings (Ostrom and Kauder, 1998). From 1989 to 1998, domestic violence filings in state courts increased 178% (Ostrom and Kauder, 1999). From 1971 to 1995 arrest rates for drug offenses increased by 122% (Ostrom and Kauder, 1998). Weary of recycling cases, proactive judges are departing from the traditional model of reactive judging, and seeking partnerships with other legal actors and communities to change the way courts and the judiciary conduct business. The objective is to become more effective problem-solvers, to improve results for victims, litigants, defendants, and communities, and to instill an 'ethic of care' into the legal system (Schma, 2000). While the results of proactive judging are clearest in the growing number of specialized courts (Fritzler and Simon, 2000a; Hora, Schma and Rosenthal, 1999), it also occurs on systemic and policy levels.

Handbook of Psychology in Legal Contexts, Second Edition
Edited by D. Carson and R. Bull. © 2003 John Wiley & Sons, Ltd.

The impetus has been the large number of cases of chronic social, human and legal problems trapped in a revolving door of court appearances and a demand by the community for deeper involvement by judges (Zimmerman, 1998). Many judges are seeking more information and options to respond to the complexities of drug addiction, mental illness, families in crisis, and domestic violence. To address the 'revolving door' nature of these cases, proactive judges have adopted the approach that originated in community policing (Kelling and Moore, 1988; Rottman and Casey, 1999). Just as some police forces have decided to tackle the underlying problems, rather than simply process cases (Moore, 1992), proactive judges have been forming court and community collaborations to problem-solve at both the community and individual case level (Fritzler and Simon, 2000b; Rottman, Efkeman and Casey, 1998). They embrace neighborhoods as clients and targets of intervention as well as litigants, ensuring that the justice system serves citizens and communities (Fritzler and Simon, 2000a, 2000b). Proactive judges broaden the focus of legal proceedings from simply adjudicating past facts and legal issues, to changing the future behavior of litigants and ensuring the welfare of the communities. The court/community collaboration has, in the case of specialized courts, created 'communities of care' in the form of networks of court and community resources applied to court participants such as families in crisis, domestic violence victims and offenders, drug abusers, mentally disordered defendants, and distressed communities.

The growth in the number of intractable cases flooding the courts occurs at a time when concerns about access to justice and public dissatisfaction with the courts prevail in American communities (Rottman et al., 1998). Only 23% of Americans surveyed have a great deal of trust and confidence in the 'courts in your community' (National Center for State Courts, 1999). Respondents reported less trust and confidence in the courts than in doctors, the police, the US Supreme Court, the state governor, and public schools. Of those surveyed, 40% believe that court participants do not understand court rulings in their cases, and that courts are not in touch with their communities (National Center for State Courts, 1999). Proactive judges, who develop partnerships with their communities to problem-solve, can educate the public, make courts more accountable, and develop a supportive constituency.

This chapter explores the phenomenon of proactive judges and the paradigm shift that is occurring in American courts. The terms 'proactive judges' and 'problem-solving judges' will be used interchangeably to denote judges who actively seek to change the court system to respond to social, psychological, and community problems.

> Problem-solving requires a shift in what is valued in the adjudication process: outcomes (rather than outputs), flexibility in decision-making, listening to people's concerns, participation by community organizations, and consideration of what is best for communities as well as for individual defendants or victims. Problem-solving also places greater emphasis on post-adjudication events, a significant change in focus from traditional models of case processing. (Rottman, 2000, p. 22)

The chapter concludes with the implications of proactive judging for future practice and policy.

PROACTIVE JUDGING AND SPECIALIZED COURTS

Problem-solving judges, and the paradigm of therapeutic courts, recently emerged as a result of the war on drugs and its effects on the courts (Lipscher, 1999). Drug courts, designed to deal with the overflow of drug cases in the late 1980s, attracted judges who sought 'a treatment-based alternative that also mandated judicially supervised sanctions' (Gebelein, 2000, p. 2). Policy-makers saw an innovative opportunity and established federal funding for drug courts in the 1994 Crime Act (Gebelein, 2000). The key elements include integration of treatment with court processing; use of a non-adversarial approach; early identification and placement; access to a continuum of services; frequent drug and alcohol testing; a coordinated team approach; ongoing judicial interaction and monitoring; continuing interdisciplinary education; and partnerships with community agencies. Proactive judges are an integral part of drug courts (Gebelein, 2000), and the relationship between drug-addicted defendants and the judge may account for a major part of the court's effectiveness (T. Merrigan, personal communication, June 7, 2001).

With drug courts as a precedent, judges have been developing problem-solving courts to test new approaches in other difficult cases (Rottman et al., 2000). Proactive judges have been motivated by frustration with the ineffective traditional judicial response to marginalized yet chronic types of cases that overwhelm the courts with their increasing numbers, high recidivism rates, and needs for social and psychological services (Fritzler and Simon, 2000a, Hora et al., 1999; Lurigio et al., 2001). These courts and judges are often the average citizen's sole point of contact with the justice system, and the experience can determine his or her respect for, or alienation from, the legal system in its entirety (Ross, 1998). By providing needed services and solutions to court users, proactive judges can improve community satisfaction with the courts (Svidiroff et al., 1998).

Specialized courts provide a forum for more individual attention to, and resources for, cases that are inadequately handled in courts of general jurisdiction (Rottman et al., 1998). Typically the catalyst for the development of a specialized court is an individual judge, who has grown deeply dissatisfied with the available diagnostic and treatment services, or with the degree of coordination among service providers for an increasing number of cases (R. Fritzler, personal communication, May 4, 2001). Proactive judges, who create specialized courts, seek out new expertise for themselves and their staff. For example, a unified family court is conducted by a specially trained and interested judge who addresses the legal and accompanying emotional and social issues of the family by coordinating resources and social service agencies (Ross, 1998; Williams, 1995). This contrasts sharply with traditional family court judges who have little or no special expertise. Moreover, the unified family court judge is assisted by every person who works in the court, from clerks to intake personnel to case managers to lawyers, who also have specialized training (Ross, 1998). A unified family court encompasses a single court with comprehensive jurisdiction over all cases involving children and relating to the family that have traditionally been handled by different judges in different courts (Babb, 1998a, 1998b). But even specialized courts differ between jurisdictions. For example, mental health courts may differ in their adaptation of the problem-solving model to their particular local systems. 'These differences include the timing and method of resolving the underlying criminal charges, the responses to non-compliance by participants, and the effect of a defense request for a trial' (Goldkamp and Irons-Guynn, 2000, p. 69). Indeed the variety of specialized courts highlights the importance of understanding how narrowly or broadly to define the subject matter jurisdiction of the court for maximum effectiveness. 'If the specialization is too broad, it is diluted. If the specialization is too narrow, the volume of cases may be too low to warrant a specialized court. And if the court shares jurisdiction of a particular subject matter, the court system becomes more complex for the user' (Rottman and Casey, 1999).

ELEMENTS COMMON TO PROACTIVE JUDGES AND SPECIALIZED COURTS

While drug, domestic violence, mental health, unified family, and community courts address different problems, they share common elements. Proactive judges and specialized courts first seek to achieve improved outcomes for victims, offenders, and society. Outcomes often stressed include reductions in the incidence of domestic violence, enhanced victim safety, increased accountability of batterers, reduced recidivism, increased sobriety for addicts, improved mental health services for mentally disordered offenders, and healthier families and communities.

Second, judicial authority is actively used to solve problems and change litigants' behavior. Instead of passing off cases to other judges, probation offices, community-based treatment programs, or to no one, judges stay involved with each case throughout the post-adjudication process (Berman and Feinblatt, 2000). Drug court judges, for example, closely supervise the performance of offenders in drug treatment programs, requiring them to return to court frequently for urine testing and courtroom progress reports.

Third, proactive judges and specialized courts employ a collaborative approach, relying on partnerships with criminal justice agencies, social service providers, and community groups to help achieve their goals. For example, many domestic violence courts have developed relationships with batterer programs, victim advocates, and probation officers to help improve the monitoring and compliance of batterers and the safety of victims.

Fourth, they have altered the dynamics of the courtroom and the adversarial system (Berman and Feinblatt, 2000). For example, in many drug courts, judges, attorneys, and treatment providers work as a team to devise systems of sanctions and rewards for offenders in drug treatment. By using the court's authority to coordinate the work of other agencies, judges assume untraditional roles as case managers. They balance fairness with increased effectiveness by observing traditional due process protections during the adjudication phase but emphasizing therapeutic outcomes post-adjudication.

> Generally, adversarial procedures are employed at the screening and admission stage (with different procedures for diversion or guilty plea courts), and at the conclusion of drug court, when participants are terminated and face legal consequences or graduate. During the drug court process, however, formal adversarial rules generally do not apply.
> (Goldkamp, 2000, p. 952)

Fifth, proactive judges have influenced actual system change. They have begun to interest the chief judges and administrators who make decisions about court policies and operations (Conference of Chief Justices and the Conference of State Court Administrators Task Force on Therapeutic Justice, 2000).

EXAMPLES OF SPECIALIZED COURTS

Domestic Violence Courts

One example of a specialized court is the Vancouver, Washington Misdemeanor Domestic Violence Court. At monthly meetings of the Clark County Domestic Violence/Sexual Assault Task Force, which included a wide array of community members and professionals (including Judge Randal Fritzler), there was a consensus that domestic violence was as much a community problem as a victim issue. Judge Fritzler decided to create a specialized domestic violence court and forged a partnership with a collaborative team that included Washington State University, probation officers, city and county prosecutors, city and county law enforcement, Young Women's Christian Association (YWCA) victim advocates, and offender treatment providers (Fritzler and Simon, 2000a, 2000b). The court has centralized the services that victims and offenders need in the courthouse, with the judge coordinating provision of legal, social, and psychological services. For example, battered women are able to get civil protection orders from the same judge who hears the criminal cases involving battering. Court clerks and YWCA victim advocates assist battered women in filling out the paperwork. The court integrates batterer intervention/treatment with alcohol and drug abuse treatment services as well as victim advocacy and support services for victims from the YWCA. The court addresses issues of economic support for battered women and their children by including specific provisions in the sentence orders of offenders. After sentencing offenders, the court schedules periodic reviews to ascertain compliance with its orders. If violations are found, the court imposes immediate graduated sanctions that include more frequent reviews, electronic home confinement, work crews, alternative community service, more restrictive terms of probation, more intensive treatment, or actual jail time (Fritzler and Simon, 2000a).

The social service providers like YWCA victim advocates, and the batterer treatment providers that assist the Vancouver Court, do not have actual offices in the court building itself, although they appear regularly in court. Most of the Vancouver Court social service providers are independently funded: The YWCA is a non-profit organization that receives funding from a variety of sources; the batterer treatment providers are private therapists who derive most of their income from fees paid by the batterers or private practice. Although independent from the Court, they readily accept direction from the judge on a case by case basis because they are allowed input into the proceedings, and because they respect the judge and judicial authority. In fact, prior to the implementation of the Court, these service providers had difficulty coordinating their services and communicating with each other, often resulting in additional violence for battered women. For example, batterer treatment providers would often recommend to the court that orders of protection be lifted based on batterer self-reports that the victim wished to resume contact. Frequently, victim advocates, who could have provided information that the victim did not wish to resume contact with the batterer, were not consulted. This was one of many problems discussed in planning and implementation meetings for the new Court. It resulted in judicial inquiries of victim advocates, prior to the lifting of orders of protection. Before the Court the judge would refer convicted batterers to the probation department which was expected to coordinate batterer treatment needs. Batterers in treatment would insist that the judge had not ordered the treatment, fueling their denial and resistance. After the Court was formed referrals came directly from the judge, resulting in less resistance. Service providers had long been frustrated with these types of problems that allowed batterers to manipulate the system. They readily welcomed and respected the active involvement by and strong leadership of the judge.

Without a formal evaluation, it is difficult to gauge the success of the Vancouver Court and the proactive judging that developed it. However, although national statistics indicate a decrease in domestic violence cases the Court has achieved an increase in the number of cases processed. In 1998 the court processed 1396 domestic violence cases, 978 civil domestic violence protection orders, and 478 anti-harassment orders (R. Winsor, personal communication, March 12, 2000). In 1999, the court processed 1631 domestic violence cases, 1028 civil domestic violence protection orders, and 486 anti-harassment orders. This suggests that, contrary to past legal practices that tended to treat domestic violence as a private matter, domestic violence cases are being treated more seriously by legal actors, and that batterers are being held accountable. A formal evaluation could determine what impact the Court and its proactive judge has had on victims, batterers, legal and social service providers, and the community. Evaluators might specifically address the effectiveness of the Court by interviewing victims and victim advocates to measure victim safety and satisfaction.

Drug Courts

Drug courts evolved out of earlier unsuccessful, often fragmented, efforts to link drug offenders with treatment services. There are over 1000 drug courts in the planning and implementation phases in the United States and beyond (National Drug Court Institute, 2001). They are 'dedicated courtrooms that provide judicially-monitored treatment, drug testing and other services to drug-involved offenders' (Belenko, 1998, p. 4). These courts seek to craft custom-designed sentences for drug offenders that

incorporate both supervision and treatment components. Drug courts take a therapeutic, non-adversarial approach that promotes public safety while promoting the
treatment of drug dependency. They rely on community-based treatment options and
supervision and require cooperation between various elements of the justice system
and the community at large. In a study of one drug court, all drug felony defendants
were randomly assigned to one of three dockets (lists or calendars of cases to be
tried at a specified date and time) (Harrell, Cavanagh and Roman, 2000). The evaluation found reductions in drug use during pretrial release for defendants in both the
treatment and sanctions docket. It found reductions in arrests during the year after
sentencing for sanctions program participants, and reductions in drug-related social
problems (such as car accidents) for treatment program participants. (Selection bias
could not be ignored because program participation was voluntary and may have
attracted defendants motivated to change.) Several factors were stressed for successful outcomes. First, combining treatment with graduated sanctions was important
for reducing drug use during the period of supervision. Second, the evaluation indicated the importance of getting the defendant's 'up-front' commitment to the rules
(Harrell et al., 2000). Defendants' knowledge of, and commitment to, the sanctions
gave them a feeling of control and a sense they were treated fairly. 'This "contingency contract" between judge and defendant clearly differentiates these sanctions
from imposed penalties using poorly understood or inconsistently enforced rules'
(Harrell et al., 2000, p. 11). Third, Harrell and her colleagues noted that 'strong and
cohesive leadership was important to the success of the programs. The judges' commitment to the program implementation was one of the strengths of the experimental
demonstration' (Harrell et al., 2000, p. 11). Lastly, the judges had state-of-the-art technology that was immediate, accurate, and accessible to judges via computers on the
bench.

Mental Health Courts

Thousands of mentally disordered individuals pass through the criminal justice system
each year. Mental health courts have access to representatives of relevant justice and
treatment agencies 'to form a cooperative and multidisciplinary working relationship
with expertise in mental health issues' (Goldkamp and Irons-Guynn, 2000, p. viii). The
judge is at the center of the treatment and supervision process, providing therapeutic
direction and overall accountability for the treatment process.

The first mental health court, the Broward County Mental Health Court in Fort Lauderdale, Florida, grew out of a recommendation of a multi-agency Criminal Justice
Mental Health Task Force (Goldkamp and Irons-Guynn, 2000). The Court serves
primarily as a pre-adjudication, diversion program for misdemeanants. Clinicians,
advanced doctoral students in psychology at a local university assigned to the Public
Defender's Office, screen jailed offenders for mental health issues prior to the first
hearing. When mental health symptoms are found, the Defender informs the Court
at the first hearing. Other mentally ill offenders are identified by Emergency Medial
Services Associated, which is a private provider that contracts with the jail to provide
mental health, medical, and dental services to the inmates. Other judges, defense

lawyers, police, the defendant's family, or mental health caseworker also makes referrals. The Court uses both county and private service providers to respond to the treatment needs of its defendants.

When the referral to the Court is first made, the court employs a monitor who interviews the defendant. If the defendant is not already in treatment, he or she is referred to a community clinic or the university community mental health clinic. Offenders requiring long-term hospitalization are not returned to the Court but typically have their charges dismissed. Other offenders, who are or have been stabilized, are returned to the Court. In the Court, the offender is given the option of entering treatment under the supervision of the Court. The judge and a team of court and treatment representatives have considerable background, experience, and interest in the problems of the mentally ill in the justice system. Services provided include short and long-term residential treatment, including supportive housing, substance abuse treatment, and mental health treatment. During the treatment process, offenders regularly report to the Court so that the judge can review their progress. 'An observer of status reviews is struck by the problem-solving nature of these hearings, as the judge draws on the staff to help first solve any treatment-related concerns and criminal justice issues defendants may be facing and to encourage the defendant's full participation in the individualized, therapeutic treatment process' (Goldkamp and Irons-Guynn, 2000, p. 15). After the participant has been found to be stable, and has performed consistently in treatment long enough to demonstrate responsibility, the criminal charges are dismissed. The success of this type of court and judge can be measured by how well the court is able to locate appropriate services in the community for each defendant, the defendant's compliance with a treatment regimen, and the ability of such diversion to permanently keep the defendant out of the criminal justice system.

Unified Family Courts

Many cases involving families are heard in disparate courts involving different types of proceedings. The current divorce process may involve up to 14 different hearings before eight different judges (Ross, 1998). A unified family court remedies this problem and has jurisdiction over all, or most, cases involving children and families and includes a broad range of cases including matrimonial, domestic violence, juvenile delinquency, and child protection matters (Kuhn, 1998; Town, 1998).

> Typically this includes all juvenile cases (delinquency, status, detention, waiver and child abuse), divorce, paternity, adoption, nonsupport, guardianship of adults and children, civil restraining orders, civil commitment in mental health cases, and in some jurisdictions crimes within the family ranging from domestic violence to intra-familial murder. Traditionally, one judge hears all cases affecting one family and the judge has a broad array of services to assist these families. (Town, 1998, p. 671)

Although broader in scope than drug and domestic violence courts, a unified family court utilizes a 'one-team-to-one family' approach to managing all cases that involve a particular family (Kuhn, 1998, p. 78). The underlying principle is therapeutic justice, empowering families with skills development, assisting them, in resolving their own disputes, enhancing coordination of court events within the justice system, providing direct services to families when and where they need them, and building a system of dispute resolution that is more cost efficient, user-friendly, and time conscious. (Kuhn, 1998, p. 68)

Because family court cases are often complex, emotional, and volatile, special expertise on the part of the judge and his/her staff is desirable. Many judges believe they serve in a variety of roles including those of 'adjudicator, mediator/peacemaker, convener, clinician, and teacher' (Town, 1998, p. 673).

Community Courts

Cities around the country have, in recent years, involved courts in solving complex neighborhood problems and building stronger communities (Lee, 2000). Community courts stem from collaborations that address the low-level crime that is part of daily life. Offenders are required to compensate neighborhoods, through community service, as well as to engage in social services that will help them to address their problems. The court establishes a partnership with the community, setting up community advisory boards and responding to particular concerns of individual communities. The community court is used as a gateway to treatment and social services for low-level offenders.

Launched in 1993, the Midtown Community Court began to target quality-of-life offenses such as prostitution, illegal vending, graffiti, shoplifting, fare avoidance, and vandalism in downtown Manhattan in New York (Lee, 2000). The decision to establish the Court grew out of a belief that the traditional court response to these low-level offenses 'was neither constructive nor meaningful to victims, defendants, or the community', resulting in community dissatisfaction with the courts and producing 'revolving door justice' (Sviridoff et al., 1997, p. 1). Instead of the usual sentence of credit for time already served in jail, the Midtown Court sentences low-level offenders to pay back the neighborhood through community service while offering them help with problems that include addiction, mental illness, and lack of job skills. The Court promotes a community-focused, problem-solving approach to solving quality-of-life community problems by collaborating with court administrators and community and criminal justice agencies. Social workers from the court, for example, join police officers on the beat to engage homeless and other street people and encourage them to come to the court voluntarily for social services. The Court has devoted an entire floor for the scheduling and monitoring of alternative sanctions and the provision of court-based social services. Separate space has been allocated to service providers from city and community-based agencies to respond to defendants' problems with substance abuse, housing, health, education, and employment. With the Midtown Court as a model, cities around the country are crafting their own community courts based on the needs of their individual communities.

An evaluation of the Midtown Community Court found that the court was effective in meeting most of its objectives (Sviridoff et al., 1997). First, low-level offenders, who in the past had received little attention and few sanctions, were now receiving longer sentences that frequently combined community service with social services such as referrals to drug treatment. Community service compliance rates by offenders were high and accompanied by substantial reductions in concentrations of prostitution, unlicensed vending, and graffiti. Community attitudes and perceptions were transformed from initial skepticism to enthusiastic confidence in the court's ability to reduce local quality-of-life problems and to change patterns of offending. Judges reported that they did things differently at Midtown because expanded information and strict accountability promoted the use of court-based alternative sanctions programs. They were confident that they could find out what happened when they sentenced an offender to social service programs, including long-term treatment, and were therefore more willing to take risks. Defendants generally perceived the Midtown Court as cleaner, faster, and tougher than the downtown court. They were aware that Midtown Court monitored compliance closely, and viewed sentencing as consistent and fair, even if tougher. They particularly noted that the Midtown program staff treated them like human beings.

THE ROLE OF THE JUDGE IN SPECIALIZED COURTS

A common feature of specialized courts is the problem-solving strategy in which the judge occupies a central role in a team process (Fritzler and Simon, 2000b). Strong and cohesive judicial leadership is essential to the success of court programs (Harrell et al., 2000). The judge represents a respected authority figure and has responsibility for all legal and treatment-related actions undertaken. Many see the judge's most important contribution as a case manager at the center of the treatment process. He or she has regularly scheduled contacts with participants, encouraging progress and responding to performance with graduated rewards and sanctions. Many believe that court users benefit therapeutically from the special relationship with the judge, both during and after adjudication (T. Merrigan, personal communication, June 7, 2001). Judge William Schma, Circuit Judge in Kalamazoo, Michigan, describes his experience presiding as a drug court judge:

> My experience is that so many people in the court system have been beaten down for so long by society and by the court system that they don't expect to receive respect from the judge. When the judge, in particular, believes in them, it has a profound impact because of prior negative experiences they have experienced. Offenders respond to a judge who has expressed an interest in helping them and is not threatening. People come back to see me all the time. I let them know that they can tell me if they are using without punitive consequences, and they tell me if they are using. They are willing to be open with me because all they have experienced before appearing in my court has been a punitive criminal justice system. Because this is a positive and not a negative relationship, they accept consequences readily. Once they have been given the experience with a positive judge, they accept the consequences that may include putting them in prison, which I have done; and they thank me for it. The judge creates for offenders what people ordinarily experience in healthy relationships: There needs to be trust, the setting of limits, and insistence on personal responsibility. In this context, the consequences are expected without whining. Denial is not helpful to them. They can start being honest.

Their social relationship with the judge reinforces their recovery. (W. Schma, personal communication, March 16, 2001)

Judge Peggy Fulton Hora, a Superior Court Judge in Alameda County, California, also has observed the powerful effect drug court judges can have on offenders before them:

Judges in drug courts are successful because they are in a position of authority and they care. People see the judge as an empathic person who cares, and they want to please the judge. Offenders need praise. One guy said, 'I got my nudge from the judge.' When you see what addicts go through to change, you begin to see your own problems. One person who worked in the courtroom said that she had a hard enough time staying on a diet, and was impressed with how drug addicts are able to break the habit. It may be that judges are just human and are responding in a human way. (P. Hora, personal communication, March 21, 2001)

Judge Randal Fritzler, District Court Judge in Vancouver, Washington, sees the therapeutic role of the judge differently depending on the subject matter of the court.

The therapeutic role of the judge was not as clear in the domestic violence court. I see it more in the mental health court. I found domestic violence offenders to be very manipulative and deceptive. Because the offense of domestic violence is looked down on in society, the offenders feel that they have to hide their offenses. They lie to themselves and everyone else. Mental health court is different. People bring me Valentines on Valentine's Day. They want to please me. If they miss a court day, they come in a few days later and apologize. Mentally ill offenders respect the fact that I am wearing a black robe. The idea of someone in authority that cares about them is very powerful in these cases. Some sort of bonding seems to occur. (R. Fritzler, personal communication, March 19, 2001)

In addition to therapeutic benefits to offenders, judges themselves benefit therapeutically from participation in therapeutic courts such as drug courts. In their study, Chase and Hora (2000) observe that drug treatment court judicial officers are significantly more likely than family law court judicial officers to have stopped drinking or using other substances. Drug treatment court officers are significantly more likely than family court officers to witness change for the better in the litigants, and this highly correlates with job satisfaction.

PROACTIVE JUDGES AND COURT/COMMUNITY COLLABORATION

Recent Trial Court Performance Standards have sought to address the problem of low public confidence by suggesting that judges improve their image in the community (Commission on Trial Court Performance Standards, 1997). The Conference of Chief Justices and the Conference of State Court Administrators have passed a joint resolution that pledges to 'support training on the principles and methods of problem-solving courts and collaboration with other agencies and organizations' (Conference of Chief Justices etc., 2000). Individual states have also taken steps in this direction. For example, 'the California Judicial Council, working with the American Judicature Society, recently revised its code of judicial ethics to make involvement in problem-solving with the community an expectation' (Rottman and Casey, 1999).

Proactive judges and specialized courts rely on criminal justice and outside agencies to provide services as well as to give the court information and essential feedback. Like community policing (Kelling and Moore, 1988), such partnerships allow the court and community to tackle the types of cases that trouble the community. Coordinating task forces and committees are established for the locality served by the court. New programs are initiated and modified with experience. While decisions on individual cases remain the sole province of the judge, decisions on the nature and governance of coordinating bodies and programs are made collaboratively (Rottman et al., 1998). Such collaboration often results in improved public confidence in the courts.

Rottman and his colleagues (1998, p. 2) distinguish between programmatic and systemic court and community collaborations.

> On the programmatic level, collaboration is a blueprint for establishing court programs or special courts or for dedicating a judge and a courtroom to a particular set of cases. . . . Thus, far, such collaborations have been forged primarily between communities and courts of limited jurisdiction: those that process misdemeanor criminal cases and juvenile delinquency cases. . . . The systemic joint venture seeks more global discussions about how the judiciary can better serve the community. . . . One consequence of systemic change is the extension of collaborative programs to courts of general jurisdiction and, indeed, to appellate courts.

Thus, the current wave of community/court collaborations seen in specialized courts is only one possibility for adding a community perspective to the justice system.

PROACTIVE JUDGES AND THEIR MOTIVATION TO CHANGE THE WAY COURTS DO BUSINESS

Court and community collaboration relies heavily on judicial initiative and support (Rottman et al., 1998). However some courts and judges are highly resistant to change or innovation (J. Kuhn, personal communication, January 11, 2000). Judge Fritzler sees the motivation for proactive judges in the following way:

> People are motivated by job satisfaction, and judges are no different. As a proactive judge, one is fighting against the values instilled by traditional legal education. Some judges are not satisfied by just processing cases—they want to see positive outcomes and receive positive feedback from court users and the community. Also, attorneys become judges later on in life. It is where attorneys come to finish out their careers. People seem to become more conservative as they age. Because many judges are serving out their time, they are not motivated to seek out change. It is unusual for a judge to be a risk-taker.

> Before I developed the Domestic Violence Court in Vancouver, I had been interested in changing the court system for a long time. I wanted to increase my job satisfaction—I

was frustrated by seeing that we were not dealing adequately with many types of cases. Originally, I was more moved by the many mentally ill people processed through the court than by the domestic violence cases. However, I noticed that while the volume of other cases was decreasing, the number of domestic violence cases we were seeing was increasing. Then I met you and others in the community on the Domestic Violence/ Sexual Assault Task Force who were willing to collaborate to better respond to domestic violence cases. I decided to start a domestic violence court to improve outcomes with these cases. (R. Fritzler, personal communication, March 19, 2001)

Judge Schma explains the motivation this way:

The judiciary is generally discouraged from doing anything new by appellate courts that will kick back cases that depart from precedent. Some judges stop being intellectually curious. They get comfortable and sometimes lazy. The Canons of Judicial Ethics also discourages judges from getting out of the mold. The Canons of Judicial Ethics emphasize judicial neutrality. Judges buy into this role. Judging is a reactive type of job. Judges who are reluctant to try something new are not necessarily bad-willed. There are differences in the types of courts the judges sit on. Courts of general jurisdiction are conservative and don't experiment much. On the other hand, probate judges and family court judges are generally interested in hands-on approaches. The adversarial system has made us gun-shy of appearing to take sides. Judges are not trained to think outside of the box. Continuing judicial education does a good job on more traditional legal updates. However, there is evidence that things are changing. The Conference of Chief Judges and other such organizations are key to making changes. They are taking more of an active interest in innovation.

I first got involved with drug court because on the bench, I felt overwhelmed by the revolving door of substance abusers. It didn't make sense—it's a matter of common sense. Then I discovered therapeutic jurisprudence and that made sense—the law as a healing agent. I'm a liberal-minded, social worker type. I was invited to a seminar on sentencing alternatives for drug offenders put on by the Michigan Judicial Institute, the division for educating the judiciary and court personnel. They had picked up on drug courts. This seminar preceded and initiated my involvement with the drug court. Presiding over a drug court has changed me. I have been a cigarette smoker and a drinker. Sitting on the bench in drug court, I woke up and made changes to my life. I was at a stage where I could quit drinking and smoking. I have learned I can't touch chemicals. (W. Schma, personal communication, March 16, 2001)

Having struggled with their own addictions may make judges more effective and credible. In addition, proactive judges are intellectually curious and interested in developing new expertise. Judge Hora describes how her involvement in a drug court came about:

Fifteen years ago, after one year on the bench, I realized that I was seeing a lot of drug addicts and alcoholics, and that I knew nothing about the subject matter. I set out to educate myself. We formed the Oakland Drug Court, the second drug court after Miami, around 1991. We had a committee of judges study the subject of alcohol and other drugs. We were interested in what we were doing that made sense, and more importantly, what we were doing that did not make sense. We educated ourselves by bringing in experts. We found out that treatment with the threat of jail is more effective.

The major difference between judges who get involved with specialized courts is that judges who are innovators are problem solvers. They see the big picture. Innovative judges see the possibility of systemic changes. They are people who are bucking the way things have always been done. This is due, in part, to personality differences, partly local legal culture, and partly the security the individual feels as a judge. I feel very secure as a judge which allows me to do a lot of things. I do not think I will be voted out. Generally, judges tend to be status-quo types of people who are afraid of venturing too far from tradition. (P. Hora, personal communication, March 21, 2001)

Although there is no research on personality differences between proactive judges and their peers, research suggests that those law students who come to law school with an 'ethic of care' adopt a rights orientation by the end of the first year (Janoff, 1991). The 'ethic of care' orientation values interpersonal harmony, maintaining relationships, people's feelings and needs, and preventing harm. In contrast, a rights orientation focuses on rights, rules, standards, individuality, justice fairness, objectivity, accomplishments, ambitions, principles, personal beliefs, and freedom from others' interference (Janoff, 1991). Generally, the research finds that people go to law school for intellectual stimulation as well as money and prestige (Daicoff, 1997). They are uniformly less interested in people, emotions, altruism, and interpersonal concerns, tending to prefer 'logic, thinking, rationality, justice, fairness, rights, and rules', with humanistic, people-oriented individuals not faring well psychologically or academically, in law school or in the legal profession (Daicoff, 1997, p. 1405). Consequently, lawyers who become judges generally will not endorse an 'ethic of care' perspective. Proactive judges appear to be the exception to the rule.

Mills (2000) argues that the objective, dispassionate, traditional practice of law—that ignores the emotional dimensions of a case—renders lawyers less effective, and in some cases, incompetent. She suggests that being attuned to the emotional aspects of clients and their cases improves outcomes and satisfaction. Lawyers, judges, and law school professors follow the formalistic approach to law that ' . . . seek[s] only the details they need to formulate their narrow arguments and clients are, through this process, rendered emotionally silent and stifled by the weight of a fact-gathering and precedent oriented system, which its objectivity, produces an allegedly just result' (Mills, 2000, pp. 427–428).

> Affective Lawyering can provide lawyers with the emotional skills necessary for doing a more therapeutically-engaged and psychologically-oriented practice. . . . Affective Lawyering provides the impetus and the emotional desire to grow personally from our work with the clients we meet, and to reflect on that growth as a method of mutual understanding (Mills, 2000, p. 446).

It appears that proactive judges are moving away from the more formalistic, precedent-based, detached manner of judging, in favor of a more Affective Judging mode that allows them to connect emotionally with court participants and community members.

Proactive Judges Increase Trial Court Performance

Until recently court reform focused on the needs of judges and court personnel instead of the individuals served by the courts. The Bureau of Justice Assistance (BJA), of the US Department of Justice and the National Center for State Courts (NCSC), has developed 22 standards to assess and improve the performance of State general jurisdiction trial courts (1997). The standards are grouped into five performance areas: (1) access to justice; (2) expedition and timeliness; (3) equality, fairness, and integrity; (4) independence and accountability; and (5) public trust and confidence. Once developed, measures of performance were constructed and tested in three courts (Casey, 1998).

Proactive judges and specialized courts may increase the performance of their courts according to these standards. For example, the standards that aim to improve access to justice require that trial courts 'eliminate unnecessary barriers to . . . services' (Bureau of Justice Assistance, 1997, p. 7). In the Vancouver Domestic Violence Court battered women are helped by court clerks to fill out the necessary paperwork. Standards on safety, accessibility and convenience have been achieved by setting up safe waiting areas for victims and their children awaiting their appearance in court. The Midtown Community Court may have ensured compliance with this standard by offering social services in the courthouse. The standards aiming to increase timeliness are also more likely to be satisfied by a specialized court with a judge who knows that delays can have fatal consequences for battered women. Traditionally, delay in the courts has been one of the reasons battered women have decided to drop charges and pursue other strategies (Hart, 1996).

JURISPRUDENTIAL BASE

Proactive judges, and the problem-solving approach, have developed in a trial and error manner without a jurisprudential base (Rottman et al., 1998). However, the shift is supported by three complementary jurisprudential paradigms. All three paradigms seek to instill an 'ethic of care' in the practices of the justice system.

Therapeutic Jurisprudence

Some judges have adopted the schema of therapeutic jurisprudence (TJ) (Hora et al., 1999; Fritzler and Simon, 2000a, 2000b; Town, 1998) and TJ academics have cited specialized courts as an example of the successful application of TJ (Winick, 2000; Lurigio et al., 2001). TJ examines the impact of laws, legal policies, and legal actors on the emotional health of participants in the legal process (Casey and Rottman, 1998; Simon, 1995, 1999). Laws, legal procedures, and legal actors can have positive or negative emotional consequences for litigants, defendants, and victims (Schma, 2000). TJ encourages policy-makers and legal actors to be sensitive to the often unanticipated harmful effects of the legal process without diminishing legal rights of the parties (Slobogin, 1995). Proponents of TJ do not 'suggest that therapeutic considerations should trump other considerations' (Wexler and Winick, 1996, p. xvii). 'Rather, therapeutic jurisprudence places the psychological and emotional health of persons affected by the law and by legal actors as one important consideration among many'

(Stolle, 2000, p. xv). While advocating more sensitivity to the aitrogenic effects of the legal process, TJ also proposes more radical changes to the legal culture by supplanting the argument culture of law with alternative dispute resolution mechanisms that minimize distress of litigants and legal actors (Wexler, 2000). TJ is interested not only in law reform, but also in how existing law may be most therapeutically practiced (Wexler, 2000). In application to courts, TJ emphasizes transforming the judicial role from a more traditional, adversarial one to that of trying to satisfy the needs and interests of all parties in a collaborative, informal manner, thereby increasing public confidence in the courts (Rottman and Casey, 1999). At the same time, the practice of TJ by courts should not overshadow additional values of our legal system, such as due process, which are integral to it (W. Schma, personal communication, July 31, 2001).

TJ can be applied by proactive judges on a continuum of court levels ranging from individual cases, to organizational level of the court, to law and court policy (Rottman and Casey, 1999). Judges can facilitate individuals' healing by being attuned to the emotional dynamics of the courtroom and making appropriate empathic or supportive comments. For example, judges can take advantage of therapeutic opportunities in individual cases, as in praising an individual drug court defendant when she has ejected an abusive, drug-using, boyfriend from her home. But most TJ studies reflect a systematic approach that anticipates problems and develops strategies that can be applied to more than one individual or case at a time (Rottman and Casey, 1999). A more systematic approach to the use of TJ would be for judges handling domestic violence and sexual offense cases (committed by family members and acquaintances) to treat the offenses as seriously as if they were committed by a stranger (Simon, 1995, 1999). In domestic violence cases, judges can develop a means of monitoring compliance with criminal and civil orders, communicating to the offenders that 'they cannot escape liability for single lapses in compliance' (Simon, 1995, p. 75). In acquaintance rape cases, handing out sentences commensurate with ones received by stranger rapists will help to ease the confusion and self-blame that many acquaintance rape victims feel (Simon, 1999).

Proactive judges can, at the organizational level, create special programs or specialized courts. A drug court program in Washington, DC, provides court-based interventions using psychological principles. 'Because the sanctioning rules were simple and clearly explained in advance, defendants viewed the penalties they received as fair' (Harrell et al., 2000, p. 6). Judicial access to sophisticated computers with up-to-date information allows them immediate access to drug test results, and the application of graduated sanctions is swift and certain. Evaluation of this program, and its use of graduated sanctions for drug defendants, demonstrated reduced drug use during the period of supervision (Harrell et al., 2000).

At the policy level, TJ could call into question strict adherence to the adversarial system of law and the neutral, detached role of judges in that system. For example, some proactive judges find that the adversarial process inadequate in problem-solving certain types of cases, such as drug offenses and domestic violence cases. The requirement that judges strictly adhere to a neutral, detached role in all cases may hinder their effectiveness in working with therapeutic courts where mentally disordered offenders or drug offenders may respond better to some form of affective judging. Recognizing that the courts can effect cognitive restructuring, by encouraging batterers to plead guilty instead of plea bargaining or going to trial, plea bargaining in domestic violence cases could be abolished in all but the most exceptional cases (Simon, 1995).

Regardless of what level of the court system applies TJ, the practice of TJ requires that judges follow three steps. 'The first step is to become sensitive to the fact that we, as participants, do produce such results in our daily routines and in the discharge of our professional duties' (Schma, 1997, p. 81). Although TJ is something that many good judges do intuitively, TJ practice reform requires that judges make this intuitive process deliberate and systematic (Wexler, 1999). 'The second step, practice, involves systematically exploring where and when problems (i.e. psychojudicial soft spots) arise and how they can best be addressed' (Casey and Rottman, 1998, p. 13). Psychojudicial soft spots, for example, require the identification by judges of social relationships and emotional issues that ought to be considered in order to avoid conflict, stress, or hurt feelings. For example, Judge Fritzler describes that when defendants come to the Mental Health Court, he collects all their existing files. Many of the files may be dead, but defendants often owe a substantial amount in fines. He typically dismisses all the old fines and tells defendants he hopes that they can get a fresh start. To defendants weighed down by the obligation of substantial old fines, this small gesture allows them to feel that a huge burden has been lifted from their backs and that they can start anew. This is an example of a psychojudicial soft spot—recognition that an old legal obligation that a mentally ill defendant could never hope to satisfy is creating additional stress for him, and devising a strategy (dismissing the fines) that alleviates the stress and worry. The process of identifying such soft spots and strategies to address them requires continual modification of the soft spots and their strategies (Wexler, 1998). The third step in adopting a TJ approach is evaluating the effectiveness of strategies and their consistency with other values. This is a continuing process that selects strategies for soft spots based on social science information, and modifies the strategies after evaluation (Casey and Rottman, 1998).

Preventive Law

Preventive law (PL) primarily addresses how practicing lawyers can proactively improve the practice of law so as to minimize and avoid adversarial legal disputes and increase legal and emotional outcomes through careful client counseling and planning (Brown and Dauer, 1978; Hardway, 1997; Richards, 1992). Like preventive medicine that seeks to keep people healthy, PL seeks to keep people litigation-free (Hardway, 1997). PL encourages periodic 'legal checkups', updates on clients' lives, so as to improve legal planning to prevent future problems and conflicts (Dauer, 1990; Hardway, 1997). PL encourages identification of 'legal soft spots', anticipated legal trouble points, and seeks to develop strategies to avoid or minimize them (Casey and Rottman, 1998; Hardway, 1997). 'It emphasizes the lawyer's role as a planner and proposes that careful private ordering of affairs as a method of avoiding the high costs of litigation and ensuring desired outcomes and opportunities' (Stolle et al., 1997, p. 17). When problems do crop up, preventive law encourages a 'rewind technique' (Hardway, 1997, p. xlii) using the benefit of hindsight to discuss what could have been done at an earlier point to avoid legal problems. When combined with a TJ approach, PL encourages that legal actors look not only to 'legal soft spots' (areas that can lead to future legal trouble) but also to 'psycholegal soft spots' (Stolle et al., 1997; Wexler, 1998). These are areas where legal processes may not lead to a lawsuit, but may instead result in anxiety, depression, hurt feelings, family disruption, or general psychological distress (Wexler, 1998). 'Parallel to the preventive law field, judges who apply therapeutic jurisprudence principles look for *psychojudicial soft spots*, areas in which judicial actions could lead to anti-therapeutic consequences. The recognition of these soft spots provides a *therapeutic moment*—an opportunity to promote a more therapeutic outcome' (Casey and Rottman, 1998, pp. 3–4).

Scholars have integrated TJ and PL to complement the strengths of each approach. 'Therapeutic jurisprudence alone lacks the practical procedures for law office application. Preventive law alone lacks an analytical framework for justifying emotional well-being as one priority in legal planning' (Stolle et al., 2000, p. 9). In combination with TJ, PL allows judges to practice in a way that prevents harm to and encourages healing of litigants, court participants, and the community.

Restorative Community Justice

The restorative and community justice paradigm can work in tandem with TJ/PL by adding the community/problem-solving philosophy of proactive judges and specialized courts. At its core, restorative justice (RJ) rejects the criminal law's focus on culpability and retribution and views punitive responses to criminal conduct as aggravators of the harm already done (Smith, 2001, p. 3):

> In the paradigm of RJ, the purpose of justice is to restore the victim and the victim's family (who suffer the harm), the community (whose fabric is torn by the crime), and the offender (who will remain part of that community, or will reenter it before long, and who, if unrestored, represents a continuing threat to it). The key restorative practices are respectful listening to the victim's story of the harm done, voluntary acceptance of responsibility by the offender (also heard respectfully, lest stigmatization and self-loathing block the offender's return to full membership in the community); and voluntary undertakings by the offender to make amends for the harms resulting from his crime.

RJ recognizes that crime damages people, communities, and relationships (Office of Victims of Crime, 2001). RJ emphasizes repairing the harm while striking a balance among the needs of victims, offenders, and communities. An RJ system ensures that the offender is held accountable for the damage and suffering caused both to victims and communities by supporting, facilitating, and enforcing reparative agreements. RJ elevates the role of the victim in the justice process by giving high priority to victim involvement and reparation. Although much of the RJ literature rejects traditional treatment or rehabilitation of the offender, relying instead of on informal social control and the socialization process (Bazemore and Schiff, 2001), other aspects of current RJ concepts are consistent with the proactive judging movement.

The paradigm of RJ has recently been integrated with community justice into a restorative community justice (RCJ) paradigm (Bazemore and Schiff, 2001). Community justice is:

> ... all variants of crime prevention and justice activities that explicitly include the community in their processes. Community justice is rooted in the actions that citizens, community organizations, and the criminal justice system can take to control crime and social disorder. Its central focus is community-level outcomes, shifting the emphasis from individual incidents to systemic patterns, from individual conscience to social mores, and from individual goods to the common good. (Clear and Karp, 1999, p. 25)

Community justice programs seek to be explicitly preventive and attempt to employ a problem-solving focus to intervention (Bazemore and Schiff, 2001; Clear and Karp, 1999).

The rise of community justice can be attributed primarily to developments in community policing being applied to other components of the criminal justice system. Community justice advocates want the criminal justice system to serve citizens and communities in lieu of or in addition to the traditional case processing that is out of touch with community needs (Bazemore and Schiff, 2001). The accessibility and problem-solving focus of specialized courts is analogous to the pragmatic problem-oriented and service provision emphases of many community policing advocates (Clear and Karp, 1999). In essence, community and restorative justice embody both a critique of existing formal legal procedures and practices and a quest to revive community involvement (Crawford and Clear, 2001).

TJ, PL, RCJ, AND PROACTIVE JUDGES

Clearly, there is a natural fit between TJ, PL, and RCJ and the transformed nature of judging and courts currently underway. Some of the best examples of TJ/PL/RCJ practice can be seen in specialized courts that, even if not always based explicitly on these principles, implicitly employ them as the underlying paradigms. Judges see many similar types of cases and acquire special expertise. They are well placed to identify and develop strategies for psychojudicial soft spots. A unified family court, for example, can anticipate and develop strategies to protect battered women when deciding visitation issues. Mental health courts may facilitate one-on-one contact between the judge and defendant to develop a therapeutic working alliance associated with positive change.

CONCLUSION

Proactive judges are changing the way courts conduct business and initiating a paradigm shift. By responding to their own idealism, wanting courts to produce better outcomes and being receptive to community input and collaboration, they are addressing social problems. These proactive judges appear particularly adept at connecting with court participants and creating a therapeutic alliance with individuals the court is designed to help. By combining their mantle of authority with approval of positive change, proactive judges are encouraging chronic court users like mentally disordered offenders and drug abusers *to want* to heal. By combining TJ, PL, and RCJ, proactive judges are infusing courts with an 'ethic of care' and creating communities of care. By their problem-solving strategies, these judges are improving access to justice and enhancing confidence in the courts.

Proactive judges in specialized courts typically work collaboratively with social service providers and legal actors to develop the courts. Because this collaboration begins in the planning stages, the relationship between the judge and social service providers is a symbiotic one where the judge relies on professionals for expertise and the professionals rely on the judge for leadership. The team approach ensures a mutually supportive relationship between the judge and service providers and other legal actors, with judicial decisions being informed by community and justice professionals. Because the collaborative approach overcomes the insular, out-of-touch nature of traditional judging, other members of the team welcome the 'hands-on' approach of proactive judges. They tend to be successful due to their skills in negotiating with participants, social service providers, and other legal actors. A few evaluations, cited in this chapter, suggest that proactive judging has been successful in engaging communities to become involved in problem-solving with the courts, improving outcomes for court participants, and increasing public confidence in the courts.

Because of their success, the resourcefulness and creativity of proactive judges is being tested in a new innovation, re-entry courts, designed for convicts being released from prison. By one estimate, 600 000 inmates are released from adult prisons or juvenile institutions into the community each year (Petersilia, 2000).

> In a project sponsored by the U.S. Department of Justice, nine jurisdictions are serving as pilot sites of the Reentry Partnership Initiative, whose goal is better risk management via enhanced surveillance, risk and needs assessment, and prerelease planning. The Department's new Reentry Courts Initiative is based on the drug court model and taps the court's authority to use sanctions and incentives to help released offenders remain crime free. (Petersilia, 2000, p. 5)

Policy-makers recognize that no effective means of reintegrating offenders released from prison into the community exits (Travis, 2000). Borrowing many of the principles of drug courts, judges are being called on to sit on re-entry courts from the time of sentencing of an offender (Travis, 2000).

> The judge-centered model described here obviously borrows heavily from the drug court experience. Both feature an ongoing, central role for the judge, a 'contract' drawn up between court and offender, discretion on the judge's part to impose graduated sanctions for various levels of failure to meet conditions imposed, the promise of the end of supervision as an occasion for ceremonial recognition. (Travis, 2000, p. 8)

The new development seeks to utilize judges as case managers and agents of change. Clearly, the success of proactive judges and specialized courts has instilled confidence in policy-makers and the public that judges may be better able to integrate offenders into the community than parole officers and community programs of the past. Perhaps their newly enhanced roles as problem-solvers and respected coordinators of social and psychological services will generalize to re-entry courts as well as more traditional courts. The integration of TJ, PL, and RCJ can serve as a jurisprudential basis for such an 'aftercare' court by applying needed social and psychological services to released convicts with many social, educational, and psychological disabilities.

ACKNOWLEDGMENT

I wish to acknowledge the helpful guidance of Randal Fritzler, Peggy Fulton Hora, Thomas Merrigan, David Rottman, and William Schma, the comments of David Carson, Ray Bull, and Richard Lamma, and the research support of ETSU library staff, particularly, Kelly Hensley.

REFERENCES

Babb, B.A. (1998a). Fashioning an interdisciplinary framework for court reform in family law: A blueprint to construct a unified family court. *Southern California Law Review, 71*, 469–545.

Babb, B.A. (1998b). Where we stand: An analysis of America's family law adjudicatory systems and the mandate to establish unified family courts. *Family Law Quarterly, 32*, 31–65.

Bazemore, G. and Schiff, M. (2001). Introduction. In G. Bazemore and M. Schiff (eds), *Restorative community justice: Repairing harm and transforming communities*. Cincinnati, Ohio: Anderson Publishing Co.

Belenko, S. (1998). *Research on drug courts: A critical review*. NY: National Center on Addiction and Substance Abuse (CASA) at Columbian University.

Berman, G. and Feinblatt, J. (2000). *Problem-solving courts: A brief primer*. NY: Center for Court Innovation.

Brown, L.M. and Dauer, E. (1978). *Perspectives on the lawyer as planner*. Mineola, NY: Foundation Press.

Bureau of Justice Assistance (1997). *Trial court performance standards*. Washington, DC.

Casey, P. (1998). Defining optimal court performance: The trial court performance standards. *Court Review, 35*, 24–29.

Casey, P. and Rottman, D. (1998). *Therapeutic Jurisprudence: A Court Perspective*. A white paper presented to the California Judicial Council. Williamsburg, VA: National Center for State Courts.

Chase, D.J. and Hora, P.F. (2000). The implications of therapeutic jurisprudence for judicial satisfaction. *Court Review, 37*, 12–20.

Clear, T.R. and Karp, D.R. (1999). *The community justice ideal: Preventing crime and achieving justice*. Boulder, CO: Westview Press.

Commission on Trial Court Performance Standards (1997). *Trial Court Performance Standards with Commentary*. Washington, DC: US Department of Justice.

Conference of Chief Justices and the Conference of State Court Administrators Task Force on Therapeutic Justice (2000). *Resolution supporting 'problem-solving courts'*, adopted Aug. 3, 2000, Task Force on Therapeutic Justice of CCJ/COSCA.

Crawford, A. and Clear, T. (2001). Community justice: Transforming communities through restorative justice? In G. Bazemore and M. Schiff (eds), *Restorative community justice:*

Repairing harm and transforming communities (pp. 127–149. Cincinnati, Ohio: Anderson Publishing Co.

Daicoff, S. (1997). Lawyer know thyself: A review of empirical research on attorney attributes bearing on professionalism, *American University Law Review, 46*, 1333–1427 (esp. pp. 1401–1403).

Dauer, E.A. (1990 March). Future of the legal profession lies in utilizing preventive law. *Preventive Law Reporter*, 20–27.

Fritzler, R.B. and Simon, L.M.J. (2000a). Creating a domestic violence court: Combat in the trenches. *Court Review, 37*, 28–39.

Fritzler, R.B. and Simon, L.M.J. (2000b). The development of a specialized domestic violence court in Vancouver, Washington utilizing innovative judicial paradigms. *University of Missouri-Kansas City Law Review, 69*, 139–177.

Gebelein, R.S. (2000). *The rebirth of rehabilitation: Promise and perils of drug courts.* Washington, DC: US Department of Justice.

Goldkamp, J.S. (2000). The drug court response: Issues and implications for justice change. *Albany Law Review, 63*, 923–1006.

Goldkamp, J. and Irons-Guynn, C. (2000). *Emerging judicial strategies for the mentally ill in the criminal caseload: Mental health courts in Fort Lauderdale, Seattle, San Bernardino, and Anchorage.* Washington, DC: National Institute of Justice.

Hardway, R.M. (1997). *Preventive law: Materials on a non-adversarial legal process.* Cincinnati, Ohio: Anderson Publishing Co.

Harrell, A., Cavanagh, S. and Roman, J. (2000). *Evaluation of the D.C. Superior Court Drug Intervention Programs.* Washington, DC: US Department of Justice.

Hart, B. (1996). Battered women and the criminal justice system. In E. Buzawa and C.G. Buzawa (eds), *Do arrests and restraining orders work?* (pp. 98–114). Thousand Oaks, CA: Sage Publications.

Hora, P.F., Schma, W.G. and Rosenthal, J.T.A. (1999). Therapeutic jurisprudence and the drug treatment court movement: Revolutionizing the criminal justice system's response to drug abuse and crime in America. *Notre Dame Law Review, 74*, 439–537.

Janoff, S. (1991). The influence of legal education on moral reasoning. *Minnesota Law Review, 76*, 193–238.

Kaye, J.S. (1999, Oct. 11). Making the case for hands-on courts. *Newsweek*, p. 13.

Kelling, G.L. and Moore, M.H. (1988). *The evolving strategy of policing.* Washington, DC: US Department of Justice.

Kuhn, J.A. (1998). A seven-year lesson on unified family courts: What we have learned since the 1990 National Family Court Symposium. *Family Law Quarterly, 32*, 67–93.

Lee, E. (2000). *Community courts: An evolving model.* Washington, DC: US Department of Justice.

Lipscher, R.D. (1999). The judicial response to the drug crisis: A report of an executive symposium involving judicial leaders of the nation's nine most populous states. *State Court Journal, 13*, 13–17.

Lurigio, A.J., Watson, A., Luchins, D.J. and Hanrahan, P. (2001). Therapeutic jurisprudence in action: Specialized courts for the mentally ill. *Judicature, 84*, 184–189.

Mills, L.G. (2000). Affective lawyering: The emotional dimensions of the lawyer–client relation. In D.P. Stolle, D.B. Wexler and B.J. Winick (eds), *Practicing therapeutic jurisprudence: Law as a helping profession* (pp. 419–446). Durham, North Carolina: Carolina Academic Press.

Moore, M.H. (1992). Problem-solving and community policing. In M. Tonry and N. Morris (eds), *Modern policing* (pp. 99–158). Chicago: University of Chicago Press.

National Drug Court Institute (2001) at http://www.ndci.org/courtfacts.htm

National Center for State Courts (1999). *How the public views the state courts: A 1999 national survey.* Williamsburg, VA: Author.

Office of Victims of Crime (2001). *Victims, judges, and juvenile court reform through restorative justice.* Washington, DC: US Department of Justice.

Ostrom, B.J. and Kauder, N.B. (1998). *Examining the work of state courts, 1997: A national perspective from the Court Statistics Project*. Williamsburg, VA: National Center for State Courts.

Ostrom, B.J. and Kauder, N.B. (1999). *Examining the work of state courts, 1998: A national perspective from the Court Statistics Project*. Williamsburg, VA: National Center for State Courts.

Petersilia, J. (2000). *When prisoners return to the community: Political, economic, and social consequences*. Washington, DC: US Department of Justice.

Richards III, E.P. (1992 June). Should preventive law, like some medicine, be mandated by government? *Preventive Law Reporter*, 28–31.

Ross, C.J. (1998). The failure of fragmentation: The promise of a system of unified family courts. *Family Law Quarterly, 32*, 3–30.

Rottman, D.B. (2000). Does effective therapeutic jurisprudence require specialized courts (and do specialized courts imply specialist judges)? *Court Review, 37*, 22–27 (esp. p. 22).

Rottman, D.B. and Casey, P. (1999 July). Therapeutic jurisprudence and the emergence of problem-solving courts. *National Institute of Justice Journal*, 12–19.

Rottman, D., Efkeman, H.S. and Casey, P. (1998). *A guide to court and community collaboration*. Williamsburg, VA: National Center for State Courts.

Rottman, D.B., Flango, C.R., Cantrell, M.T., Hansen, R. and LaFountain, N. (2000). *State court organization 1998*. Washington, DC: US Department of Justice.

Schma, W.G. (1997). Review [Review of the book *Law in a therapeutic key*]. *Judges, 36*, 81–82.

Schma, W. (2000). Judging in the new millennium. *Court Review, 37*, 4–6 (esp. p. 4).

Simon, L.M.J. (1995). A therapeutic jurisprudence approach to the legal processing of domestic violence cases. *Psychology, Public Policy and Law, 1*, 43–79.

Simon, L.M.J. (1999). Sex offender legislation and the antitherapeutic effects on victims. *Arizona Law Review, 41*, 485–533.

Slobogin, C. (1995). Therapeutic jurisprudence: Five dilemmas to ponder. *Psychology, Public Policy, and Law*, 193–219.

Smith, M.E. (2001). *What future for 'public safety' and 'restorative justice' in community corrections?* Washington, DC: US Department of Justice.

Stolle, D.P. (2000). Introduction. In D.P. Stolle, D.B. Wexler and B.J. Winick (eds), *Practicing therapeutic jurisprudence: Law as a helping profession* (pp. xv–xvii). Durham, North Carolina: Carolina Academic Press.

Stolle, D.P., Wexler, D.B., Winick, B.J. and Dauer, E.A. (1997). Integrating preventive law and therapeutic jurisprudence: A law and psychology based approach to lawyering. *California Western Law Review, 34* 15–51.

Stolle, D.P., Wexler, D.B., Winick, B.J. and Dauer, E.A. (2000). Integrating preventive law and therapeutic jurisprudence: A law and psychology based approach to lawyering. In D.P. Stolle, D.B. Wexler and B.J. Winick (eds), *Practicing therapeutic jurisprudence: Law as a helping profession* (pp. 5–44). Durham, North Carolina: Carolina Academic Press.

Sviridoff, M., Rottman, D., Ostrom, B. and Curtis, R. (1997). *Dispensing justice locally: The implementation and effects of the Midtown Community Court*. Washington, DC: National Institute of Justice.

Town, M.A. (1998). Court as convenor and provider of therapeutic justice. *Revista Juridica Universidad de Puerto Rico, 67*, 671–675.

Travis, J. (2000). *But they all come back: Rethinking prisoner reentry*. Washington, DC: US Department of Justice.

Williams, P.M. (1995). A unified family court for Missouri. *University of Missouri–Kansas City Law Review, 63*, 383–427.

Wexler, D.B. (1998). Practicing therapeutic jurisprudence: Psycholegal soft spots and strategies. *Revista Juridica, 67*, 317–342.

Wexler, D.B. (1999). The development of therapeutic jurisprudence: From theory to practice. *Revista Juridica Universidad de Puerto Rico, 68*, 691–705.

Wexler, D.B. (2000). Therapeutic jurisprudence and the culture of critique. In D.P. Stolle, D.B. Wexler and B.J. Winick (eds), *Practicing therapeutic jurisprudence: Law as a helping profession* (pp. 449–464). Durham, North Carolina: Carolina Academic Press.

Wexler, D.B. and Winick, B.J. (1996). Introduction. In D.B. Wexler and B.J. Winick (eds), *Law in a therapeutic key: Developments in therapeutic jurisprudence* (pp vii–xx) Durham, North Carolina: Carolina Academic Press.

Winick, B.J. (2000). Applying the law therapeutically in domestic violence cases. *University of Missouris–Kansas City Law Review, 69,* 33–91.

Zimmerman, M.D. (1998). A new approach to court reform. *Judicature, 82,* 108–111.

Part 4

Perspectives on Policy: Psychology and Public Debate

Chapter 4.1

Drugs, Crime and the Law: An Attributional Perspective

John B. Davies
University of Strathclyde, UK

THE LOGIC OF CLASSIFICATION

Much has been written on the logic underlying the Misuse of Drugs Act 1971. The illegality which surrounds the sale and use of certain specified substances is based on assumptions about their dangerousness to the health of the user, particularly the likelihood that the user will become 'addicted', and the desire to protect society as a whole from these effects. Fears that drugs threaten to undermine Western society have been voiced, and serve as the justification for 'the war on drugs' on both sides of the Atlantic, and on a broader world scale. Such is the national and international concern about drugs that the involvement of the Taliban in the drug (opiate) trade has recently been used as an argument in support of the anti-terrorist bombing raids in Afghanistan. The assumption is that 'addiction' is, to varying and specifiable degrees, a property of the drugs and that consequently all steps have to be taken to eliminate the drug menace from our midst.

Due to accidents of history, certain other psychoactive substances and products do not fall into this pattern and are covered by legislation outwith the Misuse of Drugs Act, most notably alcohol and tobacco. It is worth noting however that there is little consensus over time, or in terms of geography, about what the most dangerous and least dangerous drugs are. Alcohol is forbidden in many middle-Eastern countries; on the other hand, there have been recent moves in the UK to reclassify cannabis—a substance described by the US Drugs Commissioner Harry Anslinger in the 1950s as one of the most dangerous and addictive substance known to mankind (Anslinger and Tomkins, 1953, pp. 21–22)—from Class B to Class C. On the other hand, two reports on smoking by the US Surgeon General (1982, 1988) saw nicotine reclassified from the status of a non-addictive drug in 1982 to being comparable in addictive potential to heroin and cocaine by the time of the second report in 1988 (p. 9). Meanwhile, strong

Handbook of Psychology in Legal Contexts, Second Edition
Edited by D. Carson and R. Bull. © 2003 John Wiley & Sons, Ltd.

evidence shows that the number of individuals who experience health problems as a consequence of the use and misuse of legal drugs and pharmaceuticals outnumbers those who experience similar problems from the use and misuse of illegal drugs by an order of magnitude. It should be apparent from the outset, therefore, that the drug laws seek to defend a state of affairs based on a set of classifications which is not under laid by any formal or scientific logic, but whose basic structure is dictated by political and social forces, acting within historical, geographical and economic contexts.

CHANGING ONES STATE OF CONSCIOUSNESS; A MOTIVATED ACT

This chapter argues that people generally use drugs (legal and illegal) on purpose, because they wish to, because it makes them feel good or better, rather than because they are forced to do so by the pharmacology of the drugs they choose to take. People, it is argued, use drugs to make the world an easier place to live in, to assist coping with a painful mental state, for pure fun, to help with a physical infirmity, and so forth. Taking drugs is a motivated act; people do it to achieve certain ends, both desirable and undesirable. Some people use drugs to alleviate withdrawal symptoms. This too is a motivated act, comparable to taking paracetamol for a headache, except that the symptoms are caused *in part* by the drug itself in the first place. We say *in part* since there is clear evidence that severity of withdrawal symptoms is context dependent (e.g. Hinson et al., 1986; McRae and Seigal, 1990). In the McRae and Seigal study, for instance, rats that lever-pressed to receive opiates suffered worse behavioural signs of withdrawal than rats that passively received the same drug at the same dose to the same site at the same time.

The notion of addiction, however, invites us to take an alternative view. Namely, a view based on the supposition that there are no motives for use, that the person uses the drugs for no reason at all of their own, and that there is some magical and mysterious essence in the illegal drugs, something about the pharmacology, which enables them to compel their own use regardless of the motives and purposes of the user.

If such were the case then environmental, circumstantial, and individual difference variables would have no bearing on the problem. Furthermore, population estimates of the numbers of people who have 'ever used' an 'addictive drug' should closely reflect the population figures for 'addicts'. Prevalence of use should reflect incidence of problems. That is to say, they should not merely predict in terms of regression; they should roughly approximate to the totals. Even taking into account variations in the supposed addictiveness of different drugs, this is simply not the case. A student survey in my own university showed that 69% of male students and 37% of female students had used illicit drugs at some time (*Strathclyde Telegraph*, 1994). The number of these who fall foul of addiction problems per annum is tiny by comparison. The vast majority of students, whether they take drugs or not, complete their studies and graduate successfully with the current completion rate, over the whole university, being in excess of 80%.

In a similar way, data cited by Frenk and Dar (2000) compare 'lifetime use' of supposed addictive drugs with 'last month' use, and produce results which lead to the same type of general conclusion. For example, a prevalence figure of 7.7% for lifetime use of all opiates translates into a figure of 0.7% for use last month. For cocaine, the comparable figures are 6.9% and 0.7%. Continuation rates for samples of drug users show a similar picture. Of a sample (100%) of lifetime opiate users, 8.6% reported using last month. For cocaine, the comparable figure was 10.8%. A recent Scottish Office-funded study also demonstrated stable controlled use of heroin in a Scottish sample of users, over a two year period of time (Shewan et al., 1998). Finally, a study by Leitner, Shapland and Wiles (1993) showed a clear effect of social class on problem drug use by young people. Rates of 'ever having tried' an illegal drug were roughly the same for all social classes; but a higher rate of escalating, heavy and problem use was found among those in classes 4 and 5. The conclusion is clear; most users of drugs (the vast majority in fact) do not end up as 'addicts', and consequently the idea that drug pharmacology is a sole and sufficient cause for the state we refer to as 'addicted' is simply untenable.

On the other hand, evidence shows that whether a drug habit becomes an 'addiction' is a function of the environment, as shown by the Leitner, Shapland and Wiles study cited above. Interestingly, analagous data are also found in certain animal studies. For example, a number of studies (e.g. Alexander, Coambes and Hadaway, 1978; Alexander et al., 1981) have shown a 'housing' effect in rats. In broad terms, rats became 'addicted' when lever pressing for drugs in a Skinner box, but 'unaddicted' when transferred to a more naturalistic and 'ratty' setting (the so-called 'rat park') where drugs were still available. In the light of these kinds of findings, it is reasonable to conclude that 'addiction' involves more than simply a pharmacologically active drug.

There is nothing new about such a conclusion. Some years ago Zinberg (1984) invoked the idea that 'addiction' had three necessary components, namely *drug* (a pharmacologically active substance); *set* (the mental 'set' of the user; their expectations, motives and reasons for use); and *setting* (the social and environmental context of use). The remainder of this chapter focuses on the set and setting aspects of drug use, with particular emphasis on the contribution made to 'setting' by the illegality surrounding drugs, and the ways in which this affects the 'set'of the user in ways which make the problem worse rather than better.

DISEASES, LAWS AND SOCIAL CONSTRUCTS

The process of categorisation is functional. Thus, calling something a 'disease' has both a purposive as well as a scientific function. It signals not only what something is, but also how we wish to see it in social terms, and how we intend to deal with it. While the 'presence of an invading organism' is a key feature of many things we term 'diseases', it is by no means the case that all 'diseases' have this 'scientific' feature. 'Addiction' and 'alcoholism' for example are both regularly conceptualised as diseases (signalling that 'treatment' is appropriate) although there is no invading organism and the main 'disease' symptoms consist of an organised, planned and generally well integrated sequence of behaviours directed towards the goal of acquiring the next fix. These arguments have been discussed elsewhere (Davies, 1997a). 'Gambling addiction' is perhaps the most striking example of this type of functional labelling, possessing neither an invading organism nor an external pharmacology (see Davies, 1997a, pp. 71–73, for a critique of the argument that there is an internal pharmacology) and thereby opening the door to the labelling of any other type of doggedly determined behaviour as an 'addiction' (e.g. shopaholism, computer-game addiction, internet addiction).

How, then, have 'addictions' come to be conceptualised within a disease framework, while lacking such a central feature, and when the main 'symptom' is an integrated goal-directed series of actions (i.e. to obtain more supplies) rather than some incapacity or deficit? (It should be noted that intoxication is not a required component of 'addiction'. The fact that some drugs can disrupt behaviour is irrelevant to definitions of 'addiction'. Thus being 'drunk' is not the same as being an 'alcoholic'. So-called addiction to nicotine, on the other hand, produces neither intoxication nor intoxication-related performance deficit, but may even improve performance on certain tasks. The answer lies in the history of the word itself and the observation that the term 'addiction' was originally a socially functional label rather than a scientifically derived concept. Its purpose was to change the public attitude towards the problems of substance abuse away from one of moral censure and 'disease of the will' and create, in its place, a framework within which help/treatment rather than blame would be deemed appropriate. The historical development of the notion of addiction and the related concept of alcoholism have been described comprehensively by Berridge (1979) and succinctly summarised by McMurran (1994). In a historical sense, therefore, the addiction notion was a classic case of functional attribution; that is, a description that had certain linguistic connotative meanings that would change the perception of a phenomenon in a way that hopefully would lead to a desired behaviour change; namely a move towards humane treatment in contrast to the whippings and cold plunges advocated by Rush (1785). The aim was to change the perceptions about, and treatment of, people who took too much of a particular psychoactive substance to their own and possibly society's detriment. Problems arose because this functional attribution began to be researched as if it were a scientifically derived 'truth'. McMurran (1994, p. 9) quoting from Szasz (1974) suggests 'that the medical profession may well have started by treating "disagreeable conduct and forbidden desire" as if they were diseases, that is using disease as a metaphor. However, over time, the metaphor became literal and the medical profession came to insist that "disapproved" behaviour was not merely like a disease, but that it was a disease—thus confusing others, and perhaps themselves as well, regarding the differences between bodily and behavioural abnormalities.' (The issue of what really is a disease raises epistemological issues that go beyond the scope of this text.)

If the scientific logic of applying the disease label to a certain type of planned behaviour is a little obscure, the epistemological status of 'laws' is equally problematic. Laws and moral codes of conduct are not engraved in the stuff of the universe for all too see. Different people and societies see moral behaviour, human 'rights' and the codes and laws that are put in place to preserve and defend these things in quite different ways. There is no international consensus in terms of legislation regarding such diverse things as sexual conduct, adultery, alcohol use, what clothing to wear, going to school, family size and so forth. It is clear that the laws of different societies are based on social and political forces rather than on 'laws of the universe' or any sort of absolute 'rights'. In fact they appear to be put together with a greater or lesser degree of caprice by politicians and others with their own social world view, which the laws are intended to enshrine, but which are not universally shared. Laws are thus socially constructed to take into account differing local beliefs, priorities and social/economic conditions.

A prime example of the almost whimsical nature of certain laws is illustrated by the recent history of the law regarding homosexual behaviour in the UK. Prior to 1973, such behaviour in a public place constituted a criminal offence. At that time, people 'suffering' from the condition could volunteer for 'treatment' in order to obtain remission from a gaol sentence or a more lenient dispensation in a court of law. The treatment, it may be recalled, was normally some variant of aversion therapy; consisting of showing male 'sufferers' pictures of same-sex nudes. If signs of physiological arousal were observed, then electric shock was administered. Subsequently, with the legalisation of homosexual behaviour (i.e. the decision to *socially construct* gay behaviour as socially acceptable rather than as a crime) the need for 'treatment' disappeared and would now be regarded in many quarters as homophobic. Nowadays, there are TV programmes for gay audiences, same-sex marriages have taken place, and books by Carol (1994, ch. 6) and many others proclaim homosexuality as a normal act of preference, sometimes with a clearly political motivation. No one goes to gaol any more for the 'crime' of homosexuality, and consequently no one is signing up for electric-shock therapy in order to get a reduced sentence.

The point being made is very simple. Conceptualising (socially constructing) an integrated, organised and goal-directed sequence of behaviours as 'crime' can, and often does, lead to a secondary construction of the behaviours in question as 'disease' in order to escape or mitigate the consequences of the first categorisation. This is purely an exercise in damage limitation, exactly analogous to the minimax solution in a prisoner's dilemma game or similar mixed motive game (e.g. McClintock, 1972). There is a functional relationship between conceptualising something as a crime and its second-order classification as a disease; a premium being placed on the latter as it removes the issue of *mens rea*, or personal responsibility. The relationship is functional, not formally logical. What could be more ridiculous than conceptualising a 'disease' within a basically criminal framework?

It could be argued that the above proposition is flawed, because it is not the 'disease' of addiction *per se* which is illegal but the possession and supply of the substances which cause it. But even so, the formal logic of the situation still creates problems. The notion is that the 'disease' of addiction derives from physiological/pharmacological states that ultimately *require* the person to use the substance in order to preserve biological normality. However, if the theoretical basis is correct, the proposal to make illegal the possession and supply of the substance(s) necessary to 'normalise' the condition still merits some logical scrutiny. What seems baffling from a treatment perspective is the idea that because one has a specific vulnerability to a substance such that one's metabolism requires the substance in order to maintain normality (homeostasis), one should therefore abstain from it for life.

DRUGS AND THE LAW

The problem with the notion of 'addiction' is that it confounds two different types of epistemology within a single definition. Specifically, it involves two mutually exclusive conceptualisations of man/woman-kind; namely man/woman as machine (i.e. as a biological *mechanism*, the nature of which mechanism determines all activity, both mental and physical) and man/woman as decision-making entity capable of making autonomous choices and exercising acts of will. It should be clear from the outset that no individual responsibility can be attributed under the first model; whereas this is possible under the second, with the very notion of *mens rea* being central to certain aspects of the law. However, this illogical bringing together of two exclusive models is precisely why the 'addiction' concept has such social value, since it enables interested parties to hop between models to excuse or blame according to personal wish and circumstance. These issues have been specifically explored by Heim and colleagues (2001).

These issues have been discussed in detail in Davies (1998) but to cut a lengthy philosophical discussion short, we tend to regard people who (for example) drink normally as being able to make choices about whether to drink or not, when to stop, when to carry on. In other words, to behave like thinking beings capable of exercising acts of will in controlling their consumption; that is, doing 'what they want to do'. On the other hand, we tend to think of 'alcoholics' (an unpopular word these days) as using alcohol because they *have to* due to an underlying compulsive mechanism. In a similar way, drug 'addicts' are felt to use drugs compulsively even though they may be 'trying to stop'; that is, against their 'will'.

The problems and contradictions that arise in the legislation around drugs and drug use come about precisely because they attempt to tackle drug problems from both these perspectives simultaneously. The 'war on drugs' seeks to eradicate the supply of and trade in certain illegal substances, using all the powers of the law (up to and including the death penalty in some countries), on the mechanistic grounds that these substances have capacities to enslave and addict due to their particular pharmacologies. On the other hand, we hold individuals responsible for possession and for drug-related crimes, on the basis that they are responsible for these acts and therefore merit punishment. To put this very succinctly, the definition has nothing to do with 'science', but represents the cobbling together of two exclusive social constructions; namely, drug use as mechanism, and drug use as act of choice or volition.

DETERMINISM VERSUS VOLITION

The issues surrounding the free-will/determinism debate as they apply to the notion of addiction and drug use are fully discussed in Davies (1996, 1998). It is sufficient to say that *choice* of a paradigm within which to study humankind is exactly that; a *choice*. The wish to conceptualise people in a certain way in order to study them is not an act of science based on empirical observation and inductive reasoning *à la* Popper (Popper, 1959) but a choice based on what you wish to achieve and how you wish to frame your questions. Determinism is not truth. An excellent book by Fernandez-Armesto (1997) outlines the different species of knowledge espoused by different societies and exposes the myopia behind the view that the Western empirical view of knowledge represents some absolute 'truth'.

It is probably worth pointing out at this stage that the mechanistic conception of addiction, which is the one universally favoured by politicians and the media, does not receive anything like unanimous support from many of those involved in the counselling and treatment of drug problems. The idea of drug use as a motivated and active choice on the part of the user is not the territory of madmen and maverick academics but receives support at the grass roots level among many agency workers and others involved at the sharp end. Books by Cohen (1989, 1990), Cameron (1995), Schaler (2000), Coomber (1998), Frenk and Dar (2000) and others all express drug problems from a multi-causal perspective rather than a monolithic pharmacological viewpoint. All see individual motivation and choice as a dimension of the problem to a greater or lesser extent. They all put the pilot back in the aeroplane.

If the choice of the best philosophical model of humankind within which to study drug problems is indeed a choice, then what criteria are available to help to guide the decision? In the opinion of the author, the best bet here is some version of the pragmatics espoused by Dewey (1933). In very broad terms, this means choosing one's approach on the basis of what it achieves, rather than searching for some absolute 'truth' which may or may not exist. The 'drug, set and setting' argument is preferred, it is argued, because it takes into account three important components of addiction which have been repeatedly shown in the literature to be related to outcomes. It assumes a motivated basis for drug use, and conceptualises the problem as one whereby individuals choose to use drugs as a logical (if unwise) response to circumstances at a community and individual level (including use for fun) rather than as a simple consequence of a mechanistic drug pharmacology. On the other hand, from a political perspective, such a view receives limited or no support as it implies that the problem of harmful and damaging drug use has to be tackled on a number of fronts with implications that are far reaching in terms of political policy. Tackling set and setting, for example, promises to be both a costly and lengthy enterprise requiring the reorganisation of some basic priorities in terms of schools, health care, education, family functioning, jobs, housing and so forth.

The problem also transmutes in most unfortunate ways to a local level. It is, in practical terms, easy enough to write academic papers about risk factors from the safety of one's desk in a university. Such a list might include truancy, theft, early onset of substance use, greater peer-group attachment, lack of parental supervision, poor attachment/relationships with parents, high community unemployment rates, poor school performance, high population density, high community crime rate (see, for example, Bukstein, 1995, for coverage of risk factors), and a number of other frequently encountered risk-factors, most of which are associated with social class. It is a very different matter to put these arguments in person, in a local community centre, to the parents of young 'addicts', some of whom may have died, on their own turf in a deprived inner-city area, especially where the local people have formed themselves into dynamic 'action groups', and where the focus, perhaps understandably, is on the drugs themselves and the evil pushers in their midst. Small wonder that politicians generally side with their constituents in areas where these issues arise.

Faced with a problem of this magnitude it is much simpler, and cheaper, to adopt an approach based on the assumption that drug problems are caused by drugs and that the best solution, albeit unachievable, is to 'stamp out drugs'. In general terms, it remains only to point out that in all countries of the world where data have been collected, the use (prevalence) of illicit drugs has increased more or less steadily since the late 1950s. 'Drug Prevention', it might be argued, is thus revealed as the name of a job that people do rather than the name of something that actually happens.

THE EFFECTS OF THE LAW ON SET AND SETTING

There is a developing literature on drug use and misuse from the standpoint of attribution theory. Some of the earliest classic studies in this area were carried out by Eiser and colleagues (e.g. Eiser, Sutton and Wober, 1977, 1978; Eiser and Sutton, 1977; Eiser, 1982) with samples of smokers. Several of these studies showed that belief that one was 'addicted' to smoking was associated with a reduced likelihood of making an attempt to quit; and a lowered probability of success if the attempt was made. Although Eiser never explicitly stated such a conclusion, the implication is that the attribution of addiction to one's smoking is a self-handicapping attribution. More recently, the same type of dimension has emerged as a component of the DiClementi and Prochaska (1985) model in the form of self-efficacy, whereby low self-efficacy (belief that one is not in a position to change one's own behaviour) again predicts inability to quit. The whole point about the 'addiction' attribution, as mentioned earlier, is that the behaviour in question is construed as compulsive, i.e. compelled by forces outwith one's control (i.e. external/stable/uncontrollable). In a similar vein, McAllister and Davies (1992) showed strategic shifts in the attribution of addiction among smokers as a function of clinical classification. After their scores on an 'attribution of addiction' scale had been taken at a first interview, those who were told they were 'heavy smokers' at a second interview shifted their attributions towards 'more addicted', while those who were told they were light smokers shifted in the opposite direction. The study suggests that the smokers in the study selected explanations for smoking that 'made sense of' what they had learned about *how seriously the clinician viewed their habit.*

More recently, work has been carried out looking at the strategic nature of attribution among users of illicit drugs. The main difference here is that while smoking is an increasingly disapproved of activity in social terms, it remains legal. By contrast, illicit drug use is an illegal activity, and as a consequence no one engaged in this activity is keen to advertise the fact, especially where the 'harder' drugs (opiates, cocaine) are concerned. Studies have revealed that users of heroin and cocaine exist in the community, that such use may not necessarily involve behaviours that one would call 'addicted' (i.e. the use appears to be stable and controlled over considerable periods of time); but the samples are difficult to find as they do not advertise their presence (Shewan et al., 1998). In this study, 74 people were identified who had used opiates at least 20 times in the last two years, but 'who had never been in addiction treatment or served a custodial sentence'. A study by Ditton (1990) similarly identified cocaine use among non-clinical samples from middle-class backgrounds; but had to use a covert 'snowballing' technique.

It is argued that because of the illegal status of drug use, known drug users present themselves differently in different contexts much like the smokers in the McAllister and Davies study (1992). For example, Davies and Baker (1987) and Ball (1967) both showed systematic lack of reliability in drug users' answers to questions about their habit. In the Davies and Baker study, heroin users reported lower consumption, more enjoyment, less need for 'treatment', and a greater degree of control over the habit when interviewed in a place of their own choosing by a fellow heroin user, but presented as 'helpless addicts' when interviewed formally in a clinical setting by a suit-wearing psychologist. With regard to another illegal activity, theft by adolescent boys, ground-breaking studies by Belson, Millerson and Didcott (circa 1968) showed systematic effects on interviewees responses even when interviewers were seated behind screens and questions were passed on cards!

Where an activity is illegal, the above studies, and common sense, suggest that the answers to questions provided by those involved in the activity become strategic and context dependent. They vary according to the threats perceived by the interviewee in the interview situation, its possible purposes and consequences. Furthermore, personal experience, as an expert witness in cases where a person is accused of 'possession with intent to supply', repeatedly shows that where the accused possesses drugs in a quantity which is judged too large for personal use (this is frequently a contentious issue, with police experts' estimates of what is possible for personal use often being very much smaller than the estimates of defence witnesses) the best defence strategy (in terms of a reduced sentence; for example, community service instead of gaol) is to play the 'addiction' card. The attribution of addiction is assumed to indicate compulsive use for reasons which are outwith the individual's control, and consequently they may not be held responsible for their actions. Furthermore, the 'addiction' attribution goes some way to explaining the quantities possessed.

Unfortunately, there is a limited literature on how specific groups of people, or people in general, construe the addiction concept. However, a study by Walters and Gilbert (2000) showed that a sample of 'addiction experts' (all of Fellow status within the American Psychological Association) and a sample of inmates in a drug education class at a medium security federal US prison, all saw diminished/loss of control as a key feature of addiction. The experts also cited 'compulsive use'. Davies (1998) has argued elsewhere that the central feature of lay and media perceptions of 'addiction' is the idea that the person is in some sense *forced* to use the drug and *can't stop*. This view is, supposedly, supported by the fact that the pharmacological substrate for certain drugs is known (e.g. inhibition of dopamine re-uptake in the acumbens by cocaine). However, a pharmacological approach assumes a deterministic/pharmacological mechanism for *all* behaviours and thus cannot be used to differentiate between addicted and non-addicted states. From that standpoint there is no such thing as a behaviour that does not have a pharmacological (deterministic) basis. It is important to note, however, that this perception (i.e. *can't stop*) is wrong in terms of clinical criteria. Whilst both lay and expert perceptions of 'addiction' focus on lack of ability to control the behaviour, perhaps the most influential document detailing diagnostic criteria explicitly rules out this dimension. The Diagnostic and Statistical Manual of the American Psychiatric Association (APA, 1994, p. XXIII) explicitly states that 'the fact that an individual meets the criteria for the DSM-IV diagnosis does not carry any necessary implication regarding the individual's degree of control over the behaviours that may be associated with the disorder'. It is also interesting to note that the contemporary academic refereed literature almost exclusively uses the term 'dependence' rather than 'addiction', precisely because of the connotations of the latter term. 'Dependence' on the other hand at least leaves the door ajar with respect to issues of free-will and compulsion. Unfortunately the popular social construction of 'addiction' as 'compelled' carries more weight with politicians and the media than more careful scientific statements. In the popular imagination the most salient feature of being a drug addict is that 'you can't stop', and that it's the drugs themselves that bring that state of affairs about. The question now arises as to why this particular construction is so pervasive when the evidence that 'addiction' in those terms is a flawed concept is so strong.

ADDICTION: A FUNCTIONAL ATTRIBUTION IN A CONTEXT OF ILLEGALITY

It is probably worth while starting this section with some quotes from one of the classic texts, *Living with Drugs* (Gossop, 1987). Despite celebrating its twentieth birthday, this text still contains material that is as fresh and radical as the day it was written. The cover to the second edition (1987) bears the text: 'One way or another, we must all learn to live with drugs.' An even more telling comment appears under the section on 'Junkie Myths', and takes the form 'but the addict is often a fiction even to himself. The fascination of the addict attaches not to the person who is dependent on drugs, but to his fabulous shadow.' This conclusion from Gossop, based on experience with drug users, closely resembles conclusions from Bem (1972) arrived at via the route of self-perception theory. According to Bem, the statement 'I can't stop' is not a statement of fact but an inference based on the self-observation that I reliably fail to do so.

Taken together, these two statements more or less summarise the concluding arguments to this chapter. Firstly, Gossop strongly argues that the only realistic option in the modern world is to learn to live with drugs, managing their use and reducing or minimising the dangers and harms associated with their use through whatever means are available. Eliminating drugs and their use from society, it is argued, is not a realistic option. This is a matter of opinion, of course, since empirical evidence cannot shed light on the likely success or otherwise of the 'war on drugs'. However, it is the view here that ease of international travel, cheapness of production at source, and increasing prevalence over a 40-year period, all suggest that the drug problem is here to stay and that we have to learn to cope with it positively rather than hoping to banish drugs from our midst.

The more subtle point is made in the second quote from Gossop, which suggests that users ('addicts') are in some sense victims of their own propaganda. The 'junkie' myth is believed and endorsed by users themselves, who in a sense live up to their own stereotype. If this is the case, then any research or enquiry which makes use of a method relying on the verbal reports of 'addicts' in order to find out 'the truth' about what addiction is 'really like', is bound to be flawed. This is of particular significance where qualitative research makes use of the discourse of 'addicts'; but instead of (correctly) construing this material as simply representing how individuals view the world, dangerously assumes that the discourses represent 'facts' from which normative statements can be derived.

Davies (1997b, 1997c) describes studies of the discourses of drug users, and shows how different broad attributional (explanatory) styles occur with great reliability and may be easily recognised. The studies also then go on to indicate that these identifiable types of drug discourse occur most often in particular settings; and that the meaning of the discourses derives as much from the setting in which they are uttered as from the words themselves. To put this another way, the meaning of an utterance is defined by the context within which it occurs (Edwards and Potter, 1992), a point of view reminiscent of Wittgenstein's later approach to meaning and language (Hartnack, 1962). The Davies studies thus attempt (i) to identify regularly occurring types of discourse and (ii) to locate the contexts within which they most often occur, and thereby to identify their meaning.

DRUG DISCOURSES: FUNCTIONAL OR DYSFUNCTIONAL?

A Scottish Office-funded study reported by Davies[1] (1997b, 1997c) analysed minimally structured conversations with drug users in the Central Belt of Scotland, South-West Scotland, and the North-East of England. Initial (first) interviews were carried out with 275 subjects; second follow-up interviews with 197 of these; and third interviews with 76. All interviews were cued by the question 'So what are you on, what are you using at the moment?' Thereafter, the interview took its own course, but with the interviewer exploring any attributional statements that emerged. All interviews were tape recorded, transcribed in full, and coded for attributional content. The full details of the process are given in Davies (1997c) together with the dimensions derived, and the inter-rater reliabilities.

Regression analysis of the dimensions suggested that five different conversational types could be identified reliably. The full typology is given in Davies (1997c) but may be summarised briefly as follows.

- *Type 1.* Drug use is characterised as fun, problem free, as having no harmful effects in any life area, and as deliberate. Some of these discourses see drug use as positive ('the best thing since hot dinners') and some of these users are drug enthusiasts.

- *Type 2.* This is an unstable and contradictory type of discourse. Part of the time the discourse resembles Type 1 (above); but at other times in the conversation problems associated with the drug use are also described (e.g. problems at school, with teachers, with parents, with social workers). The individual possesses two discourses; a positive hedonistic type for peers and fellows, and a problem-oriented discourse for disapproving others. The notion of 'addiction' is still absent from this discourse, however.

- *Type 3.* This is the 'helpless addict' box. There is said to be no control over the habit, the person 'can't stop', there is low or negative hedonism. The drug use is described as a logical and inevitable consequence of physiological or constitutional factors over which the individual has no control; or as a logical and inevitable consequence of negative life events or situations with a lengthy and more or less inexorable history.

- *Type 4.* This resembles Type 2 in being contradictory and context dependent. The addiction concept starts to break down temporarily or fundamentally for the individual concerned, due to tension between the requirements of the 'addict' role and growing discontent with those requirements. The 'addict' stereotype is still endorsed, but the drug use is again viewed positively and favourably. This is the

[1] Thanks are due to David Best, Linda Wright and Maria Crugeira for fundamental contributions to this piece of research.

stage when 'lapse' or 'relapse' occurs or is made to occur. (Data from Christo (1995) show that relapses do not simply 'happen' as part of an inevitable process but may often be planned in advance, sometimes in considerable detail.)

- *Type 5+ (positive)*. This is a positive type of discourse, in which 'addiction' is seen as something that occurred in the past. The person, however, is no longer an 'addict' (this is fundamentally different from AA-type or 12-step philosophies, where the individual is always 'recovering' but can never actually do so) and their addiction is a thing of the past. Both the addictions, and the attributions behind it, are seen as over and done with. A new lifestyle is described, with a positive focus, and is not predicated on any need to constantly guard against the reinstatement of addiction.

These types are recognisable with high degrees of reliability. There also may exist a Type 5− *(negative)* discourse on which further research is necessary. However, for the purposes of this chapter it is sufficient to focus on the above types, and examine their strategic nature by looking at the circumstances in which they occur. Once again, only a partial coverage of the data is given; a full account being available in the reference cited above.

The first thing to note about the discourses is that they are sensitive to the difference between clinical and non-clinical contexts. Drug users in agency contact are more likely to use Type 3 and Type 4 discourse; those not in agency contact are more likely to use Type 1 discourse, or to describe any problems they have in terms of Type 2. Data were collected on three occasions, and the same pattern emerged each time as can be seen in Table 4.1.1.

Table 4.1.1 shows a natural, but probably undesirable, tendency of drug users to talk the 'addict' script when in agency contact. It demonstrates that in the real world the results of the Davies and Baker (1987) study are reproduced (albeit within a between-subjects

Table 4.1.1   Discourses of drug users in agency contact, and not in agency contact, on three different occasions (raw frequencies)

		Discourse type				
		1	2	3	4	5+
Time 1	Agency contact	3	12	117	85	6
	No agency contact	27	18	3	4	0
Time 2	Agency contact	2	3	74	79	8
	No agency contact	17	9	1	4	0
Time 3	Agency contact	3	1	26	33	2
	No agency contact	5	3	1	2	1

Chi-square for 4 d.f.; $p < 0.0001$ in each case.

design). There is nothing strange about this; when one goes to the doctor one describes oneself as ill or sick in one way or another, in order to get the treatment one requires. The same is true for drug users. Furthermore, this discursive style also signals that the individual expects the doctor to fix things. However, describing *addiction* as a 'disease' encourages the same type of external/stable/uncontrollable attributional style but this time in an inappropriate context. There is a large volume of research attesting to the importance of personal motivation as a predictor of success in kicking a drug habit, even where there is pharmacological intervention. Thus Baekeland, Lundwall and Kissin (1975, p. 305) write, 'Over and over we were impressed with the dominant role of the patient, as opposed to the kind of treatment used on him'; and Vaillant (1995, pp. 353–354) in his classic, and unique, 45-year follow-up study writes, 'To change a maladaptive habit, be it smoking or getting too little exercise or drinking too much alcohol, we cannot "treat" or compel . . . the person. Rather, we must change the person's belief system . . .' and later, '. . . if you can but win their hearts and minds, their habits will follow. . .'. In a sense, therefore, individual cognitive reappraisal is the key factor. One makes a decision to quit and one implements it; and therefore a form of self-perception is required that will allow this course of action. This is not the case with 'real' diseases where the expectation that the doctor can (to a greater extent) fix it usually has more substance, and is a reasonable one.

The point raised earlier now becomes particularly salient, namely that the self-attribution of addiction is self-handicapping; and it is particularly worrying if there exist agencies who actually encourage or require this type of stable, external and uncontrollable attribution for drug use from their clients. From such a standpoint, the liberating Type 5+ discourse whereby addiction has been left behind, is simply not possible.

Table 4.1.2 shows data from subjects in the same study who were not in agency contact at time of first interview (Time 1) but *who came into agency contact during the course of the 18-month project*, and compares their discursive style with a group who *never* came into agency contact during that period.

It should be said at the outset that the data in Table 4.1.2 require support from other sources; but the implications could in principle be extremely disturbing. A group of 27 drug users who saw themselves as non-addicted, volitional and hedonistic users,

Table 4.1.2   Subjects not in agency contact at Time 1, and subjects who never came into agency contact during the study, by discursive stage

	Discourse type				
	1	2	3	4	5+
Not in agency contact at Time 1	27	22	33	19	0
Never in agency contact	27	18	3	4	0

stayed out of treatment/agency contact for the duration of the study. One is inclined to think that this subset represents a group like the students referred to in the early paragraphs, or perhaps the non-symptomatic heroin users in the Shewan et al. study (1998); a group of people for whom the combination of set and setting did not come together with their drugs of choice to produce 'addiction'. By contrast, the attrition rate for those who constructed themselves in the 'helpless addict' role is little short of alarming. Of 33 people, not in treatment but believing they were indulging in an addictive activity (i.e. Type 3 discourse) at the start of the study, only three were not in some type of treatment or agency contact 18 months later.

CONCLUSIONS

It has been argued that the classification of certain types of behaviour as 'diseases' is an act of social construction, indicating not only what something 'is', but also how one intends to deal with it. In some instances, things which lack salient features that characterise many diseases are still so described for reasons which are primarily social. The disease of addiction is an example of this, having its roots in historical and social factors whose primary function was to change the perception and treatment of those with problems of substance use.

There is convincing evidence that viewing ones drug use as a disease manifestation results in a form of addicted attribution that actually lessens the capacity to successfully manage, or quit, the habit. In short, once one has called the behaviour a disease, and that construction is supported by a body of opinion one believes to be expert, one understandably treats the problem as if it 'really is' a disease and expects someone else to fix it. This is unfortunate, since personal motivation and self-efficacy are among the predictors of success in controlling substance use problems.

In the area of human factors research, a type of analysis caused 'root-cause' analysis is often used. A root-cause is a factor or group of factors in the absence of which a particular situation would not have come about. With respect to what is in fact the *mis*-attribution of addiction to substance misuse, the status of drug problems within the current UK drug laws is, it is argued here, the root-cause. Convincing arguments have been written criticising in particular US and UK legislation, making use of cogent economic, social, and civil rights arguments (see Coomber, 1998; Stevenson, 1994; Friedman and Szasz, 1992). The value of drugs on the market, and the huge profits to be made by the Mafia and others, are supported or even stimulated by the illegality of the drug trade. The notion of treating what is effectively a health problem within a framework of illegality, of imprisoning drug offenders for a species of self-medication, and so forth, have all been well argued elsewhere (see Coomber, 1998). Mill (1859) has also often been cited as a source from which to derive support for civil rights arguments, and the rights of individuals to do what they wish provided it does not interfere with the rights of others to do the same.

The current argument supports these lines of thinking in principle, although the argument itself is none of these things. The root-cause of the sticky and intransigent nature of drug problems is the way drugs are seen in the eyes of the law. Because drug use is an illegal activity, a premium is placed on modes of explanation that remove personal responsibility. The 'addiction' notion does precisely that. Therefore, when one falls foul of the law because of ones use/misuse of drugs, a body of respectable but functional/socially constructed evidence exists to show that this is due to a disease, rather than as arising from acts of choice that, wisely or unwisely, one has made. That is the single most important reason why the addiction notion survives despite its lack of logical coherence. It is perhaps *the* classic self-serving attributional bias where an activity is surrounded by a climate of moral and legal censure. Unfortunately, however, the belief that one is 'addicted' is the one thing that removes the capacity to change the behaviour. Only a change in the drug laws can provide the fertile ground for a new construction of drug problems that leaves those individuals who experience problems with the cognitive liberty to save themselves.

It is worth finishing with a quote from one of our anonymous drug users who took part in the discourse study. This extract is from a female volunteer, and represents a section of a Type 5+ discourse.

I think what, to me, what's happened is instead of saying your addiction is selfish and it's self abuse, they've said your addiction is an illness. And I think people have used the illness thing to, you know, be easier on themselves and say 'I'm ill' instead of 'It's my own fault,' you know. But maybe, you know, that works with people but really its such a taboo subject anyway. I think you've really got to be straight and hard with people and say 'Well yeah, it is your own fault,' you know, 'cause it is. Nobody says you have to stick a needle in your arm or you have to take this, you know. It's your own choice. So if it works, if people come off thinking it was an illness then fine . . . but I mean we all know really it's not an illness . . . it's a self-induced thing, that only you can get out of, you know, I mean . . . yeah . . . you can get help and counselling all the rest of it but its you at the end of the day who has to say, right, you know, I'm going to do it.

This chapter argues that the current drug laws make it harder for people to take the kind of dynamic and personal responsibility for their actions described vividly in the above excerpt. When the law catches up with you in connection with drugs, it's best to be a helpless addict, even if that cognition divorces you from the roots of your own behaviour and makes it less likely that you can take a personal and dynamic role in your own salvation.

REFERENCES

Alexander, B.K., Coambes, R.B. and Hadaway, P.F. (1978). The effect of housing and gender on morphine self-administration in rats. *Psychopharmacology*, *58*, 175–179.
Alexander, B.K., Beyerstein, B.L., Hadaway, P.F. and Coambes, R.B. (1981). Effect of early and late colony housing on oral ingestion of morphine in rats. *Pharmacology, Biochemistry and Behaviour*, *15*, 571–576.

Anslinger, H. and Tomkins, W. (1953). *The traffic in narcotics*. New York: Funk & Wagnalls.

APA (1994). DSM-IV: *Diagnostic and Statistical Manual of Mental Disorders* (4th edn). Washington, DC: American Psychiatric Association.

Baekeland, F., Lundwall, L. and Kissin, B. (1975). Methods for the treatment of chronic alcoholism: A critical appraisal. In R.J. Gibbons (ed.), *Research advances in alcohol and drug problems* (vol. 2). New York: John Wiley & Sons.

Ball, J.C. (1967). The reliability and validity of interview data obtained from 59 narcotic drug addicts. *American Journal of Sociology, 72*, 650–659.

Belson, W.A., Millerson, G.L. and Didcott, D.J. (circa 1968: undated). *The development of a procedure for eliciting information from boys about the nature and extent of their stealing.* Survey Research Centre: London School of Economics.

Bem, D.J. (1972). Self-perception theory. In L. Berkowitz (ed.), *Advances in experimental social psychology*. Hillsdale: Erlbaum.

Berridge, V. (1979). Morality and medical science: concepts of narcotic addiction in Britain. *Annals of Science, 36*, 67–85.

Bukstein, O.G. (1995). *Adolescent substance abuse: Assessment, prevention, and treatment.* New York: John Wiley & Sons.

Cameron, D. (1995). *Liberating solutions to alcohol problems*. New Jersey: Jason Aronson.

Carol, A. (1994). *Nudes, prudes and attitudes*. Cheltenham, UK: New Clarion Press.

Christo, G. (1995). *Understanding the process of relapse and recovery: A longitudinal study of drug users in abstinence oriented treatment*. PhD thesis. London: Institute of Psychiatry.

Cohen, P. (1989). *Cocaine use in Amsterdam in non-deviant subcultures*. Amsterdam: University of Amsterdam.

Cohen, P. (1990). *Drugs as a social construct*. Amsterdam: Universeteit van Amsterdam.

Coomber, R. (1998). *The control of drugs and drug users*. Reason or reaction? London: Harwood Academic Publishers.

Davies, J.B. and Baker, R. (1987). The impact of self-presentation and interviewer bias effects on self-reported heroin use. *British Journal of Addiction, 42*, 907–912.

Davies, J.B. (1996). Reasons and causes: Understanding substance users' explanations for their behaviour. *Human Psychopharmacology, 11*, 39–48.

Davies, J.B. (1997a). *The myth of addiction* (2nd edn). London: Harwood Academic Publishers.

Davies, J.B. (1997b). Conversations with drug users: A functional discourse model. *Addiction Research, 5*, 53–70.

Davies, J.B. (1997c). *Drugspeak: The analysis of drug discourse*. London: Harwood Academic Press.

Davies, J.B. (1998). Pharmacology versus social process: Competing or complementary views on the nature of addiction? *Pharmacology and Therapeutics, 80* (3), 265–275.

Dewey, J. (1933). *How We Think*. New York: Heath.

Diclementi, C.C. and Prochaska, L.O. (1985). Processes and stages of self-change: Coping and competence in smoking behaviour change. In S. Shiffman and T.A. Wills (eds), *Coping and substance use* (pp. 319–343) New York: Academic Press.

Ditton, J. (1990 September). *The Scottish Cocaine Research Group, Scottish Cocaine Users: Yuppie Snorters or Ghetto Smokers?* University of Glasgow: Update 6. Internal Memorandum.

Edwards, D. and Potter, J. (1992). *Discursive psychology*. London: Sage.

Eiser, J.R., Sutton, S.R. and Wober, M. (1977). Smokers, non-smokers and the attribution of addiction. *British Journal of Social and Clinical Psychology, 16*, 329–336.

Eiser, J.R. and Sutton, S.R. (1977). Smoking as a subjectively rational choice. *Addictive Behaviours, 2*, 129–134.

Eiser, J.R., Sutton, S.R. and Wober, M. (1978). Smokers and non-smokers attributions about addiction: A case of actor–observer differences? *British Journal of Social and Clinical Psychology, 17*, 189–190.

Eiser, J.R. (1982). Addiction as attribution: Cognitive processes in giving up smoking. In J.R. Eiser (ed.), *Social psychology and behavioural medicine*. Chichester: John Wiley & Sons.

Frenk, H. and Dar, R. (2000). *A critique of nicotine addiction*. Boston: Kluwer Academic Publishers.

Fernandez-Armesto, F. (1997). *Truth: A history and a guide for the perplexed*. St Ives: Clays Ltd.

Friedman, M. and Szasz, T. (1992). *On liberty and drugs*. Washington: Drug Policy Foundation

Gossop, M. (1987). *Living with drugs*. London: Wildwood House.

Heim, D., Davies, J. Cheyne, W. and Smallwood, J. (2001). Addiction as a functional representation. *Journal of Community and Applied Social Psychology*, *11*, 57–62.

Hartnack, J. (1962). *Wittgenstein and modern philosophy*. London: Methuen.

Hinson, R.E., Poulos, C.X., Thomas, W. and Cappell, H. (1986). Pavlovian conditioning and addictive behaviour—Relapse to oral self-administration of morphine. *Behavioural Neuroscience*, *100* (3), 368–375.

Leitner, M., Shapland, J. and Wiles, P. (1993). *Drug usage and drugs prevention*. London: HMSO.

McAllister, P. and Davies, J.B. (1992). Attributional bias as a function of clinical classification. *Drug Issues*, 22.5.

McMurran, M. (1994). *The psychology of addiction*. London: Taylor & Francis.

McRae, J.R. and Siegel, S. (1990). Differential effects of morphine in self-administering and yoked-control rat. In D.J.K. Balfour, *Psychotropic drugs of abuse* (p. 81). New York: Pergammon.

McClintock, C.G. (1972). *Experimental social psychology*. New York: Holt, Rinehart & Winston.

Mill, J.S. (1859). 'On liberty'. Cited from M. Friedman and T. Szasz (1992) *On liberty and drugs*. Washington: Drug Policy Foundation.

Popper, K. (1959). *The logic of scientific discovery*. London: Hutchison.

Rush, B. (1785). An inquiry into the effect of ardent spirits upon the human body and mind. Cited in M. McMurran (ed.) (1994) *The Psychology of Addiction* (pp. 9–10). London: Taylor & Francis.

Shewan, D., Dalgarno, P., Marshall, A., Lowe, E., Campbell, M., Nicholson, S., Reith, G., McLafferty, V. and Thomson, K. (1998). Patterns of heroin use among a non-treatment sample in Glasgow (Scotland). *Addiction Research*, *6* (3), 215–234.

Stevenson, R. (1994). *Winning the war on drugs: To legalise or not?* London: Institute of Economic Affairs.

Szasz, T. (1974). *Ceremonial chemistry*. New York: Anchor Press.

Schaler, J.A. (2000). *Addiction is a choice*. Chicago: Open Court.

Strathclyde Telegraph (1994). Students drug Survey. Issue 3, volume 35.

US Surgeon General (1982). *The health consequences of smoking*. A report of the Surgeon General. Maryland: Department of Health and Human Services.

US Surgeon General (1988). *The health consequences of smoking*. A report of the Surgeon General. Maryland: Department of Health and Human Services.

Vaillant, G. (1995). *The natural history of alcoholism re-visited*. Cambridge, MA: Harvard University Press.

Walters, G.D. and Gilbert, A.A. (2000). Defining addiction: contrasting views of clients and experts. *Addiction Research*, *8* (3), 211–220.

Zinberg, N. (1984). *Drug, set and setting: The basis for controlled intoxicant use*. New Haven: Yale University Press.

Chapter 4.2

Psychological Research and Lawyers' Perceptions of Child Witnesses in Sexual Abuse Trials

Emily Henderson
Researcher, Cambridge, UK

INTRODUCTION

Historically, scientists, the courts and the general public have regarded children who made allegations of sex abuse extremely sceptically. Scientists in the now-distant past estimated that the vast majority of such complaints were false (which term includes both deliberate deception and mistake), with some studies putting false accusations at 93% and 94% (see Spencer and Flin, 1993). This attitude prevailed among many psychologists until very recently. Even in 1981, it was still possible to find English estimates of false accusations of sexual offences generally set at 90% (Spencer and Flin, 1993). However, since the late 1970s researchers have challenged this scepticism and in a number of studies reversed earlier 'findings', estimating the percentage of children's false allegations of sexual abuse in single figures (Spencer and Flin, 1993). Simultaneously, researchers found that children's reliability and accuracy as witnesses *per se* was far higher than had previously been believed and that children's abilities are not dissimilar to those of adults, if their interviewing is appropriate (Goodman, Aman and Hirshman, 1987; Milne and Bull, 1999).

This chapter considers the impact of these advances in psychologists' knowledge of children on the ways in which lawyers imagine and discuss child sex assault complainants in criminal trials. Many commentators have criticised defence counsel for continuing to advocate implausible and prejudicial stereotypes of children as unreliable witnesses (see Spencer and Flin, 1993). This chapter also discusses the findings of the author's qualitative study of a small sample of 14 experienced New

Zealand and five English barristers regarding their attitudes to child witnesses in child sex trials, contrasting their opinions with the psychological research. It argues that despite the changes legislation has introduced to the trial as the result of psychological research, the respondents were relatively unaware of advances in psychological knowledge, and retained outmoded views of child complainants as unreliable witnesses.

The Study

Fourteen New Zealand advocates and five English barristers were interviewed between 1995–96 and 1997–98 respectively concerning a range of issues relating to child sex abuse trials. The individual interviews lasted between one and three hours each. The New Zealand group included four specialist prosecutors and ten defence counsel. The English counsel, as is conventional in England, all acted on both sides. This chapter discusses the respondents' opinions concerning the plausibility of a series of possible defences in court. Such a small sample cannot, of course, be regarded as representative of lawyers in each country but it may give some indications as to views within each profession.

In the study the respondents were asked to comment on four defences to child sexual abuse allegations that are often criticised by researchers as implausible and prejudicial. The defences were, first, that an adult had misled the child by suggestion into believing he or she had been abused; second, that the child was coached to make false allegations knowingly; and, third, that the child fantasised the attack. The fourth defence was that the child lied deliberately and maliciously. The respondents were invited to suggest any other common defences but all agreed that the list comprised the main defences. Any additional reasons volunteered appeared to be subsets of the main four.

This chapter argues that the respondents' discussions of the defences are indicative of a negative view of childhood generally and a sceptical view of child sex assault complainants especially. This viewpoint contrasts strongly with current psychological research suggesting that children are capable witnesses. The chapter also charts some significant correspondences between defences to children's allegations of abuse and defences to adult women's allegations of rape.

EXCULPATING DEFENCES

I argue that there are two basic categories of defence outlined by the respondents. In the first category—which contains the defences of suggestion, coaching, fantasy and that the child has lied deliberately without comprehending that lying is unethical (a version of the defence of lies)—the defence counsel takes pains to exculpate the child of blame for the allegedly false allegations. Instead, counsel lays responsibility for the allegations on childhood developmental deficiencies or manipulative adults.

Conversely, the defence that the child has lied deliberately and maliciously blames the child unequivocally.

SUGGESTION

The first of the exculpating defences is that the child had been influenced by suggestions (unconscious or deliberate) to believe she or he was abused when in fact she or he was not. Both nationalities appeared to regard suggestion as a serious issue, although the English were less reliant on it as a defence than the New Zealanders.

Literature Review

The research leaves no doubt that children can be influenced by suggestion. The relevant questions however are, first, whether they are more suggestible than adult witnesses, in whom we regularly put our trust and, second, about what are children suggestible?

Concerns about children's suggestibility need to be put into context. Numerous studies have established that adult witnesses are extremely suggestible (Ceci and Bruck, 1995; Lindsay and Read, 1994; Wells and Loftus, 1984). Although very young children are much more suggestible than adults (Spencer and Flin, 1993), studies also show that by 7 years old children can generally perform as well as adults (Ceci and Bruck, 1995). We need to be careful not to overemphasise the dangers of suggestibility in the child witness unless we also subject adults to the same scrutiny.

Accepting that children are suggestible, the crucial issue is whether they are susceptible to suggestion about sexual abuse (Spencer and Flin, 1993). A distinction must be drawn between different topics. Research strongly suggests that while unimportant events not strongly present in the child's memory are relatively easily altered, memories of significant events, such as sexual assault, are difficult to alter or implant (Goodman, Aman and Hirshman, 1987; Saywitz et al., 1991).

Although some studies, notably those of Ceci (e.g. Ceci and Bruck, 1995), have been able to implant memories of physical touching, arguably analogous to sexual abuse, closer examination reveals that these studies required repeated interviews using extremely suggestive language and heavy pressure (Ceci and Bruck, 1995). Even in Ceci's study, which brought significant pressure to bear on its (preschool) subjects, 55% of the children resisted the interviewer's pressure successfully and no child made false allegations of genital touching (Ceci and Bruck, 1993). Even so, the dangers of heavy-handed, repetitive interviewing are well recognised and are contrary to practice guidelines in both New Zealand and England (Home Office and Dept. of Health, 1992; Milne and Bull, 1999). Ceci and Bruck themselves admit to 'focus[ing] disproportionately on [children's] weaknesses' and on poor investigative practice disproportionate to its actual occurrence (Ceci and Bruck, 1995; Goodman and Schaff, 1997).

A further general point is that, even were a child to be influenced to believe he or she had been assaulted, without actual experience of abuse children are highly unlikely to be able to report it in sufficient detail. Studies suggest that children are unlikely to be able to incorporate realistic details of sexual activity or to display appropriate emotional responses without personal experience (Steller and Boychuk, 1992). For example, Saywitz and colleagues (1991) found that the three children who made false allegations of genital touching provided little, if any, detail in support. Ceci and Bruck fail to say whether the participants who eventually made false allegations of touching could support their assertions in the face of continued questioning (Ceci and Bruck, 1995; see also MacFarlane et al., 1986).

Overall it is fair to say that unless there are certain high-risk factors, including seriously poor interviewing practices, suggestibility is not a significantly higher risk to the reliability of a child complainant's account of sexual abuse than it would be to an adult's evidence of similar events.

Findings

Nine of the 14 New Zealand respondents stated that children are highly vulnerable to suggestion and that suggestion was a major cause of false allegations of child sexual abuse. Only three discounted suggestion as a realistic defence.

> They're suggestible, I've no doubt about that, and I think the process can make them suggestible too. If they've had lots of interviews and [have been] asked leading questions, something ends up being drummed into them by interviewers or parents.

Emma Davies's contemporaneous study of cross-examination transcripts, from trials in the same area as that in which the New Zealand lawyers in this study practised, also shows how often suggestion is blamed. Davies found that suggestion was raised in 11 of 13 New Zealand cross-examination transcripts of children aged 12 and under, and in six of 13 transcripts of children between 13 and 17 (Davies, Henderson and Seymour, 1997; see also Brennan and Brennan, 1988). However the English lawyers, while still concerned with suggestion, reported using it less in court than did the New Zealanders. Four of the five commented on suggestion, all apparently endorsing it as a serious issue, all giving detailed descriptions of possible situations in which it could become a risk.

> [A] complaint by a child is only as good as the circumstances that generated it. . . . Supposing you . . . find out that at the time when the child went to the police, the parents were in the middle of a divorce battle and there was a raging custody battle over the child. I don't think I need to say any more.

Both nationalities attribute responsibility for suggestion to (in order) evidential inter-viewers, counsellors, parents, and the police. Of the New Zealanders, three blamed parents (especially mothers) for suggestion, two blamed the police, and nine attributed responsibility to evidential interviewers and other clinicians. Similarly, two of the English blamed family members, invariably identified as mothers, who are often blamed by ex-partners for making false allegations (Kennedy, 1992), and four blamed evidential interviewers, police and social workers generally.

Additionally, four New Zealanders and three English respondents described a scenario in which *something* 'the child . . . has said . . . has been taken out of context, and in the present climate of believing everything . . . has then become . . . a whole big criminal trial all these months later'. This defence was often referred to as 'snowballing'.

> It's usually a sort of throw-away line [where] the child might have said to Mummy 'Daddy does this' or 'I've seen Daddy sexing' . . . the mother, will interpret that to mean Daddy has somehow interfered with the son or daughter, and that can snowball.

In addition to adult misinterpretations, one New Zealander and three English also cited a defence which the English called 'horseplay', in which a hypersensitive and suspicious child misinterprets innocent touching. Two of the English described this as one of the most common defences to child abuse.

> The other [main] defence is [this]: . . . mistake and misinterpretation. . . . I don't confront child witnesses 'head on' if I can, I prefer to run a case on the basis 'yes, he put his hand on your knee, but you misunderstood, you misinterpreted. . . . As soon as the defendant put his hand on your knee, as soon as he put his arm around you, and gave you a kiss, because you have never known that from another human, it totally threw you and you misinterpreted it.' . . . That's the way I like to defend.

This comment is similar to several indicating some respondents believed that even occasional exposure to educational information about sex abuse was suggestive.

> [They say] where you get these things taught to you at school . . . [children] are so much on the look-out for them that they tend to see abuse where there is none.

An English respondent threw her net even wider:

> Whether that's suggestibility by the influence of a single adult, or whether it is suggestibility by the present climate we live in, there's quite a bit of it about, I'd suspect. It's something that's discussed in schools as openly as anti-drugs projects, there've been so many campaigns that have had high-profile TV, media generally [exposure]. Go into a telephone box and you see numbers for Childline [an English telephone helpline for abused children]. There's a climate that's out there to receive this.

It is unfortunate for real child victims if they are likely to be viewed suspiciously merely because they are educated to complain if abused. These comments, about the suggestiveness of educational materials, also raise interesting parallels with the well-recognised prejudice against sexually experienced women who complain of rape. Experienced women are less likely to be believed (and if believed their injuries are likely to be assumed to be lesser) than sexually ignorant women (Kennedy, 1992;

Lees, 1996). It is possible that a similar attitude prevails among some lawyers with regard to children so that an aware child is *prima facie* a less trustworthy complainant than an ignorant child. The equation of ignorance with innocence in the following comment is interesting in this context.

> [S]ometimes that may come down to the hypersensitive awareness. Maybe now a child in close proximity to an older, usually male, who picks them up or something, may perceive that something that's innocent to be abusive in a way where once when they were left in their more innocent frame of mind they never thought of it as being abuse.

Overall, it is clear that the overwhelming majority of the lawyers interviewed believed children to be far more suggestible than modern research has found them to be, envisaging children as fragile witnesses whose reality is able to be swayed by relatively little. The findings in this study parallel those of Leippe and colleagues (1989) to some extent in that 91% of their defence lawyers and 70% of their prosecutors believed that children were much more suggestible than adults.

COACHING

The easily influenced child described in the respondents' discussions of suggestibility also appears in their discussions of coaching as a defence. The respondents were asked their assessments of the defence that an adult had deliberately coached the child to make false allegations of sexual abuse (as opposed to the child unconsciously absorbing suggestions).

Literature Review

There is little to support the argument that children can be coached to make false allegations of sexual abuse and particularly not convincing and sustainable allegations (Bussey, Lee and Grimbeek, 1996). Bussey et al. (1996) discuss Tate and Warren-Luebecker's study, which examined the likelihood that 3 to 7-year-olds would lie after intensive coaching by their mothers to tell the interviewer that the child had played with a certain toy when they had not. Although 11 of the 20 children did lie, only three were able to sustain the lie to the end of the interview. Clinicians also report that young coached children who are asked how they know daddy abused them will often simply admit 'because mummy told me he did' (MacFarlane et al., 1986).

Further, the absence of actual experience is significant to the quality of the child's account, even with coaching. Tate and Warren-Luebecker found significant differences between the stories told by those children asked to lie and those who had actually played with the toy. The truthful children gave far more elaborate and far longer descriptions of playing, a finding which is consistent with the expectations of content-based statement analysis (see Vrij, 2000). It therefore appears that although some children can be coached it is difficult to do so and their lies, especially when very young, are unconvincing (see also MacFarlane et al., 1986).

Findings

The respondents generally stated that coaching was unlikely, although six of the 14 New Zealanders and four of the five English were prepared to argue it as a defence in court.

Five of the 14 New Zealand respondents rated coaching as very unlikely, generally because children do not have the requisite knowledge to sustain the story.

> Kids can't sustain [a coached story]. Children haven't got sophisticated processes. [...] You will get some coaching along the lines of 'Daddy's a bad man' [but] that's not so much [...] me sitting you down and saying 'repeat after me: "Daddy's a bad man".'

However, six lawyers, although still considering coaching rare, thought that it did sometimes occur, or would advance it in court.

> If they're going to make stuff up, particularly with younger kids, it's probably because some adult has put them up to it.

Further, two from the group who were ostensibly unenthusiastic about coaching, believed refreshing a child's memory of their statement before court is a form of coaching and can contaminate their evidence. In 1994 the English Court of Appeal supported this position, stating that children should not be allowed to re-read their police statements before testifying. (*R. v. Thomas* [1994] Crim LR 745). As adults routinely re-read their statements before court, it appears that these respondents require a higher standard of memory from children than from adults.

Four of the English respondents said that they believed coaching is an uncommon occurrence. However all five stated that they had encountered instances of coaching in their practice.

One English respondent suggested that if a child looks at his or her mother during cross-examination that may indicate coaching. Both nationalities considered that legal wording, sophisticated terminology or phrasing, 'parroting out exactly the same phrases that are on page two, paragraph three of the witness statement' and appearing glib or 'extremely pat in what they say' were indicative of coaching.

> Sometimes when you hear very young children talking about their 'vaginas' you are very, very sceptical because you know that that's been put there by somebody... [who] has spoken to the child before she has actually gone on video and equipped her with the necessary language skills to explain her complaint.... [Even with] a six or seven year old... I still don't necessarily think that 'vagina' would be a kid's own word at a very young age. I've got a case at the moment where an 11 year old is talking about somebody having 'fondled her breasts'. Well, it sounds like police language to me; it doesn't sound like the way an 11 year old would say it.

However, it is also plausible that some children might learn the police terminology during the pre-trial process or even from television and so use an unusually sophisticated vocabulary in an attempt to communicate correctly. To regard a child with such a vocabulary at the end of the trial process as not credible may be unrealistic.

It does seem unfortunate that children who know the correct terms for their bodies are likely to attract suspicion in this way. This tendency may also suggests that, to be seen as innocent, children must also be seen as ignorant.

FANTASY: CONFUSING REALITY AND IMAGINATION

One of the most common and most criticised stereotypes in adult rape trials is that of the would-be victim who fantasises the assault and subsequently confuses the fantasy with reality (Kennedy, 1992; Lees, 1996). Fantasy is also a common defence in child sex abuse trials according to commentators (Spencer and Flin, 1993). That fantasy is often tried as a defence is supported by the responses garnered in this study. Eight of the 14 New Zealand lawyers appeared willing to use fantasy as a defence, as were three of four English practitioners.

Literature Review

The theory that children imagine abuse has been accepted by many since Freud promulgated it in the late nineteenth century. However, Freud's theory has largely been discounted. Modern researchers argue strongly that children cannot imagine or fantasise that which they have not experienced (MacFarlane et al., 1986; Spencer and Flin, 1993; see also, more generally, Crew, 1995). Modern studies suggest that children are not generally prone to confusing reality with imagined events (Johnson and Foley, 1984; Lindsay and Johnson, 1987). Both the main studies, by Johnson and Foley (1984) and by Roberts and Blades (1995), discounted age differences between children's and adults' ability to distinguish imagined and real events. Johnson and Foley found that only the very youngest children perform less well than adults and then are only inferior in distinguishing their own real and imagined actions, not those of other people. Roberts and Blades' methodologically superior study, however, found almost no age differences at all.

It is possible that a child with psychotic delusions might confuse reality and imagination but such delusions are so rare in children that the risk is negligible. Further, even a delusional child would need experiences on which to base allegations of sexual abuse (Nurcombe, 1986).

Findings

Eight of the 13 New Zealanders who answered this question believed fantasy was a viable defence to child sex abuse allegations. Whether they meant by this that they believed such fantasies occur or merely that a defence of fantasy would probably be accepted by the jury was unclear, but the former appeared more likely. While for the majority of these respondents, fantasy was seen as a rare phenomenon, several perceived it as quite common.

> A lot of child abuse is imagination: . . . imagination and childhood fantasies which extend into a sexual fantasy world.

One believed that children did not have enough information to invent allegations entirely but could elaborate lesser happenings into serious allegations.

Teenagers and very young children were seen as most likely to fantasise attacks. One respondent believed that 'the youngest children, up to about seven' have 'a high ability to fantasise about events which may not have occurred, but . . . after, it's less likely'. Two others believed that teens are more likely to fantasise about abuse because 'how does a three year old make up [abuse]?' whereas teenagers were seen as unbalanced because of 'hormones' and 'periods and things'.

Two New Zealand lawyers blamed psychology professionals for encouraging fantasy, just as many had blamed them for suggestion. Dolls, diagnostic games, anatomical drawings and the allegedly relaxed atmosphere of interviews were seen as encouraging children to invent stories of abuse. However, a strong minority of six New Zealanders believed that fantasy was highly unlikely or impossible because children lack the requisite knowledge on which to base it.

> [T]hey can confuse fantasy and imagination with reality sometimes, but I don't think that in relation to . . . sexual abuse . . . because what they are normally describing is something way outside their normal experience.

Additionally, eight New Zealanders suggested a version of the basic fantasy defence in which the child complainant unconsciously transfers blame from the actual offender to the accused. One respondent believed that this phenomenon was well-established among clinicians.

> [W]hat does from time to time happen is that those complaints are directed at the wrong person. Psychologists call it the 'transferancy syndrome'.

This phenomenon was seen as the result of suggestion. One counsel stated that a major tactic was to argue the children have been abused but they have been told 'that's the bad guy' and some adult has wanted to push all the blame onto [the accused] for reasons of their own. Children were also seen as transferring blame to protect the offender or their families.

> Because at the time my client [the mother's common law husband] and the mother had a fall-out so . . . she [the child] probably directed the abuse against the *de facto* [husband], preferring not to direct it against the father. . . . [The child] loved [the father] and vice versa . . . and somehow things got confused in her mind and she has confused the [husband] with the [father].

However, no support has been found in the research literature for this theory. Experienced clinicians were also extremely sceptical when asked about it. None had heard of a transferancy syndrome.

Three of the four English respondents, who commented explicitly on the issue, stated fantasy was unlikely to succeed as a defence.

> It's not put to the child [in court] that 'this is all a fantasy' like a film in your head, that you can see in your head. It's put to the child 'you're just lying'. . . . If you're delving into psychology and [saying] 'you're literally fantasising it and you have convinced yourself that he did this', no.

One nonetheless stated that some children fantasise '30%' of the complaint in 'nightmares and dreams'. He and two others later discussed how fantasy could arise and how to introduce it in cross-examination.

> [C]hildren from a very early age know when someone isn't telling the truth . . . [and] what's right and what's wrong. Except, and it is a big exception, there are children . . . who just are the most outrageous romancers: fantasists. And they love it, I'm not sure how conscious they are that they're doing it. I met . . . a boy, . . . I said 'you're on holiday'. He said 'yes, I'm actually a jet pilot'. It wasn't a joke. In his head he was a jet pilot who was on holiday. Now, in court you don't always know when you've got one of those. So, the defending advocate's job, if there are seeds of this, is to let the little boy (it's usually little boys) blossom into this fantasy world. . . . [Y]ou might start by saying 'hello, John, are you keen on football?' 'Yes.' 'Who do you play football for?' Usually he will say 'St Barnabas Primary School'. Occasionally you will get little boys who will say 'Oh, I play for England.' And you say, 'You mean, you like watching England play?' 'Oh no, I play for England.' And then all of a sudden, this edifice that the prosecution has built is in tatters. And they do exist, and you've got to give them an opportunity to show that they are romancers.

Overall, eight of the 13 New Zealanders and three of the four English respondents who discussed the issue saw fantasy as a rare but still plausible scenario. However, the research already discussed suggests that fantasy is almost totally implausible unless, exceptionally, the child is psychotic (see MacFarlane et al., 1986; Spencer and Flin, 1993; Johnson and Foley, 1984; Lindsay and Johnson, 1987; Roberts and Blades, 1991; Nurcombe, 1986). It may be that the lawyers draw support for their beliefs from the long-standing but equally implausible belief that adult women fantasise rape allegations. Whatever the cause of the lawyers' views, their readiness to deploy such narratives in the courtroom, as several obviously had done, is a matter of some concern.

DELIBERATE LIES

In both the final two defences discussed with the respondents, the child complainant is said to have fabricated sexual abuse allegations deliberately. In one scenario, the child knows lying is morally wrong and acts out of malice. Alternatively, some New Zealanders suggested the child might not understand lying is wrong.

Lying as a defence is remarkable for the first significant difference in opinion between the two nationalities. Unless they could use the ignorance defence, only five New Zealanders were prepared to argue a child had lied. Conversely, four out of five English respondents supported using lying as a defence, two rating it as the main defence in child sex abuse trials.

Literature Review

Researchers suggest children are unlikely to deliberately fabricate sex abuse allegations for three main reasons. First, it is not until around 4 years old that most children understand how to lie and that it is morally wrong, although generally children will not be called as witnesses until they are older (Morton, 1988; Perner, 1997).

Second, researchers argue that the fear of embarrassment discourages children from fabricating sexual abuse. Goodman et al. (1987) found that children as young as 7 refuse to admit to having had an actual genital examination by a doctor, apparently due to embarrassment. Even pre-schoolers reacted with embarrassment or amusement to leading questions about genital touching (Saywitz et al., 1991). Goodman et al. also found that children's accounts of genital examinations varied depending on their emotional states. Embarrassed children gave less information than self-confident, relaxed children (Goodman and Schaff, 1997).

Finally, as discussed in relation to coaching, a lie about sexual abuse is extremely difficult for a child to sustain plausibly because of the lack of supporting detail and appropriate emotional response (Vrij; 2000).

Findings

Most of the New Zealanders' beliefs about the likelihood of child witnesses lying deliberately and spontaneously about sexual abuse were consistent with the research. This defence was the least popular among the New Zealanders, although all stated that all children could lie. Four New Zealanders stated that lies almost never occurred (or at least did not reach court where these lawyers could experience them) because children cannot sustain a lie for the length of time required and under the scrutiny child sexual abuse attracts before a court case is brought.

> It's very difficult for a child to sustain a deliberate lie. [It] would be a very risky task for an adult to rely on a child to lie again. A child . . . will invariably not do or say anything to get itself into trouble.

Further, they argued that few children would wish to hurt a parent: 'Why would a child wish to . . . imagine all these sorts of things? . . . This is the man they [complainant and siblings] love.'

However, five New Zealanders believed that children did occasionally fabricate allegations. One also believed that children were 'very capable of expanding on a truthful fact'. Further, even those who stated that deliberate lies were unlikely, willingly volunteered scenarios in which children might lie.

By contrast, four of the five English respondents rated lying highly as a defence, two referring to it as the 'main' and 'normal' defence, suggested in about 50% of the cases. Even the one respondent who stated that only a 'tiny number' of children 'go to court deliberately telling lies' described cases which he had defended on that basis. The English respondents appeared to see lying as the only logical defence to the charges.

> It is not something that you make a mistake about, whether somebody has put in penis in your mouth or whatever. Either it has been made up or it hasn't.

Both nationalities appeared to see older children and teenagers as more likely than younger children to lie maliciously. This unanimity of opinion among the lawyers appeared to be sustained over gender and age differences as well as those of nationhood.

> [T]here is a the teenage or older child who may or may not be disaffected with what's going on in her family life for whatever reason, big or very, very trivial . . . It's widely known, isn't it, the older the child the more reason for examining the circumstances of the complaint and to check out whether there is a motive for a bad complaint, a false complaint. But with the younger child . . . I don't think you'd be pitching it right to attribute the sophistication of lying for some oblique motive to a child of tender years . . . But if you are getting into the grown-up children-end, the 10s and . . . teenagers, then there might be all sorts of things that lurk behind a complaint.

Reasons for Lies

The English and New Zealanders also generally agreed on the reasons a child might be said to invent an abuse allegation. First, five New Zealand respondents suggested that children sometimes lie as the result of indirect pressure from one parent—especially the mother—during a family dispute. This was the reason for children lying New Zealanders nominated most frequently.

> [T]hey may have been primed up by somebody to win . . . their affections. Like if Mum has had a serious split with Dad, Mum wants to get back at Dad using the child, then the child because he or she is in the custody of Mum will want to win her affection and do what she is told.

Several English respondents also suggested that 'lying . . . to support one side of the family is universal' among even young children, and 'not uncommon' in the courtroom.

Second, the most commonly suggested reason for lying among the English barristers was one where the child acts spontaneously out of a personal grudge against a family member, unprompted by others. This scenario was suggested by just one

New Zealander. The revenge/grudge thesis was seen as covering a wide variety of situations, with two English respondents describing cases of children victimising neighbours.

> [I]t's nearly always said to be girls who don't get on with their step-father or their mother's boyfriend and have made it up for that reason or occasionally it would be someone . . . who visits the household who is not liked. Even more occasionally, and very recently I've had a very graphic example of this, it's somebody who's in the neighbourhood but who is seen by the kids in the neighbourhood as a bit of a loner, as a bit of a pervert, and he will get picked on.

One English respondent also described children attacking unpopular babysitters.

> I've had male babysitters accused . . . [who] say 'their parents used to let them stay up 'til midnight. I said "No, in bed by half past eight". They wanted to get me out of the job.'

Third, paralleling the unconscious 'transferancy syndrome' theory already discussed, three New Zealand respondents suggested that children will protect an offender they love by transfering blame to someone else deliberately.

> The classic situation in sexual abuse cases is that they don't want anyone to find out what's going on in the family so that there's denial . . . [they] don't want to face up to accusing a family member . . . [so] they accuse another person.

The rationale behind this theory is that the child wishes to stop the abuse but:

> can't bring themselves to say it was their father or their uncle, or anyone in their family. . . . It's like a cry for help: they go to the police and say 'Oh, my next door neighbour did it'.

This argument is, however, somewhat counter-intuitive, at least in the context of interfamilial abuse (which comprises the vast majority of child abuse). To accuse another person is highly unlikely to protect the child from the actual abuser, a consequence which a child sophisticated enough to realise that his or her disclosure of abuse will galvanise the authorities against abusers must logically grasp. In a custody dispute, for example, accusing the stepfather rather than the father is more likely to see the child placed with the offending dad full-time.

Fourth, two New Zealanders and two English respondents suggested that older children lie in order to avoid punishment, a rationale Lees found frequently employed against adult women rape complainants (Lees, 1996, 125):

> Let's suppose Carol is now 15, she's gone out for the evening, met a chap and the truth is Carol had too much to drink, she was inexperienced, thought it was going to be a bit of a snog in the car and it went on and on and on. She didn't like to admit her experience was so limited she'd never done anything like this before. And . . . . they're driving back and she says to the bloke 'um, I'm 15', and he . . . . shouts at her and threatens her that 'if you breathe a word of this to anyone, I'll kill you'. He drops her three doors away

from home. She should have been in at nine. It's now half past ten. She has to make a decision . . . if she says 'sorry mum, I got drunk, I've been a fool, I had intercourse with this bloke' she's in deep trouble. Hence 'I've been raped'. And a process has started that won't stop until she's . . . gone to court.

Conversely, one respondent from each group stated that some children lie about sexual abuse to get attention because 'victim status' has 'a certain celebrity status. Some children . . . who are denied attention in other ways enjoy perhaps a little more cosseting' as a result.

While not a reason to lie in itself, two New Zealand respondents listed previous complaints of abuse as a strong reason to believe the current allegations are lies. One commented that in one case the jury 'turned against her when it started to come out that she had been saying things about other people as well'. Four English respondents also suggested collaboration between complainants encouraging each other 'off to even greater heights', making one lawyer 'very, very sceptical':

> [Y]ou may have two sisters sharing the same bed: 'He did it to me. Did he do it to you?' 'Oh, he did it to me': [There is a risk of] collaboration between children.

However research shows that some children and women are the victims of multiple abuse, and so prior allegations should not be taken as prima facie evidence of lying. Moreover, sex offenders are often recidivists and that one offender should have multiple victims is not unlikely (Berliner, 1990; Vinson, 1992).

Finally, three New Zealanders, but no English respondents, spontaneously suggested the scenario I have labelled 'ignorant lying', where the child fabricates either a whole story or elaborates on an incident for fun, unaware of the moral wrong or possible practical consequences, 'without realisation of the danger that that could create'. One respondent also argued that children do not see the story they are telling as a lie if they have been told by their mother to say it. This is not supported by the research, however. As Bussey et al. (1996) discuss, studies show that even 4-year-olds can distinguish lies from truth despite a parent's directions to lie.

This new, 'ignorant liar' defence fits into the model of the exculpatory defence, particularly in the context of its proponents' open desire not to accuse children of deliberate wrong-doing. The knowing liar defence, however, is new territory for the present study because it blames the child directly. This idea, especially given the malice usually attributed as the child's motive, suggests an affinity with the common accusation levelled at adult women complainants in which they are accused of lying deliberately to obtain revenge on the defendant (Kennedy, 1992; Lees, 1996). Lees points out the strong element of irrationality and of a lack of moral understanding and self-control ascribed to the woman's actions in this defence, which is often accompanied by suggestions that she has a history of mental instability. This irrational element of the defence recalls the way in which children in the exculpatory defence are seen as mentally deficient.

DISCUSSION

On the basis of the research discussed above, it appears that many of the respondents interviewed used or believed defences to child sex abuse which research says are actually unlikely in the absence of very special circumstances.

I have argued that the defences correlate with two ways of defending child sex abuse charges. First, the defence might blame the child explicitly, alleging that he or she lied deliberately and with understanding of the moral quality of the act. Conversely, the defences of suggestion, coaching, fantasy and that the child lied deliberately but without comprehending the moral nature of the act all exculpate the child from blame for making a false allegation and blame either Machiavellian adults or the child's own developmental deficiencies.

Defences which include a claim that the child is not to blame for the allegedly false accusation are qualitatively different from those which present the child as acting with deliberate evil intent. On one level, it may be preferable that the child is not viewed as morally blameworthy. However, exculpating defences deny the child has agency or indeed a meaningful level of sentience. The evil child at least is a powerful figure in his or her own life. More practically, the lawyers interviewed, especially the New Zealanders, chose to use the exculpating defences because they saw them as more palatable and less likely to alienate juries. Thus the very inoffensiveness of such defences renders them more harmful to the child under attack.

Overall, however, whether children are exculpated or excoriated by individual defences, all of these defences present children as less than fully rational, fully functioning humans. Children, in either set of arguments, are not merely developmentally limited but are presented as fundamentally irrational and/or amoral, without ability to participate in (courtroom) discussions of their own lives at any meaningful level. Three of the defences—suggestion, coaching and fantasy—all suggest that the child complainant is not responsible for the accusations but has made them due to a mental deficiency, either unable to withstand adult manipulation or unable to distinguish reality. Conversely, the idea that a child has lied maliciously, or, another scenario suggested by respondents, because he or she does not realise lying is wrong, suggests that the child complainant is morally deficient. A further correspondence occurs between the defences of malicious lies and fantasy: in both the child is presented as dominated by overwhelming emotions—sexual or vengeful—to the point of irrationality.

These negative images of childhood stand in sharp contrast to the view of children given by psychological research in which they appear as developmentally limited but still capable of understanding and articulating their experiences.

Just why these lawyers appear to adhere to these older, derogatory stereotypes about children and disregard advances in psychological knowledge is an interesting question. I suggest that there are three reasons. First, lawyers often do not know that such advances have been made. Second, they distrust psychology to such a degree that they are unlikely to accept its information. Third, and most fundamentally, lawyers do not work in laboratories finding facts, but in theatres of persuasion: they aim to persuade their audience, be it judge or jury. Until their audiences are no longer persuaded by outdated stereotypes lawyers will continue to find such stereotypes useful.

A reading of the main journals for legal practitioners shows that these do not often publish psychological research on children. Even where there is literature readily available to lawyers, they do not necessarily absorb enough to change their practice significantly. For example, almost every lawyer interviewed understood there was a need to modify their language to accommodate young children. However, their understanding of what modifications were required was simplistic and they tended to believe that the need for modification ceased when a child of normal intelligence reached 10 or 12. When lawyers research outside their field they research only as part of a case and that research will be limited to finding material to support the client's position. If lawyers are to be educated, writers need to focus on disseminating information where lawyers are likely to stumble across it.

The second reason I suggest that psychology's concepts of children have not filtered through to lawyers is that lawyers often distrust psychology and see it as having little relevance to their work. There is not space in this chapter to detail the growing literature documenting the conflicted relationship between lawyers and psychologists (e.g. Wrightsman, 1999; Kassin and Wrightsman, 1985; Jackson, 1995; Carson and Bull, 1995; Kennedy, 1992). However, many of the respondents were suspicious of psychology professionals (including diagnosticians, evidential interviewers and therapists). Criticisms ranged from lack of training—a greater concern to New Zealanders than to the English—to bias and overzealous interviewing.

> There can be suggestion from overzealous professionals, particularly departmental social workers who are appallingly badly trained; blunder in; trample all over the evidence as much as a rookie cop, and by that stage, the damage is done.

Another New Zealand respondent was critical of clinicians' failure to differentiate between the roles of therapist and evidential interviewer.

> Evidential interviewers, particularly social workers, really are not sorted out about their role as evidential interviewer.... That's just totally unsatisfactory.... If you've got the kind of therapy and lots of positive reinforcement and that sort of thing being given to a child during the course of an evidential interview then it looks like there's amazing rapport being built up ... and she's just moulding the child to say whatever they want them to say.

The English respondents had similar criticisms to make of evidential interviewers, criticising them for creating suggestion through bias, credulity and insufficient challenge.

> [Q]uestioning now by and large is very good. There are still rare examples, and I have got a case at the moment where the child is very reluctant to disclose and in fact says

time after time 'can I stop now' and the officer simply doesn't stop. It's a very serious case and the officer is determined to try and get something and says 'well, didn't you tell so and so x, y & z?' and in the end the child eventually says 'yes, well, alright then'. Now that's the kind of prompting you will see on video.

The English saw the problem as stemming from ignorance rather than malice and believed the police were better trained than social workers.

Further, there was a perception that there is an inherent bias in the role of social worker.

> It is almost always in my experience not done deliberately to persuade the child into a worse story or different story. It is done with warmth and enthusiasm with a gut belief that the child is telling the basic truth and it is just, really, ignorance of how easy it is to suggest to a vulnerable witness what the answer is or what the next answer should be.

A strong characteristic of the New Zealanders' criticisms of parents and mental health professionals was the tendency to see support for a child's allegations as a MacCarthyite witch-hunt against defendants.

> I don't want to get hung up in a sex attack; men against women; women against men; but there are too many people out there that want to turn the issue into that, and divert it away from its true focus . . . to find [whether there is] reasonable doubt . . . . So I'm sorry, I'm very cynical about the way these things are dealt with . . . . It's a clique of women that have—unfortunately, it is women—that have the hold on the purse-strings.

Whether women—whose control over the major institutions of our society is notoriously weak—really monopolise control of psychological services and court-ordered appointments in the field of sexual abuse in New Zealand or anywhere else is questionable, however.

There was also a strong feeling among some respondents that the involvement of clinicians or psychological researchers, male or female, as expert witnesses disadvantages defendants. Such witnesses were seen as coming up with answers to every objection, of manipulating data, of manipulating or exploiting a position of power.

> According to the so-called experts, a child will either disclose and retract partially or fail to disclose . . . [and] the child has actually told the truth but then she retracted because she felt guilty or whatever, and then they'll say she refused to disclose because she feels guilty about what he's done to her. What that doesn't leave [room for] is what happens if someone actually isn't disclosing because it didn't happen. . . . They've got you boxed in, and that's sort of playing with a loaded deck. . . . I just see it as inherently unfair.

Both the allegations of bias and of ineptitude are serious and, if true, they threaten the outcome of child sexual abuse trials and may invalidate many evidential interviews and expert testimonies. However, I suggest that the lawyers' views are based on their long-established distrust of psychologists and in many instances on their misunderstanding of the dynamics of children's suggestibility, as shown in their overly anxious discussions about what might constitute suggestion.

The final reason, I suggest, that lawyers appear so divided from psychologists' concepts of children is that lawyers are fundamentally disinterested in providing a factually correct view of the evidence. This is not to say that lawyers deliberately deceive the courts. To do so would contravene legal professional ethics. My point is that in the theory of the adversarial system espoused by most of the legal profession, the task of advocacy is not to present the scenario that the lawyer believes, on objective examination, is most probably true. The lawyer's task is to make a convincing presentation of the scenario most favourable to his or her client in order to suggest reasonable doubt (Henderson, 2000). That the probable truth coincides with this scenario is, under this theory, largely irrelevant, so long as the lawyer does not actively seek to mislead the court. Thus, even if, for example, all evidential interviews were very substantially improved lawyers would continue to suggest bias, etc., because in their eyes their task is to manufacture criticism.

Thus the crucial element in advocacy is what is convincing to public opinion. One example of its effect are the two nationalities' different approach to the defence of malicious lying. Whereas the New Zealanders preferred to avoid accusing children of lying, the English were relatively unconcerned about doing so. This discrepancy appears to relate to the respondent's perception of the jury's view of children. Many New Zealand lawyers viewed juries as heavily biased in favour of child witnesses:

> [B]y the time you come to cross-examine the child, you, the lawyer, and your client are definitely the villains of the piece. The jury look at you with contempt. How could you ask this beautiful little girl, this lovely little child, this sweet little boy about these things?

Conversely, the English thought there was little or no such bias. They therefore apparently felt confident in blaming the child because they did not believe the jury would be offended. One English woman barrister commented that there had been a backlash in public opinion against child complainants:

> [Juries] once were [overly sympathetic to children]. Now they are much more amenable to defence suggestions that there's been overkill. Now they are kicking back against it. They've seen it on the TV, they've seen it portrayed in soap operas, they've seen it in the media, and they are up to saturation point with it. And you don't have to push them much harder than that to make them nod in agreement with you: 'Well, there's a lot of it about, isn't there, ladies and gentlemen?'

This rather unfortunate example at least suggests that a swing towards children in public opinion would cause lawyers to abandon some of their more negative portrayals of children in the witness box.

In conclusion, despite the fact that the legislature has made significant advances to bringing psychological research to bear in the courtroom, enhancing the opportunities children have to give evidence, it appears that some practising counsels continue to employ outdated stereotypes of those children in their arguments to the court. Psychology has had a significant impact on the legislature but not on the practitioners.

It is not the purpose of this chapter to suggest what should be done about this situation. It could be said that nothing should be done since within an adversarial system defence counsel have to be free to do their duty to advance all arguments likely to advance their client's interests, provided counsel does not actually know that an argument is false. However, it can also be argued that where a defence is exceptionally unlikely and yet might have great influence over the jury, its use should be controlled unless counsel can show some foundation. Something similar has already been done in relation to the questioning of rape complainants about their sexual history on the grounds that juries gave undue weight to that information in assessing the complainant's credibility (Sexual Offences (Amendment) Act 1976, s. 2). There is also the question of whether it is economic to allow lawyers to carry excess baggage into the system in the form of irrelevant defences. In these days of overloaded court calendars, this is perhaps not a minor consideration. Overall, however, we may have to wait until the public is more accepting of children's capabilities before lawyers stop using these outdated and damaging stereotypes.

ACKNOWLEDGEMENT

I wish to thank Professor John R. Spencer, Selwyn College, Cambridge, for his kindness in reading this chapter in draft and for his many suggested improvements.

REFERENCES

Berliner, L. (1990). *The special sex offender sentencing alternative: A study of decision-making and recidivism.* Washington, DC: Report to the Legislature.

Brennan, M. and Brennan, R. (1988). *Strange language: Child victim witnesses under cross-examination.* Wagga Wagga: CSU Literacy Studies Network.

Bussey, K., Lee, K. and Grimbeek, E.J. (1996). Lies and secrets: Implications for children's reporting of sexual abuse. In B. Bottoms and G. Goodman (eds), *International perspectives on child abuse and children's testimony: Psychological research and the law* (p. 147). Newbury Park, CA: Sage.

Carson, D. and Bull, R. (1995). Psychology in legal contexts: Idealism and realism. In R. Bull and D. Carson (eds), *Handbook of psychology in legal contexts* (p. 3). Chichester: John Wiley & Sons.

Ceci, S. and Bruck, M. (1993). Child witnesses: Translating research into policy. *Social Policy Report, 7,* 1.

Ceci, S. and Bruck, M. (1995). *Jeopardy in the courtroom: A scientific analysis of children's testimony.* Washington, DC: American Psychological Association.

Crew, F. (ed.) (1995). *The memory wars: Freud's legacy in dispute.* London: Granta Publications.

Davies, E., Henderson, E. and Seymour, F. (1997) In the interests of justice? The cross-examination of child complainants of sexual abuse in criminal proceedings. *Journal of Psychiatry, Psychology and the Law, 4,* 217.

Goodman, G. and Schaff, J. (1997). Over a decade of research on children's eyewitness testimony: What have we learned? Where do we go from here? *Applied Cognitive Psychology*, *11*, 5–20.

Goodman, G., Aman, C. and Hirshman, J. (1987). Child sexual and physical abuse. In S. Ceci, M. Toglia and D. Ross (eds), *Children's eyewitness memory* (p. 155). New York: Springer-Verlag.

Henderson, E. (2000). *Cross-examination: A critical examination.* Unpublished PhD Dissertation: Cambridge University Law Faculty.

Home Office and Department of Health (1992). *Memorandum of good practice on video recorded interviews with child witnesses for criminal proceedings.* London: HMSO.

Jackson, J. (1995) Evidence: The legal perspective. In R. Bull and D. Carson (eds), *Handbook of psychology in legal contexts* (p. 163). Chichester: John Wiley & Sons.

Johnson, M. and Foley, M. (1984). Differentiating fact from fantasy: The reliability of children's memory. *Journal of Social Issues, 40*, 3.

Kassin, S. and Wrightsman, L. (eds) (1985). *The psychology of evidence and trial procedure.* Beverly Hills, CA: Sage.

Kennedy, H. (1992). *Eve was framed.* London: Chatto & Windus.

Lees, S. (1996). *Carnal knowledge: Rape on trial.* London: Penguin.

Leippe, M., Brigham, J., Cousins, C. and Romanczyk, A. (1989). The opinions and practices of criminal attorneys regarding child eyewitnesses: A survey. In S. Ceci, D. Ross and M. Toglia (eds), *Perspectives on children's testimony.* New York: Springer-Verlag.

Lindsay, D.S. and Johnson, M.K. (1987). Reality monitoring and suggestibility: Children's ability to discriminate among memories from different sources. In S. Ceci, M. Toglia and D. Ross (eds), *Children's eyewitness memory.* New York: Springer-Verlag.

Lindsay, D.S. and Read, J.D. (1994). Psychotherapy and memories of childhood sexual abuse: A cognitive perspective. *Applied Cognitive Psychology, 8*, 281–338.

MacFarlane, K., Waterman, J., Connerly, S., Damon, L., Durfee, M. and Long, S. (1986). *Sexual abuse of children: Evaluation and treatment.* London: Holt Rinehart and Winston.

Milne, R. and Bull, R. (1999). *Investigative interviewing: Psychology and practice.* Chichester: John Wiley & Sons.

Morton, J. (1988). When can lying start? In G. Davies and J. Drinkwater (eds), *The child witness: Do the courts abuse children?* Issues in Criminological and Legal Psychology, 13 (p. 35). Leicester: British Psychological Society.

Nurcombe, B. (1986). The child as witness: Competence and credibility. *Journal of the American Academy of Child Psychiatry, 25*, 473.

Perner, J. (1997). Children's competency in understanding the role of a witness: Truth, lies and moral ties. *Applied Cognitive Psychology, 11*, 21–36.

Roberts, K. and Blades, M. (1995). Children's discrimination of memories for actual and pretend actions in a hiding task. *British Journal of Developmental Psychology, 13*, 321.

Saywitz, K., Goodman, G., Nicholas, E. and Moan, S. (1991). Children's memories of genital examinations: Implications for cases of child sexual assault. *Journal of Consulting and Clinical Psychology, 59*, 682.

Spencer, J.R. and Flin, R. (1993). *The evidence of children: The law and the psychology* (2nd edn). London: Blackstone Press.

Steller, M. and Boychuk, T. (1992). Children as witnesses in sexual abuse cases: Investigating interview and assessment techniques. In H. Dent and R. Flin (eds), *Children as witnesses* (p. 47). Chichester: John Wiley & Sons.

Vinson, T. (1992). *An evaluation of the New South Wales pretrial diversion of offenders programme (child sexual assault).* Sydney: University of New South Wales Press.

Vrij, A. (2000). *Detecting lies and deceit: The psychology of lying and its implications for professional practice.* Chichester: John Wiley & Sons, Ltd.

Wells, G. and Loftus, E. (eds) (1984). *Eyewitness testimony: Psychological perspectives.* Cambridge: Cambridge University Press.

Wrightsman, L. (1999). *Judicial decision-making: Is psychology relevant?* Perspectives in Law and Psychology, 11. New York: Kluwer Academic/Plenum Publishers.

Further reading

Bull, R. and Carson, D. (1995). *Handbook of psychology in legal contexts.* Chichester: John Wiley & Sons.

Ceci, S., Toglia, M. and Ross, D. (eds) (1987). *Children's eyewitness memory.* New York: Springer-Verlag.

Henderson, E. (1997). *Reckless disregard: The cross-examination of children in sexual abuse trials.* Unpublished Masters Thesis: Auckland University Law Faculty.

Westcott, H. and Jones, J. (eds) (1997). *Perspectives on the memorandum: Policy, practice and research in investigative interviewing.* Aldershot: Arena.

Chapter 4.3

Alleged Child Sexual Abuse and Expert Testimony: A Swedish Perspective

Clara Gumpert
Karolinska Institute, Sweden

INTRODUCTION

No crime seems to evoke as much concern and controversy as child sexual abuse. Fergusson and Mullen (1999) named child sexual abuse as 'one of the defining cultural themes of our age' (p. 1). Not only has child sexual abuse gained, by far, the most attention of all crimes against children (Jones and Finkelhor, 2001), but virtually every aspect of this crime has been a focus of debate and controversy (Hallberg and Rigné, 1995, 1999). One of the most heated arguments has been connected with professional efforts to determine whether a child has been sexually abused or not (e.g. Berliner and Conte, 1993). Professionals involved in evaluating children have been accused of 'overdiagnosing' sexual abuse (Quinn, 1989) due to the lack of integrity and appropriate assessment procedures (Edvardsson, 1996; Horner, Guyer and Kalter, 1993). Others have claimed that the majority of cases remain undetected (Berliner, 1989).

Evaluation of abuse allegations is a matter of concern to all professionals involved in caring for children. Such evaluation may be of great influence in several parallel but different decision-making procedures, such as placing a child in foster care, arranging treatment for children and families or determining whether a case should be brought to trial. Naturally, the most delicate task for psychological professionals involves the forensic evaluation of alleged victims of child sexual abuse, when a psychologist or psychiatrist is asked to take on the role of an expert witness.

From a legal perspective, criminal cases concerning suspected child sexual abuse are among the most complicated (Diesen and Sutorius, 1999). Usually, there is no other evidence except the statement from the child. Numerous circumstances may influence the quality of this statement, such as the linguistic skills of the child, his or her willingness to talk and trust in the interviewers, and the skills of the interviewer. Despite differences with regard to legal traditions and cultural norms, professionals all over the world involved in evaluating alleged sexual abuse have to face such challenges. In Sweden, as well as in many other countries, the issue of abuse assessment is the subject of an ongoing public and scientific debate. It is our belief that these experiences may be of interest for an audience outside Sweden, as well. The objective of this chapter is to describe both the Swedish debate and some of the research performed during the past decade. Special attention will be given to psychological expert evidence and the interplay between the fields of law and psychology.

THE SWEDISH LEGAL SYSTEM

The Swedish legal system differs from the adversarial system of the United States and Great Britain. Within the adversarial system each side is permitted to present data supporting its position. It is the task of the judge or the jury to listen to both sides presenting their evidence and then to 'decide where the truth lies' (Myers, 1998, p. 43). The responsibility to investigate and seek facts lies on the parties. In the inquisitorial system (applied, for example, in Germany), the court has more of an investigative responsibility. It is allowed to gather information and question those involved (including the defendant). The Swedish system is something of a compromise between the adversarial and the inquisitorial systems. The prosecution and the defence are responsible for investigating the case and presenting the evidence to the court. But the prosecutor is required to be neutral; he or she must present facts supporting both the prosecution and the defence. In addition, the court has a responsibility to ensure that the investigation is of an acceptable standard.

Expert Testimony

Within the Swedish legal system, an expert witness is defined as an individual who has been consulted by the court or either one of the parties to give an opinion on a matter that requires special knowledge (Edelstam, 1991). The object is that the expert will provide knowledge to increase the court's competence. As recently described by two representatives of the legal profession (Diesen and Sutorius, 1999), an expert witness statement is to be viewed as 'an additional source of information in the court's decision making process' (p. 44).

Most expert witnesses are officially appointed, based on the accepted view that a court appointment will guarantee the expert's neutrality (Diesen and Sutorius, 1999). This custom seems to be followed in the majority of sexual abuse cases, but experts engaged by either of the parties occur as well (Gumpert and Lindblad, 2001). When assigning an expert witness, the court 'shall describe the framework and the conditions for the evaluation task' (Edelstam, 1991).

Contrary to legal rules in some other countries, an expert witness in Sweden is allowed both to present facts and to give an opinion on facts, such as the reliability of a witness statement or the credibility of a witness. The role of expert witnesses is often more restricted in adversarial legal systems (Bala, 1994; Myers, 1993). An issue of importance both in Sweden and other countries is whether the expert witness violates the court's role by expressing an opinion on legal issues. Even though a Swedish expert witness is allowed to give an opinion on facts, there is a broad consensus within the forensic literature, that the expert is not allowed to give an opinion on a suspect's guilt (Diesen and Sutorius, 1999; Insulander, 1996; Nyström, 1996; Wiklund, 1990).

In a thesis dealing with the rules on, and use of, expert evidence in Sweden, Edelstam (1991) argued that it is reasonable to expect that the courts will increasingly need expert evidence. The author referred to the overall trend in society towards greater complexity, and the constant development of new and better scientific methods. However, the difficulty in deciding whether issues involving *psychological* judgements require expert evidence ('special knowledge') was especially mentioned.

Psychological Expert Testimony and Child Sexual Abuse

In cases concerning child sexual abuse, the issue of psychological expert testimony has been particularly controversial. The role and mandate of the expert witness, as well as the reliability of the assessment methods have been discussed (Berliner and Conte, 1993; Burton and Myers, 1992; Melton and Limber, 1993; Wiklund, 1999). Some psychologists have asserted the benefits of their expertise. For example, the well-known German forensic psychologist Udo Undeutsch claimed in 1982 that 'in his area of speciality the expert is not merely an assistant [to the court] but a veritable master' (Undeutsch, 1982, p. 52). By way of contrast, the view during the 1990s appears to be that the role of the expert witness is to educate and inform the court rather than to provide conclusions (Allen and Miller, 1995; Diesen and Sutorius, 1999; Insulander, 1996; McAnulty, 1993; Thomas-Peter and Warren, 1998). Closely connected to this question of the expert's role is the issue of the expert's responsibility to recognise the limits of his or her knowledge and assessment procedures (Gregow, 1996; McAnulty, 1993; Myers, 1993), and the duty not to 'engage in irresponsible speculation' (Schetky, 1991, p. 403).

Within the professional community of psychologists and psychiatrists, an area of debate has been the difference between performing a forensic as opposed to a clinical evaluation. Numerous authors have emphasised the importance of recognising this distinction (Borum and Grisso, 1996; Campbell, 1997; Heilbrun et al., 1994; Skeem et al., 1998; Wiklund, 1999). In fact, some have even contended that mental health professionals should be prevented from testifying about their patients (Shuman et al., 1998). Part of this discussion emanates from the observation that many reports presented before the courts have failed to address the legally relevant issues (Borum and Grisso, 1996). Another reason why this distinction is emphasised is the failure of some experts to recognise the different responsibilities of a legal as opposed to a clinical decision-making process (Campbell, 1997; Horner, Guyer and Kalter, 1993). Some authors are of the opinion that it is inappropriate to combine a therapeutic relationship with a forensic evaluation, due to the risk of identifying too strongly with the patient (Shuman et. al., 1998; Wiklund, 1999).

THE SWEDISH DEBATE

In Sweden the controversy, on a clinical as opposed to a 'strict forensic' perspective in proposed sexual abuse cases, has been closely connected to the issue of whether statement analysis or a child psychiatric/psychological evaluation is the most appropriate evaluation procedure. Whereas the importance of experience in working with children has been emphasised by some authors (Nyström, 1992), others have criticised 'child professionals' for underestimating the risks that are involved in interviewing children (e.g. Edvardsson, 1996). Such risks include, for example, the suggestibility of the child or the possible impact of the relationship between the child and the evaluator.

'Statement analysis' refers to the practice of analysing the content of witness statements as well as the context in which the statement was given. The hypothesis underlying statement analysis is that truthful statements differ significantly from unfounded or falsified stories. The statement is evaluated by applying a set of principles commonly referred to as 'reality-criteria', assessing, for example, the amount of detail in the statement. The original version of this methodological framework was called Statement Reality Analysis (Undeutsch, 1982). According to the German forensic psychologist Udo Undeutsch, reality-criteria are 'designed to constitute a guarantee that the statement is factual' (p. 43). Statement analysis has a long tradition in Sweden, due to the close collaboration between German and Swedish forensic psychologists (Holgerson, 1990; Trankell, 1971; Undeutsch, 1982).

Two attempts to further develop Undeutsch's work have been made. In Sweden, professor Arne Trankell (1971) outlined the so-called Formal Structure Analysis (FSA), and in the United States, the Statement Validity Analysis (SVA) was described by Raskin and Esplin (1991). Both of these applications of statement analysis are combinations of different partial assessment approaches, of which the analysis of the statement constitutes just one element. In addition, other information is incorporated into the assessment model. This may include, for example, data regarding the context in which the statement evolved, the quality of the interview, or data related to the individual who is assessed. But the two assessment models differ in the sense that the FSA is based on a qualitative paradigm (hermeneutics), and the SVA is constructed to be available for empirical, quantitative validation.

Several efforts have been made to test the reliability and validity of parts of the SVA (for a review, see Lamb et al., 1997). The validity of the FSA is said to be guaranteed by the thorough documentation of each step of the analytic procedure, which makes it possible for the reader to judge whether the reasoning is acceptable (Holgerson, 1990).

Proponents of statement analysis have claimed that witness psychologists are better educated to perform forensic evaluations than child psychologists, psychiatrists, or social workers (Holgerson, 1995; Wiklund, 1990, 1991, 1992, 1999). In addition, it has been suggested that the method is superior because it provides a systematic method that can help 'reveal the reliability as well as the unreliability of statements in the individual case' (Holgerson, 1990, p. 127). Others have expressed more sceptical views. Wells and Loftus (1991), as quoted in Berliner and Conte (1993), claimed that what is measured is 'convincingness' rather than 'truthfulness'. It has been pointed out that these concepts do not necessarily mean the same thing (Edvardsson, 1996). It has also been argued that an assessment procedure based on language may systematically disqualify children. Insulander (1996) noted that statement analysis has been questioned as an evaluation tool for younger children. Christianson (1992) categorised it as 'lacking scientific character' (p. 315), and Lindblad (1991) challenged witness psychologists' claim that the method is 'objective'. In an attempt to address the need for a systematic evaluation method that also integrated psychological and psychiatric expertise, Lindblad (1989) presented an assessment model based on a hermeneutic approach.

QUALITY ASSURANCE IN PSYCHOLOGICAL ASSESSMENTS OF ALLEGED SEXUAL ABUSE

In the absence of generally accepted and validated assessment instruments of alleged child sexual abuse, the approach of the professional community has been to develop standards of practice. Guidelines for practice have been developed by professional organisations (American Academy for Child and Adolescent Psychiatry, [AACAP], 1988, 1997; American Professional Society on the Abuse of Children [APSAC], 1990). In addition, initiatives to create standards or discuss consensus have been taken by groups of professionals (Lamb, 1994), or governmental agencies. In Sweden, guidelines for the evaluation of suspected child sexual abuse cases were published by the National Board on Health and Welfare (Socialstyrelsen, 1991). Such a quality assurance approach is similar to efforts in other health care areas, where an established way of addressing clinical problems has been to develop standardised procedures. This method has usually been followed by some system for reviewing professional practice (Barnum, 1993).

A dominating theme in the Swedish literature on expert testimony in child sexual abuse cases is the emphasis on theory, that is how expert witnesses' evaluations ought to (or ought not to) be performed. When the discussion has concerned empirical data, it has usually been related to individual legal cases, such as the court's and/or the expert witness's opinion on a certain case (Holgerson, 1990). Thus the degree to which the described cases represent the majority has been unknown. The lack of systematic empirical research concerning the assessment of children for forensic purposes (e.g. custody evaluations) is not unique to Sweden (Nicholson and Norwood, 2000). In areas of adult forensic assessment, both in Sweden and abroad, clinical practice and/or impact of clinical guidelines have been empirically evaluated (Borum and Grisso, 1996; Grann and Holmberg, 1999; Holmberg, 1994).

A SWEDISH STUDY OF FORENSIC EVALUATIONS OF CHILD SEXUAL ABUSE

The combination of a controversial area of practice and a lack of systematic empirical evaluations of this particular field created a demand for further inquiry of forensic assessments of alleged child sexual abuse. To meet this need, Lindblad and Gumpert initiated a study that looked into the documentation of a large number of cases of alleged child sexual abuse in Sweden. All cases tried in Swedish district courts during four different years (1985, 1989, 1992, and 1997) were included ($n = 800$). The aims were to explore the pattern of expert witness participation, and to document assessment methods and style of reporting in forensic evaluations and to compare these to the recommended guidelines. Furthermore, we wanted to explore the communication between the courts and the expert witnesses (Gumpert, 2001). Over this period (1985–1997) the number of expert witnesses consulted on issues related to the credibility of child witnesses declined (Table 4.3.1). It was more common to consult experts in cases that involved preschool children (< 7 years of age), and cases in which the suspect denied the charges (Gumpert, Lindblad and Johansson, 1999).

To compare the existing expert witness reports to recommended guidelines, a quality assessment protocol was created. This protocol, 'Structured Quality assessment of eXpert witness testimony' (SQX-12) included a set of criteria by which to evaluate the formal structure and the content of written expert witness testimony. The 'checklist' included 12 items, based on recommendations made by Swedish authorities (Social-styrelsen, 1991), but also general principles for forensic evaluations mentioned in the literature. Five items referred to formal aspects, such as whether the expert had stated the referral question(s), what information had been used for the assessment and whether more than one evaluator had been involved during the assessment procedure (as was recommended). Five items referred to the content of the written statement, for example whether the expert had included a description of the allegations (what

Table 4.3.1 Total number of court cases each year of the study

Verdict	1985		1989		1992		1997		Total	
	n	%	*n*	%	*n*	%	*n*	%	*n*	%
Convictions	146	92	214	90	231	92	134	88	725	91
Acquittals	13	8	24	10	20	8	18	12	75	9
Total	159	100	238	100	251	100	152	100	800	100

did the child say? when? to whom? in what situation? etc), and had assessed the developmental status of the child. One item checked if alternative interpretations were discussed, and one referred to the overall quality of the written statement. For a more detailed description of the development of the procedure, see Gumpert, Lindblad and Grann (2002a).

The main finding from this study was that experts giving written testimony related to child credibility and/or reliability only partly followed the recommended standards (Gumpert, Lindblad and Grann, 2002b). The statement quality according to the SQX-checklist was found to be poor, but there were differences among professional groups. Generally, the group of experts applying statement analysis produced reports of higher quality than did the more clinically oriented representatives of child psychiatry. These experts more thoroughly identified data sources and included information regarding the referral questions. They discussed alternative interpretations more often than other groups. Despite recommendations, team evaluations were rarely used, and descriptions of allegation content and context were not always included.

Communication between Courts and Expert Witnesses

Within the Swedish legal system an accepted view is that the purpose of consulting an expert witness is that the court shall get a better basis for decision-making (Edelstam, 1991). Thus, there is an expectation that the expert's testimony (written and/or oral) shall add something to the legal process. With this perspective in mind, a smaller sample of the cases was explored with regard to the interplay between experts and courts (Gumpert and Lindblad, 2001). This analysis revealed signs of impaired communication between these two parties; for example when expert evaluations did not focus issues relevant to the legal process, or when the court appeared to have misunderstood the message from the expert.

Statement Analysis

In Sweden, the use of statement analysis for evaluating children's accounts of abuse is accepted within the legal system. One advantage of this assessment method is the more structured evaluation procedure, with hypothesis building and testing in a logical order. As a consequence it is possible for an external audience (i.e. the court) to follow and evaluate the assessor's line of reasoning. However, despite its status within the legal system, the Swedish tradition of witness psychology/statement analysis has not been without critics (Christianson, 1992; Lindblad, 1991). Thus, as a part of the research project, one study focused particularly the current use of statement analysis in Swedish courts.

This study (Gumpert and Lindblad, 1999) revealed that different assessors varied with regard to what information related to statement characteristics and contextual circumstances was pointed out and how it was judged. For example, one expert judged the fact that a child's account of abuse expanded between interviews as a sign of unreliability, whereas another concluded that the presence of an expanding story was logical and coherent with other information in the case. Given the basic principle of the Swedish way of using statement analysis (Trankell, 1971; Holgerson, 1990), this diversity may not be in opposition with the theoretical model. Within the hermeneutic framework it is emphasised that 'the question at issue in a particular case must be considered in the light of the context of that particular case' (Holgerson, 1990, p. 127). However, the courts must be aware of possible variation among experts and cases, and should not regard witness psychologists as homogenous group applying criteria in a uniform way.

Hypothesis testing has strong support in the literature (Dammeyer, 1998; Munro, 1999; Holgerson, 1990; Plous, 1993), and is seen as an 'effective debiasing technique' (Plous, 1993, p. 256). Most experts applying statement analysis worked according to such a procedure. However, a possible logical miscalculation appeared to be related to the way in which experts formulated their hypotheses. The first hypothesis usually suggested that the child's statement referred to either 'self-experienced' or 'real' events, thus indirectly making propositions as to the underlying *background*. By contrast, many of the alternative hypotheses touched on both the issue of underlying background ('not based on real events'; 'some other person') and on issues of *possible disturbing events* related to statement history and context, such as the presence or absence of previous influence, leading questions etc. Despite the different focus of the hypotheses, they appeared to be regarded as equally weighted and mutually exclusive (Figure 4.3.1). Such a practice appeared to allow for confusion with regard to what circumstances should be regarded as causal factors as opposed to conditions capable of complicating the evaluation of the child's statement. The way experts posed hypotheses seemed to assume a 'mono-causal' explanatory model, where all the hypotheses were viewed as theoretical explanations for the mere existence of a statement of sexual abuse.

A recurrent discussion in the research on Statement Validity Analysis is the difficulty to interpret low scores, that is, how to evaluate statements that are vague or of low quality in some sense. Suggestive or leading interview techniques may produce answers from children that go beyond their own experiences (e.g. Ceci and Bruck, 1993),

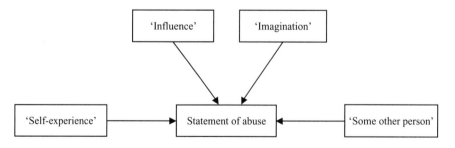

Figure 4.3.1 A 'mono-causal' explanatory model (example)

but other studies suggest that such improper interview techniques may also elicit 'low-quality' statements (e.g. lacking detail) (Hershkowitz et al., 1997; Lamb et al., 1997). The need to evaluate interview quality prior to drawing conclusions based on the quality of the child's account has been pointed out.

Interview quality was indeed an issue among Swedish witness psychologists, but in a slightly different way. Several of the witness psychologists in this study observed associations between leading questions and the presence of 'weak' or ambiguous statements, and suggested that the leading or suggestive question had produced a false answer, thus indicating causality. Given possible alternative explanations of the existence of a weak statement, a more reasonable approach would be to evaluate interview technique prior to analysing a statement, and avoid making strong conclusions based on the statement if the interview quality was judged to be low.

DISCUSSION

A major finding in this study was the declining use of expert witnesses consulted on issues related to child credibility and/or reliability. Furthermore, it appears as if the professional community of psychological expert witnesses failed to meet many of the recommended standards on how expert evaluations should be performed. In addition, there were signs of impaired communication between courts and expert witnesses. Together, these findings may be interpreted as if the attempt of collaboration between the fields of law and psychology in Sweden has not been particularly successful. When two organisations collaborate to reach a desired goal—in this case, to give the court a better basis for decision-making—the responsibility for the failure to reach that goal can be regarded as mutual. The courts have failed to direct and inform psychological expert witnesses to the extent that they can produce reports of use to the legal process. The psychology professionals, on the other hand, have failed to provide the legal system with relevant information presented in a reliable way.

Apart from insufficient report quality and communicative difficulties between courts and experts, other factors may also be responsible for the decline in cooperation. During the late 1980s and early 1990s, there was a heated public debate in Sweden concerning professional evaluations of suspected child sexual abuse. This debate revealed a severe intra-professional conflict (Hallberg and Rigné, 1995, 1999), which probably undermined the confidence in psychological evaluations as such. For example, a member of the Swedish Supreme Court (Gregow, 1996) pointed out the paradox in that a psychological expert witness could seem very self-confident with regard to his or her conclusions, despite the fact that another psychologist consulted in the same case might be of an opposite opinion.

The issue of psychological expert testimony in child sexual abuse cases has also been commented on in a case published by the Swedish Supreme Court (NJA, 1992). In this decision, the Supreme Court summarised the debate on whether a psychological expert could be of potential benefit to the court, and concluded that the courts should 'thoroughly consider if there really is a need for expert testimony' (p. 465). It was suggested that expert witnesses should contribute mainly by providing background information, and that the courts should not uncritically accept their opinions. Interestingly, the Supreme Court decision was published the same year as the trend towards declining expert participation began. Thus, the Supreme Court's view may be interpreted as an expression of an ongoing change of attitudes and procedural practices rather than as the sole cause of the decline. A similar view was expressed by Edelstam (1991), who suggested that the demand for expert evidence does not emanate from the courts themselves. Rather the courts adjust to a growing body of knowledge by incorporating those aspects of the 'new' knowledge that supposedly may add competence to the legal process. Theoretically this process may also be reversed. If representatives of such 'new' knowledge fail to establish confidence for their expertise then the legal system withdraws.

EXPERT EVIDENCE: WHAT IS GOOD QUALITY?

Although the overall report quality improved slightly after national guidelines were published in Sweden in 1991, many experts only partly followed these recommendations. It appears as if the guidelines did not influence practice to the extent that was hoped for. If the guidelines are to be seen as an expression of what is considered 'good quality' in expert evidence, this finding indicates that different or complementary types of interventions are needed in order to achieve a reasonable level of quality in forensic assessments of alleged victims of sexual abuse.

On the other hand, the concept of 'quality' in forensic assessment is complicated. The most complicated issue in a legal case relating to alleged child sexual abuse is naturally whether there is information pointing at a need for intrusive decisions that may have serious consequences for those involved, such as convicting the accused. Thus, the most important aspect of quality must be that an evaluator who is consulted on such a crucial matter as to give an opinion on the credibility of a witness draws the *correct* conclusion. However neither the Swedish national guidelines, nor guidelines or recommendations published elsewhere, set up guarantees of correct conclusions if the guidelines were followed. Instead government authorities or professional organisations approach the issue of quality indirectly, in the sense that the recommendations made are supposed to guarantee transparency. Transparency increases the demands on the evaluator and decreases the possibility of unfounded speculation. A transparent evaluation creates a possibility for external validation, that is, when the receiver of the report is given an opportunity to follow the reasoning and judge the strength of the conclusions.

When measuring report quality using criteria based on the national guidelines, it is important to have in mind that what is measured is only transparency. Although it is unlikely, it is possible for an expert witness to follow many of the guideline recommendations and still draw the wrong conclusions regarding the credibility of the child's account, just as it is for a court to get it wrong. However transparency is an accepted quality indicator in many different fields, for example science, and should be able to serve as one of several quality indicators.

Another aspect of quality concerns whether the court and the expert witness collaborate in a constructive and mutually fruitful way. To evaluate such a quality aspect, one must have a view of what is to be considered 'constructive' or 'fruitful'. In the particular study, the norm to which practice was compared was the opinion within the Swedish legal system that an expert evaluation shall supply the court with relevant information and competence, contributing to well-informed decisions. In other countries, or other jurisdictions, other norms for assessing quality of communication may have to be used.

The requests from courts to experts were often similar and brief, using standard expressions such as asking for opinions on credibility or reliability of the witness or the witness's statement. As a contrast, the expert evaluations were very diverse. Some experts focused exclusively on the child's account, such as when and where the child had disclosed abuse. In such reports, there were no comments on family situation, the child's developmental level, cognitive abilities or language skills. Other experts focused mainly on the emotional and intellectual functioning of the child, the social and family situation, without discussing what the child had actually said or in which circumstances the disclosure was made. It appeared as if experts interpreted the requests from the courts in line with their preferred practice. Despite these different perspectives, different experts claimed to be in a position where they could give an opinion on the credibility of the child or the reliability of a statement. This observation indicates a severe lack of consensus among different psychological experts with regard to concepts such as 'credibility' or 'reliability'.

Most likely, the court has not formed any opinion of its own with regard to what should be included in an evaluation of 'credibility' or 'reliability', but rather has viewed this as the expert's responsibility. The dilemma occurs when two parties communicate through vaguely defined concepts that can be interpreted differently according to the norms of different professional groups. There is a major risk that such concepts are filled with different content, and as a result thus create an arena for misunderstanding. A consequence is that even in cases where the court has assigned the expert, this does not seem to be a guarantee for relevant and legally useful expert reports.

FUTURE PERSPECTIVES

Every time suspicion rises that a child has been sexually abused, the child's competence as an informant is being judged. It should be in the interest of all those involved that evaluations aiming at assessing such competence are as thorough and professionally performed as possible. There is no doubt that the evaluation of children suspected of being victims of abuse involves many issues of psychological character. In addition, there is a broad consensus regarding the fact that these crimes are among the most difficult to investigate. Both these circumstances may be regarded as incentives to strive for collaboration and a mutual exchange of knowledge between the fields of law and psychology. However, such collaboration is far from unproblematic. In a way, one could consider forensic psychology with regard to child sexual abuse as an immature field, where issues such as 'when' and 'how' are not yet established.

From a legal point of view it is necessary that all parties involved have an opportunity to share any information that is presented in the legal process, including psychological expert evidence. Thus, there is need for clarity and openness. The presence of clear and distinct consultation agendas, agreement on what should be evaluated, experts with the necessary qualifications, and reports of high quality, are all circumstances that theoretically would add to clarity and openness. As has been illustrated, many of these goals have yet to be reached in Sweden. However, exploring previous failures is necessary in order to learn what needs to be changed. Rather than just using observed shortcomings as reasons for pessimism, they should be regarded as opportunities for the continuing process of improving the collaboration between law and psychology.

Improving the Consultation Agenda

The process of a forensic evaluation may be divided into three parts; the delineation of the consultation problem, the actual conduct of the evaluation, and the delivery of the report (Barnum, 1993). A possible improvement connected to the delineation phase would be if the courts would express their wish for assistance in a more elaborated way. Barnum suggested that defining the consultation agenda not only included the formulation of clear and distinct questions for the expert to address, but also defining the purpose of the consultation in the individual case. Similar suggestions were made in the Swedish national guidelines, where it was recommended that the expert and the court communicated prior to the evaluation with regard to the focus and content of the assessment. Although not new, these recommendations still seem reasonable.

Given the fact that the courts' assignments often were brief, it is possible that the complexity of this phase has been underestimated. There may be a need for more knowledge of the decision process preceding the consultation of an expert witness. For example, who takes the initiative and on for what reason? Who formulates the assignment? Even though a Swedish court theoretically has the initiative to inform the consulted expert, they may not have the necessary competence. If that is the case, an alternate form of support to the court could be to offer consultation from psychological expertise during the delineation phase. For example, the court could turn to an independent group of experts, whose task was to identify any relevant psychological issue that would require expert evaluation. Similar propositions have been made by LaFortune and Carpenter (1998), in relation to child custody litigation, who suggested a 'court services unit' that would assist in monitoring evaluations. The common theme in these ideas is to strengthen the 'consumer side' of the collaboration between courts and experts, without giving up the demand for openness.

Improving Evaluation Procedures

The improvement of the actual procedure of doing forensic evaluations may be approached in different ways. The most important part of any evaluation of suspected child sexual abuse is the formal interview. Given the crucial role of this event, education of interviewers as well as evaluation of such training should constitute an essential part of any action taken to improve evaluation procedures.

As noted, a common measure to improve quality in forensic assessment has been to develop guidelines for practice. An alternative (and possibly supplementary) way would be to require minimum threshold qualifications for evaluators. When the Swedish National Board of Forensic Medicine was given responsibility for the so-called §7-evaluations (a screening evaluation for assessing mental status among offenders), each evaluator was individually contracted. This limited the number of evaluators, and also permitted regular organised training and a joint discussion on crucial aspects of these forensic evaluations (Rättsmedicinalverket, 1994). A list of experts who meet some recommended qualifications would also assist the court in choosing an expert. However, quality improvement actions of this kind would probably require support from an organisation independent of the courts and the mental health services, such as a governmental agency.

Improving Report Quality

The external control, that is, the possibility for the court to make an independent analysis of the expert's reasoning, is directly dependent on the quality of the written (or oral) testimony presented before the court. Just as the court may be more elaborate when defining the consultation assignment, a basic principle of forensic assessment is that the expert includes a detailed account of how the conclusions were reached. Given the lack of consensus in Sweden on what should be evaluated in order to assess concepts such as 'credibility' or 'reliability', a professional discussion on these and other issues is warranted. A matter to discuss could be, for example, whether experts should refrain from using terms such as 'credibility' or 'reliability,' since there may be a risk that 'translating' the evaluation performed into what supposedly represents the legal construct of credibility/reliability may create misunderstandings. Another possible benefit from a professional exchange of ideas could be a clearer delineation of what psychological or psychiatric knowledge could—and could not—add to a legal process, thereby facilitating the court's choice on whether to consult an expert or not.

An indirect control of evaluation conduct as well as report quality would be to allow peer-review of written expert testimony. Such a practice is used in Norway regarding forensic medical reports, where all reports are sent to an independent committee for quality control (Edelstam, 1991). A more limited alternative would be to allow peer-review only for those reports that were questioned in some way, or to create a possibility for the parties to appeal expert testimony. A peer-review process could also be a way of initialising a professional discussion on important aspects of forensic assessment of proposed victims of sexual abuse. It would permit an ongoing comparison between theory and practice, if necessary allowing for a revision of standards or recommendations. Furthermore, the possibility that written expert testimony could be referred for peer-review would probably create an incentive to provide reports of higher quality. The opportunity to get an opinion from another professional/group of professionals would also indirectly imply that there is no 'truth' in forensic assessment, but instead more or less well-grounded opinions. Given the complexity involved in all forensic assessment of proposed child victims, a moderate view on the possibilities and limitations on what is possible to achieve is undoubtedly called for. A peer-review process should not be regarded as a substitute for the court's responsibility to independently analyse the reasoning of the expert witness. Instead, it could be viewed as the responsibility of the psychological professionals to provide some kind of 'internal' control, as opposed to the court's 'external' control of expert evidence.

In the future, alternate and improved forms of consultation need to be developed in Sweden. A theme in many of the suggestions mentioned above is the need for some kind of organisational framework to support professionals of both psychology and law in their effort to collaborate. Given the declining numbers of expert consultations, some kind of organisational support may actually be necessary in order to allow for a mutually beneficial partnership.

REFERENCES

American Academy of Child and Adolescent Psychiatry (1988). Guidelines for the clinical evaluation of child and adolescent sexual abuse. *Journal of the American Academy of Child and Adolescent Psychiatry*, *27*, 655–657.

American Academy of Child and Adolescent Psychiatry (1997). Practice parameters for the forensic evaluation of children and adolescents who may have been physically or sexually abused. *Journal of the American Academy of Child and Adolescent Psychiatry*, *36*, 655–657.

American Professional Society on the Abuse of Children (APSAC) (1990). *Guidelines for psychosocial evaluations of suspected sexual abuse in young children*. Chicago, IL: American Professional Society on the Abuse of Children.

Allen, R.J. and Miller, J.S. (1995). The expert as educator: Enhancing the rationality of verdicts in child sex abuse prosecutions. *Psychology, Public Policy, and Law*, *1*, 323–338.

Bala, N. (1994). Children, psychiatrists, and the courts: Understanding the ambivalence of the legal profession. *Canadian Journal of Psychiatry*, *39*, 323–338.

Barnum, R. (1993). An agenda for quality improvement in forensic mental health consultation. *Bulletin of the American Academy of Psychiatry and the Law*, *21*, 5–21.

Berliner, L. (1989). Resolved: Child sexual abuse is overdiagnosed. *Journal of the American Academy of Child and Adolescent Psychiatry*, *28*, 789–797.

Berliner, L. and Conte, J.R. (1993). Sexual abuse evaluations: Conceptual and empirical obstacles. *Child Abuse and Neglect*, *17*, 111–125.

Borum, R. and Grisso, T. (1996). Establishing standards for criminal forensic reports: An empirical analysis. *Bulletin of the American Academy of Psychology and the Law*, *24*, 297–317.

Burton, K. and Myers, W.C. (1992). Child sexual abuse and forensic psychiatry: Evolving and controversial issues. *Bulletin of the American Academy of Psychiatry and the Law, 20*, 439–453.

Campbell, T.W. (1997). Indicators of child sexual abuse and their unreliability. *American Journal of Forensic Psychology, 15*, 5–17.

Ceci, S.J. and Bruck, M. (1993). Suggestibility of the child witness: a historical review and synthesis. *Psychological Bulletin, 113*, 403–439.

Christianson, S.Å. (1992). Psykologisk expertis i domstolarna—får vi bättre domstolsbeslut? [Psychological experts in the courts—do we get better court decisions?]. *Svensk Juristtidning* [*Swedish Law Review*], *4*, 312–333.

Dammeyer, M.D. (1998). The assessment of child sexual abuse allegations: Using research to guide clinical decision making. *Behavioral Sciences and the Law, 16*, 21–34.

Diesen, C. and Sutorius, H. (1999). *Sexuella övergrepp mot barn: Den rättsliga processen* [*Child sexual abuse: The legal process*]. Expertrapport, Socialstyrelsen. [Expert report, The National Board on Health and Welfare.]

Edelstam, H. (1991). *Sakkunnigbeviset. En studie rörande användningen av experter inom rättsväsendet.* [*Expert testimony. A study concerning the use of experts in the judicial system*]. Doctoral dissertation, University of Uppsala. Uppsala: Iustus.

Edvardsson, B. (1996). *Kritisk utredningsmetodik.* Stockholm: Liber Utbildning. [Critical evaluation.]

Fergusson, D.M. and Mullen, P.E. (1999). Childhood sexual abuse: An evidence based perspective. *Developmental Clinical Psychology and Psychiatry*, Vol. 40. Thousand Oaks, CA: Sage.

Grann, M. and Holmberg, G. (1999). Follow-up of forensic psychiatric legislation and clinical practice in Sweden 1988–1995. *International Journal of Law and Psychiatry, 22*, 125–131.

Gregow, T. (1996). Några synpunkter på frågan om bevisprövning och bevisvärdering i mål om sexuella övergrepp mot barn [Some standpoints on the issues of evidence testing and evidence evaulation in cases concerning child sexual abuse]. *Svensk Juristtidning* [*Swedish Law Review*], *7*, 509–523.

Gumpert, C.H. (2001). *Alleged child sexual abuse: The expert witness and the court.* Doctoral dissertation. Stockholm: Karolinska Institutet.

Gumpert, C.H., Lindblad, F. and Johansson, A. (1999). Child sexual abuse: Expert testimony in Swedish district courts. *Child Maltreatment, 4*, 343–352.

Gumpert, C.H. and Lindblad, F. (2001). Communication between courts and expert witnesses in legal proceedings concerning child sexual abuse in Sweden: A case review. *Child Abuse and Neglect, 25*, 1497–1516.

Gumpert, C.H., Lindblad, F. and Grann, M.A. (2002a). A systematic approach to quality assessment of expert testimony in cases of alleged child sexual abuse. *Psychology, Crime and Law, 8* (1), 59–75.

Gumpert, C.H., Lindblad, F. and Grann, M. (2002b). The quality of written expert testimony in alleged child sexual abuse: An empirical study. *Psychology, Crime and Law, 8* (1), 76–92.

Gumpert, C. H. and Lindblad, F. (1999). Expert testimony in child sexual abuse: A qualitative study of the Swedish approach to statement analysis. *Expert Evidence, 7*, 279–314.

Hallberg, M. and Rigné, E.M. (1995). Varför är experter oeniga om sexuella övergrepp mot barn? [Why do experts disagree on child sexual abuse?]. *Svensk Juristtidning* [*Swedish Law Review*], *7*, 563–578.

Hallberg, M. and Rigné, E.M. (1999). *En studie av debatten om sexuella övergrepp mot barn 1994–1998* [*A study of the debate on child sexual abuse 1994–1998*]. Expertrapport, Socialstyrelsen [Expert report, National Board on Health and Welfare].

Heilbrun K., Rosenfeld, B., Warren, J. and Collins, S. (1994). The use of third-party information in forensic assessments: A two-state comparison. *Bulletin of the American Academy of Psychiatry and the Law, 22*, 399–406.

Hershkowitz, I., Lamb, M.E., Sternberg, K.J. and Esplin, P.W. (1997). The relationship among interviewer utterance type, CBCA scores and the richness of children's responses. *Legal and Criminological Psychology, 2*, 169–176.

Holgerson, A. (1990). *Fakta i målet. Vittnespsykologins bidrag vid bedömning av sakfrågan i enskilda rättsfall* [*Questions of fact—the use of psychology in the evaluation of evidence*]. Doctoral dissertation. Stockholm University, Pedagogiska Institutionen.

Holgerson, A. (1995). Professionals as evaluators or indoctrinators in sex abuse cases. *Nordisk Sexologi*, *13*, 163 169.

Holmberg, G. (1994). *Rättspsykiatriska undersökningar i Sverige 1991–1993*. RMV Rapport. [*Forensic psychiatric evaluations in Sweden 1991–1993*]. (English abstract). Stockholm, Sweden: The National Board of Forensic Medicine.

Horner, T.M., Guyer, M.J. and Kalter, N.M. (1993). The biases of child sexual abuse experts: Believing is seeing. *Bulletin of the American Academy of Psychiatry and the Law*, *21*, 281–292.

Insulander, S. (1996). Psykologmedverkan i brottmål [Psychologist participation in legal cases]. In Christianson, S.-Å. (ed.), *Rättspsykologi* [*Forensic psychology*]. Stockholm: Natur och Kultur.

Jones, L. and Finkelhor, D. (2001). *The decline in child sexual abuse cases*. Crimes Against Children Series. US Department of Justice: Office of Juvenile Justice and Delinquency Prevention.

LaFortune, K.A. and Carpenter, B.N. (1998). Custody evaluations: A survey of mental health professionals. *Behavioral Sciences and the Law*, *16*, 207–224.

Lamb, M.E. (1994). The investigation of child sexual abuse: An interdisciplinary consensus statement. *Child Abuse and Neglect*, *18*, 1021–1028.

Lamb, M.E., Sternberg, K.J., Esplin, P.W., Hershkowitz, I. and Orbach, Y. (1997). Assessing the credibility of children's allegations of sexual abuse: A survey of recent research. *Learning and Individual Differences*, *9*, 175–194.

Lindblad, F. (1989). Child sexual abuse. Evaluation of Allegations—A hermeneutical approach. *Acta Paediatrica Scandinavica*, supplement 358.

Lindblad, F. (1991). Sexualbrott och rättssäkerhet—en replik [Sexual offenses and the due process of law—a commentary]. *Svensk Juristtidning* [*Swedish Law Review*], *10*.

McAnulty, R.D. (1993). Expert psychological testimony in cases of alleged child sexual abuse. *Archives of Sexual Behavior*, *22*, 311–324.

Melton, G.B. and Limber, S. (1993). Psychologists' involvement in cases of child maltreatment. Limits of role and expertise. *American Psychologist*, *44*, 1225–1233.

Munro, E. (1999). Common errors of reasoning in child protection work. *Child Abuse and Neglect*, *23*, 745–758.

Myers, J.E.B. (1993). Expert testimony regarding child sexual abuse. *Child Abuse and Neglect*, *17*, 175–185.

Myers, J.E.B. (1998). *Legal issues in child abuse and neglect practice*. Thousand Oaks, CA: Sage.

NJA (1992). *Nytt Juridiskt Arkiv* [*New Legal Archives*], *67*, 446–470.

Nicholson, R.A. and Norwood, S. (2000). The quality of forensic psychological assessments, reports, and testimony: Acknowledging the gap between promise and practice. *Law and Human Behavior*, *24*, 9–44.

Nyström, I. (1992). *Brottmålet i domstol—krav och svårigheter* [*The criminal case in court—Demands and difficulties*]. Brottsförebyggande rådet [The Swedish Council for Crime Prevention]. PM 1992:4.

Nyström, I. (1996). Sakkunnig i domstol [An expert witness in court]. In S.-Å. Christianson, (ed.), *Rättspsykologi* [*Forensic Psychology*]. Stockholm: Natur och Kultur.

Plous, S. (1993). *The psychology of judgement and decision making*. New York: McGraw-Hill, Inc.

Quinn, K.M. (1989). Resolved: child sexual abuse is overdiagnosed. *Journal of the American Academy of Child and Adolescent Psychiatry*, *28*, 789–97.

Raskin, D. and Esplin, P.W. (1991). Statement validity analysis: Interview procedures and content analyses of children's statements of sexual abuse. *Behavioral Assessment*, *13*, 265–291.

Rättsmedicinalverket [National Board on Forensic Medicine] (1994). *Rättspsykiatrisk undersökningsverksamhet 1991–1993*, Vol. 2 [*Forensic psychiatric evaluations 1991–1993*]. RMV-rapport [Report]. Stockholm: National Board on Forensic Medicine.

Schetky, D.H. (1991). Ethical issues in forensic child and adolescent psychiatry. *Journal of the American Academy of Child and Adolescent Psychiatry*, *31*, 403–407.

Shuman, D.W., Greenberg, S., Heilbrun, K. and Foote, W.E. (1998). An immodest proposal: Should treating mental health professionals be barred from testifying about their patients? *Behavioral Sciences and the Law*, *16*, 509–523.

Skeem, J.L., Golding, S.L., Cohn, N.B. and Berge, G. (1998). Logic and reliability of evaluations of competence to stand trial. *Law and Human Behavior*, *22*, 519–547.

Socialstyrelsen [National Board on Health and Welfare] (1991). *Sexuella övergrepp mot barn* [*Child sexual abuse*]. Allmänna Råd.

Thomas-Peter, B.A. and Warren, S. (1998). Legal responsibilities of forensic psychologists. *Expert Evidence*, *6*, 79–106.

Trankell, A. (1971). *Vittnespsykologins arbetsmetoder* [*The methodology of witness psychology*]. Stockolm: Liber.

Undeutsch, U. (1982). Statement reality analysis. In A.Trankell (ed.), *Reconstructing the past: The role of psychologists in criminal trials*. Stockholm: Norstedts.

Wells, G.L. and Loftus, E.F. (1991). Is this child fabricating? Reactions to a new assessment technique. In J. Doris (ed.), *The suggestibility of children's recollections: Implications for eyewitness testimony*. Washington, DC: American Psychological Association.

Wiklund, N. (1990). Sexualbrott och rättssäkerhet [Sexual offenses and the due process of law]. *Svensk Juristtidning* [*Swedish Law Review*], *12*, 792–730.

Wiklund, N. (1991). Vittnespsykologerna sex år för sent [Witness psychologists six years too late]. *Svensk Juristtidning* [*Swedish Law Review*], *5*, 202–206.

Wiklund, N. (1992). Domstolarna granskar vittnespsykologer [The courts examine witness psychologists]. *Svensk Juristtidning* [*Swedish Law Review*], *2*, 159–160.

Wiklund, N. (1999). Oskyldigt dömda: erfarenheter och lärdomar [Innocent and convicted: Experiences and lessons]. *Svensk Juristtidning* [*Swedish Law Review*], 562–567.

Chapter 4.4

Eyewitnesses

A. Daniel Yarmey
University of Guelph, Ontario, Canada

Eyewitness misidentifications are the single most common cause of wrongful convictions (Huff, Rattner and Sagarin,1986). Next to an actual confession, eyewitness testimony has been described as the most incriminating evidence that can be introduced against an accused (Brandon and Davies, 1973). Although there is no authoritative method to determine the actual number of false convictions, Cutler and Penrod (1995a) estimate that there may be 4500 erroneous convictions each year in the United States arising from faulty eyewitness identification. These estimations—based mainly on case studies, archival data, and surveys of criminal justice officials—have recently been supported by 'hard' evidence. With the support of the US Department of Justice, an analysis of the applications of DNA technology to forensic issues has challenged the reliability of some eyewitness identifications (Connors et al., 1996). As of 1996, 28 men who were found guilty for various criminal acts were exonerated through the analysis of DNA typing. Eyewitness identification was the single most common factor accounting for these erroneous convictions. Two years later another 12 cases were added to this list (Wells et al., 1998). Of these 40 cases, 36 (or 90%) involved from one to five eyewitnesses making false identifications of innocent suspects. Note, these are the first 40 cases in the US which dealt with DNA typing, not the first 40 cases because they happened to involve eyewitness identifications as the primary evidence. Clearly, eyewitness evidence presented from well-meaning and confident citizens is highly persuasive but, at the same time, can be highly unreliable.

In 1986, Elizabeth F. Loftus described her 10-year-long experiences and tribulations, including backlashes from some psychologists, as an expert witness on eyewitness memory. Loftus reported that she received countless number of letters over the years from inmates, family and friends of prisoners who claimed that they or their loved ones had been falsely convicted on the basis of erroneous eyewitness identification. Two of these letters are presented here:

Handbook of Psychology in Legal Contexts, Second Edition
Edited by D. Carson and R. Bull. © 2003 John Wiley & Sons, Ltd.

April 24, 1980

Dear Dr. Loftus,

...I've written eons of letters to many different people trying to get somekind of assistance, but all to no avail. I've been in prison now for seven years fighting a case that I nor my brother knew nothing about. We were given life sentences for a crime that we didn't commit. And we were convicted mainly on shady identification. There is a law library here at the prison, but it's not equipped with the correct legal material ... It would be greatly appreciated if you would take or may I say find a small portion of time and send me some recent Federal Law pertaining to this matter.

Sincerely,
(name)
Jackson State Prison
Jackson, Michigan

June 7, 1980

Dear Professor Loftus,

My son has been 'positively' identified by a rape victim as the rapist. He is innocent, and was even home at the time.... Can you PLEASE send us any information you have regarding the 'mistaken positive identification'? Thank you so much.

Sincerely,
(name)
Union City, Tennessee

[*sic*: all spelling and grammar preserved]

Whether or not these letters reflect men who actually are innocent of the crimes for which they were convicted cannot be determined by this writer. Nevertheless, no one disputes the fact that some incarcerated individuals convicted on the basis of eyewitness evidence are innocent (Borchard, 1932; Gross, 1987). Although Anglo-American law is based on the principle first declared by William Blackstone (1765/1962) that it is better to acquit 10 guilty persons than to convict one innocent person, it appears that many legal jurisdictions are still uncertain about the admissibility of expert eyewitness testimony. This is not new. In the dawn of the twentieth Century Hugo Münsterberg (1908) argued that because experimental psychology concerns itself with the scientific study of human behaviour and experience, the results of laboratory studies on human perception and memory should be of particular importance to the courts' evaluations of witness testimony. However enlightened Münsterberg may have been on matters of applied psychology, he failed to appreciate the importance of proper social influence and persuasion techniques as well as the necessity for valid scientific proof. Münsterberg attacked the legal establishment for its lack of appreciation and endorsement of psychology's offerings. Worse still, he failed to provide the courts with sufficiently rigorous results from laboratory experiments and theoretical evidence, let alone naturalistic observations, field experiments, and archival data to support his proposals. These limitations were aptly underscored and ridiculed by Justice Wigmore (1909). In spite of this relatively poor introduction to an integration of the psychology of eyewitness testimony and law, Wigmore and other legal scholars of that period encouraged the application of scientifically valid research findings to the courts' better understandings of witness testimony (Sporer, 1982).

Approximately 15 years ago Loftus and Schneider (1987) declared that the 'battle rages on'; many American courts still refuse to allow expert testimony concerning eyewitness identification. This battle may be going in opposite directions in the United States and Canada. On May 8, 2001, the New York Court of Appeals in *People* v. *Lee* ruled that expert testimony on the reliability of eyewitnesses could be admitted at trial. The Court reasoned that expert testimony is not so much a matter of being 'necessary', instead, the test for admissibility is whether the jury would be benefited by the specialized knowledge of an expert and whether the expert's testimony would aid a lay jury in reaching a verdict. Further, the Court stated that although the expert's assistance may to some degree invade the province of the jury, it is 'a kind of authorized encroachment'. The Court recognized that although jurors may have some common knowledge about factors that influence the reliability of eyewitness observation and identification, the psychological research literature regarding the accuracy of an identification is beyond 'the ken' of the typical juror. However, such expert testimony is not inadmissible, per se; the decision whether to admit rests in the sound discretion of the trial court. Also, the Court indicated that trial judges should determine whether the proffered expert testimony is generally accepted by the relevant scientific community.

In contrast to the direction taken by the New York Court of Appeal, the Ontario Court of Appeal in 1997 upheld the decision of the trial judge not to admit expert testimony on eyewitness identification (*R* v. *McIntosh and McCarthy*). This action has effectively stopped all expert testimony on eyewitness identification on lower courts in this province. Whether or not this judgement will set a trend for other trial or appellate courts in other parts of Canada, or other common law countries, remains to be seen (Saunders, J., 2001).

In *R* v. *Mohan* (1994) the Supreme Court of Canada established a four-fold test for the admission of expert evidence. Sopinka, J., writing for the Court, stated that the admissibility of expert evidence depends on (a) relevance; (b) necessity in assisting the trier of fact; (c) the absence of any exclusionary rule; and (d) a properly qualified expert. Because the decision in *R* v. *McIntosh and McCarthy* (1997) has had a chilling effect on expert testimony in Ontario, several excerpts are presented in the next section citing the judgement of Mr Justice J.A. Finalyson, writing for the Ontario Court of Appeal.

REGINA V. McINTOSH AND McCARTHY (1997)

Owen McIntosh and Paul McCarthy were charged with numerous offenses arising from the robbery of a dry cleaning store in which the victim was beaten with a metal rod by one assailant and shot by a second assailant. The two accused men were arrested approximately three months after the incident. Circumstantial evidence was available which linked the accused to the scene of the crime and the getaway car. The Crown's case with respect to the robbery consisted primarily of three eyewitnesses: the victim who was black, the owner of the store who was Chinese, and a white passerby. The two accused were black.

At trial the defendants sought to call this writer as an expert on eyewitness identification. On a *voir dire* to test whether this expert evidence was admissible the defense proposed evidence related to: the factors present at the time of the robbery that would impair the witnesses' ability to make an accurate identification, the problem of cross-racial identification, the quality of memory recall for perceived events of different time spans, the influence of 'post event information' on memory, the validity of the photographic lineup, the misconception of jurors with respect to photographic line-ups, the difficulties with 'in dock' identifications and police procedures relating to the identification of the two accused persons. The trial judge, Madame Justice Wein, refused to admit this evidence.

Mr Justice Finlayson of the Ontario Court of Appeal summed up the tenor of my evidence in my own words:

> Well, the understanding of jurors, and how they perceive is what psychologists spend their lives doing. We hope to assist the judge or the jury on the various levels and factors of what would lead to a good or a poor identification. It is not my job to decide whether or not that is the answer. All I can do is assist the trier in understanding. Here are the reasons why it could be a good identification or a poor one. (p. 391) (On reflection, and after approximately five years, this writer would give a similar response in court.)

Mr Justice Finlayson continued:

> I am astonished at the passivity of the Crown at trial and on appeal with respect to this type of evidence. At trial, Crown counsel contented himself with the early observation that the witness had said nothing that would convince him that a psychologist would know what information would be 'probative' to the trial. However, he did not cross-examine Dr. Yarmey on his qualifications, or at all, and seemed to accept that the substance of his testimony was properly the subject-matter of expert evidence. On appeal, Crown counsel limited his argument to the submission that we should defer to the trial judge who rejected the evidence in the exercise of her discretion. He was careful, however, to state that there could be cases in which this evidence could be admitted. This posture is not surprising given the reliance by the Crown on the 'soft sciences' in other cases . . . I do not intend to leave the subject without raising some warning flags. In my respectful opinion, the courts are overly eager to abdicate their fact-finding responsibilities to 'experts' in the field of the behavioural sciences. We are too quick to say that a particular witness possesses special knowledge and experience going beyond that of the trier of

fact without engaging in an analysis of the subject-matter of that expertise. I do not want to be taken as denigrating the integrity of Dr. Yarmey's research or of his expertise in the field of psychology, clearly one of the learned sciences, but simply because a person has lectured and written extensively on a subject that is of interest to him or her does not constitute him or her an expert for the purposes of testifying in a court of law on the subject of that speciality. It seems to me that before we even get to the point of examining the witness's expertise, we must ask ourselves if the subject-matter of his testimony admits of expert testimony. Where is the evidence in this case that there is a recognized body of scientific knowledge that defines rules of human behaviour affecting memory patterns such that any expert in that field can evaluate the reliability of the identification made by a particular witness in a given case?

Paraphrasing freely from the definition of 'science' in *The Shorter Oxford English Dictionary on Historical Principles*, it seems to me that before a witness can be permitted to testify as an expert, the court must be satisfied that the subject-matter of his or her expertise is a branch of study in psychology concerned with a connected body of demonstrated truths or with observed facts systematically classified and more or less connected together by a common hypothesis operating under general laws. The branch should include trustworthy methods for the discovery of new truths within its own domain. I should add that it would be helpful if there was evidence that the existence of such a branch was generally accepted within the science of psychology.

... I have some serious reservations as to whether the 'Psychology of Witness Testimony' is an appropriate area for opinion evidence at all. I acknowledge that the subject is interesting and Dr. Yarmey's presentation is informative. I also applaud his evidence that he lectures on the subject to police officers. We should all be reminded of the frailties of identification evidence. However, I would have to be persuaded that the subject is a recognized branch of psychology. Even if it is, I do not think that it meets the test for relevance and necessity.

... This opinion evidence is noteworthy in that, unlike most expert psychological or psychiatric testimony, it is not directed to making the testimony of a particular witness more understandable to the trier of fact and therefore more believable (e.g. an explanation of repressed memory syndrome or battered spouse syndrome). This opinion evidence is directed to instructing the jury that all witnesses have problems in perception and recall with respect to what occurred during any given circumstance that is brief and stressful. Accordingly, Dr. Yarmey is not testifying to matters that are outside the normal experience of the trier of fact; he is reminding the jury of the normal experience ... Writings, such as those of Dr. Yarmey, are helpful in stimulating an ongoing evaluation of the problem of witness identification, but they should be used to update the judge's charge, not to instruct the jury.

... Dr. Yarmey was prepared to testify as to the problems of 'cross-racial identification': the perception that members of one race tend to think that members of another race 'all look alike'. Dr. Yarmey's research supports this popular perception and his opinion on the subject is hardly surprising. But before this opinion evidence could be outside the normal experience of the jurors, would he not have had to conclude that the perception was false and that a cross-racial identification problem did not exist?
(*R* v. *McIntosh and McCarthy*, 1997, pp. 391–395)

In addition, the Court was concerned that expert evidence would be misused and distort the fact-finding process, and that jurors may be overwhelmed by the 'mystic infallibility' of the expert evidence. In sum, the Court held that the 'science' of the psychology of witness testimony had not advanced sufficiently far from the common experience of jurors to warrant its admission.

A reply to Mr Justice Finlayson

With respect, the judgement of Mr Justice Finlayson should not and has not gone unchallenged. In a direct response to the learned justice, Peters (1997, 2001), an Ontario criminal lawyer, raised several criticisms of this judgement. First, the Court did not significantly question the relevance of the expert testimony, i.e. 'We should all be reminded of the frailties of the identification evidence.' However, the Court concluded that the testimony would not assist the trier of fact without allowing the jury to hear the testimony of the expert. Second, most of the proposed testimony including such factors as jurors' misconceptions with respect to photographic lineups and police procedures related to identification would be outside the common knowledge of the average juror. More critical was the Court's solution that any identification could be addressed by the trial judge in her summation. In contrast, Peters argues that the scope of identification issues proffered by the expert witness would have been far beyond the standard charge of a trial judge to the jury on the dangers of identification evidence. The only way that the trial judge could have knowingly addressed all the relevant issues based on the most current scientific understandings was to allow the expert evidence and then to have charged the jury on the fact that they could accept all, some, or none of what the expert testified. Next, the statement of 'warning flags' raised by the Justice is confusing. That is, the Court made a distinction between two types of psychological evidence. Evidence which would inform jurors about the scientific understandings of perception and recall and associated problems was considered not relevant. In contrast, expert opinion evidence on such factors as repressed memory syndrome or battered spouse syndrome which is 'directed to making the testimony of a particular witness more understandable to the trier of fact and therefore more believable', would be relevant. However, both of these types of evidence depend on a scientific understanding of perceptual and memory processes, and both are influenced by similar interference factors, such as 'post-event misinformation' effects. Furthermore, unlike the intensive scientific attention given over the last century to perception and memory in general and to the practical applications of memory to eyewitnesses in particular, there is limited scientific evidence on the repressed memory syndrome (e.g. Read and Lindsay, 1997) and the battered spouse syndrome (e.g. Jasinski and Williams, 1998).

Mr. Justice Finlayson's recommendation that expert evidence on eyewitness testimony and identification is not a proper subject-matter and should not be admitted is shared by some jurists, lawyers, and cognitive psychologists (see Bartolomey, 2001; Clifford, 1997; Ebbesen and Konecni, 1996; Lindsay, MacDonald and McGarry, 1990). The fact that appellate judges disregard research psychologists' robust empirical results or statistical findings is not unusual. Some scholars have suggested that judges are only interested in those social science theories and empirical findings that confirm their own beliefs (see Wrightsman, Nietzel and Fortune, 1994). In contrast, other courts have readily accepted social science research (Monahan and Walker, 1991). A question that needs to be addressed is whether the decision of those Courts which reject the results of eyewitness memory research is based on sound reasoning, constitutional considerations, or ideological bias? In the next section a general review of these issues is addressed, although this question remains unanswered.

LEGAL REASONS FOR EXCLUSION

The courts have given many different reasons for their decision to exclude expert testimony on eyewitness reliability. Some of these reasons been summarized by Fulero (1993):

> (1) eyewitness unreliability is a matter of 'common sense', 'ordinary experience', or 'common knowledge'; (2) the issue can be adequately addressed in cross-examination; (3) the testimony invades the province of the jury; (4) doubt as to the scientific basis of the testimony; (5) miscellaneous procedural problems; (6) the exclusion was harmless or did not affect the results; (7) there was no abuse of discretion in the exclusion of the testimony; (8) the individual who was to testify was not an expert; (9) the matter can be adequately addressed by jury instruction; (10) methodological problems with the empirical studies; (11) the prejudicial effect of the testimony outweighs its probative value; (12) the testimony would 'amount to a lecture to the jury on how to do its duty'; (13) expert psychological testimony is not admissible to impeach the credibility of a witness.

In addition, since the late 1960s several US higher court decisions (see the listing provided by Ebbesen and Konecni, 1996) and some eyewitness memory researchers (e.g. Ebbesen and Konecni, 1996; Elliott, 1993; McCloskey and Egeth, 1983) have questioned whether expert testimony on eyewitness reliability is: a proper subject matter; a waste of the court's time; conforms to a generally accepted explanatory theory; would assist the trier of fact; whether the scientific research findings are reliable and accurate and are based on forensically-related situations and populations; whether admitting the evidence would overwhelm, confuse or mislead the jury; whether such evidence would make jurors overly skeptical and inclined to reject the testimony of eyewitnesses (thereby lowering the number of false convictions but also increasing the number of erroneous acquittals); and whether the possibility that admitting expert testimony would open the gates to conflicting testimony which would degenerate into an acrimonious, confusing, and uninformative 'battle of experts'.

When trial judges' judgements to exclude are appealed, appellate courts seldom find that there has been an abuse of discretion because of the wide latitude trial judges are given in making evidentiary rulings (Fulero, 1993). In contrast, when courts permit expert testimony on eyewitness reliability they do so because: the research is seen as reliable and valid; is generally accepted by the scientific community; the research would assist the average juror in that it would contradict lay persons' common-sense beliefs; there would be no invasion of the province of the jury as the jury remains free to reject the expert testimony in whole or part; and the eyewitness identification of the defendant is a key element of the prosecution's case but is not substantially corroborated by evidence giving it independent reliability.

EYEWITNESS RESEARCH AS A 'SOCIAL FRAMEWORK'

The justice system readily admits the testimony of clinical psychologists and psychiatrists (Melton et al., 1997). It also makes use of and admits social science evidence in selected fields such as trademark cases, obscenity litigation, employment discrimination suits, and in adjudicating damages in mass tort cases, among other areas (Monahan and Walker, 1991). Note, these areas of social science can be characterized as supportive of an idiographic approach, that is, they often operate on a case-by-case basis with specific facts. Part of the reason that there is judicial resistance in some jurisdictions to expert testimony on eyewitness reliability is the fact that the law is idiographic whereas eyewitness research is nomothetic. That is, the goals of eyewitness researchers, which are consistent with the goals of science, are to describe, explain, understand, and predict general principles, relationships, and patterns of behaviour and experience. Anglo-American courts are adversarial and search for certainty, consistency and finality. In contrast, eyewitness research is based on the scientific method and searches for increasingly better understandings of representations of truth (see Haney, 1980; Schuller and Ogloff, 2001).

The courts justifiably may ask how the trier of fact can be assisted by an expert witness who draws her or his conclusions from data based on the responses of large samples of research participants? Furthermore, such opinions are based on data expressed in terms of statistically significant differences between group means, standard deviations, and effect sizes. Such expert testimony will not provide scientific evidence and theoretical explanation about a particular victim or witness to a particular criminal event.

Expert testimony on eyewitness reliability cannot and does not address the accuracy and completeness of the testimony of single eyewitnesses. However, this does not mean that the opinions of an expert cannot be of assistance to the trier of fact. Expert eyewitness testimony can provide a *social framework* in which general conclusions from social science research are presented as a means of helping the trier of fact determine factual issues in a specific case (Monahan and Walker, 1988). That is, expert testimony can provide scientific information which could assist the trier of fact in interpreting and evaluating eyewitness statements of 'what happened' and 'who did it' (Leippe, 1995). Expert testimony can provide a context for evaluating what eyewitnesses report, but the trial judge or jurors do the evaluating. Eyewitness researchers do not attempt to predict behaviour from single cases, but this is no different from that of other sciences, e.g. botanists do not predict the behaviour of falling leaves from a specific tree (Wells and Turtle, 1987). Instead, empirically-validated aggregate data on situational factors, witness factors, and procedural factors are presented which may assist in the understanding of the single instance. To the extent that a particular variable or set of variables were present at the time of the witnessing, and those variables are known through scientific research to have a particular effect or set of effects, then it is possible that expert testimony on those witnessing conditions could be relevant and of assistance to the trier of fact in evaluating particular points at issue.

The possible benefits of expert testimony for increasing jurors' awareness of factors that influence eyewitness memory and give assistance in the evaluation of an eyewitness's testimony has been cleverly described by Devenport, Penrod and Cutler (1997). They draw an analogy between jurors hearing expert testimony and a car buyer's purchase of an automobile. Car buyers enter the selection process by already having some basic commonsense knowledge about the general capabilities and expected performance of the particular cars they are considering for purchase. Customers evaluate a car by giving it a look over, kicking the tires, reading the manufacturer's advertisements, and taking the car for a test drive. Those persons wishing to avoid buying a 'lemon' may seek expert opinion on product quality from periodicals such as *Consumer Reports* which publishes annual evaluations on most automobile manufacturers' newer and older cars and their different models. Assume for argument sake that jurors are much like car buyers. Next, suppose that a particular eyewitness giving testimony at trial is the equivalent of particular make and model of car manufactured in a particular year. How trustworthy is that eyewitness (car)? And finally, assume that expert testimony on eyewitness reliability is similar to 'expert' consumer information. Through reading *Consumer Reports* or hearing expert testimony both car buyers and jurors can learn the most current and most reliable information about those factors in general which will influence the performance of a car or an eyewitness under different conditions. However, neither car buyers or jurors are forced to accept or to depend upon their respective experts' opinions. Their understandings of experts' reports may modify their commonsense evaluations and assist their decision-making, but the availability of this information does not guarantee that the decision will be correct (i.e. the purchased car may be a lemon, and the believed eyewitness may be wrong). Thus, testimony of those factors known to influence eyewitness reliability provided by an expert witness, similar to knowledge gained from expert sources regarding automotive quality, can assist jurors (car buyers) by giving probabilistic knowledge about accuracy (product quality) and minimize the risk of error.

THE UNRELIABILITY OF EYEWITNESS RECALL AND IDENTIFICATION

Not all eyewitness reports by any one witness or across witnesses necessarily are inaccurate. However, the corruption of eyewitness descriptions and identification can occur at several stages. First, errors can occur at the acquisition stage in which information about the crime is perceived and encoded as memorial representations. Second, errors may be introduced at the retention stage (storage stage) which is the period of time that passes between the acquisition of selected information and its recollection. And third, errors occur during the retrieval or narration stage in which the witness recalls and/or recognizes stored information. Information cannot be accurately retrieved if it was not perceived. Information that is misperceived during acquisition also will be incorrectly remembered. Information can be forgotten, altered, or supplemented by factors that occur during the retention stage and retrieval stage. Finally, accurate and complete information may be available in memory but may not be accessible because of inappropriate questioning techniques. Memory is not the equivalent of a videotape recorder. Rather, memory is constructed and reconstructed from available bits and pieces of information into narrative wholes. Sometimes these constructions are reproduced relatively accurately, at other times they can be faulty and incomplete. Witnesses may fill in gaps and omissions through the use of inferences about what 'probably' must have happened. Theoretical understanding of eyewitness memory is based on research conducted in highly controlled laboratory settings, staged crimes, and field experiments involving store clerks, bank tellers, students and ordinary citizens ranging in age from young children to elders. In addition, the results of empirical research can be compared and contrasted with archival analyses of police records (e.g. van Koppen and Lochun, 1997; Yuille and Cutshall, 1986). Scientific knowledge about eyewitness memory is based on over 2000 empirically-based studies conducted in systematic research programs located in North America, the UK and other parts of Europe, Australia, New Zealand, and the Far East (Cutler and Penrod, 1995a). The same concern for hypothesis testing, objectivity, research design, measurement, explanation, and prediction cuts across all these research endeavours (Maass, 1996). The present knowledge of eyewitness identification does meet the general acceptance standards specified by law.

REVIEW OF THE LITERATURE

Several recent reviews of the literature on eyewitness testimony are available ranging from single chapters (e.g. Cutler and Penrod, 1995b; Read, Connolly and Turtle, 2001; Vrij, 1998; Yarmey, 2000) to entire books and monographs (e.g. Cutler and Penrod, 1995a; Sporer, Malpass and Koehnken, 1996; Ross, Read and Toglia, 1994; Thompson et al., 1998). The contemporary literature has been thoroughly critiqued and there is no need to simply add one more review. Instead, following the reasoning and judgement of Mr Justice Finlayson in *R* v. *McIntosh and McCarthy* (1997), I will focus on a few selected factors starting with the issue that expert eyewitness testimony is merely a matter of common sense. Next, a discussion of cross-racial identification, or what is now called the 'other-race effect' or the 'own-race bias (ORB) in memory for human faces' is offered. And finally, a summary of the recommendations of the US Department of Justice, Technical Working Group for Eyewitness Evidence (1999), for the gathering of accurate eyewitness reports and identification decisions is presented.

Common-sense Evaluations of Factors Influencing Eyewitness Reliability

In those cases considered serious enough for a jury trial, the law places its confidence in the common sense understandings of jurors regarding whether or not eyewitnesses' evidence is likely to be accurate. Thus, the trier of fact organizes information related to reported witnessing factors and police procedures and findings, rules out unlikely events, and selects the most acceptable explanation because it best fits the circumstances or most completely accounts for the issues. Jurors and trial judges do this on the basis of the evidence presented at trial, which is then evaluated against their years of personal experience and acquired formal and informal knowledge. This approach is not so different from scientific thinking, except that this is only the first step in empirical research, not the final conclusion. Eyewitness researchers in part draw upon, test, and attempt to clarify those common sense ideas which underlie eyewitness testimony. Furthermore, although common sense is a process of reasoning by which jurors construct beliefs and truths regarding eyewitness reliability and share these common knowledge understandings with each other, these conclusions are often based on misconceptions about the accuracy and completeness of memory. Expert testimony on factors affecting eyewitness reliability which challenges common-sense reasoning would disrupt decades, if not centuries, of legal tradition in dealing with eyewitness evidence. To paraphrase one trial judge who excluded my expert testimony in an Ontario Supreme Court . . . *jurors have been deliberating about questions regarding perception and memory for over 200 years and there is nothing new a psychologist can tell us about these processes* (Yarmey and Jones, 1983). Those who challenge these judicial assumptions risk being categorized as prejudicial, unreliable, confusing, misleading, artificial, and so forth. The discipline may be seen as pseudo-science or junk science. Researchers may be perceived as spending a lot of time and effort in proving what is obvious and already known. Those findings that are not labelled common sense may be regarded as esoteric, dealing mainly with jargon-filled statistical minutia of social and cognitive behaviour (see Furnham, 1983).

Even if lay persons are competent in understanding themselves and others, and highly adept at describing, explaining, and understanding human behaviour based on common knowledge, does this effectiveness extend to understanding the impact of estimator variables (factors over which the criminal justice system exerts little or no control, e.g. lighting, witness age) and system variables (factors that are under the direct control of the criminal justice system, e.g. lineup instructions, lineup fairness) on eyewitness descriptions and identification? Furthermore, do lay persons have an intuitive sense of the likely correct identification rate and false alarm rate in eyewitness identifications?

'AVERAGE' PERFORMANCE IN THE ACCURACY OF EYEWITNESS IDENTIFICATIONS

Given the caveat that accuracy of performance in eyewitness research depends upon the theory and methodology of the investigator, it is still possible to talk about base rates in accuracy of identification (Cutler and Penrod, 1995a). Although a complete review would include laboratory experiments, staged crimes, and archival data, I will limit the initial discussion only to those field experiments conducted in realistic settings such as in convenience stores (e.g. Brigham et al., 1982; Krafka and Penrod, 1985, Platz and Hosch, 1988) and local banks (Pigott, Brigham, and Bothwell, 1990). In these four experiments customers (targets) were engaged in non-stressful transactions with clerks for one or more minutes and were tested after short delays. These studies (total $N = 291$, with 536 separate identification tests) yielded an average percentage accuracy of identification of 42% when the targets were present in the photo lineups, and an average percentage of 36% false alarms when the targets were not present. Thus, participants identified the target less than half of the time when he/she was present, and falsely identified an innocent person slightly more than one third of the time when the target was not present.

Similar results have been found by this writer in slightly different but still realistic contexts. The research design that we have used involves a target walking up to an adult person on a city street, shopping centre, or other public place and asking for directions or assistance in finding some lost jewellery. The encounter lasts for approximately 15 seconds. Two minutes later the witness is approached by an experimenter and asked to participate in a university study on person perception and memory. If the participant agrees, testing for descriptive recall for physical and clothing characteristics (Yarmey, 1993; Yarmey, Jacob and Porter, in press; Yarmey and Yarmey, 1997), and photo identification and/or voice identification of the target is done immediately or an appointment is made for testing within the next two days (Yarmey, Yarmey and Yarmey, 1994, 1996).

In our first study which involved a two-minute retention interval, the percentage identification accuracy for a six-person target-present photo lineup was 41% and the percentage false alarm rate in the target-absent lineup was 28% ($N = 169$). Identification from a one-person photo lineup or showup also was examined. The stimulus person in the target-absent condition, of course, was highly similar in appearance to the target in the target-present condition. Percentage accuracy in the target-present condition was 57%, which just exceeded chance (50%), and the percentage false alarm rate in the target-absent condition was 12% (Yarmey et al., 1994, $N = 651$).

In a follow-up study, using a similar research design, accuracy of identification for a six-person target-present photo lineup was 49% with a two-minute retention interval. However, accuracy of identification dropped significantly to 39%, 36%, and 32% after delays in testing of 30 minutes, two hours, and 24 hours, respectively. Correct identifications were significantly different ($p < 0.05$) from chance only on the immediate test ($N = 286$). The percentage of false alarms in the six-person target absent lineups were 62%, 72%, 69% and 71% across the four retention intervals. Accuracy of identification in the target-present photo showup condition differed significantly from chance only on the immediate test (70%), but not after delays of 30 minutes (64%), two hours (54%) and 24 hours (55%). Note, although the delay of 30 minutes was 14% greater than that expected by chance (50%), which may seem substantial, this difference was not statistically significant. The corresponding false alarm rate in the target-absent showup was 18% on the immediate test, but false alarms increased significantly to 44%, 58%, and 53% for each of the respective delayed tests ($N = 279$) (Yarmey et al., 1996).

To test the hypothesis that identification performance would have been significantly different if live persons were used at the test instead of photos, an additional 376 persons were given a target-present live showup, and 348 persons were given a target-absent live showup. (The target and the highly-similar foil were sisters). Accuracy of live showup identification at the 2-minute, 30-minute, 2-hour, and 24-hour retention intervals was 52%, 69%, 62% and 62%, respectively. The false alarm rate in the target-absent live showup was 17%, 33%, 38%, and 31% across the four retention intervals, respectively. No significant differences were found in accuracy of identification as a function of the same targets being presented live or presented by photograph. A comparison of the frequency of false identifications could not be conducted because of methodological limitations, that is, the foils were different individuals in the photo and live target-absent conditions. Averaging the results across these two studies and collapsing across treatment conditions reveals that accuracy of identification in the lineup condition was 39%, and the false alarm rate was 60%. In the showup condition accuracy of identification was 61% and the false alarm rate was 34%.

POSTDICTION STUDIES

Would most people, many of whom could be potential jurors, have predicted (actually postdicted) the results of the studies reviewed above? Following the same research design and a two-minute retention interval our latest study showed an average percentage accuracy of identification rate of 49% ($N = 293$) when the target was present in a six-person photo lineup, and an average false identification rate of 69% ($N = 297$) when the target was not present (Yarmey, unpublished). A separate group of undergraduate students (mean age $= 19$ years) enrolled in an introductory psychology course was given written summaries of the research design and asked to estimate the performance of the 'average' witness between the age of 18 and 65. Note, it is unlikely that the responses of these students would be biased or different from that of other young university students because no formal instruction on the psychology of eyewitness identification had been given to this point in their psychology course. One subgroup ($N = 206$) postdicted that 62% of witnesses would correctly identify the target (significant overestimation). Another subgroup ($N = 173$) postdicted that the average false alarm rate would be 53% (significant underestimation, but still surprisingly high). Further questioning revealed that students expected an average correct identification rate in 'real-world' police lineups of 57% ($N = 206$), and an average false alarm rate of 51% ($N = 173$). Again, this estimation of false identifications of innocent persons is surprisingly high. Sixty-two percent of the participants agreed with the statement that the courts place too much emphasis on the results of lineup identifications, 23% stated that the courts give the appropriate amount of emphasis, and 15% believed too little emphasis was given. These results, if general, suggest that a substantial proportion of the public, or at least Canadian university psychology students, are skeptical about the accuracy of, and the weight given by the courts, to lineup identifications. It is uncertain whether these potential jurors would be made even more skeptical about the importance of eyewitness evidence if they heard expert testimony on such issues.

Postdiction studies about potential jurors' knowledge about the accuracy of person identification also includes research on voice identification. We recently tested the hypothesis that most people can correctly identify the voice of a familiar speaker and correctly reject the voice of a stranger (Yarmey et al., 2001). Eighty people (listeners) between the ages of 18 and 65, sampled from the community at large, were given four different tape-recorded voices. One of the speakers was a highly familiar person, such as their spouse, son, daughter, sibling, or best friend; the second voice was that of a person with whom they were moderately familiar, such as a co-worker or teammate; the third speaker was a low familiar person or mere acquaintance who would be expected to have talked with the listener for only a few minutes on different occasions over the last year; and the last voice was that of a stranger. Listeners were given up to nine segments of normal conversational speech of increasing duration, ranging from the single word 'Hello' to two minutes of spontaneous speech. Listeners were told they could hear increasingly longer voice samples of the same speaker, but were to state the name of the speaker, or indicate that they did not know the speaker, or that it was the voice of a stranger as soon as possible. A separate group of 59 undergraduate psychology students was given a written summary of the procedures just described, and were asked to estimate the percentage of listeners between the ages of 18 and 65 who would accurately identify by name, the voice of the high, moderate, and low familiar speakers, and correctly reject the voice of the unfamiliar speaker. The mean percentage correct response rates, false identification rates, and misses, and the mean postdicted correct percentage response rates for each condition were: high familiar, 85, 5, 10, and 99; moderate familiar, 79, 13, 8, and 96; low familiar, 49, 23, 28, and 89; and stranger, 55, 45, (NA), and 84. These results showed that 85% of high familiar speakers were accurately identified but 15% of listeners misidentified or stated they did not know the voice of a most significant other. Both low familiar speakers and strangers voices yielded significantly high percentages of false identifications. Students' postdictions of correct earwitness performance were significantly greater than the listeners' actual performance in each of the four categories. These results indicate that common sense or common knowledge is not an adequate basis for estimations of percentage accuracy of identification of familiar and unfamiliar voices.

In general, postdiction studies of juror knowledge reveal that potential jurors often overestimate the accuracy of eyewitness identification; they are insensitive to the impact of crime seriousness on identification, fail to appreciate the problems of biased lineup instructions, and are insensitive to the issues that contribute to inaccuracy of cross-racial identifications (Devenport et al., 1997).

SURVEYS OF COMMON-SENSE KNOWLEDGE

Assessments of the common-sense knowledge of factors which influence the accuracy of eyewitness descriptions and identification have been conducted since the early 1980s in Australia, Canada, the United Kingdom, and the United States. These assessments have included samples of *attorneys* (Brigham and WolfsKeil, 1983; Rahaim and Brodsky, 1982; Stinson et al., 1996; Winterdyk, 1988; Yarmey, 1986; Yarmey and Jones, 1983), *trial judges* (Stinson, 1997), *police* (Bennett and Gibling, 1989; Brigham and WolfsKeil, 1983; Kebbell and Milne, 1998; Winterdyk, 1988; Wogalter, Malpass and Burger,1993; Yarmey and Jones, 1982), *law students* (McConkey and Roche, 1989; Noon and Hollin, 1987; Yarmey and Jones, 1983), *undergraduate students* (Brigham and Bothwell, 1983; Deffenbacher and Loftus, 1982; Labelle, Lamarche and Laurence, 1990; McConkey and Roche, 1989; Noon and Hollin, 1987; Shaw, Garcia and McClure, 1999; Yarmey and Jones, 1983), *members of the general public* (Bennett and Gibling, 1989; Noon and Hollin, 1987; Yarmey, 1986; Yarmey and Jones, 1983), and *eyewitness psychology experts* (Kassin and Barndollar, 1992; Kassin, Ellsworth and Smith, 1989; Winterdyk, 1988; Yarmey and Jones, 1983). The results of these surveys have been consistent. Relative to psychology experts other respondents have poor understanding of many issues involved in eyewitness memory. For example, attorneys are unaware of several factors which influence the accuracy of eyewitness identification evidence such as the presence of a weapon and presentation bias in lineup procedures. Attorneys also were found to be unaware of the low correlation or lack of a relationship between witnesses' subjective confidence in the accuracy of identification and the objective accuracy of identification. Furthermore, potential jurors lack common-sense knowledge about the influence of such factors as violence, witnessing conditions, and lineup suggestiveness on the accuracy of identification (Devenport et al., 1997). It is not only potential jurors who fail to appreciate the subtleties of proper lineup procedures; both lawyers and trial judges improperly recognize some of the biases in lineup procedures (Stinson et al., 1996, 1997). Empirical studies show that cross-examination, opening and closing arguments, and trial judges' instructions cannot be relied upon to counter mistaken eyewitness identification (Leippe, 1995).

Expert psychological knowledge on the fairness of lineup procedures is not a normal, everyday process, understood on the basis of common sense. Reliability and helpfulness are interrelated concepts. The better the proof as to scientific reliability, the greater the likelihood that the courts will find the expert's opinion helpful to the trier of fact.

CROSS-RACIAL IDENTIFICATION: THE OTHER-RACE EFFECT

Both expert psychology witnesses and lawyers (particularly defense attorneys) acknowledge the importance of the courts' clarification of the other-race bias in eyewitness identification (Brigham and WolfsKeil, 1983; Kassin et al., 1989; Yarmey and

Jones, 1983). Four meta-analyses have confirmed the hypothesis that eyewitnesses are more likely to identify correctly someone of their own race than another race, and are more likely to misidentify someone of another race than someone of their own race (Anthony, Cooper, and Mullen, 1992; Bothwell, Brigham and Malpass, 1989; Meissner and Brigham, 2001; Shapiro and Penrod, 1986). This effect is robust and consistent. According to Meissner and Brigham (2001), who based their calculations on 39 research papers involving 91 independent samples and nearly 5000 participants, there is a 56% greater chance of a mistaken identification in other-race than in same-race conditions. There is no reason to assume that this high error ratio is restricted to research studies and is not to be found in actual criminal cases. As mentioned earlier, DNA analysis is now available to facilitate the discovery of possible wrongful convictions. Of 77 cases involving mistaken identifications, 35% of the cases involved white witnesses misidentifying black suspects, in contrast, only 28% of the cases involved whites misidentifying other whites. Note the proportionately greater percentage of misidentifications which occurred across racial groups (Scheck, Neufeld and Dwyer, 2000). The significance of this difference in percentage misidentifications may be better appreciated when it is recognized that most victimization occurs within race categories rather than across race-categories. That is, most white-victims are victimized by white perpetrators. Thus, proportionately more misidentifications should occur when white victim-witnesses attempt to identify white suspects (Wells and Olson, 2001).

INTERPRETATIONS

Several theoretical explanations have been proposed to account for the other-race effect. First, there may be less physiognomic variability between faces of one race and of another race. Because of the supposed fewer differences in features or patterns of variability in features of faces, other-race faces are said to be inherently more difficult to recognize. This hypothesis, that is, 'other-race faces all look alike' has not been supported. Goldstein and Chance (1979) found no significant differences in physiognomic variation among black, white and Japanese faces. Second, because of continuous experience with one's own racial group it is possible that certain features of same-race faces are given particular attention because of their high information value. Thus, as Ellis, Deregowski and Shepherd (1975) showed, whites are more likely to report descriptions of hair colour and texture and the colour of the eyes in describing other whites whereas blacks more frequently mention hair position, eye size, skin tone, eyebrows, ears, and chin of other blacks. If witnesses attend to these types of features and use these characteristics to distinguish one person from another because they are effective in own-race recognition, this habitual processing would probably be used in other-race recognition as well, but with much less effectiveness because of the features' lesser information value. It also has been proposed that accuracy of recognition of other-race faces is inferior to own-race faces because of social attitudes and prejudice which interfere with perception and memory. Although Meissner and Brigham (2001) found no relationship between participants' self-reported racial attitudes and other-race identification, other observers are not so quick to dismiss this influence. Wells and Olson (2001) note that it is not politically correct today to admit racial prejudice. Such attitudes and prejudices may simply have gone underground and may still influence identification decisions. This more subtle-type prejudice may be shown for example in the greater willingness of white American eyewitnesses to guess or use lax criteria in lineup identifications of black suspects than white suspects (Doyle, 2001). Doyle suggests that white witnesses might believe that there are less costs to misidentification of a black than of a white. Another theoretical possibility is that witnesses may spontaneously adopt an inferential orientation (involving more elaborate encoding) when observing members of their own race and a superficial orientation when looking at other race persons (Goldstein and Chance, 1981). Although this proposal is appealing it has not been supported in research (Barkowitz and Brigham, 1982; Devine and Malpass, 1985). Finally, the amount and quality of interracial contact or differential experience with members of own versus other racial groups has been proposed to account for the other-race effect (see Brigham and Malpass, 1985). Support has been found for this hypothesis by some researchers (e.g. Carroo, 1986; Chiroro and Valentine, 1995; Li, Dunning and Malpass, 1998; Platz and Hosch, 1988) but not by others (e.g. Brigham and Barkowitz, 1978; Ng and Lindsay, 1994).

None of the above theoretical interpretations is considered sufficient explanations for the other-race effect at this time (see also, Sporer, 2001; Valentine, 1991). This is not surprising because face recognition in itself, regardless of any race effects, is in need of further investigation and explanation. Also, there probably is more than one simple explanation for the other race-effect, that is, interpretations will probably include explanations of both underlying cognitive processes and associated social-emotional processes (Wells and Olson, 2001).

Findings, Concerns and Recommendations

The own-race recognition effect is reliable and found both in laboratory experiments (e.g. MacLin and Malpass, 2001; Malpass and Kravitz, 1969) and in more ecologically valid field situations (e.g Platz and Holtz, 1988; Wright, Boyd and Tredoux, 2001). The accuracy of face recognition in general is known to be influenced by a number of factors such as changes in hairstyle, facial hair, and the addition or removal of glasses (Patterson and Baddeley, 1977), disguises (O'Rourke, Penrod and Cutler, 1989), exposure duration (Ellis, Davies and Shepherd, 1977), the presence of a weapon (Steblay, 1992), crime seriousness (Leippe, Wells and Ostrom, 1978), retention interval (Shepherd, 1983), and so forth. Similarly, the size of the other-race effect is moderated by several variables. Meissner and Brigham's (2001) meta-analysis revealed that the other-race effect is influenced by the quality of interracial contact, i.e. the different levels of experience and equal-status contact with other-race persons. Also, limited observation time, such as a brief glimpse lasting only a few seconds, has been found to produce an increase in false alarms to other-race faces. The length of the retention interval also has been shown to moderate the other-race effect, that is, when retention periods are relatively long participants adopt an increasingly lax response criterion (i.e. more guessing) with other-race faces (see also, MacLin, MacLin and Malpass, 2001).

Smith and colleagues (2001) have shown that eyewitness confidence, decision time to make an identification from a lineup, and the use of a sequential lineup versus a simultaneously presented lineup are moderated by same-race versus other-race factors. In the sequential lineup procedure witnesses are forced to make an absolute judgement decision about each individual as they are serially presented. In contrast, in the simultaneous procedure witnesses follow a relative decision-making strategy whereby all suspects are compared with each other. Whereas confidence, decision time, and the relative versus absolute judgement strategy can be used to postdict accuracy of identification in own-race faces, this was not found to be true with other-race faces. The fact that some factors have a differential effect on own- and other-race face recognition is probably not appreciated by most lay persons and potential jurors. Smith et al. (2001) reinforce the point that unlike own-race identifications once other-race suspects have been selected by an eyewitness from a lineup it is impossible to determine by any postdictor factors whether the decision is likely to be correct or incorrect.

SOME RECOMMENDATIONS

In terms of policy implications there are a number of suggestions to be made. Testimony on the strength and weaknesses of the empirical evidence, and the different theoretical interpretations of the other-race effect, may be of assistance to the trier of fact in cases involving disputed eyewitness evidence. Expert testimony on the other-race effect would draw jurors' attention to the fact that a cross-racial identification could be highly problematic.

Expert testimony in itself will not resolve the other-race problem, however. Attention has to be directed to the initial identification stage not to the trial stage. Wells and Olson (2001) suggest that the six-person lineup, for example which is used in many jurisdiction, be increased by adding more fillers in other-race cases. The use of a large numbers of fillers who are known to be innocent persons would serve to protect an innocent suspect by increasing the chances that a filler and not the innocent suspect would be selected. Also, blank lineups in which the suspect is not present, followed by the presentation of an actual lineup containing the suspect, could be used in the case of other-race suspects. If an eyewitness selected someone from a blank lineup the identification would be incorrect and harmless. However, if the blank lineup was correctly rejected, the suspect-present lineup could then be given without the concern that the witness was overly willing to just identify someone. Furthermore, if an identification of the suspect was made with the second lineup more confidence could be attached to the reliability of the identification. It has also been suggested that the selection of fillers in the construction of the lineup should be done by persons who are the same race as the suspect (Brigham and Ready, 1985). Wells and Olson (2001) would even go so far as to suggest that if there is a question of a biased lineup at trial that the trial judge be of the same race as the defendant. Otherwise, the Court may fail to appreciate the potential biases of why the other-race defendant would stand out as distinctive.

US DEPARTMENT OF JUSTICE GUIDELINES ON EYEWITNESS EVIDENCE

At the request of US Attorney General Janet Reno, the Department of Justice was given the goal to recommend uniform practices in the collection and preservation of eyewitness evidence. In 1999 the Technical Working Group for Eyewitness Evidence consisting of a 34-person group of specialists representing the police, prosecutors and defense lawyers, and social scientists/eyewitness researchers brought forward a handbook of national guidelines. If further proof was needed that there has been an integration of social science research and the law, the *Guide* (1999) provides that evidence. Eyewitness research findings and practices refined over the last 20 years have been integrated into several recommendations to promote proper police procedures in gathering and preserving reliable and accurate eyewitness evidence. Similar to the law's concerns with the proper chain of custody of physical trace evidence, there is now an acknowledgement of the crucial importance for a proper chain of custody of psychological eyewitness evidence, or memory-as-trace-evidence (Wells, 1995). This can only be accomplished through the use of skilful witness interview techniques, valid procedures in the preparation and conduction of eyewitness identifications, and a heightened awareness by members of the criminal justice system in the evaluation of the strength and accuracy of eyewitness evidence.

The *Guide* covers and makes recommendations for all stages of a criminal investigation involving eyewitness evidence starting with the emergency call from a witness to a call taker/dispatcher, preparing and using mug books and composites, interviewing witnesses, and conducting showups and lineup identifications. To give an example of the recommendations found in the *Guide* the following subsection details the proposals for composing a live lineup.

Live Lineup: In composing a live lineup, the investigator should:

1. Include only one suspect in each identification procedure.

2. Select fillers who generally fit the witness's description of the perpetrator. When there is a limited/inadequate description of the perpetrator provided by the witness, or when the description of the perpetrator differs significantly from the appearance of the suspect, fillers should resemble the suspect in significant features.

3. Consider placing suspects in different positions in each lineup, both across cases and with multiple witnesses in the same case. Position the suspect randomly

unless, where local practice allows, the suspect or the suspect's attorney requests a particular position.

4. Include a *minimum* of four fillers (nonsuspects) per identification procedure.

5. When showing a new suspect, avoid reusing fillers in lineups shown to the same witness.

6. Consider that complete uniformity of features is not required. Avoid using fillers who so closely resemble the suspect that a person familiar with the suspect might find it difficult to distinguish the suspect from the fillers.

7. Create a consistent appearance between the suspect and fillers with respect to any unique or unusual feature (e.g. scars, tattoos) used to describe the perpetrator by artificially adding or concealing that feature. (pp. 30–31)

Instructing the Witness Prior to Viewing a Lineup

Live Lineup: prior to presenting a live lineup, the investigator should:

1. Instruct the witness that he/she will be asked to view a group of individuals.

2. Instruct the witness that it is just as important to clear innocent persons from suspicion as to identify guilty parties.

3. Instruct the witness that individuals present in the lineup may not appear exactly as they did on the date of the incident because features such as head and facial hair are subject to change.

4. Instruct the witness that the person who committed the crime may or may not be present in the group of individuals.

5. Assure the witness that regardless of whether an identification is made, the police will continue to investigate the incident.

6. Instruct the witness that the procedure requires the investigator to ask the witness to state, in his/her own words, how certain he/she is of any identification. (p. 32)

The *Guide* continues by detailing recommendations for conducting the identification procedure both for the simultaneous live lineup and sequential live lineup, and the proper steps to be taken in recording of identification results. Similar recommendations are made for the use of photo lineups. The scientific foundations to support the above passages and all of the other recommendations found in the *Guide* for eyewitness identifications in lineups and photospreads may be found in Wells et al. (1998). A similar review for the evaluation of the accuracy of eyewitness information has

EYEWITNESSES   553

been made in the United Kingdom with the support of the Home Office (Kebbell and
Wagstaff, 1999).

CONCLUSIONS

Further research on eyewitness evidence will continue to inform the police and the
courts and will necessitate constant revisions of *Guidelines*. It is hoped that those
factors and practices which can minimize mistaken identifications can be understood
and acted upon before they occur at any of the different points in the chain of custody
of eyewitness evidence. If this were to happen there would be less need for expert
evidence on the reliability of eyewitness evidence. At the same time, errors in police
procedures can and do occur: eyewitness evidence is not infallible. Expert psychological testimony on eyewitness reliability if admitted can assist the trier of fact without
usurping the traditional role of the trier in determining the reliability of testimony.

REFERENCES

Anthony, T., Cooper, C. and Mullen, B. (1992). Cross-racial facial identification: A social
    cognitive integration. *Personality and Social Psychology Bulletin, 18*, 296–301.
Barkowitz, P. and Brigham, J.C. (1982). Recognition of faces: Own-race bias, incentive, and
    time delay. *Journal of Applied Social Psychology, 12*, 255–268.
Bartolomey, D. (2001). Cross-racial identification testimony and what not to do about it: A com-
    ment on the cross-racial charge and cross-racial expert identification testimony. *Psychology,
    Public Policy, and Law, 7*, 247–252.
Bennett, P. and Gibling, F. (1989). Can we trust our eyes? *Policing, 5*, 313–321.
Blackstone, W. (1765/1962). *Commentaries on the laws of England*. Boston: Beacon.
Borchard, E.M. (1932). *Convicting the Innocent*. Garden City, NY: Garden City Publishing Co.
Bothwell, R.K., Brigham, J.C. and Malpass, R.S. (1989). Cross-racial identification. *Personality
    and Social Psychology Bulletin, 15*, 19–25.
Brandon, R. and Davies, C. (1973). *Wrongful imprisonment*. London: Allen & Unwin.
Brigham, J.C. and Barkowitz, P. (1978). Do 'They all look alike'? The effect of race, sex, expe-
    rience, and attitudes on the ability to recognize faces. *Journal of Applied Social Psychology,
    8*, 306–318.
Brigham, J.C. and Bothwell, R.K. (1983). The ability of prospective jurors to estimate the
    accuracy of eyewitness identifications. *Law and Human Behavior, 7*, 19–30.
Brigham, J.C., Maass, A., Snyder, L.D. and Spaulding, K. (1982). Accuracy of eyewitness
    identifications in a field setting. *Journal of Personality and Social Psychology, 42*, 673–680.
Brigham, J.C. and Malpass, R.S. (1985). The role of experience and contact in the recognition
    of faces of own- and other-race persons. *Journal of Social Issues, 41*, 139–155.
Brigham, J.C. and Ready, D.J. (1985). Own-race bias in lineup construction. *Law and Human
    Behavior, 9*, 415–424.
Brigham, J.C. and WolfsKeil, M.P. (1983). Opinions of attorneys and law enforcement personnel
    on the accuracy of eyewitness identification. *Law and Human Behavior, 7*, 337–349.
Carroo, A.W. (1986). Other race recognition: A comparison of Black American and African
    subjects. *Perceptual and Motor Skills, 62*, 135–138.
Chiroro, P. and Valentine, T. (1995). An investigation of the contact hypothesis of the own-race
    bias in face recognition. *Quarterly Journal of Experimental Psychology, 48A*, 879–894.
Clifford, B.R. (1997). A commentary on Ebbesen and Konecni's 'Eyewitness memory research:
    Probative v. prejudicial value'. *Expert Evidence, 6*, 140–143.

Connors, E., Lundregan, T., Miller, N. and McEwan, T. (1996). *Convicted by juries, exonerated by science: Case studies in the use of DNA evidence to establish innocence after trial.* Alexandria, VA: National Institute of Justice.

Cutler, B.L. and Penrod, S.D. (1995a). *Mistaken identification: The eyewitness, psychology, and the law.* Cambridge: Cambridge University Press.

Cutler, B.L. and Penrod, S.D. (1995b). Assessing the accuracy of eye-witness identifications. In R. Bull and D. Carson (eds), *Handbook of psychology in legal contexts* (pp. 193–213). Chichester: John Wiley & Sons.

Deffenbacher, K.A. and Loftus, E.F. (1982). Do jurors share a common understanding concerning eyewitness behavior? *Law and Human Behavior, 6,* 15–30.

Devenport, J.L., Penrod, S.D. and Cutler, B.L. (1997). Eyewitness identification evidence: Evaluating commonsense evaluations. *Psychology, Public Policy, and Law, 3,* 338–361.

Devine, P.G., and Malpass, R.S. (1985). Orienting strategies in differential face recognition. *Personality and Social Psychology Bulletin, 11,* 33–40.

Doyle, J.M. (2001). Discounting the error costs: Cross-racial false alarms in the culture of contemporary criminal justice. *Psychology, Public Policy, and Law, 7,* 253–262.

Ebbesen, E.B. and Konecni, V. J. (1996). Eyewitness memory research: Probative v. prejudicial value. *Expert Evidence, 5,* 2–28.

Elliott, R. (1993). Expert testimony about eyewitness identification: A critique. *Law and Human Behavior, 17,* 423–437.

Ellis, H.D., Davies, G.M. and Shepherd, J.W. (1977). Experimental studies of face identification. *Journal of Criminal Defense, 3,* 219–234.

Ellis, H.D., Deregowski, J.B. and Shepherd, J.W. (1975). Descriptions of white and black faces by white and black subjects. *International Journal of Psychology, 10,* 119–123.

Fulero, S.M. (1993). *Eyewitness expert testimony: An overview and annotated bibliography, 1931–1988.* Unpublished manuscript. Sinclair College, Dayton, Ohio.

Furnham, A. (1983). Social psychology as common sense. *Bulletin of the British Psychological Society, 36,* 105–109.

Goldstein, A.G. and Chance, J.E. (1979). Do foreign faces really look alike? *Bulletin of the Psychonomic Society, 7,* 407–408.

Goldstein, A.G. and Chance, J.E. (1981). Laboratory studies of face recognition. In G. Davies, H. Ellis and J. Shepherd (eds), *Perceiving and remembering faces* (pp. 81–104). London: Academic Press.

Gross, S.R. (1987). Loss of innocence: Eyewitness identification and proof of guilt. *Journal of Legal Studies, 16,* 395–453.

Haney, C. (1980). Psychology and legal change: On the limits of a factual jurisprudence. *Law and Human Behavior, 17,* 371–398.

Huff, R., Rattner, A. and Sagarin, E. (1986). Guilty until proven innocent. *Crime and Delinquency, 32,* 518–544.

Jasinski, J.L. and Williams, L.M. (eds) (1998). *Partner violence: A comprehensive review of 20 years of research.* London: Sage.

Kassin, S.M. and Barndollar, K. (1992). The psychology of eyewitness testimony: A comparison of experts and prospective jurors. *Journal of Applied Social Psychology, 22,* 1241–1249.

Kassin, S.M., Ellsworth, P.C. and Smith, V.L. (1989). The 'general acceptance' of psychological research on eyewitness testimony: A survey of experts. *American Psychologist, 44,* 1089–1098.

Kebbell, M.R. and Milne, R. (1998). Police officers' perceptions of eyewitness performance in forensic investigations. *Journal of Social Psychology, 138,* 323–330.

Kebbell, M.R., and Wagstaff, G.F. (1999). *Face value? Evaluating the accuracy of eyewitness information.* Police Research Series, Paper 102. London: The Home Office.

Krafka, C. and Penrod, S. (1985). Reinstatement of context in a field experiment on eyewitness identification. *Journal of Personality and Social Psychology, 49,* 58–69.

Labelle, L., Lamarche, M.C. and Laurence, J.R. (1990). Potential jurors' opinions on the effects of hypnosis on eyewitness identification: A brief communication. *The International Journal of Clinical and Experimental Hypnosis, 38,* 315–319.

Leippe, M.R. (1995). The case for expert testimony about eyewitness memory. *Psychology, Public Policy, and Law, 1*, 909–959.

Leippe, M.R., Wells, G.L. and Ostrom, T.M. (1978). Crime seriousness as a determinant of accuracy in eyewitness identification. *Journal of Applied Psychology, 63*, 345–351.

Li, J.C., Dunning, D. and Malpass, R.S. (1998 March). Basketball fandom and cross-racial identification among European-Americans: Another look at the contact hypothesis. Paper presented at the biennial meeting of the American Psychology-Law Society, Redondo Beach, CA.

Lindsay, R.C.L., MacDonald, P. and McGarry, S. (1990). Perspectives on the role of the eye-witness expert. *Behavioral Sciences and the Law, 8*, 457–464.

Loftus, E.F. (1986). Ten years in the life of an expert witness. *Law and Human Behavior, 10*, 241–263.

Loftus, E.F. and Schneider, N.G. (1987). 'Behold with strange surprise': Judicial reactions to expert testimony concerning eyewitness reliability. *UMKC Law Review, 56*, 1–45.

Maass, A. (1996). Logic and methodology of experimental research in eyewitness psychology. In S.L. Sporer, R.S. Malpass, and G. Koehnken (eds), *Psychological issues in eyewitness identification* (pp. 279–293). Mahwah, NJ: Lawrence Erlbaum Associates.

MacLin, O.H. and Malpass, R.S. (2001). Racial categorization of faces: The ambiguous race face effect. *Psychology, Public Policy and Law, 7*, 98–118.

MacLin, O.H., MacLin, M.K. and Malpass, R.S. (2001). Race, arousal, attention, exposure, and delay: An examination of factors moderating face recognition. *Psychology, Public Policy, and Law, 7*, 134–152.

Malpass, R.S. and Kravitz, J. (1969). Recognition for faces of own and other races. *Journal of Personality and Social Psychology, 13*, 330–334.

McCloskey, M. M. and Egeth, H.E. (1983). Eyewitness identification: What can a psychologist tell a jury. *American Psychologist, 38*, 550–563.

McConkey, K.M. and Roche, S.M. (1989). Knowledge of eyewitness memory. *Australian Psychologist, 38*, 550–563.

Meissner, C.A. and Brigham, J.C. (2001). Thirty years of investigating the own-race bias in memory for faces: A meta-analytic review. *Psychology, Public Policy, and Law, 7*, 3–35.

Melton, G.B., Petrila, J., Poythress, N.G. and Slobogin, C. (1997). *Psychological Evaluations for the Courts: A Handbook for Mental Health Professionals and Lawyers* (2nd edn). New York: Guilford.

Monahan, J. and Walker, L. (1988). Social science research in law: A new paradigm. *American Psychologist, 43*, 465–472.

Monahan, J. and Walker, L. (1991). Judicial use of social science research. *Law and Human Behavior, 15*, 571–584.

Münsterberg, H. (1908). *On the witness stand*. New York: Clark, Boardman.

Ng, W. and Lindsay, R.C.L. (1994). Cross-race facial recognition: Failure of the contact hypothesis. *Journal of Cross-Cultural Psychology, 25*, 217–232.

Noon, E. and Hollin, C.R. (1987). Lay knowledge of eyewitness behaviour: A British survey. *Applied Cognitive Psychology, 1*, 143–153.

O'Rourke, T.E., Penrod, S.D. and Cutler, B.L. (1989). The external validity of eyewitness identification research: Generalizing across subject populations. *Law and Human Behavior, 13*, 385–397.

Patterson, K.E. and Baddeley, A.D. (1977). When face recognition fails. *Journal of Experimental Psychology: Human Learning and Memory, 3*, 406–407.

Peters, M. (1997). Case Comment: *R v McIntosh. Criminal Lawyers' Association Newsletter, 18*, No. 3. (www.criminallawyers.ca/newslett/18-3/peters.htm)

Peters, M. (2001). Forensic psychological testimony: Is the courtroom door now locked and barred? *Canadian Psychology, 42*, 101–108.

Pigott, M.A., Brigham, J.C. and Bothwell R.K. (1990). A field study of the relationship between quality of eyewitnesses' descriptions and identification accuracy. *Journal of Police Science and Administration, 17*, 84–88.

Platz S.J. and Hosch, H.M. (1988). Cross racial/ethnic eyewitness identification: A field study. *Journal of Applied Social Psychology, 18*, 972–984.

PERSPECTIVES ON POLICY

Rahaim, G.L. and Brodsky, S.L. (1982). Empirical evidence versus common sense: Juror and lawyer knowledge of eyewitness accuracy. *Law and Psychology Review*, 7, 1–15.

Read, J.D., Connolly, D. and Turtle, J.W. (2001). Memory in legal contexts: Remembering events, circumstances, and people. In R.A. Schuller and J.R.P. Ogloff (eds), *Introduction to psychology and law: Canadian perspectives* (pp. 95–125). Toronto: University of Toronto Press.

Read, J.D. and Lindsay, D.S. (eds) (1997). *Recollections of trauma: Scientific evidence and clinical practice*. New York: Plenum Press.

Ross, D.F., Read, J.D. and Toglia, M.P. (eds) (1994). *Adult eyewitness testimony: Current trends and developments*. Cambridge: Cambridge University Press.

Saunders, J.W.S. (2001). Experts in court: A view from the bench. *Canadian Psychology*, 42, 109–118.

Scheck, B., Neufeld, P. and Dwyer, J. (2000). *Actual innocence: Five days to execution and other dispatches from the wrongly convicted*. New York: Doubleday. (Cited in Wells, G.L. and Olson, E.A. (2001). The other-race effect in eyewitness identification. *Psychology, Public Policy, and Law*, 7, 230–246.)

Schuller, R.A. and Ogloff, J.R.P. (2001). An introduction to psychology and law. In R.A. Schuller and J.R.P. Ogloff (eds), *Introduction to psychology and law: Canadian perspectives* (pp. 3–56). Toronto: University of Toronto Press.

Shapiro, P.N. and Penrod, S. (1986). Meta-analysis of racial identification studies. *Psychological Bulletin*, 100, 139–156.

Shaw, J.S., Garcia, L.A. and McClure, K.A. (1999). A lay perspective on the accuracy of eyewitness testimony. *Journal of Applied Social Psychology*, 29, 52–71.

Shepherd, J.W. (1983). Identification after long delays. In S.M.A. Lloyd-Bostock and B.R. Clifford (eds), *Evaluating witness evidence* (pp. 173–187). Chichester: John Wiley & sons.

Smith, S.M., Lindsay, R.C.L., Pryke, S. and Dysart, J.E. (2001). Postdictors of eyewitness errors: Can false identifications be diagnosed in the cross-race situation? *Psychology, Public Policy, and Law*, 7, 153–169.

Sporer, S.L. (1982). A brief history of the psychology of testimony. *Current Psychological Reviews*, 2, 323–340.

Sporer, S.L. (2001). Recognizing faces of other ethnic groups: An integration of theories. *Psychology, Public Policy, and Law*, 7, 36–97.

Sporer, S.L., Malpass, R.S. and Koehnken, G. (eds) (1996). *Psychological issues in eyewitness identification*. Mahwah, NJ: Lawrence Erlbaum Associates.

Steblay, N.M. (1992). A meta-analytic review of the weapon focus effect. *Law and Human Behavior*, 16, 413–424.

Stinson, V., Devenport, J.L., Cutler, B.L. and Kravitz, D.A. (1996). How effective is the presence-of-counsel safeguard? Attorney perceptions of suggestiveness, fairness, and correctability of biased lineup procedures. *Journal of Applied Psychology*, 81, 64–75.

Stinson, V., Devenport, J.L., Cutler, B.L. and Kravitz, D.A. (1997). How effective is the motion-to-suppress-safeguard? Judges' perceptions of the suggestiveness and fairness of biased lineup procedures. *Journal of Applied Psychology*, 82, 211–220.

Technical Working Group for Eyewitness Evidence (1999). *Eyewitness evidence: A guide for law enforcement*. Washington, DC: United States Department of Justice, Office of Justice Programs.

Thompson, C.P., Herrmann, D.J., Read, J.D., Bruce, D., Payne, D.G. and Toglia, M.P. (eds) (1998). *Eyewitness memory: Theoretical and applied perspectives*. Mahwah, NJ: Lawrence Erlbaum Associates.

Valentine, T. (1991). A unified account of the effects of distinctiveness, inversion, and race on face recognition. *Acta Psychologia*, 61, 259–273.

van Koppen, P.J. and Lochun, S.K. (1997). Portraying perpetrators: The validity of offender descriptions by witnesses. *Law and Human Behavior*, 21, 661–685.

Vrij, A. (1998). Psychological factors in eyewitness testimony. In A. Memon, A. Vrij and R. Bull (eds), *Psychology and law: Truthfulness, accuracy and credibility* (pp. 105–123). London: McGraw-Hill.

Wells, G.L. (1995). Scientific study of witness memory: Implications for public and legal policy. *Psychology, Public Policy, and Law, 1*, 726–731.

Wells, G.L. and Olson, E.A. (2001). The other-race effect in eyewitness identification: What do we do about it? *Psychology, Public Policy, and Law, 7*, 230–246.

Wells, G.L., Small, M., Penrod, S.D., Malpass, R.S., Fulero, S.M. and Brimacombe, C.A.E. (1998). Eyewitness identification procedures: Recommendations for lineups and photospreads. *Law and Human Behavior, 22*, 603–647.

Wells, G.L. and Turtle, J.W. (1987). Eyewitness testimony research: Current knowledge and emergent controversies. *Canadian Journal of Behavioral Science, 19*, 363–388.

Wigmore, J. (1909). Professor Munsterberg and the psychology of testimony. *Illinois Law Review, 3*, 399–445.

Winterdyk, J. (1988). Canadian police officers and eyewitness evidence: A time for reform. *Canadian Police College Journal, 12*, 175–191.

Wogalter, M.S., Malpass, R.S. and Burger, M.A. (1993). How police officers conduct lineups: A national survey. *Proceedings of the Human Factors and Ergonomics Society, 37*, 640–644.

Wright, D.B., Boyd, C.E. and Tredoux, C.G. (2001). A field study of own-race bias in South Africa and England. *Psychology, Public Policy, and Law, 7*, 119–133.

Wrightsman, L. S., Nietzel, M.T. and Fortune, W.H. (1994). *Psychology and the Legal System* (3rd edn). Pacific Grove CA: Brooks/Cole Publishing.

Yarmey, A.D. (1986). Perceived expertness and credibility of police officers as eyewitnesses. *Canadian Police College Journal, 10*, 31–52.

Yarmey, A.D. (1993). Adult age and gender differences in eyewitness recall in field settings. *Journal of Applied Social Psychology, 23*, 1921–1932.

Yarmey, A.D. (2000). The older eyewitness. In M.B. Rothman, B.D. Dunlop and P. Entzel (eds), *Elders, crime, and the criminal justice system: Myth, perceptions, and reality in the 21st century* (pp. 127–148). New York: Springer.

Yarmey, A.D. (no date). *Common sense and eyewitness identifications in field settings*. Unpublished. Department of Psychology, University of Guelph, Guelph, ON, Canada.

Yarmey, A.D., Jacob, J. and Porter, A. (in press). Person recall in field settings. *Journal of Applied Social Psychology*.

Yarmey, A.D. and Jones, H.P.T. (1982). Police awareness of the fallibility of eyewitness identification. *Canadian Police College Journal, 12*, 113–124.

Yarmey, A.D. and Jones, H.P.T. (1983). Is the psychology of eyewitness identification a matter of common sense? In S. Lloyd Bostock and B.R. Clifford (eds), *Evaluating witness evidence: Recent psychological research and new perspectives* (pp. 13–40). New York: John Wiley & Sons.

Yarmey, A.D. and Yarmey, M.J. (1997). Eyewitness recall and duration estimates in field settings. *Journal of Applied Social Psychology, 27*, 330–344.

Yarmey, A.D., Yarmey, A.L. and Yarmey, M.J. (1994). Face and voice identifications in showups and lineups. *Applied Cognitive Psychology, 8*, 453–464.

Yarmey, A.D., Yarmey, M.J. and Yarmey, A.L. (1996). Accuracy of eyewitness identifications in showups and lineups. *Law and Human Behavior, 20*, 459–477.

Yarmey, A.D., Yarmey, A.L., Yarmey, M.J. and Parliament, L. (2001). Common sense beliefs and the identification of familiar voices. *Applied Cognitive Psychology, 15*, 283–299.

Yuille, J.C. and Cutshall, J.L. (1986). A case study of eyewitness memory of a crime. *Journal of Applied Psychology, 71*, 291–301.

Cases

People v. *Lee* (2001), WL 493349.
R v. *McIntosh and McCarthy* (1997), 117 CCC (3d) 385 (Ont. CA)
R v *Mohan* (1994), 89 CCC (3d) 402 (SCC)

Psychological and Legal Implications of Occupational Stress for Criminal Justice Practitioners

Jennifer Brown
University of Surrey, UK
and
Janette Porteous
University of Lincoln, UK

INTRODUCTION

Concerns for the welfare and well-being of staff have, in recent times, become a more focused responsibility for employers in both the public and private sectors. The Health and Safety Executive (HSE), a United Kingdom statutory agency charged with policing health and safety at work, has identified stress at work to be a significant source of workers' ill health. In a recent epidemiological survey of 17 000 workers, 20% reported that they suffered very high or extremely high levels of stress at work (Smith et al., 2000). Police and prison officers were identified among the occupational groups most likely to report stress. Greater attention has been placed on acknowledging a duty of care, with the courts recognising and compensating individuals if employers can be shown to have been negligent. There is no specific legislation controlling it, but the fact that an employee suffers from stress as a result of workplace bullying or harassment, or indeed excessive workload, may mean that the employer has breached his or her legal duty. This duty is to take reasonable care to ensure that the health of the employee is not at risk through excessive and sustained levels of stress arising from the way, for example, the work is organised. Ill health, resulting from stress at work, is to be treated the same as ill health due to other physical causes at work. It is now settled law that, even if there is no independent physical injury, a claimant can

Handbook of Psychology in Legal Contexts, Second Edition
Edited by D. Carson and R. Bull. © 2003 John Wiley & Sons, Ltd.

recover damages for purely psychiatric illness caused by a defendant's negligence (*Page* v. *Smith*, 1996). This chapter will outline the legal framework governing the duty of care, describe the contemporary context within which criminal justice practitioners are working, and discuss some present thinking about work related stress and legal remedies. Our examples derive mostly from British legal and criminal justice practice, and will be limited to police and prison services. However the issues we discuss do extend to criminal justice practice elsewhere, and similar analyses may be extended to other professionals within the legal and criminological fields.

STRESSORS AND STRESS REACTIONS

Modern conceptualisation of the stress concept derives from the pioneering origins of Hans Seyle who described distress, meaning adverse emotions like anger and aggression said to have destructive impacts, and eustress which are constructive emotions associated with positive-striving (summarised in Lazarus, 1999, p. 31). Of the many approaches to stress that developed thereafter, the interactive approach—largely deriving from the work of Lazarus (Lazarus, 1966, 1999)—has been most influential. This approach conceives situations not to be stressful in themselves but adverse reactions can result when there is an imbalance between perceived environmental demands on the individual and his or her response capability. Conceptual distinctions tend to be made between 'stressors' and 'stress reactions'.

Stressors have been categorised as routine, traumatic and vicarious (Brown, Fielding and Grover, 1999). Routine work stressors tend to include those that are intrinsic to the job (e.g. work overload, time pressures and deadlines); relate to role in organisations (e.g. ambiguity or conflict); to career development (e.g. promotion, job rewards); to relationships at work (e.g. with supervisors, delegation); and to organisational structure and climate (e.g. participation in decision-making, consultation). Specific sources of routine organisational stress look common across criminal justice practitioner groups (Bromley and Blount, 1997). Stress associated with high work loads (especially when demand peaks at times there is much to do with little time for recovery, together with low levels of decision authority), role problems (ambiguity and conflict), and with concerns about career prospects (perceived unfairness in promotion, little recognition and low pay) have been found in research on prison officers (Schaufeli and Peeters, 2000), on police officers (Brown and Campbell, 1990) and on probation staff (Slate, Johnson and Wells, 2000). Changing criminal justice philosophies and institutional practices has exacerbated these problems. Role problems, and low levels of control in decision-making, are predictors of burnout (Schaufeli and Peeters, 2000). While some potential stressors, such as shift work, are part of the contractual features of working within the criminal justice system which requires 24 hour cover, other sources of stress such as poor communication, lack of support, and perceived unfair promotion opportunities are within the province of management practice. Poor or mis-management has been implicated in stress-inducing rather than stress-reducing work environments (Henderson, 1981). Remedial intervention, to alleviate stress, often invokes better management practices such as clarity of purpose, devolved decision-making, and upward-as well as downward-directed communication (Brown and Campbell, 1994; Bromley and Blount, 1997; Schaufeli and Peeters, 2000).

Traumatic stressors tend to be those that are less likely to occur, but may have a high adverse impact when they do. Brown, Fielding and Grover (1999) find operational tasks, which police officers self-report as being highly stressful, include having to deal with the death of a colleague, child or multiple road fatalities, and shooting incidents. The latter is rare in Britain but a more frequent occurrence in jurisdictions where officers are routinely armed (Bromley and Blount, 1997). The psychological effects of being the victim of a shooting incident, or having to shoot someone in the line of duty, have been the subject of considerable research effort in the United States. Stratton, Parker and Shibbe (1984) found about a third of their sample of 60 officers reported severe reactions that included flashbacks, sleep problems and fear of legal proceedings. A low-frequency high-impact stressor that may occur in the prison service is the risk of being taken hostage. A study of 27 hostage victims, by the Correctional Service of Canada (not dated), found that 10 (37%) suffered severe distress and dysfunction. Officers who experienced the longest periods of captivity had symptoms including feelings of powerlessness, shock, fear, and isolation. Hostage survivors also reported feelings of embarrassment, critical reactions from fellow officers and lack of management support. Some survivors felt that they had been inadequately prepared for such incidents and were critical of their management for a lack of preparedness.

Vicarious or secondary stress has been associated with those whose work brings them into contact with victims, where distress spills over to the professional assigned to work with them. Thus specialist police officers working in child protection or with rape victims have been found to suffer flashbacks and intrusive thoughts relating to the victim's trauma which they themselves experience as debilitating (Martin, McKean and Veltkamp, 1986).

Schaufeli and Peeters (2000) have summarised stress reactions or strains as follows: physiological distress (such as heart palpitations, high blood pressure), psychological distress (e.g. job dissatisfaction, burnout, anxiety), and behavioural strains (e.g. quitting job, substance misuse). In addition Wilkinson and Campbell (1997) suggest that stressed individuals may suffer some cognitive impairment in terms of ability to concentrate or organise thoughts. Burnout is considered to be the result of long-term exposure to routinely occurring stressors and particularly occurs in professionals who have intensive interactions with people. Maslach and Leiter (1997) define the evolving stages of burnout and associated states as an imbalance between resources and demands (resulting in the depletion of emotional reserves), and the development of negative attitudes resulting in a detachment from, and cynicism towards, recipients of one's services (depersonalisation). This distancing represents a poor coping adaptation resulting in a cycle of increasing distress and increasing professional effectiveness. Exposure to traumatic incidents may result in post-traumatic stress disorder (PTSD) defined by DSM-IV (APA, 1994) in terms of witnessing, experiencing or being confronted with an event, or events, that involve actual or threatened death or serious injury or threat to the physical integrity of one's self or others. Symptoms after exposure include intense fear, helplessness or horror, recurrent intrusive and disturbing thoughts and images, persistent avoidance of thoughts and feelings regarding that event and increased arousal. Reactions to extended exposure to the distress of others can result in a distinguishable stress reaction termed secondary traumatic stress or secondary victimisation (Figley, 1995). Symptoms such as re-experiencing traumatic material, avoidance of reminders of the traumatic event and persistent arousal, typical in PTSD have been found in police officers (Martin, McKean and Veltkamp, 1986; Brown and Andersen, 2000). Pertinent to legal implications, discussed later, is the notion of proximity to the event and its victims.

Lazarus (1999), in a recent review, argues that the concepts of stress, emotion and coping 'belong together and form a conceptual unit with emotion being the super ordinate concept because it includes stress and coping' (p. 37). This notion has spawned an increasing number of research studies that link stress reactions to emotional intelligence when managing exposure to work stressors (Bar On et al., 1999). They report that police officers scored higher on measures of emotional intelligence and had greater stress tolerance compared with care workers. These findings were thought to be related to aspects of the informal culture of police and care workers' occupations.

As well as extending notions of stress to emotions and occupational cultures, Lazarus (1999) locates the stress experience in an historical and sociocultural context. He argues that a sense of powerlessness, brought on by anomie and/or alienation, plays an important role in motivation, identity and social commitment. This can be translated into ideas about organisational change and the potentially disruptive effects that this may have in managing work demands, especially if the identity of the profession is undergoing transformation as with the increasing professionalisation of those working in criminal justice agencies. Additionally the personal identity of officers may be under threat if they belong to minority groups within the occupation, e.g. gender or ethnic minority. The tensions between occupational socialisation and individuals' attempts to preserve personal identity, if these are counter to the dominant norm of the majority of staff, has been associated with psychological distress (Brown 2000; Wootten and Brown, 2000). In more extreme cases individuals may experience sexual or racial discrimination and harassment, involving grievance procedures and industrial tribunals, with concomitant adverse impacts (Gregory and Lees, 1999).

These ideas resonate with emerging critiques of stress concepts (e.g. Briner, 1997) which argue that stress is not unidimensional and it is usually so ill defined that definitions are unduly simplistic and confound cause and effects with little or no specificity of the pathway between these. He also convincingly argues that stress interventions are often designed in the absence of detailed analysis or evaluation with little understanding of why they may or may not work.

OCCUPATIONAL CULTURE

Organisational and occupational psychologists have begun to examine corporate culture in order to look at success and failure in business practice (Payne, 1991). In a change environment, organisations need time to manage and absorb the change. This requires clear direction from management, good communication and senior staff keeping in touch with grass roots. Callan (cited in Brown and Campbell, 1994) notes that police organisations can use the concept of stress to blame an individual's failure, rather than implicate organisational structures, and seek to indemnify themselves against corporate failures. The case of the Hillsborough football disaster (where many people were killed and injured in the crush of fans attempting to get into a penned area of the stadium) provides an example of the singling out of individuals upon whom to lay blame. It also illustrates some issues with respect to the suffering of PTSD which are discussed later in terms of legal remedies.

The occupational culture of law enforcement has been described as a potentially discriminatory environment for those who belong to minority groups. Analyses have been presented arising from theoretical work of Kanter (1977). Her thesis proposes that distortions in the gender balance of organisations have an impact on opportunities for advancement. In order to foster good communications and stability there is a tendency to appoint similar individuals to senior positions. Thus in organisations which have been historically male dominated, managers will be appointed who share common features, thereby sustaining male (white) hierarchies. This process excludes those who are different (e.g. women, ethnic minorities, homosexuals), from upward mobility and sets up a cycle of lowered motivation and discouragement which inhibits performance, reduces organisational recognition, and limits chances of advancement. Critical to Kanter's argument is the concept of 'token'. This reflects one's status as a symbol of one's kind. Three perceptual phenomena have been identified to account for behaviour of the majority towards tokens: visibility, polarisation and assimilation. The highly visible token will attract a disproportionate share of attention and is susceptible to an exaggeration of difference because the small numbers exacerbate the application of social stereotyping. The generalisations that follow from such stereotyping are made to fit the particular individual. These processes lead to job performance pressures in terms of lack of privacy within the organisation where competence was taken as a measure of the general ability of the person's social category rather than individual achievement. As a consequence tokens may cope by working harder and overachieving or attempting to limit their visibility and avoid risks or controversy. Thus tokens are sensitive to making mistakes, have an exaggerated fear of failure at important tasks or key events, and worry about retaliation by envious dominant group members. Dominants in organisations assert or reclaim group solidarity by exaggerating those occupational symbols and values that differentiate them from the tokens. Parker, Holdaway and Griffin (1998) suggested that harassment of policewomen in the workplace is linked to work performance anxieties. They found an association between harassment, as experienced by women in the police, and heightened work anxiety and psychological distress. For men harassing behaviour was actually associated with positive mental health.

Martin and Jurik (1996) summarise research on discrimination and harassment within police and prison services and find common threads in both environments that are male (and white) dominated. Sexual harassment ranges from outright assault to subtler persistent joking, teasing and name-calling. Women who advance in seniority report blatant forms of resistance to their authority. Women are accused of emotional weakness in that they become over-involved with prisoners or are too fearful to be effective in potentially dangerous situations. They report a number of studies linking these experiences to job-related stress. The irony is that the very weaknesses eschewed by male colleagues are very much the desired attributes of newer human resources orientated approaches which attempt to professionalise police and prison service delivery.

CONTEMPORARY CONTEXT FOR WORKING IN CRIMINAL JUSTICE PRACTICE

In order to make sense of the demands falling on criminal justice practitioners and their capabilities to cope, it is important to present an analysis of the changing environment in which they work. Change, and the management of change, in criminal justice organisations can be stressful in themselves (Audit Commission, 2001). The Commission notes that change can result in adverse impacts on staff morale, difficulties for staff to maintain quality of service delivery whilst responding to new demands, greater levels of public expectation and scrutiny of criminal justice practitioners' actions (Audit Commission, 2001). They comment that senior managers face difficult challenges in managing people and resources. Similar pressures can be found elsewhere. The Correctional Service of Canada (not dated), for example, observe that changes in management principles mean that senior members of staff are expected to manage rather than operate a command and control system. In addition, fiscal restraint and changing gender balance of prison staff have been associated with new job pressures for senior prison managers. Brown, Cooper and Kirkcaldy (1999) document the work pressures on senior police managers at times of change within the British police service.

Both public and private sector working styles and environments have changed somewhat dramatically in recent years. Globalisation of markets, business re-engineering, and customer focus have resulted in new management styles and organisational practices. Criminal justice agencies were later than most organisations to be subjected to such restructuring. Key factors in Britain were the introduction, in the 1980s, of new public sector management, the citizens' charter, and the establishment of the Audit Commission as an external agency to carry out best value inspections, and often from the user's perspective. Brown, Cooper and Kirkcaldy (1999) review the progress of the British police service in this regard. Organisational innovations have resulted in significant changes to traditional management practices within the police service such as variable working hours, proactive management of sickness absence, active pursuit of equal opportunities policies, introduction of part-time working and job-sharing arrangements.

The Prison Service in Britain faced similar radical changes. And these are not unique to Britain (Schaufeli and Peeters, 2000). They suggest that, underpinning much of the change occurring with this sector, was a demand for a more sophisticated professionalisation of the role of prison officers throughout liberal democracies in the Western world. They note the following pressures within the prison system: growing size and changing composition of inmate populations; increase in the numbers of drug addicts, mentally ill and aggressive prisoners; introduction of a new raft of rehabilitation programmes; liberalisation of regimes for prisoners, such as conjugal visits and access to telephones; introduction of new treatment specialists, such as forensic psychologist managing sex offender treatment programmes; middle level supervision and new career structures within the service; better educated officers; financial cutbacks and reduction of staff.

LEGAL REMEDIES

Legal Remedies as a Result of Being Involved in a Single Life-Threatening Situation

In the absence of specific legislation relating to a possible claim for PTSD which the employee alleges was caused while at work, we must turn to the common law for assistance. The tort of negligence is essentially concerned with compensating people who suffer from the careless acts (or sometimes omissions) of others. It does not provide a remedy, however, for everyone who suffers loss. Negligence liability will only arise where the law provides that the defendant owed the claimant a duty of care (*Donoghue* v. *Stevenson*, 1932). In many cases the fact the claimant owes the defendant a duty of care will be beyond argument, for example in the case of the employer and employee relationship. Perhaps what is more problematic is for the employee to prove that his or her employer has breached that legal duty, by falling below the appropriate standard of care, and that it was the employer's negligent act or omission which caused the damage to the employee.

Claims can be made if the damage was psychological, rather than physical, resulting in a psychiatric illness. The courts have, nevertheless, been cautious in awarding compensation for psychiatric damage for several reasons. First, in the past, psychiatric illness or injury was not properly described, so there could be no duty if the type of damage concerned was not recognised. Second, there was a fear that a person making such a claim could actually be faking the symptoms (*Hevicane* v. *Ruane*, 1991). Third, there was the 'floodgates' argument, that once one claim was accepted it would lead to a multitude of claims (*Victoria Railway Commissioners* v. *Coultas*, 1888). Fourth, the difficulty of assessing the 'injury' in financial terms, although the courts have always seemed to cope with assessing physical injuries. Finally, the difficulty of proving that the defendant's negligent act *caused* the claimant's psychiatric damage (*Bourhill* v. *Young*, 1943).

Notwithstanding initial reservations, the courts are now more willing to recognise that despite the fact the claimant has actually suffered no physical injury, a defendant may be liable for the 'pure' psychiatric injury caused to the claimant (*Page* v. *Smith*, 1996).

That said there appears to be two important aspects to determine whether liability should be imposed. First, the injury alleged must be a recognised psychiatric disorder that is more than a claim purely for a temporary upset such as grief or distress or fright from which we all suffer at times (*Hinz* v. *Berry*, 1970; cf. *Tredget* v. *Bexley Health Authority*, 1994). Examples of psychiatric illness would include: clinical depression, personality changes, PTSD. Second, the person claiming the psychiatric harm must fall within a category accepted by the courts as being entitled to claim. This latter restriction may present difficulties for the 'professional' rescuer, such as a police officer, as we shall see shortly.

Those who have duties of care, for example employers, will know, or be able to discover, those to whom they owe a duty, their employees. But they do not, similarly, know who will come to the rescue if there is a problem for which they are responsible. But it has been established that a rescuer will be able to recover compensation when suffering from psychiatric harm. However, such cases can be largely explained on the basis that the rescuer was a *primary victim* and as such at risk of being injured (*Chadwick* v. *British Railways Board*, 1967; cf. *Duncan* v. *British Coal*, 1990). Usually only professional rescuers will be able to claim if present at the scene of the accident. Such was the case in *Hale* v. *London Underground* (1992) where a fireman claimed successfully for PTSD he suffered following the Kings Cross fire. However, claims for psychiatric damage suffered at the scene of a disaster will not be successful in the case of those people who are not directly involved in the rescue but are merely described as bystanders (*McFarlane* v. *E.E. Caledonia*, 1994).

The House of Lords, the most senior appeal court in the UK, does appear to be hostile towards claims by the emergency services for psychiatric injury suffered while in the course of their duty in the aftermath of a disaster. In *Alcock* v. *Chief Constable of South Yorkshire* (1992) the House of Lords had the opportunity to review the law in this area and to identify restricted circumstances in which a claim can succeed. This was the Hillsborough football disaster. A number of claims for psychiatric harm were made from a variety of people. Some were present at the incident and others had family or friends at the football grounds. The House of Lords refused all claims and identified factors that must be present in determining whether an individual could recover compensation. These were: the proximity in time and space to the negligent incident; the proximity of the relationship with the party who was a victim of the incident (this will depend on the existence of a close tie of love and affection with the victim), or presence at the scene as a rescuer and the cause of the psychiatric harm being a result of witnessing or hearing the horrifying event or the immediate aftermath.

The *Alcock* (1992) case identifies the classes of claimant who will be successful. Primary victims are those present at the scene and themselves injured—this injury can be either physical, psychological or both (*McFarlane* v. *E.E. Caledonia*, 1994). Alternatively, it would cover those who were present at the scene and their own safety was threatened (*Dulieu* v. *White & Sons*, 1901). Secondary victims are those who are not primary victims of the accident but who are able to show a close enough tie of 'love and affection' to a victim and witnessed the accident or its immediate aftermath.

Such ties would include parents and children. Rescuers may well be primary victims and themselves at risk as in the case of the fireman who suffered from PTSD as a result of the Kings Cross fire.

A fairly recent decision indicates that the courts continue to be hostile towards claims made by the emergency services, who merely deal with the aftermath of a disaster in the course of their duty, and who are later psychologically harmed. In *White* v. *Chief Constable of South Yorkshire* (1998) police officers who claimed to have suffered PTSD following their part in the rescue operation at the Hillsborough disaster were denied a remedy by the House of Lords (by a majority). The reasons appear to be two-fold. First, the police officers did not actually put themselves at risk (i.e. primary victims); these police officers dealt with the dying and injured on the pitch. Second, public policy dictates that it would be unfair for them to recover damages when relatives of the victims could not. The House of Lords added that police officers at Hillsborough were not entitled to damages for psychiatric illness, merely by virtue of their status as employees of the negligent defendant. Nor were those who merely assisted in the aftermath to be seen as rescuers.

Lord Steyn, referring to the policy argument in *White* (1998), felt that it was a 'weighty moral argument: the police perform their duties for the benefit of all of us' (p. 1545). He felt the difficulty was two-fold. First, the pragmatic rules governing the recovery of damages for pure psychiatric harm do not at present include police officers who sustain such injury while on duty. If such a category were to be created by judicial decision, he said, the new principle would be available in many different situations, for example, doctors and hospital workers who are exposed to the sight of grievous injuries and suffering. This is a powerful 'floodgates' argument and the House is thus indicating the importance of keeping some kind of restriction on this area. The second point made by Lord Steyn was that police officers traumatised by such encounters as Hillsborough had the benefit of statutory schemes that permit them to retire on a pension. In this sense, he said, they were already better off than bereaved relatives who were not allowed to recover in the *Alcock* (1992) case. The *White* (1998) case altered the position taken in the earlier case of *Frost* v. *Chief Constable of South Yorkshire* (1997) where 14 police officers shared £1.2 million damages for the mental trauma of trying to save fans from the crush. The difference in *Frost* being that the police officers were, in effect, *primary victims* and in possible danger themselves whereas in the above case they were 'merely' assisting the injured on the pitch and in no direct danger themselves.

Another chapter of the Hillsborough disaster unfolded in March 2001. It was reported that a retired police officer, Mr Long, who claimed he began suffering PTSD nine years *after* the Hillsborough disaster, received an out-of-court settlement of £330 000. Mr Long helped to rescue fans trapped in the crush on that fateful day. He successfully sued the police on the grounds that he suffered *delayed* PTSD, his argument being that PTSD did not have to be immediate. This argument was accepted. This case is not dissimilar to the *Frost* case above in that here, Mr Long had been 'actively involved in rescuing trapped fans' as opposed to assisting with the injured. Nevertheless, such a claim has raised further reaction from the families of victims who were not entailed to claim. While every sympathy is to be given to officers and their families it could be argued, in line with Lords Steyn and Hoffmann, that Mr Long has been given 'appropriate benefits' in the form of an enhanced pension. (See also *R* v. *(1) Joy Madeline Court (2) Dr Ian G Bronks, ex parte Derbyshire Police Authority* (1994), where it was held that psychological stress caused as a result of events which occurred in the course of a police officer's work was capable of amounting to an injury. It entitled the police officer to an award of a pension under the Police Pensions Regulations 1987.)

Calls for reform of the law in this area have made been made amid much criticism. One of the main focuses of criticism (e.g. Stephenson, 2000, p. 250) has been on the severe barriers to recovery placed by the heavy-handed proximity requirements facing *secondary victims*. These requirements it will be recalled are stated in the *Alcock* case above. Todd (1999) finds that the law is 'in a dreadful mess' (p. 349). Even Lord Hoffmann in *White* (1998) said: 'the search for principle in this area of the law has been called off' (p. 1557). The argument now has to be that, if there are to be any further changes to the law in this area, it should be up to Parliament to make those changes and not the judges. The Law Commission (1988), a statutory law reform agency, saw no need for legislation specifically dealing with the entitlement of employees to recover damages for psychiatric illness suffered as a result of death, injury or imperilment of another (paragraph 7.10).

Legal Remedies as a Result of Being Involved in a Series of Incidents at Work

Here we examine two separate situations. First, where the victim is saying he or she is suffering stress as a direst result of work pressure or other work-related reason; second, where the victim of harassment and/or bullying at work claims they are suffering from stress as a direct result. As previously mentioned, there is no specific legislation on controlling or preventing stress at work, nevertheless, employers do have legal duties under both statutory and common law. Employers have a statutory duty under section 2(1) the Health and Safety at Work, etc., Act 1974 to ensure, so far as is reasonably practicable, that their workplaces are safe and healthy. Further, Regulation 3 of the Management of Health and Safety at Work Regulations 1999, requires employers to make a suitable and sufficient assessment of health and safety risks in order to identify the preventative and protective measures necessary to reduce them. These assessments must be kept under review. These regulations apply to occupational stress, so assessments must take stress into account. Although not explicitly stated, the employer's duty to protect employees' health extends to both physical and psychological health and when identifying hazards in the workplace the employer should include causes of stress. In other words, stress should be treated like any other health hazard.

Working long hours and shift work are both clearly linked to stress. The Working Time Regulations 1988 (as amended) cover these issues. Their provisions entitle most workers to:

- a 48-hour ceiling on the maximum average working week (Reg. 4(1) and (2));

- a ceiling on night workers' normal hours of an average of eight hours in every 24 (Reg. 6(1) and (2));

- an absolute eight-hour ceiling for hazardous night work (Reg. 6(7));

- a daily rest period of 11 hours (Reg. 10 (1) and weekly rest periods (Reg.11(1) and (2));

- a rest break of 20 minutes after six hours of work (Reg 12(1)); and

- paid annual leave of four weeks (Regs. 13 and 16).

The regulations, which came into force on 1 October 1998 as a result of a European Directive, impose legal obligations on employers. They are enforceable by the Health and Safety Executive on local authorities. The regulations also establish rights for eligible workers that can be pursued through the employment tribunal system (Reg. 20). Workers can, however, opt out of the 48-hour maximum. Some sectors are specifically excluded, under Regulation 18, from almost all of the regulations. The civil protection services are among those excluded, and that would include the police and prison service. So it would seem that these two services are not protected by the regulations. The Safety Representatives and Safety Committees Regulations 1977 give safety representatives extensive legal rights to investigate and tackle workplace stress. They have rights to investigate potential hazards, inspect the workplace, take up members' health and safety complaints, and are consulted by the employer about health and safety matters. Additionally, they can conduct membership surveys to build up awareness at work and reveal the extent of the problem. Inspectors can be charged to identify the causes of stress.

Under the common law employers have a legal duty of care to their employers to make sure they are reasonably safe at work and to ensure that health is not placed at risk through excessive and sustained levels of stress arising from, for example, the way work is organised. Employers should have a coherent policy, which takes account of the way work is organised, working conditions, the working environment and any relevant social factors. Employers had been aware that they may be sued by employees for causing them physical injury while at work. However, it was not until the case of *Walker* v. *Northumberland County Council* (1995) that it was confirmed that they also have a duty of care for their employees' psychiatric well being. In other words, they may be liable for a stress-related illness due to conditions in the workplace sometimes known as 'occupational stress'. Mr Walker successfully sued his former employer for breaching their duty by failing to take reasonable precautions to avoid the claimant suffering a health endangering workload. He had suffered two breakdowns. The first was not caused by a breach of the defendant's duty of care as it was not, at that stage, reasonably foreseeable that Mr Walker's workload would give rise to a material risk of mental illness. However the second breakdown was caused by his employers' breach of duty to provide a safe system of work, and protect him from an unnecessary risk of injury, which was now reasonably foreseeable. Clearly the court had no doubt that the employers should have foreseen that there was a serious risk that Mr Walker would suffer mental illness if again exposed to the same or indeed heavier workload as before. The County Council decided not to proceed with their appeal against the decision in the High Court and Mr Walker was awarded around £175 000 in an out-of-court settlement. (See also *Johnstone* v. *Bloomsbury Health Authority*, 1992.)

It should, however, be remembered that the law requires reasonable care and not *all* possible care of employees. In reality the circumstances where an employee can bring a successful claim of this sort are and have been fairly limited. The Court of Session, in Scotland, has provided useful clarification of the limits for personal injury claims for stress. In *Rorrison* v. *West Lothian College and Lothian Regional Council* (1999) a nurse was, allegedly, subjected to a campaign of sustained bullying by her line manager. As a result she suffered anxiety and depression. She had six weeks off work and when she returned to work the bullying continued. She suffered further symptoms of stress. Ms Rorrison argued, following the *Walker* (1995) case, that while she did not have a psychiatric illness she had suffered two 'nervous breakdowns' and that this was sufficient injury upon which to base her personal injury. The Court disagreed. It held that there was a distinct difference between a nervous breakdown and a psychiatric illness. To bring a claim it had to be shown that the applicant was suffering from a condition which is recognised in the *Diagnostic and Statistical Manual of Mental Disorders* (either DSM-III or DSM-IV (APA, 1994)) or its international equivalent, the World Health Organisation's *International Classification of Diseases* (ICD-10). Ms Rorrison failed to show that her illness fell into either of these categories.

Janet Leach v. *Chief Constable of Gloucestershire Constabulary* (1999) concerned an appeal against a claim for compensation which had been struck out as improper. Janet Leach, in 1994, was a voluntary worker on a Young Homeless Project in Cheltenham. The police asked her to attend interviews of a murder suspect. As the suspect was thought to be mentally disordered the Code of Practice for police interviewing (issued under section 66 of the Police and Criminal Evidence Act 1984) required that he had an 'appropriate adult' with him in the interview room. Janet Leach was only told that the suspect was aged 52. In fact he was Frederick West and this was the beginning of the discovery that he was a notorious, sadistic, serial murderer. Janet Leach acted as the appropriate adult for West for many weeks, accompanying the investigating officer and suspect to murder scenes and on several occasions was left alone in a locked cell with him. She alleged negligence in that, *inter alia*, she was not warned of what the case involved nor given counselling or support until West committed suicide in custody. She claimed to be suffering from PTSD and psychological injury, as well as a stroke, as a result of her experiences. The Court of Appeal had to decide a number of issues, not least whether a duty of care was owed to Janet Leach. Initially the Court said that the police had created a situation in which it was foreseeable that Janet Leach would be subject to the risk of psychiatric injury. In such circumstances the police assume responsibility to Janet Leach in the inevitably stressful situation in which they placed her and the element of proximity was established. However, the Court went on to say a duty of care could not be established on the grounds alleged. Such a concept, it said, should not be extended to cover a given case, if the result of so doing would hamper the operations of the police. It was for Parliament, or the House of Lords, to create a new category of duty of care in those circumstances. Being an appropriate adult was an unpaid task, not a contractual obligation. There was no requirement to pre-select or warn appropriate adults as to the nature of the case. They could withdraw at any time. Lord Justice Pill, dissenting, considered that it was fair, just and reasonable that the law should impose an unrestricted duty of care on police in respect of a member of the public of whom they had requested that kind of assistance.

Bullying/Harassment at Work and Stress

While there is no legal framework in place dealing specifically with bullying at work, we do have legislation that deals with sexual or racial harassment. Bullying at work can be linked to sexual or racial harassment, or indeed a person's disability, so the victim could claim under the Sex Discrimination Act 1975, Race Relation Act 1996 or Disability Discrimination Act 1995. There appears to be no reason why a victim of overwork, and thereby suffering from a stress-related illness as in the *Walker* (1995) case, cannot also make a claim against his or her employer for the stress suffered as a result of harassment/bullying. In other words, there is no reason why a breakdown suffered as a result of bullying/harassment at work should be treated any differently to a breakdown as a result of overwork.

It was said in *Alexander* v. *The Home Office* (1988), in the Court of Appeal, that in discrimination cases damages for injury to feelings should reflect compensation for the consequences of discrimination and that it should not be minimal. This head of damages is in additional to other awards. Record compensation for injury to feeling of £100 000 together with an additional sum of £25 000 for aggravated damages was awarded to an Asian police officer discriminated against on grounds of sex (*Virdi* v. *The Commissioner of Police of the Metropolis* (Case no. 2202774/98)). *LSM* v. *Royal Navy* (Case no. 55542/95) involved a woman sailor, in the Royal Navy, who had been sexually assaulted, forced to mimic oral sex, and bullied. She suffered clinical depression. She received an award of £65 377. The industrial tribunal said £25 000 was awarded 'for injury to feelings, for humiliation and stress suffered, an element relating to the personal injury arising from the harassment in the form of depression, and an element for the loss of congenial employment'. A further example of an award for injury to feelings can be found in *Armitage, Marsden and HM Prison Service* v. *Johnson* (1997) where it was argued that an auxiliary prison officer, at Brixton Prison, was ostracised and subjected to racist remarks by fellow prison officers. He was awarded £21 000 compensation for injury to feelings.

What is the situation when the employer fails to deal with complaints from a victim or does not properly deal with a complaint? In the *Armitage* (1997) case an additional sum of £7500 was awarded because of the poor way in which the employers investigated the complaint. Indeed in *Hatrick* v. *City Fax* (COIT 3041/138) the industrial tribunal said that the employer's failure to act on a complaint was a fundamental breach of contract entitling the victim to resign and claim constructive dismissal.

In *Waters* v. *Commissioner of Police of the Metropolis* (2000) a woman police officer alleged that she had been raped and buggered in her police residential accommodation by a fellow officer when they were both off duty. In the proceedings she alleged that her complaint had not been dealt with properly by her superiors. They had allowed other officers to harass, victimise 'and otherwise oppress her' and that she had suffered psychiatric injury as a result. Her claim had been struck out, so she appealed. The House of Lords decided that it should not have been struck out. Lord Slynn said:

> I do not find it possible to say . . . that this is a plain and obvious cases that (a) no duty analogous to an employer's duty can exist; (b) that the injury to the appellant was not foreseeable; and (c) that the acts alleged could not be the *cause* of the damage. As to the last of these I accept that many of the individual items taken in isolation are at the least very unlikely to have caused the illness alleged, the appellant's case puts much emphasis on the cumulative effect of what happened under the system as it existed. (p. 938)

This latter comment is sometimes know as the 'last straw' whereby bullying consists of a series of incidents which, although trivial in themselves, the insidious behaviour is carefully calculated to undermine or humiliate the employee over a period of time. Case law has established that individual actions taken by an employer, which do not in themselves constitute fundamental breaches of any contractual term, may nevertheless have the cumulative effect of undermining trust and confidence. That could entitle the employee to resign and claim constructive dismissal (*Garner* v. *Grange Furnishings Ltd.*, 1977; *Wright* v. *Holt Jackson Book Co. Ltd.*, 1985; *Hatrick* v. *City Fax*, COIT 3141/138).

The *Waters* (2000) case raises the issues of vicarious liability and causation. Vicarious liability is where one person is liable (usually) for the torts of another, even though the former does not have the primary liability, i.e. is not at fault. Employers are liable for the torts of their employees, providing the employees are acting 'within the course of their employment'. Will the employer also be liable for the acts of harassment or bullying by one of his or her employees against a fellow employee? The interpretation by the courts to the phrase 'course of employment' is wide. If an employer can show that the act(s) complained of are outside the employee's course of employment, then the employer will not be vicariously liable for the acts of the employee. This means that the employee will be personally liable. But will an employer be responsible for the acts of an employee that are performed *outside* working hours and not 'in the workplace'? Should the employer, in *Waters* (2000), be responsible for a criminal act (alleged rape and buggery) committed outside work hours and off work premises? The industrial tribunal, Employment Appeals Tribunal and Court of Appeal all agreed that the alleged assault was not committed 'in the course of employment' since both parties were off duty. Therefore the employer would not be vicariously liable. The tribunals and court are thus placing limits on the employer's liability for acts of harassment. Employers can avoid vicarious liability, in relation to sex or racial discrimination, if they 'took such steps as were reasonably practicable to prevent the employee from doing that act or from doing in the course of his employment acts of that description' (section 32(3) Race Relations Act 1976 and section 41(3) of the Sex Discrimination Act 1995).

A further issue is causation. Simply put, did being bullied or harassed at work, cause the victim to suffer stress and thereby trigger or precipitate the mental breakdown or other psychiatric illness complained of? The issue of causation arose in *R* v. *Dr A.M.P. Kellam, ex parte South Wales Police Authority & Paul Julian Milton* (*Interested Party*) (2000). The question to be decided was whether a psychiatric illness to a serving police officer was an injury received in the execution of 'police duty', for the purposes of regulations A11(1) and A11(2) of Police Regulations 1987. Here M. went on sick leave in July 1996 suffering from anxiety and stress and was retired on grounds of ill health. In April 1997 the Force Medical Officer, in respect of M.'s illness, issued a certificate of permanent disablement under the 1987 Regulations. The certificate found that M. was made permanently incapable of carrying out police duties, but that the disablement was not a result of any injury received in the execution of his duty as a police officer. M. appealed. He argued that his depression started when his wife (also a police officer) had problems at work and he was supporting her, but his depression was largely to do with subsequent treatment by other officers he received at work. Was there was a direct causal connection between the injury and M.'s duty as a police officer? The Court held that the correct test to apply was whether the person's injury 'is directly and causally connected with his service as a police officer' (see also *Garvin* v. *Police Authority for City of London*, 1944 and *Police Authority for Huddersfield* v. *Watson*, 1967). This related to 'work circumstances' as well as operational duties and the Court was of the opinion that it was sufficient to find a causal connection with events experienced by the officer at work, which included the things said or done by his colleagues. It was not necessary to establish the work circumstances as the *sole* cause of the injury as long as the work circumstances had a causative role.

In *Commissioner of Police* v. *Stunt* (2000), the Court of Appeal held that a police officer could not claim a gratuity and injury pension after retiring as a result of a permanently disabling psychiatric injury. It was suffered in reaction to disciplinary proceedings brought against him. Such proceedings were 'not part of the execution of his duty'. The Court, referring to *R* v. *Dr A.M.P. Kellam* (2000), said that police officers, whose depressive illness developed from the accumulated stresses of work, qualified for an award provided that their ultimately disabling mental state had been materially brought about by stresses suffered through actually being at work. Stunt's psychiatric injury did not result from the execution of duty, rather, it was caused through the exposure to disciplinary proceedings.

CONCLUSIONS—THE WAY FORWARD

What emerges from this review, of previously disparate literature, is the clear message that work-related stress represents a huge problem for both employer and employee. Evidence shows us that it is now the second largest occupational health problem in the

UK, after back pain (Smith et al., 2000). In addition to the detrimental health effects on the individual, stress has a financial and economic impact on the employer through illness of their employees, poor productivity and so on. We have seen some of the causes of stress at work, through long hours, bullying, and harassment or through a one-off major disaster.

While there is no specific legislation relating to stress in the workplace, however caused, employers do have legal duties under both statute law and the common law to their employees to make sure they are reasonably safe while at work. This duty extends beyond physical safety and includes the mental well-being of the employee. Indeed even if there was specific legislation the question remains: Would any laws actually prevent work-related stress? Probably not. More importantly perhaps is the issue as to how employers can prevent and tackle work-related stress.

The Health and Safety Executive (HSE) has produced a number of guides on stress and states the importance of employers in assessing the risk of stress at work (HSE, not dated, and 1995). The Trades Union Congress (TUC) emphasises that the key to the implementation of a stress at work policy is risk assessment. First then, the employer should undertake a risk assessment of the workplace. Indeed every employer has a legal duty, under the Management of Health and Safety at Work Regulations 1999 (Reg. 3), to make a suitable and sufficient assessment of the risks to the health and safety of their employees, to which they are exposed while at work, so that they can introduce the appropriate preventive and protective measures. The Labour Research Department (2002) provides a useful checklist (*Tackling Stress at Work*) of the kind of things an employer should consider when undertaking this assessment. Following on from this is to implement a 'stress policy'. There are a number of model stress policies from various trade unions. This would include procedures for complaining about, say, incidents of bullying or harassment, both informal and formal, emphasising that confidentiality is guaranteed. Any policy should be monitored and kept under review and above all communicated effectively to all employees.

Further guidance from the HSE outlines several points of 'good management', which should be followed to prevent stress from becoming a problem. Indeed the best way to protect employees from stress and stress-related illnesses is good management. As the HSE points out 'ordinary plain good management and regard for people may well be as effective a way of dealing with stress and reducing its effects as a high profile approach to stress such as a company stress programme' (HSE, 1995, p. 10). Employers should take stress seriously and understand when people say they are under too much pressure. They should ensure that people are treated fairly and consistently and that bullying and harassment are not tolerated. In short, there is a number of positive actions an employer can do to prevent stress occurring in the first place and if it does occur to respond effectively and efficiently to the problem.

In the absence of specific laws on stress would a Code of Practice suffice? An approved code of practice may be introduced in the next few years. A consultation exercise has been carried out between the HSC and the HSE with the HSC asking the HSE to develop standards of management practice for controlling work-related stressors. At this time no approved code of practice has emerged.

To conclude, workplace stress is not going to be eliminated merely by passing legislation or having workable policies in the organisation. A thorough analysis of the sources of stress- and evidence-based stress management interventions will help to alleviate this problem in the workplace.

[*Editor's comment*—After this chapter was submitted the Court of Appeal, in London, issued an important judgement. Four cases, concerning employers' liability for employee's psychiatric illness caused by stress at work, were brought together (*Sutherland v. Hatton* [2002] 2 All ER 1]. It has made the tests stricter. Injury to the specific person must now be reasonably foreseeable. That would require study of the individual's characteristics and the job. Relevant factors for the employer to consider include the nature and extent of the work (with employers being more alert where jobs are intellectually or emotionally demanding), and the employee's behaviour. Employers could, in the absence of being told otherwise, assume that employees could cope and did not need to make searching enquiries. Employees returning to work, after sickness breaks, could be assumed to be fit but uncharacteristic regular or long illness breaks could put them on guard. The employer's duty to act arose when it would be plain to any reasonable employer that there were problems. When deciding what the employer should do, account should be taken of the size and scope of the business as well as available resources.]

REFERENCES

APA (1994). *Diagnostic and statistical manual of mental disorders* (4th edn; DSM-IV). Washington, DC: American Psychiatric Association.

Audit Commission (2001). *A change of direction: Managing changes in local probation areas.* London: HMSO.

Bar On, R., Brown, J.M., Kirkcaldy, B.D. and Thome, E.P. (1999). Emotional expression and implications for occupational stress: an application of the Emotional Quotient Inventory (EQ-I). *Personality and Individual Differences, 28*, 1107–1118.

Briner, R. (1997). Improving stress assessment: Toward an evidence based approach to organizational stress interventions. *Journal of Psychosomatic Research, 43*, 61–71.

Bromley, M.L. and Blount, W. (1997). Criminal justice practitioners. In W.S. Hutchison and W.G. Emenor (eds), *Employee assistance programs* (2nd edn). Springfield, IL: Charles C. Thomas.

Brown, J.M. (2000). Occupational culture as a factor in the stress of police officers. In F. Leishman, B. Loveday and S. Savage (eds), *Core issues in policing* (2nd edn). Addison Wesley.

Brown, J.M. and Andersen, K. (2000). Adapting a compassion fatigue questionnaire to measure vicarious stress in a sample of police officers. *Forensic Update, 62*, 6–11.

Brown, J.M. and Campbell, E.A. (1990). Sources of occupational stress in the police. *Work and Stress, 4*, 305–318.

Brown, J.M. and Campbell, E.A. (1994). *Stress and policing: Sources and strategies.* Chichester: John Wiley & Sons.

Brown, J., Cooper, C. and Kirkcaldy, B. (1996). Occupational stress among senior police officers. *British Journal of Psychology*, *87*, 31–41.

Brown, J.M., Cooper, C. and Kirkcaldy, B.D. (1999). Stressor exposure and methods of coping among senior police managers at time of organisational change. *International Journal of Police Science and Management*, *2*, 217–228.

Brown, J.M., Fielding, J. and Grover, J. (1999). Distinguishing traumatic, vicarious and routine operational stressor exposure and attendant adverse consequences in a sample of police officers *Work and Stress*, *13*, 312–325.

Correctional Service of Canada (n.d.). *Hostage taking of CSC staff: Psychological and institutional management* (www.csc-scc.gc.ca/text/pblct/sexoffender/hostage/toc_e.shtml).

Figley, C. (1995). Compassion fatigue as secondary traumatic stress: An overview. In C. Figley (ed.), *Compassion fatigue: Coping with secondary traumatic stress disorder in those who treat the traumatized*. New York: Brunner Mazel.

Gregory, J. and Lees, S. (1999). *Policing sexual assault*. London: Routledge.

Henderson, G. (1981). *Police human relations*. Springfield, IL: Charles C. Thomas.

HSE (n.d.). *Five steps to risk assessment*. London: Health and Safety Executive.

HSE (1995). *Stress at work*. London: Health and Safety Executive.

Kanter, R. (1977). Some effects of proportions on group life: Skewed sex ratios and response to token women. *American Journal of Sociology*, *82*, 965–990.

Labour Research Department (2002). *Tackling stress at work*. London: Trades Union Congress.

Law Commission (1988). *Liability for psychiatric illness*. London: HMSO (Law Com. No. 249).

Lazarus, R.S. (1966). *Psychological stress and the coping process*. New York: McGraw-Hill.

Lazarus, R.S. (1999). *Stress and emotion*: *A new synthesis*. London: Free Association Books.

Martin, C.A., McKean, H.E. and Veltkamp, L.J. (1986). Post traumatic stress disorder in police and working with victims; a pilot study. *Journal of Police Science and Administration*, *14*, 98–101.

Martin, S.E. and Jurik, N. (1996). *Doing justice, doing gender*: *Women in law enforcement and criminal justice occupations*. Thousand Oaks: Sage.

Maslach, C. and Leiter, M.P. (1997). *The truth about burnout. How organisations cause personnel stress and what to do about it*. San Francisco: Jossey-Bass.

Parker, S.K., Holdaway, S. and Griffin, M.A. (1998). Why does harassment cause distress? The mediating role of work performance anxiety. Paper presented to First International Conference of Institute of Work Psychology. July.

Payne, R. (1991). Taking stock of corporate culture. *Personnel Management*, July 26–29.

Schaufeli, W.B. and Peeters, M.C. (2000). Job stress and burnout among correctional officers: A literature review. *International Journal of Stress Management*, *7*, 19–47.

Stratton, J.G., Parker, D.A. and Shibbe, J.R. (1984). Post traumatic Stress: Study of police officers involved in shootings. *Psychological Reports*, *55*, 127–131.

Slate, R.N., Johnson, W.W. and Wells, T.L. (2000). Probation officer stress. Is there an organizational issue'? *Federal Probation*, *64*, 56–59.

Smith, A., Brice, C., Collins, A. Matthews, V. and McNamara, R. (2000). *The scale of occupational stress*: *A further analysis of the impact of demographic factors and type of job*. Contract Research Report 311/2000. Cardiff: Centre for Occupational and Health Psychology Cardiff University.

Stephenson, G. (2000). *Sourcebook on torts*. London: Cavendish Publishing Ltd.

Todd, S. (1999). Psychiatric injury and rescuers. 115 *Law Quarterly Review*, 345.

Wilkinson, J.D. and Campbell, E.A. (1997). *Psychology in counselling and therapeutic practice*. Chichester: John Wiley & Sons.

Wootten, I. and Brown, J.M. (2000). Balancing occupational and personal identities: The experience of lesbian and gay police officers. *BPS Lesbian and Gay psychology Section Newsletter*, *4*, 6–13.

Cases

Alexander v. *The Home Office* [1988] IRLR 190
Alcock v. *Chief Constable of South Yorkshire* [1992] 4 All ER 907
Armitage, Marsden and HM Prison Service v. *Johnson* [1997] IRLR 162
Bourhill v. *Young* [1943] AC 92
Chadwick v. *British Railways Board* [1967] 1 WLR 912
Commissioner of Police v. *Stunt* (Case no. C/2000/2242)
Donoghue v. *Stevenson* [1932] AC 562
Dulieu v. *White and Sons* [1901] 2 KB 669
Duncan v. *British Coal* [1990] 1 All ER 540
Frost v. *Chief Constable of South Yorkshire* [1997] 1 All ER 1036
Garner v. *Grange Furnishings Ltd.* [1977] IRLR 297
Garvin v. *Police Authority for City of London* [1944] 1 KB 358
Hale v. *London Underground* [1992] 11 BMLR 81
Hatrick v. *City Fax* (COIT 3041/138)
Hevicane v. *Ruane* [1991] 3 All ER 65
Hinz v. *Berry* [1970] 2 QB 40
Irving & Another v. *The Post Office* [1995] IRLR 529
Janet Leach v. *Chief Constable of Gloucestershire Constabulary* [1999] 1 WLR 1421
Johnstone v. *Bloomsbury Health Authority* [1992] QB 333
LSM v. *Royal Navy* (Case no. 55542/95)
McFarlane v. *E.E. Caledonia* [1994] 2 All ER 1
Page v. *Smith* [1996] 3 All ER 372
Police Authority for Huddersfield v. *Watson* [1967] 1 KB 842
R v. *Dr A.M.P. Kellam, ex parte South Wales Police Authority & Paul Julian Milton (Interested Party)* (2000) ICR 632
R v. *(1) Joy Madeline Court (2) Dr Ian G Bronks, ex parte Derbyshire Police Authority* [1994]
Rorrison v. *West Lothian College and Lothian Regional Council* [2000] IDS 655
Tredget v. *Bexley Health Authority* [1994] 5 Med. LR 178
Victoria Railway Commissioners v. *Coultas* [1888] 13 App. Cas. 222
Virdi v. *The Commissioner of Police of the Metropolis* (Case no. 2202774/98)
Walker v. *Northumberland County Council* [1995] IRLR 35
Waters v. *Commissioner of Police of the Metropolis* [2000] 4 All ER 934
White v. *Chief Constable of South Yorkshire* [1998] 3 WLR 1509
Wright v. *Holt Jackson Book Co Ltd.* [1985] IRLR 465

Legislation

Disability Discrimination Act 1995
Health and Safety at Work, etc., Act 1974
Management of Health and Safety at Work Regulations 1999 (SI 1999/ 3242)
Police and Criminal Evidence Act 1984
Police Regulations 1987
Race Relation Acts 1996
Safety Representatives and Safety Committees Regulations 1977 (SI 1977/500)
Sex Discrimination Act 1975
Working Time Regulations 1988 (SI 1988/ 833)

Chapter 4.6

Therapeutic Jurisprudence: An Invitation to Social Scientists

Carrie J. Petrucci
California State University Long Beach
Bruce J. Winick
University of Miami School of Law, Coral Gables, Florida, USA
and
David B. Wexler
University of Arizona, USA and University of Puerto Rico, Puerto Rico

Therapeutic jurisprudence—the study of the role of the law as a therapeutic agent—is a vehicle for bringing mental health insights into the development of law. (For a full description and explanation of the theory and application of therapeutic jurisprudence, see: Wexler, 1990; Wexler and Winick, 1991, 1996; and Winick, 1997b.) Therapeutic jurisprudence began in the late 1980s and grew out of mental health law, which is the body of law designed to deal with people with serious mental illness. Mental health law has traditionally been concerned with issues such as voluntary and involuntary hospitalization standards and procedures and the right to refuse treatment. Considered to be one of the most important influences on mental health law (Perlin, 2000), therapeutic jurisprudence has since grown to become a truly interdisciplinary enterprise that has emerged as a broad-based approach for examining law generally. It proposes that we explore ways in which, consistent with the principles of justice, the knowledge, theories, and insights of mental health and related disciplines can help to shape the development of the law (Wexler, 1994). Therapeutic jurisprudence provides a useful framework for generating law and policy-relevant questions for empirical research. It integrates psychological theory to frame proposals for improving law's functioning by diminishing antitherapeutic outcomes and improving emotional well-being. It is an interdisciplinary approach to legal scholarship and law reform that is increasingly international in character (Tomkins and Carson, 1999, 2000). A recent therapeutic jurisprudence conference emphasized its connections with a myriad of fields and disciplines, including mental health law, criminal law, problem-solving courts, children's issues, legal education, health care, domestic relations, judging, social work, nursing, emotional responses within law, allied movements in law, ethical concerns, legal practice, and policing, and included presenters from several continents (see http://www.therapeuticjurisprudence.org/).

The purpose of this chapter is to introduce the reader to several key concepts in the definition of therapeutic jurisprudence that are important in its conceptualization and practice, and to invite further empirical research to contribute to its future development. The scope of therapeutic jurisprudence will be discussed first. Several factors, including how 'therapeutic' is defined, how competing therapeutic outcomes can be weighed and balanced, and for whom are therapeutic outcomes considered, will be addressed. The next section takes a look at the role that empirical research can play in the development and practice of therapeutic jurisprudence. It is not possible to cover all aspects of therapeutic jurisprudence in one chapter but it is hoped that this discussion will serve as a springboard for further exploration by interested readers.

THERAPEUTIC JURISPRUDENCE DEFINED

The Scope of Therapeutic Jurisprudence

Therapeutic jurisprudence builds on the insight that the law can be seen to function as a kind of therapist, or therapeutic agent. Legal rules, legal procedures and the roles of legal actors (such as lawyers and judges), constitute social forces that, whether intended or not, often produce therapeutic or antitherapeutic consequences. Therapeutic jurisprudence calls for the study of these consequences with the tools of the behavioral sciences to identify them and to ascertain whether the law's antitherapeutic effects can be reduced, and its therapeutic effects enhanced, without subordinating due process and other justice values (Winick, 1997a).

Therapeutic jurisprudence does not suggest that therapeutic considerations should trump other considerations. Therapeutic considerations are but one category of important factors, as are autonomy, integrity of the fact-finding process, and community safety. Therapeutic jurisprudence does not itself propose to resolve the value questions; instead, it sets the stage for their sharp articulation (Schopp, 1993; Wexler, 1992a).

How to choose between competing therapeutic effects, and between conflicting values when therapeutic considerations conflict with other considerations valued by law, has been raised as a concern in discussions of therapeutic jurisprudence (Kress, 1999; Schopp, 1999; Slobogin, 1995; Wexler, 1995; Winick, 1997a). The insanity defense, by producing self-attributional effects that may make it more difficult for an individual relieved of criminal responsibility on this basis to control his future antisocial conduct, may be antitherapeutic, but abolition of the insanity defense may undermine the moral authority of the criminal law. A victim's sense of vengeance and safety may seem best served by a sentence including a long period of incarceration, but does this ultimately contribute to a defendant's rehabilitative efforts and to long-term victim safety (Wiebe, 1996)? Can an ordering of values be predetermined? How should conflicts between therapeutic and other values be resolved? Because therapeutic jurisprudence endorses psychological health as a good, but does not consider other goods irrelevant or unimportant, in cases in which these other values converge with positive therapeutic effects, the direction of law reform will be clear. When there is conflict among them, however, therapeutic jurisprudence is not a method of resolving the conflict.

Winick (1997a, 2000a) emphasizes that therapeutic jurisprudence highlights that competing values exist, but the role of therapeutic jurisprudence is to make these competing values visible rather than prescribing a resolution for which values have greater importance. When the therapeutic dimensions of a legal issue have been clarified (a task that requires both theoretical speculation and empirical study), law reform will be indicated when there is a convergence between therapeutic and other normative values (Winick, 1997b). It may also be required, even in the absence of such convergence, when therapeutic considerations strongly outweigh other values. This involves a weighing of therapeutic against other normative values, a task that some might describe as weighing apples and oranges. But as Kress (1999) has recently demonstrated, differing values can be weighed and balanced, even those thought of as incommensurable. When therapeutic and other normative values do not converge, Kress suggests that creative solutions often can be found that will permit maximizing the balance among such values with a minimization of conflict.

Kress (1999) argues for using a normative or behavioral theory to present the moral, political, and public policy perspectives to resolve competing values on a case-by-case basis. He suggests that values be made visible through the normative theory used, which provides the reasoning that competing values are weighed and balanced against one another. Seldom would two people, using the same normative theory, come up with the same resolution to generate a hierarchy of values. Therefore, it is unrealistic to expect therapeutic jurisprudence to dictate a resolution, and more useful to emphasize making the steps of the argument visible based on the normative theory being used.

Kress (1999) also states that therapeutic jurisprudence should not be linked to one particular normative theory but, instead, can be used in conjunction with a host of various theories. This makes having a strict hierarchy of values that much more unrealistic. This line of thinking is echoed in Schopp's (1999) analysis of competing values, in which he argues that therapeutic jurisprudence does not address the normative question of whether law ought to consider the value of psychological well-being. Instead, it stresses how the law can address values through analysis of how legal rules, legal procedures, and legal actors affect well-being. By avoiding the normative question, therapeutic jurisprudence leaves itself open to work in conjunction with many theoretical and analytical strategies, giving it that much more versatility in practice and in research (Schopp, 1999). Therapeutic jurisprudence focuses on how the law can achieve psychological well-being for instrumental rather than prescriptive purposes. Therapeutic jurisprudence is prescriptively neutral while providing instrumental recommendations; it 'prescribe[s] means to ends rather than ends' (p. 601). This highlights the importance of the merging of the empirical inquiry with conceptual and normative analyses (Schopp, 1999).

An example drawn from the practice of mandatory arrest law in domestic violence cases may help to illustrate this process of weighing and balancing when competing values occur. Saccuzzo (1999) uses therapeutic jurisprudence to argue for mandatory arrest laws, insisting that these laws are needed to protect women who cannot protect themselves and will come to harm or even death if the police do not intercede. Mills (1999), on the other hand, also based on therapeutic considerations, argues that mandatory arrest laws disempower the victim and reinforce many of the negative psychological effects of domestic violence, essentially revictimizing victims. Winick (2000a) suggests a creative solution to maximize balancing between the considerations that Saccuzzo commends in support of his defense of mandatory arrest and those that Mills cites in support of her conclusion condemning it. Winick suggests a law enforcement policy of presumptive arrest rather than mandatory arrest. Under presumptive arrest, police generally would be required to effect an arrest when probable cause exists that domestic violence has occurred, but would not be required to do so when countervailing considerations argue strongly against arrest in the circumstances. In such cases, the police would be required to justify a decision not to arrest by stating in writing the reasons they relied upon.

Such a presumptive arrest policy arguably would convey a similar message to both batterers and victims as that communicated by a mandatory arrest policy, but without as many of the antitherapeutic consequences that Mills (1999) warns about. A similar societal message that domestic violence is wrong and will not be tolerated could be conveyed. The message that domestic violence will usually result in arrest could also have a similar deterrent effect on future acts of violence. Yet, a policy of presumptive arrest would permit the police to take into account the victim's perspective on whether arrest should occur in these circumstances, thereby providing her with a sense of voice and a measure of empowerment that can help her in the healing process. Presumptive arrest, then, would seem likely to produce therapeutic value for both batterers and victims.

The therapeutic jurisprudence lens generates empirical questions: one may speculate on the therapeutic consequences of various legal arrangements or law reform proposals, but empirical research is often necessary to determine with confidence whether the law actually operates in accordance with the speculative assumption (Wexler, 1994). Much like law and psychology, and social science in law, therapeutic jurisprudence looks at law with the tools of the behavioral sciences (Winick, 1997a). But therapeutic jurisprudence has a more narrow focus. Unlike these other interdisciplinary approaches, it does not seek *generally* to examine law to test its assumptions or measure its effectiveness of impact. Much of law and psychology and social science in law have been dominated by research into law's consequences (O'Reilly and Sales,

1987; Sales, 1983; Sarat, 1985), although not all such work, of course, has been in this tradition (O'Reilly and Sales, 1986). Therapeutic jurisprudence is concerned with a more narrow set of consequences. It seeks to apply social science to examine law's impact on the mental health of the people it affects (Slobogin, 1995). Therapeutic jurisprudence seeks to utilize psychological and behavioral science research to explore these questions empirically. It uses such research to delineate how legal rules, legal procedures, and legal actors impact a therapeutic or antitherapeutic consequence for those affected by the legal process. This need for empirical research is the niche that social science research can fill.

The Expanding Scope of Therapeutic Jurisprudence

Therapeutic jurisprudence makes a contribution by bringing under one conceptual umbrella many legal areas that previously had not been thought to be related (Wexler, 1995; Wexler and Winick, 1996). Moreover, its principal power is to generate questions that otherwise might well go unasked. Perhaps the best way to approach the question of the distinctiveness of therapeutic jurisprudence is to ask how likely, *without* a therapeutic jurisprudence perspective, it would have been that we would ask the following questions which are representative of therapeutic jurisprudence:

- Can a judge's colloquy with a criminal defendant at a plea hearing influence the defendant's acceptance of responsibility (Wexler and Winick, 1992)?

- Can a judge conduct a sentencing hearing in a manner likely to increase a criminal defendant's compliance with conditions of probation (Wexler, 1993c)?

- Is 'sentence bargaining' less likely to interfere with later efforts at offender rehabilitation than 'charge bargaining' (Wexler, 1993c; Wexler and Winick, 1992)?

- How can a judge's functioning in domestic violence court act so as to facilitate the healing of victims of spousal abuse (Winick, 2000a)?

- Can 'teen courts' increase empathy in delinquent youths by having those youths serve as attorneys for victims in teen court proceedings (Shiff and Wexler, 1996; Wexler, 2000)?

- How can a judge's functioning in drug treatment courts minimize the perception of coercion on the part of those electing this form of diversion from the criminal process (Winick and Wexler, in press)?

- Might a fault-based tort system promote recovery better than a no-fault system (Shuman, 1994)?

Like law and economics, therapeutic jurisprudence is essentially a consequentialist approach to law. Both evaluate law on the basis of its consequences. Therapeutic jurisprudence focuses on a particular kind of consequence—the therapeutic—and calls for study of the law's impact on health and mental health. This assessment should be scientific, based on empirical research.

But what is therapeutic? Therapeutic jurisprudence has been criticized for not offering a clear-cut definition of the term therapeutic (Melton, 1994). As a mere lens or heuristic for better seeing and understanding the law, however, therapeutic jurisprudence has opted not to provide a tight definition of the term, thereby allowing commentators and researchers to broadly roam within the intuitive and common-sense contours of the concept (Wexler, 1993a).

There remains, however, the question of what therapeutic should mean for the purposes of researchers and academics. At the outset, it is important to consider the involvement and input of consumers-recipients at the research stage (Shuman, Hamilton and Daley, 1994; Zito, Vitrai and Craig, 1993; Wexler and Winick, 1993). A tight definition of 'therapeutic' should be avoided. A restrictive definition might simply be ignored by the research community or, far worse, might be taken seriously and might prematurely eclipse the issues that may be subject to research (Wexler, 1995).

Of course, working within the broad intuitive boundaries of the concept, each individual researcher or academician writing about therapeutic jurisprudence must settle on a definition of therapeutic and ought to be fairly explicit about what definition is being used and why (Cohen and Dvoskin, 1993; Slobogin, 1995). Making the definition reasonably explicit will ease the empirical measurement of dependent variables or outcome measures and will also raise the issue for normative debate in the political arena. Naturally, empirical researchers will bear the brunt of this obligation, but even articles of a more theoretical and speculative nature need to be sensitive—more sensitive than they have been—to the definitional matters. For example, is rehabilitation defined by attitudinal changes or by the absence of criminal activity (itself measured by self-reports or by official records)? Should one care about achieving rehabilitation if it is manifested only by attitudinal change? Why or why not? How is emotional stress to be measured? Should one be concerned with the law's impact on emotional stress in the short-term, in the long-term, or both? Why? Thus, it is important for each writer, commentator, or researcher to come to grips with the therapeutic dimension so that research and debate might best proceed (Wexler, 1995).

Although the definition of the term 'therapeutic' thus needs to be left very flexible for purposes of promoting research, it is also probably true that, to preserve the camaraderie (and efficient work) of a common scholarly community, there ought to be some notion about the core concept and its rough bounds. In that connection it is noteworthy that the therapeutic jurisprudence literature to date has overwhelmingly conformed to areas within the ordinary mental health/health connotations of the term therapeutic: mental health/mental illness and health, illness, injury, disability, treatment, rehabilitation, and habilitation. Moreover, because therapeutic jurisprudence conceptualizes the law itself as the therapeutic agent, the focus has been on sociopsychological ways in which mental health, health and mental illness might be promoted or inhibited by the law (Wexler, 1995).

Therefore, what is meant by 'therapeutic' far exceeds the reversal of ill health. On the other hand, the term 'therapeutic' has not yet become (and for research purposes ought not to become) synonymous with simply achieving intended or desirable outcomes. Therapeutic jurisprudence seeks to retain its distinctiveness as a discipline relating to mental health and psychological aspects of health. Thus, certain matters central to law and psychology generally, such as the accuracy of eyewitness identification or the impact of jury size on jury decision-making, would not in and of themselves be of interest to therapeutic jurisprudence. Such areas could be brought into therapeutic jurisprudence, however, if they were expanded to ask certain questions about impact on emotional life. It would be interesting to know, for example, whether in traumatic criminal cases six-person juries suffer greater or less stress than 12-person juries (Wexler, 1995).

More to the point, it will be helpful to the therapeutic jurisprudence community if a relatively discrete literature is regarded as principally relevant to the enterprise (Wexler, 1995). Of special interest should be those articles, whether expressly related to law or not, that are written on cognitive-affective-behavioral topics by and for mental health professionals—psychiatrists, psychologists, social workers, counselors, and criminal justice and correctional professionals. In that way efficiency will be promoted, for therapeutic jurisprudence scholars will have a handle on the kind of literature they need to keep up with and examine through the legal lens of therapeutic jurisprudence. When one looks through a therapeutic jurisprudence lens at behavioral science literature on the cognitive distortion of sex offenders, one is tempted to ask how the law might promote or inhibit cognitive distortions. Similarly, when one approaches the psychological principles of health care compliance through a therapeutic jurisprudence lens, one might want to ask whether those principles might somehow be imported into the legal system (Wexler, 1992b).

Therapeutic for Whom?

When one mentions for whom the law might be therapeutic, the therapeutic jurisprudence lens again provides no answer and no particular limit. Growing as it did out of mental health law (Wexler, 1993a), therapeutic jurisprudence began its exploration with the impact of the law on respondents in commitment cases and on mental patients within the legal system. However, scholarly interest soon spread to examining the law's therapeutic or antitherapeutic impact on criminal defendants (Gould, 1993; Wexler, 1993c, 2001), victims (Feldthusen, 1993), jurors (Shuman et al., 1994), mental health professionals (Poythress and Brodsky, 1993), personal injury plaintiffs (Shuman, 1993), and employees with disabilities (Daly-Rooney, 1996).

There may, of course, sometimes be a clash whereby a legal rule is therapeutic for one person or participant and antitherapeutic for another (Wexler, 1995). Once again, therapeutic jurisprudence merely sheds light on this issue and does not resolve the normative debate. Instead, that normative analysis can be undertaken and then addressed to the legal or political arena. Of course, finding a convergence of interests—for example, the earlier example of presumptive arrest rather than mandatory arrest to balance the therapeutic effects between defendants and victims of domestic violence—is the hoped for goal, although it is understandably not always reachable (Slobogin, 1995).

Therapeutic Jurisprudence's Expanding Conception of Law

When therapeutic jurisprudence speaks of looking at the law as a potential therapeutic agent, it refers to looking at both legal (and administrative) rules and procedures and at the roles of legal actors or 'players' (Dorfman, 1993) which typically include lawyers and judges but may include many other actors, such as therapists (Klotz, 1991) and employers (Daly-Rooney, 1996). Accordingly therapeutic jurisprudence scholarship is addressed not only to the appellate judiciary, through policy arguments grounded in empirical and clinical insights as well as psychological theory, but also to legislators (Rubin, 1993), administrative agencies and, importantly, trial courts (Wexler, 1993b; Wexler, 1993c) and practicing lawyers (Stolle, Wexler and Winick, 2000).

More recently specialized courts have become an arena for therapeutic jurisprudence to be practiced by judges (Casey and Rottman, 2000; Wexler, 2001). These specialized courts, or problem-solving courts as they increasingly are becoming known, include drug treatment courts (Hora, Schma and Rosenthal, 1999; Winick and Wexler, in press); domestic violence courts (Fritzler and Simon, 2000; Winick, 2000a); mental health courts (Fritzler, in press; Lurigio et al., 2001); teen courts (Schiff and Wexler, 1996; Wexler, 2000); and others. Compared to conventional courts, these problem-solving courts play a more direct and proactive role in the treatment and rehabilitative process. Wexler (2001) discusses the role of the judge in criminal court settings, borrowing on mental health compliance principles, cognitive self change programs to address relapse prevention, and a desistance model springing from recent research that sees rehabilitation as a 'maintenance process' that can be aided by a judge's public endorsement of an offender's changed behavior. Moreover, in addition to these specialized courts, trial judges serving in more general courts and appellate judges have increasingly become sensitive to the fact that the way they play their roles have therapeutic consequences for those affected (Seattle University Law Review, Symposium Issue, 2000; Rottman, 2000). (See Chapter 10 by Simon in this volume.)

Research is just beginning to surface emphasizing that, within these courts, the therapeutic effects of judges, defendants, and victims are important and should be studied. The components of the court process itself, from administrative/organizational concerns to what was actually said and how this might impact the therapeutic nature of the exchange for the judge and the defendant was studied in a domestic violence court ethnographic study (Petrucci, 2002). Therapeutic effects of the judicial process on the judges' themselves was the focus of another recent study. Chase and Hora (2000) compared judicial attitudes across two groups of judges: drug treatment court judges using therapeutic jurisprudence and family court judges who did not. They asked several questions of the 194 judges who participated in their survey. Did drug treatment court judges hold a more positive view of drug offenders appearing before them? Did they feel more personally motivated by their assignment than family court judges? Among their key findings was a positive correlation between having an opportunity to see the offenders appearing before them improve and overall judicial satisfaction. Drug treatment court judges, using therapeutic jurisprudence techniques, had more positive attitudes about litigants in general than did family court judges, felt more positive about their jobs, and also felt a greater sense of gratitude from the offenders in their court. Combined, this made for a more therapeutic working environment for drug treatment court judges compared to family court judges. In a field in which burnout runs high, but consistent and fair decision-making is essential, therapeutic jurisprudence research can shed light on the therapeutic process for judges and can make a valuable contribution to understanding judicial best practices.

A recent study of mental health tribunals in the UK compared the impressions of participating patients as well as professionals in an exploratory design (Ferencz and McGuire, 2000). Here, rather than being used within the court, therapeutic jurisprudence was used as the lens to ask how the process was viewed from these two perspectives. Patients described a 'cycle of stress', made worse by the tribunal process itself. Moreover, patients and tribunal members differed in their opinion of fairness of the process (with patients feeling the process was unfair), in their opinion of whether the tribunal was an independent body (with patients feeling it was not), and in their opinion of their overall impressions of the tribunal (with patients feeling more negatively than tribunal members). The therapeutic jurisprudence analysis allowed the authors to include a broader scope of who ought to be considered as part of the research question, and to compare across two apparently disparate groups (patients and professionals) as a step toward a remedy for the situation.

The emphasis on roles of legal actors, especially when the actors operate in a relatively unconstrained legal field (Wexler, 1993b)—i.e. with great discretion—is particularly ripe for therapeutic jurisprudence analysis. Because these various legal actors, implementers, enforcers, and administrators of the law have a great potential for influencing outcomes therapeutically or antitherapeutically, their actions should appropriately fall within the scope of therapeutic jurisprudence study. There is great potential for study here and great interest to legal scholars because of important, albeit nuanced, subtle, and often completely hidden, therapeutic or antitherapeutic consequences. Moreover, whether any rule of law or legal procedure, in the traditional sense, will succeed or fail may depend as much or more on these 'implementation' matters as on anything else (Wexler, 1995).

When considering how legal actors impact, and are impacted by the legal process, therapeutic jurisprudence has much in common with a multitude of current theories in both law and social science. Sometimes these links have been made explicit in research and analyses, as is the case for preventive law and restorative justice, and in other instances research and practice connections have yet to be developed. Cognitive-behavioral theory has been linked with therapeutic jurisprudence as a means to incorporate offender attitudes and behavior into judicial decision-making in domestic violence courts (Simon, 1995) as well as attorney relationships with defendants (Winick, 2000a). Therapeutic jurisprudence is also consonant with such theoretical frameworks as Braithwaite's (1989) theory of crime, shame and reintegration, restorative justice (Braithwaite, 2000, 2002; Scheff, 1998), community justice (Bazemore and Schiff, 2001), preventive law (Stolle et al., 1997; Winick, Wexler and Dauer, 1999) and procedural justice (Thibaut and Walker, 1978; Tyler, 1992; Winick, 1999). Lawyering practice theories can also work in conjunction with therapeutic jurisprudence (Stolle et al., 2000).

Daicoff (2000) ties these legal theories together under one umbrella concept that she calls the 'comprehensive law movement'. She traces the dissatisfaction of both lawyers and society from an overly-adversarial approach in law that has led to a growing acceptance of a 'more comprehensive, humane, and psychologically optimal way of handling legal matters' (p. 466). She identifies 10 vectors of the comprehensive law movement: therapeutic jurisprudence, preventive law, therapeutic jurisprudence/preventive law, restorative justice, procedural justice, facilitative mediation, transformative mediation, collaborative mediation, holistic law, and creative problem-solving. Each of these has two things in common. First, psychological well-being is considered from the standpoint of individuals, relationships and communities. Second, each vector considers a larger view than the traditionally narrow scope of the law. The 10 vectors can be split into two groups based on their functionality: theoretical lenses and concrete processes. Specialized courts and preventive law are examples of concrete processes or mechanisms. Procedural justice, the holistic perspective, creative problem-solving, restorative justice and therapeutic jurisprudence are examples of the lenses through which practice can be evaluated. Daicoff puts forward that therapeutic jurisprudence is the most developed among these theories, and may actually be fueling the popularity of these many developments within law practice and theory. She suggests that therapeutic jurisprudence ought to be the overarching theory of the comprehensive law movement, given its ability to capture these many perspectives and work in conjunction with them (Daicoff, 2000). Whether or not therapeutic jurisprudence is accepted as the undergirding theory of the comprehensive law movement, the point is well taken that it converges well with a host of current behavioral practice theories related to lawyering.

THERAPEUTIC JURISPRUDENCE'S INVITATION TO EMPIRICAL RESEARCH

Social Science Research in a Therapeutic Jurisprudence Context

There are several inherent qualities of therapeutic jurisprudence as a theory that make it an exciting and pertinent enterprise for social science researchers: defined and measurable constructs, a focus on process and the link to outcomes, and an emphasis on context each make it amenable to research. Broadening the scope of who is included in the research is another inherent quality. Lastly, therapeutic jurisprudence provides a rationale for incorporating behavioral science into legal practice.

First, therapeutic jurisprudence specifically lays out the constructs to be studied. From a research perspective, the four main constructs are: legal rules, legal procedures, legal actors, and emotional well-being. These constructs can be studied separately or together. Operationalizing these constructs for research purposes is a reasonable task given the tangible nature of the constructs themselves. The first three constructs would generally constitute the independent or predictor variables, with emotional well-being as one outcome variable (among others). For example, Poythress and Brodsky (1996) examined how hospital staff and hospital procedures were affected by a negligent release lawsuit against hospital staff. Here, the authors looked retrospectively at change in staff attitudes and behavior, and at change in hospital procedures as an indicator of therapeutic or antitherapeutic consequences of a lawsuit. Arguably, the dependent and independent status of the constructs is less important when the research design does not capture causality; that is, we cannot say that the effects on staff are a direct result of the lawsuit, and the authors specifically note this. Thus, a cause–effect order cannot be assumed. Therapeutic jurisprudence as a theory presents an order of cause and effect (i.e. what a legal actor does affects a therapeutic or antitherapeutic outcome whether it produces emotional well-being or its opposite). For research purposes, however, as long as the basis of the research method is relational (Rosenthal and Rosnow, 1991) or establishing correlations, as is often the case, the predictor and outcome status of the variables being studied is essentially interchangeable.

Furthermore, these constructs are measurable in a host of ways. How a judge interacts with a defendant can be measured through quantitative instruments that measure attitudes or behaviors. Qualitative methods can also be used, including observation or interviews. One of the authors observed a judge–defendant interaction, as it occurred in the courtroom, then conducted open-ended interviews with defendants and the judge (Petrucci, 2002). The effects of legal rules or legal procedures can also be observed in action or documented through surveys, questionnaires, or document review. Poythress and Brodsky (1996) examined how hospital procedure had changed by interviewing hospital staff and by examining hospital release records. Contrast this with general deterrence theory which states that certainty, severity, and swift punishment will deter individuals from offending. Volumes have been written on the difficulties of measuring these concepts (see Von Hirsch et al., 1999, for a recent review), and from whose perspective, not to mention how to measure the outcome of deterrence. How does one measure what people do *not* do (in the case of general deterrence, do not offend) while also considering the counterfactual, or what they would have done if deterrence were not at work?

From a research perspective, therapeutic jurisprudence does not have these theoretical and practical difficulties because the constructs themselves are reasonably concrete and are present. The possible exception to this would be how to define and measure emotional well-being as it relates to therapeutic and antitherapeutic effects, which results in the value conflict previously discussed.

Second, therapeutic jurisprudence has an inherent focus on process and the link to outcomes. This is useful from both a research and a practice perspective. In the research enterprise, from the outset, this sets up the boundaries of the research hypotheses or research questions themselves. Among the most commonly researched questions is: How does the judge or authority figure interact with defendants or how do plaintiffs impact the emotional well-being of those involved? Susman (1996) looked at whether psychiatric patients were equally satisfied across two methods of dispute resolution for mandatory medication. Anderson and her colleagues (1996) examined how therapists integrated the mandatory child abuse reporting laws, and how it affected their interactions with clients. Chase and Hora (2000) flipped this question around and asked whether judicial satisfaction varied across specialized court judges who did and did not use therapeutic jurisprudence. Holmberg and Christianson (2002) analyzed the perceptions of convicted murderers and sexual offenders and linked these attitudes to how likely offenders were to deny or admit their behavior during police interrogation.

Therapeutic jurisprudence suggests that the process itself has meaning and may affect outcomes, and therefore deserves consideration. From a theoretical standpoint therapeutic jurisprudence suggests that how the process occurs may have meaning for the outcomes or consequences of the process (through how legal rules, legal procedures, and legal actors are experienced). Social science research has the task to prove this.

A third aspect of therapeutic jurisprudence, of interest to social science researchers, is its inherent focus on the context of the legal process and the ramifications this has for research methodology. The focus on context also allows the multiple units of analysis suggested by the constructs, from the micro-level interactions between legal actors, to the macro-level interaction between a set of legal rules or procedures and well-being and, ultimately, law reform (Wexler, 1995). This has implications for the creative use of an array of research methodologies. Research questions can lend themselves to strictly quantitative methodologies to explore questions one construct at a time. For example, Susman (1996) used an instrument measuring aspects of procedural justice developed by Tyler (1992) to assess whether patients who refused medication felt they were treated fairly in two contrasting dispute resolution methods.

Any number of well-being measures could be used to analyze the well-being of patients, defendants, victims, attorneys, or judges as an outcome on its own. Qualitative methods can also be utilized to look at one construct at a time or multiple constructs (Petrucci, 2002). Semi-structured and open-ended interviews have been used in several therapeutic jurisprudence studies (Anderson et al., 1996; Poythress and Brodsky, 1996; Zito et al., 1993). Document analysis could also be used to take a more macro-level look at how legal rules or legal procedures affect outcomes by analyzing case records and court decisions. Zito et al. (1993) reviewed official records to analyze the administrative process conducted when patients refused medication. Poythress and Brodsky (1996) examined hospital release records as evidence for change in hospital procedure after a lawsuit. A comprehensive analysis of the process and outcomes could be accomplished through a mixed methodology such as a case study that permits multiple units of analysis (Yin, 1993), or through the use of quantitative or qualitative methods on their own.

From an epistemological stance, through its emphasis on context, therapeutic jurisprudence can be firmly placed within several current context-focused frameworks. Based on their work in experimental psychology, Rosenthal and Rosnow (1991) argue that human behavior is complex and embedded in the context in which it takes place, making it difficult for one theory or method to provide a complete explanation of a phenomenon. Pluralistic theories and methods are needed to fully understand and explain behavior. They locate their point-of-view within the philosophical framework of contextualism, based on Pepper's work (1942, 1967). Contextualism accepts that behavior is active and always changing. The researcher is seen as an active participant. The meaning of an event is linked to the context in which it occurs, making multiple methods a natural outgrowth of this philosophy.

Education researchers Tashakkori and Teddlie (1998) place their mixed model work within the philosophical framework of pragmatism, based on the work of several authors (see Cherryholmes, 1992; Greene, 1994; House, 1994; Howe, 1988; Murphy, 1990 and Rorty, 1982—as cited in Tashakkori and Teddlie). The research question is the primary determinant of the methods used. Tashakkori and Teddlie see pragmatism as the best philosophical fit for mixed methods because it avoids the 'either–or' approach of positivism and constructivism and advocates the use of the best methods to best answer the research question.

Additional frameworks have been developed by various scholars to support the use of mixed methods with a concomitant emphasis on context. Examples include falliballistic realism (Manicas and Secord, 1983), scientific realism (Kazi, 2000), and a developmental approach (Bronfenbrenner, 1979). Therapeutic jurisprudence fits well within each of these.

A fourth inherent quality of therapeutic jurisprudence is that it provides an invitation to look at the legal process from a multitude of perspectives often previously overlooked. It broadens the 'who' of who is studied, to include each person directly or indirectly involved in the legal process itself. In many cases, this means considering those who previously had no voice, such as involuntary patients (Perlin, 2000) and victims of domestic violence (Winick, 2000a). Or it can include a practitioner, a criminal defendant, a victim, or society as a whole. Empirical research, thus far in therapeutic jurisprudence, has focused mostly on how mental health professionals and plaintiffs perceive an aspect of the legal process (Anderson et al., 1996; Ferencz and McGuire, 2000; Greer, O'Regan and Traverso, 1996; Kennedy, 2001; Poythress and Brodsky, 1996; Susman, 1996; Zito et al., 1993). Interestingly, conflict between practitioners' and clients' views within the same study have already emerged (Ferencz and McGuire, 2000; Susman, 1996; Zito et al., 1993), bringing what might be important differential perspectives in plain view for reform.

Therapeutic jurisprudence provides the opportunity to expand our research subject pool beyond the much-studied lawyers, judges, and juries, to include a broader array of practitioners directly and indirectly involved with the legal process itself. This allows interdisciplinary discussion as the needs of the legal process and the medical or mental health fields (or juvenile justice, corrections, social work, substance abuse treatment, etc.) are illuminated.

It is just as important to gather information from the people being 'acted upon' by the legal system itself—defendants/plaintiffs, victims/respondents, and their families. Holmberg and Christianson's (2002) study looks at the perceptions of 83 men convicted of murder or a sexual offense. The work in procedural justice (Thibaut and Walker, 1978; Tyler, 1992) easily integrates within a therapeutic jurisprudence approach (Greer et al., 1996; Kennedy, 2001; Susman, 1996) and insists on gaining the perspective of the defendants themselves due to the constructs of the theory itself (having voice and participation). Winick (1999) uses procedural justice in the realm of civil commitment hearings. To increase the therapeutic effects of the commitment process, Winick emphasizes the importance of patients being able to tell their story in an environment that supports dignity, trust, and respect. He outlines how the roles of the legal actors involved in the commitment process can be changed to adhere to the principles of procedural justice not only to enhance a patient's experience of the commitment process, but to contribute to the patient's acceptance of the outcome of the hearing. Therapeutic jurisprudence also emphasizes the importance of how victims perceive the legal process, allowing a merging with the growing victimology research (Wright, 1996), and placing a much needed focus on how the legal system responds to victims. The well-being of families can also be considered. Borrowing on procedural justice, Kennedy (2001) looked at 226 family members who were also petitioners in an involuntary commitment hearing to see if their perceptions of fairness affected their willingness to care for their committed family member after the hearing. As can be seen, the 'who' of whose emotional well-being is considered can be quite broad.

Finally, therapeutic jurisprudence provides a rationale for the integration of behavioral science research into the legal process. Through its inherent focus on process, it permits and even encourages discussion of constructs of interest to social science research and practice. These include areas such as compliance (Wexler, 2000), rehabilitation (Wexler, 2001), coercion (Winick, 1999; Winick and Wexler, in press), denial (Winick, 2000a, 2000b), and relapse prevention (Wexler, 2000). For example, in his analysis of teen courts, Wexler (2000) combines a cognitive-behavioral approach with a relapse prevention plan. With the help of a probation officer or social worker, youths develop a plan that identifies how they will recognize a high-risk situation in the future, and what they will do about it if faced with it. The youth's ability to develop the plan is suggested as one piece of information for release decisions.

Therapeutic jurisprudence supports the use of these constructs as a means to accomplish emotional well-being. Social science research is well poised to take a closer look at how these constructs can be operationalized and what influence they have on the process and outcomes. Thus, therapeutic jurisprudence, and the research and practice enterprise, share common goals of achieving a court process that is as therapeutic as possible for those going through it. Social science research and practice can provide the operationalization of the constructs suggested by therapeutic jurisprudence.

We've described the ways that social science research can be useful to a therapeutic jurisprudence approach, but is there also a role that social science researchers can play in the development and implementation of therapeutic jurisprudence? One of the most important roles that social science research can play in therapeutic jurisprudence is empirical support or disproof of the theory itself. This involves observing, documenting, and explaining how therapeutic jurisprudence operates in practice within legal forums.

Therapeutic jurisprudence researchers can also contribute to the definition and measurement of what differentiates a therapeutic jurisprudence approach from other approaches. The development of measurable process components would be a natural consequence. This can serve to both disentangle competing theoretical approaches as well as to provide a sophisticated triangulation of theoretical mechanisms. Specifically, how do judges carry out therapeutic jurisprudence in their day-to-day interactions with defendants and victims, and how does this differ from a judge in a specialized court who does not subscribe to therapeutic jurisprudence? Are there differences in outcomes across different judicial approaches? What does a lawyer utilizing therapeutic jurisprudence actually do or say in his or her interactions with clients? Are there measurable differences between a lawyer using a therapeutic jurisprudent approach and one not using it? How is a therapeutic jurisprudence approach different from deterrence? Social science research can begin to name and measure these factors, with input from those actually 'doing' therapeutic jurisprudence in their day-to-day practice. This process of disentangling and triangulating competing theories is important if we are to understand which approach brings about the most effective outcomes.

Another key role for social science research is to develop measurable outcomes of therapeutic jurisprudence. This would include analysis of emotional well-being as well as legal reform as the outcome. Emotional well-being is fertile ground in social science, with a multitude of directions in which to go, depending on who is considered: an individual, a family, a community, or society at large (Kress, 1999). It is not intended that any one particular outcome measure be declared 'the one and only', but that a constellation of measurable outcomes be developed that reflect various units of analysis. These outcomes can then be linked to specific aspects of therapeutic jurisprudence (legal actors, rules, procedures).

In short, therapeutic jurisprudence and social science research can work in tandem to explore and document how therapeutic jurisprudence is practiced, how implementation is defined in operationalizable constructs, and in linking these constructs to outcomes. This combination of tasks will allow empirical research to make its most important contribution: to achieve meaningful law reform that is carefully thought out from multiple perspectives, and to contribute to best practices for practitioners working in the legal arena.

Caveats

Therapeutic jurisprudence is not intended as a panacea for all that is wrong with the legal system. It suggests law reform in a step-by-step process, based on empirical behavioral research and legal analysis of therapeutic and antitherapeutic effects. Law reform can occur through changing a procedure or by actually changing laws. If laws are to be changed, then empirical research can serve as a partial basis for the change, based on how legal rules, legal procedures, and legal actors contribute to or detract from the emotional well-being of concerned parties. This is not anticipated to be an easy or clear-cut process. We can look to previously learned lessons in the social science literature for caveats to consider in this process.

The hope of law reform could be hindered by two extremes: either too quickly incorporating research findings without clearly understanding their implications or by not incorporating findings at all. Sherman and Berk's (1984) seminal work in arrest in domestic violence provides an apt example of research being translated into policy too quickly, based in large part on the findings of one study. Before the National Institute of Justice could complete six additional replication studies (Berk et al., 1992; Dunford, Huizinga and Elliott, 1989; Hirschel et al., 1991; Pate and Hamilton, 1992; Sherman et al., 1992), none of which fully reproduced Sherman and Berk's work, arrest policies across the United States had dramatically changed to incorporate various forms of mandatory arrest (Buzawa and Buzawa, 1996). The additional studies uncovered the complexities of arrest, including the heightened risk it posed to certain groups of domestic violence victims (NIJ Research Report, 1998). These findings emerged long after policy changes had already been implemented. Sherman and Berk's (1984) study was not solely responsible for a nationwide move to mandatory arrest, but it was interpreted as powerful empirical evidence advocating it, without fully considering the unintended consequences that emerged in the other studies. Could this now controversial influence of one study have been averted?

One answer can be found in the social science and law scholarship. Monahan and Walker (1986, 1998) set out four parameters for courts to evaluate social science research. They stress the importance of utilizing empirical studies that have been critically reviewed by the scientific community, that have utilized valid research methods, that have generalizable findings, and that are supported by a body of research. If lawmakers had followed these steps, when the mandatory arrest for domestic violence laws were changed, evaluation of the research might have been questioned perhaps more than it was on the grounds that the research was not supported by a body of evidence—meaning it had not been replicated prior to the decision to change the laws. It is true that several other political factors influenced the change in the domestic violence arrest laws and the research was clearly not the only factor (Buzawa and Buzawa, 1996). However, at least to the extent that the research was used as evidence for change in the laws, its connection might have been more carefully analyzed. Based on Monahan and Walker's recommendations, one study, even a rigorous one, is not enough to change policy. They actually make the point that they expect that *less* social science research will be integrated into law if their recommendations are followed precisely because *only rigorous research* that has withstood the test of time would be considered by judges. This approach risks erring on the side of conservatism, however, since replicating studies and publication of findings can take years. Meanwhile, judges must make decisions that impact defendants, victims, and communities on a day-to-day basis.

The mandatory arrest example reveals the ambiguities that must be faced as the integration of empirical research findings into law reform is considered. Timing and context become key considerations. Empirical work can occur prior to a legal reform, as Monahan and Walker suggest. However, it can also occur simultaneously with a policy change. Incorporating the context, or integrating the legal process in its entirety within one study, also becomes important, particularly for purposes of generalization. Studies on domestic violence arrest and coordinated court approaches provide examples of both of these issues. The arrest studies failed to produce a uniform conclusion as to whether arrest was a deterrent (NIJ Research Report, 1998). It was not until research designs incorporated additional components of the arrest process, including sentencing and probation (Thistlethwaite, Wooldredge and Gibbs, 1998) that a consensus began building in the research literature around the usefulness of arrest if it was followed by conviction and an order for court-ordered treatment (Steinman, 1990; Syers and Edleson, 1992; Tolman and Weisz, 1995). Considering this larger context becomes a key factor for generalizing findings to real-world practice settings. The arrest studies initially looked at only one piece of a domestic violence offender's experience—that is, the arrest—without considering how prosecution, jail time, probation, or offender characteristics may affect offender outcomes. Later work did a better job, incorporating a greater portion of the context of an offender's experience from arrest to post-conviction, and that research seems to be standing up to the test of time as far as consistent findings. In addition, these studies could not have occurred if court reforms had not already taken place. Coordinated community responses in domestic violence have been implemented around the nation, though not on a large scale basis (Keilitz, 2000). Conducting research in these settings simultaneously with their new implementation has permitted researchers to provide useful findings that can build on or confirm what judges in these settings are learning. This research can then be accessed by those about to embark on similar projects, and becomes useful prior to implementation. Empirical research does not have to pre-date law reform, but can work simultaneously with changes in the legal process, particularly when they occur on a smaller scale.

Turning to the opposite scenario of research being overlooked, the previous discussion has shown how research can be left out of the process of law reform through a conservative approach of waiting for consensus from multiple rigorous studies—a process that can take easily 10 years or more. It can also be left out if it contradicts a study already referenced by a higher court. To avoid this scenario, Monahan and Walker (1986) suggest that research be considered similar to legal precedent. Legal precedent changes, and so does research. This allows lower courts to introduce new research, or to bring in empirical studies that contradict existing research that a higher court might already have used. In this way the door remains wide open between research and courtrooms rather than funneling down to only those studies that are accessed by the higher courts.

The relationship between research and policy implementation can be a tenuous one, at best, particularly in criminal justice. This makes the need for integration of pertinent, meaningful research findings as early as possible that much more pressing. Having a process in place to do this can only improve the relationship between social science research and law.

CONCLUSION

Therapeutic jurisprudence is an exciting and functional approach to social science research in legal settings for a host of reasons. It provides a framework useful to both social science practice and research and a rationale for the integration of mental health and behavioral science research into the legal arena. The types of research questions that it generates expand the boundaries of what is asked of whom, often including voices previously not heard. It gives attention to constructs often used in practice such as compliance, coercion, dealing with denial, and relapse prevention. It can work in conjunction with theories that explain behavior, with an implicit emphasis on how interactions between actors occur—what a judge says and how he or she says it matters. It links the process to the outcome. The goals of therapeutic jurisprudence and social science practice/research are the same—to assure that the court process is as therapeutic as possible for those going through it, with the underlying assumption that this will result in the most positive consequences for the parties involved and society. By gaining an understanding of these therapeutic consequences, the cause of legal reform can be furthered through empirical support from a much needed interdisciplinary approach of research, law, and practice.

REFERENCES

Anderson, E., Levine, M., Sharma, A., Feretti, L., Steinberg, K. and Wallach, L. (1996). Coercive uses of mandatory reporting in therapeutic relationships. In D.B. Wexler and B.J. Winick (eds), *Law in a therapeutic key: Developments in therapeutic jurisprudence* (pp. 895–906). Durham, NC: Carolina Academic Press.

Bazemore, G. and Schiff, M. (2001). *Restoring community justice.* Cincinnati, OH: Anderson Publishing Co.

Berk, S.F., Campbell, A., Klap, R. and Western B. (1992). Bayesian analysis of the Colorado Springs spouse abuse experiment. *Criminal Law and Criminology*, *83*, 170–200.

Braithwaite, J. (1989). *Crime, shame and reintegration.* Melbourne: Cambridge University Press.

Braithwaite, J. (2000). Decomposing a holistic view of restorative justice. *Contemporary Justice Review*, *3* (4), 433–440.

Braithwaite, J. (2002). Restorative justice and therapeutic jurisprudence. *Criminal Law Bulletin*, *38* (2), 244–262.

Bronfenbrenner, U. (1979). *The ecology of human development: Experiments by nature and design*. Cambridge, MA: Harvard University Press.

Buzawa, E.S. and Buzawa, C.G. (1996). *Domestic violence: The criminal justice response* (2nd edn). Thousand Oaks, CA: Sage Publications.

Casey, P. and Rottman, D.B. (2000). Therapeutic jurisprudence in the courts. *Behavioral Sciences and the Law*, *18* (4), 445–458.

Chase, D.J. and Hora, P.F. (2000). The implications of therapeutic jurisprudence for judicial satisfaction. *Court Review*, *37* (1), 12–20.

Cherryholmes, C.C. (1992). Notes on pragmatism and scientific realism. *Educational Researcher*, *21*, 13–17.

Cohen, F. and Dvoskin, J.A. (1993). Therapeutic jurisprudence and corrections: A glimpse. *New York Law School Journal of Human Rights*, *10*, 777–804.

Daicoff, S. (2000). The role of therapeutic jurisprudence within the comprehensive law movement. In D.P. Stolle, D.B. Wexler and B.J. Winick (eds), *Practicing therapeutic jurisprudence: Law as a helping profession* (pp. 465–492). Durham, NC: Carolina Academic Press.

Daly-Rooney, R.A. (1996). Designing reasonable accommodations through co-worker participation: Therapeutic jurisprudence and the confidentiality provision of the Americans with Disabilities Act. In D.B. Wexler and B.J. Winick (eds), *Law in a therapeutic key: Developments in therapeutic jurisprudence* (pp. 365–383). Durham, NC: Carolina Academic Press.

Dorfman, D. (1993). Effectively implementing Title I of the Americans with Disabilities Act for mentally disabled persons: A therapeutic jurisprudence analysis. *Journal of Law and Health*, *8*, 105–120.

Dunford, F.W., Huizinga, D. and Elliott, D. (1989). *The Omaha domestic violence police experiment: Final report to the National Institute of Justice and the City of Omaha*. Boulder, CO: Institute of Behavioral Science.

Feldthusen, B. (1993). The civil action for sexual battery: Therapeutic jurisprudence? *Ottawa Law Review*, *25*, 203–234.

Ferencz, N. and McGuire, J. (2000). Mental health review tribunals in the UK: Applying a therapeutic jurisprudence perspective. *Court Review*, *37* (1), 48–52.

Fritzler, R.B. (in press). How one misdemeanor mental health court incorporates therapeutic jurisprudence, preventive law, and restorative justice. In J.M. Moore (ed.), *Management and administration of correctional health care: Policy, practice, administration*. Kingston, NJ: Civic Research Institute.

Fritzler, R.B. and Simon, L.M.J. (2000). Creating a domestic violence court: Combat in the trenches. *Court Review*, *37* (1), 28–39.

Gould, K.A. (1993). Turning rat and doing time for uncharged, dismissed, or acquitted crimes: Do the federal sentencing guidelines promote respect for the law? *New York Law School Journal of Human Rights*, *10*, 835–875.

Greene, J.C. (1994). Qualitative program evaluation. In N.K. Denzin and Y.S. Lincoln (eds), *Handbook of qualitative research* (pp. 530–544). Thousand Oaks, CA: Sage.

Greer, A., O'Regan, M. and Traverso, A. (1996). Therapeutic jurisprudence and patients' perceptions of procedural due process of civil commitment hearings. In D.B. Wexler and B.J. Winick (eds), *Law in a therapeutic key: Developments in therapeutic jurisprudence* (pp. 923–934). Durham, NC: Carolina Academic Press.

Hirschel, J.D., Hutchison, I.W., Dean, C.W., Kelley, J.J. and Pesackis, C.E. (1991). *Charlotte spouse assault replication project: Final report* (Grant No. 89IJ-CK-K004). Washington, DC: National Institute of Justice.

Holmberg, U. and Christianson, S.A. (2002). Murderers' and sexual offenders' experiences of police interviews and their inclination to admit or deny crimes. *Behavioral Sciences and the Law*, *20* (1/2), 31–45.

Hora, P.F., Schma, W. and Rosenthal, J.T.A. (1999). Therapeutic jurisprudence and the drug court movement: Revolutionizing the criminal justice system's response to drug abuse and crime in America. *Notre Dame Law Review*, *74*, 439–555.

House, E.R. (1994). Integrating the quantitative and qualitative. In C.S. Reichart and S.F. Rallis (eds), *The qualitative–quantitative debate: New perspectives* (pp. 13–22). San Francisco: Jossey Bass.

Howe, K.R. (1988). Against the quantitative–qualitative incompatibility thesis or dogmas die hard. *Educational Researcher, 17,* 10–16

Kazi, M.A.F. (2000). Contemporary perspectives in the evaluation of practice. *British Journal of Social Work, 30* (6), 755–768.

Keilitz, S. (2000). *Specialization of Domestic Violence Case Management in the Courts: A National Survey*. National Center for State Courts.

Kennedy, C.J. (2001). *The perception and role of the involuntary civil commitment hearing through the eyes of the petitioner: Procedural versus distributive justice.* Unpublished doctoral dissertation. The Fielding Institute, Santa Barbara.

Klotz, J.A. (1991). Limiting the psychotherapist–patient privilege: The therapeutic potential. *Criminal Law Bulletin, 27,* 416–433.

Kress, K. (1999). Therapeutic jurisprudence and the resolution of value conflicts: What we can realistically expect, in practice, from theory. *Behavioral Sciences and the Law, 17,* 555–588.

Lurigio, A.J., Watson, A., Luchins, D.J. and Hanrahan, P. (2001). Therapeutic jurisprudence in action: Specialized courts for the mentally ill. *Judicature, 84* (4), 184–189.

Manicas, P.T. and Secord, P.F. (1983). Implications for psychology of the new philosophy of science. *American Psychologist,* 399–413.

Melton, G. (1994). Therapy through law. *Contemporary Psychology, 39,* 215–216.

Mills, L.G. (1999). Killing her softly: Intimate abuse and the violence of state intervention. *Harvard Law Review, 113,* 550–587.

Monahan, J. and Walker, L. (1986). Social authority: Obtaining, evaluating, and establishing social science in law. *University of Pennsylvania Law Review, 134* (3), 477–517.

Monahan, J. and Walker, L. (1998). *Social Science in Law* (4th edn). Westbury, NY: The Foundation Press, Inc.

Murphy, J.P. (1990). *Pragmatism: From Peirce to Davidson*. Boulder, CO: Westview.

NIJ Research Report (1998 July). *Legal interventions in family violence: Research findings and policy implications*. US Department of Justice, Office of Justice Programs. NCJ 171666.

O'Reilly, J. and Sales, B.D. (1986). Setting physical standards for mental hospitals: To whom should the courts listen? *International Journal of Law and Psychiatry, 8,* 301–309.

O'Reilly, J. and Sales, B.D. (1987). Privacy for the institutionalized mentally ill: Are court-ordered standards effective? *Law and Human Behavior, 11,* 41–53.

Pate, A. and Hamilton, E. (1992). Formal and informal deterrents to domestic violence: The Dade County Spouse Assault Experiment. *American Sociological Review, 57,* 691–697.

Pepper, S.C. (1942). *World hypotheses: A study of evidence*. Berkeley: University of California Press.

Pepper, S.C. (1967). *Concept and quality: A world hypothesis*. LaSalle, IL: Open Court.

Perlin, M.L. (2000). *The hidden prejudice: Mental disability on trial*. Washington, DC: American Psychological Association.

Petrucci, C. (2002). Respect as a component in the judge–defendant interaction in a specialized domestic violence court that utilizes therapeutic jurisprudence. *Criminal Law Bulletin, 38* (2), 263–295.

Poythress, N.G. and Brodsky, S.L. (1993). In the wake of a negligent release law suit: An investigation of professional consequences and institutional impact on a state psychiatric hospital. *Law and Human Behavior, 16,* 155–173.

Poythress, N.G. and Brodsky, S.L. (1996). In the wake of a negligent release law suit: An investigation of professional consequences and institutional impact on a state psychiatric hospital. In D.B. Wexler and B.J. Winick (eds), *Law in a therapeutic key: Developments in therapeutic jurisprudence* (pp. 875–894). Durham, NC: Carolina Academic Press.

Rorty, R. (1982). Pragmatism, relativism, and irrationalism. In R. Rorty (ed.), *Consequences of pragmatism* (pp. 160–175). Minneapolis: University of Minnesota Press.

Rosenthal R. and Rosnow, R.L. (1991). *Essentials of behavioral research: Methods and data analysis* (2nd edn). Boston, MA: McGraw-Hill.

Rottman, D.B. (2000). Special issue on therapeutic jurisprudence [Special issue]. *Court Review*, *37* (1).

Rubin, E.L. (1993). Public choice in practice and theory. *California Law Review*, *81*, 1657–1672.

Saccuzzo, D.P. (1999). How should the police respond to domestic violence? A therapeutic jurisprudence analysis of mandatory arrest. *Santa Clara Law Review*, *39*, 765–787.

Sales, B.D. (1983). The legal regulation of psychology: Professional and scientific interactions. In C.J. Scheirer and B.I. Hammonds (eds), *Psychology and the law* (pp. 9–35). Washington, DC: American Psychological Association.

Sarat, A. (1985). Legal effectiveness and social studies of law: On the unfortunate persistence of research tradition. *Legal Studies Forum*, *9*, 23–31.

Scheff, T.J. (1998). Therapeutic jurisprudence forum: Community conferences: Shame and anger in therapeutic jurisprudence. *Revista Juridica Universidad de Puerto Rico*, *67*, 97–119.

Schopp, R.F. (1993). Therapeutic jurisprudence and conflicts among values in mental health law. *Behavioral Sciences and the Law*, *11*, 31–45.

Schopp, R.F. (1999). Therapeutic jurisprudence: Integrated inquiry and instrumental prescriptions. *Behavioral Sciences and the Law*, *17*, 589–605.

Sherman, L.W. and Berk, R.A. (1984). The specific deterrent effects of arrest for domestic assault. *American Sociological Review*, *49*, 261–272.

Sherman, L.W., Schmidt, J.D., Rogan, D.P., Smith, D.A., Gartin, P.R., Cohn, E.G., Collins, D.J. and Bacich, A.R. (1992). The variable effects of arrest on crime control: The Milwaukee Domestic Violence Experiment. *Journal of Criminal Law and Criminology*, *83*, 137–169.

Shiff, A. and Wexler, D.B. (1996). Teen court: A therapeutic jurisprudence perspective. *Criminal Law Bulletin*, *32*, 342–357.

Shuman, D.W. (1993). Making the world a better place through tort law: Through the therapeutic looking glass. *New York Law School Journal of Human Rights*, *10*, 739–747.

Shuman, D.W. (1994). The psychology of compensation in tort law. *University of Kansas Law Review*, *43*, 39–77.

Shuman, D.W., Hamilton, J.A. and Daley, C.E. (1994). The health effects of jury service. *Law and Psychology Review*, *18*, 267–307.

Simon, L.M.J. (1995). A therapeutic jurisprudence approach to the legal processing of domestic violence cases. *Psychology, Public Policy and Law*, *1* (1), 43–79.

Slobogin, C. (1995). Therapeutic jurisprudence: Five dilemmas to ponder. *Psychology, Public Policy and Law*, *1*, 193–219.

Steinman, M. (1990). Lowering recidivism among men who batter women. *Journal of Police Science and Administration*, *17* (2), 124–132.

Stolle, D.P., Wexler, D.B. and Winick, B.J. (2000). *Practicing therapeutic jurisprudence: Law as a helping profession*. Durham, NC: Carolina Academic Press.

Stolle, D.P., Wexler, D.B., Winick, B.J. and Dauer, E.A. (1997). Integrating preventive law and therapeutic jurisprudence: A law and psychology based approach to lawyering. *California Western Law Review*, *34*, 15–51.

Susman, Jack (1996). Resolving hospital conflicts: A study on therapeutic jurisprudence. In D.B. Wexler and B.J. Winick (eds), *Law in a therapeutic key: Developments in therapeutic jurisprudence* (pp. 907–922). Durham, NC: Carolina Academic Press.

Syers, M.S. and Edleson, J.L. (1992). The combined effects of coordinated criminal justice intervention in woman abuse. *Journal of Interpersonal Violence*, *7* (4), 490–502.

Symposium Issue (2000). Therapeutic jurisprudence: Issues, analysis, and applications. *Seattle University Law Review*, *24* (2), 215–689.

Tashakkori, A. and Teddlie, C. (1998). *Mixed methodology: Combining qualitative and quantitative approaches*. Applied Social Research Methods Series, Vol. 46. Thousand Oaks, CA: Sage Publications.

Thibaut, J. and Walker, L. (1978). A theory of procedure. *California Law Review*, *66*, 541–566.

Thistlethwaite, A., Wooldredge, J. and Gibbs, D. (1998). Severity of dispositions and domestic violence recidivism. *Crime and Delinquency*, *44* (3), 388–398.

Tolman, R.M. and Weisz, A. (1995). Coordinated community intervention for domestic violence: The effects of arrest and prosecution on recidivism of woman abuse perpetrators. *Crime and Delinquency, 41* (4), 481–495.

Tomkins, A.J. and Carson, D. (eds) (1999). International perspectives on therapeutic jurisprudence, Part One [Special issue]. *Behavioral Sciences and the Law, 17* (5).

Tomkins, A.J. and Carson, D. (eds). (2000). International perspectives on therapeutic jurisprudence: Part Two [Special issue]. *Behavioral Sciences and the Law, 18* (4).

Tyler, T. (1992). The psychological consequences of judicial procedures: Implications for civil commitment hearings. *Southern Methodist University Law Review, 46,* 433–445.

Von Hirsch, A., Bottoms, A.E., Burney, E. and Wikstrom, P.O. (1999). *Criminal deterrence and sentence severity: An analysis of recent research.* Oxford: Hart Publishing.

Wexler, D.B. (1990). *Therapeutic jurisprudence: The law as a therapeutic agent.* Durham, NC: Carolina Academic Press.

Wexler, D.B. (1992a). Justice, mental health, and therapeutic jurisprudence. *Cleveland State Law Review, 40,* 517–526.

Wexler, D.B. (1992b). Putting mental health into mental health law: Therapeutic jurisprudence. *Law and Human Behavior, 16,* 27–38.

Wexler, D.B. (1993a). New directions in therapeutic jurisprudence: Breaking the bounds of conventional mental health law scholarship. *New York Law School Journal of Human Rights, 10,* 759–776.

Wexler, D.B. (1993b). Therapeutic jurisprudence and changing concepts of legal scholarship. *Behavioral Science and the Law, 11,* 17–29.

Wexler, D.B. (1993c). Therapeutic jurisprudence and the criminal courts. *William and Mary Law Review, 35,* 279–299.

Wexler, D.B. (1994). An orientation to therapeutic jurisprudence. *New England Journal on Criminal and Civil Confinement, 20,* 259–264.

Wexler, D.B. (1995) Reflections on the scope of therapeutic jurisprudence. *Psychology, Public Policy and Law, 1,* 220–236.

Wexler, D.B. (2000). Just some juvenile thinking about delinquent behavior: A therapeutic jurisprudence approach to relapse prevention planning and youth advisory juries. *UMKC Law Review, 69* (1), 93–105.

Wexler, D.B. (2001). Robes and rehabilitation: How judges can help offenders 'make good'. *Court Review, 38* (14), 14–19.

Wexler, D.B. and Winick, B.J. (1991). *Essays in therapeutic jurisprudence.* Durham, NC: Carolina Academic Press.

Wexler, D.B. and Winick, B.J. (1992). Therapeutic jurisprudence and criminal justice mental health issues. *Mental and Physical Disability Law Report, 16,* 225–231.

Wexler, D.B. and Winick, B.J. (1993). Patients, professionals, and the path of therapeutic jurisprudence: A response to Petrila. *New York Law School Journal of Human Rights, 10,* 907–914.

Wexler, D.B. and Winick, B.J. (1996). *Law in a therapeutic key: Developments in therapeutic jurisprudence.* Durham, NC: Carolina Academic Press.

Wiebe, R.P. (1996). The mental health implications of crime victims' rights. In D.B. Wexler and B.J. Winick (Eds.) *Law in a therapeutic key: Developments in therapeutic jurisprudence* (pp. 213–241). Durham, NC: Carolina Academic Press.

Winick, B.J. (1997a). The jurisprudence of therapeutic jurisprudence. *Psychology, Public Policy and Law, 3* (1), 184–206.

Winick, B.J. (1997b). *Therapeutic jurisprudence applied: Essays on mental health law.* Durham, NC: Carolina Academic Press.

Winick, B.J. (1999). Therapeutic jurisprudence and the civil commitment hearing. *The Journal of Contemporary Legal Issues, 10,* 37–60.

Winick, B.J. (2000a). Applying the law therapeutically in domestic violence cases. *University of Missouri–Kansas City Law Review, 69* (1), 33–91.

Winick, B.J. (2000b). Redefining the role of the criminal defense lawyer at plea bargaining and sentencing: A therapeutic jurisprudence/preventive law model. In D.P. Stolle, D.B. Wexler and B.J. Winick (eds), *Practicing therapeutic jurisprudence: Law as a helping profession* (pp. 245–308). Durham, NC: Carolina Academic Press.

Winick, B.J. and Wexler, D.B. (in press). Therapeutic jurisprudence and drug treatment courts: A symbiotic relationship. In A.W. Graham and T.K. Schultz (eds), *Principles of addiction medicine* (3rd edn). Chevy Chase, MD: American Society of Addiction Medicine.

Winick, B.J., Wexler, D.B. and Dauer, E.A. (1999). Therapeutic jurisprudence and preventive law: Transforming legal practice and education [Special issue]. *Psychology, Public Policy and Law, 5,* 793–1210.

Wright, M. (1996). *Justice for victims and offenders: A restorative response to crime* (2nd edn). Winchester: Waterside Press.

Yin, R.K. (1993). *Applications of case study research.* Applied Social Research Methods Series, Volume 34. Newbury Park, CA: Sage Publications.

Zito, J.M., Vitrai, J. and Craig, T.J. (1993). Toward a therapeutic jurisprudence analysis of medication refusal in the court review model. *Behavioral Sciences and the Law, 11,* 151–163.

Part 5

Legal Psychology, Psychological Science and Society

Chapter 5.1

Methodology: Law's Adopting and Adapting to Psychology's Methods and Findings

Brian Clifford
University of East London, UK

As Clifford (1995) indicated, on the surface it would seem as if law and psychology share common concerns in that they are both trying to understand and predict human behaviour. However, beyond this commonality of focus, law and psychology can be seen to diverge at the level of value, basic premises, their models, their approaches, their criteria of explanation and their methods.

Tapp (1969) has gone as far as to argue that while law is value-laden and subjective, relying upon tradition and precedent, psychology is value-free and objective, relying upon empirical research. Further, while law is a practical art, a system of rules, a means of social control concerned with solving practical problems, psychology is a science, concerned with description, explanation, understanding, prediction and (benign) control of human behaviour.

At the deepest level the beliefs that psychologists hold most dear are disputed by law. Philosophically, both psychology and law struggle with causation and free will as core concepts, but whereas psychology talks of causes of behaviour, law talks of reasons for behaviour. The law assumes that people freely and consciously control their own behaviour, choosing their actions and thus taking responsibility for them. As Bentley (1979) points out, consciousness and free will are axiomatic in legal theory. Psychology, on the other hand, regards conscious intent and free choice as far from axiomatic in the real world. Psychologists argue that genetic inheritance, mental abnormality, crushing social structures, either by themselves or in combination, can render free will a luxury that cannot be countenanced or engaged in the full explanation of behaviour.

Handbook of Psychology in Legal Contexts, Second Edition
Edited by D. Carson and R. Bull. © 2003 John Wiley & Sons, Ltd.

A major battleground of law and psychology is that of 'common sense' generalisations about human behaviour. Law relies upon such generalisations fuelled by speculation, introspection, intuition, reflection, culturally transmitted beliefs and personal anecdotal observation. Psychology, in contra-distinction, favours empirical research and where feasible, and ethically practicable, experimental or systematic testing to lay bare the 'facts of the matter'.

Now if these stark polarised oppositions were reflective of the truth then the possibility of a fruitful reciprocity and fertilisation of law and psychology would be a forlorn hope. Fortunately, the reality is a little more promising. In other words, law is less ossified and tradition-bound than the above characterisation would suggest, and psychology is a more applied discipline than the above would imply. Indeed, psychology claims to be both a theoretical science and at the same time an applied discipline, able to serve in the practical affairs of the world (Clifford, 1981), because it sees itself as objective, empirical, eclectic and humane.

As a method, psychology accepts that science is but one approach to the discovery and ordering of knowledge, but one which is unique by virtue of its method and logic of discovery. Specific techniques vary between and within different sub-disciplines of psychology, but the basic method remains the same—careful, controlled observation, rational and constrained reasoning, and the subjecting of theories to empirical test. As Clifford (1995) pointed out, description is the empirical goal of psychology: explanation is its theoretical goal.

The axiomatic substructure of psychology involves beliefs that nature is orderly and regular, thus we can know human nature, because humans are just as much a part of nature as are other natural objects, and although they possess unique and distinctive characteristics they can yet be understood and explained by the same methods as all science. That is, individuals and groups exhibit sufficiently recurring, orderly and empirically demonstrable patterns as to be amenable to scientific study. Another tenet of psychology is that claims for truth must be demonstrated objectively—be intersubjectively verifiable—and that tradition, subjective belief and common sense are not sufficient for verification or falsification.

These pre-theoretical assumptions are enshrined in the 'rules of scientific enquiry' which, it must be admitted, are ideal descriptions of psychological endeavours based upon the 'hard' physical sciences. Indeed, there is a backlash against psychology's overweening 'aping' of such sciences and a strong argument that, because the subject matter of psychological study—human beings—is very different from the subject matter studied by the physical sciences, so the methods should be very different also. While this argument has eventuated in novel, and different, paradigms in psychology, such as evolutionary and critical psychology, none the less the dominant paradigm continues to be that based upon cultural borrowing from the physical sciences with a genuflection to the need to adapt methods to the nature of our subject matter. The chief 'rules' are that operational definitions must be made clear. That is, terms that are used must be defined by the steps, or operations, used to measure them. Another rule is that of generality. Discussion is about abstract variables, not particular antecedent or consequent conditions. Specifically, descriptions are stated in terms of variables, not the specific stimuli that instantiate the variable values. Thus, discussion centres on 'punishment', not 'a smack on the back of the hand'.

Another rule of science is controlled observation that is predicated upon the concept of causality. Assuming causality, the way to uncover such causality is to hold constant all variables not under test, while varying the variable that is under investigation—the hypothesised causal agent. The logic of this rule is that variables that do not vary cannot explain changes in observed behaviour.

Yet another 'rule' is replication—the backbone of science. If data (findings) are not reliable then any verification predicated upon them is likewise unreliable. Proper and sufficient replication underpins generalisability.

Over and above the procedural rules of operationalisation, controlled observation and replication, there are rules of scientific reasoning that need to be adhered to. These are parsimony, consistency and confirmation. Parsimony dictates that a more complicated explanation should never be accepted when a simpler or less complicated explanation exists. Consistency dictates that an explanatory statement must not contradict any other explanatory statement that has been confirmed. Lastly, explanatory statements must admit of predictive statements and these statements must be verifiable or, more stringently, falsifiable.

These then are the premises upon, and the methods by which, psychology operates. It believes that the scientific method is the most powerful calculus yet devised to produce verifiable and, more importantly, falsifiable knowledge. Its stress on being both a pure and an applied scientific endeavour ensures that it does not operate in a vacuum but believes it has the potential to inform and perhaps improve practical concerns in the world. One such practical concern is that of law. Having begun to interact with this practical concern, has psychology been probative or prejudicial?

In the concluding chapter of an earlier edition of this book, Carson and Bull (1995) conclude: 'It is no longer a question of whether psychology has a contribution to make to the law and its practices: psychology is making a significant contribution in a number of different ways' (p. 645). They go on to aver that 'The important questions now concern how the relationship will flourish' (p. 645).

These authors appreciate that the relationship between law and psychology is a challenging one, and largely for the reasons laid out above. The practising lawyer desires a firm answer or prediction to a particular question about human behaviour that he or she is dealing with currently: the practising experimental psychologist stresses the impossibility and, more importantly, the inappropriateness of making statements of such specificity. The science of psychology cannot offer ready made answers for the legal system, except on the rarest of occasions. Rather, it is a perpetual cycle of law adopting or adapting to psychological methods and, as will be argued below, more importantly, their findings when particular legal questions are being addressed, and of psychology using the richness of legal issues to formulate, test and verify or falsify extant and evolving applicable theory.

But, it could be objected that law and psychology are such different beasts that adoption and adaptation are inherently problematic and unrealisable. Such, I believe, is not the case. Both psychology and law ask: what is the reality? Law answers in terms of probability—beyond reasonable doubt or on the balance of probabilities. Psychology answers in terms of probabilities also, as enshrined within statistical tables, that calculate the probability of the event (reality) being due to chance. Thus both psychology and law deal with uncertainty and both end up with a decision or judgement despite this uncertainty. Law clearly has to deal with perceived subjective probabilities (e.g. how certain can we be that the person heard three shots and not two?); psychology deals with more apparently objective data (such as numbers ascribed to behaviours or responses). However, this objectivity may be more illusory than scientists like to admit, in two senses. Numbers can have different mathematical properties (level of measurement) and psychology rarely if ever achieves the most powerful level (ratio measurement). Secondly, while tables can be read off to give estimates of the occurrence of the event of interest being due to chance, and thus being statistically significant (reliable) or not, statistical significance does not necessarily mean psychological significance. Further, statistical treatment is required to establish effect size (i.e. the magnitude of the difference between conditions or the strength of a relationship). However, when we come to evaluate effect size then we are into subjective territory. Effect sizes can be judged as 'small', 'medium' or 'large'. This trichotomy—while given numerical values—is completely subjective, not objective.

In truth then, the formal methods of law and psychology are not very different—both depend upon reasoning with uncertainty. When we come to ask whether law should adopt and adapt to the methods of psychology the wrong question may be being asked. The more appropriate question may be: Should law adapt to and adopt the *content* of psychology's findings concerning reasoning and decision-making rather than the formal *nature* of that enquiry? The *findings* of psychology in the field of reasoning have much greater potency for law and its evolution than has the *method* of enquiry that psychology has applied in this field.

Let us look at a number of supposed crisis-points inhibiting the desired reciprocity between law and psychology. King (1986) argues that psychologists and psychological research purportedly concerned with legal issues fail to take sufficient account of the context of legal processes. Thus, he notes, psychological research is designed to establish universal truths about human behaviours or general flaws in procedural methods employed by criminal justice personnel, but which do not, necessarily, relate to the reliability of a particular piece of evidence or a particular witness. This assertion, however, is countered by psychologists who point out that it is the law itself which prevents the scientific investigation of the applicability of universal statements to particular cases or the probative value of general procedural doubts applying to particular instantiations of those procedures, by, for example, too slavish an adherence to the Turner rule. This rule (*R* v. *Turner*, 1975) enshrined the view of the 'transparency' of normal behaviour that can be traced back to the eighteenth century when it was argued that an expert's opinion was admissible only if it furnished the court with information that was likely to lie outside the common knowledge and experience of the jury or trier of fact. The Turner ruling argued that everyday processes such as memory, thinking and perception lay within common knowledge and experience and thus were not the proper subject matter of expert testimony. There is evidence that the courts in Britain are becoming a little more willing to admit experimental psychologists who are not proffering evidence about mental abnormality but rather are being asked about general issues. Empirical evidence shows that ordinary people generally have a very poor knowledge and understanding of psychological functions and phenomena (Furnham, 1992). This evidence suggests that the transparency assumption about normal behaviour, according to which the Turner rule has been used to exclude psychological evidence of non-clinical psychological phenomena, on the grounds that they necessarily fall within the common knowledge and experience of ordinary jurors, is due for revision. King's (1986) argument then is not critical. With goodwill and understanding on both sides, psychology can continue to produce findings that can inform and improve legal decision-making at both the legislative and litigation levels.

Another argument is that processes of legal proof express moral and political as well as epistemological values that cannot be impugned by any amount of scientific research (Bankowski, 1981, 1988). This proposition asserts that the validity of legal rules and procedures is independent of external scientific criteria and thus legal methods of gathering and evaluating evidence are also independent of scientific scrutiny. In other words, as Nelken (1994) puts it, 'law's truth' is not necessarily 'scientific truth' and in law fact-finding is not conducted in the spirit of scientific inquiry. In law, lawyers mould facts and the legal rules into a legal case (Morison and Leith, 1992). Further, as Hodgkinson (1990, p. 204) points out:

> There is no direct method of correlating the standards of proof in criminal and civil cases to the varying degrees of certainty which scientists and other experts ascribe to their findings. The criminal standard is susceptible of no precise mathematical description, such as 99% probability, and although the civil standard can be meaningfully described as 51% probability this is often difficult to translate into terms equivalent to those of scientific results or estimates.

The facts of a case must be constantly related to the relevant legal standards—a process that can call for different processes of reasoning from those involved in scientific reasoning. Indeed, McCormack (1974) distinguishes between the 'brute' facts of the empirical world and the 'institutional' facts of the legal world. Thus, in reality, a trial is not an active truth-finding inquiry but a contest between the prosecution which seeks to prove its case beyond reasonable doubt and the defence which seeks to raise a reasonable doubt about the case. Thus, Marshall (1966) has depicted the courtroom as a world of make believe where relevant evidence may not be presented, counter-evidence may not be made known and contradictions are left implicit, unexplored and unresolved.

And yet evidence is critical to all trials. As Twining (1990) indicates, the direct end of law is rectitude of decision-making. Rectitude of decision-making is arrived at by way of correct applications of valid, substantive laws and accurate determination of the facts proved to specified standards of probability on the basis of evidence which is relevant and reliable and presented to a competent and impartial decision-maker, albeit sifted by various rules of evidence—relevance, exclusion, opinion, hearsay and ultimate issue rules.

In court, it is realised that knowledge (truth) must be a matter of probability, not certainty; thus rules to determine what standard of proof is necessary to enable the facts in issue to be considered proven or not, have been established—beyond reasonable doubt in criminal cases, and on the balance of probability in civil cases.

Thus facts, and reasoning about these facts, are a central concern of the law. But is the method of factual reasoning in law so very different from that in science and thus psychology? Schum (1986) has argued that the inferential process of discovery, proof and deliberation are common to all fields of enquiry. Of late, however, controversy has surfaced concerning the applicability of conventional probability theory to legal processes (e.g. Lempert, 1986). Finkelstein and Fairley (1970) argue that it is not wrong to use statistical reasoning to resolve problems of evidence, but the appropriate method of statistical reasoning to be applied is crucial. They claim that the appropriate approach is that of Bayes' theorem. Others have protested that Bayes' theorem can be dangerous when applied to legal contexts because lay triers of fact may become confused and give undue weight to statistical data over other, unquantifiable, data (e.g. Tribe, 1971). A more fundamental critique has been offered by Cohen (1977) who questions the applicability of conventional probability theory to trial disputes, indicating that Bayesian probability is inconsistent with the rules of proof in legal trials. Cohen goes on to argue that inductive probability—rather than mathematical probability—fits the forensic context much better.

The issue of whether probability theory should and does underpin the reasoning and decision-making of lay fact-finders (juries), magistrates and judges has been visited by psychologists. Psychology's answer to the issue is to say that even although the context in which legal fact-finding is conducted is quite different from fact-finding in less institutionalised settings, none the less, at base, it is always humans who are reasoning about facts, inferring the probabilities, and making the decisions under conditions of uncertainty. This holds true whether we are looking at Allison's (1971) rational actor model, organisational process model, or bargaining games model of decision-making. All have human cogitation as the irreducible unit of analysis.

When the human is taken as the analytic unit of analysis, psychology has provided many counter-intuitive examples of human reasoning and demonstrated that we frequently make mistakes. Now while it can be argued (e.g. Carson, 1995) that the real issue is the quality of the decision and the decision-making process rather than the quality of the decision-maker, and faulty individual reasoning can always be subjected to the power of the (public) law, which will focus upon the former rather than the latter, at base this merely relocates the problem. For psychology, the primary issue is the decision-maker.

Reasoning can be seen to involve either hypothetico-deductive reasoning or inductive reasoning: that is, moving from the general to the particular or from the particular to the general. Many decision errors relate to, or involve, issues of probability, and thus are directly relevant to legal issues and decision-making. The key point to grasp is that psychology has long rejected the concept of rational decision-making based upon the normative economic-based belief that humans are rational actors. In situations of uncertainty, or information overload, humans adopt a number of 'heuristics' or 'rules of thumb' which help to arrive at decisions. Unfortunately these heuristics can lead to error (e.g. Kahneman and Tversky, 1972, 1973, 1984). Fundamentally, we use some of the information that is available to us, and disregard or discount other information which might be available and be more informative.

One such heuristic is that of representativeness. As an example, if all the families having exactly six children in a particular city were surveyed and it was shown that 72 of the families had a birth order of boy (B) and girl (G) of GBGBBG, what is your estimate of the number of families surveyed who would have had the birth order BGBBBB? The best estimate is again 72, because the gender of each birth is independent (at least, theoretically) of the gender of every other birth, and for any one birth the chance of a boy or a girl is 0.5, i.e. 1 out of 2. If you answered less than 72 to the above query then you have demonstrated the heuristic of representativeness. You will have judged the probability of an uncertain event according to (a) how obviously it is similar to or representative of the population from which it is derived, and (b) the degree to which it reflects the salient features of the process by which it is generated. If you estimated fewer than 72 families in the above example this was because the first sequence, GBGBBG, is more representative of the number of females and males in the population, and, secondly, that the first sequence looked more random than the second sequence. In fact, either birth order is equally likely to occur by chance.

Another example of the representative heuristic is the gamblers' fallacy—the false belief that the probability of a given random event is influenced by previous random events. Seven losing previous bets do not predict that the eighth bet will have a higher probability of being a winning bet.

The representative heuristic also is utilised when we are highly aware of anecdotal evidence based on a very small sample of the population—Nisbett and Ross's (1980) 'man who' argument. That is, we can frequently discount or ignore reliable data by recourse to a counter-argument that begins 'I know a man who...'!

One reason that people frequently use the representative heuristic is because they fail to understand the concept of base rates—the prevalence of an event or characteristic. In everyday decision-making, people often ignore base-rate information, even though it is important to effective judgement and decision-making.

Another major heuristic that humans use in decision-making is the availability heuristic (Tversky and Kahneman, 1973). Here we make judgements on the basis of how easily we can call to mind what we perceive as relevant instances of a phenomenon. Again, as an example, are there more words in the English language that begin with the letter R, or more words that have R as their third letter? In fact, there are more words that have an R as their third letter! The reason we tend to say that there are more words that begin with R is that we can easily generate such words, but find it difficult to generate words with the letter R in the third position.

The availability heuristic can give rise to the conjunction fallacy whereby an individual gives a higher estimate for a subset of events than for the larger set of events containing the given subset. As an example: estimate whether there are a greater number of words of seven letters ending in 'ing' or a greater number of words of seven letters with 'n' as the second to last letter, in any 2000 word passage. Tversky and Kahneman (1983) found that people estimated twice as many 'ing' as 'n' words. A little thought will show that this must be wrong.

A variant of the conjunction fallacy is the inclusion fallacy whereby individuals judge a greater likelihood that every member of an inclusive category (e.g. lawyers) has a particular characteristic than that every member of a subset of the inclusive category (e.g. criminal lawyers) has that characteristic. For example Shafir, Osherson and Smith (1990) showed that participants judged a much greater likelihood of all lawyers being conservative than every single criminal lawyer. Here judged likelihood that a member of a particular class will demonstrate a particular characteristic is based on the perceived typicality (i.e. representativeness) of the given characteristic for the given category, rather than judging likelihood based on statistical probability.

In addition to the two major heuristics (or biases) discussed above, other faulty reasoning strategies with specific relevance to legal decision-making have been identified.

Related to the availability heuristic is the so-called anchoring-and-adjustment heuristic. As an example, calculate mentally, and fairly rapidly, an estimated answer to $8 \times 7 \times 6 \times 5 \times 4 \times 3 \times 2 \times 1$. Now in the same way, quickly calculate your answer to $1 \times 2 \times 3 \times 4 \times 5 \times 6 \times 7 \times 8$. Tversky and Kahneman (1974) found the median answer to the former to be 2250, and for the latter 512. Now the products must be the same because the numbers involved are identical and the commutative law of multiplication applies. Why such divergent answers then? The answer lies in the fact that multiplication of the first few digits (the anchor) renders high or low estimate from which to make an adjustment to reach the final estimate. This anchoring-and-adjustment heuristic has relevance to an issue currently being debated in Britain: whether a defendant's previous conviction should be made known before the conclusion of a trial. The fact is that previous convictions do predict future convictions—but not perfectly. The relationship is probabilistic not certain. Thus by presenting a defendant's previous conviction adds in a further uncertainty factor and clashes with the presumption of 'innocent until proven guilty'. The anchoring-and-adjustment heuristic strongly supports the notion that previous convictions should not be made known until the conclusion of a trial has occurred.

The framing effect is another mental bias we exhibit in decision-making. This heuristic refers to the fact that the way options are presented influences the selection of, or decision about, an option. For example, we tend to choose options that demonstrate risk aversion when we are faced with an option involving potential gains, but exhibit risk-seeking when we are faced with options involving potential losses.

Thus, it can be concluded that human decision-makers are prone to error, and that human rationality is limited. Work on heuristics and biases shows the importance of distinguishing between intellectual competence and intellectual performance.

Another area of human weakness is in the calculation of probabilities and their use in decision-making.

Classical decision theory assumes that decision-makers are (a) fully informed regarding all possible options for their decisions and of all possible outcomes of their decision options, (b) infinitely sensitive to the distinctions among decision options, and (c) fully rational in regard to their choice of options (e.g. Edwards, 1954; Slovic, 1990), These assumptions of rationality mean that people make their choices so as to maximise something of value, whatever that something may be. Decision-makers are assumed to calculate the expected value for each option, which is the probability times the corresponding value (utility), and then choose the option with the highest expected value. Clearly, in most legal cases, the conditions do not allow of the application of classical decision theory.

A valid theory of decision-making in legal cases needs to account for the empirical reality and the normative elements involved in any trial (van Koppen, 1995). Life would be so simple if the evaluation of evidence could lead to a decision through a strictly logical process of consecutive steps. Such a process would require that the validity of presented evidence could be established in some objective manner and then an infallible process of inferential reasoning could be applied. Such clean, logical, infallible processes are impossible. Wigmore's (1937) description of specification of *probandum* into *facta probanda* which matches with *facta probantia* at some point requires legal proof to attain any desired degree of precision. Such is not possible, because there are always alternative explanations for any fact. A key point to note is that trials are not bottom-up processes (from facts to decisions) but rather are top-down (indictment justified by facts).

This perception of the structure of judicial reasoning suggests that trials are hypothesis testing situations and thus very much like science—which is the hypothetico-deductive approach *per excellence*. This approach has become popular in modelling decision-making in legal cases (Edwards, 1988; Goldsmith, 1980; Saks and Kidd, 1980). This approach is Bayesian probability. Here it is assumed that the decision-maker has a certain prior belief in the truth of the hypothesis being advanced, expressible in terms of odds (a number between zero and infinity). This prior odds is obtained by dividing the probability of the hypothesis being true by the probability of its being false. The presentation of trial evidence presents new information upon which prior odds can be advanced to posterior odds (or belief). The posterior odds is achieved by multiplying prior odds by the diagnostic value of the newly presented evidence. This new posterior odds then becomes prior odds for the next piece of evidence to be given. When all the evidence has been presented the decision-maker has arrived at a final posterior odds value which, when compared with a preset (or imposed) level of confidence, can allow a decision of guilty or not guilty. As van Koppen (1995) correctly points out this Bayesian approach seems an elegant model of judicial decision-making. However, the problem is that, psychologically, it is a nonsense.

On the assumption that a person is innocent until proven guilty the initial prior odds must be zero. Any number multiplied by zero is zero. Thus there would never be a guilty verdict! However, this iron law of mathematics is impotent in the face of psychology. Prior odds are formulated after the introduction of the case, thus the initial prior odds from which all future calculations emanate is far from zero.

The second major problem with the Bayesian approach—or any quantitative approach to decision-making—is that the value of evidence must be quantifiable. However, the diagnostic value of evidence is nowhere certain in most cases. Research has suggested certain procedures can be quantified in terms of their evidential value but much doubt and debate remains—see, for example, the use of anatomically correct dolls in sexual abuse cases; line-up diagnosticity; DNA-profiling; hypnosis; the polygraph, and so on.

A third major problem with the logical approach of Bayesian probability is the revision of probabilities from prior to posterior to final posterior odds. As Cohen (1977) and Wagenaar (1991) have pointed out: (i) compensation of one fact for another, (ii) many facts of low diagnostic value compared with one fact of high(?) diagnostic value, (iii) and the independence or interaction of one fact with another, cannot be handled by the Bayesian model.

The last problem for the Bayesian model is that it does not explain how a criterion (for conviction or acquittal) is chosen or set. What does 'beyond reasonable doubt' actually mean? What does 'on the balance of probabilities' actually mean?

From the above it should be clear that the proposing of a Bayesian model of hypothesis testing for decision-making in legal cases is both unsuccessful as a descriptive model and useless as a prescriptive model.

An alternative, more psychologically based, model to that of either Classical or Bayesian decision theory is that of subjective expected utility theory. According to this theory humans in coming to a decision seek to maximise positive utility and to minimise negative utility. To achieve this, however, we need to make calculations of both subjective utility, based on judged weightings of utility rather than on objective criteria, and subjective probabilities, based on individual estimates of likelihood, rather than on objective statistical computations. According to subjective expected utility theory, then, each person will multiply each subjective probability by each subjective positive utility, subtract the calculation of the subjective probability of each subjective negative utility, and then reach a decision which chooses the highest expected value.

However, human decision-making is even more complex than this, because the above assumes that (a) all possible alternatives are known and considered, (b) use is made of all information available, (c) careful, if subjective, weighting of the potential costs (risks) and benefits of each alternative is performed, (d) careful but subjective calculation of the probability of various outcomes is undertaken, given that the certainty of outcomes cannot be known, and (e) sound reasoning is then applied. Slovic (1990) argues that while subjective expected utility theory offers a poor description of actual human decision-making, it does offer a good prescription for enhancing the effectiveness of decision-making when confronting a decision important enough to warrant the time and mental effort required—as in legal issues. However, that subjective utility theory does or could offer a good prescription for enhancing the effectiveness of decision-making under the conditions stipulated by Slovic is, I believe, doubtful.

From earliest times psychologists have questioned the notions of unlimited rationality and information processing capacity that underlie Classical, Bayesian and subjective expected utility theory. Specifically, Simon (1957) suggested that while humans are not necessarily irrational, none the less they show bounded rationality—we are rational but within limits. Simon suggests humans typically use a decision-making strategy he termed satisficing. Rather than considering all possible options and computing which of the universe of options will maximise our gains or minimise our losses, he suggests that we consider options one by one, and select an option as soon as we find one that is satisfactory or good enough to meet our minimum level of acceptability.

In the 1970s Tversky (1972a, 1972b) built on Simon's notion of bounded rationality by suggesting a process of elimination by aspects. This is achieved by focusing upon an aspect (attribute) of the various options, and forming a minimum criterion for that aspect. We then eliminate all options that do not meet that criterion. For the remaining options we then select another aspect for which we set a minimum criterion by which to eliminate additional options. By a process of iteration we reduce all alternatives until a single option remains.

Thus we make decisions based on less than optimal strategies and within this psychological framework, we additionally utilise mental shortcuts (heuristics) and unconscious biases such as those described above. These further limit and may even distort our ability to make rational decisions. One of the key shortcuts centres on our estimation of probabilities, and has been shown to be present in all decision-making theories set out above, and must be so when uncertainty is present.

However, research has shown that humans have difficulty with simple, combined and especially conditional probability (such as Bayes' theorem). The simple probability of event A is $p(A)$; the negation of the probability of event A is $\sim(pA) = 1 - p(A)$; the combined probability of two mutually exclusive events $= p(A) + p(B)$; the combined probability of two independent events $= p(A) \times p(B)$. Confusion between the different types of probability can be crucial in criminal cases as the recent trial and conviction of a mother who was charged with the murder of her two children (at different times) shows. A key piece of evidence was the assertion that the chance of two children dying from cot-death (the alternative explanation) was 1 in 73 million. This probability statement is commonly regarded as having convinced the jury that the mother should be found guilty. This figure, it has since been argued (Watkins, 2000), was based upon the calculation of the combined probability of independent events. What would the probability estimate be, however, if it was demonstrable that they were not independent events, but rather could be linked by, for example, a cot-death gene, transmittable from the mother (or father)? The estimated probability drops precipitously, to about 1 in 4!

From all that has been said above about psychological research into human decision-making, it would be misguided to assume that jurors, judges or magistrates are fully rational, calculating machines with infallible reasoning and decision-making capabilities. When a human acts as a judicial fact-finder and decision-maker his or her human information processing limitations, cognitive biases and heuristics, and 'grounded' beliefs, values, attitudes and opinions are not somehow miraculously set aside to be replaced with unlimited rationality, cognitive capacity and infallible logical reasoning powers. Once a human, always a human: irrespective of what role ascription one finds oneself in.

But if humans are poor at hypothetico-deductive reasoning could it not be that they are good at inferential reasoning: reasoning from specific facts or observations to a general conclusion that may explain the facts? Unfortunately, such seems not to be the case. Psychology has demonstrated that humans have difficulty with causal inferences whether it be with Mill's (1874) method of agreement, or his method of difference; with the law of large numbers, or with base-rate information; and with configuration bias, illusory correlation, and correlation per se.

Holyoak and Nisbett (1988) suggest that humans use both bottom-up (evidence based) and top-down (existing knowledge) strategies when drawing inferences. More recently Sloman (1996) has suggested that humans have two complementary systems of reasoning. The first is an associative system that involves mental operations based upon observed similarities and temporal contiguities. The second is a rule-based system. The associative system can lead to fast responses that are based on well-learned patterns and general tendencies, focusing on salient typical-features of a situation. This system, however, makes use of the error-producing representativeness heuristic discussed above, belief-bias effects in syllogistic reasoning, plausibility effects in causal reasoning and enhancement of conditional reasoning in pragmatic context.

The second system is based on rules of evidence evaluation that we have built up over a lifetime and have stored away for painstaking decision-making situations. This system allows us to understand logical reasoning when it is explained to us; allows us to rule out contradiction, impossibilities and improbabilities. Sloman (1996) argues that we need both systems to fully explicate human reasoning in both everyday and specialist (e.g. legal) contexts. The issue being raised here is whether the rule-based system is, or in fact can be, used in the latter type of situation.

So, what is left as a model for the decision-making approaches seen in law if psychology rules out, on the one hand, a clean crisp hypothetico-deductive capability for humans, in terms of either conditional reasoning: stressing their difficulty with *modus ponens* and *modus tollens*, and their willingness to engage in deductive fallacies of denying the antecedent and affirming the consequent; or in reasoning with both linear and categorical syllogisms, and their known difficulties with universal and particular affirmative and negative premises; or, on the other hand, inductive reasoning in which humans have been shown to have less than ideal capability? The options are, in fact, numerous, consensual and in harmony with what goes on in court cases and other decision-making fora.

The most powerful 'explanation' of humans' attempts to deal with deductive reasoning problems is that of 'mental models' (see Johnson–Laird, 1983). A mental model is an internal representation of information that corresponds analogously with whatever is being represented. Here logical problems are being solved not logically but psychologically!

As with deductive reasoning, so with inductive reasoning, psychology rather than logic best encapsulates the pragmatic reality. This conception has been most comprehensively captured by the anchored narrative approach of Wagenaar, van Koppen and Crombag (1993). These authors articulate the key point that at trial the key finders of fact are often (if not always) confronted with a problem that has no logical solution. As Wagenaar (1995) point out there is no algorithm (step by step approach) for solving such ill-defined problems. The laws, and rules of evidence, give some guidance but the final criterion for acceptance of a solution is purely subjective. Further, this subjective criterion for decision-making is based upon the evaluation of the narrative offered by the prosecution or defence barristers. A good narrative is a story that is characterised by the presence of a coherent central action and a setting that makes the action understandable (Bennett and Feldman, 1981; Pennington and Hastie, 1986, 1988). To be accepted as a good narrative in court, however, the stories being told must be tied to reality by means of evidence. However, the evidence itself is yet another narrative, defined as either strong or weak by its consistency and the compellingness of circumstances.

Wagenaar et al. (1993) stress that legal narrative involves the themes of identity, *actus reus* and *mens rea*. Each of these themes require anchoring in generally accepted beliefs which can be argued to be knowledge of the world in the form of general rules which are usually valid. However the major problem of judicial decision-making, conceived as anchoring narratives, is that plausibility and anchoring do not require the logical exclusion of other and perhaps better narratives.

This view of how judicial decision-making actually occurs pays full homage to the psychological rather than the logic aspect of decision-making. Anchoring can countenance, and in fact implies, all the heuristics and mental shortcuts and biases that were outlined above. In this sense then psychology and law are brought closer together by this theory. The key point is that this theory of judicial reasoning can be seen as the logical end point of all the difficulties that psychology has shown humans to have with the need for infinite rationality, unlimited cognitive capacity and totally objective reasoning.

Now embedded in what has been said above, is an implicit argument against the use of expert (psychological) evidence. In many countries, and many jurisdictions, the argument has been debated that, in the light of psychological evidence, only the admission of expert opinion can help to stave off the fallible decision-making that is replete in legal cases. A case in point would be the common belief exhibited by courts in eyewitness testimony. Eyewitness evidence can have a very powerful effect in court requiring no further grounding or anchoring, especially if the Turnbull conditions have been met. However, for some time now, the veracity of eyewitness testimony has been questioned by experimental psychology (Clifford and Bull, 1978; Loftus, 1979; Yarmey, 1979) but, in turn, this questioning has been the site of contestation in several journals (e.g. *Law and Human Behaviour*, 1986; *American Psychologist*, 1993; *Expert Evidence*, 1996/7; Clifford, 1997; Yarmey, 1996; Ebbesen and Konecni, 1996). Moreover, the injection of experts into this decision-making arena may well create greater not lesser uncertainty.

But there is a more fundamental point. If lay fact-finders are inherently unreliable decision-makers, by virtue of being limited capacity humans, are not experts also unreliable decision-makers, again by virtue of being human and thus limited capacity information processors? There is nothing which stipulates that lay persons are inherently irrational while experts are inherently rational, by virtue of their expertise. All psychology-based experts, be they psychiatrists, clinical psychologists, or experimental (academic) psychologists, have to reason with, and within, uncertainty. To this extent they are no different from the lay fact-finder and decision-maker. They are all dealing with probability, not certainty.

Now it may be that these three types of expert, who may appear before the court, can be argued to be dealing with different degrees of certainty. For example, the clinical psychologist will have interviewed the defendant, have administered a number of valid and reliable tests, and would have been able to place the particular person in the particular case under review within a vector of relevant dimensions. The psychiatrist on the other hand will, again, have interviewed the defendant, but may or may not have passed him or her through a series of more or less validated and normed tests. Thus the psychiatrist's opinion is likely to be weaker (less grounded or defensible) than that of the clinical psychologist. The experimental psychologist, called, for example, on the basis of disputed testimony will not have had access to the person whose testimony he or she will be asked to offer an opinion on. Rather this type of expert will be asked to give an opinion about the general case of which the case under review may or may not be a particular instance.

In all three cases the 'evidence' presented in court is less than certain. If a clinical psychologist finds that a person has low intelligence there is some probability that he or she will be suggestible and prone to false confession. If the person is also found to be suggestible on a suggestibility scale (for example, Gudjonsson's, 1997 Suggestibility Scale), the probability of a confession being false increases, but not to unity. Thus there is still uncertainty and decisions as to whether the actual testimony was false or not is a problematic estimate. In the case of a psychiatric opinion the interview may suggest a psychopathic personality type—but this can be far from certain. If the defendant is also passed through a psychopathic checklist (for example, Hare, 1991—PCL-R) the probability of psychopathic tendencies can be spoken of with greater certitude, but not certainty. An additional problem is that a differently based assessment, predicated upon a standardised personality scale (such as the MMPI), could issue in a different conclusion. That is, the two assessment measures do not necessarily result in exactly the same classification being accorded to a particular individual (e.g. Harpur, Hare and Hakstian, 1989). Lastly, the whole issue of psychopathy has undergone theoretical and validity disputation (Howells, 1982; Grounds, 1987), and, as a concept, is probabilistic rather than certain.

In the case of the experimental psychologist giving evidence about the fallibility of eyewitness testimony a statement may be made that empirical tests have shown that 40% of eyewitness evidence is known to be wrong. However, how should the trier of fact reason from this? Is the current witness testimony to be categorised as falling within the 40% that is wrong or within the 60% that is correct? Further is this 40/60 split true for all conditions? Can error rate be massaged downwards by any known procedures? Were such procedures employed, and employed effectively in the particular case under review? This evidence may not be presented, thus leaving the trier of fact with increased uncertainty.

Clearly, in all cases the role of the expert is not to deliver certainty, it is merely to advance the reasoning of the fact-finder by the insights conveyed by the expert. The inherent difficulty in this is that the expert's opinion could merely make the fact-finder's task more difficult by adding probabilistic knowledge to the already saturated probabilistic decision space of the trier of fact.

And yet the rigour of the scientific method with which this chapter is concerned has been brought to bear on legal issues. The law frequently deals with concepts of 'incompetency' (Grisso, 1986), 'incapacity' (Law Commission Consultation Paper, 1993) and 'vulnerabilities' (Metropolitan Police, 1991). These legal concepts are amenable to psychological assessment and test. In fact one pole of the whole psychometric tradition has been concerned with psychological deficit and vulnerability.

The use of such tests that have demonstrated validity, reliability and have undergone standardisation can allow the evaluation of an individual in relation to a particular reference group, and can be expressed in various numerical terms, such as percentages, percentiles or standard deviations. This provides some clarity to triers of fact. By the use of such tests it is contended that legal issues concerning intellectual abilities, social functioning, neurological status, personality, competence to stand trial, moral development and reasoning ability, post-traumatic stress disorder, dangerousness, anger management, deception and malingering, have all been given some empirical basis upon which triers of fact can thus better formulate their reasoning and decision-making.

The point made above concerning the relative certainty injected into a trial situation by a clinical psychologist versus a psychiatrist hinges upon the use or otherwise of such standardised tests. As Gudjonsson (1995) indicates, forensic psychiatrist usually base their assessment on a clinical interview and, because they lack training and expertise in administering psychological tests, rarely on grounded empirical findings. This means their evidence is generally less factually based than the clinical psychologists' evidence, relying almost exclusively on an opinion.

But note further that even for the clinical psychologist his or her opinion is precisely that, an opinion. Psychometric tests are 'snapshots' of a person's current psychological status, and present a 'point estimate' of a multidimensional psychological being. Opponents of the psychometric movement stress that such tests are de-contextualised, attitudinal rather than behavioural, and essentially artificial paper-and-pencil extrapolations from real-life behaviour. As such, any conclusions drawn from them are probabilistic rather than certain.

CONCLUSION

The 'method' of Psychology is very different from the 'method' of Law. Broadly, the two methodologies can be cast as polar opposites on a great number of dimensions. And yet law and psychology do enrich each other. Psychology has impacted both the individual case and, more broadly, legal structures and procedure as well as appeals procedure. And this is as it should be given that the law is based upon theories and expectations of human behaviour, intentionality and judgement. The legal structure has been changed and enhanced by psychological knowledge and empirical data, operating at both the litigation and legislative levels (see Carson, 1995). Psychology has aided the court in the evaluation of such techniques as hypnosis, lie detection, the polygraph, anatomically correct dolls, and the 'live link'. It has provided evidence on issues such as the fallibility of eyewitness and earwitness testimony, false confessions, suggestibility and vulnerability. Empirical psychological research has informed in Britain the Memorandum of Good Practice (1992), the Code of Practice under the Police and Criminal Evidence Act (1984) and was informative in the Report of the Royal Commission on Criminal Justice (1993). Psychological research has also served to underpin certain new civil and criminal grounds such as Post-Traumatic Stress Disorder, Battered Wife Syndrome, Pre-menstrual Tension Syndrome and many others.

Thus the law has adopted many of the well-founded findings of the science of psychology. What remains to be seen is whether it will adapt to certain findings of psychology which strike at the very heart of the judicial system—legal decision-making in, of necessity, situations of uncertainty. Judges, jurors and magistrates have been regarded as rational, objective decision-makers: psychological research strongly suggests that this assumption lacks empirical foundation. Rather, judicial decision-making, dealing as it must in probabilities, can be characterised as, at best, quasi-rational and subjective. Evidence that humans cannot handle pure deductive or inductive reasoning, and that probabilities are dealt with by heuristic and mental shortcut strategies, and that the facts and evidence presented by opposing barristers are attended to as narratives and stories which are anchored and thus given credence in a way that obviates the need to seek further, logical, explanation, should be a cause for concern for Law.

That judicial fact-finders have difficulty with certain aspects of legal procedure has been recognised by Law itself. For example, in complex fraud cases it has been argued that juries should be dispensed with; in the States, juries have been reduced in size, for a variety of reasons; the decision rule is variable—unanimous, 10-2, simple majority. In Britain why should 2 hours 10 minutes be critical in moving from a unanimous decision requirement to one of a 10-2 majority? The research cited above suggests that a much more radical approach to understanding juries and juror behaviour is required. From a scientific view, Section 8 of the Contempt of Court Act 1981 which, in Britain, prevents asking jurors about their deliberation, must be looked at again. This would be a very important first step towards the law adapting to the method and findings of psychology.

But as Lloyd-Bostock (1995) pointed out, juries are present in Britain in only about 2% of all criminal cases, and in few if any civil cases. Thus the clear message of non-rationality, mental heuristics and subjective handling of probabilities applies to many more fact-finders than jury members. It applies to judges, magistrates, and to psychologists who present their findings in court or by way of pre-trial reports. All are dealing with uncertainty: never certainty. The purpose of this chapter has been to show that, on the surface, psychology and law both deal in uncertainty and thus probabilities; and while psychology can take refuge in statistical testing which does handle probability mathematically, systematically and logically, no such luxury is afforded the trier of fact. But when the psychologist steps outside his or her laboratory and attempts to particularise from the general then he or she is in exactly the same sea of uncertainty. In this real sense, then, it is not so much law adapting to the methods of psychology, rather it is the need for both parties to accept, at the law–psychology interface, that uncertainty is the reality and that both disciplines have to come to terms with the realisation that where uncertainty is found, psycho-logical rather than logical reasoning will predominate, with all that that entails.

REFERENCES

Allison, G.T. (1971). *Essence of decision: Explaining the Cuban missile crises*. Boston, MA: Little, Brown.
Author (1993). *American Psychologist, 48* (5), 550–580.
Bankowski, Z. (1981). The value of truth: Fact-scepticism revisited. *Legal Studies, 1*, 257.
Bankowski, Z. (1988). The jury and reality. In M. Findley and P. Duff (eds), *The jury under attack*. London: Butterworth.
Bennett, W.L. and Feldman, M.S. (1981). *Reconstructing reality in the courtroom*. London: Tavistock.
Bentley, D. (1979). The infant and the dream: Psychology and the law. In D. Farrington, K. Hawkins and S. Lloyd-Bostock (eds), *Psychology, law and legal processes*. London: Macmillan.
Carson, D. (1995). Public law decisions. In R. Bull and D. Carson (eds), *Handbook of psychology in legal contexts*. Chichester: John Wiley & Sons.
Carson, D. and Bull, R. (1995). Psychology and law: Future directions. In R. Bull and D. Carson (eds), *Handbook of psychology in legal contexts*. Chichester: John Wiley & Sons.
Clifford, B.R. (1981). Towards a more realistic appraisal of the psychology of testimony. In S. Lloyd-Bostock (ed.), *Psychology in legal context: Applications and limitations*. London: Academic Press.
Clifford, B.R. (1995). Psychology's premises, methods and values. In R. Bull and D. Carson (eds), *Handbook of psychology in legal contexts*. Chichester: John Wiley & Sons.
Clifford, B.R. (1997). A commentary on Ebbesen and Konecni's 'eyewitness memory research: Probative v. Prejudicial value'. *Expert Evidence, 5*, 140–143.
Clifford, B.R. and Bull, R. (1978). *The psychology of person identification*. London: Routledge.
Cohen, L.J. (1977). *The probable and the provable*. Oxford: Clarendon.
Ebbesen, E.B. and Konecni, V.J. (1996). Eyewitness memory research: Probative v. Prejudicial value. *Expert Evidence, 5*, 2–28.
Edwards, W. (1954). The theory of decision making. *Psychological Bulletin, 51*, 380–417.
Edwards, W. (1988). Summing up: The society of Bayesian trial lawyers. In P. Tillers and E.D. Green (eds), *Probability and inference in the law of evidence*. Dordrecht, Netherlands: Kluwer Academic.
Expert Evidence (1996/1997). Vol. *5* (1/2), 2–28; (3), 89–97; and (4), 140–143.
Finkelstein, M.O. and Fairley, W.B. (1970). A Bayesian approach to identification evidence. *Harvard Law Review, 83*, 489.
Furnham, A. (1992). Prospective psychology students' knowledge of psychology. *Psychological Reports, 70*, 375–382.
Goldsmith, R.W. (1980). Studies of a model for evaluating judicial evidence. *Acta Psychologica, 45*, 211–221.
Grisso, T. (1986). *Evaluating competencies. Forensic assessment and instruments*. New York: Plenum Press.
Grounds, A.T. (1987). Detention of psychopathic disordered patients in special hospitals: Critical issues. *British Journal of Psychiatry, 151*, 474–478.
Gudjonsson, G.H. (1995). Psychology and assessment. In R. Bull and D. Carson (eds), *Handbook of psychology in legal contexts*. Chichester: John Wiley & Sons.
Gudjonsson, G.H. (1997). *The Gudjonsson Suggestibility Scales*. Hove: Psychology Press.
Hare, R.D. (1991). *The Hare Psychopathy Checklist—Revised*. Toronto: Multi-Health Systems.
Harpur, T.J., Hare, R.D. and Hakstian, A.R. (1989). Two-factor conceptualization of psychopathy: construct validation and assessment implications. *Psychological Assessment: A Journal of Consulting and Clinical Psychology, 1*, 6–17.

Hodgkinson, T. (1990). *Expert evidence: Law and practice*. London: Sweet & Maxwell.

Holyoak, K.J. and Nisbett, R.E. (1988). Induction. In R.J. Sternberg and E.E. Smith (eds), *The psychology of human thought*. New York: Cambridge University Press.

Howells, K. (1982). Mental disorder and violent crime. In P. Feldman (ed.), *Developments in the study of criminal behaviour. Vol. 2: Violence*. Chichester: John Wiley & Sons.

Johnson-Laird, P.N. (1983). *Mental models*. Cambridge, MA: Harvard University Press.

Kahneman, D. and Tversky, A. (1972). Subjective probability: A judgement of representativeness. *Cognitive Psychology*, *3*, 430–454.

Kahneman, D. and Tversky, A. (1973). On the psychology of prediction. *Psychological Review*, *80*, 237–251.

Kahneman, D. and Tversky, A. (1984). Choices, values and frames. *American Psychologist*, *39*, 341–350.

King, M. (1986). *Psychology in and out of court*. Oxford: Pergamon Press.

Law and Human Behaviour (1986). Vol. *10* (1/2), 1–181.

Law Commission Consultation Paper (1993). *Mentally incapacitated adults and decision-making: A new jurisdiction*. London: HMSO (Papers No.128 and 129).

Lempert, R. (1986). The new evidence scholarship: Analysing the process of proof. *Boston University Law Review*, *66*, 439.

Lloyd-Bostock, S. (1995). The jury in the United Kingdom: Juries and jury research in context. In G. Davies, S. Lloyd-Bostock, M. McMurren and C. Wilson (eds), *Psychology, law and criminal justice: International developments in research and practice*. Berlin: de Gruyter.

Loftus, E.F. (1979). *Eyewitness testimony*. Cambridge, MA: Harvard University Press.

Marshall, J. (1966). *Law and psychology in conflict*. Garden City: Anchor Doubleday.

Memorandum of good practice for video recorded interviews with child witnesses for criminal proceedings (1992). Home Office/Department of Health. London: HMSO.

Metropolitan Police (1991). *A change of PACE. A guide to the changes to the codes of practice*. London: New Scotland Yard.

Mill, J.S. (1874). *A system of logic*. New York: Harper.

Morison, J. and Leith, P. (1992). *The barrister's world*. Milton Keynes: Open University Press.

McCormack, N. (1974). Law and institutional fact. *Law Quarterly Review*, *90*, 102.

Nelken, D. (1994). *The truth about law's truth*. London: Pluto.

Nisbett, R. and Ross, L. (1980). *Human inferences and short-comings in social judgment*. Englewood Cliffs, NJ: Prentice Hall.

Pennington, N. and Hastie, R. (1986). Evidence evaluation in complex decision making. *Journal of Personality and Social Psychology*, *51*, 242–258.

Pennington, N. and Hastie, R. (1988). Explanation-based decision-making: affects of memory structure on judgment. *Journal of Experimental Psychology: Learning, Memory and Cognition*, *14*, 521–533.

Royal Commission on Criminal Justice (1993). *Report* (Cmnd. 2262/3). London: HMSO.

Saks, M.J. and Kidd, R.F. (1980). Human information processing and adjudication: Trial by heuristics. *Law and Society Review*, *15*, 123–160.

Schum, D.A. (1986). Probability and the process of discovery, proof and choice. *Boston University Law Review*, *66*, 825.

Shafir, E.B., Osherson, D.N. and Smith, E.E. (1990). Typicality and reasoning fallacies. *Memory and Cognition*, *18* (3), 229–239.

Simon, H.A. (1957). *Administrative behaviour* (2nd edn). Totowa, NJ: Littlefield, Adams.

Sloman, S. (1996). The empirical case for two systems of reasoning. *Psychological Bulletin*, *119*, 3–22.

Slovic, P. (1990). Choice. In D.N. Osherson and E.E. Smith (eds), *An invitation to cognitive science: Vol. 3. Thinking*. Cambridge MA: MIT Press.

Tapp, J.L. (1969). Psychology and the law: The dilemma. *Psychology Today*, *11*, 16–22.

Tribe, L.H. (1971). Trial by mathematics: Precision and ritual in the legal process. *Harvard Law Review*, *84*, 1329.

Turner (*R* v. *Turner* [1975], All ER 70, 75).

Tversky, A. (1972a). Choice by elimination. *Journal of Mathematical Psychology*, *9*, 341–367.

Tversky, A. (1972b). Elimination by aspects: A theory of choice. *Psychological Review*, *79*, 281–289.

Tversky, A. and Kahneman, D. (1973). Availability: A heuristic for judging frequency and probability. *Cognitive Psychology*, *5*, 207–232.

Tversky, A. and Kahneman, D. (1974). Judgment under uncertainty: Heuristics and biases. *Science*, *185*, 1124–1131.

Tversky, A. and Kahneman, D. (1983). Extensional versus intuitive reasoning: The conjunction fallacy in probability judgment. *Psychological Review*, *90*, 293–315.

Twining, W.L. (1990). *Rethinking evidence*. Oxford: Blackwell.

van Koppen, P.J. (1995). Judges' decision-making. In R. Bull and D. Carson (eds), *Handbook of psychology in legal contexts*. Chichester: John Wiley & Sons.

Wagenaar, W.A. (1991). Waar logica faalt en verhalen overtuigen: Een beschouwing over het strafrechtelijk be wijs. *Onze Alma Mater*, *45*, 256–278 (in translation).

Wagenaar, W.A. (1995). Anchored narratives: A theory of judicial reasoning and its consequences. In G. Davies, S. Lloyd-Bostock, M. McMurran and C. Wilson (eds), *Psychology, law and criminal justice: International developments in research and practice*. Berlin: de Gruyter.

Wagenaar, W.A., van Koppen, P.J. and Crombag, H.F.M. (1993). *Anchored narratives: The psychology of criminal evidence*. Hemel Hempstead: Harvester Wheatsheaf.

Watkins, S.J. (2000). Conviction by mathematical error. *British Medical Journal*, *320*, 2–3.

Wigmore, J.H. (1937). *The science of judicial proof as given by logic, psychology and general experience* (3rd edn). Boston: Little, Brown.

Yarmey, A.D. (1979). *The psychology of eyewitness testimony*. New York: Free Press.

Yarmey, A.D. (1996). Expert evidence—a reply to Ebbesen and Konecni. *Expert Evidence*, *5* (3), 89–97.

Chapter 5.2

Interviewing and Assessing Clients from Different Cultural Backgrounds: Guidelines for all Forensic Professionals

Martine B. Powell *and* **Terry Bartholomew**
Deakin University, Australia

The range of people who come into contact with the criminal justice system (whether as witnesses, victims, or alleged perpetrators of criminal acts) is diverse, but minority racial and ethnic groups are overly represented in all Western judicial and penal systems (Manson, 1997; Mildren, 1997; Robin et al., 1997; Singer, 1996; Thomas, 1987). Despite their disproportionate presence, it is widely recognised that people from minority groups are systematically disadvantaged at numerous stages of criminal justice processing, and that this has ramifications at the procedural, substantive and sentencing levels (e.g. see Cain, 1994; Human Rights and Equal Opportunity Commission, 1993; Pope and Feyerherm, 1991; Poulos and Orchowsky, 1994; Siegal, 1988). This cultural diversity poses major problems for professionals such as police, lawyers, and psychologists because one of the fundamental tasks of any forensic professional is to elicit relevant, detailed and accurate information from the interviewee. Success is often mediated by the professional's ability to communicate clearly, to assess the communicative ability of the interviewee, and to make appropriate adjustments. When there are fundamental differences between the professional's and the client's language and culture, the potential for miscommunication and the risk of eliciting information that is misleading, unreliable and/or self-incriminating is elevated (Cooke, 1998; Siegal, 1988).

Given the unchallenged importance of providing equal access to due process protections, it is vital that professionals who assist in the investigation of complaints

Handbook of Psychology in Legal Contexts, Second Edition
Edited by D. Carson and R. Bull. © 2003 John Wiley & Sons, Ltd.

by and against people from cultural minority groups, adopt a 'minority perspective' in their interviewing practice (see French, 1987; Mildren, 1997). At present, there is a relative paucity of discussion in psycho-legal arenas about the varied cultural and contextual needs of clients from minority groups. Similarly, there is a concomitant lack of guidance about the specific implications of these concerns, and the numerous ways that forensic professionals should be sensitive to them. While legal research and commentary reveals an ever-increasing number of cases where the processes followed in eliciting evidence from 'minority' defendants has been questionable (e.g. see Aldridge and Wood, 1998; Criminal Justice Commission, 1996; Cronheim and Schwartz, 1976; Lawrie, 1999; Manson, 1997; Mildren, 1997; Roy, 1990), most legal psychology textbooks and training courses fail to address issues related to multicultural assessment or interviewing practice (Powell and Bartholomew, in press; Young, 1989). Despite these numerous indicators of need, coherent recommendations about how practitioners can accommodate these differences have not been forthcoming.

This chapter seeks to address these concerns by offering an overview of the critical elements required to obtain relevant and accurate information from forensic clients who are from cultural minority groups. These elements, which form the acronym 'PRIDE', include:

- Prior knowledge about the person and the wider context,

- Rapport with the client/interviewee,

- Interpretative assistance (if required),

- Diverse array of hypotheses about the alleged offence, and

- Effective techniques for eliciting a free narrative.

The PRIDE framework was first developed and discussed by Powell (2000a, 2000b) in the context of conducting investigative interviews with Australian Aboriginal people. However the model is applicable to a range of cultural groups, and to all verbal interactions where the goal is the elicitation of accurate and reliable information about a person or event. Specifically, this chapter offers a description of, and rationale for, the importance of each element of the PRIDE framework, while making specific reference to the relevant legal, linguistic, and eyewitness memory literature. Although the authors acknowledge that cultural concerns are relevant to all processing stages (e.g. the trial, sentencing, and treatment phases to name a few), the interview/assessment process is the focus of this chapter because it often represents the first (and arguably the most important) point of contact with a forensic client.

PRIOR KNOWLEDGE ABOUT THE PERSON AND THE WIDER CULTURAL CONTEXT

The first step in a productive interview or assessment with a person from a cultural minority group is the identification of the specific group the person belongs to (a group-based issue) and the *degree* to which that person identifies with a particular group (an individualized issue) (Milan, Chin and Nguyen, 1999). Without an understanding of each of these factors, it is not possible to probe issues appropriately, understand the context and meaning of the client's behaviour and verbal reports, or provide a thorough analysis of the client's problems and needs.

The reliance on (i) the clients' report of their 'cultural identity' and (ii) their level of adherence to that culture reflects a contemporary rejection of essentialistic notions of one's biological make-up (i.e. 'race') as deterministic. Relying on the construct of 'cultural identity' affords individuals a level of agency about their socio-demographic status, while terms such as 'race' and 'ethnicity' have been criticised for making behavioural attributions from physiognomic features (Zuckerman, 1990). In their critique of the use of such constructs in psychological research, Betancourt and Lopez (1993) observed that many researchers use the terms 'race', 'ethnicity' and 'culture' interchangeably, while Okazaki and Sue (1995) noted that 'confusion or a lack of differentiation among race, ethnicity, and culture at the terminology level likely reflects confusion at the conceptual level' (p. 368). Despite the gamut of unresolved questions that such uncertainty raises (see Betancourt and Lopez, 1993, for a useful outline), current practices concede a collective or 'group-based' element to the notion of culture, while also acknowledging that cultural membership is not always correlated with biological or lifestyle characteristics. This idiographic component of the information gathering exercise allows for the idea that cultural practices vary markedly across regions, generations, socio-economic subgroups, and individuals. For instance, even within siblings of similar age groups, there is considerable variation in adherence to cultural traditions and practices, as well as the level of familiarity and identification with the mainstream language and socio-legal culture (Sattler, 1998).

The implications of these concerns is that a person's cultural background and the degree to which that person identifies with the cultural group needs to be elicited *directly* from the client, or from credible persons who have a good understanding of the client's background and position in the community. The need to obtain background material first-hand from clients is a particularly important consideration for professionals who conduct forensic assessments/interviews in different regions and have little prior contact with the client and his or her family or community on a day-to-day level.

The second step in eliciting accurate and detailed knowledge from a person from a cultural minority group involves a consideration of how relevant cultural variables are likely to impact on the interview or assessment process. Specifically, the potential role of three factors relating to the clients' cultural identity need to be considered.

These include: (i) the person's dialect, (ii) the person's usual style of relating, and (iii) factors relevant to the person's kin-based network(s), cultural practices and beliefs about various situations. Each of these factors is now discussed in turn.

The Person's Dialect

Many people of minority cultural backgrounds do not speak their country's main language. In these cases, the barriers to effective communication between the (main language) professional and interviewee are obvious; an interview or assessment cannot proceed without access to an appropriate interpreter. However, there are many people who speak some of this language (i.e. enough to partake in general conversation). In these instances, the decision about whether the client's communication skills are 'good enough' to undertake an interview without the aid of an interpreter often rests with the client and/or the professional. Although both parties invariably lack definitive thresholds about what 'good enough' competency actually is (Aldridge and Wood, 1998), the professional at least has some understanding of the events that are likely to follow the interview, and the effect of the interview on those subsequent events. In most instances, the client has no such knowledge.

Determining the client's competency in the dominant language on the basis of a brief interaction is fraught with difficulty because forensic interview or assessment procedures require considerable clarity and detail about the alleged offence(s) (i.e. time, place and contextual factors), the physical and psychological symptomatology the client has experienced, and the client's perceptions of the event. Details like these are rarely provided in brief interactions. For the same reason, asking a client whether he or she can partake in the interview without the aid of an interpreter is not likely to be reliable unless the client has a thorough understanding of the major questions, what is expected in the interview, and the events that will follow. In most instances, it is unlikely that these conditions will be met.

The decision about whether a person is competent to partake in an interview/assessment without the aid of an interpreter requires an understanding of the client's performance under task demands that are similar to that required in the forensic context. Such an assessment can be performed by a qualified linguist or by any professional who has access to a tool designed specifically for determining the level of language competency of minority groups in legal contexts. Some Australian lawyers have begun using a quick, objectively verifiable questionnaire (developed by two linguists) to determine whether Aboriginal witnesses or defendants have the language skills necessary to cope with the court proceeding and to instruct legal counsel (Cooke and Wiley, 1999). However, it needs to be noted that even direct observation of the client's ability to relate details about unrelated (i.e. innocuous) events may not be totally reliable. *Production* of words does not always indicate *comprehension*, and the person's use and understanding of words may differ from that usage which is widely accepted. Legal scholarship has highlighted numerous instances where subtle differences between minority groups' use of words and standard conceptions of a language have been undetected by police and lawyers. These instances invariably lead to misinterpretation, inconsistency, and injustice (Mildren, 1997; Stefan, 1996).

To illustrate, for many people who speak English as a second language, present tense forms are used to refer to past events, and pronouns and prepositions are used in non-standard ways. For example, 'he' and 'him' may be used to refer to males, females or objects, and to more than one person, while the word 'on' is often used instead of 'in' (Gumperz, 1969; Gumperz and Cook-Gumperz, 1981). Similarly, use of words relating to crucial 'state of mind' issues may differ across cultures. Among older Warlpiri (Aboriginal) people, the term 'guilty' is used only in reference to murder. Thus, a plea of guilty (regardless of the charge) has a meaning that transcends that ascribed by Western legal systems (McKay, 1985). Among Samoan people, the word 'kill' (which translates to 'fasi') also means 'beat' or 'maim', rather than to terminate in the English sense (Lane, 1985).

It must also be noted that language barriers are by no means overcome by the use of interpreters, as there may be no meaningful equivalent for some terms. For example, in Philippine English or the native languages of the Philippines, there is no term for child abuse (Gumperz, 1982a). In Bengali, there are only very limited and general terms to describe sex or the sexual organs, as the topic of sex is rarely discussed (Gupta, 1997). Similarly, language barriers can also arise if the concept being discussed is not mean-ingful within the person's sociocultural framework. For example, in Western culture, there is a constant focus on quantified information to represent size, number, distance and time, however in many indigenous cultures, issues of time, number and distance are defined in qualitative rather than quantitative terms. In these cases, specifics about such concepts can only be elicited using references to physical, social, geographical or climatic situations rather than clock or calendar time (Eades, 1992, 1995).

Critical jurisprudential concepts such as rights, legal presumptions, and due process protections are very difficult to communicate to members of cultural groups who have no experience with such notions, and/or have grown accustomed to feeling powerless under Western systems of government (Goldflam, 1995). Indeed, an invitation to re-main silent would seem bizarre to any person who had no understanding of the legal context of this requirement. This is particularly true if that person had already ex-pressed a willingness to cooperate with the police, and was repeatedly asked questions by those in authority anyway (Roy, 1990). Further, a desire to appear competent and cooperative in the interview may lead interviewees to intentionally mask or downplay comprehension difficulties (Cooke, 1998). For these reasons, the onus remains on the professional to use information-gathering techniques that acknowledge cultural rela-tivism, identify and overcome the difficulties of the interviewee, thereby maximizing the amount and validity of the information obtained.

The Person's Usual Style of Relating

Miscommunication in forensic assessments and interviews can occur, not just be-cause of misunderstandings of *factual* statements, but due to fundamental differences between the professional's and client's use of discourse cues (e.g. listenership cues, intonation patterns, rhythm, eye-gaze, space usage, etc.). The question-and-answer style of eliciting information, typical in English-speaking cultures, is not commonly used in minority cultures. For example, among many American Indian, Australian Aboriginal, New Zealand Maori, and Samoan groups, information is commonly transmitted via observation and interaction with others rather than by prioritizing verbal means. In fact, direct questions in one-to-one interactions or group-discussion are considered highly intrusive and discourteous (Ainsworth, 1984; Eades, 1994; Lane, 1988; Sattler, 1998). Among these groups, silence is a positively valued part of conversation (indicating patience and respect), and details of stories unfold very slowly over time (Kearins, 1991; Stubbe, 1998). A high priority is placed on keeping harmonious relationships in interactional contexts, rather than on 'self-promotion' or the expression of one's individual point of view (Liberman, 1982). There is considerable evidence to indicate that these patterns of interaction are consistent across formal as well as informal settings (Sattler, 1998). One implication of this is that professionals' direct requests for information may be less effective with minority groups. Instead, interactions may be more fruitful if interviews are conducted in a less prescriptive style, and at a more leisurely pace.

Marked differences in eye-gaze and levels of explicit verbal feedback can also be displayed across different cultural groups. For example, among Native American, Aboriginal Australian and Japanese groups, avoidance of eye contact is a sign of respect or deference to a speaker (Sattler, 1998), whereas among many English-speaking listeners a lack of eye contact signals avoidance or a lack of attention. In an intensive study of listening attention among various dyads, Mayo and La France (cited in Erickson, 1979) noted the different ways in which eye gaze was used by white and black Americans. White Americans, when speaking, tended to look away from the listener and to return their gaze only intermittently, while white listeners were more likely to look continuously at the speaker. In contrast, black American speakers tended to 'look at the listener continuously, looking away only intermittently, while listeners tended to look at the speaker only intermittently, except at turn relevant moments, when both speaker and listener would show gaze involvement' (Erickson, 1979, p. 104). The implication is that if a white speaker glanced briefly at a black listener and found him or her looking away, the speaker may misinterpret the behaviour as being due to evasion, inattentiveness, indifference, or a reluctance to participate in the interview. Further, if a black speaker found that a white listener looked continuously at him or her while speaking, this behaviour might be misinterpreted as being due to hostility or insubordination. Erickson (1979) noted that this sort of communication clash caused white speakers to 'hyper-explain' (i.e. repeat the same point over and over) which to black speakers was 'at best tedious and at worst demeaning' (p. 106).

Another example of inter-racial differences in the use of subtle discourse cues was described by Gumperz (1982b) who analysed a problem that arose in a cafeteria at a British airport involving newly hired Indian and Pakistani women. The women were perceived by many native English-speaking customers as surly and uncooperative because they used intonation patterns that were considered strange in their employment context. Specifically, they used falling intonation to indicate a request (e.g. whether the customers wanted gravy on their meat). Although customers ascribed particular meaning to such intonation, this represented the normal way for questions to be asked in those cultures, and no rudeness or indifference was intended.

While miscommunications in brief encounters may be tedious or annoying, in forensic contexts they can impact the outcome of the interview process and the case in general. This is because gaze and other non-verbal behaviours can influence a professional's judgement of how credible, dominant or competent an interviewee is. In a study by Winkel and Vrij (1990), two actors (one white and one non-white) were required to play the role of a suspect being interviewed by a police officer. In one interview, both actors were trained to display gaze behaviour typical of white people, and in the other interview, they were required to display gaze behaviour typical of non-white people. Dutch police officers who observed these video-recordings rated the interviewees who displayed the gaze behaviour typical of non-white people as more tense, uncooperative and 'suspect'. This perception would have deleterious effects on the way these interviewees would subsequently be treated by the police. Strong preconceptions or bias about an alleged offender's guilt leads investigative interviewers to employ more persuasive, leading, and manipulative questioning tactics which might contaminate the statement and/or impinge on the interviewee's voluntariness—or appear to (Pearse and Gudjonsson, 1999). In a therapeutic setting, misinterpretations of silence, eye-gaze and subtle 'listening attention' cues may result in distrust, resentment and/or hypervigilence which would be detrimental to any therapist–client alliance.

The Person's Kin-Based Network, Cultural Practices and Beliefs about Relevant Issues

Different priorities regarding social commitments across different cultures, and divergent restrictions on contact and/or dissemination of information between certain categories of relatives can result in miscommunication and misunderstandings in forensic settings. For example:

- In Muslim communities, sex is not openly discussed between males and females in any circumstances (Gupta, 1997).

- In Philippino society it is regarded as inappropriate for an outsider to question the validity of any statement made by a person about their family (Gumperz, 1982a).

- In Cambodia it is taught that women must obey and respect men, and believe men are always right regardless of how they behave (Sattler, 1998).

- For many groups of Asian origin, restraint of feeling is regarded as a sign of maturity and wisdom, and considerable stigma is placed on individuals with mental or emotional problems (Sattler, 1998).

- In many Australian Aboriginal groups, it is forbidden to say the name of a deceased person, see any photograph of the person or use anything belonging to the person for approximately six months after the deceased person's death (Eades, 1992).

The fears, expectations and consequences of violating these codes would obviously have a large impact on a person's willingness to disclose relevant information to a forensic professional.

These issues are essential considerations, not only for eliciting information about offences for the courts, but also for determining accurate clinical diagnoses and appropriate treatment of clients. The importance of considering ethnicity and race when administering, scoring, and interpreting psychometric scales is well documented (e.g. see Geisinger, 1994); however, the issues being discussed here are no less important. The only difference between the testing and interviewing tasks is that the effects of ethnicity and race on psychometric performance are more quantifiable. In reality, the concerns being explicated in this chapter are likely to be contributors to cross-cultural differences on such tests. In that sense, while psychometrics identify different *performance* levels across cultures, it is the forensic interviewer's job to anticipate more subtle issues that could influence the *process* of information gathering.

To further illustrate, a client's description and perception of his or her problem (or whether he or she does in fact perceive a problem) is heavily influenced by cultural expectations and proscriptions (Okazaki and Sue, 1995). Behaviours defined as 'abuse' in one society may not be inappropriate in another, and customs and beliefs that relate to health problems vary widely (Kapitanoff, Lutzker and Bigelow, 2000). Similarly, descriptions of thoughts, perceptions, and beliefs that might be indicative of a thought disorder or psychosis among members of one culture may reflect normal thought processes in another (Milan et al., 1999). An awareness of these relativities may minimize misdiagnosis and assist the practitioner in determining how mainstream intervention programmes (when psychological problems do exist) need to be adjusted (Paniagua, 1994). Further, beliefs about the causes of illness and appropriate treatment differ widely across cultures, and these have a direct impact on the degree to which a person will accept help from members of another cultural group. Some cultural groups view illness (treatable with Western medical practices) as stemming from natural, environmental or supernatural causes, or as a form of divine punishment (Sattler, 1998). Any intervention that did not acknowledge or address the person's beliefs would be resisted by the person and/or his or her family, and this would decrease treatment efficacy and the participant's sense of well-being (Kapitanoff et al., 2000).

In summary, the elicitation of detailed knowledge about a client's language, customs and interactional style offers three immediate benefits for forensic practitioners. First, it provides the incentive and background knowledge needed to tailor assessments and interviewing styles to the needs of the interviewee. This may involve the help of other professionals who are appropriately suited to working with a particular client. The more the interviewer relies on a style of interaction that is inappropriate for the client or interviewee, the greater the cognitive demands and stress he or she places on that person. This then reduces the interviewee's ability to provide the practitioner with forensically relevant information. Second, knowledge of the interviewee's culture and styles of relating allows the interviewer to interpret the person's verbal and non-verbal behaviour within the wider sociocultural context, and to minimize misinterpretation of the listener's actions. Finally, knowledge of the social and cultural background of the interviewee and his or her community helps the interviewer to understand the full context of the offence and/or problem, and to generate fruitful leads that facilitate investigation of a crime, accurate diagnoses, and/or appropriate treatment avenues.

RAPPORT WITH THE CLIENT OR INTERVIEWEE

Most psychologists would agree that a good rapport with a client or interviewee is one of the most important assets to a professional, especially if the topic being discussed is traumatic, sensitive or embarrassing (Milne and Bull, 1999). The more trusting and at ease the client is within the interview or therapeutic setting, the greater the likelihood that he or she will engage with the professional and talk openly, without fear of criticism or judgement. While more time may be needed to develop rapport and trust with cultural minority interviewees, the time devoted to this crucial impression-making task is likely to reap significant dividends (Sattler, 1998).

The development of rapport in a cross-cultural forensic context should not be perceived as a compromise in professionalism, impartiality or authority. On the contrary, rapport is achieved by being courteous, fair, honest, reliable and respectful of the person's value systems (Powell, 2000b). A professional who shows acceptance of the person's cultural differences (beyond simple stereotypic beliefs) empowers the client and reduces his or her subjective experience of threat. This then increases the clients willingness to cooperate in the interview or assessment (Baikie-Howard, 1995). A practitioner's preparedness to engage with cultural differences is displayed by:

- taking the time to get to know the client before embarking on an interview, assessment or treatment programme;

- avoiding any behaviour, labels or terms that may be considered offensive by members of that cultural group, (but note that individuals from the same ethnic background may have different opinions about how they should be addressed, and what behaviours are considered offensive; appropriate responses to such differences are premised on the professional's ability to first ascertain their nature);

- being sensitive to the interviewee's needs and being flexible (where appropriate);

- showing goodwill (without being patronizing);

- using greetings that are culturally appropriate;

- listening carefully to the interviewee (and showing the interviewee that he or she has been understood);

- not assuming that the interviewee or client understands the role of the professional and the nature and purpose of the procedures adopted;

- an apparent willingness to incorporate (as far as practicable) the person's beliefs into treatment regimens (or other responses); and

- a willingness to consult (where legally or ethically appropriate) with family members about decisions (particularly elders, if they hold a powerful position within the community).

The early stages of contact between the professional and the interviewee or client are critical for the development of good rapport. The professional at this stage of contact should be assessing the person's preferred speech volume, accent, attitudes, cognitive skills, and language comprehension. He or she will determine the need for any modification in procedure or to consult with other professionals. At this stage, most interviewees will be learning (via the professional's behaviour) what is expected, and will try to adjust their behaviour accordingly. Thus, if the professional speaks in a relaxed and calm manner, the interviewee will also be encouraged to do so. If the professional shows concern for the interviewee's level of comfort, lets him or her talk without interruption, and responds openly and honestly without judgement, the client or interviewee will feel confident about being understood and treated fairly. If the initial interaction between the professional and client or interviewee provides indications that the process is unlikely to progress in an easy manner, it may be fruitful to postpone the session, and to conduct further research into the client's background and circumstances before re-attempting the procedure. There is no value in continuing if the session is causing anxiety, if the person will not talk, or if the professional cannot understand what the person is saying.

Rapport is also facilitated by the interview context, as well as qualities associated with the individual interviewer. An ideal physical environment is one that minimizes a sense of threat, isolation, distractibility, disorientation and physical discomfort. The factors needed to achieve this will obviously differ depending on the individual and particular cultural group. For example, with American Indian and Australian Aboriginal clients, any diminution in formality of manner and language is likely to decrease the client's sense of intimidation and anxiety. Respect is displayed by allowing the client to conduct the session at a relaxed place, where silence is tolerated and the person is free to respond (or not to respond) without pressure (Powell, 2000a). In contrast, respect among Latinos is displayed by the use of formal behaviours such as addressing clients as Señor, Señora or Señorita followed by their surnames, and by devoting much of the early contacts to talking about shared backgrounds and experiences (Organista and Munoz, 1996). Where possible, therefore, interviewers should seek advice in advance about cultural and linguistic factors that are needed to create a non-intimidating environment. Factors to consider include the seating arrangement (i.e. some cultural groups do not feel comfortable seated in a face-to-face situation), the choice of people who may be present in the interview/assessment (and whether they are permitted to hear about the situation or alleged offence), and the amount of personal space or direct eye contact.

Finally, any formal investigative or evidentiary interview procedure requires a clear explanation of the routines and ground rules for the interview. This is because the function of various rules of speech and social requirements is likely to vary markedly between the professional and the client. When interviewees do not understand the purpose of the investigative interview (and this is particularly likely if they have not experienced a forensic interview before), they are less likely to provide information that is forensically relevant (Siegal, 1991), and may be unnecessarily fearful about the interview process (Forham, 1994). Important procedures, such as the delivery of legal cautions, explanation of the function and purpose of any technical equipment, introduction of the various people who are attending the interview, and the need to elicit specific details about seemingly trivial issues, are all likely sources of stress and confusion. The interviewer should not assume that the interviewee understands any of the above issues merely because he or she has participated in such interviews previously or appears to be familiar with mainstream culture and language.

INTERPRETATIVE ASSISTANCE (IF REQUIRED)

The elicitation of accurate and detailed statements from people who have limited skills in an interviewer's predominant language is obviously largely dependent on the assistance of interpreters. A speaker with a limited vocabulary is constrained in his or her ability to link pieces of information together, and to provide detailed information, particularly in relation to evaluative and descriptive comments about an event. Although access to appropriate assistance from interpreters is a well-documented due process and human rights issue, these services are underutilized in forensic interviews and assessments (Aldridge and Wood, 1998; Lawrie, 1999; Mildren, 1997).

There appear to be three main reasons for the underuse of interpreters. First, it may simply be due to a lack of competent interpreters who are readily available at short notice (Gibbons, 1995; Social Services Inspectorate, 1994) and sometimes there is no interpreting service offered at all (Aldridge and Wood, 1988; Lawrie, 1999). In these latter cases, practitioners who require interpretative assistance in interviews often depend on a friend or relative of the interviewee (e.g. a person from the local community) or another experienced interpreter. This strategy is fraught with difficulty. Not only do untrained interpreters have a profound lack of understanding about the procedures of forensic professionals and the importance of not asking leading questions, but with small language groups and extended families, it can be extremely difficult to find an interpreter who is not compromised by his or her relationship with the interviewee. Further, untrained interpreters cannot be expected to interpret accurately without changing the structure and meaning of sentences. Such a skill requires considerable practice and critical feedback, as well as advanced knowledge of cultural and linguistic factors (Cooke, 1998). It is not an uncommon problem for interpreters to delete information, or to make changes and embellishments in the translations (see Sattler, 1998, for a discussion of this issue).

Second, because many people from minority groups can speak some of the dominant language (at least at a conversational level) there may be an overestimation of their ability to partake competently in the interview or assessment process (Lawrie, 1999). In other words, the person's ability to speak informally in the rapport-building stage of the interview may mask weaknesses that are likely to surface later in the interview when linguistic demands become more complex. Without formal training in language assessment, it is unrealistic to expect an interviewer to determine whether the person has adequate language skills for legal purposes (Cooke, 1995). With this in mind, there is a clear need for tools to be developed that allow for objective and standardized assessment of language abilities and linguistic preference (see Sattler, 1998; Stefan, 1996).

Third, there appears to be reluctance among some police and lawyers to use interpreters because they perceive such arrangements to minimize their sense of control during the interview. Indeed, the presence of an interpreter in the interview setting can alter the power dynamic in the court or interview room (especially if interpreters are viewed as quasi-advocates for interviewees) and they can deflect the full force of an aggressive questioning style (Laster and Taylor, 1994). However, research in the area of investigative or evidential interviewing does not support that intimidation and control of the interviewee's answers are effective interview tactics (Pearse and Gudjonsson, 1999). The most reliable and detailed evidence from suspects is obtained using good social communication skills; that is, allowing the interviewee to speak at a relaxed pace in his or her own words (Milne and Bull, 1999).

Even if an interpreter was sought for a completely bilingual speaker, allowing the interviewee to relate the information in his or her own language may still enhance the quality and quantity of information obtained. For instance, if an interview was being conducted about an alleged offence and the incident occurred in an environment where the foreign language is always spoken, it would facilitate the person's memory to be interviewed in that language (Tulving and Thomson, 1973). In addition, it may be necessary for bilingual speakers to code-switch (interchange their languages) within conversations—a natural process that would be restricted by the presence of a monolingual interviewer (Aldridge and Wood, 1998). For example, interviewees may not know how to translate a word, or a topic might be too upsetting to discuss in their primary language. Finally, research has demonstrated that reconstruction of a story is less accurate when a listener does not share the same cultural schemata as the storyteller, even though the listener may comprehend each of the individual sentences in the story (Bartlett, 1932; Hall, Reder and Cole, 1975; Kintsch and Greene, 1978). Therefore, the issue of language notwithstanding, there are other benefits of having access to persons from the interviewee's cultural group (Sattler, 1998; Cooke, 1998). Growing awareness of these issues among the judiciary has led to an increased propensity to exclude interview evidence obtained without the use of an appropriate interpreter (Laster and Taylor, 1994).

In conclusion, there needs to be greater use of interpreters by forensic professionals. However, this is unlikely to improve the quality of information obtained unless professional interpreters are readily available, and forensic practitioners become better versed in how to assess the need of such professionals, select and brief the interpreters, and use them effectively (Cooke, 1998). Professionals also need to be aware of the issues that interpreters cannot address. The more a professional relies on legal jargon and concepts that are not meaningful within the client's sociocultural context, the more explanation is required, and the greater the potential for misunderstanding during this interpretation process.

DIVERSE ARRAY OF HYPOTHESES

Any forensic investigation, interview or assessment should be regarded as an exercise in testing alternative hypotheses, not a confirmation of what the practitioner already knows. In other words, the professional should be flexible enough to change his or her hypothesis about what occurred as new information arises (Milne and Bull, 1999). This is important, regardless of the strength of the corroborating evidence, and whether the interviewee is an alleged victim or suspect. When a professional believes that he or she knows the truth about the client, the nature of the event, and/or the identity of the offender, relevant and vital information is overlooked, screened out, or ignored, and questioning is likely to be incomplete or inaccurate (Ceci and Bruck, 1995; Loftus, 1975). A common criticism of investigative interviewers is that they are not neutral regarding the alleged perpetrator's guilt and, as a result, have little desire to test the belief that the suspect did not commit the alleged crime (Gudjonsson, 1992; Milne and Bull, 1999). However, the likelihood of making a false assumption of guilt is even more likely to occur with a person from a minority group as behavioural differences related to an interviewee's ethnicity may be confused or misinterpreted as evidence of dishonesty or guilt (see Vrij and Winkel, 1991).

With regard to forensic psychologists, subtle misinterpretation or bias can result from the use of inappropriate assessment tools. The use of standardized psychometric instruments with different cultural groups can lead to significant under-reporting as well as over-reporting of symptoms and syndromes if the tools are not relevant, applicable, comprehensive or culturally sensitive (Geisinger, 1994). For example, the persistently higher prevalence of symptoms of depressed mood and anxiety among Puerto Ricans compared to white, middle-class Americans may represent 'culturally patterned variations in the experiential levels of these phenomena, and not necessarily higher rates of disorder' (Manson, 1997, p. 247). Among the Hopi (American Indian) Tribe, sadness and worry are so common that current diagnostic criteria derived from work with mainstream populations may lead to a relatively large number of false positives among these groups (Manson, 1997). Abnormality is a social construct and therefore the diagnosis of personality and mood-related disorders need to be undertaken with some caution.

Given the above-detailed concerns, culturally-aware practitioners who are willing to explore alternative hypotheses should adhere to the following six practices when they are conducting an interview or assessment with a client from a different cultural background. First, they should gather and consider all evidence, even details that do not fit with their assumption about what happened. This requires time to explore the interviewee's perspective, value systems, attitudes, and world views, and the ability to determine how these may affect the interview process and the conclusions drawn from it. Second, they should be flexible in the form of their questioning, and not limit the interviewee's responses. Third, they should not assume that the results from assessment tools are valid for all interviewees irrespective of their cultural identity. Even if such instruments need to be employed, the practitioner can easily note their personal reservations about the use of the tools with particular client groups. Fourth, culturally aware practitioners should routinely explore the possibility of alternative explanations, and occasionally enlist the help of expert cultural consultants. Fifth, they should recognize the prejudices they hold towards members of the interviewee's culture, and endeavour to ensure that their own values about relevant issues (e.g. child care, discipline, gender roles, family values, etc.) do not affect the information gained or the interpretations drawn. Finally, if the practitioner feels he or she cannot remain totally neutral or impartial towards the interviewee, he or she should have the case reassigned.

EFFECTIVE TECHNIQUES FOR ELICITING A FREE NARRATIVE

Research has consistently demonstrated that the most reliable and accurate method of eliciting details from a witness is via 'free narrative' (Home Office and Department of Health, 1992). A free narrative is obtained by asking interviewees to provide an account of the event or situation in their own words, at their own pace, and without interruption. This account generally proceeds with an interviewer providing a general or open-ended question, for example 'Tell me what happened.', and using non-verbal encouragers (e.g. head nods, pauses) or open-ended questions (e.g. 'What happened then?') to encourage the interviewees to provide further information (Powell, 2000c).

The importance of eliciting evidence in narrative format with cultural minority groups is four-fold. First, general prompts and open-ended questions elicit more accurate evidence and longer responses compared to specific or closed questions, provided the person is competent enough in the language being spoken (Lamb et al., 1996). Second, responses to closed questions can mask poor comprehension as the person can adopt strategies to cover up his or her limitations, e.g. repeating phrases or words used by the interviewer, providing a stereotypical response, or providing affirmative answers to yes/no questions even if the questions are not understood (Cooke, 1998). Third, questions are only effective if they cue the interviewee's mental representation of the event (Thomson, 1972), and a forensic professional's representation of the event may not be consistent with that of the interviewee. Finally, swift questioning does not allow time for either party to collect his or her thoughts and, as a consequence, this direct interrogatory style does not lend itself to elaborate retrieval of deeper memory processes. If the interviewee feels hurried, he or she will not be able to engage in an effective memory search (Powell, 2000c).

Despite the benefits of the free narrative stage, research indicates that most forensic professionals tend to adopt a question-and-answer approach to interviewing and, when free narrative approaches are employed, they are usually rushed or interrupted during the early stages (Fisher, Geiselman and Raymond, 1987; Moston, Stephenson and Williamson, 1993). In fact it is generally shown that police officers, social workers, lawyers and psychologists use relatively few open-ended questions and minimal non-verbal encouragers in investigative interviews, even when they are aware of the importance of such practices (Davies et al., 1995; Lamb et al., 1996; Warren et al., 1996). US and British studies of forensic interviews with actual witnesses have shown that professionals tend to use a very stylized speech pattern (which includes jargon and technical terms). They have also been shown to employ short-answer questions with few pauses, and ask an excessive number of leading questions (Fisher et al., 1987; George, 1991, cited in Milne and Bull, 1999). This reluctance to allow the interviewees to relay their accounts in their own words has been attributed to a professional desire to keep responses within a predefined framework. This remains one of the primary criticisms of professionals who conduct forensic interviews with minority groups (Mildren, 1997).

Given the importance of the free narrative stage, why do forensic professionals tend to avoid non-specific, open-ended questions and minimal encouragers? There are several possible reasons. First, most forensic professionals (particularly those who speak English as a first language) tend not to use these conversational techniques in their daily life; they are socialized from a very young age into the question-and-answer style of conversation (Eades, 1992). For these professionals, the elicitation of a comprehensive narrative is a skill that requires specialized training with practice and critical feedback (Davies et al., 1995). However, relatively little ongoing training is provided in this skill, and when training is offered, it is generally provided at a time when professionals have already established their interviewing styles (Ericcson and Charness, 1994; Fisher, 1995; Fisher and Geiselman, 1992). Second, if forensic interviews and assessments are not being conducted in the clients' first language, the linguistic constraints may preclude their ability to provide a free account that could be understood clearly. Third, there may be a false belief among some professionals that persuasive questioning tactics are more effective than open questions in making guilty suspects confess. To the contrary, the available research suggests that most suspects who confess do so at the beginning of the interview. Those few who confess as a result of the interviewers' tactics include 'a sizeable proportion of false confessors' (Milne and Bull, 1999, p. 89). Last, the aforementioned organizational imperatives to provide interviews that follow a predefined sequence are likely to represent a further obstacle to best practice.

Summary

Effective communication with forensic clients from different cultural groups is a complex process that is largely dependent on the skills of the interviewer. These skills address the process and substance of the interview, and include the ability to use open-ended questioning strategies, develop a culturally sensitive rapport with the interviewee, keep an open mind, appreciate the wider sociocultural context of the event and the interviewee's responses, and to make appropriate decisions about when and how to elicit the assistance of a suitable interpreter. Unless forensic professionals begin to acknowledge the multitudinous issues that clients from different cultural groups present, *and* partake in training programmes to develop the range of skills required to respond to these, it is unlikely that much needed improvements will be made to current interview and assessment practices with these diverse and often disadvantaged client groups.

REFERENCES

Ainsworth, N. (1984). The cultural shaping of oral discourse. *Theory into practice, 23* (2), 132–137.

Aldridge, M. and Wood, J. (1998). *Interviewing children: A guide for child care and forensic practitioners*. Chichester: John Wiley & Sons.

Baikie-Howard, B. (1995). 'Different coloured skin': The experiences of Aboriginal young people in the juvenile justice system. *Youth Studies Australia*, Summer, 47–52.

Bartlett, F.C. (1932). *Remembering: A study in experimental and social psychology*. London: Cambridge University Press.

Betancourt, H. and Lopez, S.R. (1993). The study of culture, ethnicity, and race in American psychology. *American Psychologist, 48*, 629–637.

Cain, M. (1994). *Juveniles in detention. Special needs groups: Young women, Aboriginal and Indo-Chinese detainees*. Sydney: Department of Juvenile Justice.

Ceci, S.J. and Bruck, M. (1995). *Jeopardy in the courtroom: A scientific analysis of children's testimony*. Washington, DC: American Psychological Association.

Cooke, M. (1995) Interpreting in a cross-cultural cross-examination: An Aboriginal case study. *International Journal of Social Language, 113*, 99–111.

Cooke, M. (1998). *Anglo/Yolngu Communication in the criminal justice system*. Unpublished doctoral dissertation. University of New England, Australia.

Cooke, M. and Wiley, E. (1999). *Interpreter need guidelines*. Darwin: North Australian Aboriginal Legal Aid Service.

Criminal Justice Commission (1996). *Aboriginal witnesses in Queensland's criminal courts*. Brisbane: Criminal Justice Commission.

Cronheim, A.J. and Schwartz, A.H. (1976). Non-English speaking persons in the criminal justice system: Current state of the Law. *Cornell Law Review, 61*, 289–311.

Davies, G.M., Wilson, C., Mitchell, R. and Milsom, J. (1995). *Videotaping children's evidence: An evaluation*. London: Home Office.

Eades, D. (1992). *Aboriginal English and the law*. Queensland: Queensland Law Society Inc.

Eades, D. (1994). A case of communicative clash: Aboriginal English and the legal system. In J. Gibbons (ed.), *Language and the law* (pp. 234–264). Essex, England: Longman Group.

Eades, D. (1995). Aboriginal English on trial: The case for Stuart and Condren. In D. Eades (ed.), *Language in evidence: Issues confronting Aboriginal and multicultural Australia*. Sydney, Australia: University of New South Wales Press.

Erickson, F. (1979). Talking down: Some cultural sources if miscommunication in interracial interviews. In A. Wolfgang (ed.), *Nonverbal behavior: Applications and cultural implications* (pp. 99–126). New York: Academic Press.

Ericsson, K.A. and Charness, N. (1994). Expert performance: Its structure and acquisition. *American Psychologist, 49,* 725–747.

Fisher, R.P. (1995). Interviewing victims and witnesses of crime. *Psychology, Public Policy and Law, 1,* 732–764.

Fisher, R.P. and Geiselman, R.E. (1992). *Memory-enhancing techniques for investigative interviewing.* Champaign, IL: Charles C. Thomas.

Fisher, R.P., Geiselman, R.E. and Raymond, D.S. (1987). Critical analysis of police interviewing techniques. *Journal of Police Science and Administration, 15,* 177–185.

French, L. (1987). The challenge of teaching the minority perspective in criminal justice, *Quarterly Journal of Ideology, 11,* 95–106.

Forham, H. (1994). Cultural difficulties in defence of Aboriginal clients: Guidelines to assist lawyers in dealing with Aboriginal clients, *Proctor Newsletter of the Queensland Law Society, 14* (2), 17–19.

Geisinger, K.F. (1994). Cross-cultural normative assessment: Translation and adaptation issues influencing the normative interpretation of assessment instruments. *Psychological Assessment, 6,* 304–312.

Gibbons, J. (1995). What got lost? The place of electronic recording and interpreters in police interviews. In D. Eades (ed.), *Language in evidence: Issues confronting Aboriginal and multicultural Australia* (pp. 175–186). Sydney, Australia: University of New South Wales Press.

Goldflam, R. (1995). Silence in court! Problems and prospects in Aboriginal legal interpreting. In D. Eades (ed.), *Language in evidence: Issues confronting Aboriginal and multicultural Australia* (pp. 28–54). Sydney, Australia: University of New South Wales Press.

Gudjonsson, G. (1992). *The psychology of interrogations, confessions and testimony.* Chichester, England: John Wiley & Sons.

Gumperz, J.J. (1969). Communication in multilingual societies. In S.A. Tyler (ed.), *Cognitive anthropology* (pp. 435–449). New York: Holt, Rinehart and Winston, Inc.

Gumperz, J.J. (1982a). Fact and inference in courtroom testimony. In J.J. Gumperz (ed.), *Language and social identity.* Cambridge: Cambridge University Press.

Gumperz, J.J. (1982b). *Discourse Strategies.* Cambridge: Cambridge University Press.

Gumperz, J.J. and Cook-Gumperz, J. (1981). Ethnic differences in communicative style. In C.A. Ferguson and S.B. Heath (eds), *Language in the USA* (pp. 430–445). Cambridge: Cambridge University Press.

Gupta, A. (1997). Black children and the Memorandum. In H.L. Westcott and J. Jones (eds), *Perspectives on the memorandum: Policy, practice and research in investigative interviewing.* Aldershot: Arena.

Hall, W.S., Reder, S. and Cole, M. (1975). Story recall in young black and white children: Effects of racial group membership, race of experimenter, and dialect. *Developmental Psychology, 11,* 628–634.

Home Office and Department of Health (1992). *Memorandum of good practice for video-recorded interviews with child witnesses for criminal proceedings.* London: HMSO.

Human Rights and Equal Opportunity Commission (1993). *State of the nation report on people of non-English speaking background.* Canberra: Australian Government Printing Service.

Kapitanoff, S.H., Lutzker, J.R. and Bigelow, K.M. (2000). Cultural issues in the relation between child disabilities and child abuse. *Aggression and Violent Behavior, 5* (3), 227–244.

Kearins, J. (1991). Factors affecting Aboriginal testimony. *Legal Service Bulletin, 16* (1), 3–6.

Kintsch, W. and Greene, E. (1978). The role of culture-specific schemata in the comprehension and recall of stories. *Discourse Processes, 1,* 1–13.

Lamb, M.E., Hershkowitz, I., Sternberg, K.J., Esplin, P.W. Hovav, M., Manor, T. and Yudilevitch, L. (1996). Effects of investigative utterance types on Israeli children's responses. *International Journal of Behavioral Development, 19,* 627–637.

Lane, C. (1985). Mis-communications in cross-examination. In J.B. Pride (ed.), *Cross-cultural encounters: Communication and mis-communication* (pp. 196–211). Melbourne, Australia: River Seine Publications.

Lane, C. (1988). *Language on trial: Questioning strategies and European–Polynesian miscommunication in New Zealand courtrooms.* Unpublished doctoral dissertation. University of Auckland, New Zealand.

Laster, K. and Taylor, V. (1994). *Interpreters and the legal system.* Sydney, Australia: Federation Press.

Lawrie, D. (1999). *Inquiry into the provision of an interpreter service in Aboriginal languages by the Northern Territory Government.* Darwin, Australia: Office of the Northern Territory Anti-Discrimination Commissioner.

Liberman, K. (1982). Some linguistic features of congenial fellowship among Pitjantjatjara. *International Journal of Sociology of Language, 36*, 35–51.

Loftus, E.F. (1975). Leading questions and the eyewitness report. *Cognitive Psychology, 7*, 560–572.

Manson, S. (1997). Cross-cultural and multiethnic assessment of trauma. In J.P. Wilson and T.M. Keane (eds), *Assessing psychological trauma and PTSD* (pp. 239–266). New York: Guilford Press.

McKay, G.R. (1985). Language issues in training programs for Northern Territory Police: A linguist view. *Applied Linguistics Association of Australia*, Series 'S' Papers No 2.

Milan, M.A., Chin, C.E. and Nguyen, Q.X. (1999). Practicing psychology in correctional settings: Assessment, treatment, and substance abuse programs. In A.K. Hess and I.B. Weiner (eds), *Handbook of forensic psychology* (2nd edn; pp. 580–602). New York: John Wiley & Sons.

Mildren, J.D. (1997). Redressing the imbalance against Aboriginals in the criminal justice system. *Criminal Law Journal, 21*, 7–22.

Milne, R. and Bull, R. (1999). *Investigative interviewing: Psychology and practice.* Chichester: John Wiley & Sons.

Moston, S., Stephenson, G.M. and Williamson, T. (1993). The incidence, antecedents and consequences of the use of the right to silence during police questioning. *Criminal Behaviour and Mental Health, 3*, 30–47.

Okazaki, S. and Sue, S. (1995). Methodological issues in assessment research with minorities. *Psychological Assessment, 7* (3), 367–375.

Organista, L.C. and Munoz, R.F. (1996). Cognitive behavioral therapy with Latinos. *Cognitive and Behavioral Practice, 3*, 255–270.

Paniagua, F.A. (1994). *Assessing and treating culturally diverse clients: A practical guide.* Thousand Oaks, CA: Sage.

Pearse, J. and Gudjonsson, G. (1999). Measuring influential police interviewing tactics: A factor analytic approach. *Legal and Criminological Psychology, 4*, 221–238.

Pope, C. and Feyerherm, W. (1991). *Minorities and the juvenile justice system: Final report.* Washington, DC: Office of Juvenile Justice and Delinquency Prevention.

Poulos, T.M. and Orchowsky, S. (1994). Serious juvenile offenders: Predicting the probability of transfer to criminal court. *Crime and Delinquency, 40* (1), 3–17.

Powell, M.B. (2000a). Interviewing of Aboriginal people. *Australian Police Journal, 54* (3), 209–212.

Powell, M.B. (2000b). PRIDE: The essential elements of a forensic interview with an Aboriginal person. *Australian Psychologist, 35* (3), 186–192.

Powell, M.B. (2000c). Guidelines for conducting investigative interviews with Aboriginal people. *Current Issues in Criminal Justice, 12* (2), 181–197.

Powell, M.B. and Bartholomew, T. (in press). The treatment of multicultural issues in contemporary forensic psychology textbooks. *Psychiatry, Psychology and the Law.*

Robin, R.W., Chester, B., Rasmussen, J.K., Jaranson, J.M. and Goldman, D. (1997). Prevalence, characteristics, and impact of childhood sexual abuse in a southwestern American Indian tribe, *Child Abuse and Neglect, 21* (8), 769–786.

Roy, J.D. (1990). The difficulties of limited-English proficient individuals in the legal setting. *Annals of the New York Academy of Sciences, 606*, 73–83.

Sattler, J.M. (1998). *Clinical and forensic interviews of children and families.* San Diego, USA: Jerome M. Sattler Pub. Inc.

Singer, S.I. (1996). *Recriminalizing delinquency: Violent juvenile crime and juvenile just reform.* Cambridge: Cambridge University Press.

Siegal, M. (1988). Culture, social knowledge, and the determination of criminal responsibility in children: Issues in justice for Aboriginal youth. *Australian Psychologist, 23* (2), 171–182.

Siegal, M. (1991). A clash of conversational worlds: Interpreting cognitive development through communication. In L.B. Resnick, J.M. Levine and S. Behrens (eds), *Perspectives on socially shared cognition* (pp. 23–40). Washington, DC: American Psychological Association.

Social Services Inspectorate (1994). *The child, the court and the video.* London: HMSO.

Stefan, S. (1996). Race, competence testing, and disability law: A review of the MacArthur competence research. *Psychology, Public Policy and Law, 2* (1), 31–44.

Stubbe, M. (1998). Are you listening? Cultural influences on the use of supportive verbal feedback in conversation. *Journal of Pragmatics, 29*, 257–289.

Thomas, C.A. (1987). *Corrections in America.* Newbury Park, CA: Sage.

Thomson, D.M. (1972). Context effects in recognition memory. *Journal of Verbal Learning and Verbal Behaviour, 11*, 497–511.

Tulving, E. and Thomson, D.M. (1973). Encoding specificity and retrieval processes in episodic memory. *Psychological Review, 80*, 352–373.

Vrij, A. and Winkel, F.W. (1991). Cultural patterns in Dutch and Surinam nonverbal behavior: An analysis of simulated police/citizen encounters. *Journal of Nonverbal Behavior, 15*, 169–184.

Warren, A., Woodall, A., Hunt, J. and Perry, N. (1996). 'It sounds good in theory, but . . .': Do investigative interviewers follow guidelines based on memory research? *Child Maltreatment, 1*, 231–245.

Winkel, F.W. and Vrij, A. (1990). Interaction and impression formation in a cross-cultural dyad. *Social Behaviour, 5*, 335–350.

Young, T.J. (1989). Treatment of multicultural counseling in correctional psychology textbooks. *Psychological Reports, 65*, 521–522.

Zuckerman, M. (1990). Some dubious premises in research and theory on racial differences: Scientific, social, and ethical issues. *American Psychologist, 45*, 1297–1303.

Psychology and Law: A Behavioural or a Social Science?

Stephen P. Savage
University of Portsmouth, UK

INTRODUCTION

The study of law and legal contexts, like any other field of research and analysis, is prone to what might be called 'territoriality'. Disciplines and schools of thought, between and within disciplines, compete to demonstrate that their own offerings constitute the only 'legitimate' or valid approach to the genuine understanding of law and legal process. This need not be the case. The justification of a particular perspective on legal contexts need not necessarily entail the denial of legitimacy of alternative frameworks for the analysis of law. It should be accepted that our appreciation of legal contexts in enriched by the proliferation of approaches to the subject, from varied disciplines and a multiplicity of conceptual and methodological paradigms. However, in the context of comparing, in our case, psychological with social scientific, or sociological, stances on the study of legal contexts, this tends not to be the case. There is indeed a high degree of territoriality at work. Thus psychologists might deride the failure of sociology to satisfy the standards of the 'scientific paradigm' in its varied methodologies; sociologists, in turn, may attack psychology for 'naivety' in aspiring to apply the strictures of the natural sciences to human behaviour or for failing to see the wood (society and social processes) for the trees (human individuals).

The view adopted in this chapter is that there should be no hard and fast boundaries between psychological and social scientific approaches to the understanding of law. At times, they stand at different points on a *continuum* of analysis and are differentiated more on the basis of the *different questions* they pose, and on *orientation*, than on any exclusive right to the 'truth'. It is argued here that in this respect psychology can be usefully *counterbalanced* by more sociologically oriented approaches to the study of law. The purpose of this discussion is to demonstrate that, by asking different questions of the law and legal process, the social and political sciences can, together with psychology, help to forge a more comprehensive understanding of this field of study. In order to do so it will draw heavily from *criminology* and will focus on the literature on the social and political analysis of *crime* and *criminal justice*, for it is in these areas that most of the social scientific analysis of law has been focused.

The chapter will be in two sections. Part One will examine the contributions which social science can make to our understanding of *crime* and *offending*. Part Two will discuss the varied ways in which the social and political sciences have furthered our comprehensions of the *legal and judicial responses* to crime.

PART ONE: SOCIAL SCIENCE, CRIME AND OFFENDING BEHAVIOUR

It is not possible to make sense of the contributions which social and political science can make to the understanding of law and legal processes without some broad appreciation of what the social sciences have to say about the behaviours which those processes seek to address. In the context of criminal law and judicial process this requires an awareness of sociological approaches to the analysis of offending behaviour. A number of these are particularly important because in different ways they tell us that *legal* interventions aimed at behaviour modification are not always appropriate and, indeed, may exacerbate problems they are designed to resolve.

It is difficult to identify where 'psychological' approaches to the study of offending behaviour end and 'sociological' approaches begin. The analysis of the linkages between crime and processes of *socialisation*, for example, draws freely from both psychological and sociological traditions (Farrington, 1997). There are nevertheless a number of quite fundamental differences in approach which mark out at least some sociological perspectives on crime from more psychologically oriented approaches. In identifying two broad theses on crime we can illustrate what social science can 'bring to the party' when it comes to understanding crime.

Crime as a Social Variable

From a sociological stance, one problem with psychology as a discipline is that it tends to presuppose that offending behaviour can be traced to some form of 'pathology' or 'abnormality' in the psychological constitution of the individual. Whether this is a fair assessment or not, a number of sociologists in very different ways have tried to undermine this assumption by locating crime firmly as a *social variable*. This is to say that over and above any psychological processes, social forces dictate the actual extent of crime, whether that be over time, between localities or across different social groupings or classes.

This thesis can be traced back to the foundations of sociology as a discipline in the works of Durkheim, who sought to trace variations in crime between societies and over time within societies to the strength or weakness of cultural bonds (Durkheim, 1964). For example, in times of rapid economic change, he argued, the disruption to the social order and breakdown in the normative framework of social life can lead to what he called 'anomie', a state of 'normlessness'. This loosening of the bonds that tie us together as a community can generate major increases in crime rates (they can also be associated with increases in suicide, that quintessentially 'individualistic' act). Interestingly, Durkheim was also famous for stating that a certain level of crime is quite *normal* in any given society and, at those levels, is even a sign of a healthy, functioning society, as we shall see later.

Others were to follow Durkheim's lead in holding crime to be very much a social, or cultural, variable. It is an established criminological premise, for example, that crime is to be seen as primarily a *male* activity. In a very real sense the 'problem of crime' may be seen as the 'problem of masculinity' (Newburn and Stanko, 1994). It could be argued, as a consequence, that no explanation of crime can be sustained if it fails to address this very basic issue: in virtually all areas of criminal behaviour males account for the vast majority of offences, upwards of 80% (Maguire, 1997). Another very strong predictor of offending is *age*: most crimes are committed by teenagers (ibid.). The age variable is doubly significant. On the one hand it associates offending with the social processes of adolescence rather than, say, with personality disorder. On the other it demonstrates that, typically, people *grow out of crime*. The very fact that offending peaks at a certain age should be seen, ironically, as a source of comfort—it would appear to be a phase which (if left unhindered!) most of those involved simply pass through. Does psychology take sufficient notice of the gender and age dimensions of criminal behaviour? Does the criminal process take sufficient notice of these factors? One suspects not.

Another attempt to identify crime as a social variable lies with *economic* analyses of crime. There is evidence that crime patterns mirror closely patterns of economic growth or recession and the changes in criminal opportunities these can generate. Field (1990) found that long-term changes in recorded crime in post-war Britain reflected changing economic and consumption patterns, so that property, or 'acquisitive' crimes, tended to rise quickly in periods of recession, whereas violent crimes against the person increased during times of relative prosperity and rising consumption—an explanation for the latter is that people go out more, drink more and as a consequence are more likely either to commit crimes of violence or be vulnerable as victims of violence. This type of approach is also associated with what is known as *situational* analysis of crime which links crime to *opportunity* (see Clarke, 1992). Put simply, this perspective proposes that crime will go up when the opportunities to commit them increase. As regards crime reduction strategies, this type of analysis would emphasise 'environmentally' based approaches, aimed at reducing 'vulnerable targets' (poorly secured housing, easily accessible vehicles, etc.) rather than 'offender-based' strategies such as those associated with the criminal process. Again, such perspectives make us think more broadly about crime and the means of controlling crime than just focusing on offenders and the law-enforcement and judicial machineries targeted at them. If crime is a social, or even economic, variable, then that should be reflected in crime control strategies.

Crime as 'Normal'

Linked to the notion of crime as a social variable is the thesis held by many sociologists of crime that criminal conduct is not that far removed from 'normal' law-abiding behaviour; as such we should be cautious not to overstate criminality as a special type of problem requiring special measures of redress. The notion of the 'normality' of crime is expressed in a number of ways, not all of which are compatible. Edwin Sutherland, one of the earliest and most influential criminologists, proposed that criminal behaviour is *learned* and learned in much the same way as law-abiding behaviour is learned (Sutherland and Cressey, 1955). Criminal conduct comes about when people are raised in an environment where there is a surplus of cultural norms favourable to law-breaking over norms favourable to law-abiding behaviour. Crime in this sense is seen not as the product of abnormality or dysfunction but more simply as the result of social environments that differ from environments where law-breaking is less the norm.

Another exponent of the 'normality' thesis was Matza, who advanced two important propositions about criminality. Matza claimed that one reason why we should not view offenders as significantly different from non-offenders is that offenders seem to try constantly to *justify* or *rationalise* their behaviour—an indication that they are not that far removed from law-abiding citizens. He called these justifications 'techniques of neutralisation', forms of rationalisation employed by offenders to excuse their actions according to some rough and ready logic. For example, offenders will seek to neutralise their behaviour by denying they had victimised anyone—a theft from a department store could be justified by claiming that 'they can afford it' (Matza, 1964). What is significant about such techniques is not that they are convincing as arguments but that offenders feel the need to employ them at all; it can be taken as evidence that they are still seeking to hold on, however precariously, to values more widely accepted in the community. In that sense they are not to be seen as too separate or different from anyone else. Matza pushed this thesis further with another proposition: that crime and delinquency, from the offenders' perspective, were only *intermittent* facets of their lives. Offenders, Matza argued, *drifted* in and out of crime—and in most cases eventually drifted out of crime altogether (what we have referred to as 'growing out of crime'). For much of their time offenders carried on as normal law-abiding citizens—delinquency was only their part-time career (ibid.). This also raised the spectre of crime (or at least some crime) as a leisure-pursuit, or *crime as* fun. This is a sobering antidote for those who see crime as an abnormality or a signifier of pathological forces at work, who see remedies and treatments as necessary as a consequence. Crime may just be something that some people do for fun at weekends! This thesis is particularly relevant to those oriented to psychological approaches to crime reduction. At least some psychologies would employ techniques of intervention for the special 'treatment' of offending behaviour, techniques which might accentuate rather than reduce any propensity to offend (as we shall see below). The message contained in the 'crime as fun' thesis is *avoid* interventions where possible and allow the process of 'drift' to operate.

Another variant of the crime-as-normal thesis lies with *control theory*. As advanced by criminologists such as Hirschi (1969), control theory stipulates that, in effect, we are all potential offenders, the task of criminology is to find out why many of us *are not*. This turns the tables on much criminology and particularly psychological branches of criminology, which put the spotlight on offenders and which poses the question of what has 'gone wrong' in their formation. Control theory asks the opposite question: given the propensity in us all, initially, to be delinquent, what is it that creates *law-abiding* behaviour in most of us for most of the time? The answer lies, it is argued, in the effectiveness of social controls, such as bonds, ties and attachments to those close to us, in inhibiting potential offending behaviour. For example, we might be tempted to commit a criminal act if it would not bring shame on those emotionally close to us. Alternatively, if we do not feel close emotional bonds to others, that would mean we do not have the level of controls that some others do have; criminal behaviour is one possible expression of that. As Braithwaite (1989) has argued, one explanation for relatively low crime rates in countries such as Japan is the power of 'shaming cultures' in controlling behaviour. This approach locates the sources of crime, or at least most crime, in the strength or weakness of variant *cultures* in controlling behaviours. This is of particular significance to strategies to reduce crime and delinquency, for control theory insists it is the *informal controls* imposed by families, neighbourhoods, communities and other social networks which are the real key to reducing offending behaviour, not the *formal* mechanisms of control we find with *legal* interventions by means of the police, courts and penal systems. Also, that insofar as formal systems can contribute to crime control it is mostly in terms of the role they can play in re-imposing *informal* controls on offenders—through, for example, *restorative justice* schemes—which serve to 'bind' the offender back into the community (see later).

We can take this point further. Not only would many sociologists argue that the crucial determinants of crime lie with wider social and cultural processes, which the imposition of sanctions through the formal agencies of control will do little to disrupt, but they go on to argue that such impositions can actually *make matters worse*. *Labelling theory*, for example, proposes that persistent offending is more likely the result of the application of criminal sanctions than any 'disorder' or 'pathology' in the make-up of the individual concerned. Such offenders are those who have come to accept the *label* which the criminal process has passed down to them, along the logic of 'give a dog a bad name'. More, rather than less, offending can result from the application of the law and the criminal process as a consequence (see Becker, 1963). Labelling theory in many ways typifies the sociological approach not just to crime but also to the study of the law and the criminal justice system. It is essentially a *critical* perspective, much concerned to undermine and debunk the established practices of law-makers and those responsible for law enforcement and criminal justice. This is a valuable role to play and offers an important counterbalance to other approaches to the study of law and legal contexts. At the very least it urges us to be cautious in the application of the law, or indeed in supporting those responsible for the application of the law, which is why one would be hard pushed to find someone who calls himself a 'forensic sociologist'! But it is more than that. The sociologist is typically looking for the *non-apparent*, for the *hidden and unseen* forces at work behind the workings of the law, or for the *unintended consequences* of the workings of the law. Let us take this case further by considering the contributions made by the social sciences to the specific area of law enforcement and criminal justice.

PART TWO: SOCIAL SCIENCE AND THE SOCIAL AND POLITICAL CONTEXT OF LAW

The Sociology of Law

The 'sociology of law' is as old as the discipline of sociology itself. Sociology tends to ask the following sorts of questions about law:

- What social factors influence *changes* in the law and legal systems?

- What *role* does law play in society?

- Does the law operate fairly and equally in society, or does it favour some groups and their interests over others?

- What are the social characteristics of those who deliver legal processes and legal services—lawyers and judges? Does their social background affect the way law is organised in society?

The sociology of law views the working of the legal and judicial systems in terms of the relationship between law and the wider society. It focuses on the *social functions of law* both in terms of the ways in which the law is *shaped* by wider social forces—how, for example, the law reflects wider social and economic change and, in turn, how the law serves to *reinforce* or *reproduce* wider social structures. For convenience we can distinguish two major perspectives within the sociology of law (for a full discussion see Cotterell, 1992), *functionalist* and *critical* approaches to law.

Functionalist theory is more concerned with discovering how 'order' is maintained in society and, above all, with the processes of '*social integration*'. Functionalists would argue that the fundamental problem facing any society is the '*problem of order*', how the individuals that make up a society are somehow held together in some form of network to constitute a social group, small or large. It is clear that law in whatever form has a role to play here. The criminal law and the punishment attached to it fulfil an important social function in maintaining social cohesion, for in punishing the 'outsider'—those who have broken the code of obedience—the law serves to draw the group closer together, to give the 'group identity' more force. This thesis is linked to the point made earlier on the 'normality' of crime. We should not assume that crime is a 'pathology' to be weeded out, because crime stimulates punishment which in turn helps to bind the social group closer together; the very process of identifying and condemning those who have threatened the social order serves to strengthen that order (Durkheim, 1964).

Durkheim's thesis is an important one for the purpose of this discussion because it expresses the view that the 'purpose' of the law is much more than the specific and technical task of administering punishment or conflict resolution. The macro-sociology of law would point to the wider social functions of law that would not be apparent in the day-to-day workings of the legal system. Indeed, the law might very well be 'working' even when, technically, or at a surface level, it appears to be failing. This view is even more apparent in some *critical* or radical approaches to the sociology of law.

Like functionalist theorists, critical sociologies of the law focus on the wider social functions of law but do so in terms of *power* relations rather than in terms of social cohesion and integration. Starting from the assumption that societies are organised around social *inequalities*—in terms of *class* or *gender* inequalities—critical perspectives examine the law in terms of the role played by law, law enforcement and criminal and penal systems in *extending* or *reinforcing* those inequalities. The notion of the law as a means of reinforcing *class* inequalities is associated with Marxist or neo-Marxist theory. For example, Quinney has agued that:

> While law is to protect all citizens, it starts as a tool of the dominant class and ends by maintaining the dominance of that class. Law serves the powerful over the weak; it promotes the war of the powerful against the powerless. Moreover, law is used by the state (and it elitist government) to promote and protect itself. (Quinney, 1978: 42)

While Quinney may be offering a rather simplistic version of this approach it does sum up the ethos of this form of analysis. To illustrate, we can consider how this perspective has been applied to the analysis of English criminal law in a fascinating study by Hay (1975) on the operation of the criminal law in eighteenth-century England. The starting point for Hay's analysis was the apparent severity of the criminal law at the beginning of the eighteenth century. It was estimated to involve more than 200 capital offences, and one piece of legislation alone—known as the 'Black Act'—established some 50 *new* capital offences. In the words of Radzinowitz (1948, p. 77):

> There is hardly a criminal act which did not come within the provisions of the Black Act; offences against public order, against the administration of criminal justice, against property, against the person, malicious injuries to property of varying degrees—all came within the statute and all were punishable by death.

There is little denying that the criminal law was used in eighteenth-century England as part of a naked attempt to defend the property of the aristocracy, the landed gentry, and those involved in trade and commerce. A massively coercive criminal code was employed to terrorise the population to respect the rights of those with property in whatever form:

> ... the gentry and merchants and peers who sat in Parliament in the eighteenth century set new standards of legislative industry, as they passed act after act to keep the capital sanction up to date, to protect every conceivable kind of property from theft or malicious damage. (Hay, 1975, p. 22).

Property and the law were thus inseparable at this time. Indeed, offences against the person were treated with less severity than offences against property. New capital offences such as forgery coincided with the rise of banking and commerce in such a way as to make clear the connection between the criminal law and economic/class interests. For Hay and his colleagues, however, there was an anomaly in the operation of criminal law during the eighteenth century—an anomaly which can be used to demonstrate the sophistication of law as a form of class rule. The anomaly was that despite the huge number of capital offences, and despite a high number of convictions under these offences, the *actual number of executions fell* during the eighteenth century (ibid.: 22). Most of those sentenced to death were granted a Royal pardon, often as they stood on the gallows awaiting execution—they were typically transported to America, and later Australia. For Hay this was part of an ideological strategy on behalf of the aristocracy and the gentry—who were, in most cases, those responsible for requesting the pardon—to create the image of a ruling class which could show *mercy* and humility to the offender. In other words, those who were most responsible for the legislation creating capital penalties were also those most inclined to support the pardon for those who broke the law! The target of such mercy was not so much the actual offender but the community at large, many of whom would gather at the gallows to watch the execution. The pardon was a means of winning their support for the ruling class by encouraging their respect and deference for their betters, who by their actions demonstrated their compassion and hence supremacy. The use of law in this fashion was one of the ways in which the ruling class 'ruled':

> ... the criminal law, more than any other social institution, made it possible to govern eighteenth century England without a police force and without a large army. The ideology of the law was crucial in sustaining the hegemony of the English ruling class. (Hay, 1975, p. 56)

This is a classic example of a *sociology* of law which goes *behind* and *beyond* the actual processes of law to uncover other forces at work. The central thesis is that the law and its operation may be fulfilling 'functions' which are not necessarily explicit but which nevertheless provide the *raison d'etre* of particular legal forms. A similar type of analysis has been levelled at the study of the *police*. Marxist historians have studied the formation and development of policing not by making the obvious association between *the police* and *crime control* but rather in terms of the role of the police in maintaining wider *social control*. For example, Storch (1976) has examined the establishment of 'modern policing' in nineteenth-century England as a response to the interests of the new capitalist class. Those with new property in manufacture in the expanding urban areas of the country, were demanding new forms of protection from the increasingly unruly communities which inhabited the cities of England. Earlier forms of social control, involving such bodies as the yeomanry (a volunteer and ad hoc outfit), were proving themselves to be ill-equipped to handle the emerging problems of order in the newly urbanised areas (Cohen and Scull, 1983). The 'solution' lay in the formation of a permanent body of officers who could impose order on the working class through regular patrols and by winning the 'assent' of the community for the police function—'policing by consent'. The police force, from a Marxist perspective, arose *out of* the class system, in the sense that the reform movement which led to the establishment of the Metropolitan Police in the early nineteenth century was backed by the new capitalist class, for they saw in the idea of a police force the answer to the problems of order. The police force, in turn, *acted on behalf of* the class system, by maintaining order and discipline of the working class in the interests of the ruling, capitalist class.

Such types of analysis are not restricted to historical analysis; a similar thesis on the 'class-based' role of the police has been advanced in relation to contemporary policing (Scraton, 1985). Critical sociologies of law have also extended to a consideration of the role of the courts and the police in reinforcing *racial inequalities* (Hall et al., 1978) and *gender inequalities*, such as in the areas of rape law and domestic violence (Burton, 1985; Benn, 1985; Jones, 1987; Lacey, Wells and Meure, 1990). If there is a common theme in this wide range of studies of the law and law enforcement it is that the functions or consequences of the law are not always apparent and that we need to look deeper into the workings of the law to gather a full picture of the contexts of law.

A similar sentiment comes from another, but related, tradition within the sociology of law which compares and contrasts *law-in-books* with *law-in-action*. This approach lays great emphasis on the role of *informal cultural* factors and practices in the operation of the law. It asks us to move beyond the formal rules and procedures which ostensibly determine legal procedure—'law-in-books'—and to study the actual workings of the legal system through an examination of the cultures and subcultures of those groups responsible for the application of the law. This would include the police, court personnel, the legal professions and the judiciary. Only by examining how such groups work 'on the ground' can we fully understand the law and its operation. One example of this level of analysis comes from Carlen (1976), who studied the social interactions within English magistrates' courts. Using observational methods and interviews with court personnel and defendants, she found that what goes on in the courts is largely meaningless to defendants, or is understood by them in a way that is different from 'court professionals'—clerks, lawyers, magistrates and so on. Whatever the formal procedures of the trial process, a 'game' is played by court practitioners which only they, not the people at issue, understand. Carlen concluded from this that trial in the lower courts is about a 'plausible public performance of justice' (Carlen, 1976, p. 64) rather than 'justice' as such. Justice in this sense is a social *ritual* between practitioners which leaves defendants powerless and marginalised. As regards the higher courts, much of the attention has focused on the *social attitudes* of the judiciary. In particular, studies have attempted to link the *social origins* of the judiciary—family and educational backgrounds (largely upper class and typically from the same elite schools and universities)—with the types of *decisions* they reach, particularly on sensitive areas such as rape trials, cases involving morality, and so on. Such studies have tended to conclude that the social origins of the judiciary, coupled with the rather isolated professional legal training they experience, is often reflected in sexist, racist or otherwise unfair decision-making (Griffith, 1997; Lee, 1988; Pattullo, 1983).

Most of the work in this area, however, has focused on *police culture*. The sociology of policing has tended to contrast the formal rules and regulations which are supposed to govern policing, such as police powers, with the 'reality' of police work on the ground. This has been expressed in terms of the way in which officers work less to the formal framework of police powers than to the 'Ways and Means Act' (see Reiner, 2000, 86), self-elected, informal sets of 'rules' governing officers' behaviour. Given the wide range of *discretion* available to police officers in any given situation, sociologists have been interested in how the 'working culture' of police officers, made up of these informal rules and other cultural artefacts, shapes police conduct and thus the delivery of law enforcement itself. Recruit officers are 'socialised' into this culture as soon as they are 'inducted' by serving officers, who will tell the officer what policing is 'really about' and how rules can be 'bent' to achieve desired results. Sociologists would argue that unless we understand the informal working culture of police officers we will never fully understand law enforcement, or indeed improve standards of policing if that were deemed necessary. Sociologists have sought to reveal the dimensions of 'cop culture' (in some cases by means of participant observational study—Holdaway, 1983) and in this respect have tended to focus on issues such as police *racism*, police *sexism* (or 'machismo') and the extent to which police decisions about, for example, stop and search, are governed by stereotypes of the 'sorts of people' who should be acted upon (for a discussion see Reiner, 2000, ch. 3). Such cultural dimensions determine how officers exercise their discretion 'on the streets'. A 'legalistic' framework for the analysis of policing, which would focus on the formal rules supposedly governing police procedure ('law-in-books), might miss a lot of what is really going on in the world of policing if police culture is really so powerful a force over officers' conduct ('law-in-action').

The sociology of law, in very different ways, encourages us to look behind and beyond the law and to the hidden, the non-apparent and the informal processes that may be at work. The law may be fulfilling certain functions which give it purpose over and above the specific tasks it is charged to fulfil. It is for this reason, to return to a point made above, that the law may be 'working' *even when it appears to be failing*. An illustration of this might be reconviction rates. If high numbers of offenders are reconvicted after serving a prison sentence we might reach the conclusion that prison is 'failing'. However, from some sociological perspectives we might reach a different conclusion: prison is not failing because of high reconviction rates because the *function* of the prison is not to reduce offending. The function of the prison for some is not to rehabilitate the offender but to take the offender away from the community and avoid that offender 'contaminating' the law-abiding community (Ignatieff, 1978). Sociologists are oriented to looking for roles and functions within the law and its agencies which are not always obvious on a first reading. If that helps us to understand the law more fundamentally then sociology does have a useful role to play in this area.

The Politics of Law

Alongside and overlapping the sociological study of law, there is a growing literature on what might be called the *politics* of law. This extends the analysis of the role of *power* and power relations by linking the organisation of the law and the criminal justice system with the political process. There are at least three levels of analysis in this regard, which focus on the role of political *ideologies*, political *parties* and *pressure groups*.

Political *ideologies* can have a powerful role in shaping the direction of legal forms and the criminal process over and above any consideration of their 'effectiveness' in addressing behavioural or other 'problems'. The adoption of particular legal strategies or interventions may be more a reflection of wider changes in ideological frameworks than the sudden acceptance of the 'rationality' of this or that approach to the law. Furthermore, those changes may be transnational developments, taking place simultaneously in many countries. One example of this is the rise of 'new right' or 'neo-conservative' political ideologies during the 1980s and early 1990s across the United States and many parts of Europe, most clearly expressed with the emergence of 'Reaganism' in the USA and 'Thatcherism' in the UK (Savage and Robins, 1990). From the point of view of law and legal contexts what was most significant about new right ideology was the re-emphasis within public policy of notions of 'personal responsibility', 'culpability', 'just deserts', 'free choice' and other concepts associated with neo-liberal thought. It reflected a view of 'human nature' which saw individuals as acting on the basis of rational choice and 'calculation' and as responsible for their own actions. This has relevance to a whole range of public policies (ibid), but as regards *criminal* behaviour therefore, new right ideology reintroduced into crime policy the notion that criminals 'choose' to act in the way they do and should be dealt with accordingly. This shifted the emphasis away from the idea of the 'treatment' or 'rehabilitation' of the offender, whereby the offender is seen as the 'victim' of his or her environment, to the principle that offenders should be held to 'account' for their actions given that they were actions for which they are fully responsible. This pointed to a legal and penal process oriented to 'just deserts', 'rational deterrence' and *retribution* (normally by means of custody). Such ideological shifts can reverberate throughout the criminal/legal process. In the case of 'just deserts' the tendency is to reorient legal decisions—pre-trial reports, evidence in court, penalty on conviction, and so on—around the nature or seriousness of the *offence* rather than around information about the *offender* (previous record, mitigating circumstances, etc.).

In these ways a whole legal machinery can be shaped by the wider ideological framework within which it operates. Different ideological frameworks can generate very different legal forms. For example, in more recent years there has been a growth of interest in the political ideology of 'communitarianism', a broad-based ideology which places emphasis on the need to build communities around social cohesion and social *inclusion* (Etzioni,1995). This entails an altogether different conception of 'human nature', one which rests on the idea of the essentially 'social' or community-oriented basis of human action (as distinct from the individualistic ethos of the new right).

This ideology generates a very different set of responses to criminal behaviour, one which is oriented to *community-based* responses to crime and which also lends support to *non-legal* or *informal* methods of dealing with offending behaviour—such as 'restorative justice' schemes, whereby offenders and victims are brought together and jointly agree ways in which offenders can attempt to repair the damage done to their victims. The full application of communitarian ideology to the problem of crime would thus have quite fundamental effects on the role of law in this area of problem-solving.

Political ideologies thus provide important contextual frameworks within which legal systems operate. Closely linked to political ideologies is the role of *party* or *electoral* politics. The focus in this case is on the influence of *political competition* on forms of law and the criminal process. More specifically, it is on the use of the law as a means of gaining political advantage for political parties, whether in power or in opposition. An example of this is the role of *sentencing* policy in the UK. As this author has argued elsewhere (Savage and Nash, 2001), from 1979 onwards the UK experienced major shifts and U-turns in sentencing policy, much of this taking place under consecutive Conservative governments. The early 1980s saw an emphasis on custodial sentencing, targeted particularly at young offenders, through an expansion in the use of imprisonment and detention orders. By the mid-1980s, however, non-custodial or *community-based* sentences came to the fore, in the form of supervision orders and an extension in the use of probation; this move was associated with a critique of the effectiveness of custodial penalties and the view that prison is 'an expensive way of making bad people worse'. This was to shift back, in the early 1990s, with a re-emphasis of the role of imprisonment as a central platform of sentencing policy, expressed in the then Conservative Home Secretary's famous claim that 'prison works'. To an extent, that 'philosophy' has been maintained under Labour since taking office in 1997. It is possible to account for these shifts and U-turns by examining the part played by political competition and electoral politics during these periods. Crudely speaking, the criminal law has been 'used' by political parties to appeal to the electorate, often doggedly attached to 'heavy' sentences for offenders. When parties feel under threat or feel that they are being out-flanked on 'law and order', they can often turn to crime policy for salvation. Considerations of the effectiveness of this or that penal strategy have played a secondary role in comparison to the political gains which a 'get tough on offenders' stance seems to be able to offer. More generally, policy on police powers, prosecution and court disposals may be heavily dictated by the political calculations made by political parties as to how well this or that policy will 'go down with the voters'. We need to appreciate this factor if we are to fully understand the wider contexts of law and legal interventions.

The politics of law also operates at a 'sub-governmental' level, in the form of *pressure group politics*. The emphasis here is how the law is shaped by different groups and associations and how forms of legal intervention can reflect *vested interests* and not just the particular issues they are apparently concerned to address. We can illustrate this with reference to UK legislation on the contentious question of the 'right to silence'. There has been much debate over the years about the appropriateness of the right of suspects to remain silent under questioning by the police and in court, without negative inferences being drawn within court about their choice to do so. The *Criminal Justice and Public Order Act 1994* amended the right to silence by allowing the judge in certain contexts to invite the jury to consider whether exercise of that right constituted some sign of 'guilt' on behalf of the defendant, effectively a major qualification on the 'unfettered right of silence', one much criticised by the civil liberties bodies. In examining this issue a psychological approach might investigate the extent to which any relaxation of this principle could place pressure on individuals to make untrue statements and assess the amendment of the right to silence accordingly. From the point of view of the *politics* of law, however, a different picture emerges, one which focuses on how the right to silence became embroiled in *pressure group politics*. Savage, Charman and Cope (2000) have documented how the amendment of the right to silence came about largely as a result of successful pressure group activity by senior police associations, who 'lobbied' for a reform of the right to silence on the grounds that, in its traditional form, it allowed many guilty defendants protection against challenging questioning and, as a consequence, enhance their chances of acquittal. The 'police case' was that this acted as an undue protection for the defendant; this was a view which, in the end, attracted the support of the government of the day and won out as a consequence over the views of civil libertarians and, indeed, the 'legal lobby' of lawyers associations (Savage, Charman and Cope 1997). In other words, the new rules governing the right to silence are in place not particularly because they secure the best forms of justice, but because 'police interests' have won out over competing interests in the criminal process. In many cases it is not evidence or research (psychological or otherwise) which directs the adoption of this or that law or this or that criminal procedure, but rather the hard world of pressure group politics.

CONCLUSION

This chapter has sought to explain how the social and political sciences have developed a range of approaches to the study of law and the criminal process which address the *wider societal contexts within which law operates*. The message is not that psychological analysis of the law is in any sense illegitimate, but that an understanding of the social contexts of law serves to counterbalance psychologically oriented perspectives on law by seeking to address different types of questions about the role and purpose of law. However, there is a point at which the social scientist might draw swords with psychology if and when psychology fails to appreciate the social forces which can underpin and influence criminal conduct, or the social forces which determine whether this or that act suddenly becomes *defined* as 'criminal'. It is sobering to recall that there was a time when homosexuality, then a crime, was considered a human pathology worthy of 'treatment' and even 'cure'. We must be careful that 'criminal conduct' more generally is not misinterpreted in the same way, as something driven by individual human pathology clearly distinct from 'normal' beahviour. In many ways it is surprising how 'normal' crime is and how 'normal' criminals are.

REFERENCES

Becker. H. (1963). *Outsiders.* New York: Free Press.

Benn, M. (1985). Policing Women. In J. Baxter and L. Koffman (eds), *Police: The constitution and the community.* Oxon: Professional Books.

Braithwaite, J. (1989). *Crime, shame and reintegration.* Sydney: Cambridge University Press.

Burton, C. (1985). *Subordination.* London: Allen & Unwin.

Carlen, P. (1976). *Magistrates' justice.* London: Martin Robertson.

Clarke, R. (1992). *Situational crime prevention.* New York: Harrow & Heston.

Cohen, S. and Scull, A. (eds) (1983). *Social control and the state.* Oxford: Martin Robertson.

Cotterrell, R. (1992). *The sociology of law.* London: Butterworths.

Durkheim, E. (1964). *The division of labour in society.* New York: Free Press.

Etzioni, A. (1995). *The spirit of community.* London: Fontana Press.

Farrington, D. (1997). Human Development and Criminal Careers. In M. Maguire, R. Morgan and R. Reiner (eds), *The Oxford handbook of criminology.* Oxford: Oxford University Press.

Field, S. (1990). *Trends in crime and their interpretation: A study of recorded crime in post war England and Wales.* Home Office Research Study No. 119. London: HMSO.

Griffith, J. (1997). *The politics of the judiciary* (5th edn). London: Fontana.

Hall, S., Critcher, C., Jefferson, T., Clarke, J. and Roberts, B. (1978) *Policing the crisis.* London: Macmillan.

Hay, D. (Ed.) (1975). *Albion's fatal tree.* London: Penguin.

Hirschi (1969).*Causes of delinquency.* Berkeley, CA: University of California Press.

Holdaway, S. (1983). *Inside the British police.* Oxford: Basil Blackwell.

Ignatieff, M. (1978). *A just measure of pain.* London: Macmillan.

Jones, S. (1987). *Policewomen and equality.* London: Macmillan.

Lacey, N., Wells, C. and Meure, D. (1990). *Reconstructing criminal law.* London: Weidenfeld.

Lee, S. (1988). *Judging judges.* London: Faber & Faber.

Maguire, M. (1997). Crime statistics, patterns and trends. In M. Maguire, R. Morgan and R. Reiner (eds), *The Oxford handbook of criminology.* Oxford: Oxford University Press.

Matza, D. (1964). *Delinquency and drift.* Englewood Cliffs, NJ: Prentice Hall.

Newburn, T. and Stanko, E. (eds) (1994). *Just boys doing business?.* London: Routledge.

Pattullo, P. (1983). *Judging women.* London: NCCL.

Quinney, R. (1978). The ideology of law. In C. Reasons and R. Rich (eds), *The sociology of law.* London: Butterworths.

Radzinowitz, L. (1948). *A history of English criminal law and its administration from 1750.* London: Stevens and Sons Ltd.

Reiner, R. (2000). *The politics of the police.* Oxford: Oxford University Press.

Savage, S. and Robins, L. (eds) (1990). *Public policy under Thatcher.* London: Macmillan.

Savage, S., Charman, S. and Cope, S. (1997). ACPO: A force to be reckoned with? *Criminal Lawyer*, April.

Savage, S., Charman, S. and Cope, S. (2000). *Policing and the Power of Persuasion.* London: Blackstone Press.

Savage, S. and Nash, M. (2001). Law and order under Blair: New Labour or Old Conservatism? In S. Savage and M. Nash (eds), *Public policy under Blair.* London: Macmillan.

Scraton, P. (1985). *The state of the police.* London: Pluto.

Storch, R. (1976). The plague of blue locusts. *International Review of Social History*, *20*, 61–90.

Sutherland, E. and Cressey, D. (1955). *Principles of criminology.* Chicago: Lippincott.

Table of Cases

Table of Statutes

Index